HANDBOOK OF RESEARCH ON ENVIRONMENTAL TAXATION

Handbook of Research on Environmental Taxation

Edited by

Janet E. Milne

Professor of Law and Director of the Environmental Tax Policy Institute, Vermont Law School, USA

Mikael Skou Andersen

Professor in Policy Analysis at the Department of Environmental Science, Aarhus University, Denmark

EE Edward **Elgar**
PUBLISHING

Cheltenham, UK • Northampton, MA, USA

Published by
Edward Elgar Publishing Limited
The Lypiatts
15 Lansdown Road
Cheltenham
Glos GL50 2JA
UK

Edward Elgar Publishing, Inc.
William Pratt House
9 Dewey Court
Northampton
Massachusetts 01060
USA

Paperback edition 2014

A catalogue record for this book
is available from the British Library

Library of Congress Control Number: 2012939922

This book is available electronically in the **Elgar**online
law subject collection
DOI 10.4337/9781781952146

ISBN 978 1 84844 997 8 (cased)
       978 1 78471 759 9 (paperback)

Typeset by Servis Filmsetting Ltd, Stockport, Cheshire
Printed and bound by CPI Group (UK) Ltd, Croydon, CR0 4YY

Contents

List of contributors   vii
Acknowledgments   x
List of abbreviations   xi

1   This book's approach to environmental taxation   1
    Janet E. Milne

PART I   CONCEPTUAL FOUNDATIONS

2   Introduction to environmental taxation concepts and research   15
    Janet E. Milne and Mikael Skou Andersen
3   Economic principles of environmental fiscal reform   33
    Jean-Philippe Barde and Olivier Godard
4   Legal authority to enact environmental taxes   59
    Michael Rodi and Hope Ashiabor (contributing author)

PART II   DESIGN

5   Design options and their rationales   85
    Pedro M. Herrera Molina
6   Earmarking revenues from environmentally related taxes   102
    Claudia Dias Soares
7   Designing environmental taxes in countries in transition: a case study of
    Vietnam   122
    Michael Rodi, Kai Schlegelmilch and Michael Mehling
8   Externality research   139
    Philipp Preiss

PART III   ACCEPTANCE

9   Regressivity of environmental taxation: myth or reality?   161
    Katri Kosonen
10 The political acceptability of carbon taxes: lessons from British Columbia   175
    Mark Jaccard
11 Gaining intergovernmental acceptance: legal rules protecting trade   192
    Birgitte Egelund Olsen
12 The double dividend debate   211
    William K. Jaeger
13 The political economy of environmental taxation   230
    Nils Axel Braathen

PART IV   IMPLEMENTATION

14   Multilevel governance: the implications of legal competences to collect,
     administer and regulate environmental tax instruments   249
     Nathalie Chalifour, María Amparo Grau-Ruiz and Edoardo Traversa
15   Transaction costs of environmental taxation: the administrative burden   273
     Jan Pavel and Leoš Vítek
16   Structuring road transport taxes to capture externalities: a critical analysis
     of approaches   283
     Teresa Palmer-Tous and Antoni Riera-Font
17   Environmental taxation in China: the greening of an emerging economy   303
     Yan Xu
18   A review of selected databases on market-based instruments   321
     Hans Vos

PART V   IMPACT

19   Decoupling: is there a separate contribution from environmental taxation?   343
     Adrian Muller, Åsa Löfgren and Thomas Sterner
20   The role of environmental taxation in spurring technological change   360
     Herman Vollebergh
21   Impacts on competitiveness: what do we know from modeling?   377
     Paul Ekins and Stefan Speck

PART VI   POLICY MIX

22   The role of environmental taxation: economics and the law   399
     Michael G. Faure and Stefan E. Weishaar
23   Regulatory reform and development of environmental taxation: the case of
     carbon taxation and ecological tax reform in Finland   422
     Rauno Sairinen
24   Bounded rationality in an imperfect world of regulations: what if individuals
     are not optimizing?   439
     Helle Ørsted Nielsen
25   Global environmental taxes   456
     Philippe Thalmann

PART VII   CONCLUSION

26   The future agenda for environmental taxation research   479
     Mikael Skou Andersen and Janet E. Milne

Index   495

Contributors

Mikael Skou Andersen, Professor in Policy Analysis, Aarhus University, Denmark, currently with the European Environment Agency

Hope Ashiabor, Associate Professor of Law, Faculty of Business and Economics, Macquarie University, Australia

Jean-Philippe Barde, former Head of the OECD National Environmental Policies Division; Lecturer, SciencesPo Paris (Paris School of International Affairs), France

Nils Axel Braathen, Principal Administrator, Environment Directorate, OECD, France

Nathalie Chalifour, Associate Professor, Faculty of Law, University of Ottawa, Centre for Environmental Law and Global Sustainability, Canada

Paul Ekins, Professor of Resources and Environmental Policy and Director, UCL Institute for Sustainable Resources, University College London, England

Michael G. Faure, Professor of Comparative and International Environmental Law, Maastricht University, and Professor of Comparative Private Law and Economics, Erasmus University Rotterdam, The Netherlands

Olivier Godard, Director of Research at CNRS, Economics Laboratory, École Polytechnique, France

María Amparo Grau-Ruiz, Associate Professor, Financial and Tax Law Department, Faculty of Law, Complutense University of Madrid, Spain

Pedro M. Herrera Molina, Full Professor of Tax Law, Spanish Open University (UNED), Spain

Mark Jaccard, Professor, School of Resource and Environmental Management, Simon Fraser University, Canada

William K. Jaeger, Professor, Department of Agricultural and Resource Economics, Oregon State University, United States

Katri Kosonen, Principal Administrator, Economist, DG TAXUD, European Commission, Belgium

Åsa Löfgren, Associate Professor, Department of Economics, University of Gothenburg, Sweden

Michael Mehling, President, Ecologic Institute, and Adjunct Professor, Georgetown University, United States

Janet E. Milne, Professor of Law and Director, Environmental Tax Policy Institute, Vermont Law School, United States

Adrian Muller, Senior Researcher at the Chair of Environmental Policy and Economics, Swiss Federal Institute of Institute of Technology ETH Zurich, Switzerland

Helle Ørsted Nielsen, Senior scientist, Political Science, Department of Environmental Science, Aarhus University, Denmark

Birgitte Egelund Olsen, Professor and Director of Study, Master of Environmental and Energy Law, Department of Law, Aarhus University, Denmark

Teresa Palmer-Tous, Associate Professor, Department of Applied Economics, University of Balearic Islands, Spain

Jan Pavel, Associate Professor, Department of Public Finance, University of Economics, Czech Republic

Philipp Preiss, Head of the section Technology Assessment, Institute of Energy Economics and the Rational Use of Energy, Department of Technology Assessment and Environment, Universität Stuttgart, Germany

Antoni Riera-Font, Chair Professor in Applied Economics and Director of the Research, Economic Center University of Balearic Islands, Spain

Michael Rodi, Professor of Law, University of Greifswald, Faculty of Law and Economics and Director, Institute for Climate Protection, Energy and Mobility (IKEM), Berlin/Greifswald, Germany

Rauno Sairinen, Professor (environmental policy), University of Eastern Finland, Finland

Kai Schlegelmilch, Environmental Fiscal Expert, Federal Environment Agency (Umweltbundesamt), Germany.

Claudia Dias Soares, Professor of Law, Law School, Portuguese Catholic University, Portugal

Stefan Speck, Project Manager, Environmental Economics and Policies, Integrated Environmental Assessments Program, European Environment Agency, Denmark

Thomas Sterner, Professor, Department of Economics, University of Gothenburg, Sweden, currently Visiting Chief Economist, Environmental Defense Fund; former President of the European Association of Environmental and Resource Economists

Philippe Thalmann, Associate Professor, School of Architecture, Civil and Environmental Engineering, École Polytechnique Fédérale de Lausanne (EPFL), Switzerland

Edoardo Traversa, Professor of Tax Law, Faculty of Law, Catholic University of Louvain, Belgium

Leoš Vítek, Associate Professor, Department of Public Finance, University of Economics, Prague, Czech Republic

Herman Vollebergh, Senior Researcher, PBL Netherlands Environmental Assessment Agency, and Research Fellow, CentER and Tilburg Sustainability Center, Tilburg University, The Netherlands

Hans Vos, independent; former Project Manager with the European Environment Agency, The Netherlands

Stefan E. Weishaar, Associate Professor of Law and Economics, Department of Law and Economics, Faculty of Law, University of Groningen, The Netherlands

Yan Xu, Assistant Professor, Faculty of Law, The Chinese University of Hong Kong, Hong Kong, China, and Senior Research Fellow, Taxation Law and Policy Research Institute, Monash University, Australia

Acknowledgments

The editors owe thanks to many who have made this book possible: Edward Elgar for suggesting the project and for his commitment to this field of research; the contributing authors for making time in their schedules to devote their talent to this undertaking; Ben Booth, John-Paul McDonald, Rebecca Hastie and Laura Seward at Edward Elgar for their guidance from start to finish; Jonathan Voegele, Ginny Burnham and Michele LaRose at Vermont Law School for their assistance with editing, manuscript preparation and research; Eric Levy for his copyediting eye; and the Environmental Tax Policy Institute at Vermont Law School.

Janet Milne thanks her husband, John Kuhns, who offers constant love and patience.

Mikael Skou Andersen dedicates his work on this book to the memory of Svend Auken, Minister of Environment and Energy in Denmark from 1993 to 2001, who gave us many environmental taxes to study.

Abbreviations

ASA	aviation service agreement
ATSDR	Agency for Toxic Substances and Disease Registry
BT	business tax
BTA	border tax adjustment
CAFE	Clean Air for Europe
CCA	climate change agreement
CCL	Climate Change Levy
CERCLA	Comprehensive Environmental Response, Compensation, and Liability Act (US)
CGE	computable general equilibrium
CIT	country in transition
CRF	concentration-response function
CT	consumption tax
dB	decibels
ECA	enhanced capital allowance
ECJ	European Court of Justice
EEA	European Environment Agency
EFR	Environmental Fiscal Reform
EKC	Environmental Kuznets Curve
ETD	Energy Tax Directive
ETR	environmental tax reform
ETS	Emission Trading Scheme
EU	European Union
FYP	five-year plan (China)
GATT	General Agreement on Tariffs and Trade
GDP	gross domestic product
GHG	greenhouse gas
GTZ/GIZ	German Development Implementing Agency
HCFC	chlorinated and fluorinated hydrocarbons
ICAO	International Civil Aviation Organization
IEA	International Energy Agency
IMF	International Monetary Fund
IPA	impact pathway approach
LCA	life cycle assessment
LCIA	life cycle impact assessment
MAC	marginal abatement costs
MBI	market-based instruments
MEA	multilateral environmental agreement
MFN	most-favored nation
MLG	multilevel governance

MSD	marginal social damage
NEEDS	New Energy Externalities Developments for Sustainability
NICs	national insurance contributions
ODC	ozone-depleting chemical
OECD	Organization for Economic Cooperation and Development
OPEC	Organization of the Petroleum Exporting Countries
PM	particulate matter
PPM	Process and Production Methods
PRF	Permanent Reforestation Fund
R&D	research and development
SARA	Superfund Amendments and Reauthorization Act
TFEU	Treaty on the Functioning of the European Union
TI	tax interaction
UNFCCC	United Nations Framework Convention on Climate Change
VAT	value added tax
WTO	World Trade Organization
WTP	willingness to pay
YOLL	years of lost lifetime

MEMBER STATES OF THE EUROPEAN UNION—OFFICIAL ABBREVIATIONS

AT	Austria		SE	Sweden
BE	Belgium		SI	Slovenia
BG	Bulgaria		SK	Slovakia
CY	Cyprus		UK	United Kingdom
CZ	Czech Republic			
DE	Germany			
DK	Denmark			
EE	Estonia			
EL	Greece			
ES	Spain			
FI	Finland			
FR	France			
HU	Hungary			
IE	Ireland			
IT	Italy			
LT	Lithuania			
LU	Luxembourg			
LV	Latvia			
MT	Malta			
NL	Netherlands			
PL	Poland			
PT	Portugal			
RO	Romania			

1 This book's approach to environmental taxation
Janet E. Milne

The field of environmental taxation is entering a stage of maturity as governments increasingly incorporate environmental tax instruments into their environmental port-folios and as a wide variety of stakeholders and scholars explore ways to address the ecological challenges that face their countries and the globe. This Handbook describes the state of the art of research on environmental taxation for a wide variety of readers, including researchers in academia and at think tanks, policymakers and analysts in government, representatives of the private sector, and people interested in the ways in which tax systems can affect behavior. This brief chapter describes the approach we have taken to the subject and an overview of the following chapters.

AN INTERDISCIPLINARY PERSPECTIVE

Because environmental taxation is inherently a topic that has warranted interest from many different sides, the Handbook takes an approach based on several areas of study. Economic theories generate the roots from which environmental taxation grows; the principles and practice of political economy and economics shape its acceptance and application; law and public finance mold the features of its design and execution. Consequently, the book is written both for and by people from a range of disciplines, including economics, law, political science, public finance and engineering. We have encouraged the contributing authors to present their topics in a way that delicately treads the line between providing sophisticated analysis and explaining research in a manner that a broad range of readers can understand. We hope that a deeper appreciation of the issues involved in environmental taxation will enhance the ability to effectively design and implement environmental tax measures and encourage research and interdisciplinary collaboration among different fields.

A LIFE CYCLE APPROACH TO ENVIRONMENTAL TAXATION

It is a statement of the obvious that environmental taxation exists to advance environmental goals. The range of these environmental goals is broad, and it grows each year as policymakers find new ways to harness tax systems for environmental protection. Science, of course, defines the environmental goals that environmental taxation serves. This book, however, does not try to start with any specific environmental goals or the science that underlies those goals. That starting point is the logical place for the development of any particular environmental tax instrument, but an issue-by-issue analysis would require a tome much larger than this one.

Instead, the following chapters focus on universal themes that affect environmental taxation, organized around what we think of as the life cycle of environment tax instruments:

- The life cycle starts with an introduction to the *concepts* underlying environmental taxation, in effect the fundamental DNA that shapes its development. It explores the vocabulary and principles of environmental taxation and the legal authority to engage in environmental taxation.
- The book then turns to the *design* of environmental taxation—the fundamental elements of the design of environmental taxation instruments that shape the details of the way the instruments look when governments create them. Environmental taxation instruments share many universal design choices. They also raise interesting issues about how to determine the cost of environmental externalities that tax rates might reflect and whether to dedicate the revenue to the environmental purpose.
- The enactment of environmental taxation instruments requires their *acceptance* in the public and private sectors. The degree of acceptance is heavily influenced by assessments of their effect on competitiveness, the extent to which tax measures disadvantage people at lower income levels, the economic and equity impacts that flow from how government can use the revenue from environmental taxes, and other aspects of political economy.
- Acceptance is followed by the realities of *implementation*. Implementation involves issues such as how countries with multiple levels of government match environmental taxes with the appropriate level of government and the level of public and private transactional costs associated with environmental taxes. Case studies illustrate how environmental elements can be incorporated into tax systems in established economies and countries in transition.
- Once in place, the ultimate merit of environmental taxation depends on its *impact*. Therein lie the challenges of determining the actual impact of environmental taxes in decoupling economic growth and environmental degradation, and assessing environmental taxation's effect on environmentally positive technological innovation. There is also the question of how environmental taxes affect competitiveness.
- It is then useful to step back and consider the role of environmental taxation amid the broad *policy mix*, which includes traditional regulation and other market-based instruments, such as tradable emissions allowances. Environmental tax instruments rarely exist in isolation, and policymakers must continually determine the most appropriate combination of instruments, each with its own unique attributes.

We hope that readers can draw lessons from this life cycle analysis that will inform the development and analysis of a broad range of environmental taxation instruments. We also hope that it can serve readers around the world. Research on environmental taxation is often country- or region-specific, but many of the principles and lessons have broad applicability. In selecting topics, we have tried to identify issues that are quite universal and will have currency in the greatest number of countries. At the same time, we have included several case studies that illustrate how specific issues have been addressed in particular countries or regions, choosing examples that offer lessons that can have broad relevance or interest.

WHAT IS 'ENVIRONMENTAL TAXATION'?

A foundational issue for environmental taxation is the question of what 'environmental taxation' encompasses. Environmental taxation is often viewed as meaning environmental taxes, such as pollution or emissions taxes. This book adopts the OECD's definition of environmental taxes, provided in Chapter 2, which considers whether an environmental tax is 'environmentally related,' a definition that provides significant latitude.

However, this book also addresses environmental tax policy more broadly. It considers tax instruments that provide government support for environmentally positive choices—such as reduced tax rates, tax credits, exemptions or deductions. As explained in Chapter 2, these tax incentives are often referred to as environmental tax expenditures. We think it is important to consider both sides of the incentive coin: the tax increases for environmentally negative actions and the tax benefits for environmentally positive actions.

The repeal of subsidies for environmentally damaging activities, such as the production and use of fossil fuels, is also a significant component of environmental tax policy viewed broadly. Environmental tax policy consists not only of adjusting the tax code to include new measures designed to promote environmental protection but also considering ways to reform the tax code to withdraw or discourage measures that work at cross purposes. While certainly important and worthy of research, a detailed inquiry into environmentally damaging subsidies lies beyond the scope of this book. With limited pages, we have chosen to delve more deeply into the environmental taxation instruments that can yield positive environmental results.

A BRIEF OVERVIEW OF THE BOOK

This Handbook seeks to serve multiple goals. Its authors capture the key literature to help researchers in the field, and in doing so, they also provide their own analytical frameworks that may assist researchers and policymakers as they consider issues. After assessing the landscape, they highlight issues that warrant future research, and the final chapter presents the editors' views on an agenda for research. In short, the book is descriptive and analytical, retrospective and prospective. Given the multiplicity of environmental taxation instruments and their potential for broad application, it cannot be comprehensive, but we hope it can help establish a framework and can be a useful reference for current and future research and exploration.

Although the wealth of material in the pages ahead defies summarization, the following brief descriptions of the subsequent chapters highlight the key issues addressed in the book and how various issues relate to each other. They also note issues that lie beyond the scope of this book, given the inevitable realities of limits on coverage, but that readers nonetheless should bear in mind.

Part I: Fundamental Concepts of Environmental Taxation

Part I introduces readers to fundamental concepts that shape environmental taxation. Janet Milne and Mikael Skou Andersen (Chapter 2) review the development of the concepts of environmental taxation and the vocabulary used to articulate those concepts. Starting with the intellectual father of environmental taxes, A.C. Pigou, they trace the evolution of environmental taxation concepts over the past century, and in so doing, they discuss semantic and conceptual issues that lurk beneath this evolution. Questions examined include: What is a 'Pigouvian tax'? How has the international community distinguished an 'environmental tax' from other taxes, fees or charges? What are the terms used to describe tax reforms of which environmental taxes are one component, and what are the other components of such reforms? And what is the place of environmental tax expenditures in environmental tax policy? The chapter builds a common foundation for the chapters that follow.

Environmental taxation is the product of economics. As a market-based instrument, environmental taxation springs from economic principles of how to affect behavior in environmentally positive ways. Consequently, understanding the economic theories is critical to appreciating the conceptual basis for environmental taxation. Jean-Philippe Barde and Olivier Godard (Chapter 3) explore the economic rationales for environmental taxes and the static and dynamic efficiency of environmental taxes. They also place environmental taxes in the important context of environmental fiscal reform, which includes the restructuring of existing taxes and the removal of environmentally damaging tax subsidies—a significant topic not otherwise addressed at great length in this book, as noted above. Finally, they distinguish the economic principles of environmental taxation and tradable permit systems and identify key criteria for choosing between these two market-based approaches. Taken as a whole, the chapter offers a comprehensive but accessible framework for considering the role of taxation in environmental protection.

Although shaped by economics, environmental taxation instruments are also creatures of the law. This legal aspect generates often underappreciated but fundamental questions about which governmental units actually have the legal authority to use environmental taxes and how legal procedures affect their ability to do so.

Michael Rodi (Chapter 4) takes on the task of analyzing the legal authority to enact environmental taxes. Because the law varies from country to country, the chapter highlights key legal issues that are common to many countries, illustrated by examples from a variety of countries, including those from Australia provided by contributing author Hope Ashiabor. The chapter starts with the basic question of whether environmental taxation instruments fall within the rules governing tax instruments or environmental instruments, given their hybrid nature. It then focuses on how a country's constitution and its more general legal principles, such as rules governing retroactivity or basic rights, can affect the use of environmental taxation. Because one governmental entity is usually part of a tiered set of governmental entities (local, state, national and possibly supranational, as in the case of the European Union), the chapter considers intergovernmental legal rules that can limit the authority to use environmental taxation. International law can also play a role in defining legal authority. It lays the groundwork for Chapter 14, which examines how environmental taxation has actually been implemented at different levels of government, and it links to the discussion in Chapter 11 about how trade agreements affect the use of environmental taxes.

Part II: Design

After adopting the concept of environmental taxation and ensuring its legal basis, a government or advocate must consider how to design the environmental taxation instrument. Economic and environmental principles motivate its use, but a variety of considerations affect the actual design details. Pedro Herrera Molina (Chapter 5) lays out the critical design decisions for environmental taxes and environmental tax expenditures. He dissects the instruments into their component parts and identifies factors that affect design decisions, which can arise from issues of law, environmental policy, economics, politics or technical administrative feasibility. As he notes, the influence of these factors will vary depending on the country and the particular circumstances, but the fundamental design choices and the need to consider each factor are universal. The chapter also addresses the important issue of who can and should administer environmental taxation instruments as a matter of law and policy—tax authorities or environmental authorities. As noted in Chapter 4, the hybrid nature of the environmental taxation instrument poses interesting challenges that traditional environmental protection instruments need not face.

A significant issue in environmental tax design is how to use the revenue from a new or increased environmental tax, a recurring element in the discussion about how to design policy packages that include environmental taxes. One design option is to dedicate the revenue to environmental purposes. Claudia Dias Soares (Chapter 6) examines the law and policy of earmarking environmental tax revenues to the environmental problem that the tax addresses. She distinguishes earmarked taxes from other arrangements, such as charges and revenue recycling, and explores the literature and range of considerations surrounding the question of whether to earmark revenues. Selected examples illustrate these distinctions and considerations. The option of using the revenue for revenue-neutral tax reform is also explored elsewhere in this Handbook, particularly with respect to the political acceptance of environmental taxes in Part III.

In a case study, Michael Rodi, Kai Schlegelmilch and Michael Mehling (Chapter 7) explore how a number of design issues played out in one specific context—when Vietnam adopted its recent environmental tax reform, which came into effect in 2012 and applies to a broad range of pollutants. Although they discuss the role of environmental tax reforms in countries in transition in general, many of the design issues are common to a broad range of countries considering enacting or reforming environmental taxes. The chapter describes and analyzes the steps that led to the enactment of Vietnam's environmental tax reform and the legal, political and policy factors that influenced its introduction and design, as well as its projected distributional impacts.

An inevitable issue for environmental tax design is how high to set the tax rate. As explained in Chapters 2 and 3, the tax rate could be set to execute the Pigouvian principle of internalizing externalities, or it might be set to achieve a given degree of environmental improvement under the Baumol-Oates approach. Alternatively, government could decide to send a softer price signal not strictly correlated with an economic theory. If government seeks to execute the Pigouvian principle, it will need to know the cost of the environmental externalities when it designs the tax, because that cost will determine the tax rate. Even if the tax rate does not achieve the Pigouvian level, it will partially internalize the externalities.

Hence, the study of the cost of externalities is very important to the theory and design of environmental taxes. Philipp Preiss (Chapter 8) presents the state of the art of assessing the cost of externalities, reviewing the history and methodologies of externality-cost models that have been developed in the United States and Europe. He then focuses on the primary method now used, the impact pathway approach, and provides examples of how monetary values are assigned to pollution. Although externality research can serve a broad range of purposes, its lessons for the design and evaluation of environmental taxation are critical.

Other chapters in this Handbook also contain discussions relevant to design considerations for environmental taxes as they consider issues of competitiveness (Chapters 11 and 21) and equity (Chapters 9 and 10), and as they provide examples of how environmental taxes have been implemented (including Chapters 16, 17 and 23).

Part III: Acceptance

The question of the economic impact of environmental taxes on commerce and households is particularly important for environmental taxes' gaining acceptance, from the perspectives of both policy and political economy. The degree of impact will depend in part on whether the new taxes represent an increase in the tax burden or are offset by other policy measures. Over the past two decades, the idea of using new environmental tax revenue to reduce other tax burdens has grown in popularity. Revenue-neutral tax reform provides interesting opportunities to serve multiple policy goals, address adverse impacts from the environmental taxes and build supportive political coalitions.

Katri Kosonen (Chapter 9) takes on the question of the impact of environmental taxes on households. Drawing on theoretical literature and empirical studies, she explores the methodologies for determining impact, given for example different definitions of the length of time over which one evaluates impacts. Decisions about how the revenue is used will also affect the impact of the tax. Experiences in the Nordic countries and studies of proposals at the European Union level offer an empirical basis for her analysis.

Mark Jaccard (Chapter 10) provides an on-the-ground case study of revenue-neutral environmental tax reform—a carbon tax adopted in British Columbia, Canada, in 2008 that generated revenues used to lower income tax rates. He assesses why the tax was politically acceptable, and how the government survived a subsequent 'axe the tax' campaign. He evaluates the design features of the revenue-neutral tax package, which applied phased-in carbon tax rates to ease the transition for taxpayers and used offsetting tax relief to help address concerns about impacts on lower-income households and businesses. He also examines the role of political and economic circumstances in the political acceptance of the tax, as well as the issue of the extent of public understanding of the revenue-neutral tax reform. As a case study, the chapter offers perspectives for other countries considering environmental tax reform.

Although revenue-neutral environmental tax reform can hold out prospects for economic improvement for the business sector or equitable relief, one country acting alone will nonetheless be concerned about whether its enactment of an environmental tax will put its products at a competitive disadvantage relative to products made in other countries. Such a disadvantage can cause domestic companies to lose business or to relocate. Conversely, countries may be tempted to place environmental taxes on imported products to protect the domestic products' competitive position. These competitiveness concerns can significantly affect the political acceptability of environmental taxes.

Here, legal rules governing international trade enter the picture. They help create an internationally uniform set of ground rules that can make environmental taxes more acceptable from an intergovernmental perspective. As Birgitte Egelund Olsen (Chapter 11) explains, the World Trade Organization's legal regime governing international trade plays a significant role in shaping environmental tax practices that could affect international trade. She examines how the General Agreement on Tariffs and Trade (GATT) prevents discriminatory practices and how countries that enact environmental taxes may be able to use border tax adjustments to equalize the tax burden on domestic and imported products. She tackles the particularly thorny questions of how these rules apply to taxes on pollution generated during the production process outside the taxing country and whether the environmental purpose of a tax provides a defense against a challenge of a GATT violation. With relatively few legal decisions directly involving environmental taxes, she draws on analogous authorities and highlights the issues that remain to be resolved.

William Jaeger (Chapter 12) delves into the theoretical 'double-dividend' hypothesis, which espouses that environmental taxes can yield both an environmental dividend and an economic dividend when their revenue is used to reduce other tax burdens, potentially increasing the tax's acceptability. This theory has generated significant analysis and debate among economists. Jaeger explains the double-dividend hypothesis and its 'strong' and 'weak' forms. He focuses on the question of how environmental taxes and preexisting taxes interact, a source of long debate among economists who have focused on the double-dividend hypothesis, and examines the strengths and weaknesses of the analysis to date.

Behind many of the aspects of the acceptance of environmental taxes lie fundamental concepts of political economy. Nils Axel Braathen (Chapter 13) surveys the theoretical and empirical literature that helps shed light on the question of when environmental taxation is used. His analysis underscores the diversity of factors at play in the political economy of environmental taxes, some favoring and some challenging the use of environmental taxes, and the significance of sectoral competitiveness issues in this mix.

Part IV: Implementation

Part IV turns to how environmental taxation instruments are actually being used around the world, focusing on a combination of broadly applicable issues and case studies.

Implementation can occur at different levels of government, depending on each level's legal authority and interest. Nathalie Chalifour, María Amparo Grau-Ruiz and Edoardo Traversa (Chapter 14) examine the implementation of environmental taxation instruments from the perspective of multilevel governance. The challenges of determining the appropriate level of government and coordinating activity among different levels of government are not unique to environmental taxation, but relatively little work has been done to date studying how these issues affect environmental taxation in particular. Hence the authors draw on both fiscal federalism literature and environmental federalism literature and, with the help of the limited literature on environmental taxation, suggest principles for allocating environmental taxation among levels of government. They review the challenges of determining actual empirical trends and provide examples of allocations of taxes to different levels of government. In addition, they identify key issues that arise from the need to coordinate actions among different levels of government and among different authorities at the same level of government. The resolution of the multi-level governance issues in any particular country will depend on its law and institutional structure, but the chapter's assessment of the potentially relevant issues offers an analytical framework for researchers.

Another issue common to implementation is the extent of transactional costs of environmental taxation instruments—the private cost of taxpayers' compliance and the public cost of tax authorities' administration. Jan Pavel and Leoš Vítek (Chapter 15) consider how to define transactional costs and then how to measure them, drawing on general literature about transactional costs of taxes in general and literature specific to environmental taxes. They summarize the results of empirical studies on the transactional costs of environmental taxes and the burden of those costs for environmental taxes relative to other taxes.

Most countries are faced with the need to reduce emissions from motor vehicles and the question of whether or how to revise their existing fuel and vehicle taxes to make them more environmentally sensitive. Teresa Palmer-Tous and Antoni Riera-Font (Chapter 16) analyze a wide range of environmental tax instruments that can help internalize the external costs of road transport, including emissions, noise, accidents and congestion. Although their work focuses on instruments used in the European Union, their analysis and the literature they cite have broad applicability for transport pricing policies around the world. This chapter serves as an analytical case study of how to translate the theoretical concepts of environmental taxation into specific taxes and how to evaluate the strengths and weaknesses of different policy approaches that are implemented.

The issue of implementation of environmental taxes is particularly timely and vivid for countries in transition to a free market, which face emerging environmental problems at the same time that they are adjusting their legal systems. Yan Xu (Chapter 17) explores the Chinese context for environmental taxation, which is now entering a second generation of environmental reforms as it considers how to address increasingly pressing environmental problems. As she explains, reforms between the 1980s and early 2000s included a number of environmentally related taxes and charges, but in 2007 the government began its effort to develop a more comprehensive, independent system of environmental taxation. The chapter presents these efforts in the context of the broader system of Chinese taxes at various levels of government and identifies and analyzes the key environmental taxes, painting a picture of the extent of environmental taxation and its impact in China to date.

A key question in assessing implementation is how to determine which instruments have been enacted, for which environmental problems, and in which countries. In other words, what is the current state of implementation? Hans Vos (Chapter 18) analyzes major databases that track the use of environmental taxes. These databases provide useful doorways to information for readers, and his analysis assesses their scope, their strengths and weaknesses, and ways to improve databases in the future.

Part V: Impact

The environmental and economic impact of environmental taxation is a product of the design of each specific environmental tax instrument, its implementation, its relationship to other governmental policies, and the economic characteristics of the society where it is being applied—factors that vary from instrument to instrument. Although ex ante and ex post evaluations of a wide range of specific instruments are a very valuable area of inquiry, they would warrant a book unto itself. Consequently, this Handbook instead addresses three specific issues that are relatively common to the question of the impact of environmental tax instruments and that, we believe, have emerged as key research areas for the future.

Adrian Muller, Åsa Löfgren and Thomas Sterner (Chapter 19) consider the need for countries to engage in economic growth without proportionately increasing environmental damage, and the role of environmental taxes in this decoupling of growth and environmental degradation. They present the theoretical concepts and literature about decoupling and identify key indicators of decoupling, using selected examples to translate a theoretical discussion into concrete terms. They then venture into the relatively new frontier of examining the extent to which environmental taxation contributes to decoupling and the merits of various economic models that seek to answer that question—a question that is significant to evaluating the future design and impact of environmental taxes.

Herman Vollebergh (Chapter 20) considers the equally complex and important issue of determining how much environmental taxes and environmental tax expenditures contribute to the use and development of new technologies. Environmental taxation instruments will be environmentally effective not only by directly reducing existing technologies' pollution but also by inspiring the development of new technologies that can function at more environmentally beneficial levels. Vollebergh reviews the literature about the static and dynamic efficiency of environmental taxes, the models used, and the nascent field of empirical analysis of the effect of environmental taxation instruments (both taxes and tax expenditures) on technological change.

Paul Ekins and Stefan Speck (Chapter 21) turn to the challenges of evaluating the competitiveness impact and environmental impact of environmental taxes, focusing primarily on environmental tax reforms enacted by European countries. Their case study of the world's longest-standing environmental tax reforms provides a window into the broader field of ex post and ex ante analysis of impacts. They discuss the economic models used to evaluate the results of European environmental tax reform at the national level and their empirical results. They also review more general literature on the competitiveness effects at the national, firm and sectoral levels, and suggest ways that environmental tax reform can be designed to mitigate adverse competitiveness effects.

Part VI: Policy Mix

Environmental taxation instruments are just one approach in a portfolio of policy instruments for environmental protection. Policymakers and researchers must consider when it is appropriate to use environmental taxation instead of some other type of instrument and when to use some combination of instruments. Hence it is important to consider the role of environmental taxation in the mix of policy instruments.

Michael Faure and Stefan Weishaar (Chapter 22) paint the big picture. They place environmental taxation among the constellation of environmental policy instruments, evaluating the relative rationales, scope, and strengths and weaknesses of each from the perspective of the discipline of economics and the law. Their discussion of the key literature and their analysis address the Coase theorem, environmental liability regimes of accident law and strict liability, regulation, environmental taxation and emissions trading. They conclude with thoughts about the factors to consider in developing instrument mixes in practice and the importance of interdisciplinary research.

Rauno Sairinen (Chapter 23) then considers the specific case of the choice of carbon taxation and environmental tax reform in Finland. He places Finland's use of carbon taxation on the continuum of the development of environmental policy as the academic literature and Finland moved beyond command-and-control regulation to examine opportunities for carbon taxation as a mode of governance. He traces several stages in Finland's use of carbon and energy taxes from the late 1980s to the present, focusing on the evolution of the design of the tax regimes, the reasons for the choice of environmental taxes and environmental tax reform and the relationship to European Union policies, including the EU's failed attempt to adopt an EU-wide carbon tax and the EU's introduction of the EU emissions trading scheme.

Helle Nielsen (Chapter 24) takes on the task of examining the relative merits of environmental taxation from the perspective of 'bounded rationality.' She tests the neoclassical economic assumptions that underlie the arguments for environmental taxation by examining the extent to which players act less rationally than assumed, given cognitive limitations. The chapter surveys the economic literature about behavioral assumptions, the models used to evaluate the theory of bounded rationality and the key issues. Nielsen extracts important lessons that apply to environmental taxes in particular and that can influence the decision about whether they are the appropriate instrument in a particular situation.

Finally, Philippe Thalmann (Chapter 25) addresses issues on the new frontier of the choice-of-instrument question—what role taxation can play in environmental issues that have global consequences and demand global solutions. He considers the role of global environmental taxes: How would one design environmental taxes to address global problems, given that no global authority exists to impose the taxes? How would its revenues be used? The chapter examines in particular the global problem of climate change and the potential role for pushing environmental taxes into uncharted international territory. Thalmann explores the design, effectiveness and implementation of a global carbon tax, closely analyzing the issues and the potential strengths and weaknesses of this approach.

Part VII: Conclusion

Mikael Skou Andersen and Janet Milne (Chapter 26) close the Handbook with their thoughts about a research agenda for the future. The authors of most chapters in the Handbook have provided their views on specific research needs in the areas about which they have written, and Andersen and Milne look more broadly at the field and identify several overarching areas that could benefit from more research as environmental taxation continues to mature. They highlight research frontiers that have emerged with the evolution of work in the areas of economics, law and policy sciences, but they also underscore the need for more interdisciplinary collaboration.

***

When economist Paul Samuelson summarized how John Maynard Keynes built on but revolutionized neoclassical economics, he wrote, 'Thomas Kuhn . . . would realize that it takes a generation for new ideas to become part of conventional wisdom. Once again it was a case where, funeral by funeral, science progressed.'[1] Environmental taxation has gone through several generations. The Pigouvian concept of internalizing externalities is now part of mainstream environmental thought; environmental taxation is more commonplace; and research continues to refine our understanding of environmental taxation instruments and their theories, design, implementation, impact and relative role. We hope that this Handbook can contribute to the continued growth of understanding.

---

[1] PAUL A. SAMUELSON, ECONOMICS 845 (10th ed. 1976).

PART I

CONCEPTUAL FOUNDATIONS

2 Introduction to environmental taxation concepts and research

Janet E. Milne and Mikael Skou Andersen

The late twentieth century marked the rise of the use of economic instruments to protect the environment. As later chapters will explore, governments started looking for ways to move beyond 'command-and-control' regulation by also harnessing market forces in a manner that would improve environmental quality. Economic instruments 'affect costs and benefits of alternative actions open to economic agents, with the effect of influencing behavior in a way that is favorable to the environment.'[1] Environmental taxes and permit trading regimes emerged as two dominant approaches.[2] They are called economic instruments because they are founded on economic theories about how adjusting price signals can influence behavior, and they are also called market-based instruments because they operate through the daily workings of the market.

Environmental taxation embodies the concept of using the tax system to adjust prices in a way that will influence behavior in an environmentally positive manner. That relatively simple concept, however, has been supported by different theories at different points in time, and environmental taxation has assumed a wide variety of names and subcategories. This chapter briefly summarizes the evolution of the theories and vocabulary of environmental taxation as the concept of environmental taxation moved from theory to practice, and highlights key developments in research that influenced this evolution.

THE PIGOUVIAN TRADITION AND ITS PROGENY

A.C. Pigou, a professor of political economy at the University of Cambridge in England,[3] laid the intellectual groundwork for environmental taxation in *The Economics of Welfare*, a well-known economics textbook he first published in 1920.[4] As he developed his theories of welfare economics, he analyzed activities to identify divergences between the net

---

[1] OECD, ENVIRONMENTAL POLICY: HOW TO APPLY ECONOMIC INSTRUMENTS 10 (1991); *see also* EUROPEAN ENVIRONMENT AGENCY, USING THE MARKET FOR COST-EFFECTIVE ENVIRONMENTAL POLICY: MARKET-BASED INSTRUMENTS IN EUROPE 13 (2006) (discussing other definitions of 'economic instruments').

[2] Environmentally related taxes range from a few percent and up to 12 percent of total taxes and social contributions in European countries. EUROSTAT, ENVIRONMENTAL STATISTICS AND ACCOUNTS IN EUROPE 332 (2010).

[3] At Cambridge, he was a tutor of Prof. John M. Keynes, who succeeded him.

[4] In his preface to *The Economics of Welfare*, Pigou noted that the book resulted from his efforts to rewrite his earlier book, *Wealth and Welfare* (1912). A.C. PIGOU, THE ECONOMICS OF WELFARE, at v (1920).

benefit or loss incurred by society (the social net product, in his terms) and the net benefit or loss incurred by the private sector entity (the trade net product). In 1920 he wrote:

> It is evident that, in general, industrialists are interested, not in the social, but only in the trade, net product of their operations. Clearly, therefore, there is no reason to expect that self-interest will tend to bring about equality between the values of marginal net social products of investments in different industries when the values of social net product and of trade net product in those industries diverge.[5]

Based on that premise, Pigou explored how both the private sector, on one hand, and neighbors or a broader community, on the other hand, can provide uncompensated services and disservices to the other, yielding divergences between the social net product and the trade net product. Among his examples are the private urban park that offers air quality benefits to the neighbors, rendering an uncompensated service, and conversely, a factory building in an urban residential area that impairs the neighborhood's amenities, yielding disservices.[6] His conclusion set the framework for what is now known as Pigouvian taxation:

> It is plain that divergences between trade and social net product of the kinds we have so far been considering cannot . . . be mitigated by a modification of a contractual relationship between any two contracting parties, because the divergence arises out of a service or disservice rendered to persons other than the contracting parties. *It is, however, possible for the State, if it so chooses, to remove the divergence in any field by 'extraordinary encouragements' or 'extraordinary restraints'* upon investments in that field. The most obvious forms, which these encouragements and restraints may assume, are, of course, those of *bounties and taxes*.[7] (Emphasis added.)

Pigou's approach was sometimes referred to as the tax-bounty[8] or tax-subsidy[9] approach. It was not confined to environmental problems, but using taxation to address environmental divergences was often the example mentioned.

Although Pigou was not the first to consider the role of social costs in economic

---

[5]   PIGOU, *supra* note 4, at 149.

[6]   *Id.* at 160–61.

[7]   *Id.* at 168. The terms 'extraordinary restraints' and 'extraordinary encouragements' may harken back to Adam Smith. In 1776, he used those terms in his book, *The Wealth of Nations*, but he argued against such government intervention. He also referred to 'restraints' and 'bounties.' ADAM SMITH, AN INQUIRY INTO THE NATURE AND CAUSES OF THE WEALTH OF NATIONS 418–19, 650–51 (Edwin Cannan ed., 1937). Paul Samuelson elegantly summarized the 'Pigouvian doctrine' in 1947: 'To Pigou, the problem is not at all one of increasing or decreasing returns; it was only a question as to whether each unit is taking account of its full effect upon social magnitudes (other than prices), or whether it is not. If it is not, and that is all that we mean by external economies, then there is of course need to interfere with the "invisible hand".' PAUL A. SAMUELSON, FOUNDATIONS OF ECONOMIC ANALYSIS 196 (4th prtg. 1955).

[8]   WILLIAM J. BAUMOL, WELFARE ECONOMICS AND THE THEORY OF THE STATE 30 (2nd ed. 1965); MIKAEL SKOU ANDERSEN, GOVERNANCE BY GREEN TAXES: MAKING POLLUTION PREVENTION PAY 37 (1994).

[9]   William J. Baumol & Wallace E. Oates, *The Use of Standards and Prices for Protection of the Environment*, 73 SWEDISH J. ECON., no. 1, 1971, 42–54, at 42 (also available in THE ECONOMICS OF ENVIRONMENT 53–65 (Peter Bohm & Allen V. Kneese eds., 1971) and THE ECONOMICS OF THE ENVIRONMENT 161–73 (Wallace E. Oates ed., 1992)).

analysis,[10] his work provided the intellectual framework for future research about 'externalities,'[11] the term that supplanted his 'services and disservices.' Pigou emphasized the concept of externalities and introduced the idea of using taxes as one way to capture, or internalize, externalities.[12] Reduced to a simplified essence, taxes equal to the externalities could equalize the private and social marginal costs. K. William Kapp's *The Social Costs of Private Enterprise* pioneered the field of environmental externalities in 1950.[13]

Analyses of taxes based on Pigou's theory followed in the 1960s. One of his most ardent critics, Ronald Coase wrote a seminal piece[14] evaluating the 'Pigovian tradition.'[15] He challenged Pigou's assumption that the polluter should always bear the cost of externalities, arguing that in some situations negotiated settlements between the polluter and the victim are preferable,[16] and his challenge sparked detailed theoretical, economic explorations and critiques of the Pigovian tradition.[17] Interestingly, the initial commentators generally did not use the term 'Pigovian tax,' a term that subsequently became more prevalent[18] (and changed to 'Pigouvian'),[19] nor did they refer to 'environmental taxation.'

Although the principle named after Pigou and developed through economists' externality theory called for a tax equal to the negative external environmental costs imposed by a product or activity (or a corresponding subsidy for the positive benefits provided), economists in the early 1970s proposed a theoretically modified application of the Pigouvian approach. This interest came at a time when governments in the United States and Europe were starting to seriously confront environmental problems and weigh the merits of various policy approaches. It was time to determine whether and how to adapt Pigou's concepts to

---

[10]   *See generally* K. WILLIAM KAPP, THE SOCIAL COSTS OF PRIVATE ENTERPRISE 26–40 (1971 ed.).

[11]   *See, e.g.*, PAUL A. SAMUELSON, ECONOMICS 477 n.10 (10th ed. 1976) (citing Pigou as the economist who 'most emphasized the problem of externalities'); David Pearce, *An Intellectual History of Environmental Economics*, 27 ANN. REV. ENERGY ENV'T 57–81, at 58 (2002). Chapter 3 in this Handbook contains a detailed discussion of the economic theory of environmental taxes.

[12]   *See* WILLIAM J. BAUMOL, ENVIRONMENTAL PROTECTION, INTERNAL SPILLOVERS AND TRADE 7 (1971) (discussing Pigou's analysis in *Wealth and Welfare* (1911) of Marshall's externality concept).

[13]   KAPP, *supra* note 10 (first published in 1950); *see also* WILLIAM J. BAUMOL, WELFARE ECONOMICS AND THE THEORY OF THE STATE (2nd ed. 1965) (originally published in 1952). For a discussion of current research on externalities, see Chapter 8 in this Handbook.

[14]   R.H. Coase, *The Problem of Social Cost*, 3 J.L. & ECON. 1–44 (1960).

[15]   *Id.* at 39.

[16]   For a discussion of Coase's theory, see Chapter 22 in this Handbook.

[17]   *E.g.*, James M. Buchanan, *External Diseconomies, Corrective Taxes, and Market Structure*, 59 AM. ECON. REV., no. 1, 1969, 174–77; Otto A. Davis & Andrew Whinston, *Externalities, Welfare and the Theory of Games*, 70 J. POL. ECON., no. 3, 1962, 241–62; D.W. Pearce & S.G. Sturmey, *Private and Social Costs and Benefits: A Note on Terminology*, 76 ECON. J., no. 301, 1966, 152–58; Ralph Turvey, *On Divergences between Social Cost and Private Cost*, 30 ECONOMICA, no. 119, 1963, 309–13. Buchanan also challenged welfare economists to consider the effect of political feasibility on Pigovian solutions. James M. Buchanan, *Politics, Policy, and the Pigovian Margins*, 29 ECONOMICA, no. 113, 1962, 17–28.

[18]   James M. Buchanan and William Craig Stubblebine used 'Pigovian tax' and 'Pigovian solution' in their 1962 article, *Externality*, 29 ECONOMICA, no. 116, 1962, 371–84, at 382. For later references, *see, e.g.*, Baumol & Oates, *supra* note 9, at 42; Agnar Sandmo, *Optimal Taxation in the Presence of Externalities*, 77 SWEDISH J. ECON., no. 1, 1975, 86–98, at 87.

[19]   For example, while Buchanan and Stubblebine referred to a 'Pigovian' tax in 1962, Baumol and Oates used 'Pigouvian' tax in 1971.

real problems. Recognizing the challenge of identifying the monetary values of externalities, as was necessary to set the tax rate for an optimal Pigouvian tax or subsidy, William Baumol and Wallace Oates proposed in 1971 that government instead could determine an acceptable level of pollution and set the tax or subsidy at a level that would achieve that standard, and adjust the tax as necessary over time.[20] They submitted that this approach, when compared with direct regulation, would result in 'least-cost' pollution reduction,[21] a theory of environmental taxation now often referred to as least-cost abatement.

With the interest in converting theory to practice, literature began emerging about how taxes or charges could address specific water and air pollution problems from the perspectives of economics, political economy and environmental science. Analyses did not adopt any consistent terminology—effluent or emissions charges, fees or taxes—but they showed a common interest in exploring the design of taxes and charges and the relative efficiency of regulation and instruments in the Pigouvian tradition.[22]

At the same time, the OECD introduced the polluter-pays principle into the environmental policy arena.[23] The principle charged polluters with the cost of pollution control measures based on two rationales: imposing the cost on polluters would protect against trade distortions that might occur if government subsidized pollution control measures, and it would promote the economically efficient use of resources. As an anti-subsidy principle, it referred specifically to abatement efforts mandated by public authorities and recommended avoiding the use of public subsidies for this purpose. In terms of the efficieny rationale, it did not go so far as to require taxes for emissions, but the OECD's discussion of the polluter-pays principle endorsed the use of a variety of means of imposing the cost of pollution prevention on the polluter, including charges, which would be consistent with the Pigouvian tradition.[24] Today, the OECD cites a concise definition of

---

[20]   Baumol & Oates, *supra* note 9, at 44–45; *see also* William J. Baumol, *On Taxation and the Control of Externalities*, 62 AM. ECON. REV., no. 3, 1972, 207–22.

[21]   Baumol & Oates, *supra* note 9, at 46. In a footnote, the authors indicate that the least-cost proposition had been suggested but not explicitly stated in other literature. *Id.* at 46 n.1.

[22]   *See, e.g.*, RALPH W. JOHNSON & GARDNER M. BROWN, JR., CLEANING UP EUROPE'S WATERS: ECONOMICS MANAGEMENT AND POLICIES (1976) (discussing effluent charges and subsidies in multiple European countries); ALLAN V. KNEESE & BLAIR T. BOWER, MANAGING WATER QUALITY: ECONOMICS, TECHNOLOGY AND INSTITUTIONS (1968) (exploring the use of standards and charges for waste discharge); ALLEN V. KNEESE & CHARLES L. SCHULTZE, POLLUTION, PRICES AND PUBLIC POLICY 87–104 (1975) (discussing water effluent charges, President Nixon's proposal for a sulfur oxides tax, a smog tax); D. EWRINGMANN UND F. SCHAFHAUSEN, ABGABEN ALS ÖKONOMISCHER HEBEL IN DER UMWELTPOLITIK [LEVIES AS AN ECONOMIC INSTRUMENT IN ENVIRONMENTAL POLICY] (1985); CHARLES L. SCHULTZE, THE PUBLIC USE OF PRIVATE INTEREST (1977); Giandomenico Majone, *Choice Among Policy Instruments for Pollution Control*, 2 POL'Y ANALYSIS, no. 4, 1976, 589–613; Susan Rose-Ackerman, *Effluent Charges: A Critique*, 6 CANADIAN J. ECON., no. 4, 1973, 512–28; Larry E. Ruff, *The Economic Common Sense of Pollution*, in ECONOMICS OF THE ENVIRONMENT 20–36 (Dorfman & Dorfman eds., 1993) (originally published in THE PUBLIC INTEREST, no. 19, 1970, 69–85) (exploring how to set prices on pollution); *Tax Recommendations of the President: Hearing Before the Committee on Ways and Means*, 91st Cong. 2d Sess. 369–379 (1970) (written testimony of the Rand Corp. proposing a smog tax).

[23]   OECD, Recommendation of the Council on Guiding Principles Concerning International Economic Aspects of Environmental Policies, Doc. C(72)128 (May 26, 1972), *reprinted in* 11 ILM 1172 (1972).

[24]   OECD, THE POLLUTER PAYS PRINCIPLE 15–16 (1975). 'The principle to be used for allocating

the polluter-pays principle: 'the principle according to which the polluter should bear the cost of measures to reduce pollution according to the extent of either the damage done to society or the exceeding of an acceptable level (standard) of pollution.'[25] In sum, the environmental taxation lexicon today includes the theories of internalizing externalities, achieving least-cost abatement and executing the polluter-pays principle, although each can have different implications for the design of environmental taxes.[26]

Continuing environmental challenges and the decline of planned economies further stimulated thinking about the virtues of market-based approaches. In 1989 the OECD published its first review of international experience with environmental charges[27] and the government of Sweden agreed to a comprehensive tax shift, where new taxes on energy and CO_2 replaced labor taxes,[28] while the German philosopher Ernst Ulrich von Weizsäcker argued the case more generally for environmental tax reform.[29] These developments provided the momentum for deliberations over Pigouvian taxation as a possible alternative to conventional schemes and spurred the debate over competitiveness and a potential 'double dividend,'[30] as discussed later in this chapter. The concept of environmental taxation and green tax reform reached the agendas of decision-makers.[31]

---

costs of pollution prevention and control measure to encourage rational use of scarce environmental resources and to avoid distortions in international trade and investment is the so-called "Polluter-Pays Principle". The Principle means that the polluter should bear the expense of carrying out . . . measures decided by public authorities to ensure that the environment is in an acceptable state. In other words, the cost of these measures should be reflected in the cost of goods and services which cause pollution in production and/or consumption. Such measures should not be accompanied by subsidies that would create significant distortions in international trade and investment.' *Id.* at 12 (Principle 4, Annex to Recommendation to the Council, Guiding, 1972). An OECD note accompanying the definition states that the principle may be implemented by various means, including the levying of pollution charges. *Id.* at 16 (Note on the Implementation of the Polluter-Pays Principle).

[25] OECD Glossary of Statistical Terms, *available at* http://stats.oecd.org/glossary/detail. asp?ID=2074.

[26] Janet E. Milne, *Environmental Taxation: Why Theory Matters, in* 1 CRITICAL ISSUES IN ENVIRONMENTAL TAXATION: INTERNATIONAL AND COMPARATIVE PERSPECTIVES 3–26 (Janet Milne et al. eds., 2003).

[27] J.B. OPSCHOOR & HANS B. VOS, ECONOMIC INSTRUMENTS FOR ENVIRONMENTAL PROTECTION 9 (1989).

[28] Thomas Sterner, *Environmental Tax Reform: The Swedish Experience,* 4 EURO. ENV'T, no. 6, 1994, 20–25.

[29] Ernst U. von Weizsäcker, *Regulatory Reform And The Environment: The Cause For Environmental Taxes, in* DEREGULATION OR RE-REGULATION?: REGULATORY REFORM IN EUROPE AND THE UNITED STATES 198–210 (Giandomenico Majone ed., 1990); ERNST U. VON WEIZSÄCKER, ERDPOLITIK: ÖKOLOGISCHE REALPOLITIK AN DER SCHWELLE ZUM JAHRHUNDERT DER UMWELT [ECOLOGICAL POLITICS AT THE THRESHOLD TO THE CENTURY OF THE ENVIRONMENT] (1990); ERNST U. VON WEIZSÄCKER & JOCHEN JESINGHAUS, ECOLOGICAL TAX REFORM: A POLICY PROPOSAL FOR SUSTAINABLE DEVELOPMENT (1992).

[30] David Pearce, *The Role of Carbon Taxes in Adjusting to Global Warming,* 101 ECON. J., no. 704, 1990, 938–48; *see also* Michael Porter, *America's Green Strategy,* 264 SCI. AM., no. 4, 1991, 168 (submitting that environmental regulation with economic instruments can enhance competitiveness); ECOTAXATION (Timothy O'Riordan ed., 1997) (discussing the double dividend debate).

[31] *See* EUROPEAN ENVIRONMENT AGENCY, ENVIRONMENTAL TAXES: IMPLEMENTATION AND ENVIRONMENTAL EFFECTIVENESS (1996); OECD, ENVIRONMENTAL TAXES AND GREEN TAX REFORM (1997).

THE CHALLENGE OF DEFINING 'ENVIRONMENTAL TAX'

As interest in and use of the economic instruments increased during the 1980s and 1990s, a debate emerged over how various instruments should be categorized. Although the term 'Pigouvian tax' remained in circulation, few if any taxes truly earned the name, given the difficulty of designing and enacting the optimal Pigouvian tax. Nevertheless, under the least-cost abatement theory and the polluter-pays principle, second-best taxes could still have significant environmental attributes and warrant recognition as legitimate environmental economic instruments. The challenge was where to draw the line. Which taxes would qualify under the label of 'environmental'—only the classical taxes on emissions and pollutants, or also taxes on resources, products and raw materials? In addition, the environmental attributes of a tax could relate to the environmentally positive behavioral impact of the tax, the environmentally damaging nature of the tax base (the commodity or activity subject to the tax), whether the revenue from the tax was used to address the environmental problem associated with the tax base, or simply the name of the tax or charge. The need to define environmental policy instruments increased as institutions started investing significant effort in surveying and evaluating the use of economic instruments in general and environmental tax instruments in particular.[32]

Whereas much of the early literature simply referred to emissions or effluent charges, Ralph Johnson and Gardner Brown[33] introduced a useful distinction between what they termed 'user charges' and 'effluent charges.' While payment for a service rendered, such as wastewater treatment, involves a user charge, the term 'effluent charge' refers to a case where a financial payment is due for a discharge or emission regardless of any public abatement effort, simply for making use of the environment as a sink. The latter case is the one that usually is understood in the economics literature to represent the principle of Pigouvian taxation.

Europeans on the continent tend to use the term 'levies' to denote the economic instruments used in environmental management (in Dutch, 'heffingen'; in German, 'abgaben'; in French, 'redevances'). European countries, notably those with schisms between upstream and downstream polluters, had in the post–World War II period prepared payment schemes for emissions that both differed from conventional user charges and implied financial penalties for using the environment as a sink for emissions. Administrated by regional and often task-specific authorities, they provided a financial basis for pollution control activities. While these schemes have been subject to some attention in the literature,[34] they are not conventional taxes. Public services are in fact provided in return for the earmarked payments, which are recycled for pollution abatement.

---

[32]   See Chapter 18 in this Handbook.

[33]   RALPH W. JOHNSON & GARDNER M. BROWN, JR., CLEANING UP EUROPE'S WATERS: ECONOMICS, MANAGEMENT AND POLICIES 14 (1976).

[34]   K. Holm, *Wasserverbände im internationalen Vergleich: Eine ökonomische Analyse der französichen Agences Financières de Bassin und der deutschen Wasserverbände im Ruhrgebiet [Water agencies in international comparison: An economic analysis of the French and German Water Agencies]*, IFO STUDIES IN ENVIRONMENTAL ECONOMICS 3 (Information and Research (IFO) Institute for Economic Research, 1988).

As the leader in globally oriented assessments of economic policies,[35] the OECD became a key arbiter in the definitional arena of economic instruments for the environment. A 1984 conference was its first initiative.[36] In line with the existing academic literature, its early surveys tended to refer to charges and to categorize the charges according to their design characteristics, such as emissions charges, user charges and product charges.[37] At the same time it grappled with the definitional relevance of the intent behind the tax or charge—whether it was intended to operate as a behavioral incentive or to raise revenue—and the actual environmental effect of the tax, but no clear cut categories emerged.[38]

In 1997 the European Union's Eurostat, along with the European Commission's Tax Directorate (DG TAXUD), joined the OECD and the International Energy Agency in an attempt to solve the dilemma. They chose to focus on the nature of the tax base— what was being taxed—rather than the environmental intent or effect of the tax. They defined an environmental tax as a 'tax whose tax base is a physical unit (or a proxy of it) of something that has a proven specific negative effect on the environment.'[39] On the basis of this definition Eurostat published a detailed guideline for the operational accounting of revenues from such taxes, dividing them into four basic categories: energy (including carbon), transport, pollution and natural resources. The United Nations subsequently integrated this definition into the System of National Accounts as the System of Environmental-Economic Accounting (the SEEA).[40]

The OECD, however, favors a slightly different terminology and has adopted the term 'environmentally related taxes.' Incorporating the traditional definition of a tax, it defines an environmentally related tax as 'any compulsory, *unrequited* payment to general government levied on tax-bases deemed to be of particular environmental relevance. Taxes are unrequited in the sense that benefits provided by government to taxpayers are not normally in proportion to their payments.'[41]

---

[35]   *See* OECD, GREEN TAX REFORM, *supra* note 31, at 13–14 (describing OECD's environmental taxation programs during the 1990s).

[36]   OPSCHOOR & VOS, *supra* note 27, at 9 (referencing the 1984 Conference on 'Environment and Economics').

[37]   OECD, EVALUATING ECONOMIC INSTRUMENTS FOR ENVIRONMENTAL POLICY 16 (1997); OPSCHOOR & VOS, *supra* note 27, at 14–15; OECD, MANAGING THE ENVIRONMENT: THE ROLE OF ECONOMIC INSTRUMENTS 18–19 (1994). The European Environment Agency, however, took a different definitional tack, preferring in 1996 to use the overarching term 'environmental taxes' rather than 'charges,' which covered cost-covering charges, incentive taxes and revenue-driven fiscal environmental taxes. EUROPEAN ENVIRONMENT AGENCY, ENVIRONMENTAL TAXES, *supra* note 31, at 8.

[38]   OECD, ENVIRONMENTAL TAXES IN THE OECD COUNTRIES 7 (1995); OECD, MANAGING THE ENVIRONMENT, *supra* note 37, at 19; *see also* EUROPEAN ENVIRONMENT AGENCY, USING THE MARKET FOR COST-EFFECTIVE ENVIRONMENTAL POLICY 5 (2006) (focusing on design intent).

[39]   EUROSTAT, ENVIRONMENTAL TAXES: A STATISTICAL GUIDE, LUXEMBOURG 9 (2001).

[40]   STATISTICS SWEDEN & EUROSTAT, REVISION OF SEEA 2003: OUTCOME PAPER: ENVIRONMENTAL TAXES (2008), *available at* http://unstats.un.org/unsd/envaccounting/londongroup/meeting14/LG14_18a.pdf.

[41]   OECD, ENVIRONMENTALLY RELATED TAXES IN OECD COUNTRIES 15 (2001). Earlier formulations of the definition of 'environmental taxes' can be found in OECD, GREEN TAX REFORM, *supra* note 31, at 18, and OECD, ENVIRONMENTAL TAXES: RECENT DEVELOPMENTS IN CHINA AND OECD COUNTRIES 26 (1999).

By focusing on unrequited payments, the definition excludes charges and fees paid to the government for services, such as waste removal and treatment fees. A charge or levy that is an unrequited payment may, despite its name, qualify as an 'environmentally related tax.' As a general rule, a payment should be classified as a tax if no link between the payment and the service rendered can be established, or if the revenue is much larger than the costs of providing the service in question. This Handbook uses the term 'environmental taxes' to mean 'environmentally related taxes,' but its editors recognize that there can be a faint line between taxes and other levies, depending upon how one interprets 'unrequited.'[42]

There are various ways to categorize environmentally related taxes, depending on whether one focuses on the design of the tax or its purpose. When focusing on design, the taxes are often classified as

- emissions and effluent taxes;
- product taxes; and
- natural resource taxes.[43]

The distinction between the first and the second is that the first taxes the emissions directly, while the second taxes products that are likely to generate environmental damage in their manufacture or use. Although some studies include natural resource taxes in the category of product taxes,[44] the difference in the rationales for the two types of taxes would seem to warrant separate categories. Product taxes attach a price to pollution while natural resource taxes place a price on the use of scarce natural resources. Each presents a different social value, although both will serve the ultimate end of environmental protection.

Alternatively, one can classify environmentally related taxes according to their relative environmental and fiscal function, such as

- incentive environmental taxes, which can also be called regulatory taxes;
- financing environmental taxes; and
- fiscal environmental taxes.[45]

The first is driven by its environmental impact, the second by its ability to finance an environmental measure, and the third primarily by the demand for revenue. One can also classify taxes as either independent or complementary by evaluating their role relative to other instruments.[46]

---

[42]   *See* OECD, Revenue Statistics 1965–2007, 311–12 (2008). The Merriam Webster Online Dictionary defines unrequited as 'not reciprocated or returned in kind.'

[43]   *See* OECD, The Use of Economic Instruments for Pollution Control and Natural Resource Management in EECCA 14, 50 (2003).

[44]   OECD, Evaluating Economic Instruments, *supra* note 37, at 16.

[45]   Kalle Määttä, Environmental Taxes 19–20 (2006). Stephen Smith has taken a hybrid of the two approaches above, using 'measured emissions taxes,' 'the use of other taxes to approximate a tax on emissions,' and 'non-incentive taxes.' Stephen Smith, *Environmental Tax Design, in* Ecotaxation 21–36, at 23 (Timothy O'Riordan ed., 1997).

[46]   Määttä, *supra* note 45, at 23.

Classifications such as these are useful for drawing attention to different features and functions of environmentally related taxes. The Pigouvian tax reflecting marginal social cost was conceived to internalize environmental burdens in the economy by providing incentives. A Baumol and Oates' standard-driven, second-best tax would qualify as an incentive (regulatory) emissions tax. Still, some environmental taxes have been introduced simply to finance specific schemes to provide relief from the environmental burdens of water, air and waste pollution. These taxes sometimes fall between the two main categories of fiscal and incentive taxes, constituting financing environmental taxes—occasionally hypothecated for predefined purposes. They are not user charges, because the revenues contribute toward a common good of pollution abatement, rather than an individual service provision of garbage collection or wastewater treatment.[47]

These classifications illustrate how current research in the field extends beyond conventional fiscal taxes, and how different disciplines may focus on different issues as they classify and evaluate taxes. The distinction between fiscal taxes and financing taxes is one that preoccupies public finance experts. Others may focus on the financing versus incentive distinction. Conventional taxes are understood as revenue-raising fiscal taxes, but the innovative feature of environmentally related taxes is that they are supposed to alter behavior in addition to raising revenues. Some tax lawyers, for instance, have been concerned that basic principles of equal standing under the law could be violated when economic instruments are used to change behavior.[48] Many economists on the other hand would expect any tax to influence behavior, whatever purpose it serves.

To add another layer to the vocabulary of environmental taxation, environmental taxes are often known by other names in political discourse and research, such as green taxes, green fees and ecotaxes. Under the internationally agreed-upon approach, however, the nature of the tax base should prevail over the name when deciding whether to admit a tax, fee or charge into the category of environmentally related taxes. The remaining differences in what Eurostat and the OECD will classify as an environmentally related tax underline the need for further attention and research on terminology issues.[49]

---

[47]   Wallace E. Oates, *Review*, 34 J. ECON. LIT., no. 2, 1996, 815–17, dubs this an Andersen tax. *Cf.* Jukka Pirttilä, *Earmarking of Environmental Taxes and Pareto-Efficient Taxation*, 56 PUB. FIN. ANALYSIS (FINANZARCHIV) 202–17 (1999); Tingsong Jiang, *Earmaking of Pollution Charges and the Sub-Optimality of the Pigouvian Tax*, 45 AUSTRALIAN J. AGRIC. & RES. ECON. 623–40 (2002).

[48]   UMWELTSCHUTZ IM ABGABEN- UND STEUERRECHT [ENVIRONMENTAL PROTECTION IN LEVY AND TAX LAW] (Kirchhof ed., 1993).

[49]   For instance, Eurostat does not consider the German wastewater tax (Abwasserabgabe) as an environmental tax, whereas the OECD does. Its revenues are hypothecated for Länder-level (regional) EPA's.

ENVIRONMENTAL TAXES IN BROADER FISCAL FRAMEWORKS

As environmental taxes emerged as a realistic environmental policy instrument in the 1980s and 1990s, researchers and then policymakers began to address them seriously in the broader fiscal context. They first focused primarily on how revenues from significant, broad-based environmental taxes, such as energy or carbon taxes, could be used to reduce other tax burdens. For example, in 1984 David Terkla published an early exploration of the efficiency of substituting revenues from air pollution taxes for labor or corporate income taxes.[50] As mentioned above, Ernst Ulrich von Weizsäcker proposed environmental tax reform in the late 1980s and early 1990s. In 1991, David Pearce coined the term 'double dividend' for this revenue-neutral approach when he wrote about carbon taxes:

> Governments may then adopt a fiscally neutral stance on the carbon tax, using revenues to finance reductions in incentive-distorting taxes such as income tax, or corporation tax. This 'double dividend' feature of a pollution tax is of critical importance in the political debate about the means of securing a 'carbon convention.'[51]

The double dividend concept has spawned a field of economic literature debating the validity and extent of the double dividend under various circumstances.[52] The first dividend refers to the environmental impact of the environmental tax and the second to the economic impact of the use of the tax revenues, but researchers can define the second dividend differently. The OECD has observed that European authors tend to concentrate on an increase in employment while American authors focus on reductions in distortionary taxes.[53]

As the economists' debate was occurring, policymakers pursued the concept of revenue-neutral tax reform that could use environmental tax revenues to reduce other tax burdens. For example, the so-called Delors White Paper on Growth, Competitiveness and Employment looked to environmental taxes as one way to reduce labor taxes,[54] and in the early- to mid-1990s several northern European countries enacted revenue-neutral tax reforms.[55] The revenue-neutral approach is often referred to as 'green tax reform,'[56]

---

[50]   David Terkla, *The Efficiency Value of Effluent Tax Revenues*, 11 J. ENVTL. ECON. & MGMT. 107–23 (1984).

[51]   Pearce, *supra* note 30, at 938, 940.

[52]   For a discussion of the double dividend theory, see Chapter 12 in this Handbook.

[53]   OECD, GREENING TAX MIXES IN OECD COUNTRIES: A PRELIMINARY ASSESSMENT 7, 17 (2000).

[54]   Commission of the European Communities, *White Paper on Growth, Competitiveness, Employment: The Challenges and Ways Forward into the 21st Century*, at 141, COM(1993) 700 final (Dec. 5, 1993).

[55]   *See, e.g.*, NORDIC COUNCIL OF MINISTERS, THE USE OF ECONOMIC INSTRUMENTS IN NORDIC ENVIRONMENTAL POLICY (1997); OECD, GREEN TAX REFORM, *supra* note 31, at 22–28. Several countries established green tax commissions. *See* OECD, GREEN TAX REFORM, *supra* note 31; GREEN TAXES: ECONOMIC THEORY AND EMPIRICAL EVIDENCE FROM SCANDINAVIA (Runar Brännlund & Ing-Marie Gren eds., 1999) (containing chapters on green tax commissions in Denmark, Norway and Sweden).

[56]   *See, e.g.*, EUROPEAN ENVIRONMENT AGENCY, ENVIRONMENTAL TAXES, *supra* note 31, at 25; OECD, GREENING TAX MIXES, *supra* note 53, at 3, 15 (also using the terms 'tax shift' and 'ecologi-

'environmental tax reform,'[57] 'ecological tax reform'[58] or a 'tax shift.'[59] While the term 'double dividend' focuses attention on the environmental and economic benefits of the tax adjustments, these terms highlight the revenue-neutrality and tax-reform aspects of the policy packages.

As analysis of the role of environmental taxation in policy packages developed, it grew beyond revenue-neutral tax reform. A broader framework, usually referred to as 'environmental fiscal reform' or 'ecological fiscal reform,'[60] drew in the issue of subsidy reform. Given that environmental taxes were intended to correct for the market's failure to recognize the cost of environmental damage or resource use, it was quite logical for researchers and policy analysts to look at the other side of the coin and consider whether government should repeal subsidies, such as spending programs or tax incentives, for environmentally harmful activities.[61] Recently, climate change has focused international attention on the problem of environmentally damaging subsidies and the benefits of their repeal.[62] As explained in Chapter 1, this Handbook does not cover in detail the issue of subsidy repeal, but that omission is not meant to diminish its significance or the significance of environmental fiscal reform.

Environmental fiscal reform can also evaluate the use of environmentally related charges that are not technically taxes. The OECD and the World Bank have defined environmental fiscal reform broadly as 'a range of taxation and pricing measures that can raise fiscal revenues while furthering environmental goals.'[63] Full-cost pricing for water services (including waste water) is one element that could contribute to this broader goal, as user fees in many countries are too low to match incurred investments and operational costs. In sum, green tax reform can be a component of environmental fiscal reform, but

---

cal tax reforms'); OECD, OECD ENVIRONMENTAL STRATEGY FOR THE FIRST DECADE OF THE 21ST CENTURY 8 (2001).

[57] *See, e.g.*, CARBON-ENERGY TAXATION: LESSONS FROM EUROPE (Mikael Skou Andersen & Paul Ekins eds., 2009).

[58] EUROPEAN ENVIRONMENT AGENCY, ENVIRONMENTAL TAXES: RECENT DEVELOPMENTS IN TOOLS FOR INTEGRATION 20 (2000); VON WEIZSÄCKER & JESINGHAUS, *supra* note 29; MICHAEL KOHLHAAS, ECOLOGICAL TAX REFORM IN GERMANY: FROM THEORY TO POLICY (2000).

[59] *See, e.g.*, ALAN THEIN DURNING & YORAM BAUMAN, TAX SHIFT (1998).

[60] *See, e.g.*, Allan Howatson, *Ecological Fiscal Reform*, The Conference Board of Canada, Report 166-96 (1996); GREEN BUDGET REFORM IN EUROPE (Kai Schlegelmilch ed., 1999).

[61] Some of the early research on environmental fiscal reform can be found in HANS G. NUTZINGER & ANGELIKA ZAHRNT, FÜR EINE ÖKOLOGISCHE STEUERREFORM [TOWARDS AN ECOLOGICAL TAX REFORM] (1990); VON WEIZSÄCKER & JESINGHAUS, *supra* note 29, at 21–22; ROBERT REPETTO ET AL., GREEN FEES: HOW A TAX SHIFT CAN WORK FOR THE ENVIRONMENT AND THE ECONOMY (1992); European Commission, Taxation, Social Security Systems and Environment: Fiscal Reform for More Employment (1993); Allan Howatson, *supra* note 60; GREEN BUDGET REFORM: AN INTERNATIONAL CASEBOOK OF LEADING PRACTICES (Gale et al. eds., 1995).

[62] *See, e.g.*, INTERNATIONAL ENERGY AGENCY, OECD & THE WORLD BANK, THE SCOPE OF FOSSIL-FUEL SUBSIDIES IN 2009 AND A ROADMAP FOR PHASING OUT FOSSIL-FUEL SUBSIDIES (2010) (a joint report prepared for the G-20 Summit in November 2010); *see also* OECD, INVENTORY OF ESTIMATED BUDGETARY SUPPORT AND TAX EXPENDITURES FOR FOSSIL FUELS (2011) (compiling data on a variety of support measures in 24 countries).

[63] OECD, ENVIRONMENTAL FISCAL REFORM FOR POVERTY REDUCTION 12 (2005); THE WORLD BANK, ENVIRONMENTAL FISCAL REFORM: WHAT SHOULD BE DONE AND HOW TO ACHIEVE IT 1 (2005).

BOX 2.1　DEFINITIONS OF SOME KEY TERMS IN ENVIRONMENTAL TAX POLICY

The **polluter-pays principle** is 'the principle according to which the polluter should bear the cost of measures to reduce pollution according to the extent of either the damage done to society or the exceeding of an acceptable level (standard) of pollution.' OECD Glossary of Statistical Terms, *available at* http://stats.oecd.org/glossary/detail.asp?ID=2074.

An **environmentally related tax** is 'any compulsory, *unrequited* payment to general government levied on tax-bases deemed to be of particular environmental relevance. Taxes are unrequited in the sense that benefits provided by government to taxpayers are not normally in proportion to their payments.' OECD, Environmentally Related Taxes in OECD Countries 15 (2001).

Environmental tax reform (ETR) 'is a reform of the national tax system where there is a shift of the burden of taxation from conventional taxes, for example on labour, to environmentally damaging activities, such as resource use or pollution. The burden of taxes should fall more on "bads" than "goods" so that appropriate signals are given to consumers and producers and the tax burdens across the economy are better distributed from a sustainable development perspective. The economic rationale is that welfare gains are generated by reducing taxes on labour or capital and increasing taxes on externalities and hence helping to avoid "welfare-reducing" activities.' European Environment Agency, Market-based Instruments for Environmental Policy in Europe 84 (2005).

Environmental fiscal reform (EFR) 'is a broader approach, which focuses not just on shifting taxes and tax burdens, but also on reforming economically motivated subsidies, some of which are harmful to the environment and may have outlived their rationale . . . . EFR is a more recent development than ETR and offers more opportunities for progress, and is more in line with the "polluter pays" principle and the concept of sustainable development.' European Environment Agency, Market-based Instruments for Environmental Policy in Europe 84 (2005).

---

environmental fiscal reform looks as well at the government's direct and indirect spending decisions—the larger fiscal framework.

BOUNTIES AND ENVIRONMENTAL TAX EXPENDITURES

The Pigouvian tradition is famous for Pigou's extraordinary restraints, which laid the theoretical foundation for environmental taxes, but in his paragraph about restraints (quoted above), Pigou also referred to extraordinary encouragements, such as bounties for the activities that generate otherwise uncompensated benefits for society. Although he did not provide details about tax subsidies that could serve as 'bounties,' his analysis raises the conceptual issue of the relative role of taxes (restraints) and subsidies (bounties), and the role of tax preferences within the sphere of subsidies.

Subsidies in general are not without controversy. Baumol and Oates have cautioned against the use of subsidies compared with taxes,[64] and the decline of Keynesianism and state intervention toward the closing of the twentieth century has generally served to cool interest in offering subsidies. For environmental policy purposes the polluter-pays principle suggests that it is better to abstain from subsidies, so as not to initiate a 'race to the bottom' to relieve polluters from their responsibilities and distort the terms of competition in free trade. From a taxation perspective the main problem is that for subsidies to be offered, offsetting taxes will have to be raised, and taxes are likely to be distorting to the economy (a deadweight loss arises)—unless the tax base refers either to externalities or to land use.[65]

In the 1930s, when Pigou's *Economics of Welfare* was a standard textbook in universities, subsidies were regarded with less skepticism, but public finance scholars have established that subsidies have undesirable side effects in the same way as many taxes do.[66] For example, paying out bounties for renewable energy may create unwanted side effects such as maintaining uncompetitive producers and yielding excess profits. To maintain support beyond the promotion phase of new technologies, it would be regarded as more preferable to tax the external costs of fossil fuels, such as carbon and air pollution, thereby providing a measured and indirect advantage to renewables according to their environmental properties (biofuels for instance also imply burdens of air pollutants and would be subject to tax according to those burdens). The problem is that what is desirable from an environmental economics perspective is often not a feasible option in the policy process.

In the past decades policymakers have become fond of an innovative and less transparent approach to subsidizing, based on modulations in tax systems. Special tax exemptions, deductions, credits or lower tax rates that reduce the cost of environmentally positive activities are being introduced. Frequently presented as targeted 'tax cuts,' they are in reality expenditures, often off-budget, that also have implications for budgets and tax bases.

As in the case of environmental taxes, finding the best vocabulary for these tax bounties or encouragements is somewhat challenging. The term 'tax incentive' is accurate because it conveys the fact that the benefit should serve as a behavioral incentive, but it is potentially confusing because environmental taxes also create environmentally positive incentives by imposing a cost. The term 'tax subsidy' captures the fact that government is providing a benefit, but it does not necessarily require that the benefit induce behavior that would not otherwise occur. Stanley Surrey took a different approach in 1967, coining the term 'tax expenditures' for tax benefits that deviate from neutral principles of

---

[64] WILLIAM J. BAUMOL & WALLACE E. OATES, THE THEORY OF ENVIRONMENTAL POLICY 211–34 (2d ed. 1988).

[65] W.J. MCCLUSKEY & R. FRANZSEN, LAND VALUE TAXATION: AN APPLIED ANALYSIS (2005); J. Backhaus, The Quest for Ecological Tax Reform: A Schumpeterian Approach to Public Finance (1995) (paper prepared for the Fifth Conference of the International J.A. Schumpeter Society).

[66] D. BEGG, S. FISCHER & R. DORNBUSCH, ECONOMICS (1991); R. PERMAN, Y. MA, J. MCGILVRAY & M. COMMON, NATURAL RESOURCE AND ENVIRONMENTAL ECONOMICS (1999).

taxation.[67] This term highlights the fact that government in effect expends public funds when it provides tax benefits. It foregoes revenues it otherwise would receive, accomplishing potentially the same result it could have achieved if it had obtained revenues and then disbursing them through spending programs. The tax-expenditure approach 'produce[s] an expenditure system described in tax language.'[68] Surrey's term applies to all forms of tax subsidies, not just those that are environmental in nature.

This Handbook tends to use the term 'tax expenditure' to describe these environmental tax benefits. It is not a perfect term because it does not convey the positive environmental incentive effect, but it is the term customarily used in tax realms, and its use in environmental tax policy research and debate can help integrate the disciplines of environmental protection and taxation. Because environmental tax expenditures send price signals and are being used by governments, this Handbook includes them in the sphere of environmental tax policy. These, instruments, however, would benefit from more research in the future.

Theoretical debate about tax expenditures in the tax literature has revolved in part around the question of whether government should provide subsidies through direct spending programs, which are subject to the governmental appropriations process, rather than through tax expenditures, which circumvent the appropriations process.[69] This fundamental choice-of-instrument question, which is not unique to environmental tax expenditures, involves theoretical and practical issues of public finance and political economy and has rightfully haunted the tax expenditure debate for decades. In the environmental tax context in particular, the debate also involves the question of whether to use tax increases rather than some form of subsidy (direct or though tax expenditures). Environmental taxes have maintained a center-stage position in environmental economists' tax theory, and direct budget subsidies have received more attention than tax expenditures.[70] Environmental economists have bestowed comparatively little theoretical attention to the potential economic properties of using tax expenditures, even though tax expenditures could be grounded on Pigou's less-touted notion of extraordinary encouragements and governments are harnessing them.

From a variety of policy perspectives, there is often a natural tension between imposing the cost of environmental protection on polluters by applying a tax and imposing the cost on society by offering tax benefits as an incentive to avoid pollution.[71] In situations where government has a choice, it will have to decide who will bear the cost of environmental protection—the polluter or the general public. With tax expenditures tapping revenue

---

[67] STANLEY S. SURREY, PATHWAYS TO TAX REFORM: THE CONCEPT OF TAX EXPENDITURES, at vii, 3–4 (1973).

[68] *Id.* at 3.

[69] Stanley Surrey triggered and stated the basic elements of this debate in his book. *See id.* at 126–54. The same chapter also discusses the alternative of using regulatory taxes and, in particular pollution taxes. *Id.* at 155–74. For references to some of the tax expenditure literature and a discussion of the use of environmental tax expenditures relative to direct spending in the US, see Janet E. Milne, *U.S. Climate Policy: A Tax Expenditure Microcosm with Environmental Dimensions, in* TAX EXPENDITURES: STATE OF THE ART 9:1 (Lisa Philipps, Neil Brooks and Jinyan Li eds., 2011).

[70] *E.g.*, BAUMOL & OATES, *supra* note 64, at 211–34.

[71] Staff of Joint Comm. on Taxation, 111th Cong., Tax Expenditures for Energy Production and Conservation 113–15 (Comm. Print 2009).

potential, other taxes have to be raised to a higher level if the loss is to be offset. One resolution might be to use environmental taxes to fund environmental tax expenditures,[72] thereby avoiding shifting the cost of tax expenditures to society and keeping it on the polluter. Pigou's examples of extraordinary encouragements involved situations that may have minimized the conflict over who pays, such as when government supported town planning:[73] no offending party was present to absorb the cost and the benefit was not otherwise likely to be compensated. These important cost-allocation decisions, which warrant more research, are made at the political level and sometimes are shaped by legal rules.[74]

As indicated above, literature about environmental fiscal reform has explicitly targeted the elimination of environmentally damaging subsidies, such as tax expenditures that support the production and use of fossil fuels, but it has hardly focused on the use of environmentally positive tax expenditures, such as the California program for wind power that in the 1980s opened a market for wind energy producers at a time critical to the industry.[75] The OECD and World Bank's definition of environmental fiscal reform, quoted above, limits environmental fiscal reform to green measures that would raise revenue, implicitly ruling out environmentally positive tax expenditures as a component of environmental fiscal reform. These tax expenditures, however, can fit under the rubric of environmental fiscal reform if the reform is viewed more broadly as the full range of ways to revise the fiscal system in order to enhance environmental protection.

TRADABLE ALLOWANCE REGIMES ARE NOT TAXES

Political rhetoric sometimes refers to tradable emissions allowances as taxes, as happened for example following the recent adoption of a cap-and-trade scheme for carbon in Australia. Allowances can share common features with environmental taxes, particularly if they are auctioned by the government rather than distributed without cost. They impose a cost on polluters, and they may generate revenue for government.

The differences between environmental taxes and tradable allowances, however, are also very marked. First, taxes establish a fixed cost for polluters, while the cost of traded allowances fluctuates according to market demand. Second, allowances do not impose a cost when they are not fully or even partially auctioned, as can happen when emissions are 'grandfathered' and awarded free allowances. Free allocation of allowances creates an implied transfer of a windfall rent to holders of these allowances that can be substantial. Under the EU's emissions trading scheme for carbon these transfers were sufficient in some member states to neutralize the desired market signal from placing a price on carbon in the first place. Moreover, under a grandfathered emissions trading scheme

---

[72]   MARTIN ENEVOLDSEN, THE THEORY OF ENVIRONMENTAL TAXES AND AGREEMENTS 109 (2005).

[73]   PIGOU, *supra* note 4, at 169.

[74]   See Chapter 4 in this Handbook for a discussion of the European Commission's state aid rules defining circumstances in which member states can use environmentally positive subsidies, European Council, Community Guidelines on State Aid for Environmental Protection, 2008 O.J. (C 82) 1–33.

[75]   PAUL GIPE, WIND ENERGY COMES OF AGE 31, 36, 50 (1995).

no revenues will be available to offset other distorting taxes, and so trading has been shown to be theoretically less efficient than a revenue-neutral environmental tax reform, which replaces a distorting tax with a non-distorting environmental tax internalizing externalities.[76]

The two approaches also differ in their theoretical basis. The theoretical roots of tradable schemes are with the so-called Coase theorem, which shows that no matter whether the polluter or the taxpayer (victim) is held responsible, it is possible to obtain an efficient solution by instituting a compensation scheme, absent transaction costs. Coase warned that the transaction costs of instituting Pigouvian taxes could be so high as to make environmental taxes rather inefficient.[77] He recommended simply defining property rights for the various commons and then allowing polluters and victims to bargain so as to achieve an optimal solution. Issuing tradable allowances is one way of defining property rights and enabling markets. Thus, the trading system operates through a property-based approach quite different from the tax approach. Unfortunately there has been little research to date that explores and compares systematically the transaction costs of the two main approaches to pricing of environmental stocks and flows.

The comparison of the tax and trading approaches also highlights the question of who pays. Under the polluter-pays principle, it is the polluter who pays, while with a victim-pays principle, taxpayers or neighbors will be compensating the polluter for abatement efforts. Environmental taxes can implement the polluter-pays principle. When the tradable allowances are not auctioned, the property rights are handed out for free and the associated loss of rents and revenues implies implementation of a 'victim-pays' principle. With auctioning, the polluter-pays principle is maintained, generating revenues that become available for wider fiscal reform.

Under traditional analysis and for the purposes of this book, tradable allowance schemes lie beyond the boundaries of the field of environmental taxation. Unlike taxes, they do not impose a set price, which is a traditional hallmark of a tax. In addition, they are usually not subject to the legal rules that govern taxation, such as the European Union's requirement that European-wide tax proposals must receive the unanimous consent of the member states. As will be seen in other chapters of this book,[78] the topic of tradable emissions allowances is nonetheless highly relevant to environmental taxation in the choice-of-instrument context. If governments want to use a market-based instrument to impose a cost on polluters, they often will consider whether to use an environmental tax or a trading regime, or both.

CONCLUSION

The chapters that follow in this Handbook explore a wealth of issues and future research needs relating to the concepts and evolution of environmental taxation surveyed here.

---

[76] Ian Parry, *Pollution Taxes and Revenue Recycling*, 29 J. ENVTL. ECON. & MGMT., no. 3, 1995, S64–S77.

[77] R.H. COASE, THE FIRM, THE MARKET AND THE LAW (1988).

[78] *See* Chapters 3, 22 and 23.

Hence these concluding remarks focus on issues that relate to the vocabulary of environmental taxation and the relationships among the components of environmental taxation described above.

The vocabulary of environmental tax policy raises several research issues for the future. It would be useful to explore in more detail the legal and practical consequences of the definitional distinctions among fees, charges and taxes and whether the definition of environmentally related taxes may inadvertently de-emphasize the potential environmental impact of charges and user fees. Several chapters in this book illuminate these questions, with new perspectives offered from Spanish literature for instance.[79] One of the purposes of this Handbook is to provide researchers with insights into a broader diversity of approaches than is normally considered in individual national contexts.

Given the significance of the issue of who pays for environmental protection—the polluters through taxes or society through direct subsidies, tax expenditures or grandfathered allowances—it will be important in the future to research in greater depth the relationship between these different approaches to a classic dilemma. For instance, as discussed earlier in this chapter, environmentally related taxes and non-tax subsidies have been explored more thoroughly in economic theory than have environmental tax expenditures. In particular, research might identify more clearly the specific situations in which one is more theoretically and pragmatically appropriate or environmentally effective than the other, drawing on the growing body of experience with environmental tax expenditures in many nations. This research can help guide the use of environmental tax expenditures and identify their place, if any, in environmental fiscal reform.

As trading regimes continue to evolve, it may be useful to revisit the question of whether certain trading programs should be incorporated into discussions of taxes if they start assuming tax-like features or fall within the jurisdiction of tax authorities. For example, some proposals for carbon trading regimes currently call for design features that limit the fluctuation in the market price of the tradable allowances; they strive to capture some of the benefit of the consistent, predictable price signal that comes with a carbon tax. When the legislative proposals call for auctioning all the allowances, they have been referred on at least one occasion to a tax-writing legislative committee as a 'revenue measure.'[80]

The survey of concepts and vocabulary in this chapter attempts to capture some of the key and more prevailing definitions and explain their relationship to each other. As noted above, however, the vocabulary is also diverse and ever-changing, and a variety of terms are used in political discourse to describe the same environmental tax policy instrument. Future research could evaluate the relative political merit of different terms and their appeal in different political settings, among different blocs of voters, and in different countries. While many types of taxes are traditionally less than popular with voters, European Eurobarometer surveys indicate that environmental taxes at times have been fairly popular with electorates.[81]

One might expect responses to differ for different countries and regions. For instance

---

[79]   See in particular Chapters 4 and 5.
[80]   Carbon Limits and Energy for America's Renewal (CLEAR) Act, S. 2877, 111th Cong. (2009) (referred to the US Senate Committee on Finance).
[81]   European Commission, Europeans' Attitudes Towards The Issue Of Sustainable Consumption And Production, Flash Eurobarometer 256 (2009); La Commission Europeenne,

in the former 'frontier economies' of the United States, Canada and Australia, environmental taxes are less used, but this usage may also depend on features of those countries' political and institutional systems. When is usage linked to the vocabulary of environmental taxation or to other considerations? Are there keywords that most effectively capture the notions in different regions across the world? And in what ways are those keywords universal or culture-specific? If environmental taxes effectively are putting a price on externalities, is it then politically—and legally—more appropriate to develop a separate label from simply 'tax' to distinguish them from conventional distorting taxes? These inquiries may be vital to the ultimate success of environmental tax policy as it moves from the realm of theories to practical implementation. Developing a common and more finely tuned language of terminology among the involved academic disciplines will also be useful to this purpose and to enabling the progress of research itself.

Les Europeens Et L'environnement En 1995 [The European Commission, Europeans and the Environment in 1995], Eurobarometre 43.1 BIS (1995).

3 Economic principles of environmental fiscal reform

Jean-Philippe Barde and Olivier Godard

INTRODUCTION

The adoption of the polluter-pays principle by OECD (Organization for Economic Cooperation and Development) member countries in 1972 occurred at the crossroads of economic, trade and environmental concerns. The principle inspired interest in economic instruments as a means of promoting a full integration of environmental and economic issues, particularly after the 1987 Brundtland report successfully advocated for the concept of sustainable development worldwide. In this context, economic instruments would be the key policy means of joining economic and environmental sustainability. Reaching a macroeconomic level of significance, environmentally related taxes could become the nexus of fiscal reform, partially switching the burden of social security from labor and capital to sources of environmental externalities. At that time the so-called 'double dividend' strategy came to the forefront of proposals for supporting an integrated approach of economic, fiscal and environmental issues. Nevertheless, despite a few success stories, in particular in Nordic European countries, implementing consistent environmental tax reforms is often fraught with difficulties and obstacles.

Environmental taxes have a long-standing intellectual history, rooted in welfare economics (for instance Pigou 1920; Baumol and Oates 1988) as well as in institutional economics (Andersen 1994). Yet despite early analyses and experiences of water charges (Kneese 1964), it took a long time before the academic literature began to influence the political sphere. Signs of a consistent use of tax instruments started to emerge during the early 1990s in a few pilot countries such as Sweden, Norway and Denmark (OECD 2002 and 2006). Although recurrent energy crises and the challenge of climate change have revived the issue, there is still a long way to go before environmental taxes will become widely used as an environmental policy instrument. This reflects the fact that citizens and consumers are not familiar with the efficiency features of the price mechanism in a market economy, and that distributive or power issues take precedence over efficiency issues in the political process, shaping the choice of environmental policy instruments.

Defining Environmental Taxes

International organizations, in particular the OECD, have strongly promoted the use of environmental taxes. Regional policies like those in the European Union have also endorsed them verbally, but with limited success. OECD (and IMF) define a tax as a compulsory, unrequited payment to general government. Taxes are unrequited in the sense that benefits provided by the government to taxpayers are not normally in proportion to their payments. The term 'environmentally related taxes' is used by OECD to describe any tax levied on tax bases deemed to be of particular environmental relevance (OECD 2002 and 2006). This is a broad concept in the sense that this category encompasses different types of taxes well beyond those designed with an explicit environmental purpose, the main example of which is energy taxes.

Therefore the name, or the expressed purpose, of a given tax is not an appropriate criterion for deciding whether or not a tax is 'environmentally related'—*inter alia* because the names used and the expressed purposes are often arbitrary, and because the purpose of a given levy can change over time. Hence, this definition of 'environmentally related taxes' is rooted in economics, that is, it focuses on the potential environmental *effects* of the given tax, which are determined by the tax's impacts on the producer and consumer prices in question, in conjunction with the relevant price elasticities.

A distinction should be made between taxes and fees (or charges). Environmental fees or charges are payments for specific services, such as waste collection and treatment or sewage and collective water treatment facilities. The term *levy* can be used to cover both taxes and fees and charges.

BOX 3.1   DEFINING ENVIRONMENTAL TAXES, CHARGES OR FEES

Charges/fees are compulsory requited payments, that is, a service is provided in proportion to the payment (for instance, sewage charges). Charges can also be paid into specific 'funds' and earmarked for specific environmental purposes, without necessarily being directly proportional to the service rendered.

An emission charge or tax is defined as a payment for each unit of pollutant discharged into the environment or for each unit of environmental damage. For instance, a thermal power plant can be charged an amount of $100 per ton of carbon dioxide emitted into the atmosphere; a pulp mill or a manufacturer of dairy products can be charged $50 dollars per ton of biological oxygen demand discharged into a river. According to specific design features, the economic meaning of a pollution tax can be interpreted in various ways: it can be just a source of fiscal resource for public bodies, with no intent to drive behaviors; it can represent the price necessary to meet a given quantitative target regarding an environmental pressure; it can be a compensation for the marginal external damage suffered by victims of external effects; it can try to mimic the market price that would derive from a competitive market confronting all demands of use for a specific environmental resource (the atmosphere, the water, soil and so on) that would be compatible with the sustainability of the resource or of the environment in which the latter is embedded, whereas this resource is actually not marketable.

Product taxes are applied to, and thus increase the relative prices of, products that create pollution when they are manufactured, consumed or disposed of. These constitute a major portion of taxes with an environmental impact in most OECD countries. Taxes on energy (such as carbon and sulphur taxes on fuels) form a large category. Other examples are taxes on fertilizers, pesticides and batteries.

The European Commission, IEA and OECD have singled out energy products, motor vehicles and transport services; measured or estimated emissions to air and water; ozone-depleting substances; certain non-point sources of water pollution; waste management; noise; and the management of water, land, soil, forests, biodiversity, wildlife and fish stocks as the most relevant (but not the sole relevant) tax bases in this context.

THE ECONOMIC RATIONALE OF ENVIRONMENTAL TAXES

Why Environmental Taxes?

The intentional use of environmental taxes has been promoted as a way of overcoming the shortcomings of the regulatory ('command-and-control') approach to environmental protection. As a matter of fact, regulation has been the main policy instrument used by governments each time they have been faced with increasing signs of critical environmental degradation. However, regulatory instruments have long been subject to strong criticism from economists, mainly in regard to the excessive costs imposed on businesses and consumers and to the instruments' poor cost-efficiency, or because of the ease with which access is given to rent-seeking lobbyists from big business or well-organized constituencies. In fact economists express a wide range of criticisms about using regulation for a majority of environmental issues.[1]

First, in addition to being costly at the enforcement level regulations are not efficient in economic terms.[2] The cause of the inefficiency can be traced back to various sources. One is the information asymmetry between regulated agents and civil servants in charge of environmental public action. Regulations impose uniform requirements on a population of agents (in a sector or in a particular place) since civil servants do not possess the appropriate information about the particular features of the agents' respective situations nor, most importantly, about the true marginal abatement cost curves of firms (see Figure 3.1). Moreover, public action must often respect the principle of equal treatment of every person standing in the same legal situation. Another criticism is the lack of incentives to reconcile private interest and collective preferences: regulations impose constraints that agents try to bypass, and they do not deliver incentives to make private interest work toward achieving public goals. A third criticism is that regulations are too easily exposed to bargaining and negotiations between public authorities and the most influential representatives of the private sector, possibly cheating the terms and conditions of a license or standard. In that case, power asymmetries entail a degradation of both economic efficiency and distributive equity. For instance, it has been documented that pushing authorities to impose new technological requirements of a certain type may

---

[1]   Based on Barde (2000).
[2]   Unless in very specific conditions that are unlikely to be met in most cases involving pollution. One typical case in which regulation is the most appropriate approach is the management of health and environmental safety faced with hazards generated by the production or use of chemicals or by nuclear activities (power generation, medicine). Nobody suggests controlling nuclear safety of nuclear plants or end of life of nuclear wastes just with the help of a tax on radioactive emissions . . .

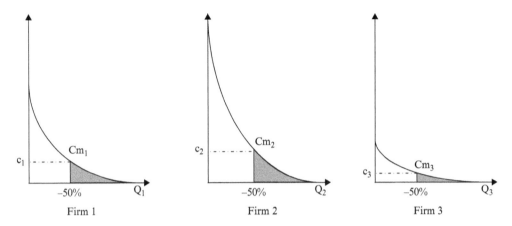

Figure 3.1   Impact of a uniform rate of abatement on three facilities

be a good strategy for raising the costs of competing technologies or for raising new barriers to entry in favor of incumbents.

Another limitation of regulations is their static character and lack of dynamic incentive regarding adoption of new technologies. Regulations and standards, laboriously negotiated, are not likely to evolve rapidly, especially when embodied into legislation. Technological progress will become embodied in new regulations and standards only after a long time. Economic agents may be reluctant to disclose technical progress as doing so may result later in more stringent regulatory requirements (the 'ratchet effect').

Figure 3.1 shows that imposing a uniform regulation of pollution on a heterogeneous population of firms will involve very unequal burdens (represented by the shaded area under the marginal abatement curve for a regulation asking to cut pollution by 50 percent), but also unequal marginal abatement costs (c_i on the Cm_i curve). In most cases where pollution generates private bads, this means that the allocation of abatement efforts is not efficient: less pollution could be obtained at the same overall cost, or the same level of overall abatement could be obtained at a lower cost.

Enforcement often proves to be difficult or weak, mainly owing to the great number of controls, administrative requirements, staff (inspectorate, engineers, lawyers and so on), legal procedures in case of noncompliance, etc. Often the lack of staff available for control and enforcement makes the probability of being caught rather small; even so, noncompliance fines are usually too low to function as a real deterrent. For businesses, a low noncompliance fine multiplied by a low probability of being caught remains preferable to having to pay the marginal cost of pollution abatement.

Static Efficiency of Taxes

Static efficiency is the main quality attributed to well-designed environmental taxes, when they apply to a responsive, flexible market economy that does not suffer from significant distortions, except for the environmental issue of concern. In particular, to keep the properties of efficiency, the existing fiscal system should be well designed, providing adequate redistribution in line with the collective preferences of society without impair-

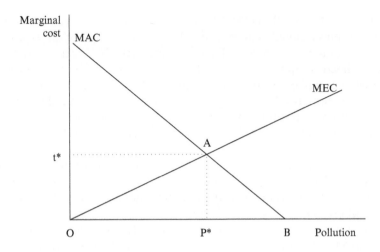

Figure 3.2   Matching marginal abatement cost and marginal external damages cost

ing the running of markets, in line with individual preferences of consumers. Then, an economically rational polluter will ideally react to the environmental tax by reducing emissions to the level where the unit rate of the tax and the marginal pollution abatement cost (that is, the cost of removing one additional unit of pollutant) are equal. On Figure 3.2 the marginal abatement cost (MAC) curve increases from right to left because the more a pollutant is abated, the higher the unit (marginal) costs for additional abatement. If a tax with a rate t^* is imposed, the polluter will abate pollution from B to P* because beyond this level (A on MAC) it is cheaper to pay the tax than to abate emissions further.

Assuming that it is possible to define an all-embracing inter-temporal social welfare function, searching for an 'optimal' level of pollution becomes accessible. Within the static framework adopted on Figure 3.2, it would correspond to the point where MAC equals marginal external (or damage) cost (MEC), defined as the marginal variation of the social welfare function. Any departure from this level (point A in Figure 3.2) implies a welfare loss, because either pollution damage exceeds abatement costs (moving to the right of A on MEC) or abatement costs are higher than damage costs (moving to the left of A on MAC). None of these situations is satisfactory from an economic point of view.

Ideally, the pollution tax should be fixed at a level corresponding to this optimal level: a tax fixed at level t^* would achieve the optimal pollution level P*. This of course implies that the marginal external/damage costs can be estimated, a condition often difficult to fulfill in reality. It is interesting to see that with a tax t^*, the payment of the polluter can be divided into three parts: surface P*AB, which is the total pollution abatement cost (the surface under MAC); surface OAP* (the surface under MEC), which covers the residual damage corresponding to the residual emission level OP*; and surface Ot*A. The latter can be interpreted as the payment of a tax on the use of scarce environmental resources, or payment of a resource rent. Thus the overall tax burden has two components, with one linked to the optimal damage and the other to the payment of a scarcity rent, assuming that the environment is globally a collective heritage of society and that the government is responsible for looking after the sound management of this heritage.

Note that surface OAB reflects the total value of the internalized environmental costs (abatement costs plus residual damage costs). To give an example of this type of framing, the Stern Review of the economics of climate change (Stern 2007) came to the conclusion that a strategy aimed at capping the atmospheric concentration of greenhouse gas (GHG) below 550 parts per million (ppm) of CO_2-equivalent would cost an expected 1 percent GDP and would entail a residual damage of about another 1 percent GDP. Provided that appropriate transfers of resources are achieved in favor of less developed and developing countries,[3] a worldwide coordinated scheme of taxation of GHG emissions could approach such a result.

Introducing a new environmental tax is an innovation involving two movements: first, the fiscal taking, which has merited much attention from both academic experts and stakeholders; and second, the use of the new fiscal resource, often overlooked by analysis and public positions. Hence the tax is treated as if it were a foreign taking entailed by a price increase of imported oil. If we consider only the first movement, leaving aside the second one, introducing a tax imposes an additional burden on the polluter who pays the abatement costs (P*AB) plus the tax (Ot*AP). If an emission standard P* were imposed, the polluter would pay only the pollution abatement costs. This feature of pollution taxes has very important financial, distributive and political consequences. Although the tax can minimize the global abatement costs, that is, the sum of the abatement costs of all polluters (see below), individual polluters may have to bear heavier costs owing to the payment of the tax in addition to abatement costs if nothing is done to neutralize the fiscal burden dimension and keep only the incentive effect for which the tax is aiming. The initial intent of a Pigovian tax is not to raise revenue for public bodies but to use a price signal to push economic agents (firms, consumers) to take account of the social costs of their activity and to make different technological and economic choices.

A key feature of taxes is that they minimize total abatement cost by equalizing marginal abatement costs across polluters. Figure 3.3 depicts three firms with different marginal abatement costs. If public authorities would like to see total emissions reduced by, say, 50 percent, they could for example require each of the three firms to halve its emissions, or they could introduce a tax t per unit of emissions. In this simple setting, the environmental impacts of the two approaches would be identical, as would the impacts on Firm 2. However, in the tax alternative, Firm 1 would increase its abatement effort so as to lower emissions from E_{11} to E_{12}. Its abatement cost increases with the light shaded area in the figure. Firm 3 would abate less than it would in the case of uniform emission reductions, so that its emissions would increase from E_{31} to E_{32} and its abatement cost decreases with the dark shaded area in the figure. As the distance between E_{11} and E_{12} is equal to the distance between E_{31} and E_{32}, it is obvious that the cost decreases in Firm 3 are larger than the cost increases for Firm 1, meaning that total abatement cost for society

---

[3]   The international climate policy should address a specific framing of decentralized production, via billions of micro-decisions of all inhabitants, of a global public good, that is, a certain state of the global climate that will be imposed on all human beings. As initially shown by Chichilnisky and Heal (1993) and developed by Heal and Chichilnisky (2000), it is not possible in that context to conceive of efficiency and distributive justice as two independent criteria or as two dimensions that can be addressed by different mechanisms. A specific distribution of compensating transfers is needed for a unique price of carbon leading to economic efficiency.

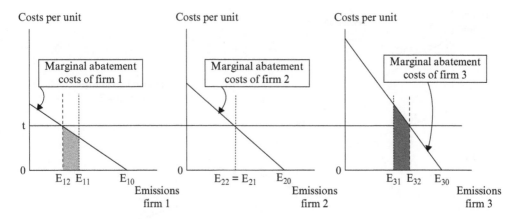

Source: Barde 2000 and OECD 2006.

Figure 3.3   Imposing a tax on heterogeneous firms

as a whole is lower when taxes are used to equalize the marginal abatement costs among the three producers.

A number of empirical evaluations of the gains achieved with economic instruments (taxes or tradable permits) have been made; they suggest that cost savings can be substantial. For example, Tietenberg (1990) indicates a number of cases where least-cost policies can be up to 22 times cheaper than command and control. But generally speaking, these gains should not be overestimated by a comparison between, on one hand, the potential achievements of a perfectly designed theoretical solution assuming perfect markets and flexible and well-informed firms and, on the other hand, a real-life, very imperfect regulation imposed on an imperfect economy. For instance, in a significant experience of emissions trading, the Acid Rain Program in the United States, real gains on abatement costs have been estimated at about 35–40 percent compared to the cost that command-and-control regulation (forcing the use of scrubbers for every power plant) would have generated (Burtraw 1999; Burtraw and Palmer 2004).

Measuring benefits of such economic instruments is difficult because it depends on the choice of the counterfactual (business as usual or another policy instrument?), and there exist at least two ranges of benefits. Direct benefits echo the situation of Figure 3.3 and are not so ambiguous if the main variables are known; indirect ones include businesses' taking advantage of new opportunities for which the economic instrument has no responsibility but that a rigid command-and-control approach would not have permitted. The main benefits of the US Acid Rain Program came from the deregulation of railway tariffs, easing the use of Western low-sulphur coal by Midwest and Eastern power plants, and from the development of competition from alternatives to scrubbers, putting new pressure to innovate on producers of scrubbers. Should these sources of benefits be considered as specific benefits of emissions trading? No, to the extent that these benefits did not come from the trading itself; yes, because the increased power of choice given to managers of power plants allowed them to fully exploit these new opportunities. The same sort of hesitation could not be avoided when assessing the benefits of an environmental tax for incentive purposes.

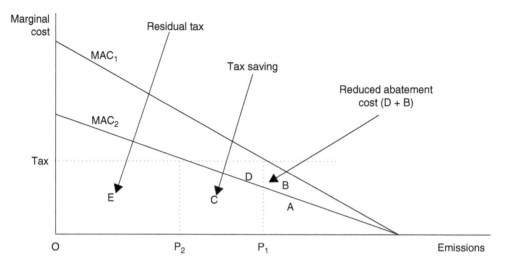

Source: Barde 2000.

Figure 3.4   Components of dynamic efficiency of a tax

Dynamic Efficiency

Taxes provide a permanent incentive to pollution abatement by giving a double stimulus. First, they stimulate reduction of pollution when abatement costs decrease. Assume that, owing to technical progress, the marginal abatement cost is reduced from MAC_1 to MAC_2 (Figure 3.4). In the case of an emission standard P_1, the level of emission will remain unchanged and the polluter will save surface **B**. If, however, a tax, *t*, is imposed, emissions will be reduced to level P_2.

Secondly, a tax is a stronger stimulus to technological change (that is, to developing more efficient pollution-abatement techniques). This is because technological change (shifting from MAC_1 to MAC_2) provides a double cost savings: abatement costs (surface **D + B**) and reduced tax (surface **C**).

In practice, this general incentive to bet on technological innovation to address environmental issues—the Porter's thesis on the positive role of well-designed environmental policies to enhance competitiveness of industrial firms when they are rather protected from market pressures (Porter and Van der Linde 1995)—should be precisely documented. Its validity may depend on several features. One is linked to the integration or distinction between the polluting firm and the one doing research to develop new technologies. If the polluter is also the producer of new technologies, the basic argument fits well. If that is not the case, the configuration of networks and relationships between the firms producing the new technologies and the polluting firms that would have to buy those new technologies really matters. If the eco-industry market is imperfect, due to an oligopolistic structure, environmental policies implemented through taxation may well be a way to enhance rents and captured markets of eco-industry as well as increase innovation. In that case, the optimal rate of taxation should be revised (Sinclair-Desgagné and David 2005), since cost savings would be less than expected.

Another consideration is the predictability of the evolution of the tax rate. When innovation is not 'end-of-pipe' but involves a retrofitting of the whole production equipment, or is incorporated when investing in a new plant, significant investments are required and the expected future tax rate is more decisive than the current one. The better-known the future rate is, the more the environmental tax can trigger technological change and innovation. On the contrary, if the prospect of a tax is very uncertain because of political mismatch or any other reason, it may have no dynamic effects at all.

Taxes Provide Revenue

To avoid a biased approach to environmental policy, it is necessary to take a complete view of environmental tax reform, including both movements, with the fiscal taking on one side and the use of the revenue on the other side. Tax is a two-sided coin; paying the levy is the first. This is a source of political complication and uncertainty. For instance, industry is often strongly opposed to environmental taxes and charges, since it does not believe that the revenue will be returned to the payers nor expect that the main taxpayers will be the main receivers. Another issue is political uncertainty, since a change of political majority may change the laws.

In OECD countries, the revenue from environmental taxes represents 6–7 percent of total tax revenue and 2–2.5 percent of GDP.[4] The revenue can be used in different ways: it may be driven to the general treasury; earmarked to a specific fund aiming at compensating victims of pollution, rehabilitating depleted environments, subsidizing activities contributing to the production of environmental public goods or financing specific expenditures not related to environmental issues (permanent education of workers, social security charges, etc.); or returned on a lump-sum basis to firms who paid the tax. If used to reduce or remove existing distortionary tax provisions in general tax structure, the tax may provide several 'dividends' in terms of both environmental benefits and increased economic efficiency.

These options deserve a detailed analysis from the points of view of efficiency and incentive-compatibility; several issues can be pointed out. First, in the case of local pollution issues that can be dealt with through private or territorial measures, a systematic compensation of victims may neutralize incentives given to victims to limit their own exposure to hazards. Also, authorities and stakeholders should avoid transforming compensation schemes in rents that victims would try to maximize.

Second, the issue of earmarking is delicate. There is often a tendency to set the tax rate according to budgetary needs and not at the efficient level. If the environmental tax revenue exceeds the financing needs of projects, the result will be economic inefficiencies and a rationale of exhaustion of the available budget, whatever the value of actions. An opposite argument is that earmarking may provide a predictability of resources that is precious when investment is at stake, thus counterbalancing the imperfections of public decision-making (uncertainty and possible instability generated by the annual rhythm

---

4   See the OECD/EEA database on environmentally related taxes (http://www2.oecd.org/ecoi nst/queries/index.htm).

of budgetary decisions by parliaments, etc.). In the end, this amounts to a question of trading off the positive and negative impacts of earmarking.

Third, there is the issue of tax shift. Since the 1990s, most countries have compensated for new environmental taxes by reducing other existing taxes in a revenue-neutral approach, keeping the counterfactual total tax burden unchanged. But since the 2008–2009 financial and economic crises, increasing the tax pressure will be a critical issue during the next decade in order to improve public finance and recover international credibility among lenders. In this setting, new non-revenue neutral environmental taxes may be considered, particularly in the context of policies aiming at mitigating climate change. An analogous outcome can be attained in this regard via a carbon tax or auctioned quotas, with the first alternative offering better predictability for public finance.

POLICY OPTIONS FOR ENVIRONMENTALLY FOCUSED TAX REFORMS

Three complementary policy options are available for implementing environmental tax reform.

Restructure Existing Taxes According to Environmental Criteria

So as to benefit the environment, many existing taxes could be changed by increasing the relative prices of the most polluting tax-bases. Since energy is one of the main sources of both pollution and tax revenue, an 'environmental' restructuring of energy taxes is essential. For instance, in most OECD countries, taxes on motor vehicle fuel can reach 80 percent of the pump price. This leaves enormous room for restructuring the fuel and mineral oil taxes on the basis of environmental parameters, such as sulphur content, as the Nordic countries, Germany, Ireland and the United Kingdom have done, or on other bases such as particles or carbon content.

Taxes on other energy products, for instance fuels used for heating purposes and in industrial processes, can also be differentiated according to environmental criteria, such as carbon and/or sulphur content. It is also possible to restructure taxes on motor vehicles (both one-off sales taxes and annual taxes on vehicle usage), for example according to the environmental characteristics of the fuel a vehicle uses, according to estimated fuel consumption and/or according to whether or not the vehicle is equipped with a catalytic converter.

Introduce New Environmental Taxes

An obvious option is to introduce new taxes whose primary purpose is to protect the environment. These may be taxes on emissions (for instance on atmospheric pollutants or water pollution) or on products that are closely related to environmental problems. The latter are more frequent. Since the early 1990s, many environmentally related taxes have been introduced on products including packaging, fertilizers, pesticides, batteries, chemical substances (solvents), lubricants, tires, razors, disposable cameras and 'white products' (refrigerators, dishwashers etc). The OECD/European Environment Agency (EEA) database provides extensive information on a large variety of such levies (over 150 taxes in all).

Remove Distortionary Tax Provisions and Subsidies

Many environmentally harmful tax provisions (tax rate variations or exemptions) exist in all countries. For instance, coal is taxed at all in only five OECD countries, and in these countries the most significant coal users are benefiting from many tax exemptions and rebates. Another type of support measure is the widespread availability of tax exemptions and rebates for diesel fuel used in road transport, farming and fishing in many countries, or the tax exemption for kerosene used in international civil aviation. The OECD database on environmentally related taxes documents 1150 exemptions and special tax provisions. A key feature, even a prerequisite, for a consistent environmental tax reform is to remove these harmful tax provisions.

Subsidies, as tax expenditures, are also an integral part of tax policy. A number of subsidies are environmentally harmful and should be removed. This is a key issue for further research and action (see below).

KEY ISSUES FOR A RESEARCH AGENDA ON ENVIRONMENTAL TAXATION

Removing Environmentally Harmful Subsidies

Subsidies as government failures

Introducing environmental taxes is not enough if environmentally harmful tax provisions, in particular harmful subsidies, are not removed. Public subsidies may be justified by distributive motives, sectoral or territorial public policy, or non-environmental market failures. A typical example is the subsidizing of scientific research: because knowledge is a public good, private investment in research and development is generally under-funded, the solution to which is a mix of public financing and extension of intellectual property rights. But very frequently public subsidies of the production of private goods entail both excess pressure on natural resources and excess pollution. In that case, it is necessary to reframe subsidies, for example as subsidies of the income of a certain class of agents, instead of subsidies of productions, in order to alleviate the perverse side effects on the environment.

In some cases, market and policy failures may result in a cumulative detrimental effect on the environment. In Figure 3.5, the marginal private cost curve MPC intersects the demand curve D so that a quantity Q_0 is produced at price P_0. Accounting for the external cost associated with the production increases the cost so that the marginal social cost curve MSC (including private plus external cost) intersects the demand curve at point B with a quantity $Q^*<Q_0$ produced at price $P^*>P_0$. The difference in output $Q-Q^*$ represents the market failure.

When a subsidy is paid to the producer, the marginal private cost curve is shifted down to MPC-SUBS corresponding to a quantity $Q_1>Q_0$ and a price $P_1<P_0$. The excess

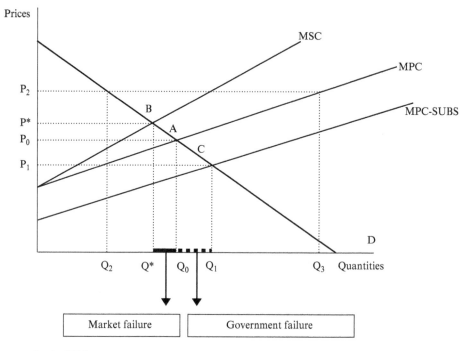

Source: Barde (1993).

Figure 3.5   Cumulative detrimental effect of market and policy failures

production represents the policy (or government) failure. In this particular case (other configurations can be conceived), the market and policy failure are added up.

If the government sets a price at P_2 to support the producer's income, the government may need to take specific measures to guarantee the purchase of the quantity Q_3-Q_2 that would otherwise not be purchased at price P_2.

Long-term effects of subsidies are generally different from the short-term ones
Removing subsidies will reduce profits in the short term and cause marginal firms to exit from the market. But removing a long-standing subsidy will open the way to the development and application of new technologies hitherto blocked by the subsidy. The technology lock-in effect will disappear in the long term, thus enabling substitution between factors of production and increases in efficiency.

Many policies providing subsidies in OECD countries are implemented in order to support environmentally sensitive sectors, particularly agriculture, the fishery industry, energy production, transport and heavy industries. These support measures often lead to increased use of (possibly polluting) inputs and increased production levels as prices for the finished good fall in response to declining costs (OECD 1998). Encouraging production augmentation through such support measures increases the risk of environmental damage from production.

Subsidies are pervasive

Subsidies are widespread throughout OECD countries (with wide variations among countries) and worldwide. Every year, OECD countries give over US$400 billion in subsidies to different economic and often environmentally sensitive sectors (OECD 2005); due to lack of data, this figure is most probably an underestimate.

Agricultural subsidies compose the lion's share of subsidies in OECD countries.[5] In 2011, estimated total support to agriculture amounted to US$406 billion, which represents 0.93 percent of GDP in OECD countries and of which 62 percent represented support to producers. Some of these support measures contribute to increasing agricultural production (such as price support), the use of land and the use of water resources (through the absence of water pricing for farmers). Market price support, output payments (per output unit produced) and input subsidies (such as fertilizer, pesticide, water and energy subsidies) have the greatest impact.[6]

Available estimates indicate that subsidies of fisheries in OECD countries have slightly declined, but they still represent 19 percent of the value of landings. Some of these subsidies are paid for R&D, surveillance and management services, which may contribute to the sustainable management of fish resources. Yet the remaining subsidies can help develop and sustain over-capacity in fishing fleets and the over-exploitation and eventual exhaustion of fish stocks.

Water use is subsidized in many different forms, such as water abstraction charges below cost recovery, external costs and resource rents; subsidies of irrigation water (irrigation accounts for 75–90 percent of total water use in developing countries and more than one third in many OECD countries); and subsidized water prices for households and industry.

Subsidies for energy production in OECD countries are intended mainly to protect domestic producers and maintain employment in given sectors. These support measures take different forms: direct grants, tax breaks for diesel and heavy fuels, and tax breaks for specific users (industry sectors, agriculture, transport, fisheries etc.). World fossil fuel consumption and production subsidies were estimated at a total of $700 billion in 2008 (1 percent of world GDP) (IEA/OECD/OPEC/ World Bank 2010). It is estimated that removing fossil fuel consumption subsidies could cut CO_2 emissions by 10 percent in 2050, compared to a 'business as usual' scenario (OECD 2009).

Industry is also subsidized, although it is difficult to obtain detailed data.

Defining transport subsidies is more complex. One definition compares total revenue of the sector with the total social cost of each transport mode. According to this definition, in most European countries revenue from fuel taxes and specific road user charges roughly covers the cost of road infrastructure (Nash et al. 2002). However, in some

---

[5]   Except in Australia and New Zealand.

[6]   During the 1990s, many OECD countries began to take steps to reduce and restructure their agricultural support policies in an effort to reduce overproduction and trade distortions, and to encourage more environmentally sound use of land, soil and water. The current reform of the EU Common Agricultural Policy is an important step in this direction. The share of market price support, output payments and input subsidies, which are potentially the types of agricultural support exerting the greatest environmental pressure, has decreased marginally since the mid-1980s, but they still account for 70 percent of the producer support in OECD countries.

BOX 3.2   DEFINING SUBSIDIES

The concept of subsidy is not straightforward. The term 'subsidy' also covers transfers, payments, support, assistance or protection associated with governmental policies. Sometimes these terms are used interchangeably, but often they are associated with different methods of measurement and thus different economic indicators. OECD defines environmentally harmful subsidies and tax concessions as including 'all kinds of financial support and regulations that are put in place to enhance the competitiveness of certain products, processes or regions, and that, together with the prevailing taxation jurisdiction, (unintentionally) discriminate against sound environmental practices' (OECD 1998). It is not necessary to make a distinction between subsidies and tax expenditures, as the latter can be regarded as implicit subsidies.

Subsidies take different forms, such as budgetary payments or support involving tax expenditures (various tax provisions that reduce the tax burden of particular groups, producers or products), market price support, subsidized input prices and preferential interest rates. This is why the more generic terminology of 'support measures' is often used. There is, however, no international consensus: different definitions prevail for specific purposes, fields (such as agriculture or transport) or contexts (such as international trade).

There has been much controversy over whether the non-internalization of external costs should be construed as a subsidy, the argument being that, as external costs are not internalized, the environment is used 'freely' by the users: in a sense, a public good is freely supplied to users. Those who object to such an expanded definition observe that the notion of a subsidy has traditionally connoted an explicit government intervention, not an implicit lack of intervention. Moreover, for these and more practical purposes, namely the difficulty of quantifying external costs, non-internalization is not regarded here as a subsidy, except regarding the transport sector, where this definition is currently used (Nash et al. 2002).

---

cases, infrastructure costs exceed revenue, thus resulting in a subsidy. Another approach compares the price paid for using transport infrastructure and the marginal social cost associated with a specific transport mode. Some estimates indicate that in urban areas, the prices for using cars and trucks are generally much too low: it is estimated that to cover social cost, prices should increase by up to 150 percent in certain urban areas (ECMT 2003).

Assessing the environmental impact of subsidies

Collecting quantitative data on subsidies, a difficult task as such, is not enough: assessing their environmental impact is a necessity and priority. The difficulty stems from the complexity and intricacy of the economic and environmental linkages. The factors determining the magnitude of environmental effects of support measures are:

- The level of protection from competition that support measures offer the recipient sector, in other words, the extent to which alternatives to the recipient sector are discouraged.
- The environmental effects of the alternative products or technologies that are discouraged by the support measures, compared with those of the supported sector.
- The circumstances that determine how sensitive the environment is to the particular change in emission or waste levels brought about by the support measures (OECD 1998).

There is no direct linkage between the volume and nature of the subsidy and the environmental impact (cf. OECD 1998). The OECD has developed a 'checklist' enabling the analysis, in qualitative terms, of the potential environmental effect of a list of subsidies (OECD 2005). However, the development of quantitative models and methodologies, adapted to different types of subsidies, is a priority on the research agenda.

Taxes vs. Tradable Quotas or Taxes and Tradable Quotas?

Taxes and tradable permits are generally seen as alternative economic instruments that can be chosen for the same purpose. At the highest level of abstraction, economic analysis generally considers both instruments to deliver the same basic efficiency properties and economic equilibriums defined by the same price and quantity values. This means that for the same level of pollution (quantity), the market price of permits will equal the tax rate (price). Differences belong to real life, where political process, institutions and transaction costs, and uncertainty do matter. Another issue regards the possibility of using both instruments jointly. Are there some combinations that make sense?

These questions are still debated and under examination in real-life policy, notably in the context of climate change mitigation policies. Following the EU Commission tax proposal in the early 1990s, which had no success either in the EU or internationally, the United Nations Framework Convention on Climate Change (UNFCCC) in 1992 and the Kyoto Protocol in 1997 opened the way to international tradable permits, under the name of 'joint implementation,' 'Kyoto mechanisms' or 'flexibility mechanisms,' designed to supplement the national efforts of Annex 1 countries to meet their quantitative targets. At the same time, many analysts (Cooper, Stavins, Nordhaus and Stiglitz, to name a few) supported a tax approach and others (Stern) have suggested an intermediate approach: a tax approach in the short run embedded within quantitative targets and international trading in the long run.

The same sort of debate recently arose domestically, both in the United States when President Obama was elected in 2008 and in the EU in 2009 because of the many pitfalls of the Emission Trading Scheme (ETS) introduced in 2005. These pitfalls included price volatility and instability; too short a time horizon for triggering investment in line with decarbonizing targets; high transaction costs for rather small-sized sources that are not exempted; value-added tax fraud (an estimated €5 billion); huge windfall profits gained by utilities involved in power generation and by some industrial sectors (iron and steel) due to the free allocation of quotas; and limited abatement of emissions, with the main source of CO_2 emission reduction being the 2008–2009 economic recession. The perception has developed among some observers and policymakers that, in order to deliver an appropriate long-run price signal to drive investment and at the same time avoid the most disturbing side effects of emissions trading, it would be necessary to install an EU system of harmonized carbon taxes and drop the ETS. Others believe the ETS should be retained for carbon-intensive sectors, whereas a carbon tax should be used for the remaining diffuse sectors for which the emissions-trading approach would generate excessively high transaction costs.

This debate was revived after the failure of the Copenhagen meeting in December 2009 to obtain legally binding quantitative commitments from the largest polluters (Cramton and Stoft 2009). In 2011 the European Commission tried to follow the trail of a revision of the directive on energy taxation, in parallel with fine-tuning the rules of the game of the ETS for the third commitment period (2013–2020).

When should we prefer a tax approach?

Taxes or emissions trading? Several real-life features offer guidelines for a response. First, legal constraints: an environmental tax belongs to the general category of fiscal measures. Only parliaments have the power to decide the introduction of a new tax. In the EU, the balance of powers between the EU institutions and member states requires that any fiscal measures be decided unanimously. As far as the law is concerned, emissions trading is a different animal: it belongs to the category of regulatory instruments and in some countries can be decided by administrative authorities. In the EU, the directive creating the ETS required not unanimity but a qualified majority of member states.

A second issue is related to transaction and administrative costs. Although progress in technology progressively changes transaction costs, it is clear that adding a carbon tax to a gasoline tax, and benefiting from the existing information infrastructure of fiscal services, will be much less costly than extending emissions trading to road transportation. The same can be said of domestic energy uses. But taxation is not popular, and acceptability depends on the level of trust that citizens feel regarding governments' promises and commitments: even if taxes are deemed to be compensated for by an equivalent cut in income tax or other measures, most taxpayers do not believe it will remain true in the long term. In this regard, an advantage of tradable permits when permits are allocated for free is that regulated agents receive a valuable asset before they have to make any transaction. They are more confident that the environmental policy will not be a pretext for an increase in fiscal pressure whereas they keep control of their choices regarding energy use.

Beyond these sociopolitical and legal aspects, the main contribution of academic analysis to the issue of choice of an economic instrument has been linked to the effect of uncertainty on the risk of inappropriate calibration of the instrument. Weitzman (1974) and Adar and Griffin (1976) studied this problem initially. Two types of uncertainty may affect the choice: uncertainty about the marginal social damage function and uncertainty about the aggregate marginal abatement cost function. As shown in Figures 3.6, 3.7 and 3.8, key results are the following: uncertainty about the damage function MD, alone, does not discriminate between a policy approach based on price (a tax) and one based on quantities (a cap), since potential error is the same with both approaches. If uncertainty affects the abatement cost function MC alone, it is quite different; in order to minimize the possible error in the calibration of the instrument, it is then preferable to choose a price entry (a tax approach, alt. a quantity approach)

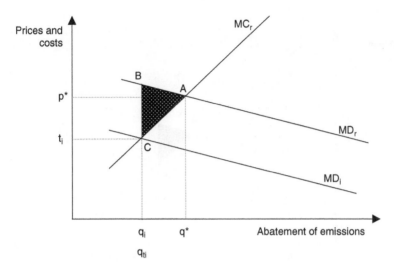

Note: In Figure 3.6, the marginal damage function is known with uncertainty, whereas the marginal abatement cost is known for sure. Hence the two curves MD_r and MD_i for, respectively, the real damage curve and the damage curve 'guessed' by the policymaker. The area inside triangle ABC is the cost of error, since real policy choices are based on the wrong position of the damage curve. The error is the same regardless of the choice of entry variable, q_i or t_i.

Figure 3.6   Tax or quota under uncertainty of marginal damage curve

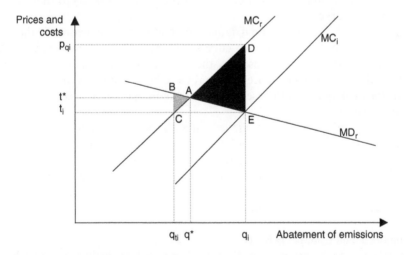

Note: In Figure 3.7, the marginal abatement cost function is uncertain regarding its exact position but is broadly known regarding its slope, that is, the increase in marginal cost when the rate of abatement becomes more stringent. Hence the two curves MC_r and MC_i for, respectively, the real abatement cost curve and the curve 'guessed' by the policymaker. Real optimal abatement quantity is q^* and optimal tax level is t^*. They are not known by policymakers. With their guessed estimates, they may choose a tax t_i or a cap q_i as policy entry. Matching the real cost curves, they will get as responses from polluters an abatement of q_{ti} in the first case and a marginal cost up to p_{qi} in the second one. The area inside triangle ABC is the cost of error with the tax entry and the area inside triangle AED is the cost of error with the cap q_i. AED is greater than ABC.

Figure 3.7   Tax or quota under uncertainty of marginal abatement cost curve (I)

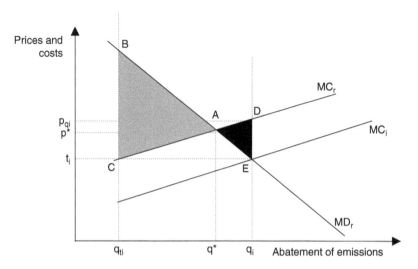

Note: In Figure 3.8, we have the same assumptions as in Figure 3.7, but for the relative slopes of the damage and abatement cost curves. The area inside triangle ABC is the cost of error with the tax entry t_i and the area inside triangle AED is the cost of error with the cap q_i. In this case, ABC is much greater than AED.

Figure 3.8   Tax or quota under uncertainty on marginal abatement cost curve (II)

when the slope of the marginal cost curve is steeper (alt. is less steep) than that of the marginal damage curve.[7]

In Figures 3.7 and 3.8, the marginal damage function is ascertained while the marginal abatement cost is not. Hence the two curves MC_r and MC_i for, respectively, the real cost curve and the cost curve guessed by the policymaker. In Figure 3.7, the MC are steeper than MD, whereas in Figure 3.8 the reverse holds. Impacts on the cost of error are straightforward and in both cases result in the comparison between the areas inside triangles ABC and AED.

On the basis of this type of analysis, several authors claimed that the climate change issue should be addressed with a carbon tax, and not with quantitative caps, even when supplemented by flexibility mechanisms. The reason is that climate change damage will be the outcome of the stock of GHG in the atmosphere and not directly of the annual flow of emissions; hence the damage function of emissions is rather flat, whereas the abatement cost curve will be sharply steep.

Combining taxes and tradable permits
Several forms of combinations may be considered. A key distinction must be drawn between schemes aiming at a full integration of both instruments in a unique mechanism imposed on the same population of agents, and those that organize a division of labor between instruments in such a way that, for example, instrument A is used for some sectors or classes of agents, and instrument B for others.

---

[7]   This argument assumes that although policymakers do not know where the cost curve exactly stands, they have enough information to compare the general forms of the two curves.

Regarding the first type, in situations of uncertainty about cost and damage functions, authorities may want both to obtain guarantees of meeting quantitative performances and to avoid exposing agents to excessive costs. Then, combining taxation and tradable permits may be an option if designed according to a method initially proposed by Roberts and Spence (1976), whereby the authorities set a cap on emissions as the basis for issuing allowances to agents; in addition, in order to limit the maximum unit cost of compliance, an optional emission tax would be introduced to allow agents to overshoot their quotas at that price and keep the price paid at this maximum level (the 'safety valve'). This level should be significantly higher than the average expectations of the market price of allowances. A tax of this type should not be confused with a penalty designed to dissuade any breaking of the rules. A bottom rate would also be set at which the authorities would buy back allowances from their holders.

As a matter of fact, this integrated approach has not been explicitly implemented in real policy life, although concerns about excessive costs of environmental policies have often been raised. In the case of climate change, the difficulties over the last 20 years in making real progress in commitments toward a low-carbon economy are generally attributed to the cost issue, which could have been resolved by the 'safety valve' solution. However, this has not been attempted and it would be useful to learn why.

What has been implemented in some cases is a pure fiscal tax as a supplement to an emissions-trading program, in order to capture the scarcity rent or windfall profits by private firms. In the United States, for example, the program to reduce CFC production combined both a quota-trading mechanism on output level and a tax. The purpose of this tax was not to encourage cuts but to prevent the scarcity rent generated by the program to be captured by industrial groups.

Another interesting case is that of EU member states that had to discover ways of combining their environmental tax initiatives with their participation in the EU ETS. Various solutions have been implemented or considered, ranging from a strict separation to a simple adding-up.

The second type of combination (i.e. applying both instruments to two different categories of actors) raises one issue: the emergence of two different price signals in one economy, since by necessity, the fluctuating market price of allowances will differ from the tax rate even if, in the medium term, the tax level is set to ensure the proximity of both prices. Due to different levels of inertia of sectors and to policy goals aimed at reaching a specific quantity target in a specified time period (such as 'factor four' by 2050), it may in fact be appropriate to introduce a higher initial price in less price-sensitive sectors like transportation. A plea in favor of differentiated prices according to the level of exposure to international competition can also be made (Hoel 1996), if the stringency of policies in different regions of the world differs and if no specific border tax adjustments are applied to restore an equal playing field between domestic and foreign producers.

The distributive consequences of a joint use of taxes and tradable permits should also be considered in order to avoid unwanted transfers. For instance, taxing final consumers and granting a free allocation of quotas to business firms is tantamount to organizing an income transfer from consumers to shareholders, since the former will have to pay taxes plus a price increase on the market for goods related to the environmental program imposed on firms, while the latter pay no tax and capture the scarcity rent generated by the environmental program.

BOX 3.3   THE CASE OF THE FAILURE OF THE FRENCH CARBON TAX

In December 2009, the Constitutional Court revoked the government carbon tax bill due to be implemented in 2010. According to the Court, the extension of exemptions and rebates granted to various sectors (agriculture, fishery, transportation, industrial activities taking part in the ETS), had two major consequences: first, the design of the project was inappropriate in regard to the stated objectives; second, it introduced an unacceptable inequality among citizens. The Court noticed that while big industries were taking part in the ETS, under present rules they received their carbon quotas for free. It has been shown (Godard 2010) that solutions exist that could avoid imposing what industry spokesmen have called a 'double punishment' on carbon-intensive emitters. By combining levy and compensation in one formula, solutions could have been designed in such a way that, at the margin, the price signal combining the market price of allowances and a net additional tax amount would equate to the tax rate imposed on non-ETS sectors, restoring an equal treatment of all sectors of the French economy. Though perhaps good for an efficient burden-sharing in the French economy, such solutions would nevertheless impose on French industry a carbon price higher than in other European countries. To be supported, such a combined approach should demonstrate a clear superiority on alternatives. In that case the quality of the price signal given by the French schemes of carbon taxes should have provided the compensation for the immediate competitiveness disadvantage. This could only come from better medium-term predictability. Government should have committed itself to an evolution of tax rates for the next 10 years or so, at least within a margin delimited by a floor and a ceiling value. It has not been the case. This certainly is a type of combination or overlapping that deserves more analysis, including of the reciprocal impacts between a region-wide system like the EU ETS and the tax choices of national states.

The Impact of Existing Taxes

In basic analytics of environmental taxes, markets are assumed to be perfect and prices reveal genuine economic scarcity of goods, without distortions. In real life, markets are incomplete and imperfect and prices altered. One source of alteration is the general tax system. In principle, an optimized tax system should be neutral, in other words, without influence on the economic choices of producers and consumers, except for externalities and public goods. In real life, tax systems are the rather contingent outcomes of a long history of innovation and partial changes reflecting the priorities of one historical moment; they are not coherent and not adapted to the priority of the 21st century, namely a reorientation of growth toward sustainability. In brief, environmental taxes will presumably often be added to incoherent and irrational fiscal taxes. To what extent does this real-life imperfection change the approach?

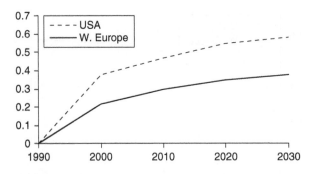

Source: Manne and Richels (1992).

Figure 3.9   Economic impact of the EC proposal of carbon-energy tax (1992)

In this regard, energy taxes and subsidies are at the forefront: are they a fiscal measure distorting economic choices or, on the contrary, a welcome correction of prices internalizing externalities? Let us give an illustration showing how important the issue can be. In February 1992, two influential American economists, Alan Manne and Richard Richels, released a draft paper analyzing the proposal made by the European Commission to other OECD countries to introduce jointly a combined carbon-energy tax. The paper was focused on the implications for the United States if the US government should accept the proposal. This draft was immediately echoed in the press. Using their Global 2100 model, these authors compared the respective impacts on the US and EC economies and concluded that the cost for the US economy would be 50 percent higher in GDP percentage than the cost for the EC economy, because Western Europe uses approximately 40 percent less energy per unit of economic output (Figure 3.9). They add (Manne and Richels 1992, 15): 'To the extent that a lower energy/GDP ratio reflects lower energy use by industry, there may be implications for international competitiveness.' The general feeling promulgated by the paper was that the EC proposal was a Trojan horse to weaken the US economy; this contributed to a dismissal of the tax approach a few months before the Rio Summit in June 1992.

When the Manne and Richels paper was published in 1993, it demonstrated no significant difference with the draft, except for one section dealing with the question of the relative cost to the EU and the US. An entirely new argument was introduced regarding the calculation of the dead-weight loss cost of a new tax when existing prices of commodities are already taxed, a point that was ignored in the 1992 model simulations. This addition resulted from the peer review of the paper. In 1993 Manne and Richels explained that 'when measured in terms of economy-wide costs, the EC proposal is likely to have an even larger impact on Western Europe than on the USA . . . the additional tax distortions would be considerably greater than those in the USA . . .We estimate that the average cost (as a percentage of GDP) would be nearly three times as high in Western Europe as in the USA' (9–10). They demonstrated what is reproduced below as Figure 3.10. The two figures depict a completely opposite reality with regard to which region would bear the highest cost.

The storytelling could be continued, because this issue of differences in existing taxation schemes and assessment of dead-weight losses has been discussed intensively since

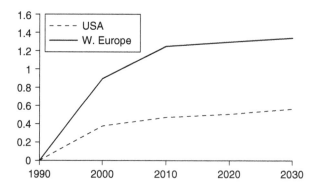

Source: Manne and Richels (1993).

Figure 3.10   Economic impact of the EC proposal of carbon-energy tax (1993)

1992. A lot of energy taxes that historically have been introduced with various motives (for example financing security stocks of oil and natural gas) have been reinterpreted as taxes internalizing the maintenance and environmental costs of transport infrastructures. Each time, it changes the analysis of dead-weight loss cost and the efficiency gains contributed by a carbon tax.

Nowadays, one debate is about what the main targeted variable should be for a long-run climate-energy policy: a carbon value to be sustained regardless of the fluctuations of oil prices, or a specific energy price for the consumer, the latter implying an adaptation of the carbon value to the fluctuation of oil prices? The climate policy cannot be envisaged without taking into account the prospect of peak oil in the rather short-term future. At the same time, a sharp increase in oil price will induce substitution by coal, the GHG rate of emissions of which is quite worse. Certainly, this intertwined relationship between the control of CO_2 emissions by a carbon tax and the evolution of market for fossil fuels is a critical issue deserving additional research.

CONCLUSIONS

There are different sorts of economic instruments designed to change the economic context (price of relative opportunities) of decentralized decision-making of the regulated agents. If the authorities wish to use such instruments, three main options are open:

- Incentive taxes, which, by correcting prices, are designed to modify current choices and behaviors in the use of certain inputs or the emission of certain pollutants. To be effective, the tax basis must be as close as possible to the behavior responsible for the environmental damage.
- A financial mechanism, which combines taxes or charges that will be paid into a special fund in order to finance or subsidize specific actions. As in the case of the regulatory instrument, the economic efficiency of this mechanism will primarily depend upon the nature of the criteria for the selection of projects to be subsidized

and the quality of the technical and economic information that managers of the system can obtain with regard to the efficiency of the projects.

- A tradable permit system based on the introduction of caps and the uprising of a new market for quotas. In this case, the economic efficiency is derived from regulated agents making trade-offs between abatement actions and payments for quotas in order to minimize costs.

Which Criteria?

What criteria might be used to choose between these three instruments? Incentive taxes and tradable permits are both based on price mechanisms. However, the public authority does not introduce this mechanism in the same way in both cases, whereas public intervention is required anyway, precluding any idea of a permit market's developing spontaneously in the absence of public action.

In economic terms, the choice is related to information, incentives, and organizational, transactional and redistribution costs. This means in particular that the designers of the new program must pay particular attention to the informational structures of the rules of the game and the incentives they provide.

In addition to the question of information, the main criteria to be taken into account are as follows:[8]

- Secure the environmental performance or limit the maximum cost? If the authorities have a very poor understanding of how agents will respond to prices but have a clearer idea of the physical performance required, they would do better to construct a regulatory system based on the physical performance targeted, which can pave the way toward tradable permits. On the contrary, if physical targets are not so clear but costs may sharply increase as a function of the stringency of the target, a tax approach should be preferred.
- Assess the ability to use existing services and capabilities. In terms of organizational and transaction costs, it is important to determine whether existing departments (such as the tax authorities) would be able to assist in implementing the chosen instrument or whether a new administration will have to be put in place. The same applies to the monitoring of the instrument, which would mean that the tax basis for the latter (emissions, inputs, equipment ratings etc.) must be reliably measurable.
- Take into account the sensitivity of the regulated agents to price versus quantity signals. The competitive structures in the regulated sector have an impact. Taxes are more appropriate if agents are sensitive to prices; in contrast, if the industry has an oligopolistic structure and product-demand elasticity is low, it might be advisable to use quantitative caps.
- Consider the opportunity to achieve an ecological tax reform. Both auctioned tradable permits and environmental taxes allow for fiscal reforms. Revenues may then be recycled to reduce economic distortions and social unbalances, or to pursue distributive goals. This potential must be considered before deciding which type of

---

[8]   The issue of international competitiveness and harmonization is also crucial.

instrument to choose. What is relevant is the net economic impact of alternative instruments, taking into account the use of fiscal resources, if any.

- Assess the distributive impacts. Although theoretically all economic instruments (taxes and tradable permits) are compatible with the full range of distributive options, there are implicit links between each instrument and a distributive strategy, so that distributive aspects play a key role in the political economy of the choice of an instrument. Many failures of tax projects have their source in distributive issues, sometimes with a huge gap between real and perceived impacts.
- From a political economy viewpoint, the choice of policy instrument should be seen in terms of problem-solving for different stakeholders. A lesson of experience is that most stakeholders do not pay much attention to cost-efficiency, focusing instead on distributive aspects and other issues. This is why the main economic argument about economic efficiency has a poor persuasive impact on the public debate and policy process. If economists think that a given instrument provides the most efficient option in a given circumstance, they have to find additional arguments, more relevant than cost-efficiency, in favor of a particular solution to the problems of various stakeholders in order to have a chance of seeing their proposal become reality (Godard 2001).

The Five Dividends of Environmental Taxes

Initial analyses of pollution problems have been set in the framework of partial equilibrium analysis of existing markets. This approach fit a general perception that environmental problems were rather minor issues to be considered at the margin of key questions related to the macroeconomic dynamics. This perception has changed, and the concept of sustainable development stresses the need for an integrated view of environmental and economic issues. In this context, a broad phased-in fiscal reform, substituting taxes on pollution and resources use to taxes on labor and capital, would be timely. Who could object to taxing bads instead of goods, if we want to minimize the first and promote the second? This is not an easy venture. As already noted, some cases had success, such as the environmental tax reform introduced in Sweden in 1992 after two years of consultation with stakeholders. But several attempts turned out to be complete failures. For instance, three times[9] during a 20-year period (1992, 2000, 2009–2010), the French government tried to introduce some form of carbon tax, but each time the project was abandoned, faced with reluctant public opinion and the intense lobbying of sectoral business organizations (see Box 3.3).

Here we come to the theme of double dividend. In fact a precise analysis should distinguish several dividends from a well-designed tax reform.

- The first dividend offers the main justification for introducing an environmental tax: the environmental performance allowed by the change in relative prices in the economy.

---

[9]   The first time, it was part of a European proposal negotiated at the EU level and supported by the Commission.

- The second dividend originates in the economic efficiency (cost-minimizing) produced by a tax scheme instead of an accumulation of disparate regulatory measures and subsidies generating many windfall profits and rents at the expense of the environment.
- The third dividend is linked to the reduction of various distortions and brakes for sustainable development that are inherent to the present state of the tax-and-subsidy system. This dividend is proportional to the unfitness of the existing tax system when matched with the goals of an emerging green economy to enhance the three dimensions of sustainable development.
- A fourth dividend would come from better social control of perverse dynamics touching land use and infrastructures: giving a price to carbon or other pollutants will dissuade producers and consumers from making decisions, the cumulative effect of which would be to install for the long term a dependency on initially low-priced (water) or unpriced (carbon) resources, with fossil fuels as the main target. Without such an early control, when environmental and economic scarcity generate huge price increases, small producers, consumers and inhabitants would be trapped in a severe social and economic position. This would politically translate into social demand for new public expenditures on welfare and assistance, in order to mitigate situations having become explosive. An early pricing of environmental assets and scarce natural resources would help to avoid socially unsustainable evolution and would subsequently moderate future pressures on public finances.
- The fifth dividend evidently comes from a reduction of the dependency on fossil fuels, subject more and more to geopolitical risks.

According to circumstances, there may be other dividends. The more the present circumstances are unsatisfactory in relation to sustainability and efficiency, the greater the potential for achieving multiple dividends through an environmental tax reform. All these dividends should be considered in real-life contexts, with more attention than was paid in the past.

REFERENCES

Adar, Z. and J.M. Griffin (1976), 'Uncertainty and the choice of pollution control instruments', *Journal of Environmental Economics and Management*, **3**, 178–88.

Andersen, M.S. (1994), *Governance by Green Taxes—Making Pollution Prevention Pay*, Manchester, UK: Manchester University Press.

Barde, J.-P. (1993), 'Economic instruments in environmental policy: lessons from OECD experience and relevance to economies in transition', OECD Development Center, Working Paper no. 92.

Barde, J.-P. (2000), 'Environmental policy and policy instruments', in H. Folmers and H. Landis Gabel (eds), *Principles of Environmental and Resource Economics*, Cheltenham, UK: Edward Elgar, pp. 157–201.

Baumol, W.J. and W.E. Oates (1988), *The Theory of Environmental Policy*, Cambridge, UK: Cambridge University Press.

Burtraw, D. (1999), 'Cost savings, market performance and economic benefits of the U.S. Acid Rain Program', in S. Sorrell and J. Skea (eds), *Pollution for Sale: Emissions Trading and Joint Implementation*, Cheltenham, UK: Edward Elgar, pp. 43–62.

Burtraw, D. and K. Palmer (2004), 'The SO_2 cap-and-trade program in the United States: A "living legend" of market effectiveness', in W. Harrington, R. D. Morgenstern and T. Sterner (eds), *Choosing Environmental Policy*, Washington DC, US: Resources for the Future, pp. 41–66.

Chichilnisky, G. and G. Heal (1993), 'Global environmental risks', *Journal of Economic Perspectives*, **7** (4), 65–86.

Crampton, P. and S. Stoft (2009), 'Global carbon pricing: A better climate commitment', Global Energy Policy Center, Research Paper No. 0906.

ECMT (2003), *Efficient Transport Taxes & Charges*, Paris, France: OECD/ECMT.

Godard, O. (2001), *Domestic Transferable Permits for Environmental Management: Design and Implementation*, Paris, France: OECD.

Godard, O. (2010), 'La Contribution carbone après la censure du Conseil constitutionnel' [The carbon contribution after the censure by the Constitutional Court], ParisTech-Ecole Polytechnique, Working document, March 18.

Heal, G. and G. Chichilnisky (eds) (2000), *Environmental Markets—Equity and Efficiency*, New York, NY, US: Columbia University Press.

Hoel, M. (1996), 'Should a carbon tax be differentiated across sectors?', *Journal of Public Economics*, **59**, 17–32.

International Energy Agency (2008), *World Energy Outlook*, Paris, France: IEA.

Kneese, A.V. (1964), *The Economics of Regional Water Quality Management*, Baltimore, MD, US: John Hopkins Press.

Manne, A.S. and R.G. Richels (1992), 'The E.C. proposal for combining carbon and energy taxes—the implications for future CO_2 emissions—draft', EPRI & Stanford University, February 24.

Manne, A.S. and R.G. Richels (1993), 'The E.C. proposal for combining carbon and energy taxes—the implications for future CO_2 emissions", *Energy Policy*, January, 5–12.

Nash, C. et al. (2002), 'The environmental impact of transport subsidies', Paper prepared for the OECD Workshop on Environmentally Harmful Subsidies, November 7–8, 2002, Paris, France, http://interprod. oecd.org/agr/ehsw/index.htm

OECD (1998), *Improving the Environment through Reducing Subsidies*, three volumes, Paris, France: OECD.

OECD (2002), *Environmentally Related Taxes in OECD Countries: Issues and Strategies*, Paris, France: OECD.

OECD (2005), *Environmentally Related Subsidies, Challenges for Reform*, Paris, France: OECD.

OECD (2006), *The Political Economy of Environmentally Related Taxes*, Paris, France: OECD.

OECD (2009), *The Economics of Climate Change Mitigation*, Paris, France: OECD.

OECD, IEA, World Bank, OPEC (2010), *Analysis of the Scope of Energy Subsidies and Suggestions for the G20 Initiative.*

Pigou, A.C. (1920), *The Economics of Welfare*, London, UK: Macmillan.

Porter, M.E. and C. Van der Linde (1995), 'Toward a new conception of the environment–competitiveness relationship', *Journal of Economic Perspectives*, **9** (4), 97–118.

Roberts, M.J. and M. Spence (1976), 'Effluent charges and licenses under uncertainty', *Journal of Public Economics*, **5**, 193–208.

Sinclair Desgagné, B. and M. David (2005), 'Environmental regulation and eco-industries', *Journal of Regulatory Economics*, **28** (2), 141–55.

Stavins, R. (1996), 'Correlated uncertainty and policy instrument choice', *Journal of Environmental Economics and Management*, **30**, 218–32.

Stern, N. (2007), *The Economics of Climate Change: The Stern Review*, Cambridge, UK: Cambridge University Press.

Tietenberg, T.H. (1990), 'Economic instruments for environmental regulation', *Oxford Review of Economic Policy*, **6** (1), 17–33.

Weitzman, M.L. (1974), 'Prices vs. Quantities', *Review of Economic Studies*, **41** (4), 477–91.

4 Legal authority to enact environmental taxes

Michael Rodi and Hope Ashiabor (contributing author)

This chapter will analyze the legal authority to enact environmental taxes, a competence that is generally vested in the national legislator. Environmental tax law is therefore subject to all the legal preconditions of the national constitution in question, and in some cases it is subject to relevant supranational law as well. For instance, a European Union (EU) Member State can implement a new national environmental law only if it is in line with EU legislation.

The issue of legal competence primarily concerns questions of vertical competence within a system of multilevel governance:[1] It can lie with a central authority, be it on a national or a supranational level, or be decentralized and lie in subdivisions like federal states and municipalities. Moreover, any relevant preconditions for the legislative procedure within parliament must be met, and the participation of other constitutional organs (such as other chambers of government) must be ensured to include a horizontal perspective of competence distribution. Finally, the legal authority enacting environmental taxes must take a variety of material restrictions into account, including constitutional principles such as basic rights and the rule of law (legality, retroactivity). Also important are the ability-to-pay principle relevant to tax law, and the polluter-pays principle relevant to environmental law. This analysis will also pay heed to possible restrictions the legislator may face that are derived from international or supranational law (such as European law).

These issues are already quite sophisticated when only regular legislation is concerned. Their complexity increases when dealing with environmental taxes, since the latter fall into two law and policy regimes: On the one hand they are taxes in a technical sense and as such must comply with all legal requirements for enacting taxes. On the other hand, as environmental policy instruments they may be subject to specific requirements governing this field, such as environmental principles. Due to this dual capacity, it is not easy to define the constitutional requirements for enacting environmental taxes. As a rule, constitutions do not provide specific guidelines for environmental taxes: It is up to the legislator and jurisprudence to derive these requirements based on general rules. This chapter will analyze and systemize the different fields in which problems may arise, and demonstrate with case studies how specific legal orders and national dogmas try to solve them. Despite a broad literature on the theory and design of environmental taxes,[2] there are almost no studies analyzing their implementation on a comparative

---

[1]   See in detail Chapter 14, *Multi-level Governance: The Implications of Legal Competences to Collect, Administer and Regulate Environmental Tax Instruments*, in this Handbook.

[2]   *See* KALLE MÄÄTTÄ, ENVIRONMENTAL TAXES: AN INTRODUCTORY ANALYSIS (2006); OECD, THE POLITICAL ECONOMY OF ENVIRONMENTALLY RELATED TAXES (2006); N. Fujiwara et al., *The Political Economy of Environmental Taxation in European Countries* (Ctr. for Eur. Pol'y Stud., Working Paper No. 245, 2006); James Alm & H. Spencer Banzhaf, *Designing Economic*

law-and-policy basis.[3] One reason for this is the time-consuming nature of quality comparative studies. This chapter alone cannot fill the comparative study vacuum. Given the diversity of law around the world, a complete and comprehensive picture of actual divisions of competence goes beyond the scope of this publication. Instead, the chapter will draw on examples that identify and illustrate key issues on a comparative basis for researchers to further pursue in any given country.

ANALYTICAL FOUNDATIONS

First, basic analytical foundations must be set in order to conduct a coherent analysis. On the one hand, the relevant terminology must be established starting with the definition of an environmental tax instrument for purposes of legal competence determination. On the other hand, some basic characteristics of tax competence in constitutional law must be clarified.

Environmental Taxes as Environmental Policy Instruments and Taxes

When analyzing environmental taxes in the realm of both tax and environmental law, problems of definition arise. They start with the definition of the term 'environment', which can be understood in a broad or narrow sense.[4] Similar problems arise with the term 'tax.'[5] If the latter is defined in a broader sense to include charges or fees,[6] the quantity of legal questions regarding, for example, competences and applicable principles will rise. For the sake of simplicity, the following analysis will focus on taxes in a technical sense, for instance as defined by the Organization for Economic Co-operation and Development (OECD). Taxes are unrequited and compulsory payments to the government that are not proportionate to the ensuing benefits provided by governments to taxpayers.[7] Earmarking and other forms of revenue recycling are—as a rule—possible within this concept.[8]

Instruments for the Environment in a Decentralized Fiscal System (World Bank, Working Paper No. 4379, 2007); ENVIRONMENTAL TAXES: A GLOBAL PERSPECTIVE (Bronwyn Spicer ed., 2008).

[3]   One exception is Scandinavia. *See* MÄÄTTÄ (2006), *supra* note 2; KALLE MÄÄTTÄ, ENVIRONMENTAL TAXES: FROM AN ECONOMIC IDEA TO A LEGAL INSTITUTION (1997).

[4]   MÄÄTTÄ (2006), *supra* note 2, at 16; JOHN SNAPE & JEREMY DE SOUZA, ENVIRONMENTAL TAXATION LAW: POLICY, CONTEXTS AND PRACTICE 13–19 (2006).

[5]   For a legal comparison approach to the concept of taxes, see VICTOR THURONYI, COMPARATIVE TAX LAW 45–59 (2003).

[6]   For the distinction between taxes and charges or fees, see Michael Rodi, *Environmental Charges, in* ENVIRONMENTAL TAXES AND CHARGES 79*ff.* (Int'l Fiscal Ass'n ed., 1995); MÄÄTTÄ (1997), *supra* note 3, at 197*ff.*; Snape & de Souza, *supra* note 4, at 164–65.

[7]   For the legal concept of taxes and its importance in tax law, see Thuronyi, *supra* note 5, at 45*ff.* It is often difficult to draw such a distinct line; for example, the question of whether the environmental compensation payments within the Brazil Nature Conservation Units (SNUC) are qualified as taxes or indemnifications is a heavily debated one. *See* P. Baracuí & M. Frohlich, *Environmental Compensation and New Perspectives for Its Application in Brazil, in* ENVIRONMENTAL TAXES: A GLOBAL PERSPECTIVE 84 (Bronwyn Spicer ed., 2008).

[8]   See Chapter 6, *Earmarking Revenues from Environmentally Related Taxes*, in this Handbook.

The next definition-related problem refers to the linkage of environmental taxes to environmental policy objectives. Some authors argue that the taxes must pursue environmental objectives by intention (purpose). However, in practice it can be quite difficult to reveal the precise purpose of a tax, since it is often not explicitly mentioned (and can even be disguised by the legislator). As it is hard to determine the purpose of the tax, it is more effective to start analyzing from the actual effect it has on the environment. Thus, the following analysis refers to environmentally related taxes levied on tax bases that are of particular environmental relevance.[9] This includes, for example, the entire sphere of energy taxes and the whole concept of 'greening' taxes.[10] In this chapter, the author will therefore follow the OECD definition of 'environmentally related taxes' as 'any compulsory, unrequited payment to general government levied on tax-bases deemed to be of particular environmental relevance.'[11]

Kalle Määttä underlined the need to distinguish incentive or regulatory environmental taxes from fiscal environmental taxes.[12] Incentive or regulatory taxes are created with the primary purpose of steering the behavior of polluters; their revenues are of secondary importance. Fiscal environmental taxes are taxes that are primarily aimed at generating revenue, but which may have significant positive effects on the environment. Although difficult, it may prove necessary to draw a distinction between these concepts. The main reason is that incentive environmental taxes are functionally equivalent to command-and-control environmental law and therefore may need to follow the corresponding legal requirements. In addition, some authors discern 'pure' incentive taxes, meaning taxes that have no additional tax (or revenue) function.[13]

In theory, we can start from the admittedly extreme case of an environmental tax that has no fiscal function at all, aiming only to reduce environmentally detrimental actions. To make the case even more extreme, the tax may be designed not just to reduce but to stop this behavior altogether.[14] In this case, there are good reasons to treat this 'tax' purely as an environmental policy instrument because it is comparable to a command-and-control regulation.[15] It may therefore be correct to require only an environmental policy competence in the constitution.[16] But, as a rule, taxes with an exclusively environmental purpose ultimately still generate revenue. There is a theory in Swiss legal literature that such taxes might still be treated as environmental policy instruments if the revenues are either dedicated to environmental state action or recycled to taxpayers, by reducing

---

[9] This is in line with OECD, IEA and European Commission practice. *See* OECD, *supra* note 2, at 26.

[10] *See* Snape & de Souza, *supra* note 4, at 13.

[11] OECD, *supra* note 2, at 26.

[12] MÄÄTTÄ (1997), *supra* note 3, at 38*ff*.; MÄÄTTÄ (2006), *supra* note 2, at 35*ff*.

[13] *See* Xavier Oberson & Jean-Frédéric Maraia, LOI SUR LA PROTECTION DE L'ENVIRONNEMENT [LAW ON THE PROTECTION OF THE ENVIRONMENT] 11*ff*. (2010).

[14] In Germany this concept is known as 'Erdrosselungssteuer' (strangulation tax), and in Switzerland as 'konfiskatorische Steuer' (confiscating tax). *See* CHRISTIAN WALDHOFF, VERFASSUNGSRECHTLICHE VORGABEN FÜR DIE STEUERGESETZGEBUNG IM VERGLEICH DEUTSCHLAND-SCHWEIZ [CONSTITUTIONAL REQUIREMENTS FOR THE TAX LEGISLATOR—A COMPARATIVE ANALYSIS GERMANY–SWITZERLAND] 321*ff*. (1997).

[15] See the discussion of Constitutional Requirements, *infra*, for an example from Germany.

[16] *Id.*

social security contributions for instance. This category is treated under the notion of 'pure steering taxes' (*'reine Lenkungssteuern'* in German or *'pures taxes d'incitation'* in French).[17] In the view of the author, this categorization is not useful for the purpose of constitutional competences: After all, these taxes finance public services with the only difference that the exact allocation of revenues is already decided in the tax law (and not, as is usually the case, via budget legislation).[18] To what extent this revenue allocation is constitutional has to be decided in accordance with constitutional principles applying to budget legislation.[19]

As a rule, states do not have one single tax, but rather a system comprising a wide variety of taxes that has developed in the course of time. They may vary considerably regarding function, justification and tax design. Each tax plays a different role in environmental tax schemes, due to the different environmental goals they target as well as the different manners in which they aim to achieve these targets. For instance, direct emission taxes are directly linked with the quality and quantity of environmentally detrimental behavior such as the emission of specific noxious substances. Consumer taxes, on the other hand, are typically linked to an environmentally neutral behavior such as selling or consuming energy, which is only roughly connected to environmental policy objectives. Furthermore, the distinction of traditional types of taxes made by economists and lawyers plays a central role in the attribution of tax competences and in the application of tax principles. The most important distinction is between direct and indirect taxes (see for instance Art. 113 of the Treaty on the Functioning of the European Union (TFEU)).[20] Income taxes (including corporate income taxes) are prototypes of direct taxes, whereas taxes on consumption (sales, VAT, or excises) are prototypes of indirect taxes. The attribution of special taxes to these categories is surrounded by many uncertainties; in principle the decisive factor is the likelihood that taxpayers will pass the tax on to others (indirect taxes) or not (direct taxes).

Tax differentiations establish different tax rates based on an environmental assessment of a variety of taxable activities. They have proven to be an effective way to influence—that is, restrict or stimulate—individual behavior.[21] A case in point: A lower mineral oil tax rate in favor of unleaded petrol has boosted the consumption of this fuel in many countries. In other cases, leaded petrol vanished from the market due to a rather small difference in tax rates. When tax rates are designed to put a price on environmentally undesirable behavior (or encourage environmentally favorable behavior), they must be classified as environmental tax schemes. This is true even if the tax rates are integrated in nonenvironmental tax codes.

---

[17]   *See* Oberson & Maraia, *supra* note 13, at 11*ff.*
[18]   *Id.* at 13.
[19]   In Germany, for instance, the Constitutional Court rules that these dedications 'ex ante' by material tax legislation are possible to a certain degree, as long as the leeway of budget legislation is not affected in a substantial manner. *See, e.g.*, Andreas Musil, *Steuerbegriff und Non-Affekationsprinzip [Tax Terminology and the Universality Principle]*, 122 DEUTSCHES VERWALTUNGSBLATT [GERMAN LAW JOURNAL] 1526–31 (2007).
[20]   *See, e.g.*, Thuronyi, *supra* note 5, at 54*ff.*; Snape & de Souza, *supra* note 4, at 6*ff.*
[21]   For tax differentiation as an instrument of environmental tax policy, see MÄÄTTÄ (2006), *supra* note 2, at 60*ff.*

Finally, the identification of tax subsidies plays an important role in attributing competences and/or applying legal principles.[22] Tax subsidies or 'tax expenditures' are an equivalent to direct subsidies and are therefore subject to the respective legal principles (like the rules on subsidies or state aid of GATT/WTO or the EU, as discussed later in this chapter). In practice, there is a broad variety of tax reliefs ranging from tax exemptions and reduced tax rates to investment allowances, tax credits and accelerated depreciation.[23] Discerning tax subsidies from tax exemptions or reductions that are a necessary part of the tax scheme is notoriously complex.

Tax Competence in Constitutional Law

Tax legislation falls to a large extent under national sovereignty. The legal authority to enact environmental taxes is therefore framed by national constitutions; supranational or international law (dealt with later in this chapter) is of secondary relevance. For this reason, this chapter will address some basic features of constitutional law regarding taxes (or finances in general).

Availability of constitutional remedies

The relevance of constitutional rules regarding taxes is heavily dependent on whether or not courts have the power to overturn acts of legislature on the basis of unconstitutionality.[24] This is generally not possible in countries that do not have a written constitution, for instance the United Kingdom or New Zealand.[25] The situation varies significantly from country to country: In Germany, only constitutional or other centralized high courts can overturn acts of legislature on the basis of unconstitutionality. This would be classified as a centralized approach, whereas a decentralized approach empowers regular courts to overturn legislation as well. Moreover, differences in the access to courts have to be considered (Germany's Federal Constitutional Court is an example of broad access and the French *Conseil Constitutionnel* is an example of rather narrow access). When a tax is declared to be unconstitutional by a court, it is also important to know whether this decision will apply prospectively only or retroactively as well (in which case already paid taxes have to be reimbursed).

Substantive constitutional tax concepts

Some constitutions contain some rules on the design of taxes, though they are often quite abstract. These rules generally concern either abstract principles of taxation like the ability-to-pay principle (as is the case in Brazil and Spain)[26] or the design of specific taxes

---

[22] *See* Rodi, *supra* note 6, at 87*ff*; Snape & de Souza, *supra* note 4, at 174–78.
[23] *See* ANUSCHKA BAKKER ED., TAX AND THE ENVIRONMENT: A WORLD OF POSSIBILITIES 20*ff*. (2009).
[24] *See* Thuronyi, *supra* note 5, at 64–69.
[25] The power of the courts, in the UK for instance, to invalidate statutes on the basis that they violate European law is, accordingly, gaining importance.
[26] *See, e.g.*, CONSTITUIÇÃO FEDERAL Art. 145 II 1 (Braz.); CONSTITUCION ESPAÑOLA, Art. 31 I (Spain).

(as in Brazil and Portugal).[27] Most constitutions do not contain special substantive rules on the design of taxes, which is the case in Germany. In the absence of such specifications, the application of general constitutional rules (such as the principle of equal treatment or the basic freedoms) to tax laws can be challenging.

Classification and allocation of tax powers

The competence to legislate taxes can be divided and attributed in different manners.[28] It can be concentrated on one level of government (such as the national government) or allocated to different levels of government in a variety of ways. In centralized states these levels are the central government and the local governments. In federal states, strong intermediate levels of government in the form of autonomous or independent regions, provinces or states can also be involved.

Certain types of taxes can be clearly distinguished: income taxes, wealth taxes, turnover taxes, excise and consumption taxes, natural resource taxes, and so on. The power of taxation with respect to one particular category of tax is often fully reserved to one specific level of government (see for instance Art. 153 of the Brazilian Constitution for taxes of the Federation). In Germany, the Federation has a broad general concurrent authority to legislate the majority of taxes, with the exception of some minor municipal taxes. States are entitled to implement taxes in areas where the Federation has not exercised its legislative power.[29] In practice, however, the Federation has enacted a rather comprehensive number of tax acts. If a state wants to introduce a new tax, it must prove that this tax is not comparable to the existing federal taxes, which is done by comparing the basic features of both tax schemes.

A second distinction can be made with respect to the basic elements of any tax: the subjects of the tax or the types of taxpayers, the tax base, the tax rate, and the tax procedure. Constitutions can reserve the power to legislate with regard to one element of taxation for one level of government, and with regard to another element of taxation for another level of government. Tax rates (in particular in the case of surcharge models)[30] and especially minimum tax rates are a good example of this approach.[31]

Finally, different functions of the legislative tax authority, such as the power to legislate, the power to administer and the right to receive the revenue, can be attributed to different levels of government. The German Constitution is an example of a sophisticated distribution system allocating these functions among federal, state and local government levels (Arts. 105, 106 and 108 of the German Constitution).

---

[27]   *See, e.g.*, CONSTITUIÇÃO FEDERAL Art. 153 (Braz.) (regarding different kinds of taxes including income tax); CONST. Art. 104 III (Port.) (wealth tax); CONST. Art. 145 IV (Port.) (consumption taxes).

[28]   *See* Frans Vanistendael, *Legal Framework for Taxation, in* TAX LAW DESIGN AND DRAFTING 15, 66*ff.* (Victor Thuronyi ed., 1996).

[29]   Concurrent tax legislation authority is also foreseen for a number of taxes in CONSTITUIÇÃO FEDERAL Art. 145 (Braz.).

[30]   *See, e.g.*, Thuronyi, *supra* note 5, at 73–76. (2003).

[31]   *See, e.g.*, CONSTITUIÇÃO FEDERAL Art. 154 (Braz.).

CONSTITUTIONAL REQUIREMENTS FOR ENVIRONMENTAL TAXES

This section examines general constitutional requirements for environmental taxes, and the competent legislative powers behind those taxes in particular. Moreover, it deals with problems related to legislative procedure, revenue allocation, and the principles of legality and rules on retroactive legislation. Finally, the limits on environmental taxes that ensue from basic constitutional rights (regarding freedom and equality) will be addressed.

Legislative Competences

Environmental taxes constitute a very specific and rather new economic instrument in the field of environmental policies. This novelty explains why constitutions contain an explicit legislative competence only in very exceptional cases. As a rule, examples can only be found in federal states, because they must provide specific legislative competences to different parts of the state. Art. 170 VI of the Brazilian Constitution is a good example, stating that products and services may deserve a different treatment depending on their environmental impact. Art. 85 of the Swiss Constitution gives the Federation the power to legislate on a traffic and transportation levy.

Thus, constitutions generally provide no specific authorization to legislate environmental taxes. However, this does not mean that it is not possible to enact environmental taxes. Rather, it is a matter of determining whether tax or environmental competence rules apply. It is well known that taxes have various effects on the behavior of individuals and especially on their environmental behavior. In a normative sense, most countries and their respective constitutions do not restrict taxes to their technical function of raising revenue. It can even be said that as a rule, taxes may primarily have steering effects.[32] In these cases, it has to be decided whether the rules on tax or environmental law (or both) apply.[33] This may cause problems for federal states, as the distribution of legislative competences may differ for tax and environmental law.[34] For example, the Australian courts have taken the view that taxation is not confined to the purpose of raising revenue. Laws with respect to a range of social and economic objectives fall within the constitutional power of the Commonwealth, as long as the relevant legislation imposes an obligation to pay taxes.[35] Against this background, there is a discernible danger that steering taxes

---

[32]   For Scandinavian countries, see MÄÄTTÄ (2006), *supra* note 2, at 40.

[33]   This would be in line with the legal practice in Belgium, where tax competences as well as environmental competences are precisely divided and attributed to the federal and the regional level, which must be taken into account. *See* Isabelle Richelle, *Environment and Taxation: A Belgian Overview, in* ENVIRONMENTAL TAXES: A GLOBAL PERSPECTIVE 25 (Bronwyn Spicer ed., 2008).

[34]   *See, e.g.*, Xavier Oberson, *Compétence des cantons en matière de fiscalité écologique, in* REFORME FISCALE ECOLOGIQUE. FONDEMENTS, APPLICATIONS [*Authority of cantons in the field of ecological taxation,* in ECOLOGICAL TAX REFORM, FOUNDATIONS AND APPLICATIONS] 67*ff.* (G. Pillet et al. eds., 2001), for an example of Switzerland, and Snape & de Souza, *supra* note 4, at 19*ff.* for an example of the UK.

[35]   *Osborne v Commonwealth* (1911) 12 CLR 321 (Austl.); *Fairfax v FCT* (1965) 114 CLR 1 (Austl.).

based on tax competences can interfere with or be in contradiction to the law and policy schemes already applicable to the substantive fields these taxes target.[36]

Thus, for steering taxes the question of whether tax law competences, environmental law competences or both apply remains unanswered.

This is generally not an issue in the case of the German Constitution, since the Federation has far-reaching competences in both fields.[37] Still, in special cases it is possible that tax law competences and environmental law competences are vested in different legal authorities. An academic debate regarding the competence requirements under these circumstances has been ongoing for decades. Some authors argued that the legislator enacting environmental taxes should possess both authorizations. Others argued that the tax competence is sufficient even in the case of steering taxes. This problem has remained unresolved for a long time. The Federal Constitutional Court had to make a decision in a case where a municipality enacted a tax on disposable tableware, which is used in fast food restaurants, for example. It was based on the exclusive municipal tax power on local taxes. It was argued that these taxes are unconstitutional, as the municipalities have no competences in environmental policies (as long as these are not delegated to them by state law). The Federal Constitutional Court decided for the first time that the tax competence allows the legislator to enact steering taxes, especially environmental ones, even if the main purpose of the tax is not a fiscal one. At the same time the Federal Court stated that the legislator should not use these fiscal instruments to interfere with the policies of another state actor in a way that conflicts with that actor's material law, based on an unwritten constitutional principle that legal rules should not contradict each other. In this case the main argument was that the local packaging tax contradicted the principles of federal waste law.[38]

A similar competence problem has to be solved in Switzerland based on a rather different set of rules regarding the distribution of competences. In this case, the Federation has restricted tax competences, for instance on consumption taxes (Arts. 86, 130, 131 of the Swiss Constitution) and on direct income taxes (Art. 128 of the Swiss Constitution). Beyond that the Federal Court decided that the Federation may legislate an agricultural steering tax merely within its competence with regard to agriculture (Art. 104 of the Swiss Constitution).[39] According to Oberson and Maraia the same approach would apply to all sorts of environmental taxes (such as a CO_2 tax) on the basis of the broad federal environmental competence (Art. 74 I of the Swiss Constitution).[40] According to the authors, this should not lead to a circumvention of restricted federal tax competences. They suggest that this can be reached by conducting a strict necessity test on the one side and applying the condition that environmental taxes may not lead to an increase of revenues of the

---

[36]   See the discussion in Chapter 14 in this Handbook about 'Integration and Coordination' and 'Administration and Costs,' for examples of conflicts between fiscal and environmental policies in Brazil.

[37]   *Id.*

[38]   *See* Monika Böhm, *Environmental Impact of Local Taxes and Fees, in* 7 CRITICAL ISSUES IN ENVIRONMENTAL TAXATION: INTERNATIONAL AND COMPARATIVE PERSPECTIVES 547–56 (Lin-Heng Lye et al. eds., 2009).

[39]   For references, see Oberson & Maraia, *supra* note 13, at 23–24.

[40]   *Id.* at 25*ff.*

Federation on the other side. To this end, taxes have to be designed in a revenue-neutral way (*'staatsquotenneutral'*) by recycling revenues to the taxpayers. Regarding the CO_2 tax, an advisory report recommended using the revenue to finance energy and environmental measures.[41] The author of this chapter is of the opinion that this recommendation is not sufficient to meet the legal standard since a financing state tax is not state budget-neutral. Rather, it functions just as a shortcut for state financing by allocating tax revenues in the state budget first and subsequently using them to finance state tasks.

Australian courts have also taken the view that taxation is not confined to the raising of revenue. Laws with respect to a range of social and economic objectives fall within the constitutional power of the Commonwealth, as long as the relevant legislation imposes an obligation to pay taxes.[42] Nevertheless, a challenging dilemma surfaces in the Australian context that may exist in other federal states as well: The Australian Constitution expressly confers powers to enact laws dealing with taxation matters to the Commonwealth. However, in environmental matters the Constitution remains rather silent on extending the necessary corresponding power. This state of affairs appears to have its genesis in the colonial history of the continent. At the time the Constitution was drafted in 1901, the question of access to the environment as a resource was seen as a matter of greater significance than issues relating to the protection and conservation of the environment. As a result, the power to manage environmental resources was vested in the states where these resources were located, and state legislation was designed to facilitate their exploitation.[43] Attempts of the federal government to intervene in environmental and resource matters within state jurisdictions were resented by the states, and often resulted in protracted litigation about its constitutionality.[44]

The framers of the Constitution included measures under the 'other heads of power' provisions of the Constitution to enable the federal government to assert its regulatory authority and avoid a stalemate in the exercise of government functions. This approach also tackled the absence of a specific constitutional mandate on environmental regulation.[45] Under these circumstances, the legislative authority of the federal government is extended into areas that historically fell under the regulatory competence of the constituent states with judicial backing. In such cases, the High Court has interpreted the Commonwealth's mandate to encompass a 'nationhood' power to enable Australia to function as a nation.[46] Most of the relevant provisions that could confer the authority to enact environmental taxes under the 'other heads of power' are set out in section 51 of the Constitution. The power to make laws with respect to trade and commerce with

---

[41]   *Rapport explicatif Taxe CO_2 prélevée sur les agents énergétiques fossiles* [*Explanatory Report CO_2 Tax on Fossil Energy Sources*] given on 23 March 1994 for the Swiss Federal Department of the Interior, 25*ff.*

[42]   *Osborne v Commonwealth* (1911) 12 CLR 321 (Austl.); *Fairfax v FCT* (1965) 114 CLR 1 (Austl.).

[43]   D. FISHER, ENVIRONMENTAL LAW: TEXT AND MATERIALS 45 (1993).

[44]   H. Ashiabor, *Constitutional Constraints to the Implementation of an Integrated Environmental Tax Management Policy: The Australian Experience, in* 1 CRITICAL ISSUES IN ENVIRONMENTAL TAXATION 125 (Janet Milne et al. eds., 2003).

[45]   J. Crawford, *The Constitution and the Environment*, 3 SYDNEY L. REV. 11 (1991).

[46]   *Murphyores v The Commonwealth* (1976) 136 CLR 1 (Austl.); *Commonwealth v Tasmania* (1983) 158 CLR 1 (Austl.).

other countries and among the states is contained in these provisions. Section 51(i) of the Constitution confers this power and has been used by the Commonwealth to regulate a whole range of environmental matters. This power is yet to be used to enact environmental tax instruments in Australia.

Similar problems may be encountered in countries that are not federal states *stricto sensu*, as far as competences are delegated. In the United Kingdom for example, the municipalities and regions dispose of environmental competences, but as a rule not environmental *tax* competences.[47]

Environmental Taxes and Revenue Allocation

Taxes should create revenues for public budgets. This revenue creation raises some legal questions in the case of environmental taxes.

As a rule, environmental taxes place a financial burden on environmentally detrimental behavior. Complete suppression of such behavior means the tax is successful from an environmental point of view, which ultimately results in a tax revenue close to zero. However, this concept is in conflict with a basic feature of taxes: Taxes that do not yield any revenue should no longer be considered taxes (based on the power to tax). They would function as command-and-control instruments and should be treated as such.[48] But how to draw a line between these categories? In Germany there is consensus that taxes lose their character as taxes when their contribution to state revenues is lower than their administrative costs.[49] The opponents of a municipal packaging tax based their case on this argument;[50] the Federal Constitutional Court unfortunately did not give a ruling on this matter as the tax was declared unconstitutional for other reasons.

As a rule, taxes are part of general state revenue and are not an instrument to finance specific tasks or objectives. This in turn is in conflict with the idea of earmarking environmental taxes.[51] There may be reasons to allocate their revenue to specific state activities, such as environmental policy measures or social security systems ('double dividend'). This can be done to increase the acceptance of the population or to fund underfinanced institutions independent of yearly budget decisions. Constitutional rules can be in place to regulate or restrict earmarking. In Germany, for example, there is no general rule that forbids the earmarking of taxes.[52] However, there is consensus that there are quantitative limits to this practice, as it interferes with the rights of the budget legislator and the function of the state budget to level state income and expenses. Of course, it is difficult to determine where exactly these limits have to be drawn.

Finally, problems may arise in federal states if the tax legislating body is not the body

---

[47]   Snape & de Souza, *supra* note 4, at 29–30.
[48]   See the discussion of 'Analytical Foundations,' *supra*, in this Chapter.
[49]   For the difficulties of assessing the costs of tax administration, see Chapter 14 in this Handbook. In the section on 'Administration and Costs,' the authors refer to the results of empirical studies that administration costs are—as a rule—higher on a regional level.
[50]   Snape & de Souza, *supra* note 4, at 29–30.
[51]   *See* MÄÄTTÄ (2006), *supra* note 2, at 70*ff.*
[52]   See Chapter 6, *Earmarking Revenues from Environmentally Related Taxes*, in this Handbook. Some countries have constitutional restrictions on earmarking.

that is entitled to the revenue. This is often the case in Germany, where the Federation has far-reaching competences regarding tax legislation. However, the revenue of many types of taxes is fully or partly attributed to the *Länder* or the municipalities (Art. 106 of the German Constitution). If the legislature provides tax subsidies for environmental purposes in this context, it would implement environmental policies at the expense of those entitled to the revenue. However, there is no constitutional rule forbidding this.

In one case this has led to a constitutional conflict in Germany. The annual vehicle tax used to be a consumption tax in a broad sense (based on the ability-to-pay of those who can afford big cars). In recent years it has been transformed into an environmental tax by integrating environmental performance criteria into the tax base.[53] Because the revenue of this tax was formerly attributed to the *Länder* budgets, the Federation's *Länder* Chamber (Bundesrat) had to take part in the legislation. The Chamber finally opposed the reform, fearing erosion of the tax base. As a result the German Constitution was amended, attributing the revenue to the national budget (while compensating the *Länder* with other income).

Legislative Procedure

When analyzing the legislative process, it is important to determine to what extent national constitutions affect the procedures to adopt new environmental tax instruments, especially if the procedural requirements to enact tax law and environmental law are different.

As a starting point, it must be stated that environmental taxes are as a rule qualified as taxes, as discussed above. In the United States, tax measures must originate in the House of Representatives pursuant to Art. 1, section 7 of the Constitution. In France, the procedures to enact tax legislation are imposed by the organic budget; according to Art. 46 of the French Constitution this type of law is higher-ranking than ordinary laws.

Environmental taxes have a dual character, qualifying as taxes on the one hand and as environmental policy instruments on the other. An example of this potentially problematic nature can be found in European Law. Decisions related to tax matters require a unanimous vote in the Council. Environmental measures, however, are enacted following the normal procedure and can therefore be adopted with a majority vote (Art. 192 I of TFEU). Still, in this case the Council has to unanimously adopt provisions of a primarily fiscal nature (Art. 192 II (a) of TFEU). As long as an environmental tax can be seen as a fiscal measure based on its main focus (and generally it can), this principle is applicable. The Commission tried to change this to qualified majority voting during the Government Conference in Nice in 2000, but without success.[54] As a result, all efforts of the Commission to enact a CO_2/energy tax have so far failed.[55]

---

[53] *See, e.g.*, the overview of CO_2-based motor vehicle taxes in the EU 2011, *ACEA Tax Guide 2011*, EUROPEAN AUTOMOBILE MANUFACTURERS' ASS'N, http://www.acea.be/news/news_detail/acea_tax_guide_2011/ (last visited Dec. 1, 2011).

[54] *See Commission Communication on Qualified Majority Voting for Single Market Aspects in the Taxation and Social Security Fields*, COM (2000) 114 final (Mar. 14, 2000).

[55] *See, e.g.*, Proposal for a Council Directive Introducing A Tax on Carbon Dioxide Emissions and Energy, 1992 O.J. (C 196/1).

Application of Substantial Legal Principles

General legal principles are often applied in a different—and as a rule more restrictive—way in the area of tax law. This is true, for instance, for the legality principle[56] or the rules on retroactive legislation.[57]

Principle of legality

The principle of legality applies to environmental taxes as long as they are set up by legislative acts.[58] In accordance with the well-known democratic claim for 'no taxation without representation,' the basic features of the environmental tax must be fixed in the parliamentary act itself (and not in implementation acts of the executive branch). Some constitutions contain special rules regarding the legality of taxes, which are—as a rule—stricter than the general legality principle.[59] In practice, constitutions differ significantly in how and to what extent they allow the legislature to delegate tax-lawmaking authority.[60]

The question of whether this legality principle is more lenient in the case of incentive taxes often arises in the field of environmental taxes.[61] For example, to ensure the effectiveness of environmental taxes, it may be required that the tax base can be adapted or modified by the executive branch. The Swiss Federal Court has supported this flexibility for incentive taxes that have been based on the legislative competence for agriculture. However, it did not follow this approach regarding incentive taxes based on tax competences.[62] Another example: The German Constitutional Court ruled that steering tax acts must be explicit with regard to their steering purpose.[63]

Since environmental taxes are part of the environmental policy instrument toolbox, their tax rates should be in line with general environmental policy objectives. For example, the Vietnamese Environmental Tax Act recently enacted ranges of tax rates to be further determined by the ministries.[64]

---

[56]   *See* MÄÄTTÄ (2006), *supra* note 2, at 46; MÄÄTTÄ (1997), *supra* note 3, at 232*ff.*; for Switzerland, Oberson & Maraia, *supra* note 13, at 33; for Europe, BESSELINK ET AL. EDS., THE ECLIPSE OF THE LEGALITY PRINCIPLE IN THE EUROPEAN UNION (2011).

[57]   MÄÄTTÄ (1997), *supra* note 3, at 243*ff.*

[58]   For a comparative legal overview, see Thuronyi, *supra* note 5, at 70–99; Vanistendael, *supra* note 28, at 16, 55*ff.*

[59]   *See, e.g.*, CONSTITUIÇÃO FEDERAL Art. 150, I (Braz.); CONST. (1976) Art. 103, sec. II (Port.); 1994 CONST. Arts 170, sec. I, 172 sec. II (Belg.); SYNTAGMA [SYN.] Art. 78 secs I, IV (Greece); RIGES GRUNDLOV § 43 (Den.).

[60]   *See* Vanistendael, *supra* note 28, at 16.

[61]   *See* Oberson & Maraia, *supra* note 13, at 34.

[62]   *Id.* at 35.

[63]   *See* Michael Rodi, *Ecological Tax Reform in Germany*, BULLETIN FOR INTERNATIONAL FISCAL DOCUMENTATION 486 (2000).

[64]   See Chapter 7, *Designing Environmental Taxes in Countries in Transition: A Case Study of Vietnam*, in this Handbook.

Retroactivity

Another problem typically associated with incentive taxes is the issue of retroactivity. Normally, legislative acts take effect after they have entered into force unless circumstances justify an earlier date. Some constitutions contain—next to the general constitutional rules—special rules on the retroactivity of taxes.[65] Often changes in taxes collected on an annual basis enter into effect at the beginning of the fiscal year in which the taxes were modified. On the one hand, legislators generally want to set new legislation into force as early as possible to avoid the use of (or even the rush to use) tax subsidies that they plan to reduce or abolish. On the other hand, the legislator must also allow taxpayers sufficient time to bring their taxable behavior in line with the new requirements. To what extent a retroactive entry into force is legally possible must be carefully analyzed based on each individual constitution, as constitutional law concerning retroactive tax legislation can vary substantially.[66]

Environmental Taxes and Basic Rights

As a rule, constitutions do not contain any specific substantive rules for or limits to environmental taxes. In fact, they rarely deal with the design of taxes at all. The challenge is therefore to apply general legal principles, such as fundamental rights, to environmental taxes. Among the most important rules and principles are those concerning equality or nondiscrimination.[67] Taxes infringe upon individual freedoms; therefore it must be decided under which circumstances they can be justified on grounds of the freedom of profession or the freedom of property. The scrutiny in the application of fundamental freedoms to tax laws differs a great deal from country to country. Germany, for example, employs a rather strict equality test whereas the United States applies a mere 'rational basis' test.[68]

When considering the principle of equality it becomes apparent that environmental taxes deviate from the ability-to-pay-principle, which concretizes the nondiscrimination principle for the field of tax law.[69] Some argue that this principle does not apply to incentive taxes.[70] More sophisticated arguments support the opinion that the ability-to-pay

---

[65]   See for instance Constitution of Portugal Art. 103 III; Constitution of Greece Art. 78 II.

[66]   For a comparative legal overview, see Thuronyi, *supra* note 5, at 76–99; Vanistendael, *supra* note 28, at 24*ff*.

[67]   For an example of a comparative tax law approach, see Thuronyi, *supra* note 5, at 82–91; Vanistendael, *supra* note 28, at 19*ff*.

[68]   *See* Thuronyi, *supra* note 5, at 82–91.

[69]   Sometimes the ability-to-pay principle is explicitly regulated in constitutions. *See, e.g.,* Constituição Federal Art. 145, III(1) (Braz.); Costituzione [Cost.] (It.) Art. 53: 'Everyone shall contribute to public expenditure in proportion to his resources'; Constitucion Española Art. 31 (Spain) holds a similar provision. Under most constitutions it is acknowledged on the basis of general considerations; see for instance Joseph M. Dodge, *Theories of Tax Justice: Ruminations on the Benefit, Partnership, and Ability-to-pay Principles*, 4 Tax L. Rev. 399 (2005). The ability-to-pay principle is less common in common-law countries. *See* Yuri Grbich, *New Modalities in Tax Decision-Making: Applying European Experience to Australia*, 2 Int'l Tax. Res. 1 (2004).

[70]   Oberson & Maraia, *supra* note 13, at 40.

principle applies to all taxes and that deviations must be justified in the light of the steer-ing objective of the tax.[71]

The same applies when incentive taxes intervene with basic freedoms.[72] In this context most countries apply the principle of proportionality: There must be some proportional relationship between the goals to be attained and the means to be used by the legislator.[73] However, this test is difficult to apply to normal financing taxes, as their purpose is just to create revenue for the state budget. This purpose is better served if the tax collects more funds from the taxpayers. As a result the principle of proportionality is generally interpreted as imposing only a marginal limitation on the taxing power of governments in the sense that they cannot impose confiscatory taxes.[74] As in the case of the equality principle, it could be argued that the proportionality test to determine if environmental taxes serve their environmental goals should be stricter to the extent that taxes deviate from ability-to-pay standards. This would allow for the proportionality of specific objec-tives of the law to be tested.

These problems can be analyzed using the example of energy and carbon taxes. These taxes generally foresee reliefs or exemptions to safeguard competitiveness of indus-try.[75] This is why the French *Conseil Constitutionnel* declared the French carbon tax unconstitutional,[76] as it exempted nearly all heavily emitting plants. The *Conseil* stated that this is not in line with the basic idea of the tax and the principle of equality, at least as long as the certificates under the European Emissions Trading Scheme are allocated for free. Recently, the German Federal Constitutional Court had to decide the constitu-tionality of the relief scheme of the Ecotax Law in the field of energy taxation.[77] Service companies (transport and cooling industry) complained that they were not entitled to tax relief, although they are extremely energy-intense as well. The Constitutional Court rejected this argument, as the service sector is not subject to as much international com-petition as the manufacturing industry.

Kalle Määttä[78] mentions another interesting case study: Vehicles for off-road use are often exempted from vehicle taxation. This may have been an expression of the benefit principle: Only those who use roads have to pay taxes. But when vehicle taxes are used as an environmental policy instrument, it no longer matters if the vehicles are used on the roads or for off-road driving. This differentiation can no longer be justified based on the modern rationality of vehicle taxes. On these grounds, one should also consider whether tax exemptions in vehicle tax schemes for public services (such as armed forces) are still legally acceptable.

---

[71]   *See, e.g., id.* at 37, 41.
[72]   *Id.* at 42.
[73]   *See* Vanistendael, *supra* note 28, at 23–24.
[74]   *Id.*
[75]   For carbon tax reliefs, see MÄÄTTÄ (2006), *supra* note 2, at 56*ff.*
[76]   *Conseil Constitutionnel* [CC] [Constitutional Court] decision No. 2009-599DC, Dec. 29, 2009, J.O. Dec. 31, 2009 (Fr.).
[77]   *See* Bundesverfassungsgericht [BVerfG] [Federal Constitutional Court] Apr. 20, 2004, ENTSCHEIDUNGEN DES BUNDESVERFASSUNGSGERICHTS [BVERFGE] 110, 274 (Ger.).
[78]   MÄÄTTÄ (2006), *supra* note 2, at 42.

ENVIRONMENTAL TAXES AND COORDINATION OF POLICIES

Environmental taxes are instruments of taxation and environmental policies, and as such must be integrated into both these policy concepts. Moreover, environmental taxes can lead to tensions and lack of coordination with other policy fields such as traffic and transport, energy or agriculture. Last but not least, environmental taxes have, as a rule, implications in the area of competition policies.

Next to these questions of horizontal or cross-sectoral integration, Chalifour et al. (Chapter 14 of this Handbook) discern challenges of vertical and time coordination from a policymaking point of view. The mentioned coordination problems become even more complicated when vertical integration is concerned. In this case, competences for the policy fields affected by the environmental tax are attributed to different levels of government. Additionally, as discussed in Chapter 14, time coordination problems may arise: For example, tax exemptions granted in favor of the production of renewable energies may reduce the use of fossil energy in the short run, but may have a negative environmental impact due to land use changes in the long run.

It is not the objective of this chapter to optimize these relationships. In its analysis of the legal authority to enact environmental taxes, the chapter merely inquires if and to what extent contradictions may invoke unconstitutionality and thus limit the legislator. On the one hand, environmental tax laws can directly conflict with constitutional rules or principles, such as constitutional rules on competition, the common market or the environment. On the other hand, conflicts of environmental tax laws with other legislation may—in exceptional cases—infringe constitutional rules and lead to constitutional challenges. In Germany, a principle of non-contradiction is derived from the Rule of Law, a concept known as *Rechtsstaatsprinzip*.[79] In some circumstances a (higher-ranking) legislator may have the competence to establish coordination rules; this is usually the case for municipal taxes.[80]

Coordination with Environmental Policies

In the case of environmental taxes, the challenge of policy coordination lies of course in the field of environmental policies. There are many examples of attempts to tackle this problem using institutional arrangements, like national climate change commissions.[81]

Since the principles of environmental policy are generally applicable to environmental taxes,[82] they could—from a substantive perspective—contribute to that coordination task. Environmental taxes have to be in line with, for example, the precautionary

---

[79] See Julian Rivers, *Rechtsstaatsprinzip and Rule of Law Revisited, in* DIE ORDNUNG DER FREIHEIT. FESTSCHRIFT FÜR CHRISTIAN STARCK ZUM SIEBZIGSTEN GEBURTSTAG [THE ORDER OF FREEDOM. COMMEMORATIVE PUBLICATION FOR CHRISTIAN STARCK FOR HIS 70TH BIRTHDAY] 891 (Grote et al. eds., 2007).

[80] See Chapter 14 of this Handbook, *Multi-level Governance*, text at note 90, with an example from Indonesia.

[81] For a discussion of coordination issues and mechanisms, see Chapter 14 of this Handbook.

[82] BAKKER, *supra* note 23, at 7*ff.*

principle[83] or the polluter-pays principle[84] as set out in an increasing number of constitutions. It must be clear however that environmental principles function more as general policy principles, and infringements on them are therefore only litigable in extreme cases.[85] Environmental principles therefore are a justification for environmental taxes, rather than a legal guideline for their design.

The role of environmental taxes as part of an environmental instrument mix becomes evident in climate change policies, when CO_2 or energy taxes are combined with command-and-control law (such as minimum requirements for fuel consumption or for energy efficiency of car fleets), information-based rules (such as product labeling for energy consuming goods), promotion schemes for renewables or CO_2 emissions trading. Designing this instrument mix in an efficient way is a big challenge;[86] a suboptimally designed combination of instruments may lead to legal conflicts. For example, if only certain parts of an industry are subject to CO_2 emissions trading, have to buy certificates within an auctioning scheme and additionally have to pay CO_2 or energy taxes, this could easily result in an infringement of the nondiscrimination rule.

Coordination within Tax Policies

Environmental taxes are part of the legal tax scheme. This raises questions with regard to consistent tax policy.[87] For instance, the legislator must take into account how the introduction of environmental taxes will shift the effective overall tax burden as well as revenue structure (in sum and possibly regarding different recipients). The financing function will be especially vulnerable to new uncertainties, given that the reaction of taxpayers to new incentives cannot easily be foreseen. Of course, all these factors can be elements of a consistent policy approach (for example, shifting tax burdens from labor to the use of natural resources, or 'tax bads not goods'). These are basically political questions that can encounter legal barriers only in exceptional cases (for instance, regarding the ability-to-pay principle).

Tax Coordination within Common Markets

Different tax schemes may impede economic activities within a common market area. This is often the case for federal states when lower levels of authority have the right to tax. For this reason, tax authorities are often restricted by an overarching constitutional

---

[83]   *See* B. de Vries & L. Francot-Timmermans, *As Good as it Gets: On Risk, Legality and the Precautionary Principle*, *in* THE ECLIPSE OF THE LEGALITY PRINCIPLE IN THE EUROPEAN UNION 83 (Leonard Besselink et al. eds., 2011)

[84]   Jonathan Verschuuren, PRINCIPLES OF ENVIRONMENTAL LAW: THE IDEAL OF SUSTAINABLE DEVELOPMENT AND THE ROLE OF PRINCIPLES OF INTERNATIONAL, EUROPEAN AND NATIONAL ENVIRONMENTAL LAW (2003).

[85]   *Id.* at 129*ff.*

[86]   *See* Paul Lehmann, *Using a Policy Mix to Combat Climate Change. An Economic Evaluation of Policies in the German Electricity Sector* (Dec. 4, 2010) (unpublished Ph.D. dissertation, University of Halle-Wittenberg) (on file with author).

[87]   *See* Louis Kaplow, *An Optimal Tax System* (Nat'l Bureau of Econ. Res., Working Paper No. 17214, 2011).

or other type of fundamental law. A similar constellation can be found in the European Union, where national tax laws may interfere with the Common Market. In federal systems, tax policy coordination can be achieved through constitutional rules or positive harmonization rules[88] legislated by a higher authority.[89]

The situation under the United States Constitution is a good example of positive tax coordination in federal states. The Constitution contains only two quite specific rules explicitly restricting the general scope of state tax powers.[90] This does not mean, however, that the framers of the Constitution did not clearly recognize the tension between the interest of the states in exercising their taxing power, and the interest of the nation in fostering economic unity.[91] Pursuant to the Commerce Clause of the US Constitution, Congress has the constitutional power to regulate foreign and interstate commerce, and can therefore limit state taxation interfering with international and interstate trade (Art. I, Section 8).[92] Despite this extensive authority to restrict or expand the taxing power of the states, Congress has enacted relatively little legislation in this respect.[93]

Thus, it was up to the US Supreme Court to develop jurisprudence on the effects of the Commerce Clause in case there is no legislation (the 'dormant' aspect of the clause) originating with *Gibbons v. Ogden*.[94] This jurisprudence has been applied to state taxes.[95] In *Complete Auto Transit*, the Supreme Court construed this Commerce Clause as permitting state taxation only where it (1) applies to an activity having a substantial nexus with the taxing state, (2) is fairly apportioned, (3) does not discriminate against interstate commerce, and (4) is fairly related to services provided by the state.[96] A tax law is discriminatory if it taxes 'a transaction or incident more heavily when it crosses state lines than when it occurs entirely within the State.'[97] In the *Jefferson Lines* case, the Court set forth the internal consistency test for the presence of discrimination: Internal consistency is preserved when the imposition of a tax identical to the one in question by every other state would add no burden to interstate commerce that intrastate commerce would not

---

[88]   For the differentiation between positive and negative harmonization, see Charles E. McLure Jr., *The Long Shadow of History: Sovereignty, Tax Assignment, Legislation, and Judicial Decisions on Corporate Income Taxes in the US and EU, in* COMPARATIVE FISCAL FEDERALISM: COMPARING THE EUROPEAN COURT OF JUSTICE AND THE U.S. SUPREME COURT'S TAX JURISPRUDENCE 123 (R. Avi-Yonah et al. eds., 2007).

[89]   See also Chapter 14, *Multi-level Governance*, in this Handbook, text at notes 76 to 81.

[90]   Import-Export Clause (U.S. Const. Art. I, § 10, cl. 2); Duty of Tonnage Prohibition (U.S. Const. Art. I, § cl. 3); *see* Walter Hellerstein, *The U.S. Supreme Court's State Tax Jurisprudence, in* COMPARATIVE FISCAL FEDERALISM: COMPARING THE EUROPEAN COURT OF JUSTICE AND THE U.S. SUPREME COURT'S TAX JURISPRUDENCE 67 (R. Avi-Yonah et al. eds., 2007).

[91]   With references to The Federalist Papers, see Hellerstein, *supra* note 90, at 68.

[92]   *See* McLure Jr., *supra* note 88, at 134.

[93]   For a comprehensive overview, see Tracy A. Kaye, *Tax Discimination: A Comparative Analysis of US and EU Approaches, in* COMPARATIVE FISCAL FEDERALISM: COMPARING THE EUROPEAN COURT OF JUSTICE AND THE U.S. SUPREME COURT'S TAX JURISPRUDENCE 67 (R. Avi-Yonah et al. eds., 2007).

[94]   22 U.S. (9 Wheat.) I (1824).

[95]   For the history of this jurisprudence, see Hellerstein, *supra* note 90, at 74*ff.*

[96]   Complete Auto Transit, Inc. v Brady, 430 U.S. 274, 279 (1977); *see also* McLure Jr., *supra* note 88, at 135–36; Thuronyi, *supra* note 5, at 74.

[97]   Chem. Waste Mgmt., Inc. v Hunt, 504 U.S. 334, 342 (1992).

also bear.[98] Although the Supreme Court has struck down some state tax laws on these grounds in the past, it has generally given the states great latitude in designing their taxes and assessing the consequences.[99]

At first sight, the situation in the European Union is quite comparable. The national states have a far-reaching competence in the field of taxation and thus on environmental taxation. European Union law and the European institutions entrusted with its implementation have to guarantee that national environmental taxation will not distort the EU's internal market. This concern is, for example, reflected in Art. 110 of TFEU on tax discrimination.[100] Taxing power is one of the key features of national sovereignty, which explains why European primary law foresees only very few specific rules directly dealing with the design (or limits) of national tax systems.

The national tax sovereignty of EU Member States is protected first and foremost by the financially weak position of the European Union,[101] whose resources basically consist of national contributions. The European Commission has argued—in vain—in favor of a genuine European tax for a long time. An environmental tax has always been a candidate for this—next to a Unionwide corporate income tax and a financial transaction tax. Today, it is more unlikely than ever that this idea will be realized.[102]

Moreover, the Treaty authorizes the European legislator to harmonize indirect taxation (explicitly in Art. 113 of TFEU) and direct taxation (according to Art. 114 of TFEU, referring to all kinds of regulation) to the extent that harmonization is needed to ensure the establishment and the functioning of the internal market and to avoid distortion of competition.[103] To protect national tax sovereignty, the European legislator can exercise these powers only if the Council unanimously decides on this matter. Needless to say, this constitutes a tremendous hurdle, especially in the light of the expansion of the Union. As a result, only few and very specific legislative acts in the area of direct taxation (not directly affecting environmental taxes) have been based on this.

However, in the field of indirect taxes remarkable legislative activity of the European Union has taken place. At first these developments stayed mainly in the area of value added tax (VAT), but later increasingly expanded into the area of consumption taxes (which seems to be counterintuitive at first glance, taking into account the requirement of unanimity). Even in the area of direct taxation an increase in secondary legislation

---

[98] Oklahoma State Tax Commission v Jefferson Lines Inc., 514 U.S. 175, 185 (1995); *see also* McLure Jr., *supra* note 88, at 135.

[99] For examples, see McLure Jr., *supra* note 88, at 136–37.

[100] 'No Member State shall impose, directly or indirectly, on the products of other Member States any internal taxation of any kind in excess of that imposed directly or indirectly on similar domestic products. Furthermore, no Member State shall impose on the products of other Member States any internal taxation of such a nature as to afford indirect protection of other products.'

[101] *See* P. Genschel & M. Jachtenfuchs, *The Fiscal Anatomy of a Regulatory Polity: Tax Policy and Multilevel Governance in the EU* 5–16 (TranState, Working Paper No. 114, 2010).

[102] *See* Jacques Le Cacheux, Funding the EU Budget with a Genuine Own Resource: The Case for a European Tax (Notre Europe Stud., Working Paper No. 57, 2007).

[103] A good overview on European tax law is provided by Thuronyi, *supra* note 5, at 100; see also the discussion of Chapter 11, *Gaining Intergovernmental Acceptance: Legal Rules Protecting Trade*, in this Handbook, text at notes 70 *et seq.*

can be observed.[104] Regarding indirect taxation, the minimum harmonization of energy taxes has to be highlighted. Although all efforts to implement a common climate change tax have failed so far,[105] the idea of such a tax is currently again under discussion,[106] as well as a common framework for environmentally oriented vehicle taxation.[107] VAT is an example of a far-reaching European harmonization. It restricts the possibilities of Member States to apply higher value added tax rates on environmentally detrimental consumption or lower tax rates on environmentally favorable consumption.[108]

Despite the unanimity requirement, secondary European legislation has contributed remarkably to tax coordination in order to achieve a 'level playing field' within the internal market, at least in the area of indirect taxes. The tax coordination has been accompanied by an intense jurisprudence of the European Court of Justice (ECJ), which interfered deeply with national tax sovereignty.[109] On the one hand this interference refers to interpretation of secondary legislation which is often the basis for national tax law (implementing EU directives). On the other hand, the ECJ has strongly interfered with national tax law on grounds of primary EU law, especially the basic freedoms and the principle of the internal market.[110] Even enormous financial consequences could not stop the Court; some say it behaved like a 'bull in a china shop.'[111] Numerous national tax measures were declared illegal on these grounds, among them promotion schemes for renewable energies.[112]

It is interesting to compare the United States and European Union frameworks for coordinating national and state legislation on taxes in general and environmental taxation in particular. Genschel and Jachtenfuchs recently conducted such a comparison.[113] In the United States, the Constitution provides vast possibilities for the Congress and the Supreme Court to restrict and shape state legislation on (environmental) taxes by legislation and court decisions. Apparently, the praxis of federal institutions is quite restrained and cautious in this respect. In the European Union, the primary law or 'constitution' is extremely restrictive regarding European Union tax competences, especially the unanimity requirement for secondary law. Nevertheless, there is an intense praxis of coordinating and shaping Member State (environmental) tax legislation through EU legislation

---

[104]   *See* Genschel & Jachtenfuchs, *supra* note 101, at 10*ff.*
[105]   *See* Michael Rodi, *Ecological Tax Reform in Germany*, BULLETIN FOR INTERNATIONAL FISCAL DOCUMENTATION 486 (2000); Paul Ekins, *Carbon Taxes and Emissions Trading: Issues and Interactions*, *in* CARBON ENERGY TAXATION. LESSONS FROM EUROPE 251 (Andersen & Ekins eds., 2009).
[106]   *See* the proposal of the European Commission for a 'Council Directive amending Directive 2003/96/EC restructuring the Community framework for the taxation of energy products and electricity', COM(2011) 169/3.
[107]   *See Commission Green Paper on Market-based Instruments for Environment and Related Policy Purposes*, COM (2007) 140 final (Mar. 28, 2007).
[108]   For details and a critical analysis, see K. Kosonen & G. Nicodème, *The Role of Fiscal Instruments in Environmental Policy* 14*ff.* (E.C. Directorate-General for Taxation and Customs Union, Working Paper No. 19, 2009).
[109]   *See* Genschel & Jachtenfuchs, *supra* note 101, at 14*ff.*
[110]   *See* Mathieu Isenbaert, EC LAW AND SOVEREIGNTY OF MEMBER STATES IN DIRECT TAXATION 229*ff.*, 275*ff.* (2010).
[111]   Grbich, *supra* note 69, at 4.
[112]   *See* Case C-379/98, PreussenElectra v. Schleswag, 2001 E.C.R. I-2099.
[113]   Genschel & Jachtenfuchs, *supra* note 101.

and an active jurisprudence of the ECJ. This especially applies to indirect taxes, which are important tools of environmental taxation (consumption taxes such as energy taxes or VAT). Further restrictions follow from a strict state aid regulation regarding environmental tax subsidies. One rather paradoxical result is that the system of unanimity may also lead to restrictions for the national legislator: Once taxes are harmonized it is quite difficult to get back to Member State sovereignty, as illustrated by the discussion on the national level to insert environmental incentives in VAT.

Examples of coordination mechanisms can be drawn from other countries as well. For example, Switzerland has an intricate regime for federalism in taxation, with substantial interdependence of taxing powers vested in the cantons.[114] In the area of direct taxation the Federation has the authority to set up principles on the harmonization of direct taxes (Art. 129 of the Swiss Constitution).

Tax Subsidies and Competition Policies

It is evident that subsidies interfere with market activities. This is also true for tax subsidies (tax expenditures). Legal orders are therefore setting up common market rules to deal with this phenomenon, which is of special relevance in environmental tax schemes. For example, (environmental) state tax incentives fall under the restrictions of the dormant Commerce Clause in the United States.[115]

In the European Union a relatively strict control scheme for subsidies is in place (Arts. 107 ff. of TFEU).[116] Art. 107 I states: 'Save as otherwise provided in the Treaties, any aid granted by a Member State or through State resources in any form whatsoever which distorts or threatens to distort competition by favoring certain undertakings or the production of certain goods shall, in so far as it affects trade between Member States, be incompatible with the internal market.' With the support of the ECJ, the Commission developed a remarkably strict test over the years to identify market distorting state aids, including (environmental) tax schemes.[117] But European law gives the Commission far-reaching discretion to consider state aids as compatible with the internal market (see Art. 107 III of TFEU), for example when the aid promotes 'the execution of an important project of common European interest' (Art. 107 III(b)).

The Commission defined the preconditions for the latter scenario and therefore when state aid is legal in the Community Guidelines on State Aid for Environmental Protection.[118] For instance, Member States can offer subsidies if the recipient reduces pollution or other negative impacts on the environment beyond European Union standards. Moreover, if Member States impose national environmental regulation going beyond European Union standards, they may grant subsidies for undertakings to avoid negative impacts for their competitive position. Additionally, the Commission defined aid

---

[114]   Thuronyi, *supra* note 5, at 75.
[115]   *See* Hellerstein, *supra* note 90, at 84*ff.*
[116]   *See, e.g.*, Thuronyi, *supra* note 5, at 106*ff.*
[117]   *See* Franz Philipp Sutter, *The Influence of the European State Aid Rules on National Tax Policy*, *in* National Tax Policy in Europe: To Be or Not to Be? 121 (Andersson et al. eds., 2007).
[118]   Community Guidelines on State Aid for Environmental Protection, 2008 O.J. (C 82/1).

designs that serve European interest, such as aids for energy saving, aids for renewable energy sources and so on. A strict proportionality test applies to all these cases to avoid distortion of competition. It becomes apparent that the Commission is steering and influencing the design of national environmental state aids through this mechanism, and thus uses its competence indirectly as an additional environmental policy instrument.

ENVIRONMENTAL TAXES AND INTERNATIONAL LAW

Environmental taxes can have an international dimension: On the one side they may tackle transboundary environmental problems such as climate change. On the other side they may conflict with principles of world trade law (or other regimes). Thus, the authority to legislate environmental taxes must also safeguard the framework of public international law.

International Tax Order

Taxes are a core aspect of national sovereignty. Although there is a clear need for an international tax order, in the area of harmful tax competition for instance, only weak elements of an international tax system can be found. The OECD, the International Monetary Fund (IMF), the World Bank and the United Nations have set up an informal International Tax Dialogue (ITD).[119] The 2003 initiative for an International Tax Organization (ITO) as a UN organization failed.[120] Against this background, it is clear that there is no legal environmental tax scheme whatsoever on an international level.

Environmental Tax Schemes and the WTO

As seen before, environmental taxation can interfere with competition and transboundary trade. An environmental tax can therefore conflict with international trade law, since it is a potential trade barrier. This is clearly the case when national environmental tax schemes contain tax subsidies, such as preferential treatment for the local industry.[121]

Possible disadvantages for the local or national industry deriving from environmental taxation can be countervailed by border tax adjustments. These lay a tax burden on imported products to off-set the financial burden on domestic producers of similar products imposed by national environmental policy. Accordingly, these schemes foresee financial reliefs in case of export of these products. On the one hand, this may level the playing field for competition between domestic and foreign products. On the other hand,

---

[119] *See* INTERNATIONAL TAX DIALOGUE, http://www.itdweb.org (last visit Dec. 1, 2011).

[120] *See* U.N. Secretary-General, *Report of the High-level Panel on Financing for Development*, U.N. Doc. A/55/1001 (June 26, 2001) ('Zedillo Report'); *see also* F.M. HORNER, 24 TAX NOTES INTERNATIONAL 179 (2001); *see generally* V. Tanzi, *Is There A Need for A World Tax Organization?*, *in* THE ECONOMICS OF GLOBALIZATION: POLICY PERSPECTIVES FROM PUBLIC ECONOMICS 173 (Razin & Sadka eds., 1999).

[121] *See* Michael Rodi et al., *Implementing the Kyoto Protocol in a Multidimensional Legal System: Lessons from a Comparative Assessment*, 16 Y.B. INT'L ENVTL. L. 3, 70*ff.* (2005).

this creates indirect pressure for other states to apply environmental policy measures themselves. They may, for example, prefer to introduce an environmental tax and receive the revenue rather than accept border tax adjustments. After all, border tax adjustments lead to a similar burden for domestic producers, but the resulting funds would flow to the importing countries rather than to the home state. In recent times, this has been an important topic in the climate change debate.[122] (See also Chapter 11 of this Handbook for a discussion of trade rules.)

Border tax adjustments are quite simple when an environmentally motivated product tax is levied on imported products in a nondiscriminating way. Far more problematic is the case that the tax compensates costs incurred during the production process (such as energy taxes or burdens from an emissions trading scheme). This leads to the delicate legal question of whether environmentally differing production and processing methods (PPMs) make products 'unlike,' with the result that discrimination may be allowed.[123]

Environmental Taxes and other International Treaties

There are many more international legal regimes that either demand and justify environmental tax action or restrict it.

International treaties serve as justification for environmental tax schemes, to the extent that they are enacted to fulfill international obligations. The ozone protection regime may serve as an example. Legislatures of contracting parties to the Montreal Protocol agreed to phase out ozone-depleting chemicals (ODCs) and passed domestic legislation to give effect to these obligations. In the United States, for instance, Congress enacted a system of excise taxes as well as production allowances for domestic manufacturers under its Omnibus Budget Reconciliation Act (1989). Under this system, taxes were levied on ODCs based on their ozone depletion potential.[124] In Australia, Parliament enacted the Ozone Protection Act 1989 (Cth). In cooperation with the states, this Act enabled Parliament to levy fees on infringing substances to meet its obligations under the Montreal Protocol. Initially, these fees were levied on an administrative cost recovery basis only. However, flagging revenue streams from these levies led the federal government to introduce the Ozone Protection (License Fees—Imports) Act 1995 (Cth) and the Ozone Protection (License Fees—Manufacturing) Act 1995 (Cth). These allowed the federal government to impose substantially higher license fees to support the Ozone Protection Trust Fund, which was set up to assist long-term ozone protection programs.[125]

A quite famous example of an international treaty restricting national legislators in

---

[122]   *See, e.g.*, M. Benjamin Eichenberg, *Greenhouse Gas Regulation and Border Tax Adjustments: The Carrot and the Stick*, 3 GOLDEN GATE U. ENVTL. L.J. 283 (2009); Roland Ismer, *Mitigating Climate Change Through Price Instruments: An Overview of the Legal Issues in a World of Unequal Carbon Prices, in* EUROPEAN YEARBOOK OF ECONOMIC LAW 2010, 205, 218*ff.* (Herrmann & Terhechte eds., 2011).

[123]   *See* Rodi et al., *supra* note 121, at 64*ff.*; Chapter 11, *Gaining Intergovernmental Acceptance: Legal Rules Protecting Trade, in* this Handbook.

[124]   Other countries that implemented environmentally related taxes to phase out ODCs include the Czech Republic, Hungary, Poland, and Sweden.

[125]   Z. LIPMAN & G. BATES, POLLUTION LAW IN AUSTRALIA 76 (2002).

environmental taxation is the Chicago Convention on Civil Aviation and related agreements imposing restrictions on the right to levy a fuel tax on international aviation.[126] Taxes on fuel supplies used in international air traffic are in conflict with the Chicago Convention and the International Civil Aviation Organization's (ICAO) Resolution on the Taxation of Aviation Fuel. The latter states that 'the fuel, lubricants and other consumable technical supplies contained in the tanks or other receptacles on the aircraft shall be exempt from customs and other duties.'[127] In addition, the imposition of a fuel tax on international aviation would be incompatible with the vast network of over 2500 aviation service agreements (ASAs) around the world—unless of course the contracting parties to the ASAs took the unlikely step of renegotiating their agreements.[128] For these reasons the EU Commission gave up its plans to integrate aviation into the energy tax scheme. Instead, it extended the ETS scheme to cover the aviation sector as well.[129]

CONCLUSION

To date, the discussion on environmental taxes has largely focused on economic questions. Ranging from effectiveness and efficiency to the design of an instrument mix, a large number of political economy aspects have been addressed. This chapter on the legal authority to enact environmental taxes highlights the manifold legal problems and restrictions in setting up environmental taxes in practice. Until now, quite a number of ideas and concepts in the field of environmental taxes were not analytically subject to these requirements. Though it can be a cumbersome undertaking, it is crucial to extend the literature on the ideal design of environmental taxes to a systematic analysis of legal frameworks to enact them. Tax design questions aside, such an analysis must be based on each individual legal order. It would certainly be desirable to have more comparative studies on legal systems, despite the time-consuming and strenuous nature of this work. This chapter tried to draw attention to some basic key features that should be analyzed in the future on a comparative basis, providing examples and case studies from both national and European legal orders. Hopefully the study will inspire and animate further research in this field.

---

[126]   For other examples, see Vanistendael, *supra* note 28, at 31*ff.*
[127]   OECD, THE POLITICAL ECONOMY OF THE NORWEGIAN AVIATION FUEL TAX 11 (2005).
[128]   *Id.*
[129]   See Chapter 14, *Multi-level Governance*, in this Handbook, text at notes 77 *et seq.*

PART II

DESIGN

5 Design options and their rationales

Pedro M. Herrera Molina

This chapter addresses the legal design of environmental taxes. At the start, it clarifies conceptual issues, and then focuses on the constitutional allocation of taxing and environmental powers, which will be exercised to implement such taxes. Next it covers several elements that build the structure: the taxable event, tax base, tax rates, tax reductions and procedural aspects. We shall try to focus on genuine legal problems without neglecting issues of environmental policy. Furthermore, the chapter addresses the legal design of environmental expenditures embodied in 'ordinary' taxes. The chapter concludes with some reflections on the codification of environmental taxes and green fiscal expenditures.

A preliminary remark is that while the chapter will try to clearly distinguish policy recommendations from legal requirements, which vary from country to country, some bias may persist as the author is an observer of the European legal system. We offer to the reader some relevant references in the English, Spanish, German, Portuguese and Italian languages, but researchers should take into account the peculiarities of their own legal systems when reading this chapter.

ENVIRONMENTAL TAXES

Starting Point

Environmentally related taxes and genuine Pigouvian taxes

Following the terminology used in Chapter 2 of this Handbook, the expression 'environmental tax' is synonymous with 'environmentally related taxes':

> OECD, IEA, and the European Commission have agreed to define environmentally related taxes as any compulsory, unrequited payment to general government levied on tax bases deemed to be of particular environmental relevance. The relevant tax bases include energy products, motor vehicles, waste, measured or estimated emissions, natural resources, etc. Taxes are unrequited in the sense that benefits provided by government to taxpayers are not normally in proportion to their payments.[1]

Accepting this starting point one can nevertheless distinguish between environmentally related taxes as defined above and more genuine *Pigouvian* taxes as a narrower concept.[2] Pigouvian taxes are a subset of environmentally related taxes characterized

---

[1]   OECD, THE POLITICAL ECONOMY OF ENVIRONMENTALLY RELATED TAXES 26 (2006).

[2]   C. Soares, *The Earmarking of Revenues within Environmental Tax Policy, in* 3 CRITICAL ISSUES IN ENVIRONMENTAL TAXATION (A. Cavaliere et al. eds, 2006).

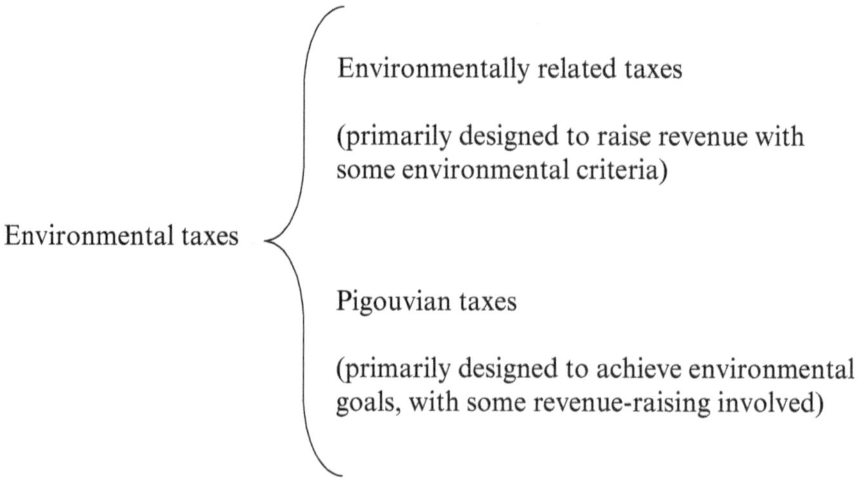

Environmental taxes

Environmentally related taxes

(primarily designed to raise revenue with some environmental criteria)

Pigouvian taxes

(primarily designed to achieve environmental goals, with some revenue-raising involved)

Figure 5.1   The goals of environmental taxes

by a special design.[3] OECD offers the following definition of a Pigouvian tax: 'A tax levied on an agent causing an environmental externality (environmental damage) as an incentive to avert or mitigate such damage.'[4] Its structure is intentionally designed to discourage environmental damage. This distinction might not always be straightforward to apply when 'inventorying' environmental taxes, because it refers to the 'purpose' or 'goal' of the tax, which is very difficult to assess. One cannot always trust the explanatory memorandum of the legislative procedure or the legal declarations on the 'purpose' of a tax, because the declared goal can be manipulated by political factors in order to increase the acceptance of the tax. Moreover, existing taxes can share several goals and therefore it is not easy to qualify them as pure Pigouvian taxes or environmentally related taxes (Figure 5.1).

The design procedure and requirements will be quite different if government is merely trying to collect revenue for the public budget by means of taxing energy resources than if it is trying to foster a most efficient and environmentally friendly use of energy.[5]

---

[3]   F. Picciaredda & P. Selicato, I tributi e l'ambiente. Profili ricostruttivi [Taxes and Environment: a Reconstruction] (1996); P. Herrera, Derecho Tributario Ambiental [Environmental Tax Law], (2000); H. Torres, Direito tributário ambiental [Environmental Tax Law] (2005); J.M. Domingues, Direito Tributário e meio ambiente [Tax Law and Environment] (2007).

[4]   OECD Glossary of Statistical Terms, http://stats.oecd.org/glossary/detail.asp?ID=2065.

[5]   K. Messerchmidt, Umweltabgaben als Rechtsproblem [Environmental Taxes as Legal Problem] 115 (1986); K.-H. Hansmeyer, *Fallstudie: Finanzpolitik im Dienste des Gewässerschutzes*, *in* Öffentliche Finanzen und Umweltpolitik II Schriften des Vereins für Socialpolitik [2 Public Finance and Environmental Policy] 50, 55, 59 (W. Benkert et al. eds, 1989); J. Jiménez Hernández, [*Taxable Event or Environmental Aim. What is the essence of an Environmental Tax?*], *in* Fiscalidad ambiental [Environmental Taxation] 374 (A. Yábar Sterling ed., 1998).

Environmental taxes and charges

Taxes are defined as 'unrequited payments,' as opposed to user charges, which are payments for a rendered service or a public cost. In the author's view, this widely accepted categorization was born in the world of fiscal-oriented levies but is not totally satisfactory in the environmental field.[6] This statement is not intended to be polemical; it suggests only that it is important to maintain a more specific notion that environmental taxation allocates the cost of environmental damage to the polluter in ways that could be seen as akin to charges, a position less emphasized in recent years by OECD.[7]

This view could be justified by the following reasoning. Genuine Pigouvian taxes are an economic instrument aimed at internalizing environmental damage. Therefore their internal logic is based on the equivalence principle: the environmental tax due should be equivalent to the external costs inflicted on the environment, in the same way that the user charge due for a service should be equivalent to the costs assumed by the public sector in order to provide the service.[8] For this reason, German literature and legal texts refer to the polluter-pays principle as the '*Verursacherprinzip*,' which literally means 'the principle of the causer.' This is the German expression traditionally used to express the equivalence principle of charges. OECD itself has stated that 'the Polluter-Pays Principle is fully satisfied, whether the polluter assumes the cost of the damage he causes or the cost of waste treatment.'[9] OECD goes on to state:

> When a charge is levied, it induces polluters to treat their effluents as long as the treatment costs remain lower than the amount of the charge they would otherwise be compelled to pay in the absence of pollution abatement. A charging policy may thus achieve an objective at least social cost to society as it would induce each of these polluters to abate pollution to the point where they each incur the same additional cost for the same reduction of pollution emission. Another advantage of charges is that they can provide a continuing incentive for improved pollution abatement.[10]

This idea has relevant implications for the design of environmental taxes: from this wider and more substantive point of view, they are not ordinary 'taxes.' Therefore, in an ideal world, their design arguably should meet the legal requirements of the equivalence principle. We say 'in an ideal world' because there are practical reasons to give up the principle and act more pragmatically: to implement a user charge we should carefully calculate the cost of the service, and in the case of Pigouvian taxes we should carefully

---

[6]   HACIENDA Y FINANZAS MUNICIPALES [MUNICIPAL FINANCES] 142 (J. Rodríguez Fernández & J.I. Gomar Sánchez eds., 2001).

[7]   However, OECD itself highlights the environmental role of some 'charges,' such as water tariffs. *Cf.* OECD, MANAGING WATER FOR ALL. AN OECD PERSPECTIVE ON PRICING AND FINANCING 81 (2009) and OECD, PRICING WATER RESOURCES AND WATER AND SANITATION SERVICES 10 (2010).

[8]   Therefore it is not always easy to differentiate environmental taxes and charges. *See* J. SNAPE & J. DE SOUZA, ENVIRONMENTAL TAXATION LAW: POLICY, CONTEXT AND PRACTICE 5, 115 (2006). Snape and De Souza suggest to use as a generic concept the term 'environmental levies' (op. cit., page 5).

[9]   OECD, THE POLLUTER PAYS PRINCIPLE 34 (1975).

[10]   *Id.* at 16. In the early 1970s the term 'charge' was often misused as a catchall phrase for both user charges and environmental taxes. 'Levy' is a better such catch-all term, *cf.* Dutch practice.

account for the specific environmental damage. The design process for environmentally related taxes is much simpler: the lawmaker can be loosely inspired by environmental criteria but does not have to justify the tax amount on Pigouvian grounds. Once it is decided by the democratic parliament, it cannot be challenged (unless there are constitutional constraints on arbitrary decisions of the parliament).

Taxing Powers

In order to design environmental taxes we must take into account the competent territorial organization: a supranational entity (such as the European Union), several sovereign nations through an international agreement, a federal state, a subcentral entity of regional scope (federated state, autonomous community) or a municipality. It would be ideal when identifying the relevant taxing power to take into account the territorial scope of the environmental problem that needs to be addressed. It does not make any sense to impose a local charge on CO_2 emissions.[11] However, logic does not rule the world and we have to take into account a real existing international and constitutional legal framework when deciding how to draft an environmental tax (Figure 5.2).[12]

As mentioned before, from a substantive point of view Pigouvian taxes are not taxes in a traditional sense but rather economic instruments designed to protect the environment based on a charge-like logic (the equivalence and polluter-pays principles).[13] Therefore one might argue that no taxing powers, but only environmental competencies, are needed to introduce environmental taxes. However, we might say that environmental taxes possess an environmental soul and a tax body. As long as they are in force, it is

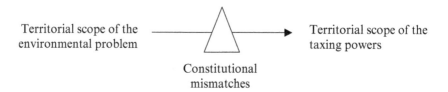

Territorial scope of the environmental problem — Territorial scope of the taxing powers

Constitutional mismatches

Figure 5.2   Territorial scopes of the environmental problem and taxing powers

---

[11]   However, we find a controversial example in Spanish law. An ordinance of the Cerceda municipality has set up a 'green charge' on CO_2 and SO_2 emissions. *See* Official Gazette of La Coruña, n° 251/2001. Moreover some local taxes for CO_2 might be justifiable based on their revenue generation, such as a tax on CO_2 in Boulder, Colorado, US, which generates revenue for the municipality's climate change mitigation programs.

[12]   R. Canosa Usera, Constitución y Medio Ambiente [Constitution and Environment] 209 (2000).

[13]   That is to say the 'principle of the causer.' *Cf.* Messerschmidt, *supra* note 5, at 87; M. Wasmeier, Umweltabgaben als Rechtsproblem [Environmental Taxes and Charges as Legal Problem] 81 (1986); R. Scholz, *Art. 20.a GG: Commentary to Article 20.a of the German Constitution, in* Grundgesetz Kommentar [Commentary to the German Constitution] ¶ 45 (T. Maunz and G. Dürig eds, 1996); B. Bender et al., 3 Umweltrecht, Grundzüge des Öffentlichen Umweltschutzrechts [Environmental Law, Fundamental Aspects of Environmental Public Law] 27 (1995).

not possible to separate their aim-oriented soul from their legal body. Therefore readers should consider whether both taxing and environmental powers are required to regulate them, because the specifics would depend on the constitutional framework of the given legal system. (See Chapter 4 in this Handbook.) Moreover, as discussed above, the difference between pure Pigouvian taxes and traditional environmentally related taxes is very important for the correct design of the tax but very difficult to determine. Therefore, in addition to the constraints of constitutional law, legal certainty may recommend that both taxing power and environmental competencies are present to enact Pigouvian taxes.

Taxable Event

According to the general tradition of legislative drafting, the tax legislation must include provisions that define the 'taxable event' (the factual situation that triggers the tax debt, *e.g.* capital gains) and the 'taxable base' (the legal quantification of such a situation, *e.g.* the difference between the acquisition price and the selling price). The taxable event must describe in legal terms the environmentally damaging circumstances that will trigger the tax burden.[14] The taxable event is one of the legal elements that delimits the real facts that are submitted to taxation, and therefore it must be coherent with the other legal elements, which comprise the tax. For example, the taxable event could be emissions of pollution into water bodies, triggering tax on those pollutants. We find a good example of a well-defined taxable event in Articles 3 and 4 of the European Commission's 1992 Proposal for a Council Directive Introducing a Tax on Carbon Dioxide Emissions and Energy.[15] The text is lengthy but defines precisely when products shall be charged under relevant circumstances in a way that is coherent with the definition of the taxable base.

However the lawmaker may stress the environmental character of the taxable event (such as polluting facilities) but distort the environmental nature of the tax through the choice of tax base. This happens when the real goal of the tax is to raise revenue but the lawmaker wants to disguise this by painting the tax green. An example is the Spanish regional tax on polluting facilities. The taxable event was described literally by the law as the 'property of polluting facilities,' but the tax base (that is, the quantification of the taxable event) referred to the gross income of certain businesses. Therefore the tax was not aimed at protecting the environment but at raising revenue in a way that was not justified by any real environmental goals. Consequently, it was declared unconstitutional.[16]

---

[14] J. JIMÉNEZ HERNÁNDEZ, EL TRIBUTO COMO INSTRUMENTO DE PROTECCIÓN AMBIENTAL [TAXES AND CHARGES AS A TOOL FOR ENVIRONMENTAL PROTECTION] 135 (1998).

[15] *Commission Proposal for a Council Directive Introducing a Tax on Carbon Dioxide Emissions and Energy*, COM (92) 226 final (June 30, 1992).

[16] We find an example in the Spanish regional tax of the Balearic Islands on polluting facilities, which was declared unconstitutional. S.T.C., Nov. 30, 2000 (R.A.J., No. 289) (Spain). *Cf.* C. Borrero Moro, *Acerca de la discutida constitucionalidad del impuesto balear sobre instalaciones que inciden en el medio ambiente [The Polemic Constitutionality of the Balearic Tax on Polluting Facilities]*, *in* FISCALIDAD AMBIENTAL [ENVIRONMENTAL TAXATION] 467 (A. Yábar Sterling ed., 1998); M.A. GUERVÓS MAILLO, EL IMPUESTO BALEAR SOBRE INSTALACIONES QUE INCIDEN EN EL MEDIO AMBIENTE [THE BALEARIC TAX ON POLLUTING FACILITIES] (2000).

Tax Base

The tax base must represent the assessment of the cause of the environmental impact that the tax seeks to discourage. Therefore the lawmaker must choose some elements that are representative of this cause. At the same time the legal design must take into account the practicability principle: the tax will be properly designed if the tax base can be assessed and controlled in an effective way without requiring disproportionate economic and technical resources. That means that the legal quantification of the 'real environmental damage' must be designed in a simplified way.

For instance, if the tax aims to discourage CO_2 emissions, the real environmental damage consists of the real emissions caused by the taxpayer, but it would be impracticable to assess diffuse emissions. Therefore it would be advisable to take into account the *potential* emissions of CO_2 corresponding to every unit of produced fuel, according to the chemical properties of the relevant fuel derivative.[17] As we can see, from the point of view of the legal design the choice of the tax base precedes the choice of the tax event (and is preceded by the fundamental choice of factual events that should be taxed). If we have decided to tax *all* emissions of greenhouse gases, the adequate tax base would be the potential emissions of such gases per unit of fuel and the right taxable event would be the production or import of such products (and not the emission itself). If for some legitimate reason we restrict the tax to large emissions of gases, the tax base would consist of the actual emissions (because in such a case it could be precisely assessed without incurring disproportionate expenses), and therefore the taxable event should be drafted as the emissions themselves. As a general rule of design, we can say that the lawmaker should achieve a balance between taxing the real environmental damage and doing so in a feasible way.

In the case of environmentally related taxes in a broad sense (that is, those that are not designed as genuine Pigouvian taxes to discourage polluting activities), the tax base loosely refers to goods or activities of particular environmental relevance (oil, vehicles, etc.). The tax base is expressed not in polluting units but in monetary units (the price of a vehicle) or in fiscal units of the taxed good (volume of oil derivatives produced). That means that the tax was not designed from the beginning with an environmental goal but merely as a means of raising revenue. From a theoretical point of view the tax base should be redesigned to convert the pre-existing environmentally related tax into a genuine Pigouvian tax (for example, changing the traditional oil excise duty into a new carbon dioxide and energy tax). If the political circumstances advise that the reform be carried out according to tax neutrality (that is, the global tax revenue should not be increased), this requirement could be met by reducing other taxes (such as environmental tax reforms) or by redesigning tax rates.

Where such radical redesign is not possible (such as for political reasons),[18] it would be

---

[17]   That was the old proposal of the European Commission, which failed because of the opposition of some Member States. *See Commission Proposal for a Council Directive Introducing a Tax on Carbon Dioxide Emissions and Energy*, COM (1992) 226 final (June 30, 1992). *See also* J. Klok, *Energy taxation in the European Union. Past negotiations and future perspectives* (Inst. de Estudios Fiscales, Working Paper No. 21, 2005). The European Commission has recently proposed the idea of introducing minimum CO_2 tax rates at EU levels.

[18]   *See* Klok, *supra* note 17, at 14.

advisable to 'green up' the traditional environmentally related tax by abolishing harmful tax expenditures (for instance tax exemptions for aviation kerosene) or by introducing environmentally related tax rates (such as tax rates based on the potential emissions of CO_2 in the registration tax[19] even if the tax base refers for historical reasons to the vehicle's price).

Tax Rates

Design criteria
What is the right level of environmental taxation? Assuming that the taxable event and the tax base are designed correctly, the lawmaker faces an alternative: to fix the tax rates based on technical criteria or to do it according to political considerations. By 'technical criteria' we mean the objective of assessing the external damage caused by the relevant polluting activity, or at least of evaluating the level of taxation that would be needed to limit the polluting emissions to the desired level. By 'political considerations' we mean the level of taxation that would be accepted by the affected taxpayers or by the electors. As suggested below, a combination of technical and political criteria is advisable.[20]

Technical criteria
Calculation of the 'ideal' Pigouvian tax should take into account the environmental damage caused by the taxed activity. Pigouvian taxes are economic instruments aimed at fixing a market failure: the market prices of certain goods or services are too low because external costs (such as environmental damage) are not taken into account, and therefore the demand of such goods and services is too high and there is no economic incentive to find more environmentally friendly alternatives. Therefore the right approach to fixing the tax rates is very similar to the procedure for setting up a charge: first the global costs must be calculated and then the individual charge due must be designed in such a way that the total charge revenue does not exceed the global costs.

This design approach is ideal from environmental, economic and policy points of view, but sometimes ideals and reality do not go hand in hand. In the first place, it may not be technically feasible to calculate the external costs of a polluting activity. For instance, what are the external costs of CO_2 emissions? Technological development and economic research can help to improve the calculation of external costs. (See Chapter 8 in this Handbook for a discussion of externality research.) For instance, the European Union

---

[19] The tax that should be paid once when a car is registered in its owner's country of residence. The notion is used in the *European Union Proposal for A Council Directive on Passenger Car Related Taxes*, COM (2005) 261 final (Jul. 5, 2005).

[20] As OECD points out, 'In practice, the design and implementation of environmentally related taxation is likely to differ from simple textbook discussions. For example, such taxes may be introduced to simply raise revenue, in which case the same environmental considerations and linkages determining the optimal tax rate generally would not apply. Where environmental goals are a central objective, measurement and estimation difficulties can be expected in practice, for example in linking a specific tax to the amount of environmental damage. Political concerns, including for example concerns over industrial competitiveness and income (re)distribution, may also figure prominently and need to be assessed.' OECD, ENVIRONMENTALLY RELATED TAXES IN OECD COUNTRIES. ISSUES AND STRATEGIES 24 (2001).

has developed detailed guidelines for the calculation of the environmental cost of the use of transport infrastructures by heavy vehicles (road charging), although they are not yet approved.[21] In the second place, even if we manage to overcome technical obstacles, the full internalization of external costs could make it impossible to carry out some polluting activities that cannot be radically suppressed under the current sociological and technological circumstances. In such cases it would be advisable to quantify the total amount of the external costs and the ideal tax rates to internalize such costs. Such information should be available to the general public. At the same time, the tax rate could be reduced to the level needed to meet acceptable environmental targets.

Political criteria
Sometimes it is technically not feasible to assess the level of taxation required to achieve certain environmental goals. It may also be that such levels are too high, so that the initial environmental goals must be scaled down, taking into account economic and social considerations.[22] When the technical basis for the tax and the grounds for the political decision are transparently conveyed to the general public, the technical and political criteria can be applied in a more balanced way.[23]

In such cases the decision regarding the initial levels of taxation often should be accompanied by a schedule of the future increase of tax rates, as illustrated by the Spanish regional tax of Galicia on SO_2 emissions.[24] Initially there were only three tax rates according to the volume of annual emissions. According to Article 12(1) of the Regional Parliamentary Act of December 29, 1995, the tax rates were:

- Up to 1000 tons: 0 percent.
- From 1001 tons to 50 000 tons: 5000 pesetas (30.05 €) per ton.
- 50 001 tons and above: 5500 pesetas (33.06 €) per ton.

The rates were too low to lead to reduced emissions, but according to Article 12(2), lawmakers would implement higher rates in 2000 in order to promote cleaner conduct. In this way the taxpayers would accept the entry into force of the new tax and have a clear signal to change their behavior in the next five years. At the same time the future rates could be adapted to technological change, which could lead to further cuts in the amount of emissions.

---

[21]   *See Commission Proposal for a Directive of the European Parliament and of the Council amending Directive 1999/62/EC on the charging of heavy goods vehicles for the use of certain infrastructures,* COM (2008) 436 final (Jul. 8, 2008).

[22]   See, regarding the Chinese case, OECD, Environmental Fiscal Reform for Poverty Reduction, Environmental Fiscal Reform for Poverty Reduction 103 (2005).

[23]   As OECD states, 'an increased carbon tax . . . might not be popular but still get support if we can explain the reasons behind these actions. And if we dare to be brave enough to implement them,' OECD, Institutionalising Sustainable Development 16 (2007).

[24]   Parliamentary Act of the Galician Region n. 12/1995 (Dec. 29, 1995); *see* J.A. Rozas Valdés, *El Impuesto gallego sobre la contaminación atmosférica [The Galician Tax on Air Pollution], in* 246 Revista Española de Derecho Financiero y Hacienda Pública 943 (1997), and C. Borrero Moro, *El impuesto gallego sobre la contaminación atmosférica [The Galician Tax on Air Pollution], in* 248 Revista Española de Derecho Financiero 305 (1997).

However, this procedure, based on technical research and the political weighing of environmental and economic goals and public information, is not always followed. Sometimes pure political criteria do prevail. That means that there are no serious calculations of the costs of external damage or of the levels of taxation needed to achieve the environmental improvements desired from taxation. There is only a vague concern for the environment, coupled with the desire to get some extra tax revenue. In such cases the design of the tax rates is based on the answer to the following question: how much can we tax the polluting activity without losing the next election?

Environmental tax rates on non-environmentally-oriented tax bases

If a Pigouvian tax is well designed from the outset, there must be coherence among the taxable event, the tax base and the tax rates. However it is also possible that a traditional environmentally related tax (such as the old circulation and registration taxes) is partially refurbished. In such a case it is possible to combine the pre-existing tax base (for example, the price or market value of a vehicle) with an environmentally oriented tariff (such as an increase in tax rates according to the theoretical CO_2 emissions of the vehicle). This was the case with the Spanish registration tax.[25]

The Taxpayer

The taxpayer may also be the polluter. However, we must take into account the possibility of shifting the tax according to the elasticity of the demand for the polluting goods and services. From an environmental economics perspective, an inelastic demand would render less significant the question of who is legally obligated to pay the tax.

Furthermore from the point of view of legal design it is not dispositive that the taxpayer is the polluter, but rather that the link of the production and consumption chain is more easily taxable, provided that the decision is consistent with the taxable event and the tax base. For instance, it would be feasible and consistent to impose a general CO_2 and energy tax on the fuel's producer or importer and not on the consumer. It would be more feasible to impose an environmental charge for domestic waste collection and management on a homeowner (giving him the right to shift the charge to the current occupant) than to charge directly the people who live there, assuming the tax authorities had direct access to land registry records and there were no trustworthy records on the actual occupants, as is usually the case in Southern Europe. However, removing the tax collection point from the actual waste producer could diminish the environmental impact, assuming that the tax is based on actual usage. Administrative feasibility plays a relevant role in the choice of whom to tax but should not lead to removing the environmental impact.

An important question of design is whether public entities should be considered taxpayers of an environmental tax. For instance, there are two main designs for

---

[25] The ecological reform of the registration tax was enacted through the Parliamentary Act 34/2007 of November 15 on air quality, and was loosely inspired by the European proposal for a directive that would require member states to restructure their passenger car taxation systems. *See Commission Proposal for a Council Directive on Passenger Car Related Taxes*, COM (2005) 261 final (Jul. 5, 2005).

waste-dumping and incineration taxes. According to the first model, only the private sector is tax-liable. However, landfill and waste incineration taxes aim to encourage waste recycling, and municipalities are the main managers of waste as well as the main users of landfills and waste incineration facilities if they are the intermediaries between the polluters and the landfills. Therefore it seems sensible to put some pressure on municipalities so that they incentivize their waste-producers to manage waste more rationally.[26] A central or regional landfill and waste incineration tax could be a good instrument for encouraging municipalities to design their waste regulations and waste charges in order to promote waste reduction and recycling.

Tax Reductions

Non-environmental tax expenditures
A well-designed environmental tax does not need additional tax incentives (tax expenditures) to promote environmentally friendly conduct. The tax is an environmental incentive in itself: its taxable event, tax base, tax rates and taxpayer rules are drafted in order to discourage pollution.

However, sometimes we find non-environmental tax expenditures within the structure of environmentally related taxes. Such expenditures are not aimed at protecting the environment. On the contrary, they are designed mostly to avoid harsh economic consequences for heavy polluters. In principle such tax expenditures clash with the polluter-pays principle,[27] because taxpayers who use more intensively polluting goods are favored over less intensive polluters. In the European Union, such tax benefits could also be considered forbidden state aid, which distorts the market.[28] In the author's view, tax benefits for polluting-intensive businesses may be justified only as a transitory measure in order to help such businesses implement higher environmental standards. Moreover, the lawmaker should provide scientific evidence that such expenditures are essential for the economic survival of the taxpayers. Public authorities should assess the effects of such tax incentives and the lawmaker should abolish them as soon as they are no longer essential.

---

[26]   *Cf.* I. Puig Ventosa, *Fiscalidad ambiental y gestión de residuos [Environmental Taxation and Waste Management]*, in 2 TRATADO DE TRIBUTACIÓN MEDIOAMBIENTAL [2 TREATY ON ENVIRONMENTAL TAXATION] 1303 (F. Becker et al. eds, 2008). *See also* I. Puig Ventosa, *Nuevo impuesto sobre la incineración de residuos en Cataluña [New Tax on Waste Incineration in Catalonia]*, 19 RESIDUOS: REVISTA TÉCNICA 68–69 (2009), and G.M. Luchena Mozo, *Impuesto sobre depósito de residuos de la Comunidad de Madrid:¿ante un nuevo impuesto ambiental? [Landfill Tax in the Madrid Region: A New Environmental Tax?]* 115 CRÓNICA TRIBUTARIA 99.
[27]   *See* T. RÓSEMBUJ, LOS TRIBUTOS Y LA PROTECCIÓN DEL MEDIO AMBIENTE [TAXES AND ENVIRONMENTAL PROTECTION] 77 (1995); C. CAMPOS DE ARAÚJO ET AL., MEDIO AMBIENTE E SISTEMA TRIBUTÁRIO [ENVIRONMENT AND TAX SYSTEM] 75 (1995).
[28]   Consolidated Version of the Treaty on the Functioning of the European Union art. 107, Sep. 5, 2008, 2008, O.J. (C 115) 47 ('Save as otherwise provided in the Treaties, any aid granted by a Member State or through State resources in any form whatsoever which distorts or threatens to distort competition by favoring certain undertakings or the production of certain goods shall, in so far as it affects trade between Member States, be incompatible with the internal market').

Coordination with other economic instruments
Some tax exemptions or reductions cannot be considered tax expenditures because they aim not to give preferential tax treatment, but to avoid a double economic burden. This is the case when certain emissions of greenhouse gases are not taxed because the relevant activity is already in the compulsory market of emission permits. There are examples, however, of a tax applying if the taxpayer has not purchased enough emission permits to cover its annual emissions.[29]

Tax Procedure

Environmentally related taxes face some special problems from the point of view of tax procedure. In a formal sense they are taxes, and therefore their assessment and collection should be carried out by the tax authorities according to general tax procedure legislation. Substantively, however, they are environmental instruments, and their assessment and control may not be possible without a certain know-how possessed only by the environmental authorities.

Who, then, should manage environmental taxes? The lawmaker might have the power to grant all administrative powers to the environmental agency, which could be financed by the earmarked environmental tax. On the one hand this choice would solve the problem regarding environmental know-how and can incentivize administrative responsibility in the management of the tax. On the other hand the environmental agency would probably lack the means and experience to manage a tax and would tend not to be impartial in their practices.

In the author's view, adequate legal design requires cooperation between tax and environmental authorities, with tax collection better left in the hands of the experts (the tax authorities). This could be provided directly by legal rules or indirectly through cooperation agreements between the two administrations. The general tax rules on tax collection should be applied to ensure transparency and legal certainty. Of course, this proposal is not a general statement of law but merely a recommendation based on the experience of European countries where difficulties have arisen in the collection of environmental taxes and charges.

Regarding tax assessment and tax audits, cooperation between both administrations is strongly recommended. In the case of traditional taxes on fuel or vehicles, the tax authorities usually have a broad experience and infrastructure that includes laboratories and technical knowledge. Therefore, even if they are revamped as genuine Pigouvian taxes, it makes no sense to set up new administrative bodies to manage them. Regarding other taxes, it could be possible to assign the assessment and audits to the environmental authorities or, if they remain in the hands of the tax authorities, to require binding reports from the environmental authorities. In such a case the lawmaker should provide for special administrative rules on tax procedures, clarify which administrative acts can

---

[29]   This is the case of the Spanish regional taxes of Andalucía and Aragón on polluting air emissions. *See* Article 16 of the consolidated text number 1/2007 on environmental taxes in Aragón of September 18, 2007, and Article 24 (b) of Parliamentary Act 18/2003 of Dec. 29, 2003, on fiscal and administrative provisions.

be challenged by the taxpayer, and define the rules applicable to the tax appeal and the competent jurisdiction. We find several examples in which a parliamentary act on environmental taxes includes special provisions on tax procedures.[30]

ENVIRONMENTAL TAX EXPENDITURES

Starting Point

One might think that environmental tax expenditures are a logical consequence of the polluter-pays principle: who pollutes must pay and who protects the environment must be subsidized. However, the reasoning is not so simple. If we subsidize those polluters who merely comply with administrative environmental standards, we are financing them through a heavier burden on nonpolluting taxpayers. Therefore, environmental tax expenditures are justified only provided that the taxpayer protects the environment beyond the binding administrative standards. Furthermore we must ensure that such standards are not made too low, which would result in a hidden breach of the polluter-pays principle.

We also must distinguish among three different design scenarios: environmental tax expenditures embedded in ability-to-pay oriented taxes, in mere tax-revenue-oriented taxes, and in equivalence-oriented taxes and charges. In the author's view, tax expenditures in the first category need a special justification to explain their deviation from the ability-to-pay principle. The second category refers to taxes that are unconstitutional or at least not justified as a matter of policy in their original situation because they are based neither on the general principle of tax justice (ability to pay) nor on non-fiscal goals. Therefore the lawmaker tries to fix them by giving them an environmental purpose through tax incentives. The last category deals with simplified charges on environmentally related activities ('equivalence-oriented taxes'), where the lawmaker initially chooses to tax simpler equivalents rather than the ideal tax base but subsequently tries to turn the equivalence-oriented taxes into genuine Pigouvian taxes by offering tax expenditures.

In ability-to-pay-oriented taxes
Ability to pay is the general principle for a fair distribution of the tax burden among the taxpayers. We must pay taxes because we are human beings with a social nature and therefore we must show solidarity with other members of the social body in order to promote the common good. Part of this solidarity requires contributing with our wealth to the public expenditure through the payment of taxes. Therefore every citizen should contribute according to his or her ability to pay.

As paying taxes is an instrument of the common good, the common interest may restrict the ability-to-pay principle. However this exception must be justified through a proportionality test, at least under most European written constitutions (Germany, Italy, Spain) and even under the law of the European Union (Article 12[b] of the Treaty on European Union). In other countries this principle may not be mandatory but can be considered a good legislative practice or preferred policy. The lawmaker should provide

---

[30]   *Id.*

evidence that the deviation is suitable, necessary and proportional for achieving the relevant environmental goals. Otherwise it would be wrong, or at least unwise, to design environmental tax expenditures.

First, the tax expenditure must be suitable for achieving the environmental goal. The suitability test should be carried out in two stages: the theoretical test and the practical test. The theoretical test is based on the analysis of the legal design and tries to decide if the legal structure is consistent with the environmental goal. The practical test is more complex: it requires ex post statistical research to assess whether the tax expenditure has worked in the real world to achieve its intended goals. This test cannot be carried out immediately after the entry into force of the tax. Some time is needed to make it possible to measure the effects.[31] Of course a good practice would request ex ante studies in order to prevent inefficient reforms.

The necessity test tries to assess whether there is any alternative measure that could achieve similar effects at similar costs without involving a distortion of the ability-to-pay principle. For instance, for a progressive income tax it would not be necessary to introduce tax expenditures through deduction from the tax base, because they would privilege taxpayers with higher income. It would be more neutral to apply the tax expenditures through tax credits. Ex ante studies would be necessary to assess the economic and environmental impact of the proposed reform.

The proportionality test in the strictest sense tries to weigh the environmental goal against the ability-to-pay principle. In our view it does not play a big role in the design of environmental tax expenditures, because the lawmaker has broad discretionary powers to decide which environmentally friendly behaviors should be fostered,[32] but it justifies compensation measures that take into account the economic effect of environmental taxes. For instance a higher tax on energy would justify higher minimums of existence (including tax rebates) within the personal income tax.

In the U.S. tax system we find some interesting experiences that differ from the European tradition and could help to implement the requirements of the proportionality test. They involve discretionary awards of capped tax expenditures, a third way between traditional tax expenditures and grants.[33]

---

[31]　A good example of this approach can be found in OECD, BETTER POLICIES TO SUPPORT ECO-INNOVATION (2011).

[32]　However, environmentally harmful subsidies should be avoided. The recent stimulus packages offer some bad examples that should be avoided in the future: 'Given that one likely effect of the crisis has been to raise risk premia and therefore lower private investment in higher-risk projects, governments could further build on these measures to move forward investments that would facilitate the development of green technologies and industries. Some countries have also invested in basic R&D to support green innovation and increased their use of environmentally-related taxes. However, not all of the stimulus measures will have been good for the environment, and some may have encouraged investments which could lock in more traditional polluting activities. For example, unless carefully designed, the significant support provided to the automobile industry in some countries, investments in road building and car-scrapping programmes, may have exacerbated pressures on the environment by increasing incentives for private car use,' OECD, INTERIM REPORT OF THE GREEN GROWTH STRATEGY: IMPLEMENTING OUR COMMITMENT FOR A SUSTAINABLE FUTURE 10 (2010).

[33]　*See* J. Milne, *US Climate Change Policy: A Tax Expenditure Microcosm with Environmental Dimensions*, *in* TAX EXPENDITURES: STATE OF THE ART 9:10 (L. Philipps et al. eds, 2011).

In mere tax-revenue-oriented taxes

As mentioned before, tax-revenue-oriented taxes exist for historical reasons but, in the eyes of this author, should be abolished or reformed. For instance, a local tax on economic activities based on average turnover could be replaced by a new tax on polluting activities. A middle way, which is used in practice, is to dignify the old tax by means of introducing certain environmentally oriented tax expenditures. For instance, the mentioned tax on economic activities can be greened through tax credits granted on expenses for sustainable transportation for employees, or on a transfer of the business to a location where its environmental impact causes less damage. These design improvements are, however, only second-bests.

In equivalence-oriented taxes

As already mentioned, certain taxes are a kind of simplified charge on activities, which impose costs on public entities or on the society. A good example is the circulation tax, which periodically taxes the ownership of motor vehicles but is justified by the expense and damage caused by driving. The ideal design would be to charge the real use of the vehicle, but practical reasons advise taxing the property itself (namely those motor vehicles suitable for driving), taking into account objective signs of their possible use (fiscal horses, maximum load, cylinder capacity and so on). These equivalence-oriented taxes may be greened via one of two possible paths: the more radical one would be to modify their quantifying criteria by introducing new bases for taxation (such as the potential emissions of the vehicle, taking into account its technical specifications). This way has been used in Portugal. A more hesitant reform, as carried out in Spain, is the introduction of tax credits for less polluting vehicles.

However, if the tax is already environmentally oriented, an exemption might be counterproductive. For instance, a tax exemption for greenhouse crops in a tax on fertilizers would not be suitable to achieve any environmental goal, but only to protect certain businesses.[34]

Taxing Powers and Environmental Competencies

The distribution of taxing powers and environmental competencies is also important for the clean design of environmental tax expenditures.[35] For instance, the essential structure of local taxes may be set up by central or regional authorities, leaving some room for fine-tuning to local regulations (as is the case in Spain, Italy and most Latin American countries). In such cases the central or regional power can provide to the local authorities the *opportunity* to implement environmental tax expenditures. The main political credit goes to the central or regional legislator, but the tax expenses should be paid by the local budget. This distribution of taxing powers tempts local authorities to implement cosmetic tax incentives that can be politically useful, without offering real tax

---

[34]　Case C-159/01, Netherlands v. Comm'n, 2004 E.C.R I-4461.
[35]　*See* C. García Novoa, *Reflexiones sobre los impuestos propios de carácter medioambiental en el ámbito de la tributación autonómica* [*Thoughts on Regional Environmental Taxes*], in LA FINANCIACIÓN AUTONÓMICA EN LOS ESTATUTOS DE AUTONOMÍA [REGIONAL FINANCING IN THE STATUTES OF AUTONOMY] 411 (A.M. Pita Grandal & J. Aneiros Pereira eds, 2008).

expenditures. The incentives do not work in practice, as they are far too low to change the taxpayer's behavior.

There is also a problem when different levels of government are responsible for designing and applying the tax expenditure and for supervising environmental requirements that have to be met in order for the tax incentive to be applied. This distribution of competencies would work only with loyal cooperation and mutual trust between both territorial levels. Otherwise the regional powers would tend to be very lax in auditing environmental requirements (given that the only consequence would be a loss of revenue for the central power) and the central power would tend to be too strict in supervising the tax credits because it would distrust the regional authorities' environmental reports on the taxpayer.

Object

Tax expenditures may be connected with investments to reduce pollution or to repair environmental damages, provided that they are not compulsory for the taxpayer (tax expenditures for compulsory investments are justified only as a transitory measure). The investments may be business-related (aimed at reducing emissions into the air or water, energy efficiency, waste management, reforestation, recovery of polluted soil and so on), or of a more private nature (for instance, those related to the home or individual cars). It is also possible to promote certain current expenditures that are environmentally friendly (such as public transportation plans for employees) or to grant tax credits for donations to public or private institutions that protect the environment.

Quantity

Tax expenditures can be used in two different ways: as an incentive to modify behavior or to help make it easier to implementing higher environmental regulatory standards. In the second case, the tax expenditure must be temporary and the lawmaker has discretion to set the quantity of the tax benefit as long as it does not exceed the costs of implementing the new standards. If the tax expenditure is designed to encourage behavior beyond mandatory standards, the quantity should be high enough to achieve that result, as justified by economic surveys. If it is not, the provision will be a cosmetic one that could bring political advantages to the ruling party, but which will overload the tax system with unnecessary rules and create opportunities for tax avoidance and tax fraud.[36]

Tax Procedure

Environmental tax incentives are usually applied at the request of the taxpayer. They may be directly applied by the taxpayer in his or her tax return or submitted for a previous declaration by the tax or environmental authorities. Moreover, the taxpayer has special

---

[36] Community Guidelines on State Aid for Environmental Protection, 2008 O.J. (C 082) 1–33, offer detailed criteria to prove the proportionality of environmental incentives. They permit, among other things, aid for undertakings that go beyond community standards or that increase the level of environmental protection in the absence of community standards, and aid for early adaptation to future community standards. *See id.* at ¶¶ 1.5.1 and 1.5.3.

documentation duties to provide evidence that he has carried out the activities promoted by the tax expenditure.

Sometimes the application of the tax incentive is dependent upon a previous arrangement with the environmental authorities. This instrument is a combination of fiscal measures and voluntary agreements. An example is the tax credit for environmentally friendly investments in the Spanish Corporate Tax Act, which is applicable only to those taxpayers who have made voluntary environmental agreements with the regional authorities.

Codification of Environmentally Related Taxes and Tax Expenditures

In the European experience environmentally related taxes are usually regulated by their own legislation, while tax expenditures are embedded sometimes in environmental legislation and sometimes in the legislation of the relevant tax. However the placement of tax expenditures in environmental and tax codes varies from country to country. For example, in the United States, environmental tax provisions may be included in environmental legislative proposals for purposes of enactment, but they are always codified in the tax code. Procedural provisions are sometimes scattered throughout different pieces of legislation. This normative dispersion is usually allowed from a constitutional standpoint, but it seems not ideal from the point of view of legal certainty and transparency in the messages sent by the lawmaker to the taxpayers. Therefore it would be advisable to reach some degree of codification in the field of environmental taxation.

Within European continental law, some countries have implemented general tax acts with common legal terminology on taxation and common rules for different tax procedures (such as assistance, tax assessment, tax audits, tax collection, tax offenses and tax claims). The same model has been followed by many Latin American countries. As a first step for the codification of environmental taxes and tax expenditures, it would make sense to introduce some specific provisions in the general tax acts for the notion of environmental taxes, charges and tax expenditures and, above all, for the procedural coordination between tax and environmental authorities for the application of environmental taxes and environmental tax expenditures. The same should apply to general tax legislation, and with a limited scope for regional or local taxes. A proposal has been drafted by a international team of tax researchers supported by the Spanish Institute of Fiscal Studies. Their *Model of an Environmental Tax Code for Latin-America* proposes reforms for the current tax codes of Spain, Argentina, Brazil, Chile, Colombia, Mexico and Panama.[37]

FINAL REMARKS

Designing environmental taxes and charges is a challenging task that involves political, economic and legal problems together with technical questions. In this chapter we have dealt with constitutional and other legal issues within a wider political framework. We

---

[37]   M. Buñuel et al., *Modelo de Código Tributario Ambiental para América Latina* [*Model of a Tax Code for Latin America*] (Inst. de Estudios Fiscales, Working Paper No. 18, 2003).

have tried to reason in a general way, but because legal science is not entirely abstract, our concepts have roots in soil that may be common among different countries. Differences, however, may emerge according to different cultural backgrounds. A European perspective probably biases the point of view of this work; therefore the researcher should adjust the route according to his or her own constitutional and legal environment.

Nevertheless, we can draw some general conclusions: the peculiarities of environmental taxes and charges require the development of a new legal dogma that differs from the traditional fiscal approach. The researcher should use the works of OECD as an excellent compass but will need to forge his or her own trail through uncharted territory, facing sometimes difficult obstacles. Furthermore, in some countries ordinary taxes have been disguised as 'environmental' in order to gain public acceptance. Legal research is essential to draft an environmental tax or charge and comparative law offers to the lawmaker a valuable starting point, but economic and environmental analysis is also indispensable. Political constraints also must not be neglected: a proper equilibrium between ideal designs and feasibility is needed.

6 Earmarking revenues from environmentally related taxes

Claudia Dias Soares*

A key issue in the design of environmental taxes is whether the revenues from the tax are to be dedicated, or 'earmarked,' to the environmental problem or used for other purposes. This chapter explores earmarking. After a short introduction, it explores the design details of earmarking, the decision about whether to earmark, the academic literature on earmarking and the pros and cons of using earmarking. It concludes with case studies that provide lessons about the use of earmarked revenues for environmentally related taxes.

INTRODUCTION

Earmarking is the practice of designating or dedicating specific revenues raised from general or special taxes to finance or offset specified public expenditures and public services. Through earmarking, governments bypass their typical budget procedure of revenue-pooling and directly tie a revenue source to an expenditure. Earmarked funds are alternatively referred to as 'special funds,' 'segregated accounts,' 'segregated budgets,' 'dedicated revenues' (Adugna 2009, 2) or 'ringfencing' (Rutherford 1995).

Earmarking revenue streams in environmental policy, often done 'off budget,' is common practice in a number of countries.[1] Earmarking revenue from environmental taxes is relevant in relation to four main policy tendencies, namely: (i) the public demand for increased transparency and efficiency in public management; (ii) the pursuit of further public intervention in the realm of environmental quality; (iii) an appeal for the use of economic instruments in order to increase economic efficiency and the effectiveness of environmental measures; and (iv) a response to the strong pressure from national and subnational authorities to contain or reduce public expenditure.

Among the most important factors influencing the worldwide adoption of taxes on polluting bases, that is, the ones that qualify as environmentally related taxes (OECD 2001), is the shift in outlook for administrative policy. New public management policy has assigned increasing importance to efficient financial incentives as instruments of regulation (Pedersen 2001, 171). Furthermore, public authorities have been instigated to look for sources of revenues that cover their new political initiatives. The increased need for new taxes provides new opportunities for earmarking.

Earmarking seems to be especially welcome in the realm of environmental policy

---

* The author gratefully acknowledges the comments provided by the editors and Steffen Kallbekken on an early draft of this chapter. The usual disclaimer applies.

[1] For a non-exhaustive list of federal US taxes that are earmarked, see Camic (2006). For examples in Spain, see Herrera Molina (2000, 280–95) and in Brazil, see Domingues (2007, 150–62).

when compared with other political domains (Bracewell-Milnes and Teja 1991, 99). Earmarking's use in environmental taxation signals a double environmental commitment from public authorities (OECD 1989): a commitment to find revenue sources consistent with the polluter-pays principle, and a commitment to environmentally positive expenditures. These commitments are exemplified by the UK Climate Change Levy, revenues of which were earmarked in part to enhance the purpose of the tax itself.

The actual design and motivation for earmarking may vary depending on the particular situation. Although typical early-twentieth-century uses of earmarking (such as the earmarking of fuel taxes to maintain and improve road structures) had a negative environmental impact, there is evidence of earmarking's improving environmental effectiveness and the economic efficiency of environmental regulation. However, its strengths and drawbacks will be discussed below.

The use of earmarking varies among countries. The UK Treasury has *de facto* earmarked on many occasions but seems keen to restrict the practice to off-budget revenues in order to avoid a *de jure* precedent (Müller 2008, 4, 10). In the Netherlands earmarking has been the rule (Paulus 1995, 205). In France earmarking has been regarded since the early 1970s as a way of implementing the polluter-pays principle (Kolm 1973, 21). In the mid-1990s, approximately 95 percent of the revenue from French taxes on polluting goods was earmarked for environmental goals (Ekins 1996, 11; Delache 1996, 67). And in Central and Eastern Europe, earmarking revenues from new environmental policy instruments has played a dominant role in terms of pollution management. It has been the main revenue source for state and municipal environmental funds, which have continued to increase, picking up in the mid- or late 1990s (Speck, McNicholas and Markovic 2004, 271–72).

CHARACTERISTICS OF EARMARKED ENVIRONMENTAL TAXES

The terms 'earmarking,' 'hypothecation' and 'dedication of the revenue' are often used interchangeably, and the literature does not distinguish precisely among them. Given this ambiguity, this chapter uses the term 'earmarking' and offers a framework for evaluating its characteristics. The chapter's conclusion notes the need for developing an academic consensus about terminology.

Earmarking requires the use of tax revenues, not revenues from user fees. A tax is an unrequited and compulsory payment to the state. As a rule, revenues from taxes go into a general fund (such as the public budget). However, the legal definition[2] of a tax does not restrict tax revenue allocation to a single and specific fund. The way revenues are used is relevant only for the application of public accounting methods and planning and control of public expenditure. Non-earmarking is conventionally acclaimed to represent sound public finance management (Musgrave and Musgrave 1989). It allows in principle for the most efficient use of tax revenues but ignores the need to legitimize tax-raising, which earmarking does when the expenditure purposes are transparent.

---

[2]   For one discussion of the legal requirements of a tax, see Snape (2007). See also Chapter 4 in this Handbook.

Taxes are different in nature than fees. Fees or user charges (or quasi-prices) are payments made by individual or commercial consumers in return for the provision of a good or service. The fees' proceeds finance the related public provisions. These fees include proxy transactions and 'indirect' charges for commodities associated with the use of public infrastructure. When the relationship between the targeted goods and the consumer behavior to be influenced is less direct, a user charge functions more as a tax than a price (Gwilliam and Shalizi 1996). User charges normally go to the service provider and finance a specific service's operation, reserve capital or both (The International Bank for Reconstruction and Development/World Bank 2005, 33). In contrast, earmarked taxes are compulsory and unrequited payments to the government that are dedicated to a specific purpose in the general interest rather than offering the individual taxpayer something specific in exchange. The earmarked taxes are then either channelled through the general treasury to a specific purpose or paid directly to a dedicated fund (Gwilliam and Shalizi 1997, 2).

Other types of measures may generate revenues earmarked for specific purposes without legally constituting taxes. For example, the UK levy associated with the Renewables Obligation, which came into effect in April 2002, was an important revenue source that subsidized renewable generation in the UK. Licensed electricity suppliers paid the levy directly to the UK gas and electricity markets regulator (Ofgem) instead of meeting their obligation to buy the required percentage of their annual supply from eligible renewable energy generators. Ofgem then distributed that revenue as a 'recycled green premium' to suppliers in proportion to their renewable purchases (Müller 2008, 10). In other instances, tariffs set by a public-private management board to recover costs or achieve other objectives (Heggie and Vickers 1998) also are not taxes.

Earmarking involves a legally mandated use of the revenue for an environmental program, which is different from simple 'revenue recycling.' Recycling implies that revenues are returned (totally or partially and with or without a legal mandate) to offset the same taxpayers from whom they have been raised, such as the revenue recycling associated with the Swedish nitrogen oxide tax. The tax was imposed on measured nitrogen oxide emissions and revenues were recycled according to the amount of final product obtained (Ekins 1996, 5; Smith 1997, 87; OECD 2010, 9, which uses the term 'refund' instead of 'recycle'). Companies with high levels of emissions per unit of energy produced were net payers, while the ones with better environmental performance were net receivers. Earmarking, on the other hand, requires by law that revenues be put to some specific expenditure by the government for one of its programs. It is possible that the entities benefiting from the earmarked spending programs may be the same as those who pay the earmarked tax, but this situation is different from revenue recycling because the taxpayers are receiving programmatic benefits, not revenue. When the use to which tax revenues are put follows only from administrative practice or financial decision-making, there is not legal earmarking. For instance, the Danish waste tax in the 1980s provided funds to improve the budget of the Ministry of Environment, but law did not mandate specific uses (Andersen 1999).

Compliance with budgetary rules of caution also cannot be considered earmarking (Soares 1998, 1185). Rules aimed at pursuing a balanced budget, such as those stating that capital revenues should cover capital expenditures, do not lead to earmarking. Those rules are aimed at improving budget management rather than restricting the powers of the authorities implementing the public budget.

Thus, earmarking occurs when a law requires government to use part or all the revenues from a specific tax toward a certain public expenditure goal. Authorities benefiting from earmarking may or may not be legally, administratively or financially autonomous. Often earmarking occurs with dedication of revenues from a single tax to a single public service within fiscal units that manage multiple taxes and services. A similar effect can be attained by assigning restricted tax powers to these units (Buchanan 1963, 458). In contrast to earmarking part of the tax revenues, allocation of taxing powers includes the ability to set tax rates in a regulated framework.

The revenue from environmentally related taxes is understood in this chapter to be used directly, in full or in part, for environmental purposes. For instance, part of the revenue of the UK's Climate Change Levy was dedicated to the Carbon Trust, which used the revenue for dedicated purposes related to the purposes of the tax (OECD 2005, 38). However, most of the revenues from this tax were recycled back to the industry according to a double-dividend rationale. It is, of course, also possible to earmark revenues from non-environmentally related taxes for environmental purposes.

Earmarking can be either weak or strong. The weak form describes those programs financed with the revenues earmarked without restrictions on the amount of revenues used for those programs. Revenue from other sources can be used to fund the programs. The latter, strong earmarking, does constrain the amount of revenues. Only revenue from the earmarked tax can be used to support the designated programs (Wilkinson 1994, 119).

A weak version of earmarking may provide the benefits of earmarking without all the costs usually associated with this technique (Gee 1997, 98), namely the inefficiency and distortion it introduces in the public finance decision-making process. The merits of each project, rather than the amount of resources available, can then be regarded as the main decision-making criterion to set revenue and expenditure priorities since revenues can flow into and out of the general budget as necessary. In theory, the strong version of earmarking is less preferable. Tax revenues seldom equal the amount deemed necessary to meet the optimal expenditure level for the specific goal pursued. While a weak version of earmarking is aimed mainly at informing the citizens about the use of public resources, thereby increasing transparency of public accounts, a strong version of earmarking is intended to restrict the budgetary capacity of public authorities. A strong version of earmarking prevents expenditure programs from expanding beyond or shrinking below the amount of revenues obtained. Excess revenues allow only a reduction of the tax, not a transfer of funds to other programs. Revenue shortage can be dealt with only through a tax increase or a constraint of the actions financed.

Moreover, due to the externalities associated with the public good and the regressive or excessively progressive impact of the tax, tax revenues might be useful to correct tax rate errors in order to attain an optimal level of output and accomplish distributive justice. Therefore, strong earmarking is also not recommended since to attain efficiency in the regulatory intervention as a whole it is usually necessary to pass revenues between the general public budget and the autonomous fund.

Earmarked revenues can accrue either from a general tax, such as an income tax, or a specific tax, such as an excise duty on polluting goods. If government increases a general tax and earmarks the revenue, however, over time taxpayers may tend to forget that the reason for the tax increase was an increased expenditure for environmental remediation. In environmental policy, earmarking specific taxes is more common than earmarking general taxes. In such cases, those benefiting from earmarked revenues can be the same ones who pay for the earmarked tax. Therefore, this kind of earmarking is commonly used to finance the provision of certain services to a group of individuals when free-riding problems make it impossible to provide them through the market. For example, in an area outside of environmentally related taxes, revenues from a municipal tax can be earmarked for cleaning public spaces within the municipality. In any case, revenues from environmentally related taxes should not be fully returned to the individual taxpayers in proportion to how much they actually paid. Instead, money should be returned to groups (classes of individuals) according to criteria that do not stimulate further pollution—for instance, road pricing revenues should not be returned to drivers as a class in proportion to car ownership or use (Litman 1996, 25–26). Otherwise the incentive provided by the tax will be washed away.

In addition to the taxpayers, others can benefit from earmarking. For instance, the public benefits when revenues from an environmentally related tax remediate residual damage for which a polluter has not been held responsible. Another example is transport-related taxes (fuel taxes, road tolls, congestion charges, car registration taxes and so on), which are levied on those who use their private cars, while the revenues, if earmarked, are often spent on public transport, thus benefiting people other than those who pay the taxes. In this example, behavior-steering concerns and the polluter-pays principle override equity concerns spurred by the income redistribution. However, sometimes when the taxpayers and revenue recipients do not overlap, distributional issues may arise and threaten the political feasibility of the tax, as exemplified by the US Superfund discussed later in this chapter.

THE DECISION ABOUT WHETHER TO EARMARK

From a legal perspective, whether countries can engage in earmarking depends on their constitutions. A country may limit earmarking. For instance, Article 31(2) of the Spanish Constitution (in the consolidated version up to the amendment of 27 August 1992) states that programming and execution of public expenditure shall be in keeping with criteria for efficiency and economy, leaving the possibility that public finance arguments about the inefficiency of earmarking might prevent its use. Article 19 of the Chilean Constitution prohibits earmarking for general taxes. Therefore any change in the Chilean tax system that includes earmarking of tax receipts to regional objectives requires, at a minimum, a presidential decree or a constitutional amendment (The International Bank for Reconstruction and Development/World Bank 2005, 27).

However, the political constitutions of most European countries (such as Sweden, Slovenia and Portugal) do not rule on the matter, thus allowing laws that introduce earmarking for specific cases. In some countries the political constitution expressly admits earmarking in very precise situations. For example, Article 86 of the Swiss Constitution (adopted in 1998, as most recently amended on 8 February 2004) states that the Federation disposes half of the net proceeds from the consumption tax on hydrocarbon fuels as well as the net proceeds of the national highway tax for the there-named tasks and expenses in connection with road traffic.

From an economic perspective, the process of deciding whether to earmark should include a comparison between, on the one hand, the benefits in terms of enhanced environmental effectiveness and the political acceptability of the regulatory intervention, and on the other hand, the costs expressed in increased economic inefficiency due to budgetary rigidity. A regulator should use earmarking only if, when compared with other options, it brings a net environmental benefit, either in effectiveness, efficiency or equity. The equity can be either horizontal, i.e. revenues benefit those who incur the cost as a class in the excess of their payments over their externalities,[3] or vertical, i.e. revenues benefit low-income taxpayers as a class at least enough to compensate for the costs they bear, and disadvantaged victims of pollution are benefited overall. Each technical option should be justified according to its own merits and not to the origin of the resources used (OECD 1985, 195). Earmarking should not be a way of escaping the normal parliamentary processes for budget control.

Another aspect to consider when deciding on earmarking is the goal pursued by the tax. Taxes aimed at different objectives should use different techniques (Garcia-Quintana 1981, 18). When the taxes primarily have a distributive goal (Osculati 1979, 35), such as the 2004 amendment to the Portuguese fuel tax discussed below, it may be reasonable to earmark revenues from an environmentally related tax.[4] However, when the taxes themselves are designed to target behavioral changes, the question arises as to whether the earmark is also necessary. In that case, a regulator should be allowed to justify the need to also earmark the revenues (among others, González 1997, 175) rather than be subject to a ban on earmarks *tout court*. Whether the tax was designed as general revenue-raising (Ramsey) tax or a Pigouvian tax might also have implications as far as earmarking is concerned, as discussed in connection with fuel taxes later in this chapter.

Some propose that criteria for subsidized financing should be developed under the polluter-pays principle (OECD 1972) and the St. Petersburg Guidelines on Environmental Funds in Economies in Transition (OECD 1995) to evaluate the economic effectiveness of earmarking (Speck, McNicholas and Markovic 2004, 272). Other guidelines that may be relevant when deciding on earmarking in European Union member states are various European Commission main policy papers, such as the Green Paper on Fair and Efficient Pricing (COM(1995) 691, 20 December 1995), the White Paper on Fair Payment for Infrastructure Use (COM(1998) 466 final, 22 July 1998), and the White Paper Roadmap to a Single European Transport Area – Towards a competitive and resource efficient transport system (COM(2011)144 final, 28 March 2011), as well as the Community Guidelines on State Aid for Environmental Protection (OJ 2008/C 82/01, 1 April 2008).

---

[3] For example, regarding earmarking of congestion pricing revenues, one can discuss whether horizontal equity requires payments just to those who actually pay the toll, or also to those who change their travel patterns in response to the toll, thereby incurring costs in terms of inconvenience and providing the congestion reduction benefit to the toll payers. Since people tolled off the road often shift to transit, bicycling or walking, road-pricing revenues could be used to benefit users of those modes (Litman 1996).

[4] Määttä (1999, 11) argues that it may be useful to earmark to environmental projects taxes without an incentive effect when the polluting demand has a low price-elasticity or the quantification of externality is too complex. See also Määttä (2006).

The pros and cons of using earmarks have been debated in the literature and are discussed at greater length later in this chapter.

THE LITERATURE ON EARMARKING REVENUES FROM ENVIRONMENTALLY RELATED TAXES

Scholarly literature on earmarking revenues from environmentally related taxes is sparse (Camic 2006, 57) and mainly revolves around the acceptability issue. Some suggest that earmarking is appropriate in special situations, but the majority subscribe to the common wisdom that earmarking is inefficient and undesirable. This section presents major publications on the topic.

Buchanan and Tullock (1975) conjecture that recycling revenues of pollution taxes in favor of polluters could cause them to lower their resistance. That view was later generalized, for example by Kirchgässner (1997), who argued that the general acceptance of green taxes depends on the mode of revenue recycling, and that citizens had to be convinced that the revenues were fully and fairly redistributed. Using data from the 2000 Swiss referendum on three energy tax proposals, Thalmann (2004) tested this hypothesis.

Drawing on lessons from World Bank case studies, McCleary (1991) attributes earmarking's limited support among economists and public administrators to the following reasons: (i) it leads to a misallocation of resources, with overfinancing of the earmarked activities and subfinancing of the others; (ii) it hampers effective budgetary control (depending to some degree on whether provisions are embedded in statutes or in the constitution); (iii) it infringes on the powers and discretion of the legislative and executive branches of government; and (iv) it introduces inflexibility into budgets, given that changes come only after a lag and earmarking systems continue after their purpose has been served.

McCleary's practical objection to earmarking rests on the observation that 'in practice, it is difficult to achieve pricing and taxation arrangements that will allocate resources appropriately for the service in question and yet require few administrative decisions. Often, efficient pricing and taxing lead to unbalanced budgets for the earmarked fund and hence to interdependence with the general budget' (McCleary 1991, 81). The paper cautions against the practice except under certain defined and restrictive conditions.

Small (1992) emphasizes the importance of the fee revenues to the net benefits, and outlines a scheme of public transit investments and tax reductions aimed at achieving a broader distribution of net benefits. While Small does not empirically test the potential improvement in public acceptability that might be provided by his proposal, his work does support the notion that the disposition of the fee revenues must be carefully designed and successfully communicated to the public. Therefore, his findings might be useful to address the earmarking of revenues from environmentally related taxes charged on congestion-related externalities.[5]

---

[5] King et al. (2007) also provide a useful insight on how to allocate the revenues from congestion pricing, but this paper proposes revenue allocation to places and people (cities) rather than earmarking, which requires allocation to programs or purposes.

Camic's paper (2006) aims to demonstrate how earmarking can trigger potent political effects, both symbolic and institutional, and the potential to increase system stability, revenue yield and progressivity. For this purpose, she introduces the following hierarchy of normative benefits of earmarking. First-order benefits include the constraint of the budget-writing process and the provision of tax policy information, while second-order benefits include increased stability, revenue yield, progressivity and predictability of spending. The paper also introduces its own taxonomy based on three characteristics, namely (i) a pre-commitment (of future leaders and generations); (ii) earmarking's being contributory, in the sense that the beneficiaries are the same as the contributors; and (iii) an entitlement, in the sense that its beneficiaries have an absolute right to a (usually monetary) benefit granted immediately upon their meeting a legal requirement.

Kallbekken (2008) assesses whether earmarking revenues from a Pigouvian tax decrease tax-aversion. This is done by letting the participants vote on three different tax schemes that differ with respect to how the revenues are redistributed. One scheme is representative of a non-earmarked scheme, while the other two are representative of targeted earmarking schemes. While experimental economists (and psychologists) have examined several features related to taxation, no experiments on earmarking taxes had previously been conducted. Experiments that combined taxation with voting decisions dealt only with voting on the tax itself, not with the use of tax revenues once the tax was in place.

PROS AND CONS OF EARMARKING

Political Acceptance of Earmarking in General

The political acceptance of earmarking is difficult. Western countries already have high levels of expenditure and widespread public resistance to tax increases (Mulgan 1997, 53). Logrolling and the lack of economic rationality in the budget processes have created a strong resistance to earmarking. The argument builds on the increasing lack of trust the layman shows government and the erosion of public consensus over social priorities that has developed since the 1970s. However, citizens now also demand more transparency and accountability in public finances. Though earmarking has been strongly opposed by economists based on efficiency criteria, it provides citizens with a sense of control over the way their contributions to society are used (Soares 2006, 249). This approach might help overcome the 'new tax revolt,' like the broad street protests in the late 1990s against European fuel tax increases.

Voters seem to demand less a contraction of public intervention than a redefinition of its goals and means. The political public demands more transparency and responsibility, stronger emphasis on efficiency and clearer separation between policy and politics (Majone 1996, 299). Earmarking might serve these interests either directly, by clarifying the connection between revenues and expenditures, or indirectly, by facilitating the formal reorganization of the public sector concerning the procedures and expertise needed and the public sector's relation to the private sector. This is because earmarking allows new forms of administrative and financial autonomy.

When coupled with the existence of public authorities that have financial or administrative autonomy, earmarking is often used to provide greater flexibility over public government and improve public performance in environmental matters. Earmarking can be a relatively stable way for governments to finance these entities while increasing transparency in the collection and use of public resources, and a more direct link between the two phases of the tax process (revenues collection and expenditure) may benefit democracy (Hills 1993).

Political Acceptance of Environmental Taxes in Particular

The transparency provided by earmarking can be especially useful within environmental policy for two main reasons. Because environmental taxes have not been in effect for a long period, it has been difficult to assess their environmental impact (Ekins and Speck 1998). In addition, the term 'environmental taxes' is often used to describe environmentally related taxes that apply to pollution tax bases but that may have little actual environmental effect. Hence, citizens are now suspicious about the environmental impact of environmental taxes. Without popular support, policies have to benefit important political actors in order to be implemented (King et al. 2007, 122).

Earmarking within environmental tax policy can have a strong image-related effect (OECD 1996, 65), reducing the political costs of a tax intervention. When revenues are earmarked to environmental programs, citizens may be more likely to trust a regulator's intention to improve environmental quality rather than primarily to collect more money. Some empirical studies show that when citizens perceive that the money they pay for environmental harm is used in ecosystems protection and rehabilitation projects, their resistance is lowered and trust builds for environmental tax interventions (Brett and Keen 2000, 315; Clinch and Dresner 2006, 960; Kallbekken and Aasen 2010, 1). Likewise, public opposition to environmentally related taxes is lower when citizens feel they are asked to pay for problems they cause than when they are asked to finance indiscriminately general public provisions (GlobeScan and PIPA 2007).

Therefore, earmarking tax revenues to environmental projects might improve social and political acceptance of environmental tax reforms. In the UK, for instance, following a vociferous campaign against the fuel tax increase, in November 1999 the government announced that future increases would be dedicated for expenditure on public transport and road-building (Dresner et al. 2006b, 931).

An alternative to earmarking the environmental tax revenues for financing environmental goals is to use them to reduce labor costs (the double dividend debate[6]) and therefore to engage in environmental tax reform. Hence, it is important to consider the relative merits of environmental tax reform's revenue recycling, on the one hand, and earmarking, on the other.

The double dividend rationale draws on a possible additional benefit to be derived from environmental taxation. While most taxes distort incentives, environmental taxes correct distortions, namely the externalities arising from excessive use of the environment. If revenues from environmental taxes are used to finance reductions in other incentive-distorting types of taxation, such as labor supply, investment or consumption,

---

[6]   For an introduction to the double dividend debate, see Goulder (1995), and Chapter 12 of this Handbook.

secondary gains could be reaped in addition to the environmental benefit (Speck and Ekins 2002, 103). However, if such a tax shift (led by concerns about political feasibility[7] or a double dividend rationale) leaves the taxpayers in an economic position equivalent to or even better than the one before the tax, it potentially annuls the tax incentive (OECD 2010, 10, 36). This might have been the case with the UK Climate Change Levy (see discussion later in this chapter).

Thus, earmarking runs counter to the basic idea of environmental tax reform, which involves a tax shift (mainly away from labor and toward environmental 'bads') and leaves less discretion for revenue allocation for specific goals. By involving revenue allocation for a specific goal, earmarking potentially enhances the environmental effectiveness of the tax. Using revenues to provide taxpayers with the know-how to change behavior in an environmentally and cost-effective manner would be especially useful when environmentally related taxes are too modest to reflect accurately the external costs, as is usually the case.

In Europe, there is resistance to the use of taxes within environmental policy and to the implementation of environmental tax reforms (PETRAS Project,[8] Thalmann 2004, 179). The fundamental problem that environmental tax reform has faced since the mid-1990s has been a lack of trust that the government would do with the revenues what it promised (Dresner et al. 2006a, 901; 2006b, 936).

In some countries, such as Denmark, France, Norway and the UK, recycling revenues to reduce labor costs has been generally considered unwarranted by the public. It was seen as confusing two separate things, one to do with the environment and another to do with labor. If revenues from a tax imposed supposedly for the sake of the environment were used for other purposes, then that was seen as a confidence trick (Dresner et al. 2006a, 901; 2006b, 938; Klok et al. 2006, 914). There is literature advocating for specific application of revenues from carbon pricing to support technology development and innovation rather than recycling (NREE 2009, 100).

Effect of Earmarking on Environmental Effectiveness and Efficiency

Increased concern over budget deficits has refocused the European tax debate on equity (avoiding shifting further burdens to the less well-off and pursuing less income inequality) and efficiency issues (getting more for each Euro spent). The share of public expenditure for environmental goals has been rising and in some EU member states it already represents a substantial part of public expenditure (OECD 2003). Hence the call for efficient and effective environmental policies. Earmarking might allow a positive effect beyond increased political acceptability; it may have a regulatory impact as well.

By more clearly linking costs and benefits for citizens, earmarking might enhance the behavioral effect that follows a regulatory tax intervention. It might increase the elasticity of demand, making polluters more responsive to the tax. Some literature (such as

---

[7]   Political feasibility concerns might still be the *ultima ratio* for revenue recycling even when other concerns, such as equity, rule the use of the tax revenues—see for example the case of the use given to the revenues of the carbon tax adopted in British Columbia (Canada) in 2008.

[8]   Available at http://www.soc.surrey.ac.uk/petras/private/six_month_report.html.

Andersen 1994) finds that the environmental results of tax measures were improved when their revenues were earmarked to the same goal. For instance, a comparative study of the German, Dutch and French systems of water pollution control concluded that earmarking enhanced the capacity of regulation to improve environmental quality (Andersen 1994, 176–77; OECD 1998, 39–41). This was evident in the French case, where effluent charge revenues were used to support industries and communities that were willing to implement pollution control measures. Earmarking compensated for the low environmental effectiveness of the charges (due to their modesty), funding a system of branch contracts under which selected industrial branches agreed to reduce pollution if they received subsidies from the River Basin Agencies (Harrison and Sewell 1980).

The expected decreasing revenue capacity associated with effective regulatory environmental taxes may allow the necessary match between revenue provided and revenue needed when earmarking addresses the same environmental problem as the environmental tax. But an automatic corrective mechanism can also be inserted in the tax design. This was done, for example, in the emission fee applied in Connecticut in the United States (Milne and Hasson 1996, 10).

Earmarking can also help to overcome some distortions introduced in the regulated industry by environmentally related taxes. This was the case with the Swedish nitrogen oxide charge. Though in that case there was only revenue recycling and no earmarking, it is reasonable to expect the same result with the extra formality provided by a legal basis.

Earmarking can also enable policymakers to set the corrective tax higher than they otherwise would, but nevertheless lower than the Pigouvian tax (Brett and Keen 2000, 315). However, earmarking might also lead to distortions in the design of environmentally related taxes. For instance, earmarking the revenues from a waste tax to waste treatment facilities might allow reductions in the waste fees and consequently lower the stimulus to recycling provided by the waste tax (and hence reduce the tax's environmental effectiveness).

Earmarking might serve efficiency concerns in what would be an application of the theory of internalization. Pigou endorsed the kind of earmarking that aims to repair the damage caused by the taxed behavior rather than fund new projects or compensate victims. He considered the British road tax a 'very incomplete and partial' application of the theory of internalization since the revenues were used to build new roads rather than to fund reparation of damages caused by drivers (Pigou 2002, 193). Thus, drivers obtained from their payment an additional service useful to them rather than to the general public. Economic efficiency requires road-pricing revenue to be used to benefit society rather than refunded to users in proportion to how much they paid. There is no efficiency requirement to dedicate revenue to road projects aimed at private driving (Litman 1996).

Furthermore, the EU's legal objections under the polluter-pays principle to environmental subsidies paid by member states for competition and equity reasons can be relaxed when the environmental subsidies are associated with earmarking.[9] Using earmarked

---

[9]   Though this is not an absolute prohibition, the European Commission has been tightening the conditions under which such aids are accepted for environmental reasons. See the 1994 Framework, OJ 94/C 72/03, 10 March 1994; its 2001 revision, OJ 2001/C 37/3, 3 February 2001; and 2008 version, OJ 2008/C 82/01, 1 April 2008.

tax revenues within the same sector where they were raised is accepted by the European Commission as a way to support the transition to full application of the polluter-pays principle and is in accordance with the EU's original idea of how member states should finance environmental policy measures.[10] Under these conditions, market distortion is considered to be minimal and the polluter pays for the damage.

Budgetary stability and caution as well as financial rationality can also explain tax-revenue earmarking when the latter is used to restrict the amount of resources applied to a certain program to the ones obtained from the individuals who cause or benefit from such expenditures. If those who cause the costs also support them (and perceive such linkage), not only will cost coverage be assured, but there may also be an effort to constrain the referred costs. A clearly different situation is the use of earmarking by interest groups to restrict their tax responsibility, resulting in a negative impact on other individuals. For example, a taxpaying industry might lobby to get its tax revenues earmarked to an expenditure program that it is able to control (for instance, investment in clean technology) in order to constrain future tax increases and break the tax linkage with pollution.

Effects of Earmarking on Geographic Balance

The argument for earmarking as a way of separating issues of allocation from distributional issues may also be applied spatially. Regional financing of regionally consumed services may be a device for avoiding overprovision in some regions at the expense of others as they all compete to maximize their share of the national budget (Gwilliam and Shalizi 1997, 9). However, some caution is necessary since regional disparities in providing environmental services may be justifiable on both efficiency and equity grounds. For instance, investment in waste treatment facilities might be more demanding depending on local soil and weather characteristics.

The Budget Flexibility Issue

Among the drawbacks usually associated with earmarking are concerns related to current OECD practices on public expenditure. Earmarking has been criticized for limiting macroeconomic flexibility and undermining stabilization programs, thereby aggravating fiscal crises and leading to inefficient allocation of resources. Due to earmarking's rigid budget process and over- or underfunding of certain programs, earmarking might lead to inefficient resource allocation and special interests pressuring for public spending. This is contrary to sound fiscal management, not only because it restricts the decision-making powers of current government, but also because it pre-commits future generations and governments. The critical issue is how to reconcile large- and small-scale efficiency considerations with criteria for evaluating trade-offs when they conflict (Gwilliam and Shalizi 1997, 2). A careful design of earmarking might assuage this criticism.

The defects cited by the critics of earmarking are the virtues for its proponents, who argue that rigidity and limitations on resource reallocation can sometimes be desirable

---

[10]   Recommendation 75/436 (EUROATOM, CECA, CEE), OJ 75/L 194/1, 25 July 1975, Point 4, b.

(McCleary 1991). Earmarking assures minimum levels of financing for public services that governments consider worthy, thus avoiding periodic haggling by bureaucrats and legislators over appropriate levels of funding. Earmarking may also protect high-priority programs from shifting majorities, inefficiency and corruption. Greater stability and funding continuity may lead to lower costs that come with faster completion of projects. In any case, while earmarking involves some pre-commitment of revenues, it does not inherently entail the long-term commitment of future actors. In this sense, earmarking in no way removes tax decisions from the democratic process (Camic 2006, 65).

The above-mentioned arguments are all the more relevant for investments with a long payback period, as environmental ones often are. The same is true when opponents can easily challenge the amount of expenditures. Since unanimously agreed-upon data on environmental damages and benefits are often not available, discussions on the correctness of investment levels have been relatively frequent (for instance the long national and international discussions on a post-Kyoto agreement and level of investment in climate change policies).

EXPERIENCES AND LESSONS WITH EARMARKING

The aims pursued through earmarking and the circumstances of its use are quite diverse. For example, in Norway, part of the revenue from a tax on lubricant oils has been used to finance the collection of used oils (Royal Norwegian Ministry of the Environment 1995, 3). In the United States, revenues from a pesticide tax have been used to support teaching sustainable agricultural practices to farmers (Barron 1995, 1). Though without formal earmarking, in Slovenia revenues from carbon dioxide taxes have been used to finance carbon-reduction projects, mainly the modernization of power plants that cannot afford upgrades due to regulations restricting energy profits (Schlegelmilch and Markovič-Hribernik 2002, 69). This section reviews five situations, exploring how some of the concepts discussed above have played out in particular instances.

The UK Climate Change Levy

In 2001, the UK Government introduced the Climate Change Levy (CCL) on the commercial use of energy to encourage businesses to find ways of reducing energy demand and greenhouse gas emissions.[11] To support business competitiveness, reduce the levy's potential economic and social impacts, and make the levy politically feasible, the CCL was accompanied by a 0.3 percent cut in employers' national insurance contributions (NICs).[12] Most of the CCL revenues were recycled back to the corporate sector in the form of employment tax refunds (OECD 2005, 37) under the double-dividend rationale.

---

[11]   As part of the CCL package, the government also introduced other measures to help business raise energy-efficiency levels, including climate change agreements (CCAs); enhanced capital allowances (ECAs) for energy-saving technologies; and funding for the Carbon Trust.

[12]   Finance Act 2000, schedule 6, paragraph 10 (climate change levy); Social Security Contributions and Benefits Act 1992, schedule 9, as amended by the Social Security (Contributions) (Re-rating and National Insurance Funds Payments) Order 2001, SI 2001 N. 477, regulation 2.

This example, often called earmarking, was rather a case of recycling, since revenues were not used for a specific purpose other than reducing other taxes imposed on the same taxpayers. It had an off-budget status and was used to mitigate the socioeconomic impact of environmentally related taxes with a double-dividend rationale. Regarding environmental effectiveness, though, depending on the counterfactuals used, different assessments of the tax have led to different results. Most now agree that a 'pure' carbon tax would have been better (OECD 2005, 5).

By recycling revenue, the CCL and NICs cuts were expected to stimulate energy efficiency while not increasing overall taxation on the business sector. In 2006, in contrast to what happened in 2003,[13] the value of the NICs reductions exceeded CCL receipts. Therefore, there was a shift of the tax burden from 'goods' to 'bads' (Müller 2008, 9) and the industry as a whole faced a lower tax burden than would have been the case in the absence of the CCL (UK Department of Energy and Climate Change 2009). Therefore, it is unlikely that the 'soft' nature of the targets from the outset (OECD 2005, 48) was compensated by any extra incentive provided by revenue recycling to reduce carbon emissions.

Another part of the proceeds of the levy was earmarked to provide environmental improvements through an Energy Efficiency Fund of £50 million and through the Carbon Trust. The latter was an independent company limited by guarantee, set up by the government 'in partnership with business,' to invest in the development and deployment of low-carbon technologies. Since July 2002, it had responsibility for the everyday administration of the tax subsidies (in the form of an enhanced capital allowances scheme) for the installation of environmentally friendly energy equipment (Capital Allowances Act 2001, section 45A) (Snape 2006, 257–299).

The Portuguese Permanent Forest Fund

The 2004 Portuguese Budget Law (31 December 2003) transposed the EU Directive on energy taxation 2003/96/EC (OJ L 283, 31 October 2003). The Budget Law set a minimum and a maximum tax rate for fuels based on their environmental impact. The Budget Law (article 38/5) also introduced an additional levy to the fuel tax (Imposto sobre Produtos Energéticos). The only regulated fuels were gasoline (euros 0.5 cents/liter) and diesel (euros 0.25 cents/liter). Revenue collected was earmarked to the Permanent Reforestation Fund (PRF) with a cap of 30 million euros per year.

This case of weak earmarking set a direct link between costs and benefits of air pollution according to the rationale of the Kyoto Protocol, namely that it is possible to store carbon in trees. It caused the main GHG emissions producers, i.e. road drivers (OECD 1993b, 88; EEA 2002, 1) to pay for afforestation, reforestation and forest management (valid climate change policy measures, according to articles 3/3 and 4 of the Kyoto Protocol). However, the PRF was not used to buy Kyoto credits since all the projects financed were located in Portugal.

Earmarking assured that a national interest project, reforestation, would have long-term financial support insulated from political changes or any temporary lack of financial

---

[13] In April 2003 HM Treasury applied a one percent 'surcharge' to all classes of NICs (National Insurance Contributions Act 2002, schedules 1–3) (Snape 2007, 148).

resources. This proved advantageous by the mid-2000s, when Portugal needed to improve its forestation policy and its financing for three main reasons: (i) fire damage to national forests; (ii) mitigating growth in national GHG emissions to maintain compliance with Kyoto obligations; and (iii) the high public deficit, which did not allow new expenditure programs absent new revenue sources.

The US Hazardous Substance Response Fund (Superfund) and the Oil Spill Liability Trust Fund

The US Comprehensive Environmental Response, Compensation, and Liability Act (CERCLA, or 'Superfund'), enacted in 1980 and amended in 1986 by the Superfund Amendments and Reauthorization Act, was designed to clean up sites contaminated by hazardous substances. CERCLA created the Agency for Toxic Substances and Disease Registry and provided broad federal authority to respond directly to releases or threatened releases of hazardous substances. The Superfund was initially funded by a broad-based business tax, a tax on raw chemicals, and an increased tax rate on crude oil.[14]

Over five years, $1.6 billion was collected and the tax went to a trust fund for cleaning up abandoned or uncontrolled hazardous waste sites when no responsible party could be identified (Müller 2008, 8). The tax ceased to be collected in 1995 and the fund was exhausted by the end of 2003. Since then the expenditures covered by the fund have been allocated by the US Congress out of general tax revenues. Following the extra burden imposed on taxpayers due to the costs of cleaning up abandoned hazardous waste sites, the option of making the polluter pay through the reinstatement of the taxes has been on the US political agenda, with the support of the US Environmental Protection Agency.

This case shows that the political feasibility of earmarking is strongly dependent on its distributional impact. It may be important that the payers overlap with the beneficiaries. Damages caused by offshore oil spills were not included in the Superfund since only coastal states suffered such damages. Noncoastal states then were unwilling to permit any net financial transfer to coastal states (Teja 1988, 530), as that would have been at odds with horizontal equity. Since the establishment of the Superfund, the Oil Spill Liability Trust Fund, funded through a dedicated tax on oil companies per barrel of oil,[15] was established to remediate any oil spill damage in offshore or otherwise navigable waters.

Fuel Taxes

Fuel taxes illustrate the dichotomy between Ramsey taxes (taxes mainly aimed at raising revenues) and Pigouvian taxes (taxes mainly aimed at internalizing externalities and consequently steering behaviors toward patterns less costly to the society). The first generation of fuel taxes, in place until the 1970s, were clearly targeted at raising revenues, whereas the second-generation taxes, used from then onward, have had a mixture of motivations. Increasingly, other concerns have been introduced into the tax design, such

---

[14] The tax provisions can be found in 26 U.S.C. §§ 59A, 4611, 4661, 4671, 9507.
[15] The tax is currently 8 cents per barrel. 26 U.S.C. § 4511(c)(2).

as, the desire early on to constrain the consumption of oil products, and more recently to improve the environment.

The willingness to earmark environmentally related tax revenues may depend on such design. For instance, the more that fuel taxes are designed as taxes aimed at raising revenues, the more averse to earmarking politicians might be, since it reduces their financial flexibility. However, this aversion may be lowered regarding earmarking revenues to expenditure items that increase future fuel consumption and (consequently) future tax revenue. Likewise, the more relevant Pigouvian features are in the tax design, the more reasonable it is to expect earmarking of the revenues, since internalization of externalities due to congestion and the fulfillment of environmental goals may require specific expenditure programs with prevention, resilience, mitigation and compensation measures.

Traditionally revenues from fuel taxes have been earmarked to road maintenance and improvement of public transports. However, the tradition of earmarking fuel taxes is quite distinct in different countries and probably influences the support for or opposition to the tax. In the US, fuel taxes are closer to Ramsey taxes than is the case in some European countries, given the low tax rates. In the US most fuel taxes are earmarked primarily for highway construction.[16] In the UK and France, efforts to hypothecate fuel tax revenues have been strongly resisted (Hammar et al. 2004, 15). Still, earmarking of the UK fuel tax escalator was announced in the late 1990s as a means to increase public acceptance of the policy measure (Dresner et al. 2006b, 931). Gwilliam and Shalizi (1997; 1999) explore in depth the governance, budget flexibility implications, and other aspects of earmarked road funds in different countries.

More recently, there are examples of fuel tax revenues being earmarked to climate change policies, as for example the additional levy in the Portuguese fuel tax since 2004. Results from polls on acceptance of urban road pricing (in London, RAC Report on Motoring 2000 and Ison 2000, 270; in California, Brett and Keen 2000; in Switzerland, Thalmann 2004; in Edinburgh, Gaunt et al. 2007; and in Stockholm, Isaksson and Richardson 2009) might allow the conclusion that earmarking fuel tax revenues could raise public acceptance of fuel taxes (Kallbekken and Aasen 2010, 1). However, it is not as certain whether this kind of hypothecation is efficient. Moreover, the most common uses of earmarked fuel tax revenues, namely road improvement and public transportation, are not equally beneficial to the environment. While the second use might drive consumption towards more environmentally sound behavior, the first one stimulates unsustainable patterns of consumption.

CONCLUSIONS AND PERSPECTIVES FOR FUTURE RESEARCH

There is a literature gap regarding the distinctions among 'earmarking,' 'hypothecation,' 'dedication' and 'recycling.' As indicated, this chapter has used the term earmarking and focused on the distinctions between earmarking and recycling. Future academic

---

[16]   The federal Highway Trust Fund does have some money for environmental mitigation and public transit.

discussions could focus on the terminology and the legal, policy and political implications of the different terms.

In spite of the criticism earmarking often faces, some principles of new public management help us to understand the importance of this practice in most developed countries. While the scholarly literature on earmarking environmentally related tax revenues is sparse and focuses mainly on financial and political aspects, one thing is apparent: the defects for earmarking's opponents are often the virtues for its proponents. Nonetheless, many research gaps exist regarding the environmental effectiveness of earmarking and environmentally related taxes. Earmarking could help to raise a tax's effectiveness through higher and more precisely targeted corrective taxes, and support the transition to a full application of the polluter-pays principle by funding subsidies acceptable to that principle.

This chapter illustrates lessons and signals the need for future research. Earmarking revenues from environmentally related taxes to specific environmental objectives might enhance the environmental effectiveness of the taxes and address concerns about political feasibility (the ones that often justify revenue recycling with a double-dividend rationale). The perception, based on experience, that taxation changes behaviors and thus reduces environmental problems seems necessary to increase public support for environmental taxes (Kallbekken and Sælen 2010, 12). But when payers overlap with beneficiaries, special caution is recommended to avoid violating the polluter-pays principle and any resulting annulment of the tax's incentive. This aspect, which would add to the financial and political reasons to earmark, should also be further investigated.

Another aspect requiring further research is the potential for earmarking revenues from emissions trading schemes, which, when in the form of a binding cap-and-trade scheme applied to all sources of emissions, parallel a GHG tax (Snoddon and Wigle 2010). Following the inevitable significant auctioning of permits in emissions trading schemes in the near future, it is expected that industry will demand earmarking that leaves it better off than it would be if revenues were to go into the general budget. In Europe, the European Commission[17] and the European Parliament[18] have addressed whether revenue from emission permits auctions in the EU ETS should be earmarked for funding climate change activities. Member states have opposed both proposals.[19] In the United States, according to the Lieberman-Warner Climate Security Act (6 June 2008), which never became law, the Administrator of the US Environmental Protection Agency would have auctioned a percentage of the annual emission allowances of the proposed US emissions trading scheme to fund some international climate change funds (Müller 2008, 8–9).

---

[17]   Commission of the European Communities (2008), Directive of the European Parliament and of the Council amending Directive 2003/87/EC so as to improve and extend the greenhouse gas emission allowance trading system of the Community, COM(2008) 16 final, Brussels, 23 January 2008. Download: http://ec.europa.eu/environment/climat/emission/pdf/com_2008_16_en.pdf.

[18]   Directive of the European Parliament and of the Council amending Directive 2003/87/EC so as to improve and extend the greenhouse gas emission allowance trading system of the Community, COM(2008) 16 final, Brussels, 23 January 2008.

[19]   For a discussion on the arguments, see Müller (2008, 4).

REFERENCES

Adugna, A. (2009), 'How much of official development assistance is earmarked?', CFP (Concessional Finance and Global Partnerships Vice Presidency) Working Paper Series No. 2.

Andersen, M.S. (1994), *Governance by Green Taxes. Making Pollution Prevention Pay*, Manchester, UK: Manchester University Press.

Andersen, M.S. (1999), 'The Waste tax 1987–1996—an ex-post evaluation of incentives and environmental effects', Working Report No. 18, Copenhagen: Environmental Protection Agency.

Barron, G. (1995), 'Consumers want pesticides out of their food . . . and are willing to pay', http://ekolserv. vo.slu.se/Docs/www/Subject/Pesticides/150-. . ./179Pesticide_Tax_Refor.

Bracewell-Milnes, B. and R.S. Teja (1991), 'The case for earmarked taxes: Government spending and public choice', London, UK: Institute of Economic Affairs.

Brett, C. and M. Keen (2000), 'Political uncertainty and the earmarking of environmental taxes', *Journal of Public Economics*, **75** (3), 315–40.

Buchanan, J. (1963), 'The economics of earmarked taxes', *Journal of Political Economy*, **71**, October, 457–69.

Buchanan, J.M. and G. Tullock (1975), 'Polluter's profits and political response: Direct control versus taxes', *American Economic Review*, **65**, 139–47.

Camic, S. (2006), 'Earmarking: the potential benefits', *Pittsburgh Tax Review*, **4**, 55–83.

Clinch, J.P., L. Dunne and S. Dresner (2006), 'Environmental and wider implications of political impediments to environmental tax reform', *Energy Policy*, **34** (8), 960–70.

Delache, X. (1996), 'Implementing ecotaxes in France: Some issues', in *European Foundation for the Improvement of Living and Working Conditions, Environmental Taxes & Charges. National Experiences & Plans – Papers from the Dublin Workshop*, European Foundation for the Improvement of Living and Working Conditions, Dublin, Ireland: European Foundation for the Improvement of Living and Working Conditions, pp. 67–95.

Domingues, J. M. (2007), *Direito Tributário e Meio Ambiente* [Tax Law and Environment], Rio de Janeiro, Brazil: Editora Forense.

Dresner, S., L. Dunne, P. Clinch and C. Beuermann (2006a), 'Social and political responses to ecological tax reform, in Europe: An introduction to the special issue', *Energy Policy*, **34** (8), 895–904.

Dresner, S., T. Jackson and N. Gilbert (2006b), 'History and social responses to environmental tax reform in the United Kingdom', *Energy Policy*, **34** (8), 930–39.

Ekins, P. (1996), *General Briefing on Environmental Taxes & Charges. National Experiences & Plans. Report of the European Workshop Held at the EFILWC*, Dublin, 7–8 February 1996, Dublin, Ireland: European Foundation for the Improvement of Living and Working Conditions.

Ekins, P. and S. Speck, (1998), 'The impacts of environmental policy on competitiveness: Theory and evidence', in T. Barker and J. Köhler (eds), *International Competitiveness and Environmental Policies*, Cheltenham, UK: Edward Elgar, pp. 33–70.

European Environmental Agency (2002), 'TERM 2002 01—Energy consumption, indicator fact sheet', Copenhagen, Denmark: European Environment Agency.

Garcia-Quintana (1981), 'Los impuestos de ordenamiento económico' [Regulatory taxes], *Hacienda Pública Española* [Spanish Journal of Public Finance], **71**, 17–29.

Gaunt, M., T. Rye and S. Allen (2007), 'Public acceptability of road user charging: The case of Edinburgh and the 2005 referendum', *Transport Reviews*, **27** (1), 85–102.

Gee, D. (1997), 'Economic tax reform in Europe: Opportunities and obstacles', in Timothy O'Riordan (ed.), *Ecotaxation*, London, UK: Earthscan, pp. 81–105.

GlobeScan and PIPA (2007), BBC World Service Poll, 'Most would pay higher energy bills to address climate change says global poll', www.worldpublicopinion.org/pipa/pdf/nov07/BBCClimate2_Nov07_pr.pdf

González, A. (1997), 'El impuesto sobre la contaminación atmosférica de Galicia' [The Galician tax on air pollutant emissions], *Revista Gallega de AdministraciónPública* [Journal of Public Administration of Galicia], **12** (5), 161–87.

Goulder, L.H. (1995), 'Environmental taxation and the double dividend: A reader's guide', *International Tax and Public Finance*, **2**, 157–83.

Gwilliam, K. and Z. Shalizi (1996), *Sustainable Transport: Priorities for Policy Reform*, Development in Practice Series, Washington, DC: World Bank.

Gwilliam, K.M. and Z.M. Shalizi (1997), 'Road funds, user charges and taxes', World Bank TWU Discussion Paper, September, Washington, DC, US: World Bank.

Hammar, H., Å. Löfgren and T. Sterner (2004), 'Political economy obstacles to fuel taxation', *Energy Journal*, **25** (3), 1–17.

Harrison, P. and W.R. Derrick Sewell (1980), 'Water pollution control by agreement: The French system of contracts', *Natural Resources Journal*, 20 (4), 765–86.

Heggie, I.G. and P. Vickers (1998), 'Commercial management and financing of roads', Technical Paper 409, Washington, DC, US: World Bank.
Herrera Molina, P. (2000), *Derecho Tributario Ambiental* [Environmental Tax Law], Marcial Pons.
Hills, J. (1993), *The Future of Welfare: A Guide to the Debate*, York, UK: Rowntree Foundation.
Isaksson, K. and T. Richardson (2009), 'Building legitimacy for risky policies: The cost of avoiding conflict in Stockholm', *Transportation Research Part A,* **43** (3), 251–57.
Ison, S. (2000), 'Local authority and academic attitudes to urban road pricing: A UK perspective', *Transport Policy,* **7**, 269–77.
Kallbekken, S. (2008), 'Pigouvian tax schemes: Feasibility versus efficiency', Steffen Kallbekken PhD thesis, University of Oslo (Department of Economics).
Kallbekken, S. and M. Aasen (2010), 'The demand for earmarking: Results from a focus group study', *Ecological Economics,* **69** (11), 2183–90.
Kallbekken, S. and H. Sælen (2010), 'Public accept for environmental taxes: Self-interest, environmental and distributional concerns', CICERO Working Paper 2010:01, Oslo, Norway: Center for International Climate and Environmental Research.
King, D., M. Manville and D. Shoup (2007), 'The political calculus of congestion charging', *Transport Policy,* **14**, 111–23.
Kirchgässner, G. (1997), 'Environmental policy in Switzerland: Methods, results, problems and challenges', in W. Wasserfallen (ed.), *Economic Policy in Switzerland*, Basingstoke, UK: Macmillan, pp. 184–212.
Klok, J., A. Larsen, A. Dahl and K. Hansen (2006), 'Ecological tax reform in Denmark: History and social acceptability', *Energy Policy,* **34** (8), 905–16.
Kolm, S.-C. (1973), 'Une économie écologique' [An ecological economy], *Revue Politique et Parlementaire,* **1**, 175–90.
Litman, T. (1996), 'Using road pricing revenue: Economic efficiency and equity considerations', *Transportation Research Record,* 1558, 24–28.
Määttä, K. (1999), 'Financing environmental taxes. A source of revenue for environmental protection', Working Paper, Helsinki, Finland: University of Helsinki.
Määttä, K. (2006), *Environmental Taxes: An Introductory Analysis*, Cheltenham, UK: Edward Elgar.
Majone, G. (1996), *Regulating Europe*, Oxford, UK: Routledge.
Markussen, P. and G.T. Svendsen (2005), 'Industry lobbying and the political economy of GHG trade in the European Union', *Energy Policy,* **33** (2), 245–55.
McCleary, W.A. (1991), 'The earmarking of government revenue: A review of some World Bank experience', *The World Bank Research Observer,* **6** (1), 81–104.
Milne, J. and S. Hasson (1996), *Environmental Taxes in New England*, South Royalton, VT, US: Vermont Law School, Environmental Law Center.
Mulgan, G. (1997), 'Functional hypothecation as a potential solution', in Timothy O'Riordan (ed.), *Ecotaxation*, London, UK: Earthscan, pp. 52–59.
Müller, B. (2008), 'To earmark or not to earmark?', Working Paper, November, Oxford, UK: Oxford Institute for Energy Studies.
Musgrave, R.A. and P.B. Musgrave (1989), *Public Finance in Theory and Practice*, 5th ed., New York, US: McGraw-Hill Book Company.
National Roundtable on the Environment and the Economy (NREE) (2009), *Technical Report on Achieving 2050: A Carbon Pricing Policy for Canada*, Ottawa, Canada: National Roundtable on the Environment and the Economy.
OECD (1972), Recommendation C(72)128, Guiding Principles Concerning the International Economic Aspects of Environmental Policies, 26 May 1972.
OECD (1985), *Environment and Economics*, Paris, France: OECD.
OECD (1989), *Economic Instruments for Environmental Protection*, Paris, France: OECD.
OECD (1993a), *Taxation and the Environment. Complementary Policies*, Paris, France: OECD.
OECD (1993b), *Environmental Performance Reviews. Portugal*, Paris, France: OECD.
OECD (1995), *Environmental Taxes in OECD Countries*, Paris, France: OECD.
OECD (1996), *Implementation Strategies for Environmental Taxes*, Paris, France: OECD.
OECD (1998), *Evaluating Economic Instruments for Environmental Policy*, Paris, France: OECD.
OECD (2001), ECO/WKP(2001)29, 17.07.2001, Paris, France: OECD.
OECD (2003), *Pollution Abatement and Control Expenditures in OECD Countries*, Paris, France: OECD.
OECD (2005), 'The United Kingdom climate change levy. A study in political economy', Paris, France: OECD.
OECD (2010), 'Innovation effects of the Swedish NOx charge', Paris, France: OECD.
Osculati, F. (1979), *La tassazione ambientale* [Environmental taxation], Padova, Italy: Cedam.
Paulus, A. (1995), *The Feasibility of Ecological Taxation*, Antwerpen/Apeldoorn, Belgium: Maklu.
Pedersen, L.H. (2001), *Miljøøkonomiske ideer i en energipolitisk virkelighed – indførelsen af CO₂-afgifter på*

erhvervene i Danmark [Environmental economics ideas in the reality of energy policy – Introduction of CO_2 taxes on the industries in Denmark], AKF Forlaget.

Pigou, A.C. (2002), *The Economics of Welfare*, New Brunswick, New Jersey, US and London UK: Transaction Publishers, originally published in 1952 by Macmillan and Co., Limited.

RAC (2000), *Report on Motoring 2000*, 12th ed., Bescot, UK: RAC.

Royal Norwegian Ministry of the Environment (1995), 'Product Oriented Environmental Policy in Norway', http://www.iisd.ca/linkages/consume/norpro.html.

Rutherford, D. (1995), *Routledge Dictionary of Economics*, Oxford, UK: Routledge.

Schlegelmilch, K. and T. Markovič-Hribernik (2002), 'Green budget reform: Case study of Slovenia', in J.P. Clinch, K. Schlegelmilch, R. Sprenger and U. Triebswetter (eds), *Greening the Budget*, Cheltenham, UK: Edward Elgar, pp. 62–83.

Small, K.A. (1992), 'Using the revenues from congestion pricing', *Transportation*, **19**, 359–81.

Smith, S. (1997), 'Environmental tax design', in Timothy O'Riordan (ed.), *Ecotaxation*, London, UK: Earthscan, pp. 21–36.

Snape, J. (2006), 'Energy taxation and sustainable development: the experience of the United Kingdom', in R. Falcon y Tella (ed.), *Estudios sobre Fiscalidad de la Energía y Desarrollo Sostenible* [Studies on Energy Taxation and Sustainable Development], Madrid, Spain: Ministerio de Economía y Hacienda de España, pp. 257–99.

Snape, J. (2007), 'The green taxes of the Brown chancellorship, 1997–2007', *Environmental Law and Management*, **19**, 143–58.

Snoddon, T. and R. Wiggle (2010), 'Carbon pricing in Canada: Options and specifics', in C. Soares et al. (eds), *Critical Issues in Environmental Taxation*, Vol. VIII, Oxford, UK: Oxford University Press, pp. 337–53.

Soares, C.D. (1998), 'A Nova Velha Problemática da Consignação de Receitas Fiscais' [New and old issues of earmarking], in Manuel Vaz e Azeredo Lopes (eds), *Juris et de Jure. Nos vinte anos da Faculdade de Direito da Universidade Católica Portuguesa – Porto* [Publication commemorating 20 years of the Portuguese Catholic University Oporto Law School], Lisbon, Portugal: Publicações Universidade Católica, pp. 1183–222.

Soares, C.D. (2006), 'The earmarking of revenues within environmental tax policy', in A. Cavaliere et al. (eds), *Critical Issues in Environmental Taxation*, Vol. III, Oxford, UK: Oxford University Press, pp. 249–65.

Speck, S. and P. Ekins (2002), 'Evaluating environmental taxes: Recent experiences and proposals for the future', in J.P. Clinch, K. Schlegelmilch, R. Sprenger and U. Triebswetter, *Greening the Budget*, Cheltenham, UK: Edward Elgar, pp. 87–106.

Speck, S., J. McNicholas and M. Markovic (2004), 'National experiences with pollution taxes: What have we learned?', in J. Milne et al. (eds), *Critical Issues in Environmental Taxation*, Vol. I, Richmond, UK: Richmond Law & Tax, pp. 269–85.

Teja, R.S. (1988), 'The case for earmarked taxes: Theory and an example', IMF Staff Papers **35** (3), 523–33, Washington, DC, US: International Monetary Fund.

Thalmann, P. (2004), 'The public acceptance of green taxes: 2 million voters express their opinion', *Public Choice* **119**, 179–217.

The International Bank for Reconstruction and Development/The World Bank (2005), *Environmental Fiscal Reform, What Should be Done and How to Achieve It*, Washington, DC, US: International Bank for Reconstruction and Development/World Bank.

UK Department of Energy and Climate Change (2009), 'Climate change agreements: The climate change levy', http://www.decc.gov.uk/en/content/cms/what_we_do/change_energy/tackling_clima/ccas/cc_levy/cc_levy.aspx.

Wilkinson, M. (1994), 'Paying for public spending: Is there a role for earmarked taxes?', *Fiscal Studies*, **15** (4), 119–35.

7 Designing environmental taxes in countries in transition: a case study of Vietnam
Michael Rodi, Kai Schlegelmilch and Michael Mehling*

Vietnam has implemented its first steps of an environmental tax reform that entered into force on January 1, 2012. This chapter will explore the background and design of this reform project, and will describe the reform process. Given the scope and the implementation of this reform, the Vietnamese example can serve as a valuable case study for the role and design of environmental tax reforms in transition countries.

THE ROLE OF ENVIRONMENTAL TAXES IN COUNTRIES IN TRANSITION

Countries in transition (CITs) are characterized by a transition economy, that is, an economy that is moving from a centrally planned economic system to a free market. Transition economies therefore undergo a process of economic liberalization, where prices are set by market forces rather than central planning, trade barriers are removed, state-owned enterprises are privatized and a financial sector is created in order to facilitate the movement of private capital.[1] This transition process goes hand in hand with a fundamental change in the role of the state, which is redefined through legal and institutional reforms by securing property rights, establishing the rule of law, introducing appropriate competition policies and developing indirect, market-oriented instruments for macroeconomic governance.

Tax policy and the introduction of a modern tax and tax administration system all play a central role in the transition process.[2] A well-designed tax system is the backbone of every functioning market economy, setting a level playing field for competition and creating sustainable incentives for investment, while guaranteeing that states actively pursue economic success. The tax tradition of CITs stands in fundamental contrast to the above, since taxes play a completely different, less important role in centrally administered economies. An entire tax system can hardly be reformed overnight, however, and CITs must therefore take a gradual approach to implementing modern tax systems, which often proves to be challenging. In the case of Vietnam, the environmental tax

---

*   This chapter reflects the author's personal opinion.

[1]   *See generally* MARTIN MYANT & JAN DRAHOKOUPIL, TRANSITION ECONOMIES: POLITICAL ECONOMY IN RUSSIA, EASTERN EUROPE, AND CENTRAL ASIA (2010); GÉRARD ROLAND, TRANSITION AND ECONOMICS: POLITICS, MARKETS AND FIRMS (2000).

[2]   With regard to practice, see Jorge Martinez-Vazquez & Robert McNab, *The Tax Reform Experiment in Transitional Countries* (Andrew Young School of Pol'y Stud., Georgia State University, Working Paper 00-1, 2000).

reform project is embedded in, and accompanied by, reform projects affecting the entire tax system.[3]

Modern tax systems do not only provide a level playing field for market actors and investments; they also aim to make optimal use of the enormous potential of taxes to set incentives and steer the behavior of private actors. Thus, taxes have become an important instrument for achieving a wide variety of political objectives, among them environmental protection. Environmental taxes are particularly useful in the transition process from a planned to a market economy, since they are part of the toolbox of indirect or market-based instruments and thus fit well in market economies.[4] Moreover, environmental problems tend to be particularly pressing in CITs, where environmental policies are often underdeveloped whilst growth is mostly strong. In this context, environmental taxes are a useful tool to internalize external environmental effects. Strong additional arguments have recently been brought forward in favor of environmental taxes in CITs; environmental fiscal reforms and good financial governance are mutually reinforcing.[5] Moreover, environmental taxes have considerable revenue potential that can be easily accessed with intelligently designed tax schemes. They can therefore help to address the ever-rising financial needs of CITs. Revenue-recycling mechanisms can also pursue social objectives, especially poverty reduction.[6]

For a long period of time European countries held a leadership position in the field of environmental fiscal policy. Asian countries are now showing growing interest in the matter and have even, in some cases, started to draft relevant laws.[7] While Indonesia and Thailand are still in an exploratory phase, preparing extensive studies, China and Vietnam have already reached a more advanced level.[8] These developments also offer

---

[3]   See, for instance, the six components of the European Technical Assistance Programme for Vietnam (ETV2), comprising Fiscal Policy and Legal Advisory Services (C1), Taxation (C2), Customs (C3), Accounting, Auditing and Insurance (C4), Statistical Analysis and Policy Tools (C5) and Standards and Quality Control (C6).

[4]   *See* for example Randall A. Bluffstone, *Environmental Taxes in Developing and Transition Economies*, 3 PUB. FIN. & MGMT. 143, 143–75 (2003); *see also* KAI SCHLEGELMILCH ET AL., OPTIONS FOR PROMOTING ENVIRONMENTAL FISCAL REFORM IN EC DEVELOPMENT COOPERATION (2010), *available at* http://www.foes.de/publikationen/studien/?lang=en/#franz3; DEUTSCHE GESELLSCHAFT FÜR INTERNATIONALE ZUSAMMENARBEIT (GIZ) GMBH, USING MODERN ECONOMIC INSTRUMENTS TO TACKLE CLIMATE CHANGE IN VIETNAM (2010), *available at* http://www.foes.de/pdf/2010-06-Vietnam_EFR%20GIZ%20copied.pdf.

[5]   Jacqueline Cottrell et al., *Environmental Fiscal Reform in Developing, Emerging, and Transition Economies*, in 6 CRITICAL ISSUES IN ENVIRONMENTAL TAXATION: INTERNATIONAL AND COMPARATIVE PERSPECTIVES 793–804 (Jacqueline Cottrell et al. eds., 2009).

[6]   OECD, ENVIRONMENTAL FISCAL REFORM FOR POVERTY REDUCTION (2005); Cottrell et al., *supra* note 5, at 800–804.

[7]   Hope Ashiabor, *Environmentally Related Taxes in the Context of High Energy Prices: Challenges and Prospects for the Developing and Emerging Economies of Asia*, in 7 CRITICAL ISSUES IN ENVIRONMENTAL TAXATION: INTERNATIONAL AND COMPARATIVE PERSPECTIVES 61–89 (Lin-Heng Lye et al. eds., 2009).

[8]   Wang Xi & Zhou Yanfang, *Greening Taxation System in China*, in 7 CRITICAL ISSUES IN ENVIRONMENTAL TAXATION: INTERNATIONAL AND COMPARATIVE PERSPECTIVES 569 (Lin-Heng Lye et al. eds., 2009). CHINA COUNCIL ON INTERNATIONAL COOPERATION FOR ENVIRONMENT AND DEVELOPMENT (CCICED), ECONOMIC INSTRUMENTS FOR ENERGY EFFICIENCY & THE ENVIRONMENT (2009), *available at* http://www.foes.de/pdf/Research_Report_EN_FINAL.pdf. This proposal

industrialized countries the unique opportunity to carefully reduce tax exemptions and other privileges for their export industries, which had concerns about competitiveness with industries in CITs. In order for that to happen, however, no such provisions should be given by CITs to industries located in Asian countries.

THE VIETNAMESE PLAN FOR THE ADOPTION OF A COMPREHENSIVE ENVIRONMENTAL TAX REFORM: BACKGROUND AND MANDATES

The Socialist Republic of Vietnam is defined as a country in transition.[9] Described by the World Bank as 'one of the best-performing developing economies in the world,'[10] Vietnam is undergoing a sweeping transformation from a planned economy to a globalized, market-based economy. This process is accompanied by a dramatic economic expansion, with real gross domestic product (GDP) growth estimated at 8.5 percent in 2007, 6.3 percent in 2008, 5.3 percent in 2009, 6.8 percent in 2010 and 5.8 percent in 2011, affording Vietnam the second-highest growth rate in Asia over the past decade.[11] Vietnam has seen two political reform waves called *Doi Moi* ('renovation'), one starting in 1986 and the other in 1999–2000, after the Asian financial crisis of 1998. Fundamental market reforms were implemented in the economic field as well. On a domestic level this translated into widespread privatization and market prices; on an international level it was manifested in the rapid integration of Vietnam into the global economy through trade agreements and accession to the WTO.[12]

Rapid economic growth was a crucial prerequisite for these positive developments. However, it also placed a heavy burden on the environment, potentially undermining the sustainability of Vietnam's continued economic success and even threatening to offset many of the benefits it offers to large segments of the Vietnamese

---

has been developed as part of the Sino-German Environmental Policy Programme, implemented by the Deutsche Gesellschaft fuer Technische Zusammenarbeit (GTZ) GmbH, commissioned by the German Ministry for Economic Cooperation and Development (BMZ). *See* SCHLEGELMILCH ET AL., *supra* note 4. For Chinese energy taxes, see Tianbao Qin, *Energy Tax: How Far Is It from Idea to Practice? Lessons Learned from the Experience in China*, in 6 CRITICAL ISSUES ON ENVIRONMENTAL TAXATION: INTERNATIONAL AND COMPARATIVE PERSPECTIVES 863 (Jacqueline Cottrell et al. eds., 2009).

   [9] IMF, TRANSITION ECONOMIES: AN IMF PERSPECTIVE ON PROGRESS AND PROSPECTS (2000).
   [10] THE WORLD BANK, VIETNAM: LAYING THE FOUNDATION FOR SUSTAINABLE, INCLUSIVE GROWTH (2009), *available at* http://siteresources.worldbank.org/IDA/Resources/IDA-Vietnam.pdf.
   [11] IMF, *Vietnam: 2007 Article IV Consultation* 4 (IMF, Country Report No. 07/387, 2007), *available at* http://www.imf.org/external/pubs/ft/scr/2007/cr07387.pdf; Helen H. Qiao, *Vietnam: The Next Asian Tiger In the Making* 5 (Goldman Sachs, Global Economics Paper No. 165, 2008); CENTRAL INTELLIGENCE AGENCY, THE WORLD FACTBOOK: VIETNAM, https://www.cia.gov/library/publications/the-world-factbook/geos/vm.html (last visited Mar. 15, 2012).
   [12] John Thoburn, *Vietnam as Role Model for Development* (World Inst. for Dev. Econ. Research, Research Paper No. 30, 2009); Thi Bich Tran et al., *Institutions Matter: The Case of Vietnam*, 38 J. SOCIO-ECONOMICS 1, 2–12 (2009).

population.[13] Increases in the discharge of industrial effluent and sanitary waste water, rising quantities of domestic and industrial waste, emissions of air pollutants from industrial processes and transportation, contamination of soil, groundwater and watercourses, and endangered biodiversity are among the considerable environmental impacts that resulted from Vietnam's economic growth. In the face of these worrying side effects, the government proceeded to take corrective action in the form of several legal measures.

Relevant environmental legislation can be traced back to the early years of the Socialist Republic of Vietnam. The Constitution of 1980 elevated environmental protection to a constitutional objective, declaring it a binding duty for all state agencies, enterprises, cooperatives and citizens. In 1993, a National Environmental Agency was established under the Ministry of Science, Technology and Environment (MOSTE). On December 27 of that same year, the IXth National Assembly passed the first general Law on Environmental Protection of Vietnam, which entered into force on January 10, 1994. On an institutional level, the Ministry of Natural Resources and Environment (MoNRE) was established by decree on November 11, 2002.

On November 21, 2007, the adoption of an Environmental Protection Tax Law was included in the official program of the XIIth Legislative Program of the National Assembly (2007–2011).[14] This mandate was embedded in a larger process of economic reform dating back to 1986 and the approval of *Doi Moi*, and clearly offered a unique window of opportunity for the introduction of innovative mechanisms to target the environmental challenges currently facing Vietnam. However, this opportunity raised key institutional challenges of its own: substantively positioned at the junction of environmental and fiscal policy, the successful elaboration and implementation of an environmental tax involved complexities beyond the ambit of more conventional areas of taxation. At the same time, it required a level of tax policy expertise not commonly found in government bodies that focus purely on environmental policy.

In 2004, Vietnamese Prime Minister Nguyen Tan Dung requested the introduction of an environmental tax reform by the year 2011.[15] Under this mandate, the framework for an environmental tax law was to be submitted to the National Assembly by

---

[13] For an overview of the main environmental pressures and their causes, see Asian Development Bank, Country Environmental Analysis for Vietnam (2005), *available at* http://www.adb.org/documents/country-environmental-analysis-viet-nam; MINISTRY OF NATURAL RESOURCES AND THE ENVIRONMENT (MoNRE), STATE OF THE ENVIRONMENT REPORT OF VIETNAM 5 (2005); THE WORLD BANK, NATIONAL ENVIRONMENT AGENCY & DANISH INTERNATIONAL DEVELOPMENT ASSISTANCE (DANIDA), VIETNAM ENVIRONMENT MONITOR 2002 20–29 (2002).

[14] National Assembly of the Socialist Republic of Vietnam, National Assembly Resolution 11/2007/NQ-QH12 dated November 21, 2007 on the XIIth Legislative Programme of the National Assembly (2007–2011), Annex 1: Law and Ordinance Projects Belonging to the XIIth Legislative Programme of the National Assembly (promulgated through Resolution No.11/2007/QH12), A. Official Programme, I. Economic Issues, No. 15: 'Law on environmental protection tax' (*Luật thuế bảo vệ môi trường*).

[15] See Decision No. 201/2004/QĐ-TTg dated 12/06/2004, *available at* http://www.chinhphu.vn /portal/page?_pageid=439,2047386&_dad=portal&_schema=PORTAL.

April 2010. To this end, an editorial committee was formed under the leadership of the Tax Policy Department of the Ministry of Finance, comprising representatives from relevant ministries. This committee was supervised at the political level by a Supervisory Committee under the leadership of the Minister for Finance. Due to the novelty of this initiative, the Vietnamese legislature had limited relevant experience and very few appropriate legal instruments at its disposal. Instead, it relied partly on existing taxes and charges that were not drafted especially for this purpose, such as the natural resource tax, petroleum and oil taxes and fees, and waste water charges. However, such isolated measures are conceptually different from a comprehensive environmental fiscal reform and render targeted capacity-building efforts an urgent priority in the short term.

The process of designing and implementing an environmental tax reform has been supported and accompanied from the outset by international donors, and all three authors of this chapter were involved in the process. The program was part of the European Union's efforts to provide technical assistance to the Vietnamese government from 2006 to 2009,[16] and was completed with a report in 2009.[17] Thereafter, the German Development Implementing Agency (GTZ, named GIZ since 2011) followed up and supported the program.[18] The process came to a successful end in November 2010 with the adoption of the Law on Environment Protection Tax by the National Assembly with a majority of around 98.7 percent, which is much greater than other National Assembly adoptions of around 85–90 percent.

EXPERIENCES AND BARRIERS ENCOUNTERED IN VIETNAM'S POLITICAL SYSTEM

Vietnam is a socialist republic where the Communist Party plays a central role.[19] Nevertheless, the National Assembly plays an important part in the design of fundamental reforms.[20] The integration of the environmental tax reform into the legislative program of the National Assembly has been an important driver of the reform process.

Still, the top-down approach has led to problems in the reform process. There were quite substantive outlines for the direction of the reform at early stages. The Law on

---

[16]   As part of this program, both Michael Rodi and Michael Mehling served as International Short-Term Experts during this phase of the reform.

[17]   *See generally* DMI Associates, Report on European Technical Assistance Programme for Vietnam-II (2008), *available at* http://www.dmiassociates.com/dmi/EN/european-technical-assistance-programme-for-vietnam-ii-etv-ii.

[18]   *See generally* GTZ, Conceptual Paper on Macroeconomic Reform Program Component 2: Public Finance (2008); *see also* GTZ, Conceptual Paper on Macroeconomic Reform Program Component 2, Module 4: Environmental Protection Tax Law (2008); Kai Schlegelmilch led these efforts.

[19]   Mark Sidel, The Constitution of Vietnam: A Contextual Analysis 86 (2009).

[20]   Mark Sidel, Law and Society in Vietnam 29, 56 (2008); Sidel, *supra* note 19, at 96; Matthieu Solomon, *Power and Representation at the Vietnamese National Assembly: The Scope and Limits of Political Doi Moi, in* Vietnam's New Order: International Perspectives on the State and Reform in Vietnam 198 –216 (Stéphanie Balme & Mark Sidel eds., 2007).

Environmental Protection of 2005 provides that 'organizations, individuals and house-holds producing and trading in some kinds of products that exert long-term adverse impacts on the environment and human health shall be liable to an environmental tax' (Article 112). The Prime Minister had already stated that an environmental protection tax law would be presented to the National Assembly in 2008 by way of a decision adopted on December 6, 2004:

> An Environment-Related Tax Law will be summated to the diet before the end of 2008, which imposes taxes on goods and services polluting the environment. The tax base will be decided on each product and service that pollutes the environment. The revenue of this tax will be used only for special purposes of environmental protection, and may not be used to cover any other needs of the state budget.[21]

As the ministries felt strictly bound by this mandate, the foregoing provision had a restrictive effect on the design of the environmental tax scheme. However, in a decision made at the end of 2011, the revenue of the environmental tax will now be used as a usual tax revenue, that is, for the general state budget. Only revenues from environmental fees and charges are earmarked for environmental purposes.

The Vietnamese government is vertically structured. As a result, the mandate to design a comprehensive environmental tax reform rests only with the Ministry of Finance. However, it is evident that an environmental tax reform must be harmonized horizontally with other policies in related areas (for example, traffic and transport taxes must be consistent with general traffic and transport policies). In the case of Vietnam this harmonization was not yet in place, and this lack of policy coordination caused considerable problems. In the initial years (under the European ETV program), it proved impossible to initiate high-ranking meetings or working groups across ministries. This experience started with the general reluctance of the Finance Ministry to fully cooperate. This was taken into account in GTZ's follow-up project, where the Ministry's cooperation was demanded from the outset as a precondition of support.

Despite the fact that Vietnam is centrally governed, local administrations, groups and other organizations have always had a strong political influence. These groups often have differing opinions on national reform projects, mostly leading to intense discussions on a regional level. This local power structure did not form an obstacle to the reform process. In fact, it turned out to be a useful source of local, in-depth information (such as on the administrative deficiencies of direct water pollution charges). It often also put pressure on the government to extend the number of intended tax bases and to increase the intended tax rates and thus to apply the polluter-pays principle more strictly, such as by including noise (here mainly blowing the horns) as a tax base. This tax base was eventually denied mainly for administrative reasons, but also because it remained unclear how a tax could really deliver targeted responses.

At the same time, the direct influence of civil society and public opinion on the policies and legislation of Vietnam should not be underestimated. This phenomenon has been described as 'motorbike constitutionalism.'[22] The reaction of the people has always

---

[21]   Prime Minister, Decision No. 201/2004/QD-TTg of 6 December 2004, approving the 'Tax Reform Strategy Toward 2010.'

[22]   *See* SIDEL, *supra* note 20, at 74.

been a major concern in the political decision-making process, sometimes even limiting available reform options. This is especially true for energy taxation that results in higher energy prices, taxes and charges that affect farmers (an important constituency in Vietnamese society and its well-vested interests), and finally, of course, traffic-related taxes and charges—with regard to motorbikes in particular.

THE DESIGN OF THE VIETNAMESE ENVIRONMENTAL TAX REFORM

The mandate for the tax reform is an essential part of the broader environmental protection strategy pursued by the Vietnamese government. It is firmly embedded in the existing framework of environmental protection legislation currently in force in Vietnam. As discussed above, the Environmental Protection Law of 1993 was revised when the Law of Environmental Protection of 2005 called for an environmental tax.[23] According to this provision, the government was to submit a list of products and commercial activities subject to the environmental tax, along with applicable tax rates, to the National Assembly for approval.[24]

Under this initial mandate, revenue from this tax would only be used for the special purpose of environmental protection, and would not be allocated for other purposes in the state budget. Moreover, according to the Plan for Tax System Reforms and Modernization in the Period 2005–2010,[25] the environmental protection tax law would regulate all subjects engaged in activities that cause environmental pollution, based on the principle that the taxable amount shall be equivalent to or higher than the extent of environmental damages incurred. Accordingly, the tax base was to be decided on an individual basis for each of the products and services that pollute the environment. Consensus could be reached that the environmental protection tax law should be designed to create the legal framework for an intensification of environmental protection and improvement. Moreover, the framework should help mitigate environmental pollution and damages, generate more income for the state budget, ensure simplicity, clarity, transparency and publicity, and approximate international common practices of environmental taxation.[26]

Pursuant to the foregoing strategy, the new environment protection tax system focuses on the following specific issues:

---

[23]   Law on the Protection of the Environment of 29 November 2005, No. 52-2005-QH11 (effective Jul. 1, 2006), *available at* http://www.dpi.hochiminhcity.gov/invest/html/Law on Environment. html. Compared to the Environmental Protection Law of 1993, the new law has been expanded both in scope and regulatory density, with 136 articles spread out in 15 chapters.

[24]   *See id.* The Law on Environmental Protection also specifies other economic instruments whose adoption should be explored, including environmental protection charges, natural resource exploitation and restoration funds, and environmental protection funds.

[25]   *See* Section III(1)(a) of the attachment to Decision No. 1629/QD-BTC of 19 May 2005 by the Minister of Finance, 'On the Promulgation of the Plan for Tax System Modernization and Reforms in the Period 2005–2010.'

[26]   *Id.*, Section III(2.9).

- Governing scope: The tax system had to cover all subjects engaged in the production, processing, use or storage of goods that cause environmental pollution. Its aim was to develop concrete and clear criteria for taxable objects, which are goods and services related to polluting activities.
- Tax base and tax rate: The tax base should be the quantity (not value) of products and goods that adversely affect the environment. The tax obligation was to be equal to or higher than the loss generated by the environmental pollution caused by the product; transparent guidance on the ensuing requirements for tax subjects would be provided to avoid undue impacts on the investment environment.
- Tax administration: Tax collection would be administered in accordance with each category of environmental pollution (production, processing, storage, use); administration of the environmental tax would be coordinated with the administration of environmental pollution.

The Ministry of Finance declared its intention to tax all types of energy consumption, including—and this set the reform apart from similar initiatives in most European countries—domestic flights and shipping.[27] Furthermore, taxes on environmentally harmful substances, HCFC (chlorinated and fluorinated hydrocarbons), soft plastic bags and tobacco would be covered as well. Legislation enacting this reform, adopted by the National Assembly on November 15, 2010 and taking effect on January 1, 2012, basically followed this broad approach (except with regard to tobacco), with concrete tax rates for 2012 fixed in the annex of the resolution on the issuance of tax rates for environmental protection adopted at the end of 2011. The exclusion of tobacco taxes is in line with the logic of an environmental tax approach in a narrower sense.[28] As advocated from the beginning of the reform process, at its core the Environment Protection Act is a comprehensive energy tax. As a consequence, the gasoline surcharge regulation was abolished when the Act entered into force.

Under the legislation, the National Assembly set ranges for the tax rates (see Table 7.1). During the legislative deliberations, it increased the lower range of the tax on coal from 6000 to 10 000 VND per ton, and shifted the tax range on plastic bags from 20–30 000 to 30–50 000 VND per kilogram. Interestingly enough, the National Assembly, along with many representatives to the regional meetings, consistently supported the law and often asked for even higher tax rates and a greater range of taxable objects, given the many environmental problems these objects cause. Hence, the Ministry of Finance was challenged during many preparatory discussions, forcing it to justify a slower pace by stating

---

[27] In this category, the tax reform will target all types of gasoline, jet fuel, diesel, kerosene, mazut, lubricating oil, grease and coal. Only Norway and the Netherlands have kerosene taxation on domestic flights. Some US states also impose kerosene taxation. At least increasingly more countries like the United Kingdom, France, Ireland, Germany and Austria have introduced a kind of air ticket tax.

[28] Still, it must be noted that in Article 2, the Environmental Protection Tax Act defines 'environment' in a broad sense, including 'natural and physical factors surrounding human beings and affecting the life, production activities, existence and development of human beings and living beings.'

Table 7.1   Environmental tax as of January 2012

No. Taxable Object	Unit	Tax rate range set by National Assembly (VND per unit)	Specific tax rates set by Standing Committee
I **Gasoline and oil**			
1 All types of gasoline	liter	1000–4000	1000
2 Jet fuel	liter	1000–3000	1000
3 Diesel	liter	500–2000	500
4 Paraffin	liter	300–2000	300
5 Mazut	kg	300–2000	300
6 Lubricating oil	liter	300–2000	300
7 Grease	kg	300–2000	300
II **Coal**	ton	10 000–30 000	10 000
III **HCFC**	kg	1000–5000	2500
IV **Soft plastic bags**	kg	30 000–50 000	40 000
V **Restricted-use plant protection chemical substances**			
1 Agricultural chemical substances	kg	500–2000	500
2 Anti-termite chemicals	kg	1000–3000	1000
4 Preservatives for forest products	kg	1000–3000	1000
5 Disinfectant chemicals used for warehouses	kg	1000–3000	1000

Note: VND is Vietnamese Dong; at the end of February 2012, 1000 Dong were equal to 0,04 Euro

that Vietnam should not overdo the first step. In the end, the draft was successfully defended in all substantial areas.

According to Article 8 of the Environmental Protection Tax Act, and in line with a long-standing Vietnamese tradition, the specific tax rates within the ranges are set by the National Assembly's Standing Committee. The following principles govern the choice of both current and future specific tax rates:

- Tax rates for taxable objects shall be in line with the socioeconomic development policies set out by the government for each period.
- Tax rates for taxable objects shall be designed based on the level of environmental pollution and degradation caused by taxable objects.

Applicable tax rates are set in the following manner: rates shall be adjusted every two to three years depending on the socioeconomic circumstances prevailing in Vietnam, or annually in the event of sufficient public support. The Ministry of Finance in the government will submit—and has first done so at the end of 2011—a proposal to the Standing Committee of the National Assembly, the official body that has to agree to a change in tax rates (not the National Assembly as such). The Ministry of Finance intends to increase the rates at a faster pace than inflation, and aims to provide long-term predictability by implementing a steady and foreseeable increase built on positive experiences with price escalators in other countries. However, socioeconomic circumstances must also be taken into account.

The level of public support is determined using opinions expressed in newspapers and other media, public hearings, and meetings with representatives during field trips organized for this purpose. Even coal suppliers, who are likely to pay a substantial share of the overall tax revenue, have so far been supportive. They stand to gain from an increase in domestic coal prices to reach a level closer to global market prices, a convergence that has not yet occurred. So far, about 50 percent of coal extracted in Vietnam has been destined for export. No price regulation applies to exported coal, whereas such regulation is in place for domestic coal use (when destined for electricity, cement, industry, construction and so on). According to recent forecasts, Vietnam is likely to become a net importer of coal by 2015. Consequently, national coal miners would be relatively less affected.

The comparison of the tax ranges and the specific tax rates in effect on January 1, 2012 shows that tax rates implemented in 2012 are generally at the lower end of the initial proposal. The rates chosen also take into account the current socioeconomic conditions (high oil prices) and the burden that the tax would place on households and businesses.

For the tax administration, the reform actually translates into a reduced burden, given that the environmental tax law—following the international standard—will apply fixed nominal tax rates, as opposed to the fluctuating product prices previously used as tax bases. This substantially facilitates the administration of the tax. In sum, the environmental tax law has garnered broad support among stakeholders and the Vietnamese public. It can therefore already be considered a success by several metrics.

THE DESIGN CHALLENGE OF A COMPREHENSIVE ENVIRONMENTAL TAX REFORM

The mandate for environmental tax reform was clearly geared toward a comprehensive system of product and service taxes. Nevertheless, discussions among representatives of the ministries and academia led to consideration of larger-scale policy instruments, such as direct emission taxes, income taxation, vehicle taxation and others.

Limiting the discussion to product taxes was deemed inadvisable. Vietnam, for example, in the past imposed high import taxes on vehicles, which are basically product taxes. A consensus emerged in the relevant discussions that such taxes strongly limit any possibility for the legislature to influence the performance of imported cars (for instance, with regard to their size or environmental features). The only effects are revenue effects, along with a dampening effect on general import figures. Thus, there are many good reasons to shift from an import tax to an annually updated vehicle tax.[29]

---

[29] These advantages have been broadly discussed in the European Union's strategy on passenger car taxation; for this see Proposal for a Council Directive on Passenger Car Related Taxes, COM (2005) 261 final (Jul. 5, 2005), and *Impact Assessment on the Proposal for a Council Directive on Passenger Car Related Taxes* SEC (2005) 809 (Jul. 5, 2005). Stephen Potter, *Using Environmental Taxation for Transport Demand Management, in* 7 CRITICAL ISSUES IN ENVIRONMENTAL TAXATION: INTERNATIONAL AND COMPARATIVE PERSPECTIVES 39 (Lin-Heng Lye et al. eds., 2009); Hope Ashiabor & Rosiati Ramli, *Managing the Shift Towards Sustainable Transportation in the South*

And yet, consensus was also reached that an environmental tax reform should not consider income taxation and direct emission taxes. Regarding personal income taxes, many general arguments can be made not to overload them with other political objectives. These taxes should be easy to understand and administer, and should concentrate on revenue effects and a fair distribution of the tax load. Moreover, it is mainly tax subsidies that integrate steering effects into direct taxation, and these lead to reverse relief effects. Relatively speaking, wealthier taxpayers are subject to a higher tax rate and therefore pay more taxes, but they are still left with a higher net income than those in lower tax brackets. These arguments are even more applicable to countries in transition than to industrialized countries.

Direct emission taxes, on the other hand, certainly have advantages from an environmental policy point of view, as they directly target the emissions that the legislator wants to reduce. Unfortunately, emission taxes also share many of the shortcomings ascribed to command-and-control regulation, especially with regard to their stringent monitoring and enforcement requirements, and for that reason there is a widespread tendency to oppose them.[30] This is particularly true for countries in transition, and a consensus was reached that this would not be a viable way for Vietnam, which lacked a well-functioning system of regulatory emissions controls. Moreover, the country's experiences with a direct water emission charge have been discouraging. Inquiries revealed that these charges are often collected on an improvised basis, relinquishing all behavioral steering effects (such as arrangements with the installation operators, or taxation according to best practices).

Yet, inspired by the fastest tax-lawmaking process ever, according to the Tax Policy Department of the Ministry of Finance, and the convincing European experiences, the Ministry of Finance also started working on legislation for regulating emissions in 2011. The respective decree on emissions shall be adopted in 2014. It is adapting the European experiences with the annual road tax to Vietnam. Another law on fees and charges may also be adopted in 2014 or 2015. And, as mentioned, the National Assembly, along with many representatives to the regional meetings, has consistently supported the law and has often asked for even higher tax rates and a greater range of taxable objects.

Hence, the environmental tax legislation comprises several elements and could thus— at least in the context of developing countries—be considered quite comprehensive. The major criteria for assessing this are not the height of the tax rates, but the number of tax bases, which go beyond energy-only to also cover energy uses often not covered (flights and shipping), the long-lasting process, and the courage to initiate and successfully implement it in such a short time, including stakeholder involvement.

East Asian Countries: Do Taxes and Other Market-Based Instruments Play a Role?, *in* 7 CRITICAL ISSUES IN ENVIRONMENTAL TAXATION: INTERNATIONAL AND COMPARATIVE PERSPECTIVES 39 (Lin-Heng Lye et al. eds., 2009).

[30] For arguments against green tax relief schemes in direct taxation see TAX AND THE ENVIRONMENT: A WORLD OF POSSIBILITIES 20–25 (Anuschka Bakker ed., 2009).

REVENUE ALLOCATION AND REVENUE NEUTRALITY

The question of revenue allocation played a central role in the discussions of the Vietnamese environmental tax reform. There are basically three options: (1) revenue could be assigned to the general state budget, (2) revenue could be used to lower other taxes, resulting in revenue neutrality, or (3) revenue could be earmarked for specific environmental protection purposes. Although a strong interest in the first option was apparent on the part of the Ministry of Finance, there had been broad consensus from the outset that this option should not be chosen, as it would discredit the environmental tax reform among the public.

By contrast, a remarkable consensus was reached on the significant advantages offered by the principles of revenue neutrality and revenue recycling ('double dividend') in the discussions among Ministry representatives, practitioners and academics. However, further deliberations revealed the many barriers these principles would encounter during the practical implementation of this policy process.

Concerning the design of taxes in the field of agriculture (such as fertilizer and pesticide taxes), it was suggested at one point that revenues be recycled back to farmers (for instance via social programs or environmental improvements, such as payment of environmental services provided by farmers). Given that the tax burden would be at least partly passed on to consumers, the agricultural sector might even emerge as a net winner under the tax reform. Nevertheless, the responsible government agencies feared the reaction farmers might have to new taxes, not least on major inputs such as fertilizers and pesticides to their production processes, and hence declined the idea. This is a good example of Vietnam's (motorbike) democracy and of how it influences political decisions. After lengthy negotiations, a moderate tax on chemical substances used in agriculture (without simultaneous revenue recycling) was included in the environmental tax reform.

To some extent, the challenges were also of a structural or technical nature. In essence, it was accepted that energy prices should be raised with the implementation of energy taxes, and that the collected tax revenues would be recycled to those most affected by the price increase. Implementing the foregoing objective within the framework of a general social security system was agreed to be the best option. However, the Vietnamese social security system does not function well enough, if at all, to allow for an adequate redistribution of tax revenues. Energy prices will therefore only be raised very slowly, after energy subsidies are removed in a first step.

The same is true for vehicle taxes. Taxation of individual traffic will be necessary. But at the same time the population's basic mobility needs have to be satisfied. Theoretically, this need could be met by recycling the revenue toward public transport. Yet this allocation would result in a time lag that cannot and will not be accepted by the public.

In the end, the foregoing constraints resulted in a pragmatic compromise to allocate revenue to environmental protection measures. Still, this decision was not legally anchored in the Environment Protection Tax Act itself; Article 12 merely states that the tax revenue shall be divided between the state budget and provincial budgets. In a broader sense, this is also a sort of 'double dividend,' and it makes an environmental tax reform even more compelling from an environmental point of view. Moreover, the Environmental Ministry (in Vietnam as in other CITs) is chronically underfinanced. However, at the end of 2011, the National Assembly voted to use the revenues of the environmental tax as general tax revenue (for the general state budget), and whether the Environment Ministry really gets more money depends on the allocation within the general budget.

IMPACTS

A simulation of the likely impacts of the environmental tax reform has been carried out by Dirk Willenbockel, a consultant recruited specifically for this task. Using figures from the year 2007, he employed a General Equilibrium Computer Model based on an updated Social Accounting Matrix and Input-Output Model. The key results of this exercise are highlighted below.[31]

Although the likely political decisions were still somewhat unclear at the time the impact assessment was carried out, the model assumes that the government distributes all additional tax revenue from environmental taxes on public investment spending, government consumption, and additional transfers to the private sector.

The reader should note that figures do *not* represent point forecasts for a particular year—they show deviations from the baseline growth path of the economy (that is, the growth path in the absence of an environmental tax). Numbers are presented in real terms, which means that quantities are valued at constant 2007 prices. Absorption is defined as total domestic demand for final goods in the economy, including imports. In other words, it comprises the sum of household consumption (C), investment expenditure including public investment (I) and government consumption purchases (G).

Ultimately, it is the household sector that bears the burden of the tax, as reflected in the noticeable drop in C (household consumption) at the high end of the tax band. The reduction in private consumption would be higher if the government failed to return part of the tax revenue to households in the form of income transfers or reductions in other taxes.

Table 7.2   Impact on real macroeconomic aggregates
Percent deviations from baseline growth path

	LOW	HIGH
Absorption (C+G+I)	0.3	0.9
Household consumption	−0.3	−0.8
Investment (public and private)	1.2	3.7
Government consumption	0.4	1.3
Exports	−0.8	−2.4
Imports	−0.6	−1.8
Real exchange rate*	−0.2	−0.8
Government revenue	1.9	5.4

Note: * Minus sign indicates real exchange rate appreciation

[31]   The following results are all taken from DIRK WILLENBOCKEL, IMPACT ASSESSMENT REPORT OF DRAFT ENVIRONMENTAL TAX LAW FOR VIETNAM (2010).

Table 7.3   Estimated environmental tax revenue in 2012 (in 2007 prices, billion VND)

	LOW	HIGH
Coal	367	1112
Refined fuels	8307	25982
HCFC	4	21
Chemicals	1	7
Plastic bags	114	170
Total	8794	27292

The government, on the other hand, can claim a higher share of productive resources as a result of the environmental tax. The increase in real government expenditure (which means an increase in demand for domestic nontradable goods and services) causes the price of nontradables relative to export goods to rise, and thus discourages exports. A drop in exports can therefore be observed.

The negative sign of real exchange rate change (price of tradables/price of nontradables) indicates a real appreciation of the VND. An important message from Table 7.3 is that the high end of the proposed tax interval implies substantial effects. If further *real* increases in the tax rates on refined liquid fuels are envisaged, it is advisable to gradually phase them in according to a pre-announced timetable. This will give investors the time to shift to more energy-efficient technologies. This was amply illustrated by the extreme high scenario presented at the first stage of the impact assessment.

Table 7.3 shows the estimated tax revenue in the year 2012 that would result from the imposition of the environmental taxes on coal, refined fuels, HCFCs, chemicals and plastic bags. The table is based on an assumed average annual real GDP growth rate of 7.0 percent between 2008 and 2012, with zero inflation.

As Table 7.3 shows, taxes on HCFCs, chemicals and plastic bags would generate relatively little tax revenue in comparison to coal and refined fuels. The impact of imposing taxes on these three products on the overall economy is also correspondingly small, and this is why the report has so far concentrated on taxes on coal and refined fuels alone.

The fact that the impact is small does not imply that the taxes should not be imposed in the first place. Imposing a tax on products that have negative environmental externalities is a worthwhile policy either way, and should therefore be encouraged. In theory, revenue from taxes on these products should eventually be driven to zero, as consumers shift their consumption to more sustainable substitutes that are not subject to an environmental tax. In other words, falling revenue from these taxes should be interpreted as a sign of success.

It is evident that an environmental tax on refined fuels constitutes the intervention with the largest potential impact on the Vietnamese economy. Figure 7.1 examines the share of refined fuel in the total cost borne by the six most fuel-intense sectors (out of a total of 33 sectors distinguished in the model).

Figure 7.1 shows that the biggest users of refined fuels are the refined fuels sector and the fishery sector. One must keep in mind that the latter is closely linked to large upstream and downstream industries (such as processing and marketing). In fact, employment in these up- and downstream industries is estimated to exceed employment in the fishery

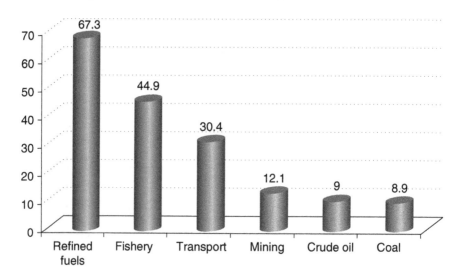

Source: Dirk Willenbockel (2011), 'Environmental Tax Reform in Vietnam: an Ex Ante General Equilibrium Assessment', Institute of Development Studies, University of Sussex, ecomod.net/system/files/EcoMod2011_VietnamEcoTax_0.pdf.

Figure 7.1   Refined fuel share in total cost for the most fuel-intense sectors (%)

sector by a factor of three. Through the fisheries sector, the environmental tax will have significant repercussions for these industries as well. In the case of the transport sector, a rising tax burden will also affect all the goods that are transported. This will in turn be impacted by a higher 'transport margin.' Finally, the intense use of refined fuels in the fuel sector itself is worth noting as an intermediate input; a rise in costs carries with it the potential danger of tax cascading effects.

The study of impacts contains a detailed analysis on a number of other points as well. In sum, the impact assessment forecast the following effects of the environmental tax reform:

- At the higher end of the proposed tax rate band, the environmental tax on fuels will have noticeable economy-wide repercussions.
- The tax-induced fuel price increase will raise the production cost and output prices of other fuel-intensive sectors to some extent—notably for the fishery, coal and transport sectors.
- The tax-induced rise in transport services spreads the impact of the fuel tax broadly across the economy through its effect on transport margins for all (nonservice) commodities.
- The refined liquid fuels tax will be the dominant source of tax revenue of all the various environmental taxes.
- At medium to high levels of the tax rate, the environmental tax shifts a significant amount of purchasing power from households to the government.
- Relative to the no-eco-tax growth path, the real exchange rate appreciates to some extent and real exports decline slightly due to the fact that the additional tax

revenue is spent on environmental protection measures (or other nontraded goods and services).

- Household welfare—narrowly defined as utility derived from the consumption of private goods—declines significantly across all household groups. However, this result does not take into account future welfare gains from beneficial environmental impacts.

- Overall, the increase in production prices of energy-dependent industries could reduce the competitiveness of Vietnam's exports and hamper the growth of national employment.[32] Nevertheless, these negative effects could be offset by the environmental benefits generated by the tax, such as reduced abatement costs and the improved health of the population. Another remedy could be to compensate certain industries using the revenues from the environmental tax.

- The analysis suggests that higher tax rates for fuels should be phased in gradually according to a transparent, pre-announced schedule. This will give firms the necessary time to plan investments in fuel-efficient technologies.

- Supportive measures are needed in order to facilitate a smooth transition to low-carbon technologies.

- The relation of coal tax rates to fuel tax rates must be taken into consideration, so as to avoid unintended substitution effects (from coal to refined fuels).

- Taxation of HCFCs, substitutable hazardous chemicals and plastic bags constitutes a good economic policy, despite the low expected revenue and insignificant economy-wide effects. A fall in tax revenue toward zero should be seen as a sign of the success of this policy.

CONCLUSIONS

Looking back from the vantage point of its recent adoption by the National Assembly, the environmental tax law and the process of its creation have turned out to be a success story in Vietnam. Within a period of two to three years, a relatively comprehensive environmental tax reform has been successfully implemented and further steps have been initiated, arguably making this one of the swiftest legislative processes ever in the area of environmental taxation. The environmental tax law will facilitate its operational administration through the introduction of international standards. Moreover, its economy-wide impacts make the tax an effective tool—both in terms of outcome and in terms of cost—to reduce greenhouse gas emissions. The fact that no tax exemptions are extended to industries is of particular importance regarding foreign states, including industrialized ones. This may—and should—have an effect on politicized debates about the competitiveness of domestic industries in Europe and North America vis-à-vis producers in low-income CITs. Also, contrary to most other environmental taxation schemes, fuels used for shipping and domestic flights will be taxed.

---

[32] Ian Coxhead & Nguyen Van Chan, *Vietnam's New Environmental Tax Law: What Will It Cost? Who Will Pay?* Univ. of Wisconsin-Madison, Dep't of Agric. & Applied Econ. 24 (Staff Paper No. 561, 2011).

The reform experience also drew attention to the value of international expert input and the importance of a coordinated approach to capacity building. In particular, the project was able to build on previous research, facilitating the consulting services provided to the Vietnamese government as well as at the onset of the legislative process. Still, not all challenges have been addressed. Stronger cooperation between different ministries, which is required, is an area with significant room for improvement. For instance, whether implementing agencies have the required capacity to actually apply the new tax rates remains to be seen. Moreover—and perhaps more importantly—it is not certain that the stakeholders' initial response to the environmental tax will remain positive once it becomes an actual cost burden, rather than a mere reform proposal. Finally, the reform process, whose underlying mandate was originally geared toward a 'comprehensive environmental tax reform,' has shown that no such thing exists. In practice it is exceptionally difficult to draft a general environmental tax act. Instead, an environmental tax law should contain certain elements, such as the coverage of as many energy products as possible, particularly in the transport sector.

8 Externality research
Philipp Preiss

INTRODUCTION

Environmental taxes are introduced to raise revenue while at the same time help reduce significantly the damages associated with pressures and emissions from polluting activities. Economists are, however, searching for environmental taxes that are 'optimal' in the sense that they reflect accurately the damages at play, not more and not less. If taxes are too low they will be insufficient to internalize environmental damages in market transactions. If taxes are too high they will penalize too extensively the market transactions and cause a loss of economic welfare. From a theoretical point of view environmental taxes need to be 'just right.' Such a tax is known as a Pigovian tax. In the debate over competitiveness effects (see Chapter 21 of this Handbook) and the double dividend (see Chapter 12), it makes an important difference whether the environmental taxes introduced are optimal or not. For this reason economists have long grappled with how to place monetary values on environmental damages. There are examples of a spillover from this preoccupation with optimality to certain legal principles codified for environmental taxation. Environmental engineers have made an important contribution by developing the 'impact pathway' approach, which is an analytical method that links the sequences leading from an emission to an impact. Models over the transport and dissemination of pollutants are required to account for the end effects and to attach a relevant price tag. While initiated in collaboration between US and European researchers, these methods have experienced a significant development over the past decade thanks mainly to a series of research projects known as the ExternE project series. Although not all relevant effects can be accounted for, we are nowadays in a much better position to fix environmental taxes that match reasonably our understanding of the external costs at play.

THE FUNDAMENTALS AND DEVELOPMENTS OF EXTERNALITY RESEARCH

Introduction

> An externality arises when the social or economic activities of one group of persons have an impact on another group and when that impact is not fully accounted, or compensated for, by the first group.[1]

This means that the side effects of any action are not taken into account, as long as they are not internalized in the market transactions of the responsible parties. Many very

---

[1] www.ExternE.info.

different effects can therefore be external; however, the focus of this chapter will be on environmental effects, especially those of air pollution such as SO_2, NO_x and primary particulate matter emissions.

An important precondition for allocating responsibility to the different groups that cause environmental pressures is the polluter-pays principle. Another common catch-phrase is 'Get the prices right' (EU Commission 2001). In international environmental law, the polluter-pays principle is mentioned in Principle 16 of the Rio Declaration on Environment and Development. Although 'internalization' does not mean that the group that is damaged necessarily has to be compensated, it does mean that externalities are internalized as soon as they are taken into account in the marketplace. In order to take them into account they have to be quantified in physical and monetary terms.

The physical impacts of air pollution, such as yield loss of crops or an increase in cases of chronic bronchitis, are here referred to as 'impacts.' The aggregated monetary value of the different physical impacts is called 'damage.' The damage costs are the external costs insofar as they are not internalized. If we assume that none of the damage costs is internalized, these costs are equal to the external cost, and the expressions can be used synonymously.

Activities such as electricity generation, heating, transportation, and industrial and agricultural production cause major environmental pressures. These pressures can lead to different effects, such as an impact on human health and the environment, which vary widely depending on the type of activity and where and when it takes place. In addition, emissions of greenhouse gases cause climate change and its consequential impacts. Regardless of the location of the emission of the greenhouse gases, the impacts of climate change vary globally. These impacts are mainly not integrated into the pricing system and therefore are not or are only partly reflected in the decisions undertaken. This may lead to suboptimal decisions regarding resource allocation. In order to avoid this, the impacts have to be quantified and taken into account in decision-making.

A significant number of scientists, covering a wide range of disciplines including the assessment of technology, risk and impact, are involved in quantifying the environmental impacts of different activities (such as production of products and/or supply of other services). Particularly worth mentioning is the community developing methodologies for performing life cycle assessment (LCA), such as the Society of Environmental Toxicology and Chemistry.[2]

LCA is necessary because one has to examine the whole chain of processes and actions that deliver the so-called 'functional unit,' for instance, one kWh of electricity. The functional unit can be delivered by different mechanisms. The generation of electricity by a photovoltaic installation itself has almost no effect on the environment at the moment of operation; however, the prior production of crystalline silicon for photovoltaic modules needs energy and hence causes pollution. On the other hand a coal-fired power station causes emissions mainly during the operation phase. The fuel supply also has considerable environmental impact, but at different locations from the power plant. One part of the LCA is the assessment of the 'life cycle inventory,' in other words the measurement or calculation of pressures such as emissions of air pollutants. Another part of LCA is the

---

[2]   http://www.SETAC.org.

'life cycle impact assessment (LCIA),' which is basically an evaluation of the impacts per pressure, and hence weighting and aggregation, of the life cycle inventory data.

Many different models are available to ascertain potential impacts such as human toxicity or acidification potential of different substances (comprehensive documentation can be found at UNEP-SETAC (2004)). One known drawback of the LCA is the lack of knowledge of the location of the pressures. Therefore, generic factors for impact assessment are usually applied that take into account average values of time and space dependence when evaluating the relation between emissions and impacts. However, on the contrary an emission of fine primary particulate matter (PPM2.5) due to shipping on the ocean has nearly no effect to human health, whereas the emission of PPM2.5 in the city center of Paris has a very large negative effect on the corresponding population. Furthermore, the different indicators derived by LCIA may lead to inconclusive results because alternative X may cause less particulate matter but more greenhouse gases than alternative Y. Hence, the different impacts have to be weighted against each other. If this weighting is based on the society's revealed preferences to avoid certain impacts, then these impacts can be monetized to damage costs.

With regard to energy supply and transport activities, and based on a concept adopted from welfare economics, the environmental 'externalities' due to emissions have been monetized and aggregated to environmental costs, also called 'external costs.' According to societal welfare principles, policy should aim to ensure that prices reflect the total costs of an activity, incorporating the cost of impacts caused by employing taxes, subsidies (in the case of positive externalities) or other economic instruments. This internalization of external costs is intended as a strategy to rebalance the social and environmental dimension with the purely economic one, and hence lead to greater sustainability. Doing so is a clear objective, for example, of the European Union, as expressed for instance in the Framework Programmes of the European Commission and in the Gothenburg Protocol of 2001. Moreover, recognizing the significance of the external effects of energy, the US Congress requested a new study in the Energy Policy Act of 2005, which was finished in 2010 (National Research Council 2010).

As shown in Table 8.1, there are several ways of taking into account the cost to the environment and health.

The policy instrument 'environmental taxes' refers to taxes intended to promote ecologically sustainable activities via economic incentives, such as ideally taxing damaging fuels and technologies according to the external costs caused. According to European Commission (2003), if the external costs of producing electricity from coal were to be internalized into the electricity bills, between two and seven euro cents per kWh would have to be added to the current price of electricity in the majority of EU member states. Another solution would be to encourage or subsidize cleaner technologies, thus avoiding environmental costs. The European Community guidelines on state aid for environmental protection explicitly foresee that EU member states may grant operating aid, calculated on the basis of the external costs avoided, to new plants producing renewable energy. An overview of market-based instruments—what they are, what drives them, what inhibits their use, etc.—can be found in EEA (2006). In their study of air pollution, Fenger et al. (2009) discuss the uses of external costs for the economy and legislation.

Quite apart from market-based instruments, the quantitative results of damage costs evaluation provide an important contribution to many other widely accepted

Table 8.1   Instruments for mitigating the external costs of electricity production

Type of policy instrument	Policy instruments
Command-and-control instruments	Technology-based command-and-control
	Performance-based command-and-control
Economic instruments	Environmental taxes
	Tradable emissions permits
	Feed-in-tariffs
	Competitive bidding processes
	Green renewable certificates
	Subsidies given to consumers who purchase renewable energy equipment or renewable energy
Voluntary instruments	Voluntary agreements
	Generation disclosure rules

Source: Markandya et al. (2005a).

evaluation methods, such as green accounting (Markandya and Tamborra 2005), life cycle assessment and life cycle costing (for example, Steen 2005), technology comparison (for example, NEEDS 2004–2009) or policy assessment (for example, CAFE CBA 2005–2007). Another application of the damage costs is their use in cost-benefit analysis. In such an analysis the costs to establish measures, for example a filter to reduce a certain environmental burden, are compared with the benefits (the damage avoided due to this emission reduction). Such a cost-benefit was conducted within HEATCO (2004–2006) and CAFE CBA (2005–2007). The avoided damage can be calculated with the methods described below.

Research on the externalities due to transport activities (road, rail, aircraft and navigation) provides just one example of how externality research applies to a sector and can be used for policy purposes. In evaluating air pollution, it focuses on the specific requirements of emission and dispersion modeling and the extension and update of dose-response functions. In addition to air pollution impacts, research considers impacts on congestion and scarcity of resources, traffic accidents, noise, nature and the landscape, and sensitive and urban areas. Besides the estimation of marginal costs of transport, aggregated costs can be calculated, for example those that refer to the entire transport sector of European countries. Several policy case studies and scenarios, such as the use of alternative fuels in city buses or the introduction of electric or natural gas-fueled vehicles, have been conducted in different countries of the European Union. A comprehensive description of general methodology and best practice per cost category is provided in Maibach et al. (2008), which also includes an overview of major studies such as UNITE (1998–2002), Recordit-Project (2000–2002), HEATCO (2004–2006), Grace (2005–2007), TREMOVE (1997–1998) and Friedrich et al. (2001).

Internalization of Externalities

As suggested above, taxes can internalize externalities. Consequently, it is useful to briefly explore internalization principles and how they apply to environmental taxation. External

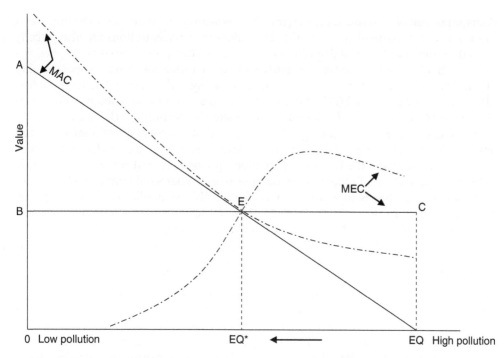

Marginal External Cost (MEC)
Marginal Abatement Cost (MAC)
Environmental Quality (EQ)

Source:　Based on European Commission (1999a).

Figure 8.1　*The socially efficient level of taxation*

effects may be positive and negative. For example, discharges to a river during production of paper pulp may have a negative external effect on a downstream fisheries company, because of a reduced number of fish. However, the waste heat may even have a positive effect on the size of the fish. An increase in the yield of fish due to certain measures at the factory, if possible, could increase the overall welfare if the positive impacts on fish stocks are larger than the costs of the abatement measures in the factory. However, why should a factory invest in abatement measures if their use to the environment has no price?

　The issues involved can be seen more clearly with the aid of a simple diagram. Figure 8.1 above plots the damages caused by each increase in the level of air pollution against the level itself, with damages measured in terms of monetary units. For most conventional cases it is generally assumed that additional or 'marginal external costs' (in the figure abbreviated as MEC) increase with pollution to a certain point. Two out of many possibilities are plotted: a) linear, without threshold (straight, horizontal line from left to right (BC)), and b) nonlinear, with threshold (dotted, s-shaped curve from low left to higher right). For emissions of pollutants, a decline implies an increase in environmental quality. There are several impacts for which this argument does not hold and where physical damages are a proportional function of concentrations (a constant additional physical damage per unit of concentration increment). This assumption is applied to health effects of radionuclides, particulates and other air pollutants. Concentrations are also directly related to emissions for most dispersion processes. The exceptions are complex phenomena that involve nonlinear effects, in particular ozone formation. Since proportionality also holds in practice for most of the economic valuations, the marginal damage curve is often likely to be horizontal (BC), but due to thresholds, or if the maximum of impacts is already reached, it may also be nonlinear as depicted by the dotted MEC curve.

On the same Figure 8.1 the additional or marginal costs of reducing pollution by a small amount (MAC) are plotted. Starting from any level of emissions, a cost-efficient strategy would be to undertake the least-cost reduction options first, and bring in more costly options as the amount of reduction required increases. That would imply a MAC curve that is sloping, as shown, more or less linear but partly also nonlinear or even stepwise. If there are no controls, and if the polluter feels no social obligation to reduce his emissions, the observed level will be the point of EQ. At that point the costs of a reduction in emissions to the level EQ* are given by the area EQ_E_EQ*. At the same time, however, the benefits of the reduction in terms of reduced damages are given by E_C_EQ_EQ*. Hence a level of emission equal to EQ represents one from which a reduction is justified. However, a level of emissions equal to EQ* does not justify further measures because at that level there is no decrease (or increase) in emissions that will generate an increase in benefits that is greater than the costs. In other words, EQ* represents the optimal level of emissions. If the polluter is already at that level, the measured damage cost should not be imposed on top of all the other regulations. However, measuring the damage cost is still useful in determining what the optimal charge or environmental tax on the polluter should be. To support this internalization, socio-environmental impacts must first be estimated and monetized.

Review of Major Projects and Methodological Developments for External Costs Estimation

Projects in the beginning

External costs have been estimated by many different institutes all over the world and corresponding tools have been developed or adjusted. In 1991 the European Commission and the US Department of Energy started a research project called the US–EC Fuel Cycle Externality Study, which was dedicated to gathering all available and useful input for a consistent calculation of external costs. In 1995 the project team of ExternE started a report series (European Commission 1995a, 1995b). There were also the reports of Oak Ridge National Laboratory and Resources for the Future (ORNL 1994). Research in estimating external costs of energy was intensified in the early-to-mid-1990s. Further, major studies were done by Hagler Bailly for the New York State Energy Research and Development Authority (Rowe et al. 1995), and by Research Triangle Institute for the State of Wisconsin. The most prominent example outside Europe and the United States is probably the South African study by van Horen (1996).

The very first studies on the externalities of electricity in Europe, done by Hohmeyer (1988) and Hohmeyer et al. (1996), used a top-down approach. According to National Research Council (2010), they calculated the total environmental burden in a region and allocated a share to electricity production. Hohmeyer estimated 'toxicity weighted' emissions from electricity generation with fossil fuels and then multiplied this fraction by estimates of total damages from pollution to various endpoints (Wicke 1986). European Commission (1999a) states that while Hohmeyer's study was a pioneering step forward, there were a number of major problems with it. For example, the relative toxicity factors were a weak link because they were derived from government regulations for maximum permissible concentrations at a place of work, rather than from exposure-response functions. Since the analysis was done in terms of national averages, effects due to variations in population density and pollutant concentration were neglected. The transport of pollutants across national boundaries was also neglected.

Therefore, due to the need to get an estimation of marginal external costs per unit of electricity and the need to attribute impacts to a certain source, a bottom-up approach was necessary. This led to development of the impact pathway approach (IPA), which attempts to model the whole chain, from emission of pollutants, to their dispersion and chemical transformation in different environmental compartments (air, water, soil) via direct exposure (inhalation, dermal contact or due to drinking water and food consumption), then to exposure of receptors (human health, ecosystems, building materials and crops). The idea of the IPA is to model the fate, i.e. dispersion, and effect of different environmental pressures, and indeed, this is the basis of most models used to calculate external costs. Ideally IPA should link with LCA to account for the whole chain of emissions involved. The steps of the IPA will be explained later in more detail.

After the first phase of externality research in Europe, the approach was further elaborated within the ExternE project-series ('External Costs of Energy,' European Research Network), which has involved more than 50 research teams in over 20 countries.[3] The projects build on each other by regional and technological extension, improvement of models and input data, and implementation of new insights in order to decrease the level of uncertainty and, therefore, the range of results. Many of these research teams have further elaborated the approach in successive projects that are still ongoing.

The effects of energy conversion are physically, environmentally and socially complex and, therefore, difficult to estimate. Calculating them involves very large uncertainties, data gaps that require certain assumptions, and unpredictable and sometimes ultimately irresolvable differences of opinion and value choices. Despite these difficulties, ExternE has become a well-recognized source for methods and results of externalities estimation. The results were published in 1999 in ExternE Volumes 7–10 (European Commission 1999a, 1999b), and during the so-called National Implementation (European Commission 1999b), the approach was applied in 15 European countries. The application of the methodology was extended to the transport sector (Friedrich et al. 2001) and to the so-called 'green accounting' (Markandya and Tamborra 2005). In successive projects NewExt (2004) and ExternE-Pol (2002–2004), the methodology was further refined by expanding the list of substances and pathways in order to reduce the level of uncertainty. The methodology is summarized comprehensively in the 2005 update (European Commission 2005). During all the ExternE projects, the methodology was continuously implemented by the computer tool EcoSense, of which the latest version is EcoSense4.0.

---

[3] All relevant information and results and a list of main institutions can be found at http:// www.externe.info/.

Apart from the ExternE project-series, external costs have been calculated in a similar way within the cost-benefit analysis of Air Quality Related Issues, led by AEA Energy and Environment (CAFE-CBA 2008). The service contract was established to support cost-benefit analysis activities under the Clean Air for Europe Programme (CAFE), including the development of a cost-benefit analysis-modeling framework. The aim of the CAFE is to establish a long-term, integrated strategy to tackle air pollution and to protect against its effects on human health and the environment in Europe. The modeling framework has been used to conduct cost-benefit analyses for the main CAFE scenarios, the Intergovernmental Panel on Climate Change's review and proposals for a revised National Emission Ceilings Directive (NECD). Documentation on methodology development and analysis undertaken can be found on the reports page of the project website. Damage costs per ton of pollutant, which can be applied for external costs calculation within Europe, were provided by the European Commission (European Commission–CAFE 2005[4]).

Furthermore, there has been a major investigation during the China Energy Technology Program, called the Integrated Assessment of Sustainable Energy Systems in China (Eliasson et al. 2003). Results are reported in Hirschberg et al. (2004) and can also be viewed at PSI (2008). The calculations have been performed with an adjusted EcoSense-China version. Also, in Japan a similar model, LIME, has been developed (Itsubo et al. 2003), which also is used to calculate damage costs. A simplified but globally applicable modeling is possible with the model RiskPoll.[5]

Recent projects
New results for the United States are provided in National Research Council (2010). The National Research Council committee formed to carry out the study was asked to define and evaluate key external costs and benefits related to health, environment, security and infrastructure that are associated with the production, distribution and use of energy (such as electricity, heat and transportation) but are not reflected in market prices or fully addressed by current government policy.

The two most up-to-date projects in Europe are the integrated project New Energy Externalities Developments for Sustainability, or NEEDS (2004–2009), and the concerted action CASES (2006–2008), which was based on input from NEEDS. The main objectives of NEEDS were further methodological improvements in the tools for energy modeling and external costs calculation (such as geographical extension and improvement in dispersion modeling) and the assessment of future internal and external costs of electricity supply technologies and strategies, with estimations until the year 2050, including improvements in LCA and energy modeling. Within the NEEDS project the EcoSense program was further developed and extended, and was updated to an online tool (EcoSenseWeb).

Within the project ExIOpol,[6] external costs per substance and per sector have been derived for countries all around the world in order to pursue three principal objectives:

---

[4]   http://www.cafe-cba.org/.
[5]   http://arirabl.org/.
[6]   http://www.feem-project.net/exiopol.

- To synthesize and develop comprehensive estimates of the external costs for Europe of a broad set of economic activities.
- To set up a detailed environmentally extended input-output (EE I-O) framework, with links to other socioeconomic models, in which as many of these estimates as possible are included. Such an EE I-O table for the EU 25 does not exist. This will allow for the estimation of environmental impacts and external costs of different economic sector activities, final consumption activities and resource consumption for countries in the EU.
- To apply the results of the external cost estimates and EE I-O analysis for the analysis of policy questions of importance, as well as to evaluate the impact of past research on external costs on policymaking in the EU.

CALCULATION OF EXTERNAL COSTS BY APPLICATION OF THE IMPACT PATHWAY APPROACH

As the primary method for calculating external costs, the impact pathway approach (IPA) warrants detailed discussion. As depicted in Figure 8.2, the IPA aims at modeling the causal chain of interactions from the emission of a pollutant to the impacts on various receptors, such as human beings, crops, building materials or ecosystems. Welfare losses resulting from these impacts are converted into monetary values based on the concepts of welfare economics.

The recommended input data and applied models for evaluating the external costs

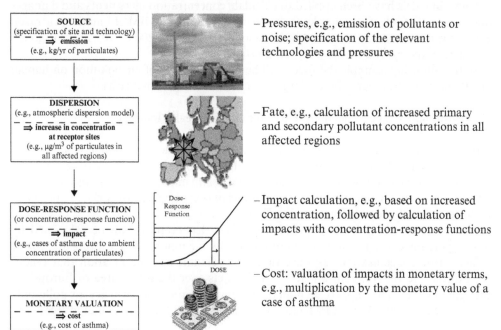

SOURCE
(specification of site and technology)
⇒ emission
(e.g., kg/yr of particulates)

– Pressures, e.g., emission of pollutants or noise; specification of the relevant technologies and pressures

DISPERSION
(e.g., atmospheric dispersion model)
⇒ increase in concentration at receptor sites
(e.g., μg/m³ of particulates in all affected regions)

– Fate, e.g., calculation of increased primary and secondary pollutant concentrations in all affected regions

DOSE-RESPONSE FUNCTION
(or concentration-response function)
⇒ impact
(e.g., cases of asthma due to ambient concentration of particulates)

– Impact calculation, e.g., based on increased concentration, followed by calculation of impacts with concentration-response functions

MONETARY VALUATION
⇒ cost
(e.g., cost of asthma)

– Cost: valuation of impacts in monetary terms, e.g., multiplication by the monetary value of a case of asthma

Source: http://www.externe.info/.

Figure 8.2   Impact Pathway Approach

will depend on the corresponding question the study wants to answer. For example, the question can refer to different environmental pressures, such as noise, global warming or air pollution, or it can refer to certain economic sectors like transport or electricity generation in a certain country or at a certain location. It is also possible to do a cost-benefit-analysis for a local hot-spot issue, such as whether to build a combined heat and power plant for a certain supply case.

The methodology of the IPA is implemented in different computer tools. Most of the relevant input data and functions (such as population figures, meteorological conditions, emission of precursors, response functions and monetary values) are site-dependent or at least country- or continent-dependent. For example, the values calculated for the United States (reported in National Research Council (2010)) are based on the APEEP model (Muller 2010), which uses a different dispersion model and different input data than the ones used in Europe.

One of the most advanced and user-friendly models in Europe is EcoSenseWeb, an online version of EcoSense. In fact, the model incorporates different modules and para-meterized results of more sophisticated models in order to cover the different pressures. The covered environmental pressures are listed in Table 8.2. Impacts with regard to human health, ecosystem damage, reduction of crop yields, material deterioration and effects of global warming have been quantified. Particulate matter (PM) are air borne particles including primary particulates, such as black carbon and other organic matter, and secondary inorganic aerosols (SIA), such as sulphate and nitrate aerosols. PMcoarse are particles with an aerodynamic diameter between 2.5 µm and 10 µm; PM2.5 are parti-cles with an aerodynamic diameter smaller than 2.5 µm.

Several models have been applied to calculate concentration increments and damages due to air pollutants, for example, for nontoxic pollutants the EMEP[7] model (Tarrasón 2009), for toxic pollutants the WATSON model (Bachmann 2006, 570), and for green-house gases the FUND model (Anthoff 2007).

In the following example the focus will be on the impacts of air pollution on human health, because these contribute a large share of the total external costs.

Concentration-Response Functions (CRF) for Human Health Impacts

Physical impacts on human health can be attributed to concentration increments of air pollutants. Since the impacts on human health contribute the majority of the damage costs, the approach to how to allocate additional health impacts to emissions is described here in some detail. Comprehensive descriptions of other impact categories are provided in, for example, European Commission (2005).

According to the IPA the physical impact on the receptors can be calculated by multiplying the concentration of a pollutant (a) by the number of receptors and (b) by a factor (the concentration response function) per unit of concentration that relates the exposure to the different impacts. The impacts over the whole area of Europe are then summed up. The impacts on human health due to the main primary air pollutants (NH_3, NO_x, SO_2, NMVOC, PPMcoarse and PPM2.5) and the corresponding secondary

---

[7]   http://www.emep.int/grid/.

Table 8.2 Impact category, pollutants and burden implemented and corresponding effects considered in the IPA

Impact Category	Pollutant / Burden	Effects
Human health—mortality	PMcoarse, PM2.5, SO_2, O_3	Reduction in life time expectancy due to short- and long-term exposure (Years of lifetime lost = YOLL)
	Heavy metal, some organics, radionuclides	Reduction in life expectancy due to short- and long-term exposure
	Accident risk	Fatality risk from traffic and workplace accidents
	Noise	Reduction in life expectancy due to long-term exposure
Human health—morbidity	PMcoarse, PM2.5, O_3, SO_2	Respiratory hospital admissions
	PMcoarse, PM2.5, O_3	Restricted activity days
	PMcoarse, PM2.5, CO	Congestive heart failure
	Some organics, radionuclides, heavy metal	Cancer risk (non-fatal) osteroporosia, ataxia, renal dysfunction
	PMcoarse, PM2.5	Cerebrovascular hospital admissions, chronic bronchitis, chronic cough in children, cough in asthmatics, lower respiratory symptoms
	Mercury	Loss of IQ in children
	O_3	Asthma attacks, symptom days
	Noise	Myocardial infarction, angina pectoris, hypertension, sleep disturbance
	Accident risk	Risk of injuries from traffic and workplace accidents
Building material	SO_2, acid deposition	Aging of galvanized steel, limestone, mortar, sand-stone, paint, rendering and zinc for utilitarian buildings
	Combustion particles	Soiling of buildings
Crops	NOx, SO_2	Yield change for wheat, barley, rye, oats, potato, sugar beet
	O_3	Yield change for wheat, barley, rye, oats, potato, rice, tobacco, sunflower seed
	Acid deposition	Increased need for liming
	N, S deposition	Fertilizing effects
Global warming	CO_2, CH_4, N_2O	Worldwide effects on mortality, morbidity, coastal impacts, agriculture and energy demand; economic impacts due to temperature change and sea level rise; and avoidance costs to reach certain targets (such as max $+2°C$)
Noise	Noise	Amenity losses and health impacts due to noise exposure
Ecosystems	Acid deposition, nitrogen deposition, SO_2, NOx, NH_3	Acidity and eutrophication, potentially disappeared fraction (PDF) of species
Land use change	Occupation and transformation	PDF of species

pollutants—nitrates, sulfates (or secondary inorganic aerosols) and due to ozone—are explained in the paragraph below. Some examples of corresponding concentration-response functions are listed in Table 8.4, together with the corresponding monetary values.

Impacts due to radio nuclides and heavy metals, and impacts on ecosystems, crop yields, and building materials are described in detail for example in European Commission (2005), Ott et al. (2006) and Preiss et al. (2008).

Corresponding Monetary Values

Different methods for monetary valuation are available, and are described in, for example, European Commission (2005, 16–29). The impact pathway requires first an estimation of the impacts in physical terms and then a valuation of these impacts based on the preferences of the individuals affected. This approach has been applied primarily to human health impacts, but in some areas of protection it cannot be fully applied because data on valuation for goods, such as cultural heritage, is missing or because estimation of all physical impacts is limited. For example, in the case of climate change, a so-called 'second best' approach is to elicit implicit values per unit of emission of greenhouse gases (GHG) from policy decisions in order to monetize the avoided impacts based on the so-called 'avoidance costs,' i.e., the costs of the implementation of a policy or technology which aims on the reduction of GHG emissions.

The willingness to pay to avoid certain impacts can be estimated for nonmarket goods, such as human health due to valuation methods based on 'revealed preference,' 'stated preference,' and by direct and indirect methods, as listed in Table 8.3.

In Table 8.4 an overview of the different health endpoints and the corresponding concentration-response function (CRF) for particulate matter (PM2.5) is given. These are the most important and updated CRFs for Europe, as provided by Torfs et al. (2007).

Additional CRFs are available for ozone and larger particulates (PM10), and other diseases such as increased mortality risk of infants, new cases of chronic bronchitis, cardiac hospital admissions, medication use (especially bronchodilator use), lower respiratory symptoms and cough days. Furthermore, the monetary values per health

Table 8.3   Classification of nonmarket valuation techniques

	Indirect	Direct
Revealed preferences	Household production function approach –Travel cost method –Averting costs Hedonic price analysis	Simulated markets Actual referenda Market price Replacement costs
Stated preferences	Choice experiments –Conjoint analysis –Contingent ranking –Contingent rating –Pair wise comparison	Contingent valuation

Source: European Commission (2005).

Table 8.4   Examples of the CRF for particulate matter (PM 2.5) – primary and secondary inorganic aerosols <2.5 μm

	Phys. impact per person per μg per m³ [1/(μg/m³)]	Unit of impact	Monetary value per case or per YOLL [Euro]	External costs per person per μg per m³ [€/(μg/m³)]
Primary and secondary inorganic aerosols < 2.5 μm				
Life expectancy reduction—years of life lost	0.000651	year	40000	26
Restricted activity days	0.00959	days	130	1.3
Work loss days	0.0139	days	295	4.1
Minor restricted activity days	0.0369	days	38	1.4

endpoints are shown in Table 8.4 (derived from European Commission 2005, Desaigues et al. 2007, and Desaigues et al. 2011). The percentages of different risk-group and age-group fractions are already accounted for in the listed factors, which are just to be multiplied by the total number of population. The reduced lifetime expectancy (years of lost lifetime, or YOLL) is the most important endpoint with regard to the share of external costs.

One Sample Calculation of how to Apply the CRF and Monetary Values in order to Derive External Costs per Unit of Emission

The following example will illustrate the application of the CRF and the monetary values. Due to the operation of a coal-fired power plant in Germany, among other pressures, SO_2 is emitted. Dispersion and a chemical reaction with NH_3, turning into ammonium sulphate, lead to a concentration increment of secondary particulate matter with aerodynamic diameter smaller than 2.5 μm (PM2.5). The yearly average concentration is calculated for each EMEP50 grid cell (50 km * 50 km across all of Europe).

The population in such a grid cell xy may be, for example, 250000 people. Assuming the yearly average concentration increment due to the emissions from Germany is 0.031 ng/m³ PM2.5 per ton of SO_2 in this grid cell, the expected years of lifetime lost (YOLL) are calculated as follows:

YOLL per ton SO_2_Ger in grid cell xy = 0.031 ng/m3 * 6.51E-04 YOLL/μg/m3/person * 250000 people = 0.005 YOLL.

The corresponding monetary value is calculated as follows:

0.005 YOLL * 40000 Euro per YOLL = 200 Euro.

This procedure is carried out for each grid cell in the whole area of Europe and for all quantifiable impacts. This calculation results to an average cost of about €9500 per ton of SO_2 emitted in Germany. For other countries and other substances, external cost

Table 8.5   *Examples of Euro$_{2000}$-per-ton damage costs from NEEDS, for high stacks such as coal-fired power stations. Year of emission 2010*

	SO$_2$	NOx	NH$_3$	PPMcoarse	PPM$_{2.5}$
Eu27 average	7300	6300	15000	580	14700
Germany	10500	10500	22800	1060	26100

Source: Preiss et al. (2008).

values have been calculated within NEEDS (Preiss et al. 2008) and CAFE (European Commission–CAFE 2005), and for the US by Muller et al. (2010).

Example for Recommended Damage Costs for Air Pollutants per Unit of Emission in Europe

The above table depicts Euro-per-ton damage costs.

The *Handbook on Estimation of External Cost in the Transport Sector* (Maibach et al. 2008) depicts external costs per ton of emission derived within the HEATCO (2006) and European Commission–CAFE (2005) projects. All of these values have been calculated based on the IPA methodology and on similar dispersion models, CRF and monetary values.

Application of Results

External costs have been calculated for a large number of European and national studies for the purpose of providing a guideline for environmental, energy and transport policies.

In addition to the different phases of the ExternE project in Europe itself, the methodology developed within the projects has been used and applied to support several policy decisions and legislative proposals, such as those by the European Commission's Directorate General Environment. It has been used to perform economic evaluations of the following:

- Draft directive on nonhazardous waste incineration;
- Large combustion plant directive;
- EU strategy to combat acidification;
- Costs and benefits of the UN-ECE Multi-pollutant, Multi-effect protocol and of proposals under this protocol (such as NOx and VOC control);
- Costs and benefits for the emission ceilings directive;
- Benefits of compliance with the EU environmental acquis: quantification of the benefits of air quality improvements;
- Regulatory appraisal of the SO$_2$, NO$_2$ and PM10 air quality objectives for the UK Department of the Environment, Transport and the Regions;
- Air quality guidelines on CO and benzene;
- The CAFE Programme—Implementation of the Thematic Strategy on Air Pollution;
- And many more.

EXTERNALITIES DUE TO ENERGY CONVERSION

One of the first objectives of externality-related research programs was to make a comparative evaluation of different technologies and fuel cycles for electricity generation. A decade of research has resulted in a detailed set of data on the impacts of a wide range of fuels, technologies and locations. Due to the ExternE project-series and other projects, the external costs of electricity supply have been calculated. The most recent results, reported within NEEDS, include a wide range of current and future technologies (up to the year 2050) that have been quantified.

According to Muller et al. (2009), economists have long advocated market-based approaches to regulating pollution. Two broad approaches have been advocated: emission taxes (Baumol et al. 1988) and tradable permits (Dales 1968; Montgomery 1972; Hirschberg et al. 2004). Denmark, Norway and Sweden have implemented uniform sulfur dioxide (SO_2) taxes, and six European countries have implemented uniform greenhouse gas taxes. The United States has used tradable permits to control SO_2 emissions from power plants and nitrogen oxide (NOx) emissions from industrial point sources.

Source-specific marginal damages of emissions can be calculated and incorporated into tax policy. Although the damage cost per ton of emission depends on the actual location of the emission, this variation is not well captured in policymaking. If the models are available, as indeed they are for many regions in the world, the effort required to perform a calculation for certain hot spots such as large combustion power plants, or for certain regions within a country, is relatively small. However, distortion may occur if not all market participants are treated equally, but one has to start somewhere. If external costs are internalized by a certain tax, either of the following may result:

(A) Damage costs are 5000 Euro per produced product, which causes 1 ton of emission of SO_2. The avoidance costs for this process may be 10 000 Euro per ton SO_2 and the tax would be 5 000 Euro. This will be paid to the state, because the polluter cannot avoid creating emissions. Ultimately the costs will be passed to the consumer, perhaps making the product less competitive because of its higher price. Perhaps a competitor (one with a process causing less emissions) will now be cheaper. Either outcome would result in somewhat lower emissions.

(B) Damage costs are 5 000 Euro per produced product, which causes 1 ton of emission of SO_2. The avoidance costs for this process may be only 2 000 Euro per ton SO_2, and the tax would be 5 000 Euro. The polluter would now prefer to avoid emissions. The additional avoidance costs may be passed to the consumer, perhaps causing a decrease in product sales because of the higher price. Perhaps a competitor (one with already a less polluting production process) will now be cheaper. Either outcome would result in considerable reduction of emissions.

From an economic perspective the preferred solution is that pollution is reduced at those sources where the lowest abatement costs can be identified. The so-called Pigouvian pollution tax is intended to correct the market outcome. It will provide a continuous incentive to polluters to consider whether some amount of control and abatement is more efficient than paying the tax. Perhaps it will even lead to a phasing-out of techniques and actors that cannot adapt to necessary environmental demands may disappear from the market.

For the fair comparison of different technologies, the quantification of the entire life cycle of a technology is important. Therefore, the analyst should look not only at the environmental pressures and externalities caused by the operation of a power plant but also at up- and downstream processes such as building power plants or solar panels, wind energy converters, fuel supply and waste treatment.

The most important substances with regard to quantifiable external costs in the area of energy conversion are the air pollutants NH_3, NO_x, SO_2, NMVOC, PPMcoarse and PPM2.5, and the corresponding secondary pollutants, namely nitrates, sulphates and ozone. Moreover, the emission of greenhouse gases and the corresponding effect on climate change are most important.

FURTHER EXTERNALITY RESEARCH NEEDS

Research is needed to reduce uncertainty and to improve the acceptability of external cost values. Therefore, it is recommended that the understanding of physical, biological and human impacts, as well as economic valuation aspects, are improved. For decision-making these aggregated estimates should be supplemented by other characteristics, for example distributional measures that describe how the burden varies among countries or even groups of population. There are large uncertainties inherent in the estimation of damage costs of greenhouse gases. However, the variability of results also depends on value choices regarding equity-weighting and discounting. Moreover, there are large uncertainties due to lack of knowledge about the consequences of loss of biodiversity. In case of loss of biodiversity, out of sight of the current concerns of society, the valuation based on willingness to pay is very difficult. With regard to nuclear power, the issue of nuclear waste and security against terrorism raise important issues and pose difficult policy challenges that can perhaps be solved only by referenda. The extent to which externalities exist is difficult to measure and the valuation including risk aversion is controversial.

The results of a life-cycle assessment depend on the technology investigated (because of the difference between state-of-the-art or average technology). Hence, the up- and downstream processes may be responsible for a smaller or larger share of the life-cycle externalities. If more effort is made to improve the performance of the operation of a coal-fired power plant, the share of up- and downstream processes will be larger unless their emissions are reduced as well.

There is also still a lack of appropriate dispersion modeling of classical air pollutants and of evaluation of the upstream impacts outside of Europe and the United States. The latter is necessary because in countries where the raw materials are extracted and pre-processed, these processes can cause large amounts of emissions due to very low environmental standards.

The uncertainty in concentration-response functions and monetary valuation must be reduced in order to achieve more and more robust results, which is necessary for the planning security of the economic actors. Nonetheless, the application of external costs in economic areas where this is already possible must be further disseminated.

REFERENCES

Anthoff, D. (2007), 'Report on marginal external costs inventory of greenhouse gas emissions', NEEDS Deliverable D5.4, RS1b – Project no: 502687.

Bachmann, T.M. (2006), *Hazardous Substances and Human Health: Exposure, Impact and External Cost Assessment at the European Scale*, Amsterdam: Elsevier.

Baumol, W.J. and W.E. Oates (eds) (1988), *The Theory of Environmental Policy*, 2nd edition, Cambridge, UK: Cambridge University Press.

CAFE CBA (2005–2007), 'Cost-Benefit Analysis (CBA) of air quality related issues, Clean Air for Europe (CAFE) Programme', http://www.cafe-cba.org/reports/.

CAFE CBA (2008), 'Clean air for Europe—Cost benefit analysis', available at http://www.cafe-cba.org/.

CASES (2006–2008), 'Cost assessment of sustainable energy systems', EU Project No 518294 SES6, http://www.feem-project.net/cases/.

Dales, J.H. (1968), *Pollution, Property and Prices: An Essay in Policy-Making and Economics*, Toronto, Canada: University of Toronto Press.

Desaigues, B. et al. (2007), 'Final report on the monetary valuation of mortality and morbidity risks from air pollution', NEEDS project, FP6, Rs1b_D6.7.

Desaigues, B. et al. (2011), 'Economic valuation of air pollution mortality: a 9-country contingent valuation survey of value of a life year (VOLY)', *Ecological Indicators*, **11** (3), 902–10.

EcoSense, 'The software system developed within the ExternE project: EcoSense—the integrated environmental impact assessment model', http://ecoweb.ier.uni-stuttgart.de/ecosense_web/ecosensele_web/ecosense4um.pdf.

EcoSenseWeb, 'EcoSenseWeb—Integrated atmospheric dispersion, exposure and impact assessment model which implements the Impact Pathway Approach developed within ExternE', http://EcoSenseWeb.ier.uni-stuttgart.de.

Eliasson, B. and Y. Lee (eds) (2003), *Integrated Assessment of Sustainable Energy Systems in China*, The China Technology Program, Springer.

European Commission (1995a), *ExternE—Externalities of Energy*, Vol. 1, Summary, EUR 16520.

European Commission (1995b), *ExternE—Externalities of Energy*, Vol. 6, Wind & Hydro, EUR 16525.

European Commission (1999a), *ExternE—Externalities of Energy*, Vol. 7, Methodology, 1998, Update EUR 19083.

European Commission (1999b), *ExternE—Externalities of Energy*, Vol. 10—National Implementation.

European Commission (2001), 'Contribution of product-related environmental policy to sustainable development—a strategy for an integrated product policy approach in the European Union', Green Paper, COM(2001)68, Brussels, Belgium: European Commission.

European Commission (2003), 'External Costs–Research results on socio-environmental damages due to electricity and transport', EUR 20198, http://www.externe.info/externpr.pdf.

European Commission (2005), 'ExternE—Externalities of Energy: Methodology, 2005 Update', EUR 21951.

European Commission—CAFE (2005), 'Damages per tonne emission of PM2.5, NH_3, SO_2, NO_x and VOCs from each EU25 Member State (excluding Cyprus) and surrounding seas', Brussels, Belgium: European Commission.

European Environment Agency (EEA) (2006), *Using the Market for Cost-effective Environmental Policy Market-based Instruments in Europe*, Denmark, Copenhagen: EEA.

ExternE-Pol. (2002–2004), 'Externalities of energy: extension of accounting framework and policy applications', project funded by the European Community under the 'EESD' Programme, CONTRACT N°: ENG1-CT2002-00609, http://www.externe.info/exterpol.html.

ExternE, 'Externalities of energy. A research project series of the European Commission', http://www.externe.info/.

Fenger, J. and J.C. Tjell (eds) (2009), *Air Pollution—From Local to Global Perspective*, London, UK: RSC Publishing.

Friedrich, R. and P. Bickel (2001), *Environmental External Costs of Transport*, Springer.

Grace (2005–2007), 'Generalisation of research on accounts and cost estimation', http://www.grace-eu.org/.

HEATCO (2004–2006), 'Developing harmonised European approaches for transport costing and project assessment', Sixth Framework Programme, Priority SSP 3.2: The development of tools, indicators and operational parameters for assessing sustainable transport and energy systems performance (economic, environmental and social), Contract No. 2002-SSP-1/502481, http://heatco.ier.uni-stuttgart.de.

HEATCO (2006), 'Derivation of fall-back values for impact and cost factors for airborne pollutants', Annex D to HEATCO Deliverable 5.

Hirschberg, S. et al. (2004), 'Health and environmental impacts of China's current and future electricity supply, with associated external costs', *International Journal of Global Energy*, **22** (2/3/4), 155–79.

Hohmeyer, O. (1988), *Social Costs of Energy Consumption. External Effects of Electricity Generation in the Federal Republic of Germany*, Berlin, Germany: Springer-Verlag.

Hohmeyer, O., R.L. Ottinger, and K. Rennings (1996), *Social Costs and Sustainability Valuation and Implementation in the Energy and Transport Sector*, Proceedings of an International Conference held at Ladenburg, Germany May 2–5 1995, Berlin, Germany: Springer-Verlag.

Itsubo, N. and A. Inaba (2003), 'A new LCIA method: LIME has been completed', *The International Journal of Life Cycle Assessment*, **8** (5), 305.

Maibach, M. et al. (2008), *Handbook on Estimation of External Costs in the Transport Sector, Internalisation Measures and Policies for All External Cost of Transport (IMPACT)*, Version 1.1. Delft, CE.

Markandya, A. and A. Longo (2005), 'Identification of options and policy instruments for the internalisation of external costs of electricity generation', Project report of MAXIMA—Making Electricity External Costs Known to Policy-Makers, http://www.feem.it/Feem/Pub/Publications/WPapers/default.htm.

Markandya, A. and M. Tamborra (eds) (2005), *Green Accounting in Europe. A Comparative Study*, Vol. 2, The Fondazione Eni Enrico Mattei (Feem) Series on Economics, the Environment and Sustainable Development.

Montgomery, W.D. (1972), 'Markets in licenses and efficient pollution control programs', *Journal of Economic Theory*, **5** (3), 395–418.

Muller, N.Z. (2010), 'The air pollution emission experiments and policy analysis model (APEEP)', https://seguecommunity.middlebury.edu/view/html/site/nmuller/node/2367900.

Muller, N.Z. and R. Mendelsohn (2009), 'Efficient pollution regulation: getting the prices right', *American Economic Review*, **99** (5), 1714–39.

Muller, N.Z. and R.O. Mendelsohn (2010), 'Weighing the value of a ton of "pollution"', *Regulation*, **33** (2), 20.

National Research Council (2010), *Hidden Costs of Energy: Unpriced Consequences of Energy Production and Use*, Washington, DC, US: The National Academies Press.

NEEDS (2004–2009), 'Integrated project NEEDS—New energy externalities developments for sustainability', Sixth Framework Programme, Priority 6.1: Sustainable Energy Systems and, more specifically, Sub-priority 6.1.3.2.5: Socio-economic tools and concepts for energy strategy, Guidelines to European Commission, Project no: 502687, http://www.needs-project.org/.

NewExt (2004), 'Final Report to the European Commission, DG Research, Technological Development and Demonstration (RTD)—NewExt—New elements for the assessment of external costs from energy technologies', Stuttgart, Germany: Universitaet Stuttgart, Institute of Energy Economics and the Rational Use of Energy (IER).

ORNL (1994), 'Estimating fuel cycle externalities: analytical methods and issues', Report No. 2, Washington DC, US: McGraw-Hill/Utility Data Institute, Oak Ridge National Laboratory and Resources for the Future.

Ott, W. et al. (2006), 'Assessment of biodiversity losses', NEEDS Deliverable D4.2, RS1b, WP4 – Project no: 502687.

Preiss, P., R. Friedrich and V. Klotz (2008), 'Report on the procedure and data to generate averaged/aggregated data, including ExternalCosts_per_unit_emission_080821.xls', NEEDS project, FP6, Rs3a_D1.1 – Project no: 502687, Stuttgart, Germany: Universitaet Stuttgart, Institute of Energy Economics and the Rational Use of Energy (IER).

PSI (2008), 'Impacts and external costs China', http://gabe.web.psi.ch/research/imp/.

Rabl, A. and J.V. Spadaro, 'RiskPoll', http://www.arirabl.com/Software/SOFTWARE.HTM.

Recordit-Project (2000–2002), 'REal COst Reduction of Door-to-door Intermodal Transport (Recordit)', http://www.recordit.org/.

Rowe, R.D. et al. (1995), *New York State Environmental Externalities Cost Study*, Vol. I and II, New York, NY, US: Oceana Publications Limited.

Steen, B. (2005), 'Environmental costs and benefits in life cycle costing', *Management of Environmental Quality*, **16** (2), 107–18.

Tarrasón, L. (2009), 'Report on deliveries of source-receptor matrices with the regional EMEP Unified model', NEEDS project, FP6, Rs1b_TP1.2 – Project no: 502687.

Torfs, R., F. Hurley, B. Miller and A. Rabl (2007), 'A set of concentration-response functions', NEEDS project, FP6, Rs1b_D3.7 – Project no: 502687.

TREMOVE (1997–1998), 'A policy assessment model to study the effects of different transport and environment policies on the transport sector for all European countries', http://www.tremove.org/.

UNEP-SETAC (2004), 'Life Cycle Impact Assessment programme, LCIA methods and links', http://lcinitiative.unep.fr/default.asp?site=lcinit&page_id=67F5A66D-9EB8-4E75-B663-297B7FD626B6.

UNITE (1998–2002), 'UNIfication of accounts and marginal costs for transport efficiency', http://www.its.leeds.ac.uk/projects/unite/.

van Horen, C. (1996), *Counting the Social Costs: Electricity and Externalities in South Africa*, Cape Town: Elan Press and UCT Press, University of Cape Town.

Wicke, L. (1986), *Die ökologischen Milliarden. Das kostet die zerstörte Umwelt – so können wir sie retten* [The ecologic billions. The costs of destruction of the environment – the way to save the environment], Munich, Germany: Kösel.

PART III

ACCEPTANCE

9 Regressivity of environmental taxation: myth or reality?
Katri Kosonen[1]

INTRODUCTION

Environmental taxes are key instruments for achieving sustainability in the economy. By increasing the prices of environmentally harmful goods in relation to other goods, they encourage consumers to shift their consumption patterns in a more sustainable direction. Environmental taxes may also increase the prices of production inputs and thus induce the producers to adopt more environmentally friendly technologies.

The most common forms of environmental taxes, and the ones that are the most fiscally important, are those on energy and transport. These taxes affect the costs of heating, electricity and transport, which can all be considered as necessities of modern life. It is often believed—and supported by empirical evidence—that imposing taxes on such goods would impose a heavier burden on low-income households than on high-income households, since the former spend a larger share of their income on these goods. This regressive impact of environmental taxes is often found politically unacceptable and makes it difficult to carry out environmental tax reforms. However, there is also empirical evidence indicating that several factors could mitigate, or even eliminate, the regressivity of environmental tax reforms, and this should be taken into account in judging the distributional effect of the a tax reform package. These factors include, in particular, the income concept used in the analysis, the use of tax revenues and the lesser regressivity of transport taxes compared with those on other energy products.

This chapter first presents an overview of the various factors that in light of the economic literature should be taken into account in the analysis of tax incidence of environmental taxation. It then explores the main empirical findings, in particular those which make a distinction between the distributional effects of transport-related taxes and those of other environmental taxes. This includes also some less well-known evidence from the Nordic countries. In the final section it presents some recent evidence on the distributional impact of energy taxation in the EU member states included in the impact assessment of the revision of the European Union's Energy Tax Directive.

---

[1] The views expressed in this chapter are those of the author and should not be interpreted as those of the European Commission or the Directorate-General for Taxation and Customs Union. It has been published by the European Commission as Taxation Paper no. 32.

FACTORS INFLUENCING THE DETERMINATION OF TAX INCIDENCE

The Analysis of Tax Incidence

Economic theory usually draws a distinction between the statutory and economic incidence of taxation. Statutory incidence refers to who legally pays the tax, while economic incidence refers to who really bears the burden of the tax. The two are not equal because of the changes in relative prices (Fullerton and Metcalf 2002).

In the partial equilibrium framework, the extent to which the burden of a commodity tax falls on the consumers depends on the price elasticity of demand relative to the price elasticity of supply. The more the demand elasticity is low and supply elasticity is high, the more the tax is shifted to consumer prices. If, on the other hand, the demand is elastic and the supply inelastic, the production side, or the factors of production, would bear the burden of the tax. In a general equilibrium framework one should also take into account the changes in prices in other commodity markets. Moreover, the tax incidence may depend on the competitiveness of the markets. When the producers have market power, it is easier for them to shift the burden of the tax to the consumers. In empirical analyses of energy taxation, it is usually assumed that a tax increase is fully passed through to consumers. This may be a fair assumption in the short run, in view of relatively low short-run price elasticities of energy demand (usual estimates vary between −0.2 and −0.3), assuming that the tax reform is implemented unilaterally without an impact on world market oil prices. In the longer run the price elasticity of demand can be assumed to be higher, however, when more substitutes for the taxed products become available (e.g. non-fossil-fuel-based energy). It is also often pointed out that in the long run the supply of crude oil in the world is inelastic, which would imply that the burden of carbon taxes, at least if they are applied globally, would fall entirely on the owners of oil resources (Stiglitz 1988). A coordinated carbon tax policy in the EU could have a similar impact, since the EU energy demand forms a relatively large share of the world energy demand. In cases where the tax burden is shared between producers and consumers, the costs to the factors of production should also be taken into account in the tax incidence analysis. Fullerton (2008) points out that these effects could also be regressive, if environmental policy increases the demand for capital and hence the price of capital relative to labor also increases (such as by increasing the demand for capital-intensive abatement technologies). The effects of environmental taxes could, however, also be contrary. By increasing the price of production inputs they could, in fact, also decrease the price of capital. Some computable general equilibrium (CGE) model simulations indicate, for instance, that in a cap-and-trade system a significant portion of the carbon price is shifted back to the owners of natural resources and capital. This makes the policy as a whole more progressive than the effects only on households would imply (Rausch et al. 2011).

Price Responsiveness

Empirical evidence regarding the distributional effects of environmental taxation is often based on a static analysis, which does not take into account behavioral changes. However, when the price of a commodity is increased by a tax, the consumers normally reduce their consumption of the commodity, depending on the availability of substitutes. These behavioral effects would as such reduce the burden of the tax. Moreover, there is empirical evidence showing that the price responsiveness would depend on the income of the households, and notably that low-income households would be more responsive to price increases and would reduce their consumption more than would higher-income households.[2] This would make the incidence of the tax less regressive, as the tax burden of low-income households would be reduced more than that of higher-income households. Smith (1992) shows, however, that the effect of allowing behavioral responses is fairly small and would not eliminate the regressivity of a carbon tax in the UK.

Indirect Effects

Most empirical analyses only take into account direct effects, that is, the increase in the costs of the taxed commodity to the consumers. Environmental taxes could also have indirect effects, if they increase the input costs and thus affect the prices of other commodities. Such indirect effects could affect the regressivity of tax policy. The evidence on indirect effects is relatively scarce. Jacobsen et al. (2001) present evidence on both direct and indirect effects of environmental taxes in Denmark. Their results indicate that although the indirect costs of environmentally related taxes to the consumers are much smaller than the direct ones (on average the direct cost is 7 percent of household disposable income and the indirect cost 1.1 percent), they are a higher burden for low-income households and thus increase the regressivity of environmental taxes as a whole.

Income Concept

The income concept used in the calculation of distributional impacts has turned out to have a relatively large impact on the regressivity results. Traditionally the households/individuals are classified in ascending order of their disposable annual income in groups of equal size (quartiles, quintiles or deciles, depending on the level of aggregation used in the study). The share of income spent on the taxed good or on taxes paid on the good is then calculated for each income group. If this share increases when moving from a low- to a higher-income group, the tax in question is progressive, and regressive in the reverse case (abstracting from all the issues that additionally may affect the economic tax incidence, as discussed above).

Poterba (1991) was one of the first to point out that it would be more appropriate to use permanent or lifetime income in the calculation than disposable annual income. This is because annual income may be lower or higher in a specific year than expected lifetime income because of transitory shocks or the lifetime variation of income. People tend to smooth their consumption over transitory shocks and determine their consumption level on the basis of their expected lifetime income. Therefore Poterba (1991) used total

---

[2]   The US evidence on the price responsiveness of different income groups is discussed in Tuuli (2009). Bureau (2010) estimates a model of car use using the data on French households and shows that rich households are less sensitive to increases in the cost of driving than poorer households. Blow and Crawford (1997) present similar evidence on UK households.

expenditures of the household as a proxy for lifetime income, divided the households into deciles on the basis of their total expenditure and calculated the shares of the taxed good (gasoline) out of total expenditure. He found out that the gasoline tax was far less regressive than could be observed on the basis of disposable income and that the low-income group actually spent a smaller share of their budget on gasoline than middle-income groups, although the top four deciles had lower shares than middle-income ones.

Similar results were obtained later in other studies. Using total expenditure as the basis of calculation instead of disposable income makes environmental taxation often appear less regressive, but does not eliminate the regressivity of taxation for the necessary household goods, such as domestic heating and electricity. Smith (1992) shows, for instance, that in the UK taxes on domestic fuels remain regressive even using expenditure shares, but that regressivity is somewhat reduced at the low end of the income scale. The results of Barker and Köhler (1998) also indicate that even using total expenditure as the income concept, the expenditure on domestic energy relative to total expenditure decreases with the level of expenditure in the 11 EU member states included in their study. On the other hand, Rausch et al. (2011) do not find any significant difference for the distributional impacts of carbon pricing when they use two different proxies for expected lifetime income instead of annual income in their model simulations.

Use of Tax Revenues

Tax instruments not only provide incentives for sustainable consumption but they also raise revenues. The way governments use the additional tax revenues can have a strong influence on the final distributional outcome of tax reform involving increases in environmental taxation. The governments can either use the revenues for consolidating public finances, in which case the distributional outcome would not be changed compared with the results of static calculations described above, or they can be recycled back into the economy through reductions of other taxes. The double dividend argument implies the governments can shift the tax burden from labor and capital toward the environment and would thus obtain efficiency gains, which would outweigh the efficiency losses entailed by environmental taxes (since taxes on labor and capital are assumed to be more distortionary than environmental taxes). The double dividend would thus consist of the environmental benefit and the efficiency gain obtained from the tax shift.[3] Reductions in labor and capital taxation would not, however, be necessarily beneficial from the equity perspective. If labor taxes are reduced by cutting marginal income tax rates equally for all income brackets, they would benefit high-income households more in absolute terms. Also, cuts in capital taxes are likely to benefit high-income and wealthy households more. In this situation there is a trade-off between equity and efficiency objectives; both cannot be achieved at the same time.[4]

Tax reductions could also be targeted to low-income households through the reduction of tax rates in low-income brackets or through the increase of basic allowances, which

---

[3]   Whether the double dividend hypothesis holds or not is a controversial issue in economic literature and depends on many assumptions used in the analysis.

[4]   See Smith (1992) for this argument.

would make the tax reform less regressive. The other form of compensation would be lump-sum transfers to all households (revenues distributed on an equal per capita basis), which in most analyses turns out to be the most progressive way of using tax revenues, although it is less efficient. Tax credits, the size of which would decrease with income level, could also neutralize the regressivity of the tax reform.[5] These results are confirmed by the model simulation of Rausch et al. (2011). They used three different assumptions of distributing auction revenues in a cap-and-trade scheme: (1) the reduction of personal income tax (by equal percentage of household income), (2) the distribution of revenues on an equal per capita basis (lump-sum transfers) and (3) the distribution of revenues in proportion to capital income. The first form of revenue recycling would have the lowest welfare costs in accordance with the double dividend argument, but would be regressive, while lump-sum transfers would have higher welfare costs but would have a progressive impact. The third form would be progressive at the low end of the income scale, but highly regressive thereafter.

EMPIRICAL EVIDENCE OF DISTRIBUTIONAL IMPACT

Different Categories of Environmental Taxes

There is now substantial empirical evidence indicating that not all environmental taxes have a similar distributional impact. This applies notably to taxes on domestic heating and electricity, on the one hand, and transport-related taxes, such as on fuels and vehicles, on the other hand. The former are found to be regressive in practically all studies, even using total expenditure as the basis of calculation, while the latter can be either less regressive or progressive depending on the country. This of course has importance for the design of environmental tax reforms, when both environmental benefit and social fairness are pursued.

The earlier evidence on this issue includes Poterba's (1991) aforementioned pioneering study, which shows that middle-income groups bear a higher burden of gasoline tax in the US than either low- or high-income groups, when total expenditure is used as the basis of calculation. Thus the gasoline tax is progressive at the low end of the income scale and regressive at the high end. Also, Smith's (1992) paper indicates that in six EU member states the budget shares on motor fuels rise steadily from the lowest to the third quartile of household equivalent income, but tend to level out between the third and fourth quartile. The evidence from the UK presented by Johnstone and Alavalapati (1998) points in the same direction: budget shares on transport expenditure rise quite strongly between the first and seventh expenditure decile, and thereafter level out. The study of Blow and Crawford (1997) shows similarly that in the UK middle-income households would be affected by fuel duty increases more than poorer or richer households. However, if only

---

[5]   Grainger and Kolstad (2009) make this point. The simulations of Bureau (2010) also demonstrate that the use of tax revenues could have a dramatic impact on the distributive effects of fuel taxation: 'income-based' recycling would be strongly regressive, while recycling revenues in equal amounts to every household or on the basis of household size would be globally progressive.

car-owning households are considered, the impact of fuel taxation would be regressive. On the other hand, the study of Bureau (2010) shows that a carbon tax on car fuels would be regressive in France, even taking into account behavioral responses, before revenue recycling,[6] but the final distributional impact would depend entirely on the form of revenue recycling.

Evidence from the Nordic Countries

The evidence on the regressivity of transport taxes referred to so far indicates that there are some differences among countries, notably that taxes on transport fuels seem to be more regressive in the US than in the EU member countries. In the following this evidence is complemented by an overview of less well-known studies done in the four Nordic countries. This evidence mostly confirms earlier findings on the absence of regressivity of transport-related taxes in the European countries. It should be pointed out that the level of transport and energy taxes is high in Nordic countries, also relative to other EU countries. The evidence presented below is based on static calculations and does not take into account behavioral responses or the use of tax revenues.

Finland
Evidence regarding the distributional effect of transport fuel taxes in Finland can be found in Tuuli (2009). He uses microdata on household consumption expenditure from the years 1985–2006. The households are divided into ten deciles on the basis of their total expenditure, and the expenditure shares of spending on motor fuels are calculated. The results show a pattern very similar to that in the UK as reported in Johnstone and Alavalapati (1998): the budget shares increase up to the sixth to eighth decile, depending on the year, and then level out, with the top decile having a somewhat smaller share than middle-income deciles. This is very much due to the fact that the share of car-owning households increases strongly with expenditure level. Among the car-owning households the budget shares spent on transport fuel are relatively equal.[7] The conclusion of the study is that taxes on transport fuels are not regressive in Finland and do not disproportionately burden low-income households. However, taxes on transport fuels would have regionally unequal impact in that they would put a higher burden on households in rural areas compared with those in urban areas.

Sweden
Ahola et al. (2009) provide similar evidence from Sweden using household expenditure survey data from the years 2004–2006. The burden of transport fuel taxes is higher in low-income deciles than in high-income deciles, when the disposable income is used as a denominator. However, using total expenditure the tax burden would increase from the lowest up to the eighth decile and slightly decrease thereafter, a pattern very similar to the one found in Finland. Including indirect effects of taxes in the calculation does

---

[6]   The results are obtained using the consumer surplus measure of tax burden.
[7]   This is different from the findings of Blow and Crawford (1997), according to which in the UK transport-related taxes would be strongly regressive among car-owning households.

not change the result. In light of this evidence transport taxes would not be regressive in Sweden either.

Norway

The paper by Aasness and Larsen (2003) applies a different methodology than the studies on Finland and Sweden. It calculates so-called Engel elasticites for several different transport modes, using consumer expenditure data from Norway (from the years 1986–1994). Engel elasticity is the percentage change in spending on a good when total expenditure increases by 1 percent. Low elasticities would imply that the good in question is a necessity and that the tax on it would be regressive. High elasticites imply that the incidence would be progressive. Aasness and Larsen find a relatively high Engel elasticity (1.21) for travel and transportation as a whole, which suggests that it is a luxury good. They then calculate Engel elasticites for different types of transport goods and find out that air flights, taxi rides, automobile purchases and road tolls have high Engel elasticities and thus taxing these goods would be progressive. In contrast, bus rides, mopeds and bicycles have very low Engel elasticites, as could be expected. Gasoline has also a relatively low Engel elasticity (0.70), implying that in Norway the gasoline tax would be regressive. This result is clearly different from those obtained in other Nordic countries. It is difficult to judge whether this is due to the different methodology applied, or to truly different consumption patterns in Norway.

Denmark

The study by Jacobsen et al. (2001) is very detailed and covers all forms of environmentally related taxes in Denmark. They calculate the shares of taxes paid in relation to household disposable income (adjusted for household size) and in relation to total expenditure, and divide the households into ten deciles on the basis of disposable income. The data is collected from different sources, with most expenditure data taken from 1997. Both the direct and indirect effects of taxes are included in the study.

The results show that all environmentally related taxes in Denmark are mildly regressive, when the tax burden is calculated as a share of household disposable income. There are, however, strong differences among different types of taxes. Transport-related taxes (including both fuel taxes and vehicle taxes) are strongly progressive, increasing from the lowest income decile to the ninth decile, while energy taxes and pollution taxes (which also include the CO_2 tax) are regressive, energy taxes somewhat more so than pollution taxes. Inside the group of transport-related taxes, registration taxes and fuel taxes are nearly equally progressive. The progressivity of transport-related taxes in Denmark seems, in fact, somewhat stronger than in Sweden or Finland. When total expenditure instead of disposable income is used as the basis of calculation, the regressivity of energy and pollution taxes nearly disappears, while the progressivity of transport-related taxes grows even stronger. The strong progressivity of transport taxes in relation to the other Nordic countries could be explained by the fact that car registration taxes are very high in Denmark (180 percent of the car price), which makes the car expensive and perhaps more a luxury good than in other countries.

DISTRIBUTIONAL EFFECTS OF ENERGY TAXATION IN THE EU

Introduction

This section presents empirical evidence on the distributional impact of energy taxation included in the impact assessment for the European Commission's potential revision of the EU Energy Tax Directive (ETD).[8] Cambridge Econometrics carried out a study for the European Commission in 2008, in which the impacts of several different policy options for the revision of the ETD were estimated. The E3ME model used in the study provided estimates on the impacts of policies on macroeconomic development, energy demand and CO_2 emissions. In addition, distributional effects on households were included in the study.

Policy scenarios were formed on the basis of policy options, which present several alternatives for the revision of the structure of the EU minimum tax rates on energy products. In the following the results of only the three most relevant policy options are reported. All of these policy options would introduce a CO_2 element to the EU energy tax framework. Options 3A and 3B would introduce a CO_2 component to the new minimum tax rates in addition to the energy component, while option 4 would set a uniform EU-wide CO_2 tax on top of the existing national tax rates. The rates are as follows:

- *Option 3A*: Energy component 0.15€/GJ for business use; 0.30€/GJ for non-business use; CO_2 component 20€/tCO$_2$ for 2013–2020 and 30€/tCO$_2$ from 2021; transport fuels 380€/1000l for both petrol and diesel (commercial diesel proposal).
- *Option 3B*: 0.15€/GJ for business use, 0.3€/GJ for non-business use; CO_2 component 10€/tCO$_2$ for 2013–2019, 20€/tCO$_2$ from 2020; transport fuels as in 3A. This option also includes transitional periods until 2020 for nine member states (BG, CZ, EE, HU, LV, LT, SK, RO, PL) to introduce the CO_2-based tax. In the model simulations it is assumed that these countries are exempted from carbon tax.
- *Option 4*: CO_2 tax 22€/tCO$_2$ for 2013–2020, 30€/tCO$_2$ from 2021.
- CO_2 tax is not levied on electricity in any of the scenarios.[9]

Policy scenarios also include other assumptions that are needed for modeling purposes but are not necessarily part of the policy options. The most important one concerns the use of tax revenues. It is assumed in all the scenarios (except one) that additional tax revenues are recycled in the form of reductions in the employers' social security contributions. This assumption turns out to have a relatively large impact on the results, including also distributional effects. To detect the effect of this assumption a scenario 3Blps was also simulated, in which revenue recycling takes the form of lump-sum transfers to house-

---

[8]   The full impact assessment can be found online at http://ec.europa.eu/taxation_customs/resources/documents/taxation/sec_2011_409_impact_assesment_part1_en.pdf.

[9]   It should be noted that the option retained in the policy proposal is not precisely any of these, but a combination of options 3A and 3B, with a new structure added for the tax rates on transport fuels (energy component of 9.6€/GJ to be reached gradually by 2018, plus a CO_2 component of 20€/tCO$_2$).

holds instead of the reduction of social security contributions, but is otherwise identical to the scenario 3B.

Another assumption of importance included in all the policy scenarios is that minimum tax rates remain constant in real terms over the period projected, implying that they are indexed to inflation.[10] The baseline scenario assumes, on the other hand, that current national tax rates stay constant in nominal terms during the projected period. Hence the difference between the tax rates in the baseline and policy scenarios grows over time and minimum rates become more and more binding on the member states.

Both the baseline scenario and policy scenario assume that an EU greenhouse gas emissions trading scheme is in place and that the price of allowances is determined endogenously on the basis of the demand for allowances and the number of allowances available. The baseline is calibrated to be consistent with the projections presented in the DG TREN publication *European Energy and Transport: Trends to 2030—Updated 2007*.

Impact on Consumer Prices

Since options 3A and 3B would affect only EU minimum rates, their impact on households depends on the extent to which they would increase national tax rates and thus consumer prices in the member states. Annex 12 of the impact assessment report presents calculations on the impact of policy options on the prices of energy products (assuming full pass-through). On the basis of these calculations the most important impact for non-business use would be on the price of natural gas, which would increase under option 3A in 21 member states and under option 3B in 11 member states, in some of them by substantial amounts (the price increases would range from 1 percent in Sweden to 87.5 percent in Bulgaria). Natural gas is the most commonly used heating fuel in the EU: it represents 36.7 percent of final non-business energy consumption in EU-27 (Annex 8). The next-most-commonly used heating oil for the households sector is gas oil (16 percent of the final energy consumption in EU-27). Under option 3A, 10 member states would experience some increase in consumer prices, but less than in the case of natural gas (from 0.04 percent in Poland to 8 percent in Lithuania). There would also be very substantial increases in the price of coal in nearly all the member states (23 member states under option 3A and 12 member states under option 3B, with the price increase exceeding 100 percent in 10 member states) due to its high CO_2 content and the low level of current national tax rates. The importance of coal as a heating fuel is small, only 2.3 percent in the EU as a whole, but it is more important in a few member states, such as Bulgaria, Ireland and Poland.

The price of electricity would not be affected under options 3A, 3B or 4.

The impact of policy options on the prices of transport fuels are not reported, but Annex 9 provides information on the impact of policy options on national tax rates on transport fuels. According to this information those rates would be increased in 15 member states under the commercial diesel proposal, which underlies the E3ME model simulations. (The number of member states affected by the new minima on diesel would be slightly higher, around 17, under the retained option in the proposal.) The national tax rate on petrol would be increased in only three member states.

---

[10]   This aspect was also retained in the final proposal.

It should be noted, however, that these numbers represent only immediate effects. In model simulations far more member states would be affected by the end of the projected periods (2020 and 2030), as the scenarios assume that the minima are indexed to inflation, while this is not the case in the baseline. On the other hand, no behavioral responses are taken into account in these calculations.

DISTRIBUTIONAL EFFECTS ON HOUSEHOLDS

Table 9.1 shows the impact of a 10 percent increase in gas and electricity prices on real household disposable income in EU-27 (percent change). In the first part the impact is given for five income quintiles and in the second part for occupational and geographical groups. It should be noted that the tables do not represent any of the policy options and are presented for the sake of comparison. They are based on a simple calculation, in which neither the use of tax revenues nor behavioral responses are taken into account.

This evidence corresponds to the findings of many other static analyses. Low-income households would lose a bigger share of their income than high-income households, when the price of domestic energy is increased and when the use of tax revenues is not taken into account. In this sense the taxes on domestic energy are regressive. Table 9.1 B reveals also that unemployed, retired and inactive households would be more affected than the active population, and that households living in rural areas would be slightly more affected than the urban population.

The distributional impacts of policy options 3A, 3B and 4 are shown in Table 9.2. These results are the outcome of the simulation of the policy scenarios described above and hence also include an assumption of the use of tax revenues, which is the reduction of the employers' social security contributions in all the scenarios except 3Blps, in which

Table 9.1A *Changes in real household incomes (percent) from a 10 percent increase in electricity and gas prices for five income quintiles, EU-27*

All households	1st quintile	2nd quintile	3rd quintile	4th quintile	5th quintile
−0.54	−0.69	−0.65	−0.59	−0.53	−0.43

Source: Cambridge Econometrics (2008), reproduced in European Commission (2011).

Table 9.1B *Changes in real household incomes (percent) from a 10 percent increase in electricity and gas prices for socioeconomic groups, EU-27*

Manual workers	Non-manual workers	Self-employed	Unemployed	Retired	Inactive	Densely populated area	Sparsely populated area
−0.53	−0.44	−0.51	−0.59	−0.67	−0.59	−0.51	−0.56

Source: Cambridge Econometrics (2008), reproduced in European Commission (2011).

Table 9.2 Change in real household incomes (percent) in 2030 in comparison with the baseline, EU-27 weighted averages

	Option 3A	Option 3B	Option 3Blsp	Option 4	Option 4bis
All households	0.11	0.09	−0.05	0.41	0.12
1st quintile	0.10	0.09	−0.01	0.39	−0.23
2nd quintile	0.10	0.09	−0.04	0.36	−0.16
3rd quintile	0.10	0.09	−0.05	0.36	−0.01
4th quintile	0.11	0.09	−0.05	0.39	0.18
5th quintile	0.13	0.09	−0.06	0.49	0.47
Manual workers	0.11	0.09	−0.06	0.39	0.21
Non-manual workers	0.13	0.09	−0.06	0.46	0.39
Self-employed	0.11	0.09	−0.06	0.42	0.22
Unemployed	0.10	0.09	0.03	0.40	−0.05
Retired	0.09	0.09	0.02	0.37	−0.24
Inactive	0.13	0.11	0.03	0.43	−0.07
Densely populated area	0.12	0.10	−0.05	0.47	0.21
Sparsely populated area	0.08	0.07	−0.05	0.31	0.02

Source: Cambridge Econometrics (2008), reproduced in European Commission (2011).

lump-sum transfers to households is assumed instead. Option 4bis is otherwise the same as option 4, but it excludes transport fuels.

The table gives rise to several observations. First, household real disposable income would increase in all income quintiles and socioeconomic groups under policy options 3A, 3B, and 4 compared with the baseline. This is largely due to the revenue recycling assumption underlying the three scenarios. The reduction of the employers' social security contributions would decrease labor costs, and in the E3ME model this would have the effect of boosting employment and decreasing domestic prices, which in turn would have a positive impact on real income, consumption and economic activity in general.

Secondly, the beneficial impact is fairly equally distributed across income quintiles and socioeconomic groups and thus the policy package as a whole is distributionally neutral. The regressivity that can be observed in Table 9.1 disappears. In scenarios 3A and 4 one can, however, observe slight regressivity in the sense that the highest-income quintile would benefit somewhat more than the other quintiles.

Thirdly, the impact of revenue recycling can be seen by comparing options 3B and 3Blps. Lump-sum transfers would make this scenario highly progressive, as the low-income groups would benefit the most, but at the same time would also be economically less efficient, as all the households would lose somewhat compared with the baseline scenario. One can also observe that socioeconomic groups usually considered to be the most vulnerable (retired, unemployed and inactive) would be the greatest beneficiaries of this policy.

A comparison of options 4 and 4bis reveals the importance of taxes on transport fuels for distributional outcome. Excluding transport fuels from option 4 makes the policy highly regressive, even taking into account the favorable effects of revenue recycling: the lowest quintiles would lose and the higher quintiles and the socioeconomic groups representing non-manual workers and the self-employed would reap the gain. The results imply that taxes on transport fuels alone are, at the EU average level, sufficiently progressive to counteract the regressivity of other types of energy taxes. These results are very much in accordance with the evidence found earlier in the other European studies.

Differences Among the Member States

Tables 9.1 and 9.2 show distributional effects only at the EU average level, and could hide substantial differences among individual countries. The same information as in Table 9.2 is contained in Annex 18 of the impact assessment report for each member state separately, except that the latter projects up to 2020 instead of 2030.

An inspection of this information reveals that options 3A and 3B would be distributionally fairly neutral in most member states with the exception of UK, Ireland, Hungary, Luxembourg and Romania, where slight regressivity can be observed. This corresponds to the findings of Barker and Köhler (1998), who also found that energy taxation tends to be more regressive in the UK and Ireland compared with other European countries. Concerning the UK and Ireland it should be noted that the exemptions from taxes on domestic energy accorded to the household sector in these two countries are not taken into account in the baseline or in the policy scenarios, so there is an impact of higher prices on domestic fuels.

The progressivity of option 3Blsp and thus the inequality-reducing effect of lump-sum transfers is confirmed in practically all countries.

With respect to options 4 and 4bis there is somewhat more variation. Option 4 would be slightly regressive in a number of countries (AU, BE, DE, EE, FR, HU, IT, LU, RO) but would be progressive in a number of other countries (CZ, DK, FI, LT, LV, NL, PL, PT, SE), while in the remaining countries it would be neutral or somewhat nonlinear. Excluding transport fuels from this scenario would make the policy option more regressive in all cases, that is, it would change from progressive to neutral or regressive or from regressive to more regressive, which is in accordance with the evidence on the progressivity of transport taxes in the EU as a whole.

CONCLUSIONS

It is often believed that ecological tax reforms are as a whole regressive, which would imply that their costs are disproportionately borne by low-income households. For this reason political resistance to such reforms is strong in many countries. The evidence presented in this chapter shows that this conclusion should be qualified in a number of ways.

First, the distributional outcome of the reform depends on the combination of tax bases on which the reform is applied. Taxes on electricity and heating tend to be regressive in most countries, while taxes on transport fuel and vehicles are not necessarily so. In fact, they seem to be sufficiently progressive in most European countries that they offset the regressivity of other energy taxes. Hence, the tax reforms which relied on both energy and transport taxation could be distributionally neutral in European conditions.

Secondly, the final distributional impact of the reforms also depends crucially on how the tax revenues are used. Cutting labor or capital tax rates without targeting low-income households, although economically efficient, would not make the tax reform more progressive, but could have an opposite impact. On the other hand, E3ME modeling results suggest that both economic efficiency and a distributionally neutral tax reform can be achieved, if tax revenues are recycled in the form of cuts in the employers' social security contributions. This is because in the model context such cuts would considerably boost employment and private consumption. It should be kept in mind, however, that the distributionally neutral outcome is achieved in this case also only if transport-related taxes are included in the reform.

Targeting income tax cuts to low-income households or using the tax revenues to finance lump-sum transfers are effective ways to ensure the distributionally fair outcome of the reform, although economically they are not as efficient as the other forms of revenue recycling.

Thirdly, the evidence indicates that with respect to regressivity there are considerable differences among countries. The US studies imply that in the US ecological tax reform would be regressive also if they include transport-related taxes, and thus energy taxation as a whole is more regressive in the US than in the European countries. There are also differences among the European countries. The results of Smith (1992) and Barker and Koehler (1998) indicate that energy taxation tends to be more regressive in the UK and Ireland compared with other European countries (Smith [1992] only compares the UK and Ireland to Southern European countries). The results of the Cambridge Econometrics study, which includes all EU-27 member states, points in the same direction. The evidence from the Nordic countries also implies that ecological tax reforms would be only mildly regressive or not regressive at all in these countries, if transport taxes are included.

There is no obvious single explanation for these differences. One factor that could play a role is pointed out in the Copenhagen Economics study of 2007. The study showed that the difference in food consumption shares between poor and rich households is greater in the countries with higher income inequality (measured by the Gini coefficient) than in the countries with lower income inequality. The countries with low income inequality and a small difference in food consumption shares include in this comparison Continental European and Nordic countries, while the countries with higher income inequality and a greater difference in food consumption shares include the UK, Portugal, Greece, Italy and Spain.

It could be assumed that this applies also to domestic energy, which is a similarly necessary good as food. If this were the case, the high equality of initial income distribution would make the tax reforms relying on energy taxes less regressive and could be one of the factors explaining the observed differences with respect to the regressivity of energy taxes among the US, the UK and other European countries. (But this could not explain the differences observed by Smith [1992] among the UK, Ireland and Southern European countries, since all these countries have higher income inequality than Continental European or Nordic countries.) If such a negative correlation between income equality and the regressivity of an ecological tax reform indeed existed, which at this stage can only be considered a working hypothesis, then the policy implication would be that progressive income taxation would be a good way to counteract the regressivity of indirect taxes levied on goods such as food and domestic energy.

Concerning the observed cross-country differences in the regressivity of transport fuel taxes, there are again several possible explanations. One of them could be the difference in the quality of public transport. The supply of good-quality public transport could make a private car more a luxury good, the use of which would increase strongly with income level. Also the high level of vehicle taxes, exemplified by Denmark, could have a similar impact. As a whole, the cross-country comparison of evidence on the regressivity of energy and transport taxation reveals some interesting patterns and could have potentially important policy implications. These observations are, however, preliminary and it would require much more empirical research to draw any firm conclusions in this regard.

REFERENCES

Aasness, J. and E.R. Larsen (2003), 'Distributional effects of environmental taxes on transportation', *Journal of Consumer Policy*, **26**, 297–300.

Ahola, H., E. Carlsson and T. Sterner (2009), 'Är bensinskatten regressiv?' [Is the gasoline tax regressive?], *Ekonomisk Debatt*, **2**, 71–77.

Barker, T. and J. Köhler (1998), 'Equity and ecotax reform in the EU: achieving a 10% reduction in CO_2 emissions using excise duties', *Fiscal Studies*, **19** (4), 375–402.

Blow, L. and I. Crawford (1997), 'The distributional effects of taxes on private motoring', London, UK: The Institute of Fiscal Studies.

Bureau, B. (2010), 'Distributional effects of a carbon tax on car fuels in France', CERNA Working Paper 2010-19.

Cambridge Econometrics (2008), 'Review of the Energy Taxation Directive: final modelling results. A report for DG TAXUD, European Commission'.

Copenhagen Economics (2007), 'Study on reduced VAT rates applied to goods and services in the Member States of the European Union. Final report to the European Commission.'

European Commission (2011): 'Impact assessment', SEC (2011) 409. Accompanying document to the proposal for a Council Directive amending Directive 2003/96/EC restructuring the Community framework for the taxation of energy products and electricity.

Fullerton, D. (2008), 'Distributional effects of environmental and energy policy. An introduction', NBER Working Paper 14241.

Fullerton, D. (2010), 'Six distributional effects of environmental policy', CESifo Working paper 3299.

Fullerton, D. and G.E. Metcalf (2002), 'Tax incidence', in A.J. Auerbach and M. Feldstein (eds), *Handbook of Public Economics*, vol. 4, Elsevier Science B.V.

Grainger, C.A. and C.D. Kolstad (2009), 'Who pays a price on carbon?', NBER Working Paper 15239.

Jacobsen, H.K., K. Birr-Pedersen and M. Wier (2001), 'Fordelingsvirkninger af energi- og miljöafgifter' [Distributional effects of energy and environmental taxes], Roskilde, DK: Risö National Laboratory.

Johnstone, N. and J. Alavalapati (1998), 'The distributional effects of environmental tax reform', International Institute for Environment and Development, Discussion Paper 98-01.

Metcalf, G.E., A. Mathur and K.A. Hassett (2010), 'Distributional impacts of comprehensive climate policy package', NBER Working Paper 16101.

Poterba, J.M. (1991), 'Is the gasoline tax regressive?', NBER Working Paper 3578.

Rausch, S., G.E. Metcalf and J.M. Reilly (2011), 'Distributional impacts of carbon pricing: a general equilibrium approach with micro-data for households', NBER Working paper 17087.

Smith, S. (1992), 'The distributional consequences of taxes on energy and the carbon content of fuels', *European Economy*, **51**, 241–67.

Stiglitz, J.E. (1998), *Economics of the Public Sector*, 2nd ed., New York, US: W.W. Norton & Company Inc.

Tuuli, J. (2009), 'Polttoaineverojen ja muiden ympäristöverojen tulonjakovaikutukset' [Distributional effects of fuel and other environmental taxes],VATT muistiot, Valtion taloudellinen tutkimuskeskus (VATT memorandum, Government Institute for Economic Research], Helsinki, Finland.

10 The political acceptability of carbon taxes: lessons from British Columbia

Mark Jaccard

INTRODUCTION

Governments seeking to reduce greenhouse gas (GHG) emissions confront a stark policy tradeoff. Noncompulsory policies like information programs and subsidies are politically acceptable, but largely ineffective by themselves. Compulsory policies that price emissions or regulate technologies and fuels can be effective, but only if their stringency is at politically risky levels. For the last two decades, most industrialized countries have favored noncompulsory policies, and this explains in part the failure to achieve emissions-reduction targets (Simpson et al. 2007).

However, the gradually emerging evidence of domestic climate policy failure has increased pressure on policymakers to seriously consider compulsory policy options, ranging from emissions pricing to regulations. Emissions pricing—via carbon taxes[1] or cap-and-trade schemes—are preferred by economists, as they should achieve environmental goals at the lowest societal cost. Regulations on technologies and fuels are likely to be less economically efficient, but their price impacts are not as readily apparent to voters, which is why some regulations are politically palatable (except when they prohibit technologies that many consumers value highly).

Emissions pricing is politically challenging, and this is especially so for carbon taxes, the most transparent instrument in terms of directly connecting, in the eyes of voters, a politician's decision and an increase in energy prices. This explains in part why cap-and-trade is often seen as a politically preferable means of emissions pricing. Even though, compared to a carbon tax, it has additional transaction costs, in the form of commissions for permit traders and extra government administration, the impact of the policy on energy prices is not as easily attributable to political decisions. Thus, politicians may favor cap-and-trade over a carbon tax when trading off between economic efficiency and political acceptability (Baldwin 2008; Harrison 2010).

In spite of the political advantages of avoiding carbon taxes in favor of noncompulsory policies or, if necessary, cap-and-trade, the Canadian province of British Columbia (BC) nonetheless introduced a substantial carbon tax in 2008, set initially at \$10 per ton of CO_2 and scheduled to rise in \$5 annual increments to \$30 by 2012. The tax is identical for all fossil fuel-related CO_2 emissions throughout the economy (residential, industrial, transportation), which collectively represent 70–75 percent of provincial GHG emissions. Remaining untaxed GHG emissions, which come from landfills, agricultural activity

---

[1]   A tax on GHG emissions is frequently called a carbon tax, which may apply only to CO_2 or to all GHG emissions.

and certain industrial processes (cement, aluminum, natural gas processing), are slated for future taxation or inclusion in a cap-and-trade scheme, but the timeline is uncertain.

In this chapter, I present political, economic and social perspectives on the design, implementation and political trials of BC's carbon tax. The chapter explains why the tax was implemented, and provides details of the tax and explains their political or social rationale. It then describes how the tax barely survived a significant political challenge in the 2009 provincial election, assesses the extent to which this anecdotal evidence from BC confirms or challenges literature on the politics of environmental taxation and the political prospects of carbon taxes, and speculates on the future of the BC carbon tax. The conclusion suggests some lessons from this policy experience and avenues for future research.

CAUSAL EXPLANATIONS FOR BC's CARBON TAX

Generic and BC-specific Drivers of Compulsory Climate Policies

Since the late 1980s, federal and provincial governments in Canada have continuously made strong commitments to reduce GHG emissions while implementing a recurring selection of voluntary policies (moral exhortations, information programs, subsidies) that they argued would achieve these targets. While some leading environmentalists and academics expressed doubts about policy effectiveness, these criticisms gained traction with the media and public as evidence showed emissions continuing to rise. The line in Figure 10.1 shows the growing level of Canadian GHG emissions since 1990, along with

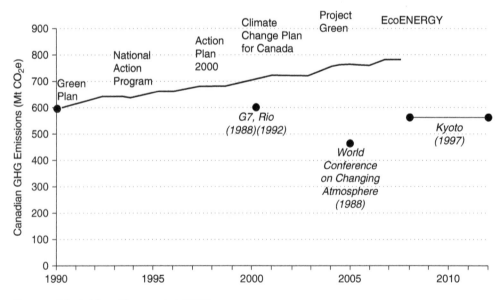

Source: Adapted from Simpson et al. (2007).

Figure 10.1 Canadian emissions targets, climate policies and emissions

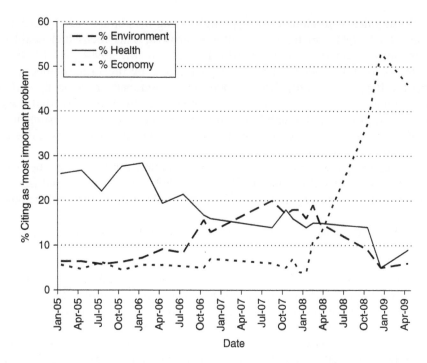

Figure 10.2   Trends in Canadians' priorities

the targets governments set below the line and the names of policy initiatives intended to achieve the targets above the line. (Dates when targets were established are in parentheses.) A similar figure could be drawn for every Canadian province, displaying the disparity between political promises and actual outcomes. By 2007, Canada's emissions were 26 percent above their 1990 levels, with no slowdown in sight.

This growing awareness of policy failure in Canada and other industrialized countries coincided in the mid-2000s with a widespread increase in concern for climate change, as witnessed by the public interest in Al Gore's movie, *An Inconvenient Truth*, the Stern report on climate change for the UK government, and the fourth assessment report of the UN's Intergovernmental Panel on Climate Change. Figure 10.2 shows the responses of Canadians to surveys asking about their priorities, taken by the Environics polling firm during the period January 2005 to April 2009. For over a year, in the 2007–2008 period, the environment surpassed health care and the economy as the leading concern for many Canadians.

In response to similar concerns in other countries, in mid-decade politicians throughout the industrialized world elevated climate policy to a prominent role in their political platforms. In North America, California's governor Arnold Schwarzenegger crusaded for aggressive GHG reductions and backed his rhetoric with legislation to enshrine emissions-reduction targets and compulsory policies to achieve them. British Columbia, a province with 4.5 million inhabitants, followed California's lead, and in some respects surpassed it, with an aggressive clean electricity requirement and then a carbon tax.

In the five years following his election in 2001, BC's premier Gordon Campbell showed little interest in climate policy, emphasizing his commitment to balance the government's budget and increase economic growth. This focus had enabled him to assemble a center-right coalition (the Liberals) in the 1990s, which, with electoral success in 2001, ended ten years of governance by the social democratic New Democratic Party (the NDP). But in 2006–2008, Campbell dramatically shifted his focus to climate-related issues, creating a 'climate action secretariat' that answered directly to him, which had a mandate to direct and coordinate all government ministries and agencies in the rapid development of ambitious provincial emissions targets and aggressive climate policies.

This represented a wholesale political transformation for both Campbell and the members of his center-right coalition. Harrison (2009) suggests additional factors that explain why such a significant political shift in BC could occur in such a short time.

- The Canadian parliamentary system concentrates political power with the prime minister federally and premiers provincially. And the first-past-the-post electoral system usually results in majority governments, which, in concert with norms of party discipline, enable political leaders and their close advisors to dominate the policy agenda and to quickly enact legislation to meet their objectives.
- In addition to this inherent concentration of power, Campbell's Liberals had won a resounding victory in 2001 and had just been reaffirmed with a second victory in 2005. With the next election not until 2009, and with a substantial lead in voter polling, Campbell's ability to drive the policy agenda was exceptionally high.
- A significant proportion of British Columbians see environmental activism and stewardship as a hallmark of their province, including initiatives of national and even international significance. There is some pride in the fact that Greenpeace was started in Vancouver. The city is also home to David Suzuki, an internationally renowned scientist, environmental activist and media personality. Environmentalists have achieved significant victories over the years in confrontations with the forest and mining industries. The Green Party, which has negligible electoral prospects in the first-past-the-post electoral system, nonetheless can receive 10 percent of votes in any given election. It would receive even more except that the mainstream political parties of both right and left have learned the importance of catering to environmentally concerned voters. Finally, some British Columbians view their province as playing a role in Canada similar to the innovative role of California in the United States.
- By the 2000s, the massive pine forests of BC's interior were being devastated by a beetle infestation, which scientists attributed to more moderate winter temperatures. Aerial photos showed huge areas of the province carpeted by 'red forests,' the color of dying pine trees. Then, a series of extreme windstorms hit the province, in one case downing many trees in Vancouver's treasured Stanley Park. Talk in the media about tangible evidence of climate change increased in step with these incidents.
- Finally, as an avid reader and new grandfather, the premier confessed to having recently shifted his literature focus to the climate risks from GHG emissions and to being profoundly affected by a recent trip to China during which he considered the effects of its growing economy on the health of the planet.

With these factors concentrating political power in his hands, supporting environmental activism in BC and raising public concern about climate change, Campbell was able to adopt an aggressive policy agenda and to carry his surprised and at times reluctant center-right party with him. In just 18 months, spanning 2007 and 2008, his government adopted aggressive GHG reduction targets and a large number of climate policies.

The Carbon Tax as One of BC's Many Climate Policies

The factors that drove Campbell to aggressive action on GHG emissions do not explain why his government specifically implemented a carbon tax. But the reason may relate more to a desire to apply all available policy tools (what some called a 'shotgun approach') rather than to any particular preference for carbon taxes over other options. By late 2008, the government's climate-related directives and legislation included (BC Government 2008):

- renewable ('clean') energy requirements for electricity generation;
- legislation to enable an emissions cap-and-trade system;
- a low carbon fuel standard;
- tighter energy-efficiency targets and regulations;
- tighter vehicle emission regulations;
- expanded investment in public transit;
- requirements for carbon neutrality in provincial government operations and facilities;
- obligations on municipal governments for GHG reductions; and
- a carbon tax.

In January 2007, over a year before the introduction of the carbon tax, the government announced its 90 percent 'clean electricity' policy for the state-owned electric utility, BC Hydro. This policy is comparable to the renewable portfolio standard applied in over half of US states and in several other countries, although in BC its application is to 'new' investments. BC's existing electricity generation is 95 percent hydropower, but large hydro dams and reservoirs are no longer politically acceptable. Since the province's plentiful natural gas and coal resources are the cheapest options for new electricity, BC Hydro had been planning to build a large natural gas plant, and in 2006 had signed letters of intent with two proponents of coal-fired power projects. The 'clean energy requirement' led to immediate abandonment of these fossil fuel pursuits, triggering a dramatic rush to small-scale hydropower projects by independent power producers. While it is not readily apparent to the public, this climate-driven policy will cause significant increases in electricity rates (Jaccard et al. 2011).[2]

Another significant policy was the passage of enabling legislation to allow the province

---

[2] Because BC has a strong lobby group for public ownership of the electric sector, which claims that rising rates are due to the high costs of electricity from new private power producers, the decision to turn away from fossil fuels is rarely mentioned in the media as causing higher electricity prices. Instead, independent power producers are accused of charging excessive rates for providing BC Hydro with wholesale electricity.

to develop a cap-and-trade system, which it intended to link with the Western Climate Initiative of US states and Canadian provinces. The assumption was that within two years BC emissions would be subject to pricing in a cap-and-trade system, which would be more ambitious than Europe's emissions trading system in that all emissions would be covered, not just those from industrial plants and electricity generators.

With everything moving so fast on the policy front, some business leaders and academics started to publicly question the potential complications and inefficiencies from policy redundancy. The government's response was that while care should be taken, speed was important and all available tools should be pursued. Once in place, policies could be integrated and coordinated.

It was within this context that the government had its climate action secretariat and finance ministry prepare a carbon tax for implementation with the annual budget in February 2008. The general assumption was that emissions pricing was coming soon to North America, so while BC would show leadership with its carbon tax, it would not be acting alone for long. The easiest way to be an emissions pricing leader was with a carbon tax because, unlike cap-and-trade, it is quick and easy from an administrative perspective. Government simply changes the rate of tax that it already applies to fuels. Implementation requires no extra bureaucrats, no extra employees for businesses, and no lengthy negotiations as would occur when determining the initial allowances in a cap-and-trade system. In fact, because of budget secrecy requirements, the government could argue that open negotiations on the tax were inadvisable.

Inside government, discussions about the design of the carbon tax needed to address several issues, including the level of the tax and the use of the revenues it generated. While environmentalists might suggest spending the tax revenues on GHG-reducing actions like transit infrastructure and energy efficiency subsidies to households, a key political consideration was how to convince voters and businesses of the benefits of the tax. This led government to the conclusion that the tax should be 'revenue-neutral' in that all revenue would be returned to firms and households via income tax cuts and direct payments to low-income households (who pay little or no income tax and thus would not benefit from a tax cut).

While Campbell and his advisors were probably aware that the carbon tax posed a substantial political risk, the counter-arguments were that the tax could be implemented quickly, the income tax cuts provided a positive upside, and, in any case, the tax would soon be superceded by or subsumed within a regional, national or North American cap-and-trade system for emissions pricing. Moreover, even the opposition NDP had spoken in favor of emissions pricing and had passed a resolution at its recent policy convention in favor of carbon taxes (Grandia 2008). This seemed to mitigate the political risks for the government.

As it turned out, however, public attention on the carbon tax was far higher than the government anticipated, skepticism about its revenue-neutrality was widespread, and shortly after its announcement the NDP made opposition to the tax the central pillar of its year-long electoral campaign. But before I describe these survival challenges of the carbon tax, the next section provides details on how its design sought to address the goal of political acceptability, especially by addressing concerns about its fairness.

CARBON TAX DESIGN AND RATIONALE

Main Elements of the BC Carbon Tax

The BC carbon tax, which came into effect in July 2008, charges a uniform tax for fossil fuel-originated CO_2 emissions in the BC economy (BC Ministry of Finance 2010a).[3] A legislated schedule increases the initial rate of $10 per ton of CO_2 by $5 in each subsequent year until 2012, when the rate will reach $30. At $10, the tax increases the price of gasoline by 2.41 cents per liter and at $30 by 7.24 cents per liter. The tax is collected using the existing fuel taxation system, with retailers collecting from final consumers, wholesalers collecting from retailers, and the government collecting from wholesalers. Exempted from the tax are (1) fuels used on ships and planes whose origin or destination is outside the province, (2) fuels used as feedstock in production processes and (3) fuels exported from the province. Other carbon and noncarbon GHG emissions are, for the time being, exempted from the tax, meaning that it applies to 70–75 percent of total provincial GHG emissions.[4]

In order to be revenue-neutral to government, in addition to the measures identified previously, incentive payments were designated for municipal governments, related to their demonstrated efforts to reduce emissions. This mechanism was created after implementation in response to municipalities' complaints that they paid the tax on fuels consumed but were ineligible for income tax recycling.

In the first two years, the specific recycling mechanisms were:

- the income tax rates on the bottom two personal income tax brackets were reduced by 2 percent for 2008 and by 5 percent in 2009;
- a quarterly payment for low-income earners (called a tax credit) was set to a possible maximum of $100 per adult and $30 per child in 2008, increasing 5 percent in 2009; and
- the corporate income tax rate was reduced by 1 percent in each of the first two years and is projected to continue falling as revenues from the tax climb (small businesses' income tax will fall from 3.5 percent down to 0 by 2012 and large businesses' from 12 percent down to 7 percent, one of the lowest rates in the G8).

In the two fiscal years from mid-2008 to mid-2010, the carbon tax generated total revenues of $848 million, while the tax credits and income tax cuts reduced projected government revenue by $1042 million (BC Ministry of Finance 2010b).[5] This shortfall of $200 million suggests that the government had erred by excessively reducing corporate and personal income taxes. However, since the revenues from the tax and the revenue

---

[3]   The tax is based on the carbon content in fuels, not actually on CO_2 emitted. The crude assumption is that all carbon in fuels will be released eventually as CO_2.

[4]   In its initial guise, the BC carbon tax is strictly a tax on fossil fuel-originated CO_2. CO_2 from other sources (cement and aluminum production, deforestation) is excluded, as are other GHGs such as methane from urban landfills, agriculture and natural gas industry leaks (called fugitive emissions).

[5]   The Canadian dollar was near parity with the US dollar in the period 2010–2011.

losses from income tax cuts are only known with certainty in hindsight, government may have deliberately erred on the side of losing revenue from the tax reform in order to avoid having opponents claim that the policy caused a net increase in taxes in any given year.

Rationale for the Design

From several perspectives, the BC carbon tax approaches the economist's ideal for economically efficient policy. First, it applies the same price for every unit of fossil fuel-originated GHG emissions everywhere in the economy. Economists argue that society has the best chance of minimizing the costs of emissions reduction if every unit of emissions faces the same price, incentivizing each potential emitter to reduce emissions up to the point where the cost of the last unit abated from each activity is equal throughout the economy.

Second, the carbon tax starts at a modest level but ramps up at a set schedule. This provides emissions price certainty for investors in GHG abatement and for innovators who are developing new ways of abating emissions. It also gives firms and households time to adjust so that they make the right investment choices (at the time of capital stock renewal) without requiring premature retirement of existing buildings and equipment because of a sudden increase in certain energy prices (Nordhaus 1992).

Third, the carbon tax revenue is used to decrease taxes on corporate and personal income, which should reduce the dampening effect that these taxes have on economic activity. This potential to use carbon taxation to achieve environmental objectives while designing the revenue-recycling mechanism to increase economic output is referred to as the 'double dividend' (Goulder 1995).

This ability of the BC government to implement a carbon tax mechanism that ranks highly in terms of an economic ideal stems in part from the fact that the tax was not negotiated with interest groups but was instead presented as a 'fait accompli' with the provincial budget. The climate action secretariat had worked closely with only the premier, his immediate policy advisors and the ministry of finance. They had confidential exchanges with some academic experts, but mostly designed the policy in seclusion from the messy world of interest group lobbying and open debate in the media.

Of course, the carbon tax system does not perfectly match the economist's ideal. The tax does not yet apply to all GHG emissions, although the expectation at the time was that it soon would. While it has a price schedule for its first five years, silence about its future growth path means that it lacks the 20-year price certainty that would be especially helpful to those contemplating long-lived investments with major GHG implications. While its recycling mechanism has double-dividend attributes by providing income tax cuts, the literature suggests that the greatest boost to economic output would occur if the tax recycling were especially directed to corporate tax cuts (Ballard et al. 1985). Instead, finance officials claim that initially two-thirds of the tax revenue comes from businesses, which receive only one-third of the recycled revenue. This may balance over time, as many businesses can raise their prices to consumers to cover higher energy input costs. But businesses that export or face strong external competition for domestic sales are price-constrained and the higher input costs could affect their performance relative to foreign competitors.

Indeed, the designers of the carbon tax faced challenges typical for any reformers of the tax system, namely determining and where desirable mitigating the policy's impact (called 'incidence') on specific groups in society and addressing perceptions of unfairness, regardless of their evidentiary basis. In the next section, I describe complaints about the fairness of the tax from specific social groups and how the government responded. I also assess the extent to which these concerns were based on evidence. Then, I describe how the tax became the prime target of partisan politics during an election campaign.

SHORT-TERM SURVIVAL OF THE CARBON TAX

Assessing and Addressing Claims of Unfair Tax Incidence

In announcing the carbon tax in 2008, the government emphasized its revenue-neutrality, and initially this induced several supportive public comments from the business community, which had previously feared the government might use carbon tax revenue to boost general spending (Vancouver Board of Trade 2008). But soon various interests expressed concerns and even hostility with respect to the incidence of the tax, and this eventually dominated the media's attention. Arguing from simple assumptions, groups claiming carbon tax unfairness included: (1) advocates for the poor, (2) northern residents who live in a colder climate, (3) rural residents with no access to public transit, (4) suburban long-distance vehicle commuters, (5) trucking firms, (6) farmers, (7) municipal governments and (8) energy-intensive industries such as cement, lime, natural gas production and coal mining.

The academic literature suggests that there are major political challenges to the application of tax policy for environmental ends, meaning that the government needed to take these concerns seriously. As Olson (1971) noted, public policies are especially at risk if their benefits are diffuse but their costs are concentrated on a much smaller number of people. Those facing concentrated costs are highly motivated to overturn the policy, while the much larger number with diffuse benefits lack the incentive to defend it. Kahneman et al. (1991) found that people tend to value losses greater than financially equivalent gains. This suggests that people would react more strongly to their losses from paying the carbon tax than from their gains from lower income taxes, even where the latter may exceed the former. Caplan (2007) extends this argument of cognitive bias to argue that democratic decision-making will frequently lead to outcomes that are counter to society's best interests and that even individual groups will push for policy outcomes that are against their own interests. Focusing on environmental taxation, Kallbekken and Saelen (2011) note that biases against certain types of evidence pose specific challenges to carbon tax reform, especially because of distrust of government claims of revenue-neutrality and widespread disbelief that the tax system can be used to change technology and behavior, and thus achieve environmental outcomes.

In the case of regressive social impacts, the designers of BC's carbon tax were determined from the outset to immunize the policy from criticism that it would increase income inequality. They set the tax credit for people who paid little or no income tax at a level that would ensure that almost all people in this category would be net winners from the tax and revenue-recycling mechanism. (They could not be certain of universal gain by low-income earners because of the chance that in rare cases a low-income person might nonetheless consume abnormally large quantities of fossil fuel products.) Within months of the tax's announcement, a left-of-center think tank (normally opposed to the Campbell government) released an analysis showing that people in the lowest income categories would be net beneficiaries for at least the first two years of the tax, but would require ongoing increases in the tax credit in years three to five (Lee and Sanger 2008). This qualified support reduced opposition from this direction and even garnered public support from some poverty activists.

Complaints against the tax by northern and rural residents were more difficult to assess because of a lack of detailed information on the relative energy use by households in different parts of the province. A simple analysis of data from energy utilities and federal government surveys showed that consumption of fossil fuel products by northern and rural residents was not particularly higher than that of other provincial residents (Rivers 2008). Buildings in the north have much better insulation standards. Rural residents use more untaxed wood for space heating and have a greater opportunity to switch to wood. Urban residents, in contrast, often commute greater distances by vehicle than northern residents in spite of having more public transit options. In fact, this was the reason for opposition to the policy from suburban commuters in greater Vancouver in the south of the province, which accounts for half the provincial population. In the face of these conflicting claims and conflicting evidence, and the potential administrative complexity of trying to do something, the government considered but eventually rejected the argument that the tax or its revenue-recycling mechanism should somehow vary by location. Those who felt harmed and the mayors of northern communities launched a campaign to overturn the carbon tax within just a few months of its announcement (Bailey 2008).[6]

The government also rejected the arguments of truckers and farmers that they should be compensated because of the importance of fuel for their businesses. The government noted that each firm and its competitors faced the same rising input costs and so eventually they should be able to pass these costs along to final consumers. Even though academic researchers supported this argument, many truckers and farmers were not convinced and their associations continued to lobby to overturn or modify the policy.

As noted, the government did eventually respond to the claim of municipal governments that they should not be excluded from the tax-recycling mechanism. It implemented a policy that returned the tax revenue paid by each municipality if it used the revenue to reduce its emissions, such as by better insulating buildings, switching heating fuels and improving the efficiency of vehicle fleets.

Energy-intensive industries also argued that the tax harmed them. While government acknowledged that GHG-intensive industries like cement and lime might be competitively threatened by foreign companies not subject to GHG emissions pricing, it refused to adjust the carbon tax policy to address this concern. Instead, it established a task force with industry involvement to consider sector-specific impacts of the rising carbon tax and options to mitigate the loss of market share to foreign competitors.

---

[6]   Later, in its 2010 budget, the government tried to address these perceptions of regional unfairness by establishing a special property tax credit for rural and northern residents, up to a maximum of $200.

Partisan Politics and Survival of the Carbon Tax[7]

The growing chorus of interest groups, prominent individuals and media pundits attacking the carbon tax helped convince the NDP opposition, led by Carol James, that the tax presented a strategic opportunity to undermine the Campbell government's popularity and perhaps win the upcoming May 2009 election. Thus, in June 2008, the NDP launched its 'axe the tax' campaign, in which it promised, if elected, to repeal the tax because it was 'unfair to working British Columbians' and 'gave breaks to industry but not ordinary people' (James 2008). The NDP and other opponents focused on the tax increase side of the policy and ignored the income tax cuts. When pressed for its position on climate policy, the NDP claimed it would replace the carbon tax with a cap-and-trade system applied only to industrial emissions, provide subsidies to help consumers reduce emissions, and yet achieve the same emission reductions promised by the government.

Through the summer and fall of 2008, the NDP campaign appeared to be successful. The Liberal lead in public opinion polls of 20 percent when the carbon tax was announced in February 2008 collapsed, and by November the NDP and Liberals were even at 42 percent. Harrison (2009) reports on detailed opinion polls showing that the carbon tax played the dominant role in the government's declining popularity. The distaste for the carbon tax was exacerbated by a coincidental steep rise in international oil prices that increased gasoline prices by 50 cents per liter in 2008. Although the first year of the carbon tax added only 2.4 cents per liter to the price of gasoline, opinion polls showed that many members of the public were unaware of this.

In this environment, the government, academics and even supportive media commentators found it extremely difficult to convince people that many of them would be net beneficiaries of the carbon tax and its recycling mechanism. Few people know what a decrease in tax rates equates to in absolute savings from one year to the next. Indeed, even government and independent experts could not estimate precisely the net effect of the tax reform on different categories of residents and businesses since this depended on future responses that were uncertain. Someone with low emissions and full potential for income tax benefits would obviously gain. But even someone who initially had high emissions might be a net beneficiary over time if their cost of reducing emissions was low because, for example, they were conveniently located next to public transit or had easy access to wood for space and water heating.

While most people were not able or interested in conducting a complex dynamic analysis of their likely costs and benefits from the carbon tax, everyone knew simply that government had just levied an additional tax on gasoline and now its price was much higher. Perhaps to encourage the thinking that government climate policy (and not high oil prices) was causing high gasoline prices, the NDP continuously referred to the carbon tax as a 'gasoline tax.'

The political challenges facing a carbon tax became more apparent when the leader of Canada's federal Liberal Party, Stephan Dion, promoted a carbon tax reform similar

---

[7]   In this section, I rely significantly on Harrison (2009), the only academic analysis I am aware of that provides a detailed review of political developments associated with the carbon tax, including media interviews, op-eds, political pronouncements, policy statements and opinion polls.

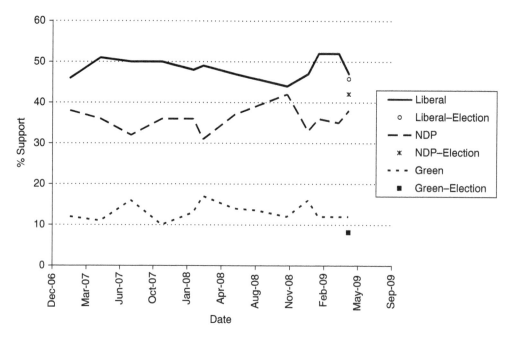

Figure 10.3   Support for BC political parties

to the BC model as the central pillar of his policy platform in the fall 2008 federal election campaign. Predictably, the competing federal parties of right (Conservatives) and left (NDP) misrepresented Dion's revenue-neutral proposal as a tax increase, with considerable success in spite of frequent efforts by the federal Liberals and independent analysts to explain the compensating benefits from income tax decreases. Dion's Liberals were soundly defeated in the election and he resigned his leadership. The victorious Conservative Party under Stephen Harper has always referred to carbon tax proposals as 'tax increase' proposals, as has the federal NDP. Harper's minority government was reelected in the 2008 election, and then won a four-year majority government in 2011, promising never to implement a carbon tax.

In BC, the political outcome was different in that Campbell's Liberals were reelected in 2009, thereby ensuring survival of BC's carbon tax for the foreseeable future. But the reasons for its survival may have had more to do with luck than a shift in public support for the carbon tax. In the latter half of 2008, the collapse of US financial markets and the ensuing global economic crisis shifted public concern strongly to the economy, an area where the Campbell government had consistently polled higher than the NDP (Harrison 2009). At the same time, the recession played a key role in reducing world oil prices, and thus gasoline prices. By the time of the 2009 election, anger at the carbon tax had dissipated relative to the public's skyrocketing concern with the economy (Figure 10.2) and Campbell's Liberals were able to gain a slight edge over the NDP (Figure 10.3). To win the close election, Campbell campaigned on his ability to steer the economy to recovery during the global economic crisis.

Some may see the political survival of the carbon tax in BC as an important symbolic event that will encourage more politicians to emulate Campbell's GHG emissions pricing strategy. But after reviewing opinion polls and media content analysis in Canada's 2008 federal election and BC's 2009 election, Harrison (2009) notes that, 'on balance carbon taxes appear to have hurt the party advocating the policy in both cases, thus offering a cautionary tale concerning the fate of politicians' "good policy" motives absent both a majority government and fortuitous timing.'

In BC, at least, the carbon tax survived and with the income tax cuts growing in importance each year, the NDP appears to have recognized the difficulty in campaigning to one day reverse the policy. Leader Carol James has stepped down and her replacement says he will keep the BC carbon tax if elected. Gordon Campbell has also stepped down (ironically because of public backlash against his 2009 reform of sales taxes) but his replacement as premier has also promised to keep the carbon tax.

LONG-TERM SURVIVAL OF THE CARBON TAX

Coordination with GHG Emissions Pricing in North America

Although it has survived a significant short-term challenge to its existence, the BC carbon tax faces an uncertain future. It was implemented at a time when many politicians assumed that some form of emissions pricing would soon be established throughout North America. During the US election campaign of 2008, both presidential candidates supported emissions pricing via cap-and-trade. Several years earlier, in fact, John McCain had co-authored an almost-successful bipartisan cap-and-trade bill in the US Senate. However, political developments in the US since the election of President Obama, and the continued governance by Canada's federal Conservative Party, have diminished the likelihood that the US or Canada will have economy-wide GHG emissions pricing in the near future.

While little is happening at the federal level, one cannot rule out the possibility that regional emissions pricing will develop. California seems intent on moving forward with a cap-and-trade approach to emissions pricing that may draw in other states and provinces in the Western Climate Initiative. If BC were to participate, it would need either to replace its carbon tax with cap-and-trade or to align in some way its carbon tax with the emissions price that would result from a cap-and-trade system. Both of these options present challenges.

Wholesale replacement of the carbon tax would create a problem for BC's tax system. Since revenue from the carbon tax enables BC to sustain low corporate and personal income tax rates, government would need either to reverse these tax cuts under cap-and-trade or to auction permits under cap-and-trade in order to raise revenues to supplant the disappearing carbon tax revenue. Uncertainties would exacerbate budget balancing as the government tried to accurately forecast revenues from auction permits. One mechanism for reducing this uncertainty involves government setting a floor and a ceiling for the price of tradable emission permits. While there are various ways of doing this, government will be challenged by the general difficulty of aligning permit prices, which would be determined in a large regional permit trading market, with the specific government revenue needs in BC related to the carbon tax.

If the government instead opted for a hybrid approach, one that mixed a carbon tax with cap-and-trade depending on the sector, it would need to decide which domestic emissions sources would shift into the cap-and-trade system and which would remain under the BC carbon tax. For competitive reasons, the most likely scenario is that large industry and perhaps fossil fuel energy products would shift to the regional cap-and-trade system while the rest of the BC economy would remain under the domestic carbon tax. Some countries in Europe find themselves in this situation as their industry operates under the European Union emissions trading system while the rest of their emission sources are subject to domestic carbon taxes.

Survival of the Carbon Tax on its Own

If, however, broad-based emissions pricing does not soon emerge at the federal or regional levels in the US and Canada, the BC carbon tax may need to survive in isolation for some time. In this case, the government must decide what happens to the tax after 2012, the last year of scheduled increases. Not surprisingly, environmentalists are lobbying for the tax to keep increasing at the same rate, if not faster, with new revenues used to subsidize emissions-reducing investments by government, consumers and industries. With equal predictability, industry is calling for the tax rate to be frozen, with perhaps a reduction or even full exemption for industries facing competitive pressures from foreign, untaxed companies.

Most likely, the government, no matter which party is in power, will not eliminate or reduce the carbon tax after 2012. Significant income tax increases would be required to offset the lost income from cutting or killing the tax. From a policy-sustainability perspective, linking the tax revenue to lower income tax rates appears to have been a clever tactic.

At the same time, neither of BC's two main political parties is likely to increase the tax by much if BC remains the lone North American bastion of direct emissions pricing. BC is already seen as the North American climate policy leader, so further tax increases would confer few political benefits. But the political costs of a rising carbon tax could be substantial, as this would drive the province's relatively high gasoline prices even further above those of neighboring jurisdictions and as its emissions-intensive industries blamed any output reductions on the tax, regardless of the real causes. The most likely outcome, therefore, is that, in the absence of strong emissions pricing elsewhere in North America, BC's carbon tax will survive into the indefinite future at or near its 2012 level of $30.

Although the chances of increasing the BC tax are small, in the absence of North American emissions pricing, small annual increases in the BC carbon tax might be possible. One approach is to justify increases of one or two dollars per year if all extra revenues from post-2012 tax increases are used to support transit, energy efficiency, fuel switching and other forms of emissions reductions in vehicles and buildings. While subsidy programs are not 100 percent effective in lowering emissions (to the extent that some subsidy recipients receive money for insulating their houses or somehow reducing emissions when they were going to do that anyway), they help build political support for climate policies like the carbon tax, which is crucial. Another approach is for government to loudly proclaim that future tax increases will not be revenue-neutral, but instead 'revenue-negative.' This was, in fact, the reality for the first two years of BC's carbon tax, when income tax cuts exceeded carbon tax revenues by $200 million. Government has not made any effort to publicize this. It might want to rethink this strategy as a way of garnering public support for future, modest carbon tax increases. The idea would be to design these as net tax decreases by ensuring that forgone revenue from income tax cuts exceeded carbon tax revenues, if only by a modest amount.

If, without a great political cost, government is somehow able to slowly raise the tax in future, it may need to introduce a partial tax exemption for trade-vulnerable industries or provide them with extra support in shifting away from GHG-emitting technologies and fuels.

In any case, a stalled emissions-pricing regime need not equate to a stalled climate effort in BC. As other regions in North America intensify regulations on technologies and fuels to reduce emissions, BC can retain its leadership role with aggressive policies to drive a growing market share for electric vehicles, electric heat pumps for buildings and expanded industrial uses of electricity—which in BC is virtually emissions-free.

ASSESSMENT AND FUTURE RESEARCH

BC's carbon tax reform has been cited as evidence that direct, open taxation of GHG emissions can be politically acceptable. But while it is true that the BC carbon tax did not cause an electoral defeat, polling evidence suggests that the tax survived only because an extreme economic crisis enabled the architect of the tax to recover just enough public support to overcome the tax's negative effects. Moreover, Canada-wide opinion polls suggest that a proposal to emulate BC's carbon tax by Canada's federal Liberal Party played a significant role in that party's resounding electoral defeat in 2008.

Since these two events, other Canadian political leaders have been careful to assure voters they will not implement a carbon tax. At the federal level, Canada's Conservative government seems content to be a policy-follower with respect to the United States. There, the taxation of carbon is not the subject of serious climate policy discussion, except among a few environmentalists, academics and maverick corporate executives. Even indirect emissions pricing via cap-and-trade is doubtful at the federal level for at least the next few years, with climate policy advocates increasingly turning to sector-specific regulations on electricity generation, industrial plants, buildings, vehicles and other components of the transport system.

Evidence from the vivid and at times vicious carbon tax debate in BC challenges the rational model of democratic policymaking, in which voters are able to comprehend the actual effects of a policy before deciding upon its value from a self-interest or societal perspective. The debate was dominated by misinformation and widespread skepticism about the intentions of government when it changes the tax system. Most respondents to opinion polls did not understand or believe claims by the government and independent analysts that the tax was revenue-neutral and that most of them could benefit by reducing their emissions with a few easy measures.

However, these possible lessons from the BC experience are largely based on anecdotal evidence, and therefore suggest several questions for further research both on emissions pricing and on other compulsory policy alternatives. Are there specific attributes of a carbon tax or its revenue-recycling mechanism that can significantly improve its chances of succeeding politically? In this regard, are there lessons that carbon tax designers can learn from cap-and-trade systems, and vice versa? Given the dramatic emissions reductions that scientists are calling for, can a carbon tax ever hope to achieve the necessary magnitude, or are complementary regulatory approaches and/or cap-and-trade systems inevitable? Can climate-motivated regulations on technologies and fuels be designed so that they approximate the cost-effectiveness of carbon taxes? How can a carbon tax best be integrated with a cap-and-trade system? What is the best strategy for assisting trade-vulnerable industries in a jurisdiction whose emissions prices are far above those of other jurisdictions?

Research into these and related questions is an urgent need. Although widespread pricing of GHG emissions appears to be a long way off in the current political atmosphere in North America, it is important to remember that the political context can change rapidly, as it did in California and British Columbia in the middle of the last decade. While such research is undertaken, perhaps the best a carbon tax advocate might hope for in the short-term is that the BC carbon tax continues to provide a functioning example of a relatively effective and efficient GHG emissions pricing policy—one that others might one day emulate.

REFERENCES

Bailey, I. (2008), 'Northern towns gang up on carbon tax', *Globe and Mail*, 9 May, S1.

Baldwin, R. (2008), 'Regulation lite: the rise of emissions trading', *Regulation and Governance*, **2**, 193–215.

Ballard, C., J. Shoven and J. Whalley (1985), 'General equilibrium computations of the marginal welfare costs of taxes in the United States', *American Economic Review*, **75** (1), 128–38.

BC (British Columbia) Government (2008), *Climate Action Plan*.

BC (British Columbia) Ministry of Finance (2010a), 'How the carbon tax works', http://www.fin.gov.bc.ca/tbs/tp/climate/A4.htm.

BC (British Columbia) Ministry of Finance (2010b), 'Tax cuts funded by the carbon tax', http://www.fin.gov.bc.ca/tbs/tp/climate/A2.htm.

Caplan, B. (2007), *The Myth of the Rational Voter: Why Democracies Choose Bad Policies*, Princeton, NJ, US: Princeton University Press.

Goulder, L. (1995), 'Environmental taxation and the double dividend: a reader's guide', *International Taxation and Public Finance*, **2**, 157–183.

Grandia, K. (2008) 'BC NDP endorsed carbon tax at 2007 provincial convention',www.desmogblog.com.

Harrison, K. (2009), 'A tale of two taxes: the fate of environmental tax reform in Canada and the province of British Columbia', presented at the Global Conference on Environmental Taxation, Lisbon, Portugal.

Harrison, K. (2010), 'The comparative politics of carbon taxation', *Annual Review of Law and Social Science*, **6** (26), 1–23.

Jaccard, M., N. Melton and J. Nyboer (2011), 'Institutions and processes for scaling up renewables: run-of-river hydropower in British Columbia', *Energy Policy*, **39** (7), 4042–50.

James, C. (2008), 'Campbell's fuel tax is unfair, ineffective and he doesn't care', *Vancouver Sun*, 29 April, A11.

Kahneman D., J. Knetsch and R. Thaler (1991), 'Anomalies: the endowment effect, loss aversion, and status quo bias', *Journal of Economic Perspectives*, **5** (1), 193–206.

Kallbekken, S. and H. Saelen (2011), 'Public acceptance for environmental taxes: self-interest, environmental and distributional concerns', *Energy Policy*, **39**, 2966–73.

Lee, M. and T. Sanger (2008), 'Is BC's carbon tax fair? An impact analysis for different income levels', Vancouver, Canada: Canadian Centre for Policy Alternatives.

Nordhaus, W. (1992), 'An optimal transition path for controlling greenhouse gases', *Science*, **258**, 1315–19.

Olson, M. (1971), *The Logic of Collective Action: Public Goods and the Theory of Groups*, Cambridge, MA, US: Harvard University Press.

Rivers, N. (2008), 'How BC's carbon tax reform defies the conventional wisdom', *Vancouver Sun*, 29 April.
Simpson, J., M. Jaccard and N. Rivers (2007), *Hot Air. Meeting Canada's Climate Change Challenge*, Toronto, Canada: McClelland & Stewart.
Vancouver Board of Trade (2008), 'BC budget: media release', http://www.boardoftrade.com/vbot_page.asp?pageid=2529.

11 Gaining intergovernmental acceptance: legal rules protecting trade

*Birgitte Egelund Olsen**

INTRODUCTION

To date, multilateral efforts to liberalize trade and prevent environmental degradation have proceeded largely along separate paths. However, these parallel regimes are more and more likely to come into closer contact with each other as environmental policies come to have significant economic effects. Environmental taxes are increasingly being used for the pursuit of environmental policy objectives. However, national environmental tax schemes may come into conflict with trade rules where they affect domestic and imported products differently.

Concerns that prospective domestic measures might breach multilateral trade rules have presumably led to less environmentally ambitious regulatory frameworks. However, opportunities exist for making trade regulation and environmental taxation more complementary, and it would be possible for trade law and environmental law to work more closely together to avoid conflicts between their different interests. One integrative step could be to facilitate a coordinated approach to the taxation of carbon or energy, for example in multilateral environmental negotiations.[1]

Although the idea of getting governments to agree sounds alluring, serious barriers exist that would make it very difficult to achieve harmonization of taxation designs, while global harmonization of tax levels must be considered impossible. Even in a supranational legal system such as the EU, where environmental considerations have high priority, only limited progress has been made in this direction.

Basically, trade-related environmental policies are driven by the need to correct market failure. If the market solution is not satisfactory, governments may use tax measures to intervene. In contrast, multilateral trade rules are not a response to market failure but a response to the failure of governments, e.g. their protectionist behavior.[2] Thus, trade rules will seek to disable trade-related environmental measures in order to ensure non-discrimination and free trade.

* This work is part of the research project 'WTO law and EU law: legal conflict and integration (2007–2011),' funded by the Danish Council for Independent Research | Social Sciences. The author would like to thank Professor Sanford Gaines and Professor Karsten Engsig Sørensen for their comments on the first draft of this chapter.

[1] O.K. FAUCHALD, ENVIRONMENTAL TAXES AND TRADE DISCRIMINATION 36 (1998).

[2] Steve Charnovitz, *Trade and Climate: Potential Conflicts and Synergies* 3 (Pew Center on Global Climate Change, Working Paper 2003).

TRADE LAW AND ENVIRONMENTAL TAXATION

Trade rules affect how governments may design and use environmental taxes on traded goods. If a government refrains from allowing tax exemptions and rebates on exports and from applying any tax on imports, then there will be no legal conflict with trade rules. However, governments will usually seek a level playing field based on fair competition, and there will be potential tension.

Of particular concern for governments when designing a tax scheme is the extent to which the international competitiveness of domestic industries will be affected. The adoption of environmental tax measures will often depend on whether similar costs are imposed on foreign products through the use of border measures, called Border Tax Adjustments (BTAs), which are duties charged at the border on imported products. An example of a BTA is an import fee levied by a carbon-taxing country on goods manufactured in a non-carbon-taxing country. However, not all types of taxes are eligible for BTAs under WTO law.[3]

An environmental tax may be applied directly on the sale of a product or the use of a natural resource, or it may be imposed on inputs into products that are either physically built into the product or physically consumed during the production.[4] Environmental taxes that have a direct influence on the free flow of trade across borders, and therefore the potential to infringe upon central tenets of international trade law, can be classified in two broad types: (1) product taxes that regulate the design, characteristics and uses of particular products, and (2) taxes that regulate the negative impacts of Process and Production Methods, or PPM taxes.

A PPM tax can be one of two sorts: product-related or non-product-related.[5] Product-related PPM taxes are levied on products on the basis of how much they pollute or degrade the environment. An example is a tax based on the fuel efficiency of cars, where a higher tax is imposed on cars with lower efficiency and vice versa. The non-product-related PPM tax is directly related to the production and the negative impact it may have on the environment, for instance taxation of the release of pollutants or the amount of energy used in production.

From a trade perspective, the product-related PPM measures are not analytically distinct from more conventional product taxation, which is exclusively concerned with the physical aspects of the product, not the product's performance or other features. In contrast, non-product-related PPM measures relate to the method of production and do not affect the characteristics of the product itself, and for this reason they are more controversial.[6]

Both WTO law and EU law categorize the above-mentioned taxes as 'internal' in the sense that they are applied once the product has entered the domestic market rather than

---

[3]   *See infra* 'Border Tax Adjustments'.
[4]   C. WOLD ET AL., TRADE AND THE ENVIRONMENT 238–39 (2005).
[5]   OECD, *PPMs: Conceptual Framework and Considerations of Use of PPM-based Trade Measures* (OCDE/GD(97)137, 1997).
[6]   *See infra* 'LEGAL FRAMEWORK FOR ENVIRONMENTAL TAXATION IN THE WTO', 'The PPM Issue' and 'LEGAL FRAMEWORK FOR ENVIRONMENTAL TAXATION IN THE EU', 'The PPM Issue'.

at the border, and as 'indirect' taxes, as opposed to direct taxes, which are imposed on income and property.[7]

This chapter focuses on the multilateral trade regime of the WTO and on the experience of the EU in the interaction between trade and environmental taxation. So far there are only a few WTO cases involving environmental issues, and to a large extent the same can be said about EU case law on environmental taxation. Therefore the analysis conducted here necessarily rests on analogies and proposed legal interpretations. As for trade liberalization, the WTO and the EU fulfill much the same function but in distinctly different contexts and through distinctly different institutional structures. Thus, there are reasons to expect a divergence of approach that may ultimately lead to legal conflicts.

LEGAL FRAMEWORK FOR ENVIRONMENTAL TAXATION IN THE WTO

The WTO is the most important international trade regime, encompassing the vast majority of all sovereign states. The General Agreement on Tariffs and Trade (GATT) deals with trade in goods and is considered the most important agreement of the multilateral trade regime. From its start in 1943, GATT Article XX contained an exception clause, referring to the protection of 'human, animal or plant life or health' and the 'conservation of exhaustible natural resources.' However, protection of the environment as such was not originally among the agreed-upon legitimate objectives.

Today the WTO has a limited capacity for coordinating policy on environmental issues, as it faces the all-important problem of achieving international consensus. WTO law is not unchangeable, but altering WTO rules presents huge difficulties. However, the role of the Appellate Body, the standing body of appeal of the WTO dispute settlement system, is crucial. The Appellate Body has shown an open and flexible approach when determining the impact of transnational policy coordination on trade restrictions. Thus, an adjustment of the provisions is more likely to be made through the interpretation of WTO law than through traditional lawmaking.

In principle, in WTO law governments are free to impose any environmentally motivated taxes on products, as long as they do not discriminate against imported products.[8] For discrimination to exist, the foreign and domestic products must be comparable

---

[7]   M. Slotboom, A Comparison of WTO and EC Law: Do Different Treaty Purposes Matter for Treaty Interpretation? 78–82 (2006).

[8]   More generally on environmental taxation and WTO law see Wold, *supra* note 4; Fauchald, *supra* note 1; M. Liang, *Green Taxes and the WTO: Creating Certainty for the Future*, 10 Chi. J. Intl. L. 359–88 (2009); R. Quick & C. Lau, *Environmentally Motivated Tax Distinctions and WTO Law*, 6 J. Intl. Econ. L. 419–58 (2003); F. Sindico, *Climate Taxes and the WTO: Is the Multilateral Trade Regime a Further Obstacle for Efficient Domestic Climate Policies?*, 3 Econ. Pol'y & L. J. Trade Envtl. Stud. 1–24 (2006); S. Zarrili, *Domestic Taxation of Energy Products and Multilateral Trade Rules: Is This Case Unlawful Discrimination?*, 37 J. World Trade 359–94 (2003); O.K. Fauchald, *Flexibility and Predictability Under the World Trade Organization's Nondiscrimination Clauses*, 37 J. World Trade 443–82 (2003); and P. Demaret & R. Stewardson, *Border Tax Adjustments under GATT and EC Law and General Implications for Environmental Taxes*, 28 J. World Trade 5–65 (1994).

products. This is laid down in GATT Article III:2, which contains the prohibition of discriminatory internal taxes. Even if a tax is discriminatory, and is thus considered a *prima facie* breach of WTO law, there are some exceptions that may be invoked to justify the discriminatory treatment, including for environmental purposes.

Basic Principles of Nondiscrimination

The national treatment principle and the most-favored-nation (MFN) principle are the two main nondiscrimination requirements in WTO law. Both the national treatment principle and the MFN principle apply to the use of internal taxes.

'National treatment' refers to the obligation to treat products equally, regardless of whether they are domestic or foreign. It thus prohibits discrimination between imported products and 'like' domestic products. The purpose of the national treatment principle is to prevent domestic taxes being used as protectionist measures to nullify the benefits of tariff concessions.[9] With respect to taxes, the principle is contained in Article III:2.

The MFN principle imposes an obligation to treat foreign products equally, regardless of their country of origin.[10] The principle is relevant where an importing country affords more favorable treatment to products originating in certain countries than to products originating in other countries. This would be the case if a tax were designed to 'punish' countries that do not participate in an international agreement.

The nondiscrimination principles prohibit both *de jure* and *de facto* discrimination.[11] *De jure* discrimination covers discrimination that is apparent on the face of a legal measure, whereas *de facto* discrimination covers regulatory measures that do not explicitly appear to differentiate between imports and domestic goods but which in fact, on closer examination, have a discriminatory effect. For example, even if on the face of it imported and domestic products are treated identically, there can be *de facto* discrimination if in fact the imported products are mainly in a category that is subject to a higher tax rate.

De facto discrimination often involves measures that distinguish between different products on the basis of their physical characteristics. An example would be a tax on cars based on their fuel efficiency. There is nothing necessarily discriminatory about such a measure. However, if in the actual market situation imported cars tend to have low fuel efficiency and domestically produced cars have high fuel efficiency, the measure may have a differential impact on imports, and it could be argued that the tax amounts to *de facto* discrimination.[12]

---

[9] Zarrili, *supra* note 8, at 370.

[10] The MFN principle is contained in GATT Art. I, which extends the principle to Art. III:2. *See* M. Cremona, *Neutrality or Discrimination? The WTO, the EU and External Trade, in* THE EU AND THE WTO: LEGAL AND CONSTITUTIONAL ISSUES (G. de Búrca & J. Scott eds 2001).

[11] B. OLSEN ET AL., WTO LAW – FROM A EUROPEAN PERSPECTIVE 169–72 (2006); L. Ehring, *De Facto Discrimination in World Trade Law: National and Most-Favored-Nation-Treatment or Equal Treatment*, 36 J. WORLD TRADE 921–23 (2002).

[12] In the 1994 *US – Taxes on Automobiles* case, DS31/R (Oct. 11, 1994), a GATT panel ruled that cars with high fuel efficiency were not 'like' gas-guzzling cars. This ruling was not adopted, and it is unclear whether the same result would be reached today.

The PPM Issue

Taxes and regulations on PPMs, especially the non-product-related, are controversial under WTO law and their legality is widely disputed.[13] The multilateral trading system has been hesitant to deal with PPMs as they may require exporters to adapt to the specific standards of the importing state and produce their products in a specific manner. The most frequent criticisms concern the issues of extraterritoriality (that is, the importing state's imposing its values etc. on exporting states), unilateralism (when the measure is an instrument of protectionism) and equity (when the products denied admittance are frequently those of developing countries).

The legality of PPM measures has been touched upon in several WTO cases, although only a few involve environmental taxes.[14] So far the suggestion is that reference to PPMs as a basis for taxation is not excluded as a matter of principle. However, there are still many questions as to what kinds of PPMs may be legitimately relied upon and to what extent. Many commentators still consider PPM measures to be justified only in a limited number of cases.[15] Some argue that non-product-related PPMs are appropriately addressed under GATT Article XX, rather than GATT Article III. Others advocate the inclusion of non-product-related PPMs in the 'like product' analysis to avoid the restrictive interpretation of Article XX.[16]

Prohibition of Discriminatory Taxation: GATT Article III:2

Internal tax measures are explicitly addressed in GATT Article III:1 and 2. Article III:1 reads as follows:

---

[13]   PPMs were first addressed in the *US – Tuna Dolphin I* case, WT/DS21/R – 39S/155 (Sept. 3, 1991) (unadopted). In the early cases, PPM measures were found to breach GATT/WTO rules. However, with the 2001 Appellate Body Report, *US – Shrimp/Turtle: Recourse to Article 21.5*, WT/DS58/AB/RW (Oct. 22, 2001) [hereinafter *US – Shrimp Recourse*], it became clear that PPM measures were not prohibited *per se*. On PPMs and the differing opinions on this issue, see D. Regan, *How to Think PPMs (and Climate Change)*, in INTERNATIONAL TRADE REGULATION AND THE MITIGATION OF CLIMATE CHANGE 97–123 (T. Cottier et al. eds 2009); J. Potts, *The Legality of PPMs under the GATT: Challenges and Opportunities for Sustainable Trade Policy* (Int'l Inst. for Sustainable Dev. 2008); *see* Wold, *supra* note 4, at 202–38; S. Gaines, *Processes and Production Methods: How to Produce Sound Policy for Environmental PPM-based Trade Measures?*, 27 COLUM. J. ENVTL. L. 383–432 (2002); S. Charnovitz, *The Law of Environmental 'PPMs' in the WTO: Debunking the Myth of Illegality*, 27 YALE J. INT'L L. 59, 91–101 (2002); and R. Howse & D. Regan, *The Product/Process Distinction—An Illusory Basis for Disciplining 'Unilateralism' in Trade Policy*, 11 EURO. J. INT'L LAW 249–89 (2000).

[14]   Panel Report, *US – Tuna Dolphin I*, WT/DS21/R – 39S/155 (Sept. 3, 1991); Panel Report, *US – Tuna II*, WT/DS29/R (June 16, 1994); Panel Report, *US – Taxes on Automobiles*, WT/DS31/R (Oct. 11, 1994); Appellate Body Report, *US – Shrimp*, WT/DS58/AB/R (Oct. 8, 1998) [hereinafter *US – Shrimp*] and Appellate Body Report, *US – Gasoline*, WT/DS2/AB/R (Apr. 29, 1996) [hereinafter *US – Gasoline*].

[15]   J. Jackson, *Comments on Shrimp/Turtle and the Product/Process Distinction*, 11 EURO. J. INT'L L. 303–7 (2000).

[16]   *See* Gaines, *supra* note 13.

> The contracting parties recognize that internal taxes and other internal charges, and laws, regulations and requirements affecting the internal sale, offering for sale, purchase, transportation, distribution or use of products, and internal quantitative regulations requiring the mixture, processing or use of products in specified amounts or proportions, should not be applied to imported or domestic products so as to afford protection to domestic production.

The paragraph is broadly formulated and does not on its own provide the basis for a claim of breach—it expresses the general objectives of Article III and has therefore been used only to interpret the other provisions of Article III.[17] The legal obligations follow from Article III:2, which prohibits discriminatory internal taxes on goods. The paragraph provides as follows:

> The products of the territory of any contracting party imported into the territory of any other contracting party shall not be subject, directly or indirectly, to internal taxes or other internal charges of any kind in excess of those applied, directly or indirectly, to like domestic products. Moreover, no contracting party shall otherwise apply internal taxes or other internal charges to imported or domestic products in a manner contrary to the principles set forth in paragraph 1.

Article III:2 is accompanied by an interpretative note (Note Ad Article III:2) that does not modify or replace the Article but aims to clarify its meaning. It provides that:

> A tax conforming to the requirements of the first sentence of paragraph 2 would be considered to be inconsistent with the provisions of the second sentence only in cases where competition was involved between, on the one hand, the taxed product and, on the other hand, a directly competitive or substitutable product which was not similarly taxed.

Taking Article III:2 together with the interpretative note and Article III:1, the provision contains two different obligations. The first sentence prohibits any discriminatory taxation of like products. Thus, if like products are treated differently, a tax that puts imports at a disadvantage will be in breach of the national treatment principle. The second sentence is less straightforward. It prohibits situations in which products that are 'directly competitive or substitutable' are taxed differently such that domestic products are protected. Article III:2 is relevant both for 'internal' taxes that affect imported products sold on the domestic market and for BTAs falling under the exception of GATT Article II:2(a).[18]

First sentence: 'like products'
The first sentence of Article III:2 prohibits any discriminatory taxation of like products. It states that imported products 'shall not be subject, directly or indirectly to internal taxes or other charges of any kind in excess of those applied, directly or indirectly, to like domestic products.' This first sentence asks two key questions: are the imported products 'like' the domestic products,[19] and are the imported products taxed in excess of the like domestic products?

---

[17]   Appellate Body Report, *Japan – Alcoholic Beverages II*, 17–18, WT/DS8,10,11/AB/R (Oct. 4, 1996) [hereinafter *Japan – Alcoholic Beverages II*].
[18]   See further on BTA *infra* 'Border Tax Adjustments'.
[19]   The GATT Agreement has several product-similarity clauses, (*e.g.* Arts I:1, II:2(a), III:4, VI:1(a), XI:2(c) and XIX:1), but nowhere does it contain a definition of what constitutes

The Appellate Body has stated that 'there [is] no one precise and absolute definition of what is like.'[20] In deciding whether products are like, the WTO tribunals have construed the concept narrowly, so that the products have to be quite similar.[21] On the other hand the concept is to some extent dynamic, and it does not require products to be identical. The question generally arises when two groups of products of the same product type are taxed dissimilarly.

Products that are different only by virtue of their origin or nationality are considered like. If the tax system distinguishes between products based on characteristics other than origin, it is harder to establish that the products are like. The likeness is determined by a case-by-case evaluation based on the following criteria identified by the GATT Working Party on Border Tax Adjustment: (1) the product's end-uses in a given market; (2) consumers' tastes and habits; and (3) the product's properties, nature and quality.[22] A fourth criterion, the tariff classification of the products, has been added in subsequent case law, implying that if two groups of products are classified under the same nomenclature, this could be an indication of likeness.[23] Thus, it is not a closed list of criteria that determines the legal characterization of products.

If the non-product-related PPM distinction is accepted, the implication is that physically identical products that have the same end-uses and tariff classification may be taxed differently. On the other hand, if the products were claimed to be like, a PPM tax that differentiated between products produced with, for example, carbon-intensive inputs and low-carbon inputs, would *per se* breach the first sentence of Article III:2. The alleged difference between the products relates only to the production process and is not perceivable in the final product. The physical properties, end-uses and classification would be the same, so the decisive criterion for a finding of unlikeness would be consumer tastes and habits. Most consumers would probably not perceive the products as different, and it is generally doubtful whether the criterion of consumer tastes and habits can overcome a strong presumption of likeness. To rely solely on the criterion of consumer tastes and habits would probably involve a high risk of the tax being perceived as an abuse for protectionist purposes, and such considerations are probably more suitable as part of the balancing exercise under Article XX rather than under the objective market analysis of Article III:2.[24]

The second question is whether imported products are taxed 'in excess of' the tax applied to domestic products. It implies that imported products need to receive at least the same or an even more advantageous tax treatment than domestic products. Accordingly, the Appellate Body has stated that '[t]he prohibition of discriminatory taxes in Article

---

like products. The term is also used in other agreements; *see* the Agreement on Subsidies and Countervailing Measures and the Agreement on Safeguards. *See* R. Zedalis, *A Theory of the GATT 'Like' Products Common Language Cases*, 27 VAND. J. TRANSNAT'L L. 36–46 (1994).

[20]   *Japan – Alcoholic Beverages II* at 21.

[21]   *See, e.g., Japan – Alcoholic Beverages II, supra* note 17, at B.2. *See also* Zarrilli, *supra* note 8, at 374–76.

[22]   Report of the Working Party on Border Tax Adjustments, ¶18, BISD 18S/97-109 (adopted Feb. 12, 1970). See further, Fauchald, *supra* note 8, at 455–57.

[23]   The criterion was added by the GATT panel in *Japan – Alcoholic Beverages I*.

[24]   *See* Quick & Lau, *supra* note 8, at 433–34.

III:2, first sentence, is not conditional on a "trade effects test" nor is it qualified by a *de minimis* standard.'[25] This implies that even the slightest difference in tax treatment that puts imports at a disadvantage would be considered discriminatory.

The answer to the second question would be fairly straightforward if there were two tax categories, one for domestic products and one for imported products. However, it becomes more complicated if domestic and imported products are found in both tax categories. In the findings in the *Japan—Alcoholic Beverages II* case it was not stated that most vodka is imported into Japan and most shochu is domestically produced.[26] The tribunals referred to taxes on vodka compared to taxes on shochu, rather than taxes imposed on imports compared to taxes on domestic products. The findings could be based on either of two approaches. Under the first approach, it would be necessary to prove that the high-tax category applies mostly to imports and the low-tax category applies mostly to domestic products. This means that it would be necessary to prove that the measure has a discriminatory effect against imports. However, the Appellate Body has rejected this 'aim and effect' test in relation to Article III:2, first sentence, and it is widely believed by most commentators that taking the regulatory purpose into account in the determination of likeness would leave Article XX redundant.[27] The alternative approach—and under current case law the most plausible interpretation—is that any differentiation between like products, even if just one imported product is taxed at a higher rate than a domestically produced product, will *per se* be a breach.

Second sentence: 'directly competitive or substitutable products'
While the first sentence of Article III:2 combines a narrow understanding of product similarity with a strict requirement for equal treatment, the second sentence combines a broader understanding of product similarity ('directly competitive or substitutable') with less strict requirements for equal treatment ('similarly taxed' and 'so as to afford protection to domestic production'). The second sentence thus extends the nondiscrimination obligation to groups of products that under the first sentence cannot be considered like. It refers back to Article III:1 and it must be understood on the basis of the interpretative note to the provision.

There are three key questions that need to be considered under the second sentence. (1) Are the imported and domestic products 'directly competitive or substitutable products'? (2) Are the products 'similarly taxed'? (3) Is the dissimilar taxation applied 'so as to afford protection to domestic production'?

As with like products under the first sentence, the determination of the appropriate range of 'directly competitive or substitutable products' must be made on a case-by-case basis.[28] The important factor is whether the products compete, and not whether they are identical. To determine whether two products are 'directly competitive or substitutable,' the physical characteristics, common end-uses and customs-related classification

---

25   *Japan – Alcoholic Beverages II, supra* note 17, at 23.
26   *Id.*
27   *Id.*
28   *Id.* at 25; *Korea – Alcoholic Beverages*, ¶ 10.38, WT/DS75,84/R.

are relevant factors to take into account.[29] These factors focus on the product as such. An additional factor to be considered is the existing competitive situation in the market, including the elasticity of substitution between the products (i.e. the likelihood that purchasers will substitute one product for the other).[30] If an increase in the price of one product will lead to higher demand for another product, it is likely that they compete.

However, it is not enough to examine the cross-price elasticity of demand merely under existing market conditions. There may be regulatory barriers, such as the discriminatory taxes themselves or consumer preferences for specific products that hinder the substitution of one product for another. But these conditions may change. Hence it is also relevant to look at the competitive situation in other markets or to make an assessment of whether one product is capable of substituting for another by focusing on the purposes for which the products can reasonably be used, and not taking into account existing consumer preferences.[31]

The second condition involves only a few difficult interpretive issues. Products will not be similarly taxed if the tax burden on imports is heavier than that on 'directly competitive or substitutable' domestic products. The assessment not only should be made of the tax rates, but should also include other aspects of the tax such as the methods of calculating the tax rate. However not all differences will constitute a breach of the second sentence. The Appellate Body has emphasized that the differences in tax rates must be more than *de minimis*.[32] Thus, an insignificant difference will not be enough for imported and domestic products to be considered not 'similarly taxed.'

The third condition is whether the tax measure is 'applied as to afford protection to domestic production.' This could be read as a requirement to prove a substantive intent behind the measure to protect domestic products. However, the Appellate Body has stated that it is not necessary to examine the subjective intentions of national lawmakers, as the protective nature of a measure can most often be revealed by 'the design, the architecture and the structure' of the tax system.[33] Consequently, the focus is on how a tax measure is applied in fact, and not on why the measure was adopted in the first place. Further evidence of a protective application may also be found in the magnitude of the differences between the tax rates.

The more discretionary obligation of equal treatment in the second sentence leaves more room for taking environmental considerations into account. If products are not like, but arguably 'directly competitive or substitutable,' dissimilar taxation for environmental matters would not *per se* be inconsistent with the second sentence of Article III:2. For example, if there were a tax on fossil fuel products, such as coal and gas, based on the carbon content of the fuel, the coal and gas would not be considered like products under the first sentence, but might be considered 'directly competitive or substitutable' under

---

[29] Panel Report, *Japan – Taxes on Alcoholic Beverages* ¶6.32, WT/DS8,10,11/R (July 11, 1996).

[30] *Japan – Alcoholic Beverages II, supra* note 17, at 25.

[31] Appellate Body Report, *Korea – Alcoholic Beverages*, ¶¶114, 124, WT/DS75,84/AB/R (Jan. 18, 1999). *See also* Olsen, *supra* note 11, at 176; Fauchald, *supra* note 1, at 148.

[32] Appellate Body Report, *Chile – Alcoholic Beverages*, ¶49–53, WT/DS87,110/AB/R (Dec. 13, 1999).

[33] *Id.* at ¶61–72; *Japan – Alcoholic Beverages II, supra* note 17, at 29.

the second sentence. They may have the same end-uses and, at least in the short term, they may have elasticity of substitution. It would thus be consistent with the national treatment principle to impose dissimilar tax rates as long as the rates would not breach the *de minimis* margin. However there could be a *prima facie* breach of the national treatment principle if the imported energy product (coal) were taxed at a much higher rate than the domestic product (gas), and if the dissimilar taxation were applied so as to afford protection to domestic production.[34] However, if there were no immediate competitive relationship between the two types of energy, a differential tax treatment would not be a breach of Article III:2.[35]

Border Tax Adjustments

To offset the adverse effects of environmental taxes on the competitiveness of domestic industries, WTO law allows for border adjustments, commonly referred to as 'border tax adjustments' (BTAs).[36] A BTA is a measure whereby a 'tax' is levied on imported products to adjust or compensate for taxes (or other impositions) levied on like domestic products. Conversely, BTAs may also be applied to exports most commonly through some form of tax relief, for example when a government generally imposes a high energy tax but exempts or rebates the tax for exports. A similar effect can be achieved by awarding subsidies or other economic benefits to affected domestic producers to offset competitive disadvantages.

According to the Working Party on Border Tax Adjustment, the aim of BTA measures is to ensure 'trade neutrality.'[37] The rules for BTAs on imports are to be found in GATT Article II:2(a) and Article III:2. If a tax is eligible for a BTA under Article II:2(a), the adjustment charge applied to imported products would still need to comply with GATT Article III:2 (cf. the discussion on discrimination under Article III:2 above). With respect to BTAs on exports, the rules are found in GATT Article VI:4 and Article XVI:4 and in the Agreement on Subsidies and Countervailing Measures.[38] Only indirect taxes on products (and not direct taxes on producers or other taxes not directly levied on products)

---

[34] Zarrilli, *supra* note 8, at 373 –75; Sindico, *supra* note 8, at 7–9.

[35] *See generally* R. Howse & A. Eliason, *Domestic and International Strategies to Address Climate Change: An Overview of the WTO Legal Issues, in* INTERNATIONAL TRADE REGULATION AND THE MITIGATION OF CLIMATE CHANGE 48, 86–93 (T. Cottier et al. eds 2009).

[36] G. Goh, *The World Trade Organisation, Kyoto and Energy Tax Adjustments at the Border*, 38 J. WORLD TRADE 395–423 (2004); Howse, *supra* note 35, at 60–62; J. Pauwelyn, US Federal Climate Policy and Competitiveness Concerns: The Limits and Options of International Trade Law, (Nicholas Inst. for Envtl. Pol'y Solutions, Duke University, Working Paper No. 07-02, 2007); F. Biermann & R. Brohm, *Implementing the Kyoto Protocol without the United States: the Strategic Role of Energy Tax Adjustments at the Border* (Global Governance Project, Working Paper No. 5, 2003); P. Demaret & R. Stewardson, *Border Tax Adjustments under GATT and EC Law and General Implications for Environmental Taxes,* 28 J. WORLD TRADE 5–65 (1994).

[37] Report of the Working Party on Border Tax Adjustments, ¶9, BISD 18S/97-109 (adopted Feb. 12, 1970).

[38] About BTAs on exported products, *see, e.g.*, WTO & UNEP, TRADE AND CLIMATE CHANGE 104–105 (2009) and M. Lodefalk & M. Storey, *Climate Measures and WTO Rules on Subsidies*, 39 J. WORLD TRADE 23–44 (2005).

are eligible for BTAs. A product-related PPM tax may thus be eligible for BTAs, whereas it is not yet clear whether non-product-related PPM taxes may be as well.

The issue has been the subject of much attention in debates on the need for more effective climate change measures and on whether such measures could be combined with BTAs to deal with the loss of competitiveness and the often-mentioned problem of carbon leakage.[39] The *Superfund* case has demonstrated that BTAs are permissible with respect to a tax on inputs to a product (such as the amount of a chemical), provided that the taxed input remains in the product.[40]

It is widely discussed whether non-product-related taxes, such as on CO_2 emitted during the production process, are eligible for BTAs. Some commentators suggest that only inputs physically incorporated into or part of the final product can be subject to BTAs.[41] Others argue that the word 'indirectly' contained in GATT Article III:2 may be interpreted as allowing the use of BTAs on taxes on inputs used during the production process even when they do not remain in the final product.[42]

Can Environmental Taxes be Saved under GATT Article XX?

In the event of a breach of GATT Article III:2, a WTO Member might justify a tax or a BTA measure under GATT Article XX.[43] Article XX gives priority to certain public policies over trade liberalization. The protection of the environment is one of the objectives that might be invoked to justify a tax that would otherwise be considered a breach of the national treatment principle. Subparagraphs (b) and (g) are of particular relevance to environmental matters. Article XX thus provides some flexibility, but how great is this room for maneuver? Article XX provides, in pertinent parts:

> Subject to the requirement that such measures are not applied in a manner which would constitute a means of arbitrary or unjustifiable discrimination between countries where the same conditions prevail, or a disguised restriction on international trade, nothing in this Agreement shall be construed to prevent the adoption or enforcement by any contracting party of measures:

---

[39] WTO & UNEP, TRADE AND CLIMATE CHANGE 103–05 (2009); O. Quirico, *EU Border Tax Adjustments and Climate Change: Reaching Consensus within the International Legal Context*, 19 EURO. ENERGY & ENVTL. L. REV. 230–38 (2010).

[40] Panel Report, *United States – Taxes on Petroleum and Certain Imported Substances*, BISD 34S/136 (June 17, 1987).

[41] An important argument against allowing countries to apply BTAs to 'neutralize' non-product-related PPM taxation is that the revenue from the environmental tax would benefit the importing country and not necessarily the country where the environmental damage takes place. However, the most serious environmental problems are regional or even global, and in such cases this argument becomes less significant; *see* Fauchald, *supra* note 1, at 173–75.

[42] See the differing opinions in Pauwelyn, *supra* note 36; Howse, *supra* note 35, at 48–93; Demaret & Stewardson, *supra* note 8, at 59; F. Biermann & R. Brohm, *Implementing the Kyoto Protocol without the USA: the Strategic Role of Energy Tax Adjustments at the Border*, 4 CLIMATE POL'Y 289, 293 (2005); F. Sindico, *The EU and Carbon Leakage: How to Reconcile Border Adjustments with the WTO?*, 17 EURO. ENERGY & ENVTL. L. REV. 328, 332–34 (2008).

[43] *See, e.g.*, Fauchald, *supra* note 1, at 269–70; Liang, *supra* note 8, at 371–73; Quick & Lau, *supra* note 8, at 438–40; Zarrilli, *supra* note 8, at 375; Sindico, *supra* note 8, at 11–13; Pauwelyn, *supra* note 36, at 33–41.

(b)   necessary to protect human, animal or plant life or health . . . [or]
(g)   relating to the conservation of exhaustible natural resources if such measures are made effective in conjunction with restrictions on domestic production or consumption.

To see whether an environmental tax can be justified under Article XX, two questions must be asked. The first is whether the environmental tax falls within one of the subparagraphs identifying the national policies for which an exception may be allowed, namely subparagraphs (b) and (g). If this question is answered affirmatively, the second issue will be whether the tax has been applied in a non-protectionist manner according to the preamble ('chapeau') to Article XX. The party that invokes Article XX bears the burden of proving that the contested tax measure satisfies the requirements of the provision.[44]

The subparagraphs: reviewing the objective

The first requirement of subparagraph (b), that a particular measure should concern the protection of human, animal or plant life or health, has been interpreted broadly in the case law.[45] For example, it would probably cover a tax on CO_2 emissions with the objective of tackling climate change, as climate change is related to health problems, even though this may not be the primary aim of the tax. The second requirement is to satisfy the 'necessity test.' The word 'necessary' was originally interpreted very strictly, but over time the approach has evolved to become the more pragmatic 'less trade restrictive' approach, supplemented by a proportionality test.[46] The question is thus whether the environmental objective of a tax is a vital interest and whether the tax measure is necessary to combat the environmental problem.

Subparagraph (g) allows trade measures 'relating to the conservation of exhaustible natural resources,' if they are used 'in conjunction with restrictions on domestic production or consumption.' The first requirement has been interpreted broadly to include, for example, clean air.[47] Thus, a 'natural resource' may be living or non-living, and it need not be rare or endangered in order to be considered potentially 'exhaustible.' The phrase 'relating to' means that there has to be a 'substantial relationship' between the tax measure and the intended resource conservation.[48] Thus, a tax aimed at combating climate change and based on the CO_2 footprint of the energy used in the production process would probably have such a reasonable means-ends relationship. The last requirement, that the measure in question should be 'made effective in conjunction with restrictions on domestic production or consumption,' implies that the tax measures should impose restrictions not only on imported products but also on domestic ones.[49] This requires, for example, that the products should not have domestic subsidies.

---

[44]   *US – Gasoline, supra* note 14, at 22.
[45]   Panel Report, *US – Gasoline*, WT/DS2/R (Jan. 29, 1966).
[46]   The modified approach was fashioned by the panel in the *US – Gasoline* case and confirmed by the Appellate Body Report, *EC – Asbestos*, WT/DS135/AB/R (Mar. 12, 2001).
[47]   *US – Gasoline, supra* note 45.
[48]   *US – Gasoline, supra* note 14, at 18.
[49]   *Id.* at 19–21.

The chapeau: reviewing the application

The chapeau is designed to ensure that measures that are inconsistent with GATT rules but are potentially allowable under the subparagraphs of Article XX do not result in 'arbitrary or unjustifiable discrimination' or constitute 'a disguised restriction on international trade.' Both conditions must be fulfilled simultaneously. The party invoking Article XX thus has to prove that the real goal of the tax is to tackle environmental problems and that the way the tax is applied to imported products is not 'arbitrary or unjustifiable' vis-à-vis domestic products. The chapeau has been described as an 'expression of the principle of good faith.'[50] In the *US-Gasoline* case, the Appellate Body noted that 'the chapeau by its express terms addresses, not so much the questioned measure or its specific contents as such, but rather the manner in which that measure is applied.'[51] Thus it is necessary to examine not only the national legal texts and implementing measures but also the manner in which a tax is in fact applied.

There are two standards for determining whether a tax measure will result in 'arbitrary or unjustifiable discrimination.' First, prior to the adoption of the tax, the Member applying the tax must have made serious efforts, in good faith, to reach a bilateral or multilateral agreement with all interested parties before resorting to unilateral measures.[52] This obligation only refers to participation in and support for negotiations, and not to the actual conclusion of an international agreement.[53] For example, the Kyoto Protocol recognizes taxes as one of the policy measures that the parties may want to use in their domestic efforts to combat climate change.[54] It has been argued that if a trade measure is provided for in a multilateral environmental agreement (MEA), this could justify the use of the measure under WTO law.[55] The measure would probably have to be specific in the sense that it should impose obligations on the parties to the MEA, and it may also make a difference whether the party affected by the measure is or is not a party to the MEA.[56] However, the question of whether MEAs may prevail over WTO rules in case of conflict has not yet been answered, although it is generally accepted that these agreements may play an important role in the interpretation of WTO obligations.[57]

---

[50]   *US – Shrimp*, *supra* note 14, at ¶ 158.

[51]   This was noted in Panel Report, *US – Spring Assemblies*, BISD 30S/107 (May 26, 1983), and confirmed by the Appellate Body in *US – Gasoline*, *supra* note 14, at 22.

[52]   In the *US – Shrimp* case, the USA had negotiated seriously with some WTO Members but not with others, so there was unjustifiable discrimination according to the Appellate Body; *see US – Shrimp*, *supra* note 14, at ¶¶172, 176. *See also US – Gasoline*, *supra* note 14, at 26.

[53]   *US – Shrimp Recourse*, *supra* note 13, at ¶¶ 132–134.

[54]   Art. 2 Kyoto Protocol.

[55]   J. Pauwelyn, Conflict of Norms in Public International Law: How WTO Law Relates to Other Norms of International Law 473, 491 (2003). On the contrary, G. Marceau, *Conflicts of Norms and Conflicts of Jurisdictions: The Relationship between WTO Agreement and MEAs and Other Treaties*, 35 J. World Trade 1130 (2001).

[56]   S. Gaines, *The WTO's Reading of the GATT Article XX Chapeau: A Disguised Restriction on Environmental Measures*, J. Int'l Econ. L. 739, 805 (2001); R. Howse, *The Appellate Body Rulings in the Shrimp/Turtle Case: a New Legal Baseline for the Trade and Environment Debate*, 27 Colum. J. Envtl. L. 491, 507 (2002).

[57]   P. Van den Bossche, The Law and Policy of the World Trade Organization: Text, Cases and Materials (2008).

Second, the measure must afford 'sufficient flexibility' in its application. Flexibility must be given to all parties,[58] and imports must be allowed if measures are adopted that are 'comparable in effectiveness.' In the *Shrimp-Turtle* recourse case, the Appellate Body held that the revised US regulations that would certify a turtle conservation program 'comparable in effectiveness' to the US program would satisfy the chapeau conditions.[59] This finding could be seen as a requirement to recognize other, equally effective tools to achieve the environmental objective.

The last requirement is that the tax measure in question must not constitute 'a disguised restriction on international trade.' The tax measure must therefore be publicly announced,[60] and the actual application of the specific measure must not amount to arbitrary or unjustifiable discrimination, which refers to the first two requirements of the chapeau and the examination of 'the design, architecture and revealing structure' of the tax measure.[61]

Although Article XX may provide some flexibility, it does not at present provide a useful escape clause in the case of non-product-related PPM taxes, whereas product-related PPM measures adhere to Article XX for the same reason as product regulations do.[62] However, it is conceivable based on analogies of existing case law that a non-product-related PPM tax taken pursuant to a MEA addressing global problems could be considered consistent with WTO law under Article XX.

LEGAL FRAMEWORK FOR ENVIRONMENTAL TAXATION IN THE EU

The economic tasks of the EU are centered around the establishment of an internal market that unites the national markets of the member states, and the abolition of obstacles to the free movement of goods, persons, services and capital.[63] Environmental taxes may distort competition and constitute an obstacle to the free movement of goods in particular. Consequently, the competence to tax is not an exclusive competence of the member states, though it comes very close to the core of national sovereignty. The Treaty on the Functioning of the European Union (TFEU) explicitly provides legal bases for the harmonization of legislation on environmental taxation. However, it is difficult to harmonize in this field and so far there are only a few examples of harmonized taxes related to the environment.[64]

In the absence of EU harmonization, the member states remain free to adopt any tax measures they want, at whatever level they wish, to achieve their environmental goals,

---

[58]   *US – Shrimp, supra* note 14, ¶¶173–175.
[59]   See *US – Shrimp Recourse, supra* note 13, at ¶¶ 140–144.
[60]   Panel Report, *US – Tuna from Canada*, ¶ 4.8, BISD 29S/91 (Feb. 22, 1982).
[61]   *US – Gasoline* at 25 and *EC – Asbestos*, ¶8.236.
[62]   Gaines, *supra* note 13, at 424–25.
[63]   Consolidated Version of the Treaty on the Functioning of the European Union art. 26, Sep. 5, 2008, 2008 O.J. (C115) 47.
[64]   An example is the Energy Taxation directive. *See* Council Directive 2003/96/EC, 2003 O.J. (L 283) (EC).

provided that such measures are compatible with the general rules of the Treaties and in particular the *lex specialis* provision in Article 110 TFEU, which prohibits discriminatory internal taxes.[65] Although the objects and purposes of the EU Treaties are different from those of the WTO, the prohibition of discriminatory internal taxes found in Article 110 imposes obligations on member states that are very similar to the obligations that GATT Article III:2 imposes on WTO members.[66] However, there is also divergence between WTO and EU law, and thus potential for conflicts.

The PPM Issue

In contrast to the WTO, the Court of Justice of the European Union ('the Court') has on several occasions accepted PPMs as a legitimate reason to restrict imports and even to make tax distinctions. It appears that the extra-territorial aspect of the tax measure only plays a minor role in the reasoning of the Court.

A most striking example of a PPM tax was in the *Outokumpu Oy* case, in which the Court reviewed a Finnish tax provision that established differentiated tax rates on electricity based on the production method.[67] Finland argued that the taxes were designed to encourage more environmentally sound methods of energy production. The Court stated:

> As regards the compatibility of such a duty with Article [110] of the Treaty, it is settled case-law that . . . Community law does not restrict the freedom of each Member State to establish a tax system which differentiates between certain products, even products which are similar . . . on the basis of objective criteria, such as the nature of the raw materials used or the production processes employed. Such differentiation is compatible with Community law, however, only if it pursues objectives which are themselves compatible with the requirements of the Treaty and its secondary legislation, and if the detailed rules are such as to avoid any form of discrimination, direct or indirect, against imports from other Member States or any form of protection of competing domestic products.[68]

Accordingly, it is legitimate for a member state to tax electricity at rates that vary according to method of production and the type of raw materials used, insofar as the differentiation is based on environmental considerations. In the *Outokumpu Oy* case the Court nevertheless concluded that the tax was incompatible with the Treaty, because imported electricity was taxed at a different rate than domestic electricity.[69]

---

[65]   The EU institutions are themselves also bound by these rules. *See* Case C-172/82 *Inter-Huiles*; Case C-341/95 *Gianni Bettani*.

[66]   F. Ortino, Basic Legal Instruments for the Liberalisation of Trade: A Comparative Analysis of EC and WTO Law (2004); M. Slotboom, *Do Different Treaty Purposes Matter for Treaty Interpretation? The Elimination of Discriminatory Internal Taxes in EC and WTO Law*, 4 J. Int'l Econ. L. 557–79; Slotsboom, *supra* note 7; Olsen, *supra* note 11, at 132.

[67]   Case C-213/96, *Outokumpu Oy*, 1998 ECR I-1777.

[68]   *Id.* at ¶ 30.

[69]   Imported electricity was taxed at a flat rate, whereas domestically generated electricity was taxed at varying rates, depending on the environmental impact of the production method.

Prohibition of Discriminatory Taxation: Article 110 TFEU

Under Article 110 TFEU, member states may not impose taxes that discriminate directly or indirectly between imported products and similar domestic products, or that afford indirect protection of domestic products.[70] It provides that:

> No Member State shall impose, directly or indirectly, on the products of other Member States any internal taxation of any kind in excess of that imposed directly or indirectly on similar domestic products.
> Furthermore, no Member State shall impose on the products of other Member States any internal taxation of such a nature as to afford indirect protection to other products.

The provision applies to taxes on both products and the use of products.[71] A tax measure is caught by this provision if the measure is meant to protect similar domestic production. If there is no similar or competing domestic production, Article 110 does not apply. In a case concerning the Danish registration tax on new vehicles, Article 110 was not applicable since Denmark did not have a domestic car industry.[72]

The prohibition of discriminatory taxes relates only to the products of other member states.[73] Accordingly, the provision is not applicable to products imported directly from third countries;[74] it applies only when products from third countries are in free circulation within the EU.[75]

In a number of cases, the Court has held that a system of taxation can be considered compatible with Article 110 only if it is arranged so as to exclude any possibility of having a discriminatory effect.[76] Accordingly, a tax measure will be discriminatory if, while applicable to all goods regardless of their origin, it falls more heavily on imported products than on domestic products. For example, a tax calculated according to the power rating of cars, which imposes a disproportionately heavy burden on more powerful cars that are all imported, would be found inconsistent with Article 110.[77] A tax measure will also be considered discriminatory if the procedure for collecting the tax is different for imported and domestic products and if it puts imports at a disadvantage.[78]

In its wording and structure, Article 110 is very similar to GATT Article III:2. Accordingly, the Article contains two different obligations in its two sentences. The first

---

[70] P. CRAIG & G. BÚRCA, EU LAW 637–65 (2007); C. BARNARD, SUBSTANTIVE LAW OF THE EU: THE FOUR FREEDOMS 45–63 (2007); and J. Snell, *Non-discriminatory Tax Obstacles in Community Law*, 56 INT'L & COMP. L. Q. 339–70 (2007).

[71] Case 252/86, *Bergandi*, 1988 E.C.R. 1343, ¶ 27.

[72] Case 47/88, *Comm'n v. Denmark*, 1990 E.C.R. I-4509.

[73] It also applies to exports to other Member States, though this is not expressly stated in the provision, *cf.* Case 142/77, *Statens Kontrol v. Larsen*, 1978 E.C.R. 1543.

[74] Case C-284/96, *Tabouillot*, 1997 E.C.R. I-7471.

[75] Case 193/85, *Cooperative Co-Frutta*, 1987 E.C.R. 2085. *See further* Cremona, *supra* note 10, at 160–161.

[76] *See, e.g.*, Case C-90/94, *Haahr Petroleum*, 1997 E.C.R. 1-4085 ¶ 34; Case C-152/89, *Comm'n v. Luxembourg*, 1997 E.C.R. 1-4085 ¶ 21.

[77] Case 112/84, *Humblot*, 1985 E.C.R. 1367. The tax rules in the *Humblot* case were revised, but once again found to be in breach of EU law in Case 433/85, *Feldain*, 1987 E.C.R. 3521.

[78] Case 55/79, *Comm'n v. Ireland*, 1980 E.C.R. 481.

sentence prohibits discrimination against 'similar' products, and the second sentence prohibits protective taxes on products which, while not exactly similar, nevertheless compete with each other. The dividing line between the first and the second sentence is not clear. However, in recent case law the Court has been more specific in its determination of whether a tax measure is examined under the first or the second sentence. As in the WTO regime, the provision has been heavily litigated, particularly in relation to alcohol and car taxes, although environmentally motivated tax schemes have also been under scrutiny.

First sentence: 'similar' products
According to the first sentence of Article 110, member states are prohibited from imposing a tax of any kind on the products of other member states in excess of that imposed directly or indirectly on similar domestic products. The sentence raises two key questions: (1) are the imported products 'similar' to the domestic products; and (2) are the imported products taxed 'in excess' of the similar domestic products?

In deciding whether products are 'similar,' the term has been interpreted in much the same way as 'like' products in the GATT regime. Accordingly, the products need not be identical. Although the Court has held that the term 'similar' must be interpreted broadly, in contrast to the interpretation of 'like' in WTO law, it nevertheless appears that on its face the Court's interpretation corresponds to the approach in WTO law.[79]

In assessing the question of similarity, the Court has focused in particular on the objective characteristics of the products, such as their origin, properties and method of manufacture, and whether they 'meet the same needs from the point of view of the consumers,' and 'whether their use is similar and comparable.'[80] The test applied by the Court combines a factual comparison of the products with an economic analysis of their use, comparable to that applied by the WTO tribunals. For example, in EU case law it has been found that fruit wines and grape wines are similar,[81] as are dark and light cigarettes.[82] In contrast, liqueur fruit wine is not similar to whiskey[83] and bananas are not similar to other fruits.[84]

The assessment of whether imported products are taxed in excess of domestic products is similar to that of the WTO tribunals. In EU law there is also no *de minimis* rule applicable to a tax imposed on imported and domestic products, and the Court does not apply an 'aims and effect' test. By contrast, the Court has been clearer in its approach than the WTO tribunals. It has interpreted the term 'in excess' very broadly, including all situations where imports are at a disadvantage.[85] An example is the above mentioned *Outokumpu Oy* case.[86]

---

[79]   Slotboom, *supra* note 66, at 569.
[80]   Case 243/84, *John Walker & Sons*, 1986 E.C.R. 875, ¶ 11.
[81]   Joined Cases C-367/93 & 377/93, *FG Roders*, 1995 E.C.R. I-2229.
[82]   Case C-302/00, *Comm'n v. France*, 2002 E.C.R. I-2055.
[83]   Case 243/84, *John Walker & Sons*, 1986 E.C.R. 875.
[84]   Case 184/85, *Comm'n v. Italy*, 1987 E.C.R. 2013.
[85]   Case C-213/96, *Outokumpu Oy*, 1998 E.C.R. I-1777. *See also* Olsen, *supra* note 11, at 186.
[86]   Case C-213/96, *Outokumpu Oy*, 1998 E.C.R. I-1777.

Second sentence: protective taxes

The member states are also prohibited from imposing on the products of other member states any tax of such a nature as to afford indirect protection to other domestic products. The second sentence is broader than the first, and is intended to cover 'all forms of indirect tax protection in the case of products which, without being similar . . . are nevertheless in competition, even partial, indirect or potential competition, with each other.'[87] There are two key conditions to the second sentence: (1) that the products are in competition; and (2) that the tax measure affords indirect protection to domestic products.

The Court has used different tests to determine whether products compete. Similarly to the WTO tribunals, the Court applies tests based on product substitutability and cross-elasticity of demand. The Court also takes other factors into consideration, such as the product properties, production process and consumer preferences, though the last factor will probably not be determinative on its own.[88] To determine whether products meet the same consumer needs, the Court has held that it is necessary to look not only at the present state of the market but also at possible developments in the market. For example, wine and beer have been found to compete with each other, as the two beverages are 'capable of meeting identical needs.'[89]

When it has been determined that certain products are in competition, the next question is whether the tax measure is 'of such a nature as to afford indirect protection to other products.' The Court has held that differences in tax rates have to be above a *de minimis* level.[90] When assessing the compatibility of a tax with the second sentence of Article 110, account must be taken of the impact of that tax on the competitive relationship between the products concerned. The essential question is whether the tax is of 'such a kind as to have the effect, on the market in question, of reducing potential consumption of imported products to the advantage of competing domestic products.'[91] It is therefore the effect rather than the aim of the tax measure that is decisive.

Can discriminatory taxes be justified?

In contrast to WTO law, there is no provision in EU law that allows an exception to the prohibition in Article 110 similar to that in GATT Article XX. In EU law, the Court has developed an 'exception clause' in case law. Under this clause, a member state may adopt tax distinctions if they pursue objectives that are recognized by the EU as legitimate and the measure taken is proportionate. Environmental protection is considered a legitimate objective.[92] The Court thus takes the regulatory purpose of a tax measure into account in the assessment of whether a measure breaches Article 110. Accordingly, member states are permitted to distinguish between even similar products for regulatory purposes.

---

[87]   Case 193/85, *Cooperative Co-Frutta*, 1987 E.C.R. 2085, ¶ 19.
[88]   Case 170/78 *Comm'n v. United Kingdom*, 1980 E.C.R. 417 ¶ 8.
[89]   *Id.* at ¶¶ 8, 12.
[90]   *See, e.g., id.*; Case 356/85, *Comm'n v. Belgium*, 1987 E.C.R. 3299.
[91]   *Id.* at ¶ 15.
[92]   Case C-213/96, *Outokumpu Oy*, 1998 E.C.R. I-1777, ¶¶ 30–31. *See also* Case 252/86 *Bergandi*, 1988 E.C.R. 1343, ¶ 32; Case 196/85, *Comm'n v. France*, 1987 E.C.R. 1597, ¶ 7.

Harmonization of Environmental Taxation

Differing approaches to environmental tax measures in individual member states may distort competition and create an immediate obstacle to the functioning of the internal market. To ensure that a similar burden falls on the same sector across the EU, the TFEU specifically provides the legal basis for the harmonization of indirect tax measures, including environmental taxes.[93] Once the EU takes action, in principle member states no longer have the power to take action in a sector governed by EU legislation.

The legal bases for the adoption of harmonized tax measures are provided for in Article 113 in the chapter on tax provisions, Article 192(2) in the chapter on the environment and Article 194(3) in the chapter on energy. This last provision is new in the TFEU.[94] The harmonization of internal taxes is subject to a unanimous vote by the Council. Although it is an objective of the TFEU to harmonize rates of indirect taxation, little progress has been made so far in the environmental area, primarily due to the requirement for unanimity.

CONCLUSION

The trade rules impose discipline on the way in which governments can design and impose environmental taxes. A mapping of trade rules and how they affect national policymakers' room to maneuver is thus of considerable importance when tax measures are considered. Governments should carefully design taxes that have a direct bearing on the free flow of trade across borders, taking into account WTO law and any regional trade rules that apply, but they should also carefully consider exploiting any room for maneuver created by legal ambiguities in the interpretation of trade rules. A core principle in designing environmental taxes so as not to risk being found in breach of trade rules is not to discriminate against imports, regardless of whether taxes are calculated on the basis of the source of energy, carbon content or otherwise, and if PPM criteria are employed it will be all-important for the tax measure to provide for recognition of similar or comparable processes used in other countries.

In this chapter, several potential legal conflicts between WTO rules and national policies for meeting environmental objectives are identified. In many cases, it will probably be only a matter of time before these arise in fact in trade disputes. Whether environmental taxes will be accepted in a trade law context largely depends on how carefully they are written to avoid arbitrary discrimination, and whether in the future there will be a more coordinated approach both to techniques and to tax levels.[95] In this 'narrow' context, looking only at WTO law and EU law, it seems possible to provide a basis for multilateral negotiations on a coordinated approach to environmental taxation, and thus to establish a common framework for developing harmonized taxation on a global level.

---

[93]   J. Jans, & H. Vedder, European Environmental Law 80–81 (2008); L. Krämer, EC Environmental Law 89–90 (2007).

[94]   It was introduced by the Treaty of Lisbon.

[95]   Charnovitz, *supra* note 2, at 16–17, 20–21.

12 The double dividend debate
William K. Jaeger

INTRODUCTION

Environmental taxes are of interest mainly because they can improve environmental quality
efficiently (at the lowest cost). A potential positive side effect from a policy perspective is
their revenue-raising potential. 'Green tax' revenues could be used in a variety of ways, such
as for environmental cleanup or for research and development of clean energy technologies. But the most widely discussed potential use of environmental tax revenues relates to
the 'double dividend hypothesis,' the idea that environmental tax revenues could be used
to finance reductions in preexisting taxes. These tax changes are assumed to be 'revenue-
neutral,' meaning that reductions in revenue from preexisting taxes would be exactly offset
by the increased revenue from environmental taxes. The notion of a 'double' or additional
benefit is achieved because this kind of 'tax swap,' or 'green tax reform,' might lower the
economic distortions from the preexisting revenue-motivated taxes. Indeed, a few observers have even raised the idea that, given this 'revenue-recycling' benefit, the need to justify
environmental taxes on the basis of their environmental benefits may be less important (see,
for example, Bovenberg 1999). It turns out, however, that the interactions between environmentally motivated taxes and preexisting revenue-motivated taxes are complex, and the
economics research on this topic since the mid-1990s has been controversial and confusing.

The issues surrounding the double dividend hypothesis arise because there are two very
different motivations for introducing a tax: one motivation is to raise revenue; the other
is to internalize the external costs of environmental externalities or market failures. Most
early economic research focused on one of these issues, but not both.

First, revenue-raising taxes represent the most common motivation for taxation. Their
primary goal is to raise revenues to finance the provision of public goods such as national
defense, public safety, transportation infrastructure, education and basic research. It is
recognized that these 'collective consumption,' or public, goods would not be provided
at optimal levels in private markets due to 'free-riding' behavior when goods are nonrival
(i.e. when an individual's consumption of the good does not subtract from its availability
for others to consume). This fact underlies the rationale, established by Paul Samuelson
in 1954, for government provision of public goods, and thus the need to raise revenues in
order to finance public expenditures.

Second, environmentally motivated taxes manifest the idea that a tax can be used to
correct a market failure, or internalize an externality efficiently. Such a tax can achieve a
'first-best,' or optimal, allocation of resources provided no other distortions exist in the
economy. Other market-based policy instruments, such as tradable emissions rights, can
achieve similar efficiencies.[1] The economist Arthur Pigou was the first to recognize that

---

[1] It should be understood that in some cases other social considerations such as equity, rights,

a tax on an externality (such as a pollution tax) will be optimal when it is set at a level (dollars per unit of pollution) that is just equal to the value of marginal social damage (MSD), i.e. the marginal damage from the pollution externality.[2] Intuitively this result suggests that abatement should be pursued up to the point where the marginal cost of further abatement is just equal to the marginal benefit from additional reductions in pollution. A tax set equal to MSD will create just the right incentive to achieve this outcome, and hence it represents the optimal, or Pigouvian, tax.

One additional element from public economics that is important for our present discussion is the notion of optimal taxation (raising revenues necessary to finance public expenditures in the most efficient way).[3] The theory of optimal taxation recognizes that taxes tend to distort behavior, which introduces inefficiencies in the allocation of resources and hence a decline in social welfare compared to the (undistorted) optimum. By contrast, the central idea behind environmental taxes is that they do not distort but correct behavior in a way that eliminates the inefficiencies from environmental damage. The basic question addressed in optimal tax theory is, how can the inefficiency, or 'excess burden,' of revenue-raising taxes be kept to a minimum?

Taxes with no distortions are possible, at least in principle. A head tax, or tax on a fixed resource such as pure land rents, would be nondistortionary because it would have no effect on resource allocation (George 1912), but such options face large political obstacles. A uniform (proportional) tax on all goods would also be nondistortionary because the relative prices of all goods would remain unchanged and thus behavior would be unaffected (Auerbach 1985). Unfortunately this option is precluded by the presence of goods that cannot be directly taxed—leisure in particular.[4] As a result, the taxation of income or consumption will distort behavior by encouraging individuals to consume more leisure (and supply less labor) in the face of taxes on their expenditures or income (Auerbach 1985).

Given that distortionary taxes are unavoidable in realistic settings where governments need to raise revenue, Ramsey (1927) solved the optimal tax problem, which minimizes tax distortions in its basic form. His results establish that it is best to introduce a tax system that is broadly based, taxing all goods at low levels rather than a narrowly based tax system with high tax rates on a few goods. In a world of identical or symmetrical demands for all goods, equal taxes on all goods would be optimal: such taxes would raise the desired level of revenue with the least distortion, the minimum negative effect on welfare. Where the demand relationships differ across goods (for example, elastic demand for some goods, inelastic for others) but are independent of one another, the 'inverse elasticity rule' holds, stating that higher tax rates should be applied to goods with

---

political considerations and enforcement costs may tip the balance toward a preference for other policy instruments despite being less cost-effective.

[2]   Estimating MSD is itself complex and at times controversial. A variety of methods are now widely used to estimate, for example, the costs to health, productivity and amenities from pollution and other forms of environmental damage (see Freeman 2003).

[3]   Other dimensions of tax policy, such as the level of taxes and their distributional impact across income groups, are also important to consider, but to a considerable degree the two sets of issues can be explored separately.

[4]   Consumption of leisure time is the main example of a good that cannot be directly taxed.

inelastic demands and low tax rates applied to goods where demand is elastic. Goods produced using 'fixed factors' should receive relatively higher taxes in order to be optimal. The objective here is to minimize the extent to which the overall set of taxes will cause individuals to shift from consumption of taxed commodities toward greater consumption of the untaxable good, leisure.

These theoretical findings have been established in the economics literature based on models with strong assumptions about the workings of the economy, including competitive markets, profit-maximizing firms, rational consumers, and, in mathematical terms, 'well-behaved' preferences and technologies for production. Thus, it should be understood that relaxing one of these assumptions can alter the conclusions reached in this standard analysis, and thus the results and interpretations reflect a base-case from which modifications can be, and in many cases have been, introduced and evaluated.

Until the 1970s, the two main strands of tax theory just described—one tax intended to raise revenue and the other intended to correct externalities—were approached independently. Ramsey's (1927) optimal revenue-raising taxes ignore the possible presence of externalities, and Pigou's (1920) optimal externality taxes ignore the possible presence of revenue-raising taxes in the economy. Although Pigou (1932) did not consider how the revenues from a pollution tax would be used, what is now known as a Pigouvian analysis typically assumes that the revenues generated by the environmental tax are returned to the economy in a lump-sum fashion (for instance, distributed as payments to all individuals in a way that will not distort behavior).

In 1975, these two optimal tax problems were combined into one and solved formally by Agnar Sandmo (1975). Sandmo derived expressions for the optimal taxes on polluting goods and nonpolluting goods in a world with both revenue requirements and externalities. His conclusions received little attention until the 1990s, however, in part because his mathematical expressions for the resulting optimal taxes are difficult to interpret in a way that sheds light on the questions raised by the double dividend hypothesis.

Indeed, this integration of revenue-raising taxation and environmental, or 'corrective,' taxation underlies the central issue at hand. At one level the double dividend hypothesis asks: if environmental taxes raise revenue, and revenue-raising taxes discourage pollution, aren't these two policy objectives complementary? Doesn't a pollution tax kill two birds with one stone? A tax that reduces pollution *and* raises revenue would be serving both environmental and public expenditure goals and, intuitively, would seem to produce two benefits, or a 'double dividend,' when the environmental tax revenues also contribute to financing the provision of public goods. Moreover, wouldn't an integrated tax program that serves both public expenditure (revenue) goals and environmental (pollution) goals make it possible to achieve more on both fronts, at a combined lower cost, than when each goal is addressed separately?

The idea of a double dividend had been presented in the economics literature well before the 1990s, but it had received little attention. Beginning in the 1990s, however, with a growing interest in carbon taxes for slowing climate change, a renewed interest in pollution taxes emerged, including some new theoretical ideas that appeared to contradict the double dividend idea (for instance Bovenberg and de Mooij 1994). This new literature suggested that the double dividend hypothesis was wrong because it overlooked a previously unrecognized 'tax interaction effect' that, the authors claimed, exists when environmental taxes are introduced in a world with preexisting revenue-raising taxes (referred to also as a 'second-best' world since not all tax distortions can be eliminated to achieve a 'first-best' world). This new tax interaction (TI) literature caught many economists by surprise, and seemed to many observers to be counterintuitive. The debate on this issue resulted in a large and complex literature that even today perplexes many professional economists who struggle to understand the reasoning behind the TI findings.

Understanding this debate is important because the policy implications of these TI findings, if correct, have profound and sweeping implications for the efficiency arguments for environmental and other kinds of policy. Authors in the TI literature suggest that standard benefit–cost approaches to environmental policy 'have unwittingly omitted from the calculations a potentially quite significant class of social costs' (Parry and Oates 2000). Indeed, Parry and Oates (2000) describe the implications of the TI results in alarming terms:

> . . . this research has found that the costs associated with corrective taxes (and other regulatory measures) can be much higher in a second-best setting, so much so that in some cases the economic improvements from the traditional prescriptions can be offset by the exacerbation of the preexisting distortions. To take one example, it has been shown that for plausible values of the key parameters, a 'perfectly' designed system of tradable emissions rights—one that precisely internalizes the environmental externality by placing the costs of the environmental damages on the polluting source—may actually result in an overall loss in social welfare! (Parry, Williams, and Goulder, 1999)

To examine these issues in an understandable manner, the next two sections summarize the double dividend hypothesis and the tax interaction (TI) literature's findings, and explain why the TI results appear to contradict the double dividend hypothesis.

THE DOUBLE DIVIDEND HYPOTHESIS

The basic hypothesis of a 'double dividend' is that a revenue-neutral substitution of environmental taxes for revenue-raising taxes might offer an additional or second benefit. This idea was first advanced by Tullock (1967) in a paper titled 'Excess Benefit.' The first benefit (or dividend) is the welfare gain resulting from an improvement in the environment (less pollution), and the second dividend or benefit is due to a reduction in the distortions of the revenue-raising tax system, which also produces an improvement in welfare. This idea received scant attention—with the exceptions of Terkla (1984) and Lee and Miseolek (1986)—until the early 1990s, when the economics of climate change attracted attention to the topic of environmental taxes.

The term 'double dividend' became widely used following its introduction by David Pearce in 1991. The idea also attracted popular attention following publications such as Repetto et al. (1992). Pearce noted that estimates of the marginal excess burden (marginal distortionary cost) of existing levels of taxation in the US economy are between 20 and 50 cents per dollar of revenue collected. He then suggested that if the revenues from a carbon tax were used to lower existing taxes dollar-for-dollar, it would be equivalent to an effective carbon tax of only 50 to 80 cents in terms of its costs. Because the revenue from the carbon tax would be recycled (used to lower preexisting and distorting taxes), the policy would be revenue-neutral, and the secondary benefit from revenue recycling would justify an even higher carbon tax.

While the double dividend hypothesis is simple, the debate surrounding its validity has become complicated. This has occurred in part because views and approaches differ on how to define the double dividend hypothesis and what it implies, and there is no consensus on any single test or experiment that would validate or repudiate it. The intuition of the double dividend can be seen by looking at the question from two alternative starting points and asking two symmetrical questions. First, does the presence of an externality (and the opportunity to internalize it with a tax) lower the cost of raising revenue for the economy generally? Second, does the presence of public goods in need of funding (and the opportunity to introduce revenue-raising taxes to finance their provision) lower the cost of environmental taxation to internalize an externality? It turns out, however, that the validity of the double dividend hypothesis depends on specific relationships in the economy (how high are preexisting tax levels? How elastic is labor supply?), and this ambiguity has made it difficult to resolve the debate.

Indeed, the double dividend hypothesis has been subdivided and redefined in several different ways, at times creating more confusion than clarity. Nevertheless, a useful distinction can be made between the 'strong form' and the 'weak form' of the double dividend hypothesis when it is applied to a typical or standard set of assumptions about an economy (for example, all goods are similar in terms of demand; tax levels and labor supply elasticities are similar to those observed in the US economy):

1. The strong form of the double dividend hypothesis has been described and defined in several different ways. The most useful of these is Fullerton (1997), who uses a thought experiment to test the strong form of the double dividend hypothesis. He starts from a first-best situation where an externality has been internalized with a Pigouvian tax set at the optimal level, but where there are no distortionary revenue-raising taxes (and indeed where no other externalities exist). Fullerton also assumes that in this initial situation the revenue from the Pigouvian tax is just equal to the amount needed to finance government services. Then Fullerton asks: If the government's revenue requirement increases so that distortionary taxes are now necessary to raise additional revenue, will it be optimal to raise the tax on the polluting, or 'dirty,' good by more, or by less, than the tax on nonpolluting, or 'clean,' goods? This question is the same as asking whether the tax differential (the difference between the tax on dirty goods and the tax on clean goods) increases or decreases as government revenue requirements increase. If the differential between the tax on the dirty good and the tax on clean goods gets larger, it means that the optimal pollution tax (differential) is getting larger in a world with preexisting taxes, and this would affirm what Fullerton calls the strong form of the double dividend hypothesis (Fullerton 1997).
2. The weak form of the double dividend hypothesis asks a simpler question: Does revenue recycling (the use of environmental tax revenues to finance reductions in preexisting distortionary revenue-raising taxes) produce a net social benefit that is higher than if those revenues are not recycled into the tax program but rather returned lump-sum to the economy (for instance, dispersed in the form of equal rebates to all households)?

There is agreement that the answer to this second question is yes (see, for example, Goulder, Parry and Burtraw, 1997). A simple thought experiment involving two different policies demonstrates this point intuitively. If the revenues from a Pigouvian tax were just equal to the total revenues required by government, then revenue recycling would completely eliminate the need for any distortionary revenue taxes, so there would be no distortions at all in the economy. If, however, the revenues from the environmental tax were simply returned lump-sum to the economy, then distortionary revenue-raising taxes would be necessary to raise revenue and welfare would be lowered due to the distortions, or excess burden, attributable to the tax system. Both alternatives can achieve a desired level of reduced pollution, but only with revenue recycling do we also eliminate the distortions from revenue-raising taxation.

Most of the debate surrounding the validity of the double dividend hypothesis, however, has hinged largely on the evaluation of the first question as framed by Fullerton. Indeed, there is general agreement that under specific circumstances (involving relatively inelastic demand for environmentally harmful goods), the optimal environmental tax with revenue recycling *could* be higher than the first-best Pigouvian rate. However, the pivotal debate and controversy has centered on models that are neutral, in the sense that the demands for environmentally benign (clean) and environmentally harmful (dirty) goods are assumed to be similar. As such, findings for these models should hold for typical or average situations.

These questions surrounding the double dividend hypothesis have generally been framed in the context of revenue-neutral environmental taxation (resulting in no net change in government funds) to avoid creating other kinds of effects, such as those that would arise if the overall level of government funding rose or fell with the introduction of pollution taxes.

THE TAX INTERACTION EFFECT LITERATURE

Beginning in 1994, the validity of the double dividend hypothesis was challenged in a set of theoretical papers that appeared to show that, despite the presence of a positive revenue-recycling effect, the optimal environmental tax would actually be *lower* than the Pigouvian rate when revenue-raising taxes are present (Bovenberg and de Mooij 1994; Parry 1995; Bovenberg and Goulder 1996). These results caught many observers and even some of the authors by surprise because they seem logically incongruous: they are at odds with the intuitive reasoning that the addition of a revenue-recycling effect would increase the benefits of green tax reform so that the optimal environmental tax would rise above the Pigouvian rate. The authors of these papers argued that their results were due to the presence of a previously unknown distortionary cost, which they dubbed the tax interaction effect. This effect, they argued, was negative and large enough that it would generally offset the positive revenue-recycling effect, resulting in a net welfare change lower than expected from revenue-neutral green tax reform, and diminishing the justification for environmental policy. Indeed, the authors of this research concluded that government's goals of providing public goods with tax revenues were in conflict with the goal of protecting the environment (Bovenberg and Goulder 1996).

The central question for both the double dividend hypothesis and the tax interaction literature has been whether the welfare gains from environmental taxation in a second-best world are larger or smaller than in a first-best setting. In the TI literature, however, this central question was framed indirectly by asking whether the second-best optimal environmental tax is higher or lower than the first-best Pigouvian rate. Bovenberg and de Mooij (1994, 1085), for example, base their conclusion on a demonstration that 'in the presence of preexisting distortionary taxes, the optimal pollution tax typically lies below the first-best Pigouvian tax, which fully internalizes the marginal social damage from pollution.'

Fullerton (1997) defines the strong form of the double dividend hypothesis as suggesting 'that a revenue-neutral switch toward a tax on the dirty good and away from taxation of clean goods can improve environmental quality *and* reduce the overall cost of tax distortions.' As noted above, Fullerton formulates the test of this hypothesis for models where only commodities are taxed, so that the environmental tax is understood—given other assumptions—to equal the differential between the optimal tax on the dirty good and the optimal tax on clean goods. He continues: 'By implication, this [double dividend] view might suggest that any additional revenue requirements should be met by raising the tax on the dirty good by more than taxes on clean goods' (Fullerton 1997, 245).

In theory, Fullerton's test should be a reliable indicator of the relative welfare changes between second-best and first-best environmental taxation. On closer examination, however, neither Bovenberg and de Mooij (1994) nor Fullerton (1997) actually performs this test. Bovenberg and de Mooij instead move this indirect test one step further away from the underlying welfare question. More specifically, rather than comparing the second-best optimal environmental tax to its first-best Pigouvian value, they observe that the first-best optimal tax equals marginal social damage (at the first-best optimum), and so they compare the second-best optimal environmental tax to the value of MSD (but measured in a second-best setting). The unstated presumption here is that the value of MSD does not change when moving from a first-best to a second-best setting, so that if the optimal pollution tax appears higher (or lower) than MSD in a second-best setting, then this means that the tax has increased (or decreased).

With the advantage of hindsight, three factors have contributed to flawed interpretations in the TI literature: an algebraic error, the use of an unreliable benchmark, and a failure to recognize compounding or double taxation. As a result, the central conclusion that a large, previously unnoticed distortionary tax interaction effect existed was based on mistaken inferences and misleading evidence (Jaeger 2011). These three factors are examined in more detail below.

An Algebraic Error

The first factor contributing to mistaken conclusions was a straightforward algebraic error. Several authors, including Fullerton (1997), Bovenberg and de Mooij (1997a) and Auerbach and Hines (2002), looked at Sandmo's (1975) seminal results, and compared his equation for the optimal tax on dirty goods to the equation for the optimal tax on a clean good. They noticed that the two algebraic expressions were similar, differing only by a separate term added to the expression for the tax on the dirty good. Let's refer to that term as M/N, where M is the marginal social damage from pollution (in utility units) and N is the marginal value of public funds. These authors defined the optimal pollution tax as the difference between the optimal tax on the dirty good and the optimal tax on the clean good. They also recognized that in a first-best world with no distorting taxes, the other terms in Sandmo's expressions disappear, leaving only M/N, which equals the marginal social damages as defined by Pigou (at the first-best optimum, N, the marginal cost of public funds equals the marginal value of income).

When revenue-raising taxes are introduced into the economy, however, the marginal cost of public funds rises due to the distortions created by taxes, and as a result M/N will get smaller as revenue-raising taxes get larger (because N increases). From this, Fullerton and the others concluded that the differential between the optimal tax on the dirty good and the optimal tax on the clean good declines with rising revenue requirements, meaning that the pollution tax gets smaller. This result was interpreted as conclusive evidence contradicting the strong form of the double dividend hypothesis, and affirming the existence of a tax interaction effect.

However, there is an algebraic error in this interpretation. These economists mistakenly assumed that the tax in these algebraic expressions was just a nominal amount, T, for example in dollars per gallon. However, Sandmo's T is not expressed in dollars, but rather as a tax ratio, meaning $T = t/(p+t)$ where p is the price without the tax, and t is the nominal tax in dollars per gallon. Given this formulation, Sandmo's expressions cannot be interpreted as casually as suggested by these observers. Indeed, as t is increased, T will rise more slowly. Thus, the conclusion that Sandmo's results provide an obvious confirmation of the TI conclusions is due to an algebraic oversight.

This error, however, only reinforced conclusions that had already been reached by other means in the initial TI literature. So let's turn to the two other ways that this initial literature was vulnerable to misinterpretation.

Reliance on an Unreliable Benchmark

The second factor arose because of the highly indirect way the TI literature tested whether the welfare changes from environmental taxation in a second-best setting were larger or smaller than in a first-best setting.

The initial logic was sound, and goes something like this: in a first-best setting, as we introduce a tax on pollution, the benefits (from internalizing the externality) outweigh the costs (the distorting effects of the tax on consumer choice) over some range. At the optimum, when the tax equals MSD, the marginal benefits are exactly equal to the marginal costs, and no further increase in the pollution tax can be justified on efficiency grounds. If, however, in a second-best setting, there is an additional benefit from revenue recycling (using the revenues to finance reductions in preexisting taxes), then the benefits from introducing and raising the environmental tax will be larger than in the first-best setting. This means that the point where the marginal benefits are just equal to the marginal costs should occur at a higher environmental tax than in the first-best case, a tax level above the first-best Pigouvian rate. Given this straightforward reasoning, if the optimal environmental tax in a second-best setting is higher than in a first-best setting, this will be an indirect indicator of the existence of these extra benefits, or a double dividend.

Rather than carry out this test, however, the authors of the TI literature made their test even more indirect. They did not compare the value of the second-best optimal environmental tax with the value of the first-best optimal environmental tax (for instance dollars per gallon). Instead they observed that the first-best optimal tax is equal to MSD, defined MSD in algebraic terms, and then set out to test whether the second-best optimal environmental tax was higher or lower than MSD. But because the value of MSD will vary when shifting from a first-best to a second-best setting, MSD is not an unvarying benchmark or standard against which to compare the level of the environmental tax (Jaeger 2002). MSD is a ratio where the numerator is the marginal social disutility from environmental damage and the denominator is the marginal utility of income, and it will vary for complex reasons involving how taxes make the private marginal value of income diverge from the social value of income, and these differences also vary depending on how the tax program is implemented (Jaeger 2011). For these models, it is reasonable to assume that the numerator of MSD is constant, but this cannot be the case for the denominator, the marginal utility of income, because its value depends on the level of taxation.

A numerical example will help illustrate the problem of using MSD as a benchmark. Let's assume that at the first-best optimum the pollution tax is $10/ton and thus MSD is, of course, also $10/ton since the optimal tax equals MSD at the first-best optimum. Now let's shift to a second-best world with higher taxes where we find that the optimal environmental tax is now $15/ton, but we also find that the value of MSD is now $20 (despite causing the same disutility or damage per unit of pollution). Using the TI approach one would simply compare the optimal environmental tax ($15/ton) to MSD ($20/ton) and conclude that the optimal environmental tax has declined—because it is now below MSD—even though it has actually risen from $10 to $15.

This is precisely the conclusion reached by Fullerton (1997): that the second-best optimal environmental tax is below its first-best value. Indeed, Fullerton then turns to Sandmo's optimal tax expressions and concludes that they reinforce his own (mistaken) findings. Thus, although Fullerton began by proposing the simplest, most transparent thought experiment with which to define the strong form of the double dividend hypothesis, in the end he did not actually test that hypothesis directly. He instead compared the optimal pollution tax to the value of an unstable expression for MSD, which resulted in mistaken interpretations.

Overlooked Compounding Effects of Direct and Indirect Taxes

The third source of confusion leading to the conclusions in the TI literature involves the way revenue-raising taxes are assumed (in the theoretical model) to be introduced into the economy—something referred to as the 'normalization' of the tax program. Revenue-raising taxes can be introduced in two ways: as a tax on income (wages) or as taxes on expenditures (consumption). With some simplifying assumptions, either one of these can be used to achieve the identical result: an optimal revenue-raising tax program with equal taxes on all goods or, equivalently, a tax on wages.

Pollution taxes must necessarily be introduced on expenditures rather than income, as a tax on the dirty good. When revenues are also collected with expenditure taxes, then the optimal pollution tax is just added to the dirty good's revenue-raising tax to give us a total tax on the dirty good. When revenues are collected using an income tax, however, it is more complicated. The presence of an income tax 'compounds' the pollution tax. One is a direct tax (on income), while the other is an indirect tax on expenditures (indirectly taxing

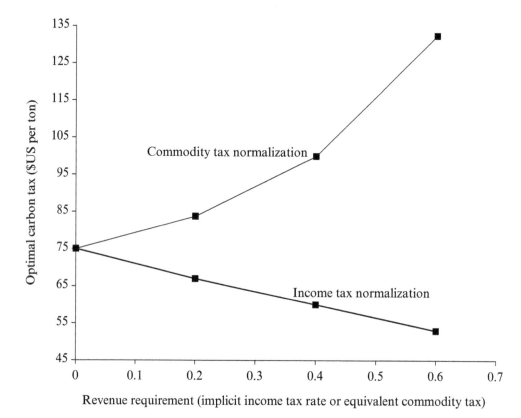

Source: Bovenberg and Goulder (1996, p. 994).

Figure 12.1   *The optimal carbon tax with rising revenue requirements under different tax normalizations*

income by taxing the things income is spent on). This magnifies the incentives to reduce pollution to a greater extent than is reflected in the pollution tax. The higher the income tax, the lower the pollution tax needs to be to achieve the same incentives and outcome. The pollution tax may look lower, but it still represents a higher 'effective' pollution tax.

Because the effective pollution tax will be higher than the nominal pollution tax in this case, the two tax normalizations (one with income taxes and one with expenditure taxes) can be viewed as identical optimal tax situations (in terms of incentives, choices and welfare), but with different taxes on pollution. Indeed, as revenue requirements increase, the optimal pollution tax will generally rise for an expenditure tax normalization, but the (nominal) pollution tax will generally decline for the income tax normalization. In fact, this divergence, due to the way the tax program is normalized, is precisely what occurs in Bovenberg and Goulder's carbon tax model (1996).

Their results can be represented for either tax normalization, as shown in Figure 12.1. Bovenberg and Goulder conclude that 'optimal environmental tax rates are generally below the rates suggested by the Pigovian principle—even when revenues from environmental taxes are used to cut distortionary taxes,' and decline as revenue requirements

rise. But this is based on a numerical model and results where the tax program was formulated using a labor tax (which is equivalent to an income tax in these models where
other sources of income are excluded) to raise revenue (lower line in Figure 12.1). Their
results can be converted to the other tax normalization (consistent with Fullerton's
framing of the strong form of the double dividend hypothesis), and we see in the upper
line in Figure 12.1 that these results confirm that the optimal carbon tax rises. But because
they normalized their model to include an income tax, they observe the opposite trend
(a declining nominal pollution tax), rather than recognizing that the effective pollution
tax is actually rising.

These issues are not transparent or easy to understand. Indeed, if they were, these
errors would have been identified long ago. Nevertheless, these three causes of mistaken
interpretation have reinforced each other, and have created confusion and puzzlement
among research economists since the mid-1990s.

In addition to these difficulties caused by somewhat obscure theoretical investigation methods, the real-world relevance of the results from the TI literature have also
been called into question by Goodstein (2002), who focuses on the assumption in the TI
models that labor supply declines with a rise in the general price level (due to taxes). The
authors of the TI literature concede that their results are dependent on a decrease in the
labor supply when pollution taxes raise the general price level. Although some empirical
evidence tends to support the assumption that labor supply declines when wages decline,
Goodstein points out that a household's labor supply response to a change in the price
level will differ from its response to a change in wages. This being the case, empirical estimates of labor's responsiveness to price level changes do not support the assumption that
labor supply will decline with a rise in the overall price level. Hence, one of the necessary
assumptions underlying the tax interaction results is without a solid empirical basis and
should thus be viewed with healthy skepticism.

To summarize, the TI literature that emerged in the mid-1990s came to be widely
accepted as valid during the subsequent decade, despite persistent and strong skepticism
on the part of many economists. With hindsight we can now see that the most surprising
conclusions of this literature appear to be largely mistaken.

Despite this state of the debate surrounding the general double dividend hypothesis
(for an average, or neutral, situation), there has been an increasing focus on specific
situations or special cases and the degree to which a double dividend can be expected in
those circumstances. We turn now to a discussion of these special cases and the direction
of recent research in that area.

DOUBLE DIVIDENDS FOR SPECIAL CIRCUMSTANCES

The two salient sources of benefits, or efficiency gains, with environmental taxation are
improved efficiency achieved by internalizing an environmental externality, and fiscal
or tax efficiency related to raising government revenues. A double dividend may arise if
tax efficiency is improved along with environmental efficiency. In the sections above the
debate was about whether we can expect this to occur in general or on average (without
assuming any special circumstances). But observers have always recognized that there
may be special cases or circumstances where introduction of an environmental tax could

have additional benefits. Fullerton (1997) points to some of these cases, including those where environmental taxes could replace regulations (that generate no revenue), or where the initial tax system includes some highly inefficient taxes that could be lowered with the environmental tax revenues.

More generally, there are several additional ways that revenue-raising tax efficiency could be improved by enlarging the tax base (so that low tax rates can be spread over a broader base, which will generally improve efficiency). To set the stage, consider the fact that in its simplest, neutral form, a double dividend is understood to depend only on economy-wide factors such as the level of taxation and the elasticity of labor supply, not on whether the polluting good is a relative complement to leisure, or whether environmental quality is a complement to leisure. The central question about the existence of a double dividend has been debated for neutral assumptions, including symmetrical demands, separability for leisure and environmental quality in the utility function, and the presumption of an otherwise efficient revenue-raising tax program. Participants in that debate, however, have long recognized that relaxing these assumptions could easily alter the central findings about the double dividend hypothesis. Such settings represent special cases where particular assumptions may make the existence of a double dividend more or less likely. In general, studies that have examined these kinds of settings fall into three categories: first, models where environmental quality affects production rather than being represented only as an environmental amenity in utility; second, models with specific assumptions about preferences, where the dirty good is no longer an average substitute for leisure, or where changes in environmental quality affect the demand for leisure; and third, models where the preexisting tax program is not optimal.

Environmental Effects on Productivity

If degrading the environment affects productivity, this represents a negative externality, and hence a justification for a corrective tax, but it will also affect the tax base by reducing the scale of taxable income. For example, when air pollution adversely affects the health of the labor force, it may also reduce labor supply due to morbidity and mortality. A pollution tax in such a case could have two beneficial effects, first by reducing pollution and second by producing an increase in labor supply which in turn raises taxable income and enlarges the tax base. A larger tax base makes it possible to collect a given level of taxes with a smaller distortionary cost.

Several studies have looked at these productivity effects in a model aimed at estimating the implications for environmental taxation. Jaeger (2002) looks at carbon taxes in a model where emissions affect production adversely, and concludes that the revenue-neutral introduction of a carbon tax would generate annual welfare gains of $3.58 billion when marginal damage is assumed to equal $40 per ton. Indeed, the optimal carbon tax is found to be $61/ton, or 53 percent above the Pigouvian rate. Williams (2002, 2003) evaluates a model where pollution affects health and labor productivity. He finds that there is significant scope for what he calls 'benefit-side tax interaction effects,' or more generally for green tax reform, to produce environmental net benefits as well as reduced distortions in the tax system. However, Williams also finds that when health benefits lead to reduced spending on medical care, this can have an opposite effect. See also Bovenberg and de

Mooij (1997b). Lower demand for medical care narrows the tax base, thereby raising the excess burden of the tax system (see also Koç 2007).

Assumptions about Individuals' Preferences

The introduction of a pollution tax may cause the tax base to expand or contract due to indirect effects that depend on individuals' preferences. In particular, if environmental quality and leisure are nonseparable (that is, if changes in one influence the marginal utility of the other), then environmental taxes may have an indirect effect on the welfare costs of the tax system because of the way that environmental quality affects the demand for leisure. Environmental quality and leisure may be complements or substitutes, so the effect can go either way: preference nonseparability can lead to higher (or lower) demand for leisure, and hence a contraction (or expansion) in the tax base. Specifically, if the environment is a close substitute for leisure, then improvement in environmental quality will cause an increase in labor supply, which enlarges the tax base and reduces the distortions in the tax system. In situations where this occurs, the introduction of an environmental tax will produce the positive effects of a double dividend.

This issue has been examined in several papers interested in how these factors may influence conclusions about the double dividend in particular settings (see, for example, Mayeres and Proost 1997; Kim 2002; and Schwartz and Repetto 2002). Intuitively, if commodities are either strong complements to pollution (such as fossil fuels) or strong complements to leisure, then making them more costly with an environmental tax will lower the demand for leisure, which in turn will increase the tax base, thereby lowering the excess burden of the tax system. For example, West and Williams (2007) find that gasoline and leisure are complements, so that raising the price of gasoline can be expected to increase labor supply (and consumption), causing a fiscal welfare gain in addition to an environmental welfare gain.

More generally, Carbone and Smith (2008) examine a range of assumptions and models in which air quality is assumed to be a complement or substitute for leisure and other market goods. They conclude that with a range of reasonable assumptions about nonseparability, the estimated excess burden estimates for a 5 percent energy tax can produce results that are 32 percent higher or 21 percent lower than under neutral assumptions. They further conclude that 'the size of the error depends on the magnitude of the assumed marginal willingness to pay for air quality improvements. The substitution pattern between air quality, leisure, and market goods is also a key determinant of the sign and magnitude of the error because it determines whether higher air quality encourages or discourages labor supply and the production of pollution-intensive goods' (1255–56). Carbone and Smith (2008) emphasize, however, that they do not have an empirical basis for gauging whether air quality is a complement or a substitute for leisure or other market goods, and they point to the need for additional empirical research focused on measuring these elasticities.

Indeed, questions have been raised about whether a positive labor supply response can be assumed to hold for tax-related price increases (that indirectly lower the real wage). There is significant debate in the literature about the effect of specific price increases on labor supply. As discussed above, Goodstein (2002) argues that the empirical literature supports the conclusion that price increases such as those resulting from environmental taxes will increase labor supply rather than decrease it, which would add to the evidence in support of a double dividend effect.

Other aspects of individual preferences could also affect the fiscal benefits of environmental taxation. For example, Howarth (2006) looks at how status-seeking, or 'keeping up with the Joneses,' behavior would affect the results. This phenomenon is described as 'relative consumption effects' because individuals' utility is dependent on their relative consumption (compared to that of their neighbors). Howarth finds that in a model with CO_2 emissions and climate change, with realistic assumptions about the empirical magnitude of relative consumption effects, the optimal emissions tax rises by 50 percent because the perceived social benefits of consumption are reduced and the social willingness to pay for environmental quality is consequently increased. Relative consumption effects also call into question the assumption that revenue-raising taxes such as income taxes create a marginal excess burden, since they may discourage the consumption externalities due to relative consumption effects (i.e. wasteful conspicuous consumption).

Preexisting Inefficient Tax Programs

When real-world tax programs are considered, the potential fiscal benefits from environmental tax reform can be significant, not necessarily because of a 'pure' double dividend, but because the revenue-neutral introduction of an environmental tax inadvertently also makes the overall tax program more efficient. For example, an optimal revenue-raising tax program, known as Ramsey taxes, will call for relatively higher taxes on goods for which demand is inelastic and for lower taxes on goods with elastic demand. So, if compared to the optimal set of taxes, the preexisting tax program includes inefficiently low taxes on dirty goods and inefficiently high taxes on clean goods, it follows that revenue-neutral environmental taxation will have the effect of moving the overall tax program toward efficiency, thus reducing the excess burden.

A number of studies identify circumstances where such opportunities to eliminate inefficient taxes exist. Parry and Bento (2001) incorporate a model with tax-favored consumption goods such as housing and medical care, and find that the efficiency gains from tax reform are larger because the preexisting inefficiencies in the tax system distorted consumption decisions and factor markets. They conclude that revenue-neutral emissions taxes (or auctioned pollution permits) produce a double dividend. It's important to be clear, however, that this kind of double dividend is one that could be achieved—at least in part—without reference to the environment. A policy change aimed simply at reducing the inefficiencies of preexisting taxes would achieve some of these gains, and so they amount to an inadvertent side effect of the environmental tax swap, or what could be called a 'quasi-double dividend.'

A different kind of tax inefficiency will be present if taxes are fairly uniform across commodities (or implicitly, with labor taxes), when in fact an optimal tax program would include higher taxes on some goods than on others. This will be the case, for example, where polluting goods are produced using fixed factors. Optimal tax theory tells us that fixed factors should be taxed (directly or indirectly) at higher rates than factors whose supply is relatively elastic. If polluting goods are produced with fixed factors, then a revenue-neutral tax swap that raises taxes on those goods will implicitly be raising taxes on fixed factors and lowering taxes elsewhere in the economy. In this kind of situation, an environmental tax swap can produce a double dividend (Bento and Jacobsen 2007). One additional example of a double dividend arising out of inefficient preexisting taxes comes from a study of Japan. Takeda (2007) finds that the weak form of the double dividend is confirmed in all scenarios, and that the strong double dividend arises when revenues are recycled by lowering capital taxes but not labor or consumption taxes. This result occurs because in Japan capital taxes are more distortionary than labor or consumption taxes. Bovenberg and de Mooij (1997b) make a similar point.

UNEMPLOYMENT AND THE DOUBLE DIVIDEND

Most of the research on environmental taxation and the double dividend hypothesis has been conducted using models that assume market equilibriums, including labor markets at full employment. In a few cases researchers have examined how unemployment might be affected by environmental tax reform for economies with involuntary unemployment. Nearly all of this research has focused on Europe, where persistent high rates of unemployment represent a central policy issue.

In an economy with 'structural' unemployment (where labor markets do not achieve a market-clearing equilibrium wage), there are a variety of ways in which revenue-neutral environmental tax reform could affect the level of unemployment. For example, if pollution taxes affect consumer prices, this could also affect the wage bargaining between unions and employers. In one model of this kind, Koskela and Schöb (1996) find that if unemployment benefits are not taxed nor indexed to the consumer price index, environmental tax reform will boost employment. In a different study, Holmlund and Kohm (1997) index the level of unemployment payments to the consumer wage, and show that in this situation environmental tax reform will boost employment if it shifts employment away from those sectors where unions have more market power.

Bovenberg and van der Ploeg (1998) look at this question and conclude that environmental tax reform will boost both environmental quality and employment in the following circumstances: if substitution between labor and resources is relatively easy, if the share of fixed factors in production is large, and if the initial tax rates on resources and profits are small. They also conclude that if the initial tax system is suboptimal with a negligible tax on resources, profits will also rise. In other studies relying on theoretical models (such as Brunello 1996; and Carraro, Galeotti and Gallo 1996), the authors find that the 'employment dividend' from environmental taxation may not persist in the long run. They also find that the environmental benefits may diminish as a result of the gains in employment and hence consumption. These studies suggest that under some circumstances, environmental quality may actually worsen, even though this change would be consistent with welfare maximization (Schöb 2003).

Overall, this research shows that it is possible to construct situations where environmental tax reform may affect employment positively or negatively, depending, for example, on the way the incentives facing the unemployed are altered relative to incentives elsewhere in the economy.

EMPIRICAL STUDIES

A basic feature of the double dividend debate is that it cannot be resolved as a general proposition through direct observation or empirical studies. The fiscal consequences of an environmental tax shift are going to be subtle and intangible. Moreover, with no way to directly observe or measure the marginal excess burden of a tax program, settling the debate will require a combination of theory and numerical models that characterizes, as best as possible, an economy. Detailed numerical computer models may have some success in estimating these interconnected effects if they are sufficiently detailed, with adequate validation in key areas such as labor supply and the cross-price effects among the environment, polluting goods and leisure, and a realistic representation of taxes, subsidies and regulations.

A number of empirical models have estimated these effects for a range of national circumstances and preexisting tax programs. For example, in a study of agricultural pollution control (Taheripour et al. 2008), a general equilibrium model that includes existing agricultural subsidies is used to evaluate the effects of nonpoint nitrogen pollution policies in the United States. The authors find that revenue-neutral changes such as removing agricultural subsidies and introducing subsidies for reduced use of nitrogen, or, alternatively, imposing output taxes on agriculture, can enhance welfare and reduce nonpoint nitrogen pollution, resulting in a substantial double dividend.

Also, in the context of climate change policy, Babiker et al. (2003) employ computable general equilibrium models to examine the welfare effects of environmental taxes with revenue recycling for a number of European countries. They find that the results differ considerably depending on the types of preexisting tax programs as well as other factors. Indeed, they find that revenue recycling through tax cuts can be welfare-reducing relative to lump-sum recycling of tax revenues. Intuitively this will occur if the tax cuts increase the relative distortions in the taxes among goods. This research strongly suggests that as a practical matter, it is important to understand which taxes are the most distorting so that a 'customized' form of revenue recycling can take advantage of specific opportunities to realize a double dividend. Given the large differences in energy taxes between the United States and European economies, Babiker et al. (2003) conclude that correctly representing the existing distortions in energy markets is essential to correctly evaluating the economic impacts of environmental taxes such as those contemplated for climate policy. However, the results from a country-specific analysis must be interpreted cautiously before applying them to other countries. And this applies especially to the need for an accurate representation of existing distortions in energy markets.

These findings are reinforced by the results of a meta-analysis that examined dozens of studies on environmental tax reform (Patuelli et al. 2005) and found that the tax type, revenue-recycling policy type, and numerical economic model used are the most important factors influencing the evidence of a double dividend. They conclude that differences in these factors should be taken into consideration when considering a tax policy, or when relying on one particular simulation study for determining the merits of environmental tax reform.

SUMMARY AND CONCLUSIONS

Despite a debate that has largely been played out on the basis of technical details in theoretical models, the concept of a double dividend fits well into a systems approach, or ecological economics framework, which emphasizes the importance of placing economic models and analyses within the larger natural systems on which they depend. Previously, the economics of optimal taxation had only recognized one untaxable endowment, namely leisure. Now we can recognize that environmental quality is clearly another such untaxable good, the consumption (enjoyment) of which cannot be directly taxed. We understand that revenue-raising taxes on income and expenditures are distortionary precisely because they discourage labor supply and encourage greater consumption of untaxed leisure; the double dividend can be seen as indicating, in a parallel fashion, that optimal taxation will discourage pollution and encourage greater 'consumption' of untaxed environmental quality. To the extent that higher revenue requirements mean higher taxes, they are also likely to mean greater consumption of both leisure and environmental quality.

The intuition that an optimal revenue-raising tax program should be as broadly based as possible is also consistent with the systems approach emphasized in ecological economics. This suggests that—like other goods in the economy—environmental goods and services should be priced at their social cost in a 'first-best' world without distortionary taxes (the Pigouvian rate in the case of emissions). In a 'second-best world,' where distortionary taxes are necessary to finance public expenditures, a broadly based revenue-raising tax should be added to all goods, raising their prices above their social cost—above the Pigouvian rate in the case of emissions.

Despite recent controversy and confusion on this topic, the conclusions that can be drawn are in keeping with economic intuition. Environmental and revenue-raising taxes are complementary tools for achieving two different kinds of government goals: the provision of public goods with revenue-motivated taxes and the protection of environmental quality with corrective taxes. Indeed, the joint pursuit of these two goals through taxation can enable government to justify doing more of each by making the optimal environmental tax higher than it would be otherwise, and by lowering the distortionary cost of financing the provision of public goods.

Still, additional research is needed on this topic. There needs to be research that will provide a better understanding of those specific circumstances where a double dividend or quasi-double dividend is most likely to arise. This kind of research could identify situations where environmental tax swaps could have particularly large positive effects on welfare. In addition, however, more attention needs to be paid to the measurement of marginal social damages, to the effect of measures based on pre-tax versus after-tax income, and to the question of when differences between the social and private marginal utility of income may be relevant. Similarly, in economies with labor taxes, policymakers need to recognize that environmental taxes may need to be set below the estimated value of MSD because of the compounding effect of direct and indirect taxes, which makes the effective tax higher than the nominal tax (Jaeger 2011).

REFERENCES

Auerbach, A. (1985), 'The theory of excess burden and optimal taxation', in A. Auerbach and M. Feldstein (eds), *Handbook of Public Economics*, Vol. 1. Amsterdam, The Netherlands: North-Holland.

Auerbach A.J. and J.R. Hines Jr. (2002), 'Taxation and economic efficiency', in A.J. Auerbach and M. Feldstein (eds), *Handbook of Public Economics*, Vol 3, Amsterdam, The Netherlands: Elsevier Science.

Babiker, M.H., G.E. Metcalf and J. Reilly (2003), 'Tax distortions and global climate policy', *Journal of Environmental Economics and Management*, **46** (2), 269–87.

Bento, A. and M. Jacobsen (2007), 'Ricardian rents, environmental policy and the "double-dividend" hypothesis', *Journal of Environmental Economics and Management*, **53**, 17–31.

Bovenberg, A.L. (1999), 'Green tax reforms and the double dividend: an updated reader's guide', *International Tax and Public Finance*, **6**, 421–43.

Bovenberg, A.L. and R.A. de Mooij (1994), 'Environmental levies and distortionary taxation', *American Economic Review*, **94** (4), 1085–89.

Bovenberg, A.L. and R.A. de Mooij (1997a), 'Environmental levies and distortionary taxation: reply', *The American Economic Review*, **87** (1), 252–53.

Bovenberg, A.L. and R.A. de Mooij (1997b), 'Environmental tax reform and endogenous growth', *Journal of Public Economics*, **63** (1), 207–37.

Bovenberg, A.L. and L.H. Goulder (1996), 'Optimal environmental taxation in the presence of other taxes: general equilibrium analysis', *American Economic Review*, **86** (4), 985–1000.

Bovenberg, A.L. and F. van der Ploeg (1998), 'Consequences of environmental tax reform for unemployment and welfare', *Environment and Resource Economics,* **12**, 137–50.

Brunello, G. (1996), 'Labour market institutions and the double dividend hypothesis', in C. Carraro and D. Siniscalco (eds), *Environmental Fiscal Reform and Unemployment,* Dordrecht: Kluwer Academic, pp. 139–70.

Carbone, J.C. and V.K. Smith (2008), 'Evaluating policy interventions with general equilibrium externalities', *Journal of Public Economics*, **92** (5–6), 1254–74.

Carraro, C., M. Galeotti and M. Gallo (1996), 'Environmental taxation and unemployment: some evidence on the "double dividend hypothesis" in Europe', *Journal of Public Economics,* **62**, 141–81.

Freeman, A.M. III (2003), *The Measurement of Environmental and Resource Values* (2nd ed.), Washington, DC, US: Resources for the Future.

Fullerton, D. (1997), 'Environmental levies and distortionary taxation: comment', *American Economic Review*, **87** (1), 245–51.

George, H. (1912), *Progress and Poverty*, Library of Economics and Liberty.

Goodstein, E. (2002), 'Labor supply and the double dividend', *Ecological Economics*, **42** (1–2), 101–6.

Goulder, L.H., I.W. Parry and D. Burtraw (1997), 'Revenue-raising versus other approaches to environmental protection: the critical significance of preexisting tax distortions', *The RAND Journal of Economics*, **28** (4), 708–31.

Holmlund, B. and A.-S. Kolm (1997), 'Environmental tax reform in a small open economy with structural unemployment', Working Paper 5.97, Milan, Italy: Fondazione Eni Enrico Mattei.

Howarth, R.B. (2006), 'Optimal environmental taxes under relative consumption effects', *Ecological Economics*, **58**, 209–19.

Jaeger, W.K. (2002), 'Carbon taxation when climate affects productivity', *Land Economics*, **78** (3), 354–67.

Jaeger, W.K. (2011), 'The welfare effects of environmental taxation', *Environmental and Resource Economics,* **49** (1), 101–19.

Kim, S.-R. (2002), 'Optimal environmental regulation in the presence of other taxes: the role of non-separable preferences and technology', *Contributions to Economic Analysis and Policy*, **1** (1), 1–25.

Koç, Ç. (2007), 'Environmental quality, medical care demand and environmental tax interactions', *Environmental & Resource Economics*, **37** (2), 431–43.

Koskela E. and R. Schöb (1996), 'Alleviating unemployment: the case for green tax reforms' CES Working Paper 106, Munich, Germany: University of Munich.

Lee, D.R. and W.S. Miseolek (1986), 'Substituting pollution taxation for general taxation: some implications for efficiency in pollution taxation', *Journal of Environmental Economics and Management*, **13** (4), 228–47.

Mayeres, I. and S. Proost (1997), 'Optimal tax and public investment rules for congestion type of externalities', *Scandinavian Journal of Economics*, **99** (2), 261–79.

Metcalf, G.E. (2003), 'Environmental levies and distortionary taxation: Pigou, taxation and pollution', *Journal of Public Economics*, **87** (2), 313–22.

Nordhaus, W.D. (1993), 'Optimal greenhouse-gas reductions and tax policy in the "DICE" model', *American Economic Review*, **83** (2), 313–17.

Parry, I.W.H. (1995), 'Pollution taxes and revenue recycling', *Journal of Environmental Economics and Management*, **29** (3), 564–77.
Parry, I.W.H. and A. Bento (2001), 'Revenue recycling and the welfare effects of road pricing', *Scandinavian Journal of Economics*, **103** (4), 645–71.
Parry I.W.H. and W.E. Oates (2000), 'Policy analysis in the presence of distorting taxes', *Journal of Policy Analysis and Management,* **19** (4), 603–13.
Parry, I.W.H., R.C. Williams III and L.H. Goulder (1999), 'When can carbon abatement policies increase welfare? The fundamental role of distorted factor markets', *Journal of Environmental Economics and Management*, **37** (1), 52–84.
Patuelli, R., P. Nijkamp and E. Pels (2005), 'Environmental tax reform and the double dividend: a meta-analytical performance assessment', *Ecological Economics*, **55**, 564–83.
Pearce, D. (1991), 'The role of carbon taxes in adjusting to global warming', *Economic Journal,* **101** (407), 938–48.
Pigou, A.C. (1920/1932), *The Economics of Welfare*, London, UK (4th ed. 1932).
Ramsey, F.P. (1927), 'A contribution to the theory of taxation', *Economic Journal*, **37**, 47–61.
Repetto, R., R.C. Dower, R. Jenkins, J. Geoghegan (1992), *Green Fees: How a Tax Shift Can Work for the Environment and the Economy*, Washington, DC, US: World Resources Institute.
Samuelson, P.A. (1954), 'The pure theory of public expenditure', *The Review of Economics and Statistics*, **36** (4), 387–89.
Sandmo, A. (1975), 'Optimal taxation in the presence of externalities', *Swedish Journal of Economics*, **77**, 86–98.
Schöb, R., (2003), 'The double dividend hypothesis of environmental taxes: a survey', Working Paper 2003.60, Milan, Italy: Fondazione Eni Enrico Mattei.
Schwartz, J. and R. Repetto (2002), 'Non-separable utility and the double dividend debate: reconsidering the tax-interaction effects', *Environmental and Resource Economics*, **15**, 149–57.
Taheripour, F., M. Khanna and C. Nelson (2008), 'Welfare impacts of alternative policies for environmental protection in agriculture in an open economy: a general equilibrium framework', *American Journal of Agricultural Economics*, **90** (3), 701–18.
Takeda, S. (2007), 'The double dividend from carbon regulations in Japan', *Journal of the Japanese and International Economies*, **21** (3), 336–64.
Terkla, D. (1984), 'The efficiency value of effluent tax revenues', *Journal of Environmental Economics and Management*, **11** (2), 107–23.
Tullock, G. (1967), 'Excess benefit', *Water Resources Research*, **3**, 643–44.
West, S.E. and R.C. Williams III (2007), 'Optimal taxation and cross-price effects on labor supply: estimates of the optimal gas tax', *Journal of Public Economics*, **91**, 593–617.
Williams, R.C. III (2002), 'Environmental tax interactions when pollution affects health or productivity', *Journal of Environmental Economics and Management*, **44** (2), 261–70.
Williams, R.C. III (2003), 'Health effects and optimal environmental taxes', *Journal of Public Economics*, **87**, 323–35.

13 The political economy of environmental taxation
Nils Axel Braathen*

INTRODUCTION

This chapter will—from an economist's angle—address the political economy of environmental taxation.[1] The first task is to define the term 'political economy.' A couple of hundred years ago, the term was used to describe anything covered by the term 'economics' today,[2] but over roughly the last century, the term has more specifically referred to economic analyses of political decision processes. Stavins (2004b, 1) stated, 'In the environmental realm, questions of political economy emerge along three fundamental dimensions, which are closely interrelated but conceptually distinct: (1) the *degree* of government activity; (2) the *form* of government activity; and (3) the *level* of government that has responsibility.'[3]

Oates and Portney (2003, 327) gave the following definition: 'The term "political economy" has come to take on a variety of shades of meaning. It is now, in fact, a rather elusive term that typically refers to the study of the collective or political processes through which public economic decisions are made.'

In order to limit the scope of the chapter somewhat, this chapter will not address the third dimension Stavins referred to, a topic discussed in Chapter 14 of this Handbook. Instead it will seek to review important parts of both the positive and normative literature addressing the first two dimensions—that is, literature that tries to explain the decisions that are being made in these areas, and literature that gives recommendations on how the decisions ought to be made. It reviews some of the theoretical literature, and then addresses some of the empirical literature. When preparing new work on environmentally related taxes some years ago, OECD sent a questionnaire to member countries, asking them to identify the main obstacles to a broader use of such taxes. Not surprisingly, a fear of negative impacts on sectoral competitiveness (and a fear that low-income households would be negatively impacted) made countries reluctant to broaden their use of environmentally related taxation. Consequently, this chapter goes on to review a number of studies addressing the competitiveness issue before closing with a few concluding remarks.

---

* The author is Principal Administrator in OECD's Environment Directorate. The views expressed are those of the author and do not necessarily reflect those of the OECD or its member countries.

[1]   In OECD's work in this area, the term 'environmentally related taxes' is used, covering all taxes levied on tax bases deemed to be of particular environmental relevance—regardless of their 'motivations' and of how the revenues raised are used.

[2]   http://en.wikipedia.org/wiki/Political_economy provides some historical anecdotes in this relation. Yandle (1990) provides additional historical information.

[3]   Stavins (2004a) is a collection of many important papers on the political economy of environmental policy. Stavins (2004b) is the introduction to that book.

EXPLAINING THE USE—OR LACK OF USE—OF ENVIRONMENTAL TAXATION

Traditionally, the view among most economists was that public policies were based on 'public interest'—largely in line with a normative viewpoint.[4] Governments were assumed to always seek to maximize social welfare, such as by taking measures to correct environmental (and other) externalities.

The positive literature on environmental taxation builds on the writings on regulation of economic actors in general, and on the literature on environmental regulations more broadly.

Stigler (1971) was a groundbreaking paper, setting out a theory of how firms could 'capture' policies to their own benefit—starting with a section called 'What benefits can a state provide to an industry?' and followed by a section called 'The costs of obtaining legislation.'[5] The tone was certainly not one of an industry sector trying to have public authorities refrain from interfering in the free markets; on the contrary, it was stated that 'regulation is acquired by the industry and is designed and operated primarily for its benefit' (Stigler 1971, 3). Commenting on this, Oates and Portney (2003, 330) stated that

> While the capture theory may describe some classes of regulatory activity reasonably well, it does not seem to us that it is very successful as a positive theory of environmental policy . . . . Environmental measures typically impose costs—sometimes quite significant costs—on the sources of polluting activities. For this reason, it seems misleading at best to describe environmental measures as instigated by regulatees—that is by polluting industries.

While Stigler (1971) looked at regulation of economic agents in general, Buchanan and Tullock (1975) looked in particular at environmental regulations, finding that firms would prefer direct regulations to a tax on emissions.[6] This famous paper stimulated much later research activity that added important nuances to their findings. For example, Dewees (1983, 55) stated that

> Buchanan and Tullock (1975) represent direct regulation as a quota allowing equal rates of discharge to all firms. In fact, such quotas are rare, represented primarily by point of impingement concentration limits. A requirement that the best available or best practicable technology be used will in the long run tend to result in a uniform rate of emission per unit of input . . . or output . . . .. An effluent concentration limit will also allow emissions in proportion to production. Some regulations explicitly relate allowable emissions to inputs or outputs. Thus it is more realistic to represent present policies as allowing emissions proportional to production than as allowing fixed total emissions per source.

---

[4]   Kalt and Zupan (1984, 279) stated more than 25 years ago that the 'economic theory of regulation long ago put public interest theories of politics to rest. These theories have correctly been viewed as normative wishings, rather than explanations of real world phenomena.'

[5]   Peltzman (1976) provided a mathematical formalization of Stigler's theory. Posner (1974, 335) gave an early, in-depth discussion of public interest and capture theories of public policies, concluding that 'while promising, the [capture] theory requires both more analytical development and new sorts of empirical investigation before it can be accepted as an adequate positive theory of regulation.'

[6]   Majone (1976) highlighted that it was unrealistic to assume that environmental taxes would be any more sheltered from lobbying by lobby groups than, for example, direct regulations.

Commenting on the same paper, Hahn (1990, 40–41) found that

> Buchanan and Tullock (1975) choose to 'explain' the choice of standards by choosing what, upon closer inspection, appears to be an unlikely alternative . . ... For example, Buchanan and Tullock (1975) do not show why industry has a marked preference for standards over taxes. They show why industry has a marked preference for a very specific standard over a very specific tax.

In contrast with the capture theory put forward by Stigler (1971), Becker (1983) presented a model in which the outcome of political processes is determined by competition among pressure groups for political favors. In this approach, the equilibrium depends on the efficiency of each group in producing pressure, the effect of additional pressure on their influence, the number of persons in different groups, and the deadweight costs of taxes and subsidies. The analysis brought together a view in the (largely normative) literature that governments primarily seek to correct market failures with a view (such as that found in the capture theories) that the governments mostly seek to favor the politically powerful. One of the findings in Becker (1983) was that governments will tend to choose mechanisms that are more efficient (in terms of the deadweight losses they create) over those that are less efficient in redistributing revenues from less powerful to more powerful groups.[7] It is, however, debatable whether this is a valid characterization of the instruments currently applied in environmental policy.

Aidt (1998) presented an alternative model, also based on competition between lobby groups. He found that the politically optimal structure of environmental taxes incorporates a Pigouvian adjustment, but since lobby groups care about the distribution of income as well as about efficiency, the equilibrium structure of taxes differs considerably from the economically optimal Pigouvian rule. Since lobby groups and the government in this model agree to pick the more efficient instrument to correct for the externality, the environmental adjustment is targeted at the source of the externality—the input that in his model causes the environmental damage, as opposed to a tax on production volumes per se. It is the presence of unorganized citizens that introduce inefficiency in an otherwise socially efficient equilibrium in this model.

While Becker (1983) was indeed a seminal contribution to the literature, the roles of voters, politicians and bureaucrats were not much elaborated in the article. Without presenting a formalized mathematical model, Dietz and Vollebergh (1999) gave a verbal discussion of the roles of polluters, environmentalists, politicians and bureaucrats in the choice of instruments for environmental policy, suggesting for instance that, compared to market-based instruments, command-and-control instruments offer politicians better opportunities to present an image as caring for the environment. They also found that bureaucrats demonstrate little interest for improving the cost-efficiency of environmental policies, and that the use of market-based instruments would shift influence from Ministries of Environment to Ministries of Finance.

In a somewhat similar line of work, Nash (2009) discussed the choice between providing new roadway capacity and using congestion charging to manage road congestion. He

---

[7]   Hahn (1990) points out that a problem with Becker's theory is that it was difficult to test because of the difficulty in specifying the 'influence functions' that it is built around.

found that 'public choice' arguments have tended to dominate over economic efficiency arguments, writing, 'New roadway construction is a politically attractive way to satisfy constituents and powerful interest groups' (308). However, despite the power of public choice, Nash also found that 'it is possible for efficiency concerns to prevail when the inefficiencies of other responses become too large' (308). He further indicated that a slight movement toward greater acceptance of congestion pricing in recent years can also be explained by public choice theories.

Haupt and Stadejek (2010) analyzed environmental policies in a situation where the market is vertically differentiated in terms of the energy efficiency of products. They found that an industry-friendly government in this case would levy an energy tax to supplement a lax product standard but would shy away from paying subsidies to firms. By contrast, a consumer-friendly government would rely heavily on a strict product standard and in addition would implement a moderate subsidy to firms, but would avoid energy taxes.

Fredriksson (1997) developed a formalized model seeking to explain the use of environmental taxes in a small open economy, and found that the equilibrium tax rate depends on lobby group membership, the government's weight on aggregate social welfare relative to lobbying activities, and the tax elasticity of pollution. In his model, the government is assumed to care only about its reelection, and the probability of electoral success depends on aggregate campaign contributions from lobby groups and on aggregate social welfare. The model was also extended to incorporate a possibility of pollution abatement and a pollution abatement subsidy, showing that total pollution may be increasing with an increasing subsidy rate. This surprising effect arose because the equilibrium pollution tax rate could be decreasing in the subsidy rate, due to altered political influence of the lobby groups in the political equilibrium.

Dijkstra (1999), using various formalized models of 'rent seeking,' sought to answer the question, 'Why are market instruments not more widely applied in environmental policy, although they are efficient?' The answer was found to lie in there being powerful interest groups that prefer direct regulation to market instruments. These interest groups have so much influence on the political decisions that they can block the introduction of market instruments. Looking at a number of specific policy situations involving an impure public good, Dijkstra found that the instrument alternative with the highest aggregate valuation could have a low, and sometimes even zero, probability of being selected.

Glachant (2002a, 4) focused on the design of environmental taxes and developed a model where 'three design parameters—tax rate, earmarking pattern and whether the tax is combined with a regulation—are simultaneously selected by a Government under the influence of a green lobby and an industrial lobby making campaign contributions.' Glachant assumed that a regulatory policy was in place at the outset, and studied the prospects of an environmental tax being introduced in situations with perfect or imperfect enforcement of the preexisting regulation. The model predicts three possible outcomes, largely determined by the share of the 'greens' in the total population and the relative political strength of the green and the industry lobbies:

- The introduction of a non-earmarked tax in combination with a regulation, at a tax rate above the regulation shadow price—when the greens are politically very influential.

- The status quo, that is, no tax is introduced—when the preexisting regulation is perfectly enforced.
- The introduction of an earmarked tax in combination with the status quo regulation at a tax rate below the regulation shadow price, with subsidies financed by the tax helping to promote compliance.

In this model, there is very little chance of seeing the introduction of a non-earmarked tax at a rate above the regulation shadow price—even if that would have been the efficient policy solution.

In a later paper, Glachant (2008) presented a somewhat different model to discuss the use of a regulation, a non-earmarked tax or a cap-and-trade system with free allocation of permits in a world where industrial polluters engage in lobbying.[8] Glachant analyzed which policy instrument would be chosen by a policymaker in a situation without any preexisting policy instruments and in a situation with a regulatory instrument already in place. In the first case, Glachant found that a cap-and-trade system would always be chosen. However, if a regulatory instrument were already in place, it would be replaced by a cap-and-trade system only if the fixed administrative costs were modest, and if the industrial lobby were strong. A tax would never be chosen in this model, due to the financial cost it would represent for the lobbying polluters.[9]

Aidt and Dutta (2004, 458) looked at the same three policy instruments as Glachant (2008), in a world where the 'conflict of interest between special-interests, representing polluters, and the electorate is resolved by an elected politician'—in a situation where the strictness of environmental policy is exogenously determined. They found that the gradual transition, observed in some countries, from emission standards to either taxes or tradable permits can be understood as a consequence of increasingly ambitious environmental targets, which cause an increased focus on the cost-effectiveness of the instruments applied.

Aidt (2010) presented a rich model with two competing political parties, an industry lobby and two groups of citizen-voters, one informed and one uninformed, where both the tax rate and the use of the revenue that the environmental tax raises is determined endogenously.[10] He showed, somewhat surprisingly, that within this model, the 'polluter lobby group may lobby in favor of a refunding rule that allocates all ecotax revenue to citizen-voters, despite the fact that it could ask for tax burden compensation for its members' (32). The reason is that by lobbying for a refunding rule that pleases the voters, the lobby group can obtain a reduction in the tax rate.

A common assumption in many models developed in this area, building on the findings of Olson (1965), is that it is easier for small groups that would be hard-hit by a given

---

[8] In this model, there is no green lobby. Glachant pointed out that if the permits had been auctioned in this model, there would not have been any difference between a tax and a cap-and-trade system.

[9] Glachant emphasized that the model used was a *partial* equilibrium model, with no benefits stemming from the use of the revenue raised by a tax.

[10] Aidt (1998) and (2010), Fredriksson (1997) and Glachant (2002a) and (2008) all built on the very influential model explaining protectionist trade policies developed in Grossman and Helpman (1994) and elaborated further in Grossman and Helpman (2001).

policy to organize their opposition than it is for a large group of actors that would obtain a small, positive benefit from a policy to organize support for it.

Boyer and Laffont (1999, 152) 'interpreted the political economy of environmental policy as an analysis of the economic implications of politicians' discretion in pursuing the private agendas of their electoral base: some voters are more concerned than others by pollution, some voters have stakes in the informational rents of the polluting firms.' They used a reelection mechanism that depended only on campaign contributions, modeled as a given percentage of rents, and found some situations where a uniform regulatory standard could be more efficient than a flexible policy instrument.

Schneider and Volkert (1999, 123), in an analysis differentiating between the behavior of voters, politicians, interest groups, and bureaucracies, concluded that 'in representative democracies, in which political entrepreneurs attempt to maximize utility, an incentive-oriented environmental policy has hardly any chance of being implemented.'

Keohane, Revesz and Stavins (1998) presented an overview of the positive literature on environmental policy and sought to explain why practical environmental policy deviated so significantly from normative prescriptions in economic textbooks, focusing on the decisions of the legislators rather than the actions of the executive branch (such as the US Environmental Protection Agency (EPA)). According to Stavins (2004b, 14), 'The authors develop their "market model" of the supply and demand of environmental policy instruments. In general, explanations from economics tend to refer to the demand for environmental policy instruments, while explanations from political science refer to the supply side.'

On the demand side, Keohane, Revesz and Stavins (1998) pointed out that standards produce rents to the affected firms, especially if coupled with more stringent requirements for new sources. In contrast, auctioned permits and taxes require firms to pay also for any remaining pollution levels. The authors also found that environmental NGOs are likely to prefer command-and-control instruments, for 'philosophical, strategic, and technical reasons' (354). The authors were of the opinion that the training and experience of legislators could make them more comfortable with direct standards than with market-based approaches. The time they would need to learn about market-based instruments could represent significant opportunity costs. For them, standards (compared to taxes, for example) could also have the advantage of tending to hide the costs of pollution control while emphasizing the benefits, and—as also touched upon by Dietz and Vollebergh— may offer greater opportunities for symbolic politics.

EMPIRICAL STUDIES OF EXPLANATIONS OF ENVIRONMENTAL POLICY CHOICES

While a number of theoretical papers provide a positive discussion of the use of environmental taxation versus less flexible policy instruments, relatively few empirical studies have sought to explain the (limited) use of environmental taxation. Stavins (2004a) included several empirical papers addressing instrument choices in environmental policy, but none of them related directly to environmental taxes.

Hahn (1989), giving examples from several countries, offered an overview of to what extent policymakers had followed recommendations from economic theory when formulating environmental policy. He pointed out that 'regulatory systems involving multiple instruments are the rule rather than the exception. The fundamental problem is to determine the most appropriate mix, with an eye to both economic and political realities' (111).[11,12]

Joskow and Schmalensee (1998, 37) discussed the allocation of emission allowances to electrical utilities under the 1990 US Acid Rain Program. They found that while 'rent-seeking behavior is apparent, statistical analysis of differences between actual and benchmark allocations indicates that the legislative process was more complex than simple models suggest. . . . Some major coal-producing states seem to have focused on benefits for miners and on sustaining demand for high-sulfur coal.'

In their edited volume, Andersen and Sprenger (2000) included some chapters discussing political economy issues related to environmental taxation in place (or not) at that time. For example, Daugbjerg (2000) discussed why a fertilizer tax had been introduced in Sweden but not in Denmark. The analysis was built on a (not mathematically formalized) model in which two political structures, policy networks and parliaments, had an important impact on environmental policymaking. Daugbjerg found that the Danish agricultural network was more cohesive than its Swedish counterpart, and that parliamentary support for the farmers was stronger in Denmark than in Sweden, in part because the Social Democratic Party in Sweden had chosen to place emphasis on consumers' interests in agricultural policy.[13] Vatn (2000) also addressed a tax on fertilizers, this time in Norway, focusing on relationships between efficiency and fairness as explanatory variables. While the initial introduction of a tax with a low rate triggered only modest resistance, opposition to a later proposal to increase the tax rate significantly grew much stronger.[14]

Kasa (2000) analyzed emission tax exemptions for heavy industries in Denmark, the Netherlands and Norway, finding that while some emission-intensive industries in Norway and the Netherlands were largely exempted from taxes, Danish industries were exempted to a more limited extent. The author tried to explain this difference by noting the economic importance and the political power and influence of these industries in the countries concerned. He concluded that explanations based on the economic importance of exempted industries are very important; however, explanations based on factors that influence the political power of the exempted industries should also be investigated. In many cases, such factors supplement explanations based on economic importance and can produce outcomes that explanations based only on the industries' economic importance fail to account for. Glachant (2002b) analyzed why the rates of the French water effluent charges are kept so low.[15] He found that the charge rate was pushed downward through three main drivers:

---

[11]   For further discussion of mixes of environmental policy instruments, see OECD (2007a) and Braathen (2007).

[12]   Bressers and Huitema (2000) provided further assessments of Hahn's discussion.

[13]   The Swedish tax on artificial fertilizers was discontinued from 1 January 2010, as part of a package of measures that also included some changes unfavorable to the agriculture sector. OECD (2007b) referred to discussions in Denmark of taxes or quota systems that would address the net nitrogen surplus going into the agricultural sector as a whole.

[14]   The Norwegian tax on artificial fertilizers was discontinued from 1 January 2000.

[15]   Barraqué (2000) also discussed the French water-charging system.

- The opposition of the Ministry for Finance to a fiscal scheme that it does not directly control due to earmarking.
- The preference of the environmental regulator (the Ministry for the Environment) to use regulation to reach the socially efficient level of pollution abatement. As regulation cannot be used alone due to problems of enforcement, it gives the water charge and subsidy a role of enforcement incentive of the water regulation.
- The reluctance of the municipalities to abate pollution beyond a regulatory constraint which approximates the socially efficient level of pollution abatement (40–41).

Glachant (2002b, 40) concluded that the 'outcome is necessarily a situation where the price signal of the charge and subsidy scheme is below the regulation shadow price.' However, this conclusion was partly based on the (not necessarily valid) assumption that the Ministry of Environment would oppose any increase in the charge rate above the regulation shadow price. Even if a higher charge rate would make the regulation the ministry administered unbinding, it is not obvious that the ministry would oppose a higher charge rate, leading to better water quality.

Daugbjerg and Pedersen (2004) sought to explain the design of taxes on pesticides and CO_2 emissions in Denmark, Norway and Sweden, with differences in the policy networks in the three countries as a major explanatory factor. The authors state that:

> In pesticide taxation, the interests of Danish farmers were accommodated to the greatest extent and the interests of Swedish farmers to the least extent. In terms of accommodating farm interests, the design of the Norwegian pesticide tax scheme lies somewhere in between the Danish and the Swedish schemes. In CO_2 taxation, the pattern is different from pesticide taxation. Norwegian industry was, in general, best off while Swedish industry was worst off. Danish industry held an intermediate position. The variation in tax schemes was explained by the existence of different established state-producer policy networks in Danish, Norwegian and Swedish agricultural and industrial politics. These networks privileged producer interests to different extents and thus affected their opportunities to influence the design of tax schemes to minimize perceived costs. (245)

STUDIES ADDRESSING SECTORAL COMPETITIVENESS IMPACTS OF ENVIRONMENTAL TAXES

As mentioned in the introduction, a major political obstacle to the broader use of environmental taxation is a fear that the competitiveness of the most affected sectors could be significantly negatively affected.[16] A number of studies have addressed this issue.[17]

OECD (2006a) discussed competitiveness impacts of environmentally related taxes

---

[16]   Certainly, what policymakers ought to focus on are the impacts on the competitiveness of the country as a whole, even if that is a concept more difficult to define (cf. OECD 2003b). Nevertheless, it tends to be the impacts on the most directly affected sectors that get most of the attention.

[17]   There is a large number of model simulations of economic (sometimes also of environmental) impacts of various environmental policies available. This survey seeks to focus on studies that in particular address political economy aspects related to sectoral competitiveness, but the choice of studies included here can certainly be found somewhat arbitrary.

from several angles, drawing on a number of ex ante and ex post case studies (OECD [2003a–2003c], [2005a–2005e]). Model simulations indicated that the use of economic instruments to reduce greenhouse gas emissions was likely to have negative impacts on the international competitiveness position of some industrial sectors, especially if such instruments were implemented in a non-global manner. This was demonstrated in ex ante case studies of carbon taxes applied in the steel and cement sectors (OECD [2003a] and [2005d]). However, both studies showed that in spite of some element of carbon leakage, significant global reductions in carbon emissions could be achieved.

OECD (2006a) indicated that unilateral policies by single regions or countries could lead to significantly larger production decreases in the countries and sectors concerned. The larger the group of countries that put similar policies in place, the more limited would be the impacts on sectoral competitiveness. OECD (2003a) and (2005e) looked at ways to limit the burden on affected firms, while maintaining the pollution abatement incentives. One option could be to recycle back to the affected firms (a part of) the revenues raised. The studies indicated that revenue recycling would reduce global emission reductions in the sector. In other words, protecting competitiveness through recycling revenues back to the affected sectors could lower the environmental effectiveness of the policy as a whole. The reports also discussed the use of border tax adjustments to reduce competitiveness impacts of taxes.

While OECD (2003a) and (2005e) presented partial equilibrium analyses of policies to address climate change, focusing on the impacts on the selected sectors, OECD (2009) presented general equilibrium model simulations of such policies. These analyses showed that while incomplete country coverage would raise the costs of achieving any global target, it does not necessarily imply significant carbon leakage—in other words, emission cuts in the participating countries would be offset by emission increases elsewhere. Unless only a few countries were to take action against climate change, leakage rates would be almost negligible. For example, if the European Union acted alone (that is, no other countries put in place *any* additional climate policies), almost 12 percent of their emission reductions would be offset by emission increases in other countries. However, if all developed countries were to act, this leakage rate would be reduced to below 2 percent.

If the coalition of acting countries is very small, OECD (2009) indicates that imposing border tax adjustments (BTAs) on the carbon content of imports from nonparticipating countries could be one way to prevent leakage. However, such tariffs would imply potentially large costs for both participating and nonparticipating countries, would be likely to be administratively burdensome, and could provoke trade retaliation, without necessarily reducing the output losses incurred by energy-intensive industries in participating countries. McKibbin and Wilcoxen (2009) also analyzed impacts of using BTAs to limit any negative sectoral competitiveness impacts of policies to address climate change, reaching results relatively similar to those of OECD (2009). They found that BTAs would be effective in reducing emission leakage but also that leakage would be very small even without BTAs. Because the BTAs would be small, they would have little effect on import-competing industries. The authors concluded that the benefits that BTAs could bring about are unlikely to justify their administrative complexity and the negative impacts on international trade. (For a discussion of the legal requirements governing BTAs, see Chapter 11 in this Handbook.)

Fischer and Fox (2009) considered four policies that could be combined with unilateral emissions pricing to counter negative effects on international competitiveness: a border tax on imports, a border rebate for exports, full border adjustment, and a domestic production rebate. While all have the potential to support domestic production, none is necessarily effective at reducing global emissions. The results were illustrated with simulations for the energy-intensive sectors in the United States and Canada.

Manne and Mathiesen (1994) was an early partial equilibrium analysis of competitiveness impacts of unilateral policies addressing an individual industrial sector. According to the authors' business-as-usual scenario, a gradual shift toward new sources of aluminium production located outside the OECD region was expected. The analysis indicated that unilateral OECD carbon restrictions could dramatically accelerate that process.

Baron (1997) showed that for energy intensive industries in most of nine OECD countries, a tax of US$100 per ton of carbon would result in a static cost increase of about 2 percent, ranging from 0.6 to 11 percent. The study noted that cost increases from carbon/energy taxation should be compared with other factors affecting price levels, such as exchange rate variations and cyclical variations of stocks of energy-intensive goods.

Morgenstern et al. (2002) examined short-term impacts of new GHG policies—both US-wide mitigation policies and ones that addressed only the electric power industry—on domestic manufacturing industries. The principal conclusion was that within the manufacturing sector, a small number of industries would bear a disproportionate short-term burden of a carbon tax or similar policy. Not surprisingly, an electricity-only policy would affect very different manufacturing industries than would an economy-wide carbon tax.

One way for policymakers to try to overcome the competitiveness obstacle is to provide compensation to the 'losers.' Bovenberg and Goulder (2003) explored various designs of CO_2-abatement policies, assessing how they could be designed to avoid 'unacceptable' effects for the most affected sectors. They found that the efficiency cost of avoiding fossil fuel industries' losses of profit could be relatively modest. The most cost-effective policies for limiting CO_2 emissions—carbon taxes and CO_2 permit trading systems in which the permits are initially auctioned—collect the most revenue and thus minimize the government's reliance on ordinary, distortionary taxes. Profits in key energy industries could be preserved if the government did forgo 10–15 percent of the potential revenue by allocating a small share of tradable carbon permits for free, by introducing minor exemptions to a carbon tax, or by providing a modest corporate income tax relief.

Goulder (2002) examined the cost of 'widening the net' to protect profits of other, downstream industries that otherwise would face significant losses from carbon-abatement policies. He found that the costs of 'insulating' a wider group of industries were modest as well.

Bjertnæs and Fæhn (2004) made a somewhat similar analysis in the case of a small, open economy, finding relatively modest welfare costs of compensating energy-intensive export industries for the losses they would suffer if the tax rate in the Norwegian electricity tax was equalized across sectors.

Bjertnæs (2006) looked at welfare impacts of possible production-dependent subsidies used to protect jobs in energy-intensive industries, finding that they were modest compared to the welfare gains of introducing uniform energy taxes across sectors.[18]

---

[18] This study was based on a similar approach as Böhringer and Rutherford (1997).

However, he also found that the welfare cost per job preserved by such a subsidy scheme would amount to about 60 percent of the wage cost per job, suggesting that these jobs are expensive to preserve.

As indicated above, OECD (2006a) mentioned (partial) refunding of tax revenues back to the most affected industries as one way of addressing sectoral competitiveness concerns. Sterner and Höglund Isaksson (2006) discussed in-depth such a tax-and-refund system, using the tax on NO_x emissions in Sweden as an example.[19] Lower net tax payments reduce resistance from the polluters and make it politically easier to implement a tax rate sufficiently high to provide significant abatement effects.[20]

Ex post assessments of environmentally related taxes (as well as other environmental policy instruments) are unfortunately rare. OECD (2005a–2005d) provided some examples. Cambridge Econometrics et al. (2005) is another example, providing an assessment of the UK Climate Change Levy (CCL) and the Climate Change Agreements (CCA), which offered an 80 percent reduction in tax rates for energy-intensive firms agreeing to negotiated targets for emission reductions or energy-efficiency improvements. One of the findings of the study was that almost all the CCA targets would have been met even if no CCL had existed, implying that the targets were not very demanding.

Martin and Wagner (2009) and Martin, de Preux and Wagner (2009) drew on firm-level data to assess the impacts of CCL and CCA, inter alia on firms' competitiveness. Their analyses showed that

> a moderate energy tax such as the CCL is more effective at promoting energy efficiency and hence mitigating climate change than a quantity target negotiated between government and industry. This is true from both a static and a dynamic perspective, since the CCL leads to more energy conservation and fosters more innovation in energy efficiency and other areas. Contrary to concerns about adverse effects on competitiveness, the CCL had no discernable effect on output and employment. (Martin and Wagner 2009, 6)

CONCLUDING REMARKS

This chapter has reviewed some parts of the literature dealing with the political economy of environmental taxes. Some of this literature has tried to explain why such taxes (or other policy instruments) are designed the way they are, while other works have made recommendations on how the taxes ought to be designed. Significant shares of the literature have in particular addressed the main political obstacle to the more widespread use of such taxes (perceived losses of sectoral competitiveness), assessing the validity of such concerns and/or suggesting ways to overcome the obstacles.

Looking across the literature, and across the existing landscape of existing environmental taxes,[21] it is clear that not just one factor explains their implementation and

---

[19]   OECD (2012) discusses in detail the political economy surrounding the introduction of this tax.

[20]   Höglund Isaksson and Sterner (2010) discussed the impacts of this tax on innovation activity. Other ex post case studies of innovation impacts of environmentally related taxes and similar instruments can be found at www.oecd.org/env/taxes.

[21]   For further information, see www.oecd.org/env/policies/database.

design. Lobby groups representing large industrial (or agricultural) emission sources will vigorously oppose such taxes, as the taxes will represent a transfer of rents from them to public authorities. However, public policies are not 'dictated' by such lobbying alone, and some countries *have* introduced such taxes (albeit normally with relatively low tax rates and major exemptions) amidst strong opposition.

The degree of (perceived) understanding of the seriousness of the environmental issue at hand, and of its underlying causes, seems likely to affect the 'climate' for introducing environmental taxes. This could inter alia influence the membership of green lobby groups, the ease with which such groups can communicate their messages to the rest of the citizen-voters, and probably also the degree of opposition from industrial lobby groups. The trust people place on information provided by environmental public authorities and environmental NGOs also seems likely to be of importance, and this is in turn likely to depend, at least to some extent, on the validity of the arguments being used. Models that explored these issues in greater detail would be welcome, as would attempts to empirically assess their importance.

On two occasions, in December 2000 and December 2009, the French Constitutional Court has turned down proposals for carbon-related taxes.[22] In the latter case, it seems clear that part of the explanation was that the Court had misunderstood the interactions between a carbon tax and the European CO_2 Emission Trading System. The Court objected to the fact that electricity use and industrial sources covered by the trading system were exempted from the proposed tax. However, given the presence of the ETS, taxing these sources would not have had any impact on total CO_2 emissions at the EU level, as long as the 'cap' of the ETS remained unchanged.[23] Further work on the best tax design in the presence of other policy instruments could hence be useful.

Additional ex post analyses of the impacts of environmental taxes that have been put in place would certainly also be welcome:[24] What have been their impacts on the competitiveness of individual sectors; what have been their overall economic impacts; how were different (income) categories of households actually affected; how were the benefits of the environmental improvements distributed etc.? Ideally, time-series of micro-level data should be used in such assessments.

Further research into the explanations of current instrument use would also seem useful. In conclusion, to pin-point one puzzle awaiting explanation: Mexico and Turkey are both OECD member countries with relatively similar income levels[25] and broadly similar total populations.[26] Is the fact that Mexico is a large petroleum producer in itself enough to explain that while Mexico (as the only OECD country doing so) provided net *subsidies* amounting to almost 0.1€ per liter of petrol sold in January

---

[22]   For further information on the former occasion, see the comments by Xavier Delache in OECD (2003c).

[23]   Similar interactions will be of importance between a cap-and-trade system and any other policy instrument applied alongside it—a major point largely ignored in practical policymaking. See OECD (2011) for further discussion.

[24]   This would obviously be easier to achieve if more such taxes were introduced, preferably with tax rates properly reflecting the relevant marginal environmental damages.

[25]   In 2008, PPP-corrected GDP per capita was US$14 500 in Mexico and US$14 000 in Turkey.

[26]   In 2007, Mexico had 107 million inhabitants, while Turkey had 71 million inhabitants.

2010, Turkey applied the highest *tax* rate on petrol of any OECD country, equalling 0.9€ per liter?[27]

REFERENCES

Aidt, Toke Skovsgaard (1998), 'Political internalization of economic externalities and environmental policy', *Journal of Public Economics*, **69**, 1–16.
Aidt, Toke Skovsgaard (2010), 'Green taxes: refunding rules and lobbying', *Journal of Environmental Economics and Management*, **60**, 31–43.
Aidt, Toke Skovsgaard and Jayasri Dutta (2004), 'Transitional politics: emerging incentive-based instruments in environmental regulation', *Journal of Environmental Economics and Management*, **47**, 458–79.
Andersen, Mikael Skou and Rolf-Ulrich Sprenger (eds) (2000), *Market-based Instruments for Environmental Management*, Cheltenham, UK: Edward Elgar.
Baron, Richard (1997), 'Competitiveness issues related to carbon/energy taxation', Working Paper 14 prepared for the Annex I Expert Group on the UN FCCC, Paris, France: OECD/IEA, www.olis.oecd.org/olis/1997doc.nsf/LinkTo/NT00000E3A/$FILE/02E88858.PDF.
Barraqué, Bernard (2000), 'Assessing the efficiency of economic instruments: reforming the French *Agences de l'Eau*', in M. S. Andersen and R.-U. Sprenger (eds) (2000), *Market-based Instruments for Environmental Management*, Cheltenham, UK: Edward Elgar, pp. 215–30.
Becker, Gary (1983), 'A theory of competition among pressure groups for political influence', *Quarterly Journal of Economics*, **XCVIII** (3), 371–400.
Bjertnæs, Geir H. (2006), 'Avoiding adverse employment effects from energy taxation: what does it cost?', Discussion Paper No. 432, Statistics Norway, Oslo, available at www.ssb.no/publikasjoner/DP/pdf/dp-432.pdf.
Bjertnæs, Geir H. and Taran Fæhn (2004), 'Energy taxation in a small, open economy: efficiency gains under political restraints', Discussion Paper No. 387, Statistics Norway, Oslo, www.ssb.no/publikasjoner/DP/pdf/dp387.pdf.
Böhringer, Christoph and Thomas F. Rutherford (1997), 'Carbon taxes with exemptions in an open economy: a general equilibrium analysis of the German tax initiative', *Journal of Environmental Economics and Management*, **32** I (2), 189–203.
Bovenberg, A. Lans and Lawrence H. Goulder (2003), 'Confronting industry-distributional concerns in U.S. climate-change policy', Les séminaires de l'Iddri, No. 6. Institut du Développement Durable et des Relations Internationales, www.iddri.org/Publications/Collections/Idees-pour-le-debat/Confronting-industry-distributional-concerns-in-US-climate-change-policy.
Boyer, Marcel and Jean-Jacques Laffont (1999), 'Toward a political theory of the emergence of environmental incentive regulation', *RAND Journal of Economics*, **30** (1) (Spring), 137–57.
Braathen, Nils Axel (2007), 'Instrument mixes for environmental policy: how many stones should be used to kill a bird?', *International Review of Environmental and Resource Economics*, **1**, 185–235.
Bressers, Hans Th. A. and Dave Huitema (2000), 'What the doctor should know: politicians are special patients. The impact of the policymaking process on the design of economic instruments', in Andersen and Sprenger (eds) (2000), *Market-based Instruments for Environmental Management*, Cheltenham, UK: Edward Elgar, pp. 67–86.
Buchanan, James M. and Gordon Tullock (1975), 'Polluters' profits and political response: Direct controls versus taxes', *The American Economic Review*, **65** (1), 139–47. Also included in Stavins (ed.) (2004a).
Cambridge Econometrics et al. (2005), 'Modelling the initial effects of the climate change levy', Report submitted to HM Customs and Excise by Cambridge Econometrics, Department of Applied Economics, Cambridge University, and the Policy Studies Institute.
Combet, Emmanuel et al. (2009), 'Economie d'une fiscalité carbone en France' [The economy of carbon taxation in France], Study undertaken for the trade union Confédération Française Démocratique du Travail (CFDT) by researchers of the Centre International de Recherche sur l'Environnement et le Développement (CIRED), www.cfdt.fr/rewrite/article/23599/nous-connaitre/nos-etudes/economie-d-une-fiscalite-carbone-en-france.htm?idRubrique=8174.
Daugbjerg, Carsten (2000), 'Explaining why the Swedes but not the Danes tax fertilizers: a comparison of

---

policy networks and political parties', in Andersen and Sprenger (eds) (2000), *Market-based Instruments for Environmental Management*, Cheltenham, UK: Edward Elgar, pp. 129–47.

Daugbjerg, Carsten and Anders Branth Pedersen (2004), 'New policy ideas and old policy networks: implementing green taxation in Scandinavia', *Journal of Public Policy*, **24** (2), 219–49.

Dewees, Donald N. (1983), 'Instrument choice in environmental policy', *Economic Inquiry*, **21**, 53–71. Also included in Stavins (ed.) (2004a).

Dietz, Frank J. and Herman R.J. Vollebergh (1999), 'Explaining instrument choice in environmental policies', in J.C.J.M. van den Bergh (ed.), *Handbook of Environmental Economics*, Cheltenham, UK: Edward Elgar, pp. 339–51.

Dijkstra, Bouwe R. (1999), *The Political Economy of Environmental Policy. A Public Choice Approach to Market Instruments*, Cheltenham, UK: Edward Elgar.

Fischer, Carolyn and Alan K. Fox (2009), 'Comparing policies to combat emissions leakage: border tax adjustments versus rebates', Discussion Paper 09–02, Washington, DC, US: Resources for the Future, www.rff.org/documents/RFF-DP-09-02.pdf.

Fredriksson, Per G. (1997), 'The political economy of pollution taxes in a small open economy', *Journal of Environmental Economics and Management*, **33**, 44–58.

Glachant, Matthieu (2002a), 'The political economy of environmental tax design', Discussion paper, Paris, France: Ecole des Mines de Paris, http://weber.ucsd.edu/~carsonvs/papers/48.pdf.

Glachant, Matthieu (2002b), 'The political economy of water effluent charges in France: why are rates kept low?', *European Journal of Law and Economics*, **14**, 27–43.

Glachant, Matthieu (2008), 'L'effet du lobbying sur les instruments de la politique environnementale' [The effect of lobbying on the environmental policy instruments], *Revue d'Economie Politique*, no. 5, www.cerna.ensmp.fr/images/stories/file/Matthieu%20Glachant/Efficacite%20des%20instruments%20et%20lobbying%20a%20paraitre.pdf.

Goulder, Lawrence H. (2002), 'Mitigating the adverse impacts of CO_2 abatement policies on energy-intensive industries', Discussion Paper 02–22, Washington, DC, US: Resources for the Future, www.rff.org/documents/RFF-DP-02-22.pdf.

Grossman, Gene M. and Elhanan Helpman (1994), 'Protection for sale', *The American Economic Review*, **84** (4), 833–50.

Grossman, Gene M. and Elhanan Helpman (2001), *Special Interest Politics*, Cambridge, MA, US and London, UK: MIT Press.

Hahn, Robert (1989), 'Economic prescriptions for environmental problems: how the patient followed the doctor's orders', *Journal of Economic Perspectives*, **3** (2), 95–114. Also included in Stavins (ed.) (2004a).

Hahn, Robert (1990), 'The political economy of environmental regulation: towards a unifying framework', *Public Choice*, **65**, 21–47.

Haupt, Alexander and Magdalena Stadejek (2010), 'The choice of environmental policy instruments: energy efficiency and redistribution', CESifo Working paper No. 2986, Munich, Germany: CESifo, www.ifo.de/pls/guestci/download/CESifo%20Working%20Papers%202010/CESifo%20Working%20Papers%20March%202010/cesifo1_wp2986.pdf.

Höglund Isaksson, Lena and Thomas Sterner (2010), *Innovation Effects of the Swedish NO_x Charge*, Paris, France: OECD, www.oecd.org/officialdocuments/displaydocumentpdf/?cote=com/env/epoc/ctpa/cfa(2009)8/final.

Joskow, Paul L. and Richard Schmalensee (1998), 'The political economy of market-based environmental policy: the U.S. acid rain program', *Journal of Law and Economics*, **41** (1), 37–83. Also included in Stavins (ed.) (2004a).

Kalt, Joseph P. and Mark A. Zupan (1984), 'Capture and ideology in the economic theory of politics', *The American Economic Review*, **74** (3), 279–300. Also included in Stavins (ed.) (2004a).

Kasa, Sjur (2000), 'Explaining emission tax exemptions for heavy industries: a comparison of Norway, Denmark and the Netherlands', CICERO Policy Note 2000:3, Oslo, Norway: Center for International Climate and Environmental Research, www.cicero.uio.no/media/1029.pdf.

Keohane, Nathaniel O., Richard L. Revesz and Robert N. Stavins (1998), 'The choice of regulatory instruments in environmental policy', *Harvard Environmental Law Review*, **22**, 313–67.

Majone, Giandomenico (1976), 'Choice among policy instruments for pollution control', Professional Papers, Vienna, Austria: International Institute for Applied Systems Analysis (IIASA), www.iiasa.ac.at/Admin/PUB/Documents/PP-76-002.pdf.

Manne, Alan S. and Lars Mathiesen (1994), 'The impact of unilateral OECD carbon taxes on the location of aluminium smelting', *International Journal of Global Energy Issues*, **6** (1/2), 52–61.

Martin, Ralf and Ulrich Wagner (2009), 'Econometric analysis of the impacts of the UK climate change levy and climate change agreements on firms' fuel use and innovation activity', Paris, France: OECD, www.oecd.org/officialdocuments/displaydocumentpdf/?cote=com/env/epoc/ctpa/cfa(2008)33/final.

Martin, Ralf, Laure B. de Preux and Ulrich Wagner (2009), 'The impacts of the climate change levy on business:

evidence from microdata', Working Paper No. 7 of the Centre for Climate Change Economics and Policy, Working Paper No. 6 of Grantham Research Institute on Climate Change and the Environment, www.cccep.ac.uk/Publications/Working%20Papers/Papers/Working_Paper7.pdf.

McKibbin, Warwick J. and Peter J. Wilcoxen (2009), 'The economic and environmental effects of border tax adjustments for climate policy', in Brainard and Sorkin (eds) (2009), *Climate Change, Trade and Competitiveness: Is a Collision Inevitable?*, Brookings Trade Forum 2008/2009, Washington, DC, US: Brookings Institution Press.

Morgenstern, Richard D. et al. (2002), 'The near-term impacts of carbon mitigation policies on manufacturing industries', Discussion Paper 02–06, Washington, DC, US: Resources for the Future, www.rff.org/documents/RFF-DP-02-06.pdf.

Nash, Jonathan Remy (2009), 'Public choice over efficiency: the case of road traffic management', in Cottrell et al. (eds) (2009), *Critical Issues in Environmental Taxation*, Vol. VI, Oxford, UK: Oxford University Press.

Oates, Wallace E. and Paul R. Portney (2003), 'The political economy of environmental policy', in Mäler and Vincent (2003), *Handbook of Environmental Economics*, Vol. 1, Amsterdam, Netherlands: Elsevier Science B.V.

OECD (2003a), 'Environmental policy in the steel industry: using economic instruments', Paris, France: OECD, www.olis.oecd.org/olis/2002doc.nsf/LinkTo/com-env-epoc-daffe-cfa(2002)68-final.

OECD (2003b), 'Environmental taxes and competitiveness: an overview of issues, policy options, and research needs', Paris, France: OECD, www.olis.oecd.org/olis/2001doc.nsf/LinkTo/com-env-epoc-daffecfa(2001)90-final.

OECD (2003c), 'Implementing environmental fiscal reform: income distribution and sectoral competitiveness issues', Proceedings of a conference held in Berlin, Germany, 27 June 2002, Paris, France: OECD, www.oecd.org/officialdocuments/displaydocumentpdf/?cote=COM/ENV/EPOC/DAFFE/CFA(2002)76/FINAL.

OECD (2005a), 'The window of opportunity: how the obstacles to the introduction of the Swiss heavy goods vehicle fee have been overcome', Paris, France: OECD, http://appli1.oecd.org/olis/2004doc.nsf/linkto/com-env-epoc-ctpa-cfa(2004)57-final.

OECD (2005b), 'The United Kingdom climate change levy: a study in political economy', Paris, France: OECD, http://appli1.oecd.org/olis/2004doc.nsf/linkto/com-env-epoc-ctpa-cfa(2004)66-final.

OECD (2005c), 'Manure policy and MINAS: regulating nitrogen and phosphorus surpluses in agriculture of the Netherlands', Paris, France: OECD, http://appli1.oecd.org/olis/2004doc.nsf/linkto/com-env-epoc-ctpa-cfa(2004)67-final.

OECD (2005d), 'The political economy of the Norwegian aviation fuel tax', Paris, France: OECD, http://appli1.oecd.org/olis/2005doc.nsf/linkto/com-env-epoc-ctpa-cfa(2005)18-final.

OECD (2005e), 'The competitiveness impact of CO_2 emissions reduction in the cement sector', Paris, France: OECD, http://appli1.oecd.org/olis/2004doc.nsf/linkto/com-env-epoc-ctpa-cfa(2004)68-final.

OECD (2006a), *The Political Economy of Environmentally Related Taxes*, Paris, France: OECD.

OECD (2007a), *Instrument Mixes for Environmental Policy*, Paris, France: OECD.

OECD (2007b), 'Instrument mixes addressing non-point sources of water pollution', Paris, France: OECD, www.olis.oecd.org/olis/2004doc.nsf/linkto/com-env-epoc-agr-ca(2004)90-final.

OECD (2009), *The Economics of Climate Change Mitigation*, Paris, France: OECD, Paris.

OECD (2011), 'Interactions between emission trading systems and other overlapping policy instruments', Paris, France: OECD, www.oecd.org/dataoecd/11/51/48188899.pdf.

OECD (2012), 'Lessons in environmental policy reform: the Swedish tax on NO_x emissions', Paris, France: OECD.

Olson, Mancur (1965), *The Logic of Collective Action. Public Goods and the Theory of Groups*, Cambridge, MA, US: Harvard University Press.

Parry, Ian W.H., Roberton C. Williams and Lawrence H. Goulder (1999), 'When can carbon abatement policies increase welfare? The fundamental role of distorted factor markets', *Journal of Environmental Economics and Management*, **37**, 52–84.

Peltzman, Sam (1976), 'Toward a more general theory of regulation', *Journal of Law and Economics*, **19** (2), 211–40.

Posner, Richard A. (1974), 'Theories of economic regulation', *The Bell Journal of Economics and Management Science*, **5** (2), 335–58.

Schneider, Friedrich and Juergen Volkert (1999), 'No chance for incentive-oriented environmental policies in representative democracies? A public choice analysis', *Ecological Economics*, **31**, 123–38. Also included in Stavins (ed.) (2004a).

Stavins, Robert N. (ed.) (2004a), *The Political Economy of Environmental Regulation*, Cheltenham, UK: Edward Elgar.

Stavins, Robert N. (2004b), 'Introduction to the political economy of environmental regulation', in Stavins (ed.), *The Political Economy of Environmental Regulation*, Cheltenham, UK: Edward Elgar. Available at www.rff.org/documents/RFF-DP-04-12.pdf.

Sterner, Thomas and Lena Höglund Isaksson (2006), 'Refunded emission payments theory, distribution of costs, and Swedish experience of NO$_x$ abatement', *Ecological Economics*, **57**, 93–106.
Stigler, George J. (1971), 'The theory of economic regulation', *Bell Journal of Economics and Management Science*, **2** (1), 3–21.
Vatn, Arild (2000), 'Efficiency and fairness: the Norwegian experience with agri-environmental taxation', in Andersen and Sprenger (eds), *Market-based Instruments for Environmental Management*, Cheltenham, UK: Edward Elgar, pp. 111–28.
Yandle, Bruce (1990), 'The decline and rise of political economy', *European Journal of Political Economy*, **6**, 165–79.

PART IV

IMPLEMENTATION

14 Multilevel governance: the implications of legal competences to collect, administer and regulate environmental tax instruments

Nathalie Chalifour,* María Amparo Grau-Ruiz and Edoardo Traversa

Motivated by a desire to minimize costs and achieve behavioural change, policymakers are increasingly implementing environmental taxes to address environmental challenges. There are numerous examples, as highlighted in this Handbook, of environmentally related taxes[1] successfully reducing pollution or addressing other environmental problems while also achieving economic gains. However, the rising use of environmental taxes around the world brings with it a number of important questions associated with their implementation and ultimate success.

The question of which level of government can implement environmental taxes is ultimately guided by a country's constitutional division of power to legislate. However, as Chapter 4 of this Handbook shows, there is often overlapping legislative jurisdiction to implement environmental taxes at the local, regional/provincial, national (state/federal) and even supranational levels. Indeed, environmental taxes are being used at all levels of government.

Given that multiple levels of government often have concurrent jurisdiction to implement environmental tax instruments, what factors determine at which level they should optimally be used? Are there adequate coordination mechanisms in the event of overlap? We have surveyed the literature to determine what is the state of scholarship on these 'multilevel governance and environmental taxation' questions, and to determine what, if any, lessons can be learned from the scholarship about the implications of concurrent legal competences to collect, administer and regulate environmental tax instruments.

In a nutshell, we have learned that the scholarship directly on this issue is very limited, but that there are various streams of literature from which we can draw theoretical principles to guide multilevel governance of environmental taxes. We have attempted to summarize the key pieces of research directly on point and provide a survey of related literature with relevant findings. Given the paucity of research on this important topic, we make numerous recommendations of areas for further study.

The chapter is divided into three sections. First, we consider what the research shows about how taxing powers at different levels should be 'matched' with different types of environmental problems. In other words, what does the theoretical research tell us about the level at which environmental taxes should ideally be implemented? This

---

* Nathalie Chalifour wishes to thank Rebecca Robb and Carla Gomez for their excellent research assistance relating to this chapter.

[1] For a definition of environmentally related taxes, see Chapter 2, text at footnote 41.

section canvases one key paper along with theoretical research on multilevel governance, environmental and fiscal federalism, and environmental governance, and attempts to summarize some of the key findings from this research base as they pertain to environmental taxation. Second, we canvas the empirical research on how countries have actually allocated competences in the area of environmental tax policy between different authorities, for example by giving access to different tax bases at different levels of government. We do not profess to provide a database of environmental tax instruments and the level at which they are implemented—rather, we point to the lack of such a database (recommending its development) and offer what gleanings we can find from existing literature. Third, we examine the research to show which implementation issues arise from multilevel governance and how they can be addressed. Most of the research we reviewed relating to implementation focused on coordination issues, so coordination is the main focus of our third section.

THEORETICAL RESEARCH ON MULTILEVEL GOVERNANCE AND ENVIRONMENTAL TAXATION

When multiple levels of government have the jurisdiction to impose environmental taxes, what theoretical research exists to guide the process of matching tax instruments to environmental problems? There is no single bundle of literature addressing the theoretical principles involved in matching environmental problems with levels of government and their tax regimes. The issues arise in a variety of disciplines, including law, economics, political sciences, tax and fiscal policy, and environmental studies, and in academic journals as well as government and other policy reports. We have, however, identified a few papers, including notably a World Bank policy research paper by Alm and Banzhaf,[2] that offer direct insight on the question. In addition, three bodies of (sometimes overlapping) scholarship offer guidance for how to match environmental problems and tax instruments: multilevel governance, fiscal federalism and environmental governance. The following section surveys this literature for the most important findings in relation to environmental taxation and identifies existing research gaps.

Brief Overview of Research Streams

As already noted, the literature addressing environmental tax policies specifically in a multilevel governance system is quite scarce. There is, however, abundant research on environment policy integration in a multilevel (and multisector) context.[3] The concept

---

[2]   James Alm & H. Spencer Banzhaf, *Designing Economic Instruments for the Environment in a Decentralized Fiscal System*, 10 J. Econ. Surveys 1 (2010).

[3]   *See*, for example, D.L. Millimet, *Assessing the Empirical Impact of Environmental Federalism*, 43 J. Reg'l Sci. 711–33 (2003); S. Walti, *How Multilevel Structures Affect Environmental Policy in Industrialized Countries*, 43 Eur. J. Pol. Res. 599–634 (2004), addressing two competing hypotheses about how federalism and other multilevel governance structures affect the environmental performance of countries, and finding that multilevel structures affect the way in which important determinants of environmental performance work. Thus, corporatist accommodation structures,

of environmental policy integration emerged from the need to develop coherent policies in an area that is 'cross-sectoral' by nature.[4] The 'multilevel governance,' or MLG, literature has also evolved in an effort to understand the EU political system.[5]

The concept of governing at multiple levels is not unique to environmental taxation, but a broad concept that has generated abundant literature on MLG. According to Marks and Hooghe, multilevel governance can be defined as 'the reallocation of authority upwards, downwards and sideways from central States,' with the result being multiple centers of authority.[6] Homeyer and Knoblauch identify three characteristics of MLG: (1) decision-making powers are increasingly shared among different levels of government; (2) new forms of networks and partnerships arise within and across different levels of government; and (3) the increasing complexity of the actors and levels involved in governance leads to a blur in the division between levels of government.[7]

Related to the concept of MLG is polycentricity, which recognizes that while environmental challenges often have global dimensions, these phenomena are an aggregation of social choices often at local or individual levels.[8] Thus it is logical that at least some of the policies to address the causes of the environmental problem have a local dimension.

There is an abundant legal and economic literature on fiscal federalism,[9] which

---

which are known to enhance environmental policy, do so primarily in multi-tiered systems. A high level of economic development, on the other hand, which has also been shown to contribute to environmental performance, does so mainly in countries that are characterized by weak multilevel structures.

[4] ENVIRONMENTAL POLICY INTEGRATION: GREENING SECTORAL POLICIES IN EUROPE (A. Lenschow ed., 2002); MULTILEVEL GOVERNANCE OF GLOBAL ENVIRONMENTAL CHANGE: PERSPECTIVES FROM SCIENCE, SOCIOLOGY AND THE LAW (Gerd Winter ed., 2006); ENVIRONMENTAL POLICY INTEGRATION IN PRACTICE: SHAPING INSTITUTIONS FOR LEARNING (Måns Nillson & Katarina Eckerberg eds, 2007); Bjorn Nykvist, *EPI in Multilevel Governance—A Literature Review* (Ecologic Inst., EPIGOV Working Paper No. 30, 2008).

[5] Nykvist, *supra* note 4, at 5. There is abundant literature on regulation of tax policy in the EU in the context of MLG. *See,* for example, Philippe Genschel & Markus Jachtenfuchs, *The Fiscal Anatomy of Regulatory Polity: Tax Policy and Multilevel Governance in the EU* (Hertie School of Governance, Working Paper No. 43, 2009), *available at* http://www.hertie-school.org/binaries/add on/1507_steuerartikel_final_komplett.pdf.

[6] Gary Marks & Liesbet Hooghe, *Contrasting Visions of Multi-Level Governance*, MULTI-LEVEL GOVERNANCE 15–30 (Ian Bache & Matthew Flinders eds, 2004), cited in Ingmar von Homeyer & Doris Knoblauch, *Environmental Policy Integration and Multi-Level Governance—A State-of-the-Art Report* (Ecologic Inst. for Int'l and European Envtl. Pol'y, Working Paper No. 31, 2008), *available at* http://ecologic.eu/projekte/epigov/documents/epigov_paper_31_homeyer_e t_al.pdf.

[7] Homeyer & Knoblauch, *supra* note 6, at 4. Some authors include non-state actors in their definition of multilevel governance. *See* Beate Kohler-Koch & Berthold Rittberger, *The 'Governance Turn' in EU Studies*, 44 J. COMMON MKT. STUD. 27–49 (2006); MULTILEVEL GOVERNANCE OF GLOBAL ENVIRONMENTAL CHANGE: PERSPECTIVES FROM SCIENCE, SOCIOLOGY AND THE LAW (Gerd Winter ed., 2006). However, in this chapter we target government actors only since we focus on environmental taxes.

[8] Elinor Ostrom, A Polycentric Approach for Coping with Climate Change (World Bank Policy Research Working Paper No. 5095, 2009).

[9] There are a number of relatively recent branches of fiscal federalism, including laboratory federalism, interjurisdictional competition, the political economy of fiscal federalism, market-preserving federalism, and fiscal decentralization in the developing and transitional economies.

complements MLG as background scholarship relevant to environmental taxation. A subset of public finance, fiscal federalism is concerned with 'understanding which functions and instruments are best centralized, and which are best placed in the sphere of decentralized levels of government. In other words, it is the study of how competencies (expenditure side) and fiscal instruments (revenue side) are allocated across different (vertical) layers of the administration.'[10] Environmental federalism can fairly be described as a subset of the fiscal federalism literature, wherein concepts of fiscal federalism are applied and discussed in the context of environmental issues. As Oates describes it, environmental federalism pertains to the question of the role of different levels of government in environmental management.[11] However, some might argue that environmental federalism is its own branch of literature that relies upon fiscal federalism for many of its theoretical foundations, but that posits a sufficiently distinct set of principles to qualify as its own literature set.[12]

Virtually none of the fiscal or environmental federalism literature tackles environmental taxes directly. However, one key paper, by Alm and Banzhaf, stands out as squarely addressing the question of how to design economic instruments, including environmental taxes, in a context of overlapping jurisdiction.[13]

To frame the discussion for designing economic instruments for the environment, Alm

---

See, for example, W.E. Oates, *An Essay on Fiscal Federalism*, 37(3) J. ECON. LIT. 1120–49 (1999); ROBIN BOADWAY & RONALD WATTS, FISCAL FEDERALISM IN CANADA (2000), *available at* http://w ww.fiscalreform.net/library/pdfs/fiscal_federalism_in_canada.pdf; R.A. Musgrave, *Who Should Tax, Where, and What?*, *in* TAX ASSIGNMENT IN FEDERAL COUNTRIES 2–19 (Charles E. McLure Jr. ed., 1983); T. Ter-Minassian, *Intergovernmental Relations in a Macro-economic Perspective: An Overview*, *in* FISCAL FEDERALISM IN THEORY AND PRACTICE 3–24 (T. Ter-Minassian, ed., 1997); R.D. Ebel & S. Yilmaz, *On the Measurement and Impact of Fiscal Decentralization* (Policy Research Working Paper no. 2809, World Bank, 2002); R. Bird, *Fiscal Federalism*, *in* THE ENCYCLOPEDIA OF TAXATION AND TAX POLICY 151–4 (J.J. Cordes, R.D. Ebel, & J.G. Gravelle eds, 2nd ed., 2005); W.O. Oates, *Toward a Second-generation Theory of Fiscal Federalism*, 13 INTERNATIONAL TAX AND PUBLIC FINANCE 349–73 (2005); B. Lockwood, *The Political Economy of Decentralization*, *in* HANDBOOK OF FISCAL FEDERALISM 31–60 (E. Ahmad & G. Brosio eds, 2008).

[10]   *See* Oates, *supra* note 9, at 1120.

[11]   *See* W.E. Oates, *A Reconsideration of Environmental Federalism*, *in* RECENT ADVANCES IN ENVIRONMENTAL ECONOMICS 1, 1 (John A. List & Aart de Zeewu eds, 2002).

[12]   For examples of literature on diverse aspects of environmental federalism, *see* Daniel C. Esty, *Revitalizing Environmental Federalism*, 95 MICH. L. REV. 570–653 (1996); M. Rauscher, *Interjurisdictional Competition and Environmental Policy*, *in* INTERNATIONAL YEARBOOK OF ENVIRONMENTAL AND RESOURCE ECONOMICS 2000–2001 197–230 (H. Folmer & T. Tietenberg eds, 2000); Oates, *supra* note 11, at 1–32; Juan Carlos Lerda et al., *Coordinación de Políticas Públicas: Desafíos y Oportunidades para una Agenda Fiscal-Ambiental* [*Coordination of public policies:challenges and opportunities for an environmental-fiscal agenda*], *in* POLÍTICA FISCAL Y MEDIO AMBIENTE: BASES PARA UNA AGENDA COMÚN [FISCAL POLICY AND ENVIRONMENT: BASIS FOR A COMMON AGENDA] 65–88 (J. Acquatella & A. Bárcena Ibarra eds, 2005); Juan Carlos Lerda et al., *Integración, coherencia y coordinación de Políticas Públicas Sectoriales (reflexiones para el caso de las políticas fiscal y ambiental)* [*Integration, coherence and coordination of sectoral public policies (thoughts related to the case of fiscal and environmental policies)*] 1–73 (CEPAL, Working Paper No. 76, 2003). The research trend has evolved recently in order to study both fiscal and environmental issues from the same perspective, S. Dalmazzone, *Decentralization and the Environment*, *in* HANDBOOK OF FISCAL FEDERALISM 459–77 (E. Ahmad & G. Brosio eds, 2008).

[13]   Alm & Banzhaf, *supra* note 2.

and Banzhaf survey the general principles of assigning tax responsibilities, and in doing so point to a number of trends that impact upon the optimal choice of government for taxes. First, the increasing mobility of tax bases due to increases in communication, technology and lower transportation costs may reduce the ability of local governments to tax these factors.[14] Second, the measurement, identification and assignment of tax bases are more difficult because of the complexity of the modern business model (for instance, businesses operate in multiple jurisdictions or make online purchases of goods and services from multiple jurisdictions) or incomes from multiple sources.[15]

These trends impact upon the ability of governments to choose their tax policies independently and may have certain effects. Alm and Banzhaf predict that the overall level of tax rates is likely to decline as mobility and complexity trends increase, though they note that the empirical evidence is mixed in this regard.[16] They predict that the composition of local taxes is also likely to change, with taxes on mobile bases such as labor and capital declining at the local level, and taxes on immobile bases such as physical capital and property increasing at the local level. They also predict that the local governments are 'likely to turn more frequently to environmental or "green taxes" . . . in attempts to replace lost revenues from mobile bases.'[17] Finally, they predict that the form of local taxes is likely to change, with subnational governments perhaps opting for a destination-based consumption tax collected at the central level or for greater coordination and harmonization (for instance, agreeing among themselves to apply a uniform local sales tax).[18]

The third stream of research identified here is environmental governance, which can be defined as 'the set of regulatory processes and organizations through which political actors influence environmental actions and outcomes.'[19] At the heart of environmental governance is the idea that some effective environmental policies must be implemented globally, through international institutions and agreements. At the same time they must involve even the most local actors, both institutional and private, in order to gain political acceptance and legitimacy.[20] The use of economic instruments, including environmental taxes, has been described as an evolution in environmental management.[21]

---

[14] *Id.* at 14, 16.

[15] *Id.* at 16–17.

[16] *Id.* at 18.

[17] *Id.*

[18] *Id.*

[19] Maria C. Lemos & Arun Agrawal, *Environmental Governance*, 31 ANN. REV. ENVT. & RES. 297–325 (2006). *See also* LAMONT C. HEMPEL, ENVIRONMENTAL GOVERNANCE: THE GLOBAL CHALLENGE (2006); EMERGING FORCES IN ENVIRONMENTAL GOVERNANCE (Norichika Kanie & Peter M. Haas eds, 2004); REFORMING INTERNATIONAL ENVIRONMENTAL GOVERNANCE: FROM INSTITUTIONAL LIMITS TO INNOVATIVE SOLUTIONS (B. Chambers and J. Green eds, 2005).

[20] Jouni Paavola, *Environmental Conflicts and Institutions as Conceptual Cornerstones of Environmental Governance Research* (Ctr. for Social and Econ. Research on the Global Envt., Univ. of Anglia, Working Paper No. EDM 05-01, 2005). For an overview of the state of research on environmental governance, *see* Paul Hendricks et al., *The Landscape of Environmental Governance Research* (Envtl. Governance Working Grp., Discussion Paper No. 1, 2009), *available at* http://egwg.colostate.edu/docs/The_Landscape_of_Environmental_Governance_Research.pdf.

[21] Andrew Jordan et al., *New Instruments of Environmental Governance: Patterns and Pathways of Change*, 12 ENVTL. POL. 4 (2003).

Principles for Allocation of Environmental Tax Powers among Different Levels of Government

Drawing upon the research in the three streams discussed above, with extensive reliance upon the Alm and Banzhaf paper, we have identified the following principles for guiding decisions about the level at which environmental instruments, including taxes, should be implemented.[22] These are scale, monitoring and enforcement capacity, mobility, effectiveness and revenue needs (or cost-heterogeneity).

Scale of the environmental externality
Alm and Banzhaf argue that the geographic scope of the externality should be the most important guiding principle in determining the level of government. This principle is in recognition of the fact that 'the standard analysis of externalities does not consider that the externality may be generated in a local, or subnational, area, with effects that may be confined to the local area or that may spill over to other jurisdictions.'[23] Oates has identified at least three 'levels' of polluting activities.[24] The first level is that of pure public goods, where the overall level of environmental quality for the nation or globe depends upon the aggregate level of waste emissions from all local areas. Examples include climate change or ozone depletion. The second level, which Oates calls local public goods, is one in which the amount of pollution in a given locality depends entirely upon the emissions generated in that area. In other words, there are no spillovers to other jurisdictions. An example of this is municipal solid waste. The third type, which Oates calls local spillover effects, is one in which local emissions have some spillover effects to nearby jurisdictions, without creating an aggregate externality as in the case of the 'pure public goods' level. An example of this level, which appears to be the most common, is acid rain. When pollution is at the level of a pure public good, Oates and Alm and Banzhaf argue that the central government should be assigned responsibility to establish standards. When pollution is at the level of a local public good, they suggest that the relevant local government should be responsible. Not surprisingly, the local spillover situation presents the most difficulty, without a single answer.[25]

The broader literature also supports the principle that scale is a critical design feature for environmental policies, including environmental taxes. MLG research is premised upon the recognition that environmental problems do not fit neatly within political boundaries. As Marks and Hooghe note, environmental 'externalities from the provisioning of public goods vary immensely, from planet-wide in the case of global warming to

---

[22] Alm & Banzhaf, *supra* note 2, at 20–23.
[23] *Id.* at 21.
[24] Oates, *supra* note 11, at 1–32. He distinguishes the first category of pure public goods by the fact that a unit of polluting emissions has the same effect on the vector of national environmental quality regardless of where it takes place. The second category of local public goods is characterized by the fact that polluting waste emissions within a given local jurisdiction have their effects solely within that jurisdiction. The third category, local spillover effects, is characterized by the case where the effects of local waste entail both local pollution and some external effects on other (most likely neighboring) jurisdictions. These three levels are identified and discussed by Alm & Banzhaf, *supra* note 2, at 21–22, but under the terms aggregate, contained and partial spillover.
[25] Oates, *supra* note 11, at 8.

local in the case of most city services.'[26] This variability of scale of problems argues for a similar variability in the scale of governance, based on research suggesting that regulating at the appropriate level can yield better results.[27] In the environmental area, there has been a recent push toward local-level governance for the many environmental problems that have a local origin. For instance, Nykvist notes that 'the literature on collective action and the governing of the commons have long argued for devolution of authority to the local level.'[28] However, some issues, such as transboundary air or water pollution and global warming, require a concerted regional or global policy response combined with policy actions at the national and subnational level, hence the multiplicity of regulatory action.

Scale is an important consideration in the environmental federalism literature. As is the case for fiscal decentralization in general,[29] where the theory of subsidiarity advocates finding the appropriate level of decentralization for a given subject, there is no consensus to indicate at which level of government an environmental tax should be assigned. Esty cautions against either a fully centralized or decentralized approach, and advocates rather for a 'multitier regulatory structure that tracks the complexity and diversity of environmental problems.'[30]

The environmental governance literature offers some insights into the complex and interrelated institutional models needed to manage environmental problems, including the need to regulate at the appropriate scale. McDaniels et al. argue that 'regulatory issues involving multiple scales of decision-making arise in virtually all significant environmental questions.'[31] They emphasize the importance of effective jurisdiction and appropriate knowledge and information flows in managing environmental issues that involve multiple scales.[32] Their research emphasizes that institutional or governance structures must be 'compatible with the multiple levels of decisions required to address an environmental problem involving multiple scales.'[33] This suggests that environmental taxes must be situated in the context of a broad strategy for tackling an environmental challenge, and that attention must be paid to the scale at which the environmental tax will be targeted.

McDaniels et al. argue that mismatched scales of environmental impact and policy regulation can lead to regulatory gaps and breakdowns in environmental management.[34] Jordan et al. identify environmental tax shifting as a concept that fits well with the ideology of smaller, less intrusive governments.[35]

---

[26] Gary Marks & Liesbet Hooghe, *Contrasting Visions of Multi-Level Governance, in* MULTI-LEVEL GOVERNANCE 15–30 (Ian Bache & Matthew Flinders eds, 2004).

[27] *See* Timothy L. McDaniels et al., *Multiple Scales and Regulatory Gaps in Environmental Change: The Case of Salmon Aquaculture*, 15 GLOBAL ENVTL. CHANGE 9–21 (2005). See also the discussion on fiscal federalism in Nykvist, *supra* note 4, and Ostrom, *supra* note 8, at 16.

[28] Nykvist, *supra* note 4, at 5.

[29] However, some orientation may be found in E.M. Gramlich, *A Policymaker's Guide to Fiscal Decentralization*, 46 NATL. TAX J. 229–35 (1993). *See also* the literature quoted *supra* note 9.

[30] Esty, *supra* note 12, at 570–653.

[31] McDaniels et al., *supra* note 27, at 20.

[32] *Id.* at 19.

[33] *Id.* at 13.

[34] *Id.* at 10.

[35] Jordan et al., *supra* note 21, at 14.

Monitoring and enforcement capacity

The monitoring and enforcement capacity of a given level of government is another factor that has been identified as important in guiding decisions about the level at which to implement environmental policies, including taxes.[36] It is important to consider which level of government has the authority and the resources to enforce penalties for violations, including which is less susceptible to corruption.

As Guideline 42 of UNEP's Manual on Compliance with and Enforcement of Multilateral Environmental Agreements notes,

> [b]ecause environmental enforcement has its foundation in action at the national level, States can and should take into account the unique nature of their legal system, as well as their culture and institutional capacity in designing and adopting enforcement measures. An effective national environmental regime will require well-developed laws and regulations, a sufficient institutional framework, national coordination, training to enhance enforcement capabilities, and public environmental awareness and education.[37]

Mobility

Third, the instrument chosen should reflect the mobility of the polluting industry. Central governments are best placed to impose taxes on mobile tax bases (such as capital) and tax bases that are not distributed equally among jurisdictions. Revenues from these can be used to redistribute fiscal capacity among the jurisdictions.[38] Local governments should impose taxes on tax bases that are immobile, and use the revenues generated to finance the provision of local services for which it is 'difficult to identify individual beneficiaries and to measure individual costs and benefits.'[39] In other words, where there is a real risk of jurisdictional competition for mobile capital, possibly leading to a 'race to the bottom' of environmental standards, centralized environmental taxes may be favorable.[40]

Effectiveness

A fourth factor to consider is the potential effectiveness of the instrument, which is influenced by many things. Some research argues that environmental taxes have their strongest advantage at the national level since the wider geographical scope increases the heterogeneity of marginal abatement costs, which is the determinant for increases in efficiency.[41]

---

[36]   Alm & Banzhaf, *supra* note 2, at 21. *See also* G. Fredriksson & Herman R.J. Vollebergh, *Corruption, Federalism and Policy Formation in the OECD: the Case of Energy Policy*, 140 PUB. CHOICE 205–21 (2009); Andrew J. White III, *Decentralized Environmental Taxation in Indonesia: A Proposed Double Dividend for Revenue Allocation and Environmental Regulation*, 19 ENV. LAW J. 43–69 (2007).

[37]   UNITED NATIONS ENVTL. PROGRAM, MANUAL ON COMPLIANCE WITH AND ENFORCEMENT OF MULTILATERAL ENVIRONMENTAL AGREEMENTS, GUIDELINE 42 (2006), *available at* http://www.unep .org/dec/onlinemanual/Enforcement/InstitutionalFrameworks/CoordinationAmongRelevant Aut horities/tabid/97/Default.aspx.

[38]   *Id.* at 21.

[39]   *Id.*

[40]   *Id.* at 32; *see also* Oates, *supra* note 11, at 1–32; Dalmazzone, *supra* note 12, at 459–77.

[41]   Alm & Banzhaf, *supra* note 2, at 21.

Another determinant of effectiveness is administration. Little will be gained in making the structure of taxes too sophisticated when the environmental costs are low, or making the tax system (in general) too complicated, thereby raising administrative costs.[42] The research suggests that effectiveness of the measure broadly defined is a relevant consideration in selecting jurisdiction, and that it is important to balance the environmental objectives to be met by the tax with the complexity and administration of the instrument. We consider the research relating to implementation in greater detail in the section on implementation issues.

Revenue needs as a driver for local environmental taxes

The need for revenue has been identified as an important motivator for local environmental taxes. For instance, a recent Canadian report proposes that environmental pricing reforms (including environmental taxes) at the local level are important to help municipalities bridge the gap between their environmental vision and its implementation, as well as the gap between fiscal constraints and fiscal flexibility.[43] Another Canadian report argues that municipalities require greater sources of revenues. While the report does not advocate environmental taxes, it suggests that taxes and fees could be more closely aligned with delivering services and offers waste management and transportation as examples of appropriate bases.[44] Similarly, a report on addressing urban finance challenges in western Canadian municipalities advocates for property tax reform and user fees and taxes, offering again justification for environmental taxation at the local level.[45]

Alm and Banzhaf argue that it is legitimate to consider the fiscal needs of the government in selecting instruments. In other words, a revenue-generating instrument such as an environmental tax is appropriate when the level of government needs revenue. They argue that local governments should have discretion over the rate of some taxes to establish a link between the services demanded and the cost of providing that service.[46] They

---

[42]   'Little can be gained from over-sophistication in the tax structure through the introduction of finely-graded tax differentials to reflect the environmental characteristics of commodities with little environmental significance. Complex tax structures are liable to be costly to operate, and the tax "boundaries" between products subject to higher and lower rates of tax are always open to socially wasteful litigation, and consequent erosion. Moreover, insufficiently large tax incentives may achieve little change in behaviour. As argued above, firms may not take account of tax incentives when making environmental technology decisions if the tax incentives are too small to justify the costs of changing established decision-making structures. It is perhaps an over-generalisation to suggest that environmental taxes should be large, or not be imposed at all. However, the costs of complexity and the risk that minor environmental taxes will simply be ignored should both caution against too much environmental fine-tuning of the fiscal system': Don Fullerton et al., *Environmental Taxes*, in Reforming the Tax System for the 21st Century 13 (Inst. for Fiscal Studies, 2008).

[43]   David Thompson & Andrew Bevan, Smart Budget: A Background Paper on Environmental Pricing Reform for Local Governments (2010).

[44]   Toronto Dominion, A Choice between Investing in Canada's Cities or Disinvesting in Canada's Future (2002).

[45]   Casey Vander Ploeg, Framing a Fiscal Fix-Up: Options for Strengthening the Finances of Western Canada's Big Cities (2002).

[46]   Alm & Banzhaf, *supra* note 2, at 12.

Table 14.1   Summary of guiding principles for the allocation of environmental taxation powers

First-level consideration	The geographic scope of the externality should lead the determination of level of government for the tax.
Second-level considerations	Monitoring and enforcement capacity should be considered in selecting the level of government for economic instruments.
	The environmental tax should reflect the mobility of the polluting or waste-generating industry to be subject to the tax.
	The advantage of national-level taxes in offering greater heterogeneity of marginal abatement costs is a relevant consideration.
	Revenue needs of various levels of government can be considered as partial justification for an environmental tax.
	The capacity to develop appropriate coordination mechanisms may be an important consideration that contributes to the feasibility and effectiveness of a policy.

also suggest that local governments have the flexibility to allow collections to grow over time with the demand of services.[47]

One of the issues that appears repeatedly in the literature, particularly in the EU, is that there may be competition for revenue between different levels of government when they each have jurisdictional authority to impose an environmental tax.[48] In some cases, governments with inadequate financial resources (often subnational or local level governments) may be tempted to use revenue-raising measures masked with an environmental objective to address fiscal needs. In cases of economic crisis, this risk may be greater.

The question of coordination as a guiding principle in the context of concurrent implementation of environmental taxes and/or coordination among environmental and fiscal authorities is an interesting one. Although the literature we surveyed did not explicitly raise coordination mechanisms as a guiding principle for allocating environmental taxation powers, the importance of ensuring that such policies are adequately coordinated is extremely important, as emphasized in the section on Implementation later in this chapter. We have thus included it in our chart of guiding principles, as an extrapolation of the discussions emerging from the literature in the section on implementation issues.

Summary and Recommendations for Further Research

While there is an abundant research base on multilevel governance, environmental federalism and environmental governance generally, the Alm and Banzhaf paper is the only

---

[47]   *Id.*

[48]   Some active authorities could motivate others, as their decisions are usually taken depending on other levels of government and private sector operators' expected or proved behaviour, *see* UNITED NATIONS ENVTL. PROGRAM, MANUAL ON COMPLIANCE WITH AND ENFORCEMENT OF MULTILATERAL ENVIRONMENTAL AGREEMENTS, GUIDELINE 40 (2006). *See also* EUROPEAN ENVT. AGENCY, ENVIRONMENTAL TAXES: RECENT DEVELOPMENTS IN TOOLS FOR INTEGRATION (2000).

paper we found that directly addresses the question of how to allocate environmental taxation powers in the context of overlapping jurisdiction. There is a need for more theoretical research on this question, but especially on the issues of how enforcement and monitoring factor into the choice, the effectiveness of instruments at different levels, and—with respect to scale—what are optimal choices in the context of 'local spillover' environmental problems.

EMPIRICAL TRENDS IN THE ALLOCATION OF POWERS TO DIFFERENT AUTHORITIES IN THE AREA OF ENVIRONMENTAL TAX POLICY

Given the theoretical research described above, what has happened in practice? How have countries actually matched their concurrent taxing powers to given environmental problems? One of the main findings of this section is that there is no simple way to ascertain the level at which environmental taxes are implemented in a global sense. There is no one database or document that offers such a synthesis. The EEA/OECD database on environmentally related taxes,[49] which is the primary source of information on environmentally related taxes around the world, offers generalized statistics on the use of environmental taxes at the country level, but without distinguishing which level of government is implementing the tax. While it is possible to ascertain the level at which a tax instrument is applied, this requires investigating each country one at a time, and then investigating each provincial/state level instrument to determine whether it is administered at the provincial/state or local/municipal level.

Of course, there are many papers that analyze and discuss a given instrument in a particular jurisdiction (or sometimes across jurisdictions), but as Geys and Revelli confirm, 'the choice of tax instruments by decentralized authorities' is an issue that has received relatively little empirical attention.[50]

In this section, we begin by summarizing some of the papers that empirically evaluate the allocation of environmental taxing powers at different levels of government, and then discuss some of the tax bases to which environmental taxes are applied locally. This is not a fulsome survey of all the empirical literature on environmental taxes and the level at which they are implemented, but rather a sampling of some studies that illustrate relationships to the framework of guiding principles identified above.

Country-specific Studies

Geys and Revelli examined 289 Flemish municipalities over eight years to determine the political and economic determinants of the local tax mix. They found that the two most powerful determinants of the local tax mix were the size of the revenue need and the size

[49] OECD & European Envtl. Agency, Database on Instruments for Environmental Policy and Natural Resources Management, *available at* http://www2.oecd.org/ecoinst/queries/index.htm.

[50] Benny Geys & Frederico Revelli, *Decentralization, Competition and the Local Tax Mix: Evidence from Flanders* (Dept. of Econ., Univ. of Turin, Working Paper No. 200902, 2009).

of the respective tax bases.[51] In other words, political variables played little role in determining the local tax mix.

In contrast, an earlier paper by Ashworth et al. identified the political context as an important determinant of local environmental taxation.[52] This study, which evaluated the elements that impacted the decision to introduce an environmental tax in 308 Flemish municipalities over an eight-year period, found that the following factors positively influenced the uptake of an environmental tax:

- Municipality 'peers' having an environmental tax positively influenced political will;
- Not being in an election year; and
- Having a left-wing or coalition government in power.[53]

The Spanish experience shows that there is a positive correlation between the degree of decentralization and the number of environmentally related taxes. Ongoing reform of the system to finance the Autonomous Communities (equivalent to regions) has led to a greater fiscal co-responsibility as well as more environmental taxes, in part to address regional revenue needs.[54]

In an empirical review of decentralized environmental taxation in Indonesia, White points to a directive from the central government encouraging local environmental taxation.[55] However, White identifies corruption as a source of constraint for effective local and provincial-level environmental taxation.[56]

Xu's chapter in this Handbook[57] provides a valuable survey of the evolution of environmental taxation in China. Her research identifies challenges relating to matching tax instruments with the scale of environmental problems. She also stresses the significant financial needs of local governments as a driver for environmental taxes, noting that the environmental goal may be secondary to the revenue needs. She notes a particular problem whereby environmentally related charges that are collected by departments that fall outside of formal budget control may 'create[] opportunities for corruption and pose[] difficulties for the coordination of governmental efforts in environmental protection.'[58]

Based on these studies, it appears that revenue needs are an important driver for the use of local environmental taxes, though the issue of scale poses challenges.

The diversity of conditions that can exist at a regional (i.e. state or local) level can influence the choice of instrument used to create an environmental tax. For instance,

---

[51]   *Id.* at 12.

[52]   John Ashworth et al., *Determinants of Tax Innovation—The Case of Environmental Taxes in Flemish Municipalities*, 22 EURO. J. POL. ECON. 223–47 (2006).

[53]   *Id.*

[54]   *See*, for example, Amparo Grau & Marta Marcos, *Impuestos propios de las Comunidades Autónomas* [*Autonomous Communities' own taxes*], *in* SISTEMA FISCAL ESPAÑOL (IMPUESTOS ESTATALES, AUTONÓMICOS Y LOCALES) [SPANISH TAX SYSTEM (STATE, REGIONAL AND LOCAL TAXES)] 373 (G. De la Peña, R. Falcón & M.A. Martínez eds, Iustel ed. 2011).

[55]   White III, *supra* note 36, at 43–69.

[56]   *Id.*

[57]   See Chapter 17.

[58]   *Id.* at text following footnote 76.

the US government's choice to implement a BTU tax may have been influenced by the vast regional disparities in energy use and type among US states. Opting for a measure with a broad tax base may help assuage these disparities, rendering the instrument more politically palatable.[59]

Specific Instruments

In an earlier, longer version of their paper in the *Journal of Economic Surveys*,[60] Alm and Banzhaf identify and discuss a number of taxes that are typically implemented at the local level and that can be appropriate for environmental taxation.

Property taxes
With respect to particular taxes, Alm and Banzhaf comment that the property tax is often viewed as most appropriately administered locally because of the immobility of the tax base. However, they identify numerous challenges with its application, including problems with valuation and political acceptability. The administration of property taxes can be 'arbitrary and idiosyncratic, especially in the procedures used to determine the value of properties,' resulting in the property tax's sometimes being viewed as unfair.[61] Kunce and Shogren build upon work by Oates and Schwab[62] and Wellisch[63] to propose that a local government can use property taxation to deliver both efficient public good provision and local environmental quality, in the case of within-jurisdiction, or 'contained,' externalities.[64]

Automobile taxes
Another tax often applied locally is a tax on automobile use or ownership, such as an annual license tax or a transfer tax.[65] Although these taxes can be administered at relatively low cost, Alm and Benzhaf note that they are underused as a source of local revenue. However, there is a risk of misuse if differences in tax rates in neighboring municipalities lead to negative outcomes from an environmental perspective.[66]

---

[59] Janet E. Milne, *Carbon Taxes in the United States: The Context for the Future*, 10 Vt. J. Envtl. L. 10, 11 (2008).
[60] Alm and Banzhaf, *Designing Economic Instruments for the Environment in a Decentralized Fiscal System* (World Bank Policy Research Working Paper No. 4378, 2007).
[61] *Id.* at 24.
[62] W. Oates & R. Schwab, *Economic Competition Among Jurisdictions: Efficiency-enhancing or Distortion-inducing?*, 35 J. Pub. Econ. 333–54 (1988).
[63] D. Wellisch, *Locational Choices of Firms and Decentralized Environmental Policy with Various Instruments*, 37 J. Urban Econ. 290–310 (1995).
[64] M. Kunch & J. Shogren, *Efficient Decentralized Fiscal and Environmental Policy: A Dual Purpose Henry George Tax*, 65 Ecological Econ. 569–73 (2008).
[65] Alm & Banzhaf, *supra* note 60, at 24.
[66] Carlos María López Espadafor, La protección del medio ambiente y el impuesto sobre ve hículos de tracción mecánica [*The protection of the environment and the tax on motor vehicles*], 1 Nueva Fiscalidad [New Taxation] 47–80 (2007); María José Portillo Navarro, El impuesto so bre vehículos de Tracción Mecánica en el contexto de la fiscalidad ambiental [*The tax on motor vehicles in the context of the environmental taxation*], 105 Revista de estudios locales [Local Studies Review] 89–99 (2007); Víctor Manuel Sánchez Blázquez, Energía, medio ambiente e I

Waste taxes

In a survey of environmental taxes in Europe, Sterner and Kohlin identify water and waste as resources for which local environmental taxes have been applied.[67] In the case of environmental taxes relating to waste, they note that the driving force was often the lack of space for landfills.[68] Environmental charges and fees are often used by state and/ or local governments as pricing mechanisms to offset the costs of collecting and managing waste.[69] However, these user charges (which relate to specific services rendered in exchange for the fees) should not be confounded with environmental taxes, which are unrequited payments that go into general revenues.

Excise taxes

Local governments often impose excise taxes on commodities such as alcohol and tobacco. These taxes are easy to collect and administer and can generate significant revenues, and they can be helpful as environmental taxes since they can reduce consumption of particular goods. However, they are unlikely to grow over time, are regressive and may not work well for goods with low response to price changes.[70] Another disadvantage is that since the goods in question are often concentrated at borders or processing locations, the tax base is unevenly distributed among local governments.

Excise taxes with an environmental goal have often been implemented at the national level, as is the case with gas or carbon taxes. Some state and local level governments have also implemented such taxes, such as the carbon tax implemented by the Canadian province of British Columbia[71] and the tax on the end users of electricity in Boulder, Colorado in the United States.[72]

Surtax

Local governments may impose a surtax or additional local tax on centralized taxes. While such taxes may generate distortions in resource use, they can be administratively efficient since the collection is left to the central government. The central government also determines the tax base, which may reduce local distortions from mobile factors. Since

---

mpuesto sobre Vehículos de Tracción Mecánica: el impuesto alemán como uno de los modelos a seguir [*Energy, Environment and the tax on motor vehicles: the German tax as one of the models to follow*], *in* ESTUDIOS SOBRE FISCALIDAD DE LA ENERGÍA Y DESARROLLO SOSTENIBLE [STUDIES ON ENERGY TAXATION AND SUSTAINABLE DEVELOPMENT] 217–30 (Ramón Falcón y Tella ed., 2007); Santiago Álvarez García & Marta Jorge García-Inés, El Impuesto sobre Vehículos de Tracción Mecánica: *implicaciones medioambientales y posibles reformas derivadas de las propuestas comunitarias* [*The tax on motor vehicles: environmental consequences and possible reforms due to the Community proposals*], 66 Tributos Locales [LOCAL TAXES] 53–62 (2006).

[67]   T. Sterner & G. Köhlin, *Environmental Taxes in Europe*, 3 (1) PUB. FIN. & MGMT. 117–42 (2003).

[68]   *Id.* at 137.

[69]   As an example, refer to the waste tire management program in Indiana. OFFICE OF POLLUTION PREVENTION AND TECHNICAL ASSISTANCE, INDIANA DEPT. OF ENVTL. MANAGEMENT, 2008–2009 ANNUAL REPORT WASTE TIRE MANAGEMENT PROGRAM (2009).

[70]   Alm & Banzhaf, *supra* note 60, at 25.

[71]   David G. Duff, *Carbon Taxation in British Columbia*, 10 VT. J. ENVTL. L. 87–107 (2008).

[72]   Milne, *supra* note 59, at 20–21.

local governments are usually implicated in determining the rate, this assists the local government with its fiscal administration.[73]

Other

Local governments use a number of other taxes, such as on forms of entertainment (for instance restaurants and gambling) and relating to disturbances, such as construction activities. These taxes are generally not administratively simple or efficient, nor do they generate significant revenues.[74] However, they may be important from an environmental perspective.

Summary and Recommendations for Further Research

The discussion of empirical trends in regions as well as with particular instruments highlights the importance of the principle of mobility, whether of the tax base itself or of the pollutant. In some cases, local level environmental taxation is suboptimal due to the mobility of the tax base or pollutant targeted by a tax. However, immobility of a tax base such as property suggests that use of local taxing authority is highly appropriate. Jurisdictional competition may in some cases lead to lower overall environmental standards (as shown in the case of automobile taxes). In addition, we see that revenue needs can be an important driver for local environmental taxation.

The findings also suggest that the recognition (or assignment) of taxing authority at local levels is not necessarily linked to environmental performance. Tax authorities at all levels face fiscal and environmental accountability. If local tax authority is not exercised, perhaps due to prudence or complexity, the federal state may choose not to compensate the ensuing revenue loss and, if the power was devolved from the federal to the local level, it could potentially lead to a reversal of the devolution.

We found that a notable gap in research exists in offering generalized statistics on the level at which environmental taxes are implemented and administered.

IMPLEMENTATION ISSUES

A number of implementation issues arise in the context of multilevel governance of environmental taxes. We focus mainly on the central issue of integration and coordination, with a few shorter points about administration, costs and competition.

Integration and Coordination

When environmental policy interventions are required at multiple levels, questions of integration inevitably arise. Similarly, the fact that fiscal and environmental policies usually originate and are elaborated in different settings can easily create contradictions, duplications, insufficiencies, gaps and imperfections not only in their design, assessment

---

[73] Alm & Banzhaf, *supra* note 60, at 27.
[74] *Id.* at 26.

and review, but also in their implementation.[75] In environmental taxation, coordination is required at three levels: horizontally, vertically and in time.

The layering of policymaking from the international to the local level raises questions of vertical integration. Vertical coordination is needed when the competences related to environmental taxation are shared between different levels of government (supranational, central, subnational/regional, municipal). Much of the literature on vertical integration is focused on the EU, with its implementation and coordination challenges and the interplay between Member States.[76]

The EU's approach to air transportation offers an illustration of how overlapping jurisdiction of environmental taxes might hamper the freedom of a jurisdiction to pursue its environmental goals, and why vertical coordination mechanisms are important for ensuring that the environmental goals behind the policies are met and avoiding unnecessary inefficiencies or duplication. Excise duties on energy products are harmonized in the European Union. Under European Union Directives, Member States are to exempt from the harmonized excise duty on inter alia 'mineral oils supplied for use as fuels for the purpose of air navigation other than private pleasure flying.'[77] This exemption does

---

[75] Coordination challenges can take different forms, including overlap and duplication between different levels of government or fragmentation of powers within one level of government (i.e. between environmental and tax agencies). As such, tax measures usually fall under the jurisdiction of tax authorities rather than environmental departments, and this can create institutional challenges. *See*, for example, Janet Milne, *New Instruments on Old Turf—The Institutional Challenges of Environmental Taxation, in* 5 CRITICAL ISSUES IN ENVIRONMENTAL TAXATION: INTERNATIONAL AND COMPARATIVE PERSPECTIVES 141 (Nathalie Chalifour et al. eds, 2008).

[76] Nykvist, *supra* note 4, at 9. The regional example of the ECLAC is also helpful as this region has worked to promote coordination between fiscal and environmental policies in Latin American and Caribbean countries. *See* M.A. Glave Testino, *Coordinación entre las Políticas Fiscal y Ambiental en el Perú [Coordination between fiscal and environmental policies in Peru]* (CEPAL, Working Paper No. 102, 2005); M. Lizardo & R.M. Guzmán, *Coordinación de las políticas fiscales y ambientales en la República Dominicana [Coordination between fiscal and environmental policies in the Dominican Republic]*, (CEPAL, Working Paper No. 100, 2005); Lerda et al. (2003), *supra* note 12. We also consider work done by the OECD. *See*, for example, OECD, THE POLITICAL ECONOMY OF ENVIRONMENTALLY RELATED TAXES (2006), *available at* http://www.oecd.org/dataoecd/27/23/36 966499.pdf; OECD, ENVIRONMENT AND TAXATION: THE CASES OF THE NETHERLANDS, SWEDEN AND THE UNITED STATES (1994); OECD, OECD ENVIRONMENTAL OUTLOOK TO 2030 (2008); OECD, ENVIRONMENTAL TAXES: RECENT DEVELOPMENTS IN CHINA AND OECD COUNTRIES (1999); OECD, *The Use of Green Taxes in Denmark for the Control of the Aquatic Environment, in* EVALUATING AGRI-ENVIRONMENTAL POLICIES DESIGN, PRACTICE AND RESULTS (2006), *available at* http:// oberon.sourceoecd.org.proxy.bib.uottawa.ca/vl=414587/cl=28/nw=1/rpsv/cgi-bin/fulltextew.pl?p rpsv=/ij/oecdthemes/99980002/v2005n11/s19/p263.idx.; OECD, IMPLEMENTATION STRATEGIES FOR ENVIRONMENTAL TAXES (1996); OECD, IMPROVING FISCAL FEDERALISM, OECD ECONOMIC SURVEYS 84–109 (2009); OECD, INSTRUMENT MIXES ADDRESSING NON-POINT SOURCES OF WATER POLLUTION (2007), *available at* http://www.olis.oecd.org/olis/2004doc.nsf/LinkTo/NT0000A5EE/$ FILE/JT03221859.PDF (part of OECD's project on instrument mixes for environmental policy); OECD, SUBSIDIES AND ENVIRONMENT: EXPLORING THE LINKAGES (1996); OECD, TAXATION AND THE ENVIRONMENT: COMPLEMENTARY POLICIES (1993).

[77] Directive 2003/96, of the European Parliament and of the Council of 27 October 2003 on Restructuring the Community Framework for the Taxation of Energy Products and Electricity, 2003 O.J. (L 283/51), art. 14, para. 1(b), and Directive 92/81, of the European Council of 19 October 1992 on Harmonization of the Structures of Excise Duties on Mineral Oils, 1992 O.J. (L

not result from a European policy on the matter but is rather inspired by international practice of the International Civil Aviation Organization (ICAO) and international law, i.e. the Chicago Convention on International Civil Aviation.[78] This exemption is a hindrance to the application of a basic principle of environmental law—also endorsed by the European Union itself[79]—at the European level, which is to ensure that polluters pay for the damage they cause to human health and the environment. And, since European Directives have primacy over national law of the Member States, they limit the margin of Member States and their policy subdivisions to design and implement their own environmental policies. In 2000, the European Commission put forward innovative ideas, such as suppressing the exemption of excise duties for aviation fuels at a European level, or, alternatively, allowing Member States to introduce their own national taxes.[80] This latter possibility was coldly received by Member States, who feared the economically damaging effects that could result from the unilateral adoption of those taxes. In this particular case, however, the European institutions partly managed to circumvent the obstacle by including aviation emissions under the EU emissions trading scheme (ETS) from 2012.[81]

Horizontal integration, or cross-sectoral integration,[82] involves the challenge of how to manage environmental policy issues that invariably transcend many government departments even at one level of government, from natural resources and transportation to agriculture and fiscal policy. Nykvist notes that integration across sectors is a central challenge.[83] To achieve horizontal coordination, the authorities (ministries or functional areas of government) in charge of tax collection, those in charge of environmental

---

316) 12–15, art. 8, para. 1 (in force until 2003). On the compatibility of this exemption with EU law, *see* Case T-351/02, Deutsche Bahn v. Euro. Comm'n, 2006 E.C.R. II-1047.

[78]   *Convention on International Civil Aviation*, 7 December 1944, 61 Stat. 1180; 15 U.N.T.S. 295 (entered into force 14 April 1947), art. 24, para.2.

[79]   *See Commission Proposal for Greening Transport*, at 2, COM (2008) 433 final (Jul. 7, 2008); *see also* EURO. COMM'N, SUSTAINABLE DEVELOPMENT IN THE EUROPEAN UNION 109 (2009).

[80]   *Commission Proposal for Taxation of Aircraft Fuel*, COM (2000) 110 final (Mar. 2, 2000).

[81]   Directive 2008/101 of the European Parliament and of the Council of 19 November 2008 on Amending Directive 2003/87/EC so as to Include Aviation Activities in the Scheme for Greenhouse Gas Emission Allowance Trading within the Community, 2008 O.J. (L 8/3) 3–21. Coordination is also essential at the international level. For example, the academic literature has addressed the issue of whether climate taxes that states adopt, among other objectives, in order to comply with the international obligations of the Kyoto Protocol are compatible with the rules on international commerce in the World Trade Organization. *See* F. Sindico, *Climate Taxes and the WTO: Is the Multilateral Trade Regime a Further Obstacle for Efficient Domestic Climate Policies?*, 8 ECON. POL'Y & L. 1–24 (2006); G. Goh, *The World Trade Organization, Kyoto and Energy Tax Adjustments at the Border*, 38 J. WORLD TRADE 395–423 (2004). On the joint work of fiscal and environmental authorities under the ECLAC, *see* J. Acquatella, *El Papel Conjunto de las Autoridades Fiscales y Ambientales en la Gestión Ambiental de los Países de América Latina y el Caribe* [*The joint role of fiscal and environmental authorities for the environmental management in Latin American and Caribbean countries*], *in* POLÍTICA FISCAL Y MEDIO AMBIENTE: BASES PARA UNA AGENDA COMÚN [FISCAL POLICY AND ENVIRONMENT: BASIS FOR A COMMON AGENDA] 25–63 (J. Acquatella and A. Bárcena Ibarra eds, 2005). For a reference to contrast the evolution of the fiscal decentralization process in the last decade, see K. FUKASAKU & L.R. DE MELLO, FISCAL DECENTRALISATION IN EMERGING ECONOMIES: GOVERNANCE ISSUES (1999).

[82]   Nykvist, *supra* note 4, at 7.

[83]   *Id.*

policies, as well as those entrusted with economic and industrial policies, or social policies must find a way to coordinate. Horizontal coordination between environmental and
social and economic policies (including tax policy) is difficult to achieve. For example,
in a period when energy prices are subject to variations and often increase, States are
reluctant to raise the level of existing taxes on energy sources. Such a policy would indeed
further expose local business to international competition, as well as have a negative
impact on poorer segments of the population (in the case of consumption taxes). This
phenomenon has been demonstrated by the 2009 Commission Report on EU Sustainable
Development Strategy.[84] Likewise, horizontal coordination among instruments (taxes,
regulations, subsidies) requires the careful attention of policymakers.

Time coordination is a peculiarity that environmental policies share with other long-
term-oriented fields of governmental activity, such as pension and retirement policies. It
covers the adjustment and the control of the different time-scales (either short- or long-
run) used in the policy processes and in the determination of the priorities. For example,
a tax exemption granted in favor of the production of renewable energies, like biomass,
may reduce the use of fossil energy on the short-term, but if accompanied by an increase
in the use of agricultural lands for biomass only, it may have a negative environmental
impact in the long run.[85]

Efficient use of environmental taxes may require all three forms of coordination to be
applied at the same time. From a juridical perspective, coordination also implies that possible incompatibilities between environmental tax legislation and other legal norms (in
particular rules concerning the areas of commerce and trade, competition, transportation
and of course taxation[86]) can be identified and, if necessary, solved.

Mechanisms for Achieving Coordination

Coordination mechanisms may take very different forms. They may be 'ex ante,' i.e.
before an environmental tax measure is adopted by one level of government, or 'ex post.'
The mechanisms may be facultative (information, consultation) or compulsory (authorization or power to quash a decision made by another authority). They may imply a hier-

---

[84]   According to the European Commission, 'the implicit tax rate on energy for the EU-27 has
been decreasing since 1999. This decrease in the effective tax burden could be seen as inconsistent
with the objective of shifting taxation from labor onto resource and energy consumption, although
there are indications that taxation may have played a role in stimulating energy conservation.
Furthermore there is greater reliance on policy instruments other than taxes, such as emissions
trading, and energy taxes were reduced to compensate for the substantial rise in the oil price
over recent years.' EURO. COMM'N, SUSTAINABLE DEVELOPMENT IN THE EUROPEAN UNION: 2009
MONITORING REPORT OF THE EU SUSTAINABLE DEVELOPMENT STRATEGY 14, 88 (2009). *See also*
EURO. COMM'N, TAXATION TRENDS IN THE EUROPEAN UNION: DATA FOR THE EU MEMBER STATES
AND NORWAY 123–4 (2009).

[85]   This example is inspired by the Hungarian experience, which was the object of a 2007
study. Márton Herczeg et al., *Environmental Concerns and Cross-Sectoral Relevance of Biomass
Utilization in Hungary* (Ecologic Inst., EPIGOV, Working Paper No. 21, 2007); Homeyer &
Knoblauch, *supra* note 6.

[86]   On the possible incompatibilities of environmental taxes with other European law, see
Commission Proposal for Environmental Taxes and Charges in the Single Market, COM (1997) 9
final (Mar. 26, 1997).

archy between levels of government (primacy), or not. They may concern the legislative, administrative or the judicial powers. In many countries, coordination is achieved by establishing common bodies or a forum between the authorities concerned. For example, in Belgium, where both national and regional levels have significant powers in the area of environment (including environmental taxation), coordination bodies have been used to deal with conflict.[87]

One fairly uncontroverted assertion is that effective coordination requires at a minimum the establishment of common objectives for all levels of government and authorities active in the area. For example, by analogy, in a 2009 technical report, the European Environment Agency examined the effectiveness of the investment made out of European funds for social cohesion in the poorer European regions in the field of environment, on the basis of empirical experience in Italian, Spanish and Austrian regions. One of the findings of the report was that the effectiveness of the environmental investments could be seen when common objectives were set for both the national and the regional levels.[88]

A set of common rules (even Codes of Conduct) can be very helpful in offering clarity and serving as a guide to the different levels of government, helping to limit duplication and overlap, and reduce litigation. Even in the absence of common rules, experience has shown that adaptive management in the implementation of environmental taxes can be helpful and that it is often necessary to adapt the institutional framework to achieve common objectives.

Coordination mechanisms can also be developed to ensure coherence of the various instruments used in a given environmental area. For example, if there is a general consensus on the fact that the ideal policy is a mix of existing instruments, one must nevertheless be aware that the various instruments can each have an impact on the effectiveness of the others.[89] For example, a labeling system may improve the effectiveness of an environmentally related tax by improving taxpayers' information about the most efficient (and thus the more environmentally friendly) behavior. On the other hand, taxes and direct regulations applied together might unnecessarily restrict the flexibility of economic actors to find the most cost-effective (tax-efficient) and less polluting scheme.

Indonesia addressed coordination issues by creating a set of conditions for new local taxes, including situating the object of the tax within the appropriate local area and avoiding duplication with provincial or central taxes.[90]

The desire for coherence between environmental tax policies may not always be

---

[87] For example, the Cellule Concertation État-Régions pour l'Énergie/Energie Overleggroep Staat-Gewesten (CONCERE/ENOVER) [Roundtable Dialogue Process between State and Regions on Energy] is an advisory body where all energy matters can be discussed. The National Climate Commission helps coordinate climate policy. It has been appointed to propose a draft National Climate Plan to the Extended Interministerial Conference for the Environment. Another example is the federal Interdepartmental Commission for Sustainable Development. OECD, ECONOMIC SURVEY: BELGIUM 74 (2009).

[88] EURO. ENVT. AGENCY, TERRITORIAL COHESION. ANALYSIS OF ENVIRONMENTAL ASPECTS OF THE EU COHESION POLICY IN SELECTED COUNTRIES (2009).

[89] OECD, THE POLITICAL ECONOMY OF ENVIRONMENTALLY RELATED TAXES, *supra* note 76, at 175.

[90] White III, *supra* note 36, at 55.

attainable, demonstrating that there is a need to do some additional research on the mechanisms for coordinating public policies where they converge in the result sought. However, in each case, the quality and quantity of these mechanisms must be carefully examined. Sometimes, even recentralization processes may be required to meet social expectations, which could be particularly difficult to reach in some states with strong centripetal dynamics, such as Spain or Belgium.

In many countries, subnational governments have taken the lead in environmental matters, because many problems related to environmental management are strongly connected to specific geographical areas or political communities and population preferences may vary among jurisdictions, which supports delegation or decentralization.[91] Consequently, on the fiscal side, assignation of revenues is defended by subnational governments.

Administration and Costs

The choice of level for environmental taxes needs to take account of both the administrative costs of different tax options and the extent to which different tax designs can achieve effective targeting of the environmental incentive. The institutional assignment of responsibility for setting the tax and the allocation of the revenues may also affect the efficiency of the outcome.[92] Empirical research also shows that the standard economic analysis has tended to neglect important distinctions and interactions among the geographic scope of pollutants, the enforcement authority of various levels of government and the fiscal responsibilities of the levels of government. For example, in many Latin American countries, fiscal decentralization has already been implemented and local governments are often the best-situated to act in environmental matters. However, vertical coordination in fiscal and environmental policies is not achieved, especially in federal states such as Argentina, Brazil and Mexico (subnational authorities have even complained about the lack of coordination with federal authorities within the same sector).[93] Sometimes

---

[91]   J. Prust, *Impuestos Ambientales en los Países en Desarrollo [Environmental taxes in Developing countries]*, *in* POLÍTICA FISCAL Y MEDIO AMBIENTE: BASES PARA UNA AGENDA COMÚN [FISCAL POLICY AND ENVIRONMENT: BASIS FOR A COMMON AGENDA] 89–104 (CEPAL, 2005).

[92]   Don Fullerton et al., *supra* note 42; M. Catenacci, *EPI at Regional and Local Level—A Literature Review* (Ecologic Inst., EPIGOV, Working Paper No. 17, 2007). There is a need to apply a more decentralized approach, enhancing the communication and interaction—both 'vertically' and 'horizontally'—among the different levels of governance. The strategies need to be integrated upstream in the policymaking processes, while the institutional ability to manage the processes toward decentralization of competencies, and an integrative approach to problems and collective learning, needs to be enhanced and coordinated at all levels of action.

[93]   An overview on financial issues for environmental management in Argentina and the use of economic and fiscal tools in Costa Rica can be read respectively in O. Cetrángolo et al., *Política y Gestión Ambiental en Argentina: Gasto y Financiamiento [Environmental policy and management in Argentina: expenditure and finance]*, (CEPAL, Working Paper No. 90, 2004); J. Echeverría, *Herramientas económicas y fiscales para la Gestión Ambiental en Costa Rica [Fiscal and economic tools for the environmental management in Costa Rica]*, *in* POLÍTICA FISCAL Y MEDIO AMBIENTE: BASES PARA UNA AGENDA COMÚN 169–96 [FISCAL POLICY AND ENVIRONMENT: BASIS FOR A COMMON AGENDA] (2005). A specific reference to the lack of coordination can be found in E. Rezk, *Fallas de Coordinación: Desafíos de Política para el Federalismo Fiscal Ambiental Argentino [Coordination*

there have been conflicts between the fiscal and environmental policies (for instance, in Brazil[94]). These are obstacles to sustainable development in the region.

Research in the well established field of fiscal federalism has shown that there are many ways to allocate legislative and management jurisdiction of fiscal policy, including the often thorny determination of who is the beneficiary of the revenues.[95] Of course, the relatively new environmental tax instruments often fit awkwardly into preexisting institutional frameworks. Because of this, there is a risk of a lack of coordination that may lead to supplementary administrative costs. Determining the costs of administering environmental taxes is not a straightforward affair. For instance, the costs for businesses to administer the taxes may or may not always be factored into analyses of costs.[96] Further, many factors that are critical to create a fair and politically acceptable measure may render a tax more expensive to administer and evaluate.[97] However, in general terms, the research seems to show that administering environmental taxes on various levels is less cost-effective than centralizing it on only one level. For example, one study found that the total costs of running regional funds for collection of charges and evaluation of environmental projects averaged 1.9 percent of revenues raised at the regional level, versus 0.9 percent at the national level.[98]

In some cases, a more efficiently targeted environmental incentive can be created through artful combination of various taxes—the so-called 'multi-part instrument'—to approximate more closely the effects of a tax on measured emissions.[99] If the competencies of each part relate to a different level of government, then the need for a stronger coordination is clear.

---

faults: Policy challenges for the Argentinian environmental fiscal federalism] (CEPAL, Working Paper No. 115, 2005).

[94] Fallas de Coordinación en el Federalismo Fiscal-Ambiental Brasileño [Coordination faults in the Brazilian environmental fiscal federalism], III Taller Regional de Política Fiscal y Medio Ambiente: Sesión III-Desafíos de la descentralización y del federalismo fiscal-ambiental en ALC [III Regional Workshop on Fiscal Policy and Environment: III Session-Challenges of decentralization and environmental fiscal federalism in Latin American and Caribbean countries], a presentation given in Santiago, 26 January, 2005, *available at* http://www.eclac.org/dmaah/noticias/discursos/1/20771/jatoba_es.pdf; J. Jatobá, *A coordenação entre as políticas fiscal e ambiental no Brasil: a perspectiva dos governos estaduais [The coordination between fiscal and environmental policies in Brazil: the State Governments' perspective]* (CEPAL, Working Paper No. 92, 2005).

[95] And these different ways may affect efficiency, as shown by D. Fullerton, A. Leicester & S. Smith, *Environmental Taxes, in* REFORMING THE TAX SYSTEM FOR THE 21ST CENTURY, THE MIRRLEES REVIEW (Inst. for Fiscal Studies, 2008), *available at* http://www.ifs.org.uk/mirrleesreview/reports/environment.pdf.

[96] OECD, THE POLITICAL ECONOMY OF ENVIRONMENTALLY RELATED TAXES, *supra* note 76, at 148.

[97] For instance, measures to create policies to counter distributional or competitive effects may be incorporated into a tax policy package to create a fair overall policy. *Id.* at 147.

[98] *Id.*

[99] A tax directly based on motor vehicle emissions may not be feasible, but it may be approximated by the combination of instruments such as a tax on petrol, a subsidy to new car purchases, or tax on older cars, and a tax on cars with low fuel-efficiency or high emission rates. D. Fullerton & S. West, *Tax and Subsidy Combinations for the Control of Car Pollution* (Nat'l Bureau of Econ. Research, Working Paper No. 7774, 2000).

Location of Environmental Tax Administration within a Level of Government

Practice varies greatly among countries with respect to the implementation of environmental taxes by administrative authorities.[100] Some countries, like the Nordic countries, rely largely on their state tax administrations to implement environmental tax policies. The advantage of having recourse to the Ministry of Finance is that its approach is usually transversal (applying all environmental taxes cross-departmentally, independently of the type of pollution that they aim to reduce), while other Ministries tend to have a sectoral view.[101]

Other countries, for example in Central and Eastern Europe, but also in developing countries such as Ghana and Uganda, tend to have established separate National Environmental Funds that are independent from state fiscal authorities (Poland's National Environmental Fund is perhaps the classical case).[102] The emergence and functions of more autonomous bodies for environmental tax purposes may be criticized because they may lead to the application of 'para-fiscal' charges. However, an autonomous approach, such as that of a water board, may create greater opportunities for environmental improvements.[103] This is a question to which more research could be devoted.

Competition

The EU experience sheds light on the role of competition in multilevel use of environmental taxes. Some research findings suggest that harmonization of environmental taxes, such as through EU level directives, may reduce the need to use exceptions to address competition concerns.[104] The European Environment Agency's 2000 report on integration of environmental taxes noted that tax harmonization at the EU level could limit differences in the competitiveness of individual Member States.[105] It also noted, however, a number of barriers to the harmonization of energy taxes. For instance, the report noted that the requirement for unanimous voting on fiscal measures at the EU level is a barrier

---

[100]   John Snape & Jeremy de Souza, Environmental Taxation Law: Policy, Contexts and Practice (2006). *See*, for example, Euro. Envt. Agency, Effectiveness of Environmental Taxes and Charges for Managing Sand, Gravel and Rock Extraction in Selected EU Countries (2008).

[101]   *Política Fiscal y Medio Ambiente* [*Fiscal Policy and Environment*], CEPAL, *available at* http://www.undp.org.cu/eventos/instruverdes/1.%20PoliticaFiscalenALC.pdf.

[102]   On environmental funds, *see* OECD, Sourcebook on Environmental Funds (2000); Convention on Biological Diversity, Reports of the Expert Group Meeting on Management of Environmental Funds for the Financial Sustainability of Biodiversity Conservation (2007), *available at* http://www.cbd.int/financial/nationalfunding.shtml (for Latin American countries).

[103]   Mikael Skou Andersen, *Governance By Green Taxes: Implementing Clean Water Policies in Europe 1970–1990*, 2 Envtl. Econ. & Pol'y Stud. 39, 52–54 (1999).

[104]   See, for example, Euro. Envt. Agency, Using the Market for Cost-effective Environmental Policy (2006), *available at* http://www.eea.europa.eu/publications/eea_report-2006_1.

[105]   Euro. Envt. Agency, *Environmental Taxes: Recent Developments in Tools for Integration* 11 (Environmental Issues Series, Working Paper No. 18, 2000).

to such harmonization.[106] The report also identified concerns about negatively impacting competitiveness.[107]

The EEA report also highlighted a barrier to unilateral introduction of environmental taxes at the EU level, namely—once again—competitiveness. In this context, the concern is that national legislation will tend to favor the national industry, but participation in the EU subjects the countries to rules about undistorted trade.[108]

Summary and Recommendations for Further Research

Our survey shows that there is a range of scholarship discussion of various aspects of implementation issues, especially coordination and competitiveness. We found that much of the literature is focused on the EU, and that while coordination and implementation issues are extremely important in the EU context, similar issues arise in federal states with concurrent jurisdiction over environmental taxation, and that more research, both theoretical and empirical, about the experience in other jurisdictions would be helpful.

CONCLUSION

This chapter has surveyed the literature related to the allocation of environmental taxing powers among different levels of government in a context of concurrent jurisdiction. Having surveyed the theoretical and empirical literature, we find that while there is abundant scholarship on related issues of multilevel governance, fiscal and environmental federalism, and environmental governance, as well as abundant research on particular tax instruments at a given level of government, there is a conspicuous lack of research directly pertaining to the central issue. We recommend the development of an empirical database of environmental tax instruments that helps build understanding of what instruments and tax bases are being targeted at what level of government. This could be achieved through the OECD's database of environmentally related taxes. Doing so will foster understanding of patterns of allocation, thereby allowing evaluations of the allocation decisions and their effectiveness. We also recommend the ongoing development of theoretical research on factors relevant to the allocation decision, such as how environmental problems with spillover externalities should be optimally addressed and how enforcement and effectiveness issues interact with allocation decisions.

With regard to implementation issues, coordination is a crucial element. Coordination mechanisms must take into account the fact that environmental taxation is a part of the tax system and not just a tool of environmental policy. This element implies that coordination must serve the objectives traditionally assigned to taxation, for example, ensuring that the various levels of government have sufficient and stable financial resources in order to carry out their policies, as well as ensuring redistribution of wealth among the various social groups. Moreover, coordination mechanisms in environmental taxation

---

[106] *Id.*
[107] *Id.* at 54.
[108] *Id.* at 55.

must avoid political and legal fragmentation and ensure that the concurring exercise of their powers by the various competent authorities do not create hindrances to companies and citizens willing to move or expand their activities from one jurisdiction to another. In other words, the internal coherence of a (sub)national environmental tax policy cannot always justify an infringement of the freedom of movement of persons from and to the territory in which this policy is implemented.

It would also be helpful to develop a stronger base of empirical research to enrich knowledge about what conditions are needed within a given governmental authority at any level in order for it to effectively and efficiently implement an environmental tax policy. This research could show the importance of several preconditions (such as enforcement and evaluation capacity, or synergy with other departments) to achieve effective environmental taxation at different levels of government.

15 Transaction costs of environmental taxation: the administrative burden
Jan Pavel and Leoš Vítek*

This chapter deals with the concept of transaction costs of environmental taxation. It analyzes the discussion about their definition, the problem of their measurement and their role in the evaluation of efficiency of the environmental taxes, and presents the results of relevant empirical studies that deal with their quantification.

STATUS OF TRANSACTION COSTS IN THE ASSESSMENT OF ENVIRONMENTAL TAXES

The commencement and development of the field of transaction costs, inseparably linked to the work of Williamson (1981), have influenced the evaluation of environment protection tools, including so-called environmental taxes (OECD 1997). The original concept of environmental taxes is based on the Pigouvian approach (1932) of a remedy tax, aimed at including external costs in economic calculations of private subjects and increasing overall allocation effectiveness.

As in the case of other types of taxes, however, the application of such a tool carries additional costs and thus results in a further drain on scarce social resources. Such additional costs are labeled as transaction costs, and their existence can complicate the tax remedy for market. Therefore, when designing environmental taxes it is necessary for a government not only to take into account the primary objective—elimination of a negative externality—but also to carry out an analysis of the size of the transaction costs.

OECD (1997) introduces the idea of including transaction costs in the practical evaluation of the effectiveness of market environmental protection tools, including environmental taxes. Given the difficulty in quantifying costs and benefits of these tools in monetary terms, OECD (1997) suggests a multi-criterion evaluation framework based on the 3E methodology discussed, for example, in Coombs and Jenkins (1994).

OECD's evaluation framework follows the input and output parameters of running interventions as well as their mutual links. The concept of the methodology is based on the model outlined in Figure 15.1. The aim of any government intervention is to modify the economic system's behavior, notably in its outputs (such as reduction of emission volumes). In order to reach this target, individual tools (taxes) are implemented. Their utilization, however, requires the consumption of certain resources (either explicit or implicit) that may be labeled as inputs.

*   The views expressed in this chapter are those of its authors. The Ministry of Education, Youth and Sports of the Czech Republic has supported this research (Registration No. 2D06029).

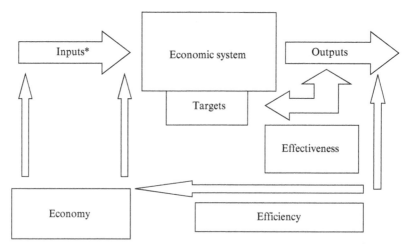

Note: * Inputs = costs related to implementation of tools.

Source: Coombs and Jenkins (1994), modified.

Figure 15.1 Model of economic tools' operation in environmental protection

For the assessment of the effectiveness of economic tools for environmental protection it is necessary to monitor several criteria, both *primary* and *supplementary*. Among primary criteria, OECD ranks the following:

- *Effectiveness.* This criterion determines to what extent the application of the evaluated tool contributed to fulfillment of the determined targets. On a general level, planned values for a target date are compared with the achieved values. Evaluations of environmental taxes monitor their impact on the behavior of economic subjects or on the rate at which external costs are being reflected in economic calculations.
- *Economy (administrative and compliance).* This criterion monitors whether the given tool has been implemented with minimal costs. Essentially it covers an analysis of transaction costs that, from an economic perspective, represent consumption of scarce resources.
- *Efficiency.* This criterion analyzes the relationship between the contributions (benefits) of the given tool and the costs of its implementation. The aim is therefore to find a tool that offers maximal contributions (in the case of environmental taxes, this translates into maximal reflection of external costs in calculations of private subjects) with minimal transaction costs. Thus, monitoring involves identifying the benefits allocated to each unit of cost.

Supplementary criteria can also be used to evaluate other effects of environmental taxes, such as the generating of public revenues, impacts on innovations, soft effects (such as the signalling effect on consumers) and broader economic effects (such as impacts on economic competitiveness, inflation, balance of trade and so on). From the above-mentioned it therefore follows that monitoring the economy and efficiency of environmental taxes essentially requires monitoring the transaction costs of the whole system of tax intervention.

DEFINING TRANSACTION COSTS OF ENVIRONMENTAL TAXES

The generally accepted definition of transaction costs is still under discussion but a rough specification may be found, for example, in Coase (1937), Demsetz (1968) and Williamson (1981). When discussing transactional costs in general (not costs for taxation in particular), these authors emphasize the concept of transaction costs particularly from the perspective of the decision-making of economic subjects (notably firms) regarding whether to organize production either internally or externally (a so-called 'make or buy' decision). They point out that this decision cannot solely take into account the savings in production costs resulting from the external production, but must also consider the additional costs associated with the market contract, such as search and information costs, bargaining costs, the keeping of trade secrets, and policing and enforcement costs.

The concept of transaction costs has also been reflected in the fundamental literature on public finance and tax policy, when for example Messere (1993), Musgrave (1989) and Stiglitz (2000) on a general level address the emergence of these costs in the implementation of state interventions. Their work therefore substantially broadened this concept's application, because transactions are considered to be costs incurred (in both public and private sectors) as a result of a state intervention. This was a quite important shift from the previous approach, in which transaction costs were relevant only for analyzing the 'make or buy' decision.

From a practical perspective and for the purposes of this subject it seems best to use a negative definition of transaction costs. The taxes' transaction costs are those costs that would not be assumed by governmental and private subjects had the system of environmental taxes not been introduced in the first place. At this point it is necessary to keep in mind that transaction costs as such do not directly produce anything (for instance, they do not represent public budgets' revenue that could be possibly used further down the line); they instead facilitate the operation of a given system. The situation under consideration is therefore that of a consumption of scarce resources not directly related to the creation of benefits. The administrator should therefore aim for their minimization—consistent with the objective of monitoring the criterion of economy within the methodological concept proposed by OECD.

Transaction costs related to the implementation of environmental taxes originate in both the private and public sectors. In the case of the public sector, transaction costs are called administrative costs and cover all costs incurred by the public sector (both central and local governments and regulatory agencies) and are related to the implementation of a given tool. This includes, for example, the costs of collecting individual taxes, monitoring costs, the costs of obtaining information, the costs of inspecting tax subjects and so on. The private sector is subjected to the second set of transaction costs, called compliance costs. Here the costs include expenses that private subjects incur for proper administration and remittance of environmental taxes, apart from the actual tax obligation. It is important to point out that both types of costs (administrative and compliance) are mutually dependent on each other since the public sector may shift a number of related activities (monitoring, reporting and so on) onto the private sector. It is therefore essential to carry out their minimization simultaneously.

The existence of transaction costs naturally affects the search for an optimal tax design. Approaches that reflect transaction costs may be found, for example, in Yitzhaki (1979) or, in the case of CO_2 taxes, in Smuldres and Vollebergh (1999). This represents a substantial shift since earlier approaches, in their quest for an optimal level of taxation, focused only on the parameter of minimizing excessive tax burdens and thus to a large extent duplicated the Ramsey (1927) approach. At the same time, Yitzhaki (1979) points out that the issue of designing an optimal tax is further complicated by the dependent nature of the relationship between the size of excessive tax burdens and transaction costs. It is therefore necessary to simultaneously carry out their minimization while respecting the mutually conditional relationship between the two quantities.

A modified approach toward incorporation of the concept of transaction costs into tax theory is presented by Slemrod and Yitzhaki (2002), who further elaborate on the relationship among administrative costs, tax avoidance and tax evasions. They prove that the efficiency of a given tax is influenced by the possibility of tax evasions that are in turn reducible through an increase in administrative costs. However, this works against an increase in efficiency. Finding an optimal level and form of a tax thus represents a complex optimization problem.

The academic literature identifies ways to classify and measure transaction costs other than the administrative versus compliance distinction. Sandford, Godwin and Hardwick (1989) provide a detailed discussion of classification and measurement. Smuldres and Vollebergh (1999) classify transaction costs of taxes as implementation costs and differentiate them not by sectors but rather by the time dimension, as ex ante (the cost of exclusion) and ex post (monitoring costs).

A more detailed classification may also be found in the case of compliance costs, aiming to factor in the fact that for taxpayers there also exist benefits related to the existence of the tax system. Sandford, Godwin and Hardwick (1989) represent this school of thought in their work with the concept of net compliance costs, defined as compliance costs less the benefits that compensate them. The most important benefit is the cash-flow benefit that taxpayers receive when they defer tax payments, because the legal obligation to pay the tax occurs later than the theoretical obligation arises. Compliance costs are in turn understood relatively broadly as costs originating with economic subjects due to the necessity of adjustment to the legal requirements of the tax system, including psychological costs.

Sandford, Godwin and Hardwick (1989) also address the necessity of analyzing compliance costs from the perspective of their duration. Similarly to Smuldres and Vollenbergh (1999), they classify transaction costs by duration into regular, relatively time-constant costs of the tax system (regular costs), and costs related to changes in the tax system (costs of change).

Despite significant advancements in transaction cost theory and its presence in the OECD's evaluation model, the application of this criterion in the assessment of environmental taxes' efficiency is far from widespread nowadays. A number of relatively detailed studies devoted to environmental taxes, such as Bayar (1998) or Millock and Nauges

(2006), either neglect to cover this aspect at all or mention it only vaguely. On a similar note, the concept of a double dividend, presented for example in Goulder (1995), assumes transaction costs only indirectly. Sadler (2001) mentioned the problem of transaction costs as a parameter of an optimal tax framework. At the same time, it is notably the size of transaction costs that to a significant extent influences the impact of the given tool on economic effectiveness.

METHODS OF MEASURING TRANSACTION COSTS

Methods of measuring the size of transaction costs related to taxation are determined by the sector incurring them. The situation is somewhat easier in the case of administrative costs than for compliance costs or even an excessive tax burden, as the former are far more visible and measurable due to the existence of budgetary data on individual public organizations, which is publicly available in democratic countries. In contrast with compliance costs, however, it is more complicated to relate administrative tax costs to individual taxes.

An ideal situation of measuring administrative costs is represented by a case in which collection of the given tax is entrusted only to a single organization that does not perform any other tasks. If such an ideal condition does not correspond with the reality and the given organization does not keep separate internal auditing systems for its individual agendas, it is necessary to carry out a cleansing of the collected data, such as via time snapshots.

The quantification of the size of compliance costs represents a substantially more difficult situation, one associated with a number of possible problems including the extensive number of taxpayers, their dissimilar structure and so on. Vaillancourt (1987), Sandford, Godwin and Hardwick (1989), Sandford (1995) and Evans (2003) analyzed the advantages and disadvantages of individual methods and arrived at the following options.

The best method is generally considered to be the use of structured surveys that can cover a relatively large number of tax subjects. In the case of surveys by mail, however, a relatively low rate of return must be taken into account. The second option is direct personal surveying, which is very costly. Other, less frequently used methods are unstructured interviews with respondents, which are useful for carrying out pilot projects measuring compliance costs, or studies of the labor and time costs of taxpayers, often associated with the method of observation. Approaches based on a deductive method require simulation and modeling, mostly operated under the concept of a 'typical' taxpayer. The relevance of results obtained in this way may be very easily challenged, however, by attacking the selected assumptions. On the other hand, it is not necessary to come into direct contact with taxpayers, which significantly reduces the financial demands of the research.

An even more complicated situation arises when we try to classify transaction costs based on their time perspective (the one-off costs associated with the change in tax versus the operational transaction costs associated with its ongoing operation). However, while segregation of costs is in theory simple, in practice it is not easy to allocate individual costs into the first or second group (particularly in the case of frequent and various changes in tax legislation). Such segregation is notably meaningful for the assessment of the compliance costs of taxation, since costs associated with changes in the tax system may in a substantial way distort the results of the compliance costs' assessment. Economically speaking, these one-off costs should be time-differentiated and should not be recorded only in the year of their origination (for example in the case of depreciable fixed assets acquired for compliance purposes). The economically ideal approach would associate costs with the year in which taxes are collected—such as through depreciation of assets associated with tax collection—and not with the year in which the asset is acquired.

However, this ideal may not always be possible in the assessment of compliance (as well as administrative) costs. In the domain of compliance costs, expenditures associated with changes in the tax system include, in particular, those for human capital investments (training of internal staff), changes in software, and other investments such as hardware. Since the length of the period throughout which these costs should be spread is not clear,[1] in practice these costs are frequently associated only with the relevant year of their origination. Due to the above-mentioned approach, in a situation where compliance and administrative costs are measured in the year of a significant tax change (or immediately before or after), the size of tax system's costs may be overrated.

The absolute size of the transaction costs of environmental taxes is influenced by several factors: the number of taxpayers, the design of the tax base, the relationship of the tax base to other taxes or reporting, and the system of monitoring and supervision. As described in Fullerton, Leicester and Smith (2010), environmental taxes designed as excises on inputs will probably have lower transaction costs than emission taxes since the former do not require a complicated system of emission measurement combined with supervision of reported emissions.

From the perspective of transaction costs, environmental taxes are advantageous when they are collected from a small number of taxpayers, as they then translate into lower administrative as well as compliance costs. It is beneficial if a tax base design is tied with already existing reporting systems or other tax bases, thereby reducing the transaction costs of reporting and control. Similarly, linking the tax base with commonly carried business transactions (purchases, sales, revenues and so on) has the same effect, as it eliminates the costly system of additional measurement or recording for the purposes of the environmental tax base.

The relative size of transaction costs is usually measured with respect to the total revenue of individual or all taxes. Tax revenues may be reported either as cash flows to the government (the cash principle) or as a tax obligation for the given year (the accrual principle). For the size of relative indicators, the level of tax rates and the extent of tax bases are also important factors. Generally speaking, countries with a higher rate of taxation (or taxes with higher rates) will, ceteris paribus, report lower transaction costs compared to other countries or taxes. This fact may distort international comparison of transaction effectiveness in environmental taxes.

---

[1]   This is due in particular to the fact that ex ante the period during which the newly introduced tax legislation will be effective (the period between two significant modifications of the relevant tax) is not known.

EMPIRICAL STUDIES OF ENVIRONMENTAL TAXES' TRANSACTION COSTS

The assessment of the administrative costs of environmental taxes is carried out in the context of other taxes. Unfortunately, tax and customs administrations do not monitor in sufficient detail the costs of administrating individual taxes, and therefore it is usually impossible from their annual reports to obtain data on the administrative costs of the collection of environmental taxes. Consequently, there are neither empirical studies of administrative costs of environmental taxes nor data from government administrations.

However, there are some cases of attempted estimation of the administrative costs for environmental taxes:

- The OECD (2006) states that the administrative costs of a collection of environmental taxes and charges in Poland vary between 0.8 and 4.5 percent of the revenue.
- According to the OECD (2005), the government's administrative costs related to Norway's aviation fuel tax are very limited.
- The Swedish National Tax Board (OECD 1997) found that the Swedish CO_2 tax incorporated into the existing petroleum tax, energy tax and environmental tax on domestic air traffic is, from the perspective of administrative costs, low (approximately SEK 3 million).
- Deutscher Bundestag (2002), on its website, publishes data from the Federal Ministry of Finance, according to which administrative costs for environmental taxes in Germany are estimated at 0.13 percent of additional revenues.
- Pavel and Vítek (2008) estimated administrative costs for energy taxes in the Czech Republic at 0.7 to 2.7 percent of the revenue.
- Convery, McDonnell and Ferreira (2007) demonstrate that administrative costs for the plastic bag levy in Ireland amount to approximately 3 percent of revenue, since it is possible to integrate its reporting and collection into existing VAT reporting systems.
- HMRC (2009) calculated administrative costs for environmental taxes in the UK during the period 2005–2009 in the range of 0.34–0.21 percent.

The OECD (2006) argues that due to improperly chosen tools and their combination, there are also occasions when some tools are not effective. According to the OECD (2006), this is the case with, for example, the combination of the Climate Change Levy, Climate Change Agreements and CO_2 emissions trading scheme in the UK, the combination of the energy efficiency agreements in Denmark and the MINAS nutrient accounting system in the Netherlands.

Still fewer empirical studies exist regarding the compliance costs of environmental taxes, due in part to (1) the relative novelty of these taxes, (2) the costly necessity of bringing questionnaire or interview surveys to taxpayers and (3) the relatively small number of taxpayers of these taxes who are more difficult to identify within broader studies of the compliance costs of taxes more generally. Fullerton (1996) discusses Slemrod and Blumental's (1996) estimates of the compliance costs for the US Corporate Environmental Tax (CET), a specific type of corporate taxation in the United States with environmentally earmarked revenues. Fullerton considers the estimate of 16.9 percent significantly underrated since it does not appropriately take into account the smaller taxpayers of CET. On the basis of a questionnaire survey, Pavel and Vítek (2010) estimated the compliance costs for energy taxes in the Czech Republic at 0.28 to 0.39 percent of tax liabilities for 2008.

Environmental taxes are usually designed as excises imposed on specific commodities. Although specific excises have been levied on a wide range of commodities, recently taxation of fuels and tobacco products has become fiscally predominant. These taxes not only generate the majority of excise duties' revenues but are also intended to influence taxpayers toward reduction of the consumption of taxable commodities. Nevertheless, the amount of the excise duties classified according to OECD (2006) as environmental taxes remains more or less stable in OECD countries. Estimates of compliance costs associated with environmental taxes in the form of excise taxes are not available. Due to structural similarities with other selective excise taxes it would be possible, assuming revenues similar to those of environmental taxes, to estimate their compliance costs using data from studies that focus on excises. The following are estimates of the respective compliance costs for specific excise duties:

- Sandford, Godwin and Hardwick (1989) estimate compliance costs for the taxation of mineral oils in the UK at 0.23 percent; the estimated administrative costs are 0.12 percent.
- Shekidele (1999) estimates the compliance costs of Tanzania's excise duties at 15.6 percent, of which mineral oils represent 28.7 percent and tobacco taxation 18.2 percent
- Vaillancourt (1987) presents the results of a study prepared by Arthur Andersen & Co. for the Department of Finance in 1985. This company estimates compliance costs for Canada's federal sales tax and excises at 0.8 percent.
- Pavel and Vítek (2009) provide an estimate for the Czech Republic in 2008 for specific consumption taxes (excises) without energy taxes at the level of 0.97 percent of revenues (including overhead costs of tax and customs administrations). Compliance costs for the Czech Republic are not available.
- Kuliš (2004) estimates compliance costs in Croatia for mineral oils at 0.25 percent of revenues and for tobacco taxation at 0.21 percent.

Despite the scarcity of surveys, some generalizations can be made. Overviews of studies presented in Vaillancourt (1987), Evans (2003) and Klun and Blazic (2004) of personal, corporate and sales taxes, on the one hand, and existing modest evidence for environmental taxes (see above), on the other hand, indicate that the transaction costs of environmental taxes are rather low compared with those of other taxes, notably income taxes. This is due mainly to their design, in the case of energy and mineral oil taxes based on the principles of excise duties (a small number of taxpayers, a tax base oriented around market transactions, and a relatively simple construction of the tax base). In this way, both the administrative costs of governments and the compliance costs of the private sector are reduced.

Today, energy taxation does not rank among the most significant sources of government revenues. As its use gradually increases, we may expect the relative transaction costs to improve. For mineral oils, relative transaction costs are lower due to the fact that these taxes are of a high-yield nature.

Environmental taxes (or levies) based on the measurement of emissions' volumes, or those that include a large number of taxpayers, would probably result in an increase in transaction costs. At the same time, this would allow them to better focus on specific environmental targets or on a fairer taxation of actual environmental damage.

FURTHER RESEARCH

It may be expected that further development in the domain of tax theory, in a quest for an optimal tax or tax mix, will not be able to avoid incorporation of transaction costs. Therefore it is necessary through further research to elaborate on factors that influence their size, and subsequently to include them in theoretical models. In this process, it is also important to clarify the definitional issue of how to reflect cost-sharing between the government and the private sector regarding various taxes and regulations, respectively. A specific problem of environmental taxes is the interaction of transaction costs and an excessive tax burden.

In assessing the efficiency, effectiveness and economy of environmental taxes it is necessary, within the sphere of empirical research, to initiate a systematic measurement based on a standard methodology of administrative costs for individual taxes and countries. Also, for purposes of a discussion on the burden of the private sector, further research should carry out more compliance cost measurements at a corporate level so that evidence-based arguments may be used. Measurement of compliance costs should be based on corporate data rather than on the estimates of researchers or state administrations. Special care should be taken to ensure that these measurements also reflect the distribution of compliance costs based on the taxpayer size, so that the total compliance costs would be correctly estimated for the entire population of relevant taxpayers. This procedure may be recommended as the most accurate one in reflecting the distribution of compliance costs among taxpayers.

For evaluations and selections of the most appropriate environmental measures it will be important to measure the administrative costs and compliance costs not only for environmental taxes but also for alternative fiscal tools. This will allow for better tuning of the system of stimulations and commands so that it becomes economically efficient and environmentally effective.

REFERENCES

Bayar, Ali H. (1998), 'Can Europe reduce unemployment through environmental taxes? A general equilibrium analysis', paper presented at the Twelfth International Conference on Input-Output Techniques International Input-Output Association New York, 18–22 May.

Coase, Ronald (1937), 'The nature of the firm', *Economica*, **4** (16), 386–405.

Convery, Frank, Simon McDonnell and Susana Ferreira (2007), 'The most popular tax in Europe? Lessons from the Irish plastic bags levy', *Environmental and Resource Economics*, **38** (1), 1–11.

Coombs, Hugh M. and D.E. Jenkins (1994), *Public Sector Financial Management*, 2nd ed., London, UK: Chapman and Hall.

Demsetz, Harold (1968), 'The cost of transacting', *Quarterly Journal of Economics*, **82**, 33–53.

Deutscher Bundestag (2002), *Antwort der Bundesregierung, Drucksache 14/9993*, 7 October, Berlin, Germany: Deutscher Bundestag.

Evans, Chris (2003), 'Studying the studies: an overview of recent research into taxation operating costs', *eJournal of Tax Research*, **1** (1), 64–82.

Fullerton, Don (1996), 'Why have separate environmental taxes?', *Tax Policy and the Economy*, **10**, 33–70.
Fullerton, Don, Andrew Leicester and Stephen Smith (2010), 'Environmental taxes', in J. Mirrlees et al. (eds), *Dimensions of Tax Design: the Mirrlees Review*, Oxford, UK: Oxford University Press.
Goulder, Lawrence H. (1995), 'Environmental taxation and the double dividend: a reader's guide', *International Tax and Public Finance*, **2**, 157–83.
HMRC (2009), *Meeting Our Challenges – Departmental Autumn Performance Report 2009*, Norwich, UK: The Stationery Office.
Klun, Maja (2004), 'Compliance costs for personal income tax in a transition country: the case of Slovenia', *Fiscal Studies*, **25** (1) 93–104.
Klun, Maja and Helena Blazic (2005), 'Tax compliance costs for companies in Slovenia and Croatia', *Finanzarchiv*, **61** (3), 418–37.
Kulis, Danijela (2004), 'The compliance costs of excise duties in Croatia', Occasional Paper No. 23, Zagreb, Republic of Croatia: Institute of Public Finance.
Messere, Ken (1993), *Tax Policy in OECD Countries*, Amsterdam, Netherlands: IBFD Publications BV.
Millock, Katrin and Céline Nauges (2006), 'Ex post evaluation of an earmarked tax on air pollution', *Land Economics*, **82**, 68–84.
Musgrave, Richard A. and Peggy B. Musgrave (1989), *Public Finance in Theory and Practice*, 5th ed., New York, US: Macmillan.
OECD (1997), *Evaluating the Efficiency and Effectiveness of Economic Instruments in Environmental Policy*, Paris, France: OECD.
OECD (2005), *The Political Economy of the Norwegian Aviation Fuel Tax*, Paris, France: OECD.
OECD (2006), *The Political Economy of Environmentally Related Taxes*, Paris, France: OECD.
Pavel, Jan and Leoš Vítek (2008), 'Revenue neutral environmental tax reform—case of the Czech Republic', in Nathalie Chalifour et al. (eds), *Critical Issues in Environmental Taxation. International and Comparative Perspectives*, Vol. V, Oxford, UK: Oxford University Press, pp. 757–81
Pavel, Jan and Leoš Vítek (2009), 'Administrative costs of the Czech system of environmental charges', in Jacqueline Cottrell, Janet Milne, Hope Ashiabor, Kurt Deketelaere, Larry Kreiser (eds), *Critical Issues in Environmental Taxation. International and Comparative Perspectives*, Vol. VI, Oxford, UK: Oxford University Press, pp. 247–61.
Pavel, Jan and Leoš Vítek (2010), 'Environmental tax reform: administrative and compliance cost of energy taxes in the Czech Republic', in Claudia Soares, Janet Milne, Hope Ashiabor, Larry Kreiser and Kurt Deketelaere (eds), *Critical Issues in Environmental Taxation. International and Comparative Perspectives*, Vol VIII, Oxford, UK: Oxford University Press, pp. 76–88.
Pigou, Arthur C. (1932), *The Economics of Welfare*, 4th ed., London, UK: Macmillan and Co.
Ramsey, Frank P. (1927), 'A contribution to the theory of taxation', *The Economic Journal*, **37**, 47–61.
Sadler, Thomas R. (2001), 'Environmental taxation in an optimal tax framework', *Atlantic Economic Journal*, **29** (2), 215–31.
Sandford, Cedric (1995), *Tax Compliance Costs—Measurement and Policy*, Bath, UK: Fiscal Publications in association with The Institute for Fiscal Studies.
Sandford, Cedric, Michael Godwin and Peter Hardwick (1989), *Administrative and Compliance Costs of Taxation*, Bath, UK: Fiscal Publications.
Shekidele, Christine M.S. (1999), 'Measuring the compliance costs of taxation excise duties 1995–96', *The African Journal of Finance and Management*, **7** (2), 72–84.
Slemrod, Joel and Marsha Blumenthal (1996), 'The income tax compliance cost of big business', *Public Finance Quarterly*, October, 411–48.
Slemrod, Joel and Shlomo Yitzhaki (2002), 'Tax avoidance, evasion, and administration', in Alan Auerbach and Martin Feldstein (eds), *Handbook of Public Economics*, 3, Amsterdam, Netherlands: Elsevier Science B.V., pp. 1423–70.
Smulders, Sjak and Herman R.J. Vollebergh (1999), 'Green taxes and administrative costs: the case of carbon taxation', NBER Working Papers No. 7298, Cambridge, MA, US: National Bureau of Economic Research, Inc.
Stiglitz, Joseph E. (2000), *Economics of the Public Sector*, 3rd ed., New York, US: Norton & Norton.
Vaillancourt, Francois (1987), 'The compliance cost of taxes on business and individuals: a review of the evidence', *Public Finance*, **42** (3), 395–414.
Williamson, Oliver E. (1981), 'The economics of organization: the transaction cost approach', *The American Journal of Sociology*, **87** (3), 548–77.
Yitzhaki, Shlomo (1979), 'A note on optimal taxation and administrative costs', *American Economic Review*, **69** (3), 475–80.

16 Structuring road transport taxes to capture externalities: a critical analysis of approaches
Teresa Palmer-Tous and Antoni Riera-Font

INTRODUCTION

The importance of the transport sector and the negative externalities it generates undoubtedly justifies the growing attention it has been attracting in terms of economic policy. Intensive use of the different means of transport (road, air, sea and rail) is associated with burgeoning environmental problems, heightened congestion situations and higher accident rates. More precisely, road transport contributes significantly to these increasing problems, given its notable weight in the formation and evolution of external costs in terms of GDP (Schreyer et al. 2004; European Commission 2007; Litman 2009). The OECD's recent studies on Central and Eastern Europe estimate that total external road transport costs account for close to 14 percent of the GDP of the countries in these areas (OECD 2003).

It is widely accepted that the presence of negative externalities means a divergence between social costs and private costs that results in suboptimal activity levels (Proost and Van Dender 1999; Borger and Proost 2001) and the need to apply corrective policies to the sector (European Commission 1995; Oberholzer-Gee and Weck-Hannemann 2002).

A diverse range of instruments is available for a policy to manage road transport problems. Specifically, we can distinguish between the administrative measures that support infrastructure to mitigate these problems and the measures that reduce external costs through behaviour modification mechanisms. The former encompass supply-side measures, which essentially attempt to reduce traffic congestion problems and, as a result, the potential environmental problems they may cause. In any case, a management policy for external problems cannot be restricted to building up infrastructure, but should also basically take the shape of demand-side policies, given the obvious limitations of the supply-side measures described.

Within this context, several mechanisms, such as the so-called regulatory ('command and control') and incentive ('market-based') instruments, can be used to internalize external road transport costs and thus achieve more efficient activity levels. While the former involve certain measures that must be adopted to comply with regulations, the latter aim to achieve the optimal use level by using price mechanisms to incentivize behavioral changes.

A brief review of European transport and environmental policy demonstrates that the regulatory vision has prevailed, as versus other kinds of instruments used to reduce negative transport impacts. A wide variety of regulatory mechanisms have been habitually applied (European Commission 1995, 1996, 1998), including measures such as traffic calming (traffic bumps, blocking off streets and so on), parking controls, regulations on air emissions and maximum vehicle noise, safety regulations, land use planning, the prohibition of the use and consumption of certain products (for example, leaded petrol), restrictions on vehicle use, vehicle maintenance and inspection programs, energy efficiency standards (kilometer per liter of fuel) and so on (Acutt and Dodgson 1997; European Commission 2001).

The objective for implementing price-based instruments, such as corrective taxes and tradable permit systems, is for vehicle users to recognize all the costs arising from use, beyond those they assume as their own. When external costs are internalized, the result is an efficient level of use, the goal of any corrective policy. Arguments in defense of market-based instruments rest on their advantages compared with regulatory instruments in terms of efficiency, and the capacity for generating revenue,[1] which allows for the emergence of the so-called 'employment dividend' when these revenues are used to reduce distortionary taxes on employment (Gago and Labandeira 1999).

At the European level, the European Commission has openly declared its support for the use of taxes or charges to ensure more efficient road transport activity levels (European Commission 1995, 1998, 2000), given the administrative and transactional costs involved in implementing a tradable permit system with a large number of mobile sources of emissions (Raux 2004).

This chapter will review the tax instruments applied to road transport in the European Union in order to examine their true corrective effectiveness. To do so, it contains four sections. After this brief introduction, the second section briefly describes road transport externalities and the most widely used valuation methodologies, which are essential to the process of internalizing external costs. The following section presents the main taxes levied on vehicles and their use. Lastly is an analysis of the taxes levied in light of certain criteria that measure the internalizing intent of the various externalities described.

Finally, it should be noted that this review of taxes on the transport sector in the European Union (EU) and the subsequent critical analysis can be applied to other countries around the world. It serves as a case study with broad applicability.

ROAD TRANSPORT EXTERNALITIES

The most important environmental road transport externalities are related to air pollution problems, exacerbated global warming and noise problems. However, in addition to these external environmental costs, there is an important series of externalities, such as accidents and congestion, that also merits study.[2]

Atmospheric Externalities

The energy consumed by road transport in Europe accounts for approximately 80 percent of the industry's total energy consumption and is by far the leading cause of the

---

[1]   In the case of the tradable markets, revenue can be obtained when the initial distribution of rights mechanism is implemented through an auction system.
[2]   Despite its probable importance in the case of freight transport, the infrastructure costs and road damage are not taken into account here.

most common air pollutants as well as CO_2 emissions, the main anthropogenic greenhouse gas effect (OECD 2001a). The relation between fuel consumption and air emissions differs according to the pollutant analyzed. Thus, while the relationship is more or less direct in the case of CO_2 emissions, other air pollutant emissions are influenced by engine technology, type of driving and so on, along with consumption. It is accepted that the transport sector's fossil fuel consumption accounts for 26 percent of all CO_2 emissions, making the sector a leading player in the escalation of global warming (Chapman 2007; EEA 2009). Furthermore, the use of cars, buses and lorries generates air pollution and is responsible for 65 percent of all NO_x emissions, 70 percent of all CO emissions, 45 percent of all volatile organic compounds (VOC) emissions and 5 percent of all SO_2 emissions, primarily because of these fuels' sulphur content (EEA and WHO 1997).[3] Moreover, approximately 40 percent of all small particle emissions comes from gases expelled by exhaust pipes.

Albeit to different degrees, each of these pollutants collaborates in the appearance of various meteorological problems at the local level (urban photochemical smog), regional level (acid rain and increased tropospheric ozone) and global level (climate change) with their consequent impacts on human health (Krzyzanowski et al. 2005), in addition to potential damage to vegetation and ecosystems, deteriorated soil productivity, forest disease, and damage to buildings, materials and cultural heritage.

To estimate the economic value of the external costs of transport-related air emissions, we recommend using a methodology with a bottom-up approach instead of a top-down one. The former handles disaggregated emissions data for a given geographical area on the basis of the area's specific values to estimate the emissions' effects. By contrast, the top-down approach handles aggregated data and then transfers the results to lower levels. The choice of the bottom-up approach is justified by, among other reasons, the influence of geographical features, such as exposed population or meteorological conditions, on transport emissions damages, which allows the marginal external costs of different transport activities to be calculated.[4]

In keeping with Bickel et al. (1997), the development of the bottom-up methodology[5] consists of a sequence of tasks that includes measuring emissions from an additional trip, modeling concentration levels and identifying dose-response functions and the corresponding economic valuation. Bickel et al. provide the cost per gram of pollutant emitted in a number of European cities, combined with emission factors (passenger-kilometer, ton-kilometer and so on) according to vehicle type (size, fuel used and emissions technology).

Also prominent are models for the economic valuation of the impact of climate change

---

[3]   At the OECD level, motor vehicles contributed 89 percent of all CO_2 emissions, 52 percent of all NO_x emissions and 44 percent of all VOCs in 1997 (OECD 2001a).

[4]   A good summary of recent studies on the economic valuation of air pollutant costs that incorporate the exposed population and local meteorological conditions can be found in Maibach, et al. (2008).

[5]   Specifically, this study uses the Impact Pathway assessment, which is a bottom-up approach in which environmental benefits and costs are estimated by following the pathway from source emissions to changes of air, soil and water quality and physical impacts, before being expressed in monetary benefits and costs (Bickel and Friedrich 2005).

that are based, on the one hand, on estimating current CO_2 emissions damage and implementing different discount rates to estimates of future damage, and on the other, on estimating a 'shadow price,' defined as the tax needed to maintain emissions on a course recommended by the modeler. Although the first option is more relevant to the purposes of this analysis, there are fundamental issues in the environmental economic valuation process, such as equity in its personal or spatial aspect (distributive weighting factors) and time aspect (social discount rate), that give any assessment a very particular character. In this sense, Tol (2005) conducted a review of several studies on estimating marginal emissions damage and achieved a widely dispersed range of valuations as a result of the different equity factors and discount rates applied. Although the second option does not achieve the economic valuation of external emissions costs, but rather the marginal costs of achieving a given environmental objective, there are many studies that focus on estimating shadow prices when determining what the price per ton should be, in compliance with the Kyoto requirements as a reference.[6]

Noise Externalities

Noise is one of the most easily perceived environmental impacts of road transport and is most often detected in urban areas (EEA 2009). Approximately 450 million people across Europe (65 percent of the population) are exposed to high noise levels[7] and around 113 million of them are exposed to levels at which the effects of noise begin to be considered harmful to health,[8] with the onset of hearing problems, cardiovascular disease and a rising number of stress and sleep disorders (WHO 1999) that adversely affect labor productivity levels. Another prominent aspect is the resulting depreciation of properties near affected zones. It has been estimated that motor vehicles now subject almost 20 percent of the population to noise levels above 65 dB in most EU countries. This is compounded by an expected worsening of the problem from the constant increase in urban traffic, despite policies to stabilize current levels.

Most studies that estimate the environmental costs of transport noise emissions use the hedonic price method, which calculates the cost of noise through changes in property values in relation to unit variations in the level of noise pollution.[9] Hence, willingness to pay (WTP) provides an approximation of the costs of noise. However, the assumption that WTP does not properly quantify the physical impacts of noise has led many studies to add estimates of damage in terms of the increased risk of heart attacks.[10] To do so, the progressive introduction of dose-response functions is recommended, including pre-

---

[6] Schreyer et al. (2004) offer a detailed summary of the estimations of the shadow price of a ton of CO_2 found in several studies.

[7] Above acoustic pressure levels equivalent to 55dB(A) within a 24-hour period.

[8] Above acoustic pressure levels equivalent to 65dB(A) within a 24-hour period.

[9] Thus, for example, Pearce and Markandya (1989) use this method to determine a change of between 0.08 percent and 0.88 percent in the price of a property per unit variation in the decibel level of certain cities in the US. Proost and Van Dender (1999) monetarily value the cost of noise based on the average values obtained in the literature of around 0.5 percent of the loss in value per increased decibel unit and an average value of the homes of 70 600 euros.

[10] Studies conducted in different countries reveal data on the effects of noise related to the higher probability of the risk of cardiac diseases and related deaths (Babisch et al. 2005).

mature deaths and disease from hypertension stemming from exposure to excessive noise levels, as well as decreased well-being. Schreyer et al. (2004) use valuations based in the WTP to reduce noise disturbances taking into account an estimate of the properties and people affected by noise.[11]

Accident Externalities

Each year approximately 40 000 people die in transport accidents, mostly road traffic accidents,[12] and more than 1 700 000 people are injured in the EU as a whole (European Commission 2001).

A key concept in identifying and assessing accident costs is accident risk, which varies according to volume of traffic, distance travelled, and type of vehicle, road and motorist. Once the probability of an accident's occurrence has been calculated, accident costs can be broken down into two broad categories in keeping with the customary terminology in transport economics (Jansson and Lindberg 1998): the material costs and the intangible costs associated with the event. The first arise as a result of the expected net loss in production related to the people injured or killed in accidents, medical costs, material damages and other clearly estimable costs in economic terms, as well as administrative costs (also called hard cost in European Commission nomenclature (European Commission 1995)). The second represent costs generated by the pain and suffering associated with injuries or death by accident, for users as well as their family and friends, which are more difficult to estimate when issues of a moral or ethical nature (also known as risk value) are introduced.

At this point, it should be noted that, unlike environmental transport costs, accident (and congestion) costs are not entirely external, since there is a cost component that users internalize when making the decision to travel. In fact, it is assumed that users internalize the risk to which they are exposed when they decide to travel, that makes it an internal component of the cost. Furthermore, internalization can be applied to the case in which representative users also take into account their families' suffering in the event of an accident, which leads again to defining these cost components as internal. Thus, the possible external costs related to a user's decision to travel are the material costs borne by the rest of society that are not covered by the insurance of a user who is entering the traffic system. Total covering of costs by the insurance occurs when increased traffic flows do not result in a higher probability of accidents, but rather remain constant, which means zero risk elasticity. However, when the incorporation of an individual user involves an increased risk of accidents for the system's other users, that is, a non-zero elasticity, all the costs related to a user's decision to travel can be identified as external.[13]

---

[11]   The updated study uses Germany as the country of reference.

[12]   Most studies focus on road traffic accidents when analyzing the external costs of transport, with references to the rest, given the relevance of this medium in the total number of accidents.

[13]   Near-zero elasticities have been verified for interurban traffic with low and average congestion levels (Rennings et al. 2001). In the case of urban traffic, accidents rise in a higher proportion than volume, which means non-zero risk elasticities (HLG 1999c) and higher external costs.

Congestion Externalities

Lastly, the ongoing growth in total number of cars is leading to congestion situations that undermine infrastructure users' well-being and natural spaces. Despite the increase in infrastructure, congestion issues are involved in the use of most transport networks.

The incorporation of one additional vehicle to the system means an increase in costs, given its impact on the average speed of all the network's users as a group. This reduced speed leads to increased individual costs, since operating costs (fuel used, vehicle maintenance costs such as tires, brakes and so on) rise, as does the cost in terms of time (depending on the value of time used). If no corrective measures are implemented, an individual motorist weighs these costs when deciding to travel. However, the introduction of an additional vehicle not only means increased individual costs, but also, owing to the appearance of congestion problems, increased costs for all the system's users, leading to rising marginal costs in terms of incremental losses of time.[14] Thus, it is usually argued that the average costs curve is equal to the private marginal cost curve, since they represent the extra costs borne and perceived by individual motorists. The marginal cost curve is like the marginal social cost curve representing the rapid rise in costs borne by both the incorporating motorist and those who are already network users. Then the difference between marginal social costs and private costs will reflect the marginal external costs of congestion at the different levels of traffic flow.

Estimating these costs requires knowledge of several variables. First, it is essential to have data on the relationship between speed achieved and different volumes of traffic,[15] which allows a marginal user's influence on speed, and therefore on costs, to be ascertained in terms of time. Second, another essential requirement in the valuation of marginal external congestion costs is the provision of a time value that represents the maximum amount an individual would be willing to spend to save time or the minimum necessary for accepting a longer trip. In fact, a key element in various studies on external congestion costs has been obtaining the marginal valuation of time made by users. This valuation is higher or lower depending on the purpose of the trip (work or leisure), time of day, urban or intercity travel, means of transport and the user's individual characteristics, especially in terms of income (Wardman 1997). Therefore, estimating the marginal time value requires a methodology that incorporates these factors to the greatest extent possible.

A number of projects have been developed in Europe to estimate external congestion costs. Banfi et al. (2000) estimated congestion costs in Europe in three possible ways, including by estimating additional costs in terms of time and operations in relation to a non-congestion situation, using the time value presented by the study coordinated by

---

[14] The weak relationship between increased fuel consumption (the main operating cost, according to most studies) and the variation in vehicle flow explains its exclusion from the additional operating costs in estimating marginal congestion costs in many studies (HLG 1999a).

[15] This depends on road characteristics as well as the number of lanes, slopes, intersections, curves, maximum speed and so on. Thus, it is necessary to use network models that incorporate these features and allow simulations to be conducted that provide estimations of the relationship among density, speed and time. The functional form that best reflects this relationship is usually exponential (Borger and Proost 2001).

Nash (1998). An updated study in 2004 (Schreyer et al. 2004) limits itself to the economic measurement of congestion costs by measuring dead weight loss.[16]

Thus, the relevance of road transport externalities and the evident desire to apply the efficiency principle in transport make it advisable to apply sector-based corrective policies that aim to achieve the optimal level of vehicle use. Levying taxes is unquestionably a possible mechanism of internalization.

TAXES LEVIED ON ROAD TRANSPORT

In view of the importance of the externalities associated with road transport, this section reviews the different fiscal measures adopted by the EU on road transport and then analyzes their true effectiveness in correcting the externalities that have been identified. The fundamental characteristic of the different measures in place at this time is that they require a vehicle's owner to pay for its acquisition, ownership and use. These measures can be classified into two major groups, based on their fixed or variable nature.

Fixed Taxes

In addition to its close relationship with the vehicle, the main feature of a fixed road transport tax is its zero variability, since payment is unrelated to distance travelled. Prominent non-variable taxes are those related to vehicle acquisition and ownership. Hence, a value added tax (VAT) payment is made once and the corresponding registration tax is settled when a new vehicle is purchased, while vehicle ownership requires a yearly payment in the form of the circulation tax.

Table 16.1 provides an overview of these taxes in EU countries.

As the table shows, all of these countries have adopted a VAT applied at the time of purchase, although with rates that vary widely from 15–16 percent in Cyprus, Luxembourg and Spain to 25 percent in Hungary, Sweden and Denmark. Furthermore, most member states levy a motor vehicle registration tax on the acquisition of cars and other means of private transport; this targets passenger vehicles, while exemptions are applied to commercial vehicles such as buses and heavy goods vehicles (except in Sweden, where the reverse is true). The applied rates vary considerably among countries in this case as well, with the high rates applied in Denmark, Malta and Cyprus standing out. In turn, 20 member states levy a yearly circulation tax on both passenger and commercial vehicles.

Variable Taxes

The variability of road transport taxes responds to the will to tax not only the purchase and ownership of vehicles, but also their use. These charges include fuel taxes as well as several other taxes related to infrastructure use.

---

[16] The loss of efficiency reflects the rise in economic costs in relation to an optimal traffic situation.

Table 16.1   Taxes on acquisition and property

Country	VAT	Registration	Ownership
Austria	20	yes	yes
Belgium	21	yes	yes
Bulgaria	20	no	yes
Cyprus	15	yes	yes
Czech Republic	19	no	no
Denmark	25	yes	yes
Estonia	18	no	no
Finland	22	yes	yes
France	19.6	yes	no
Germany	19	no	yes
Greece	19	yes	yes
Hungary	25	yes	yes
Ireland	21	yes	yes
Italy	20	yes	yes
Lithuania	19	no	no
Latvia	21	yes	yes
Luxembourg	15	no	yes
Malta	18	yes	yes
Netherlands	19	yes	yes
Poland	22	yes	no
Portugal	17	yes	yes
Romania	19	yes	yes
Slovakia	19	no	no
Slovenia	20	yes	no
Spain	16	yes	yes
Sweden	25	no	yes
United Kingdom	17.5	no	yes

Source: ACEA, 2009

Fuel taxes
Fuel taxes, mainly VAT and other consumption taxes, are applied all across the EU (ECMT and INFRAS 2000). Aside from potential environmental intentions for the taxes, fuel taxes are used because they have high revenue-generating capacity, given the low elasticity of demand for fuel, relative to price, and the size of the tax base.

These excise duties on fuel consumption create a high tax burden of these products. The differentiation that exists in specific fuel consumption taxes that tax petrol more heavily than diesel (with the exception of the United Kingdom) should also be noted. The latter fuel's favorable treatment is based on its intensive use in commercial operations, as well as theoretical environmental reasons related to its increased energy efficiency.

As shown in Table 16.2, there is also a huge disparity among different European countries in the taxes on the two kinds of fuel. In the case of Eurosuper gasoline, the tax rates range from 299 Euros/1000 liters in Cyprus to 701 in the Netherlands. Meanwhile, diesel taxes, with lower tax rates in general, range from 245 Euros in Cyprus to 481 Euros in Slovakia and 661 Euros in the UK. This disparity sets the context of the 1997 proposal

Table 16.2   Excise duties on fuels (January 2009)

Country	Unleaded Petrol*	Diesel*
Austria	442	347
Belgium	592	318
Bulgaria	350	307
Cyprus	299	245
Czech Republic	483	406
Denmark	561	382
Estonia	359	330
Finland	627	364
France	607	428
Germany	655	470
Greece	359	302
Hungary	448	368
Ireland	509	368
Italy	564	423
Lithuania	434	330
Latvia	379	330
Luxembourg	462	302
Malta	459	352
Netherlands	701	413
Poland	488	339
Portugal	583	364
Romania	336	284
Slovakia	515	481
Slovenia	403	383
Spain	360	302
Sweden	568	446
United Kingdom	661	661

Note: *In Euros/1000 litres

Source: ACEA, 2009.

to harmonize fuel taxation within Europe. This proposal led to the adoption of the 2003 directive on harmonising energy taxation, which provided for minimum taxation rates for different energy products.[17]

Charges related to infrastructure use
Along with fuel taxes, other charges related to vehicle use are applied, such as the yearly fee for infrastructure use, also known as the 'Eurovignette' (European Parliament 1999), and other taxes linked to the use of congested areas.

---

[17]   Directive 2003/96/EC established minimum rates as of 1 January 2010 that are higher than those applied to diesel fuel (330 Euros/liter compared with 302 Euros/liter). Likewise, it envisages differentiating taxes on diesel according to whether its use is professional or not.

The Eurovignette is a fixed annual fee paid by heavy vehicles for the use of certain infrastructures in countries that were not charging tolls at the time of the Eurovignette's entry into force in July 2000.[18] The tax is calculated according to the number of a vehicle's axles, given the supposed relationship between vehicle size and degree of infrastructure deterioration and environmental impact.[19]

Also prominent is the proliferation of proposals for reducing congestion through different pricing mechanisms, given the importance of these external costs, especially in urban areas. There are numerous examples of taxes directly related to the use of a congested area, including the application of licenses for driving in congested sites (area licensing schemes), tolls for entering congested areas through 'rings' (cordon tolls) and electronic road pricing systems. Licenses and tolls can be implemented through relatively simple technology, whereas electronic pricing requires the application of advanced communications systems.

Unlike circulation licenses, which allow a vehicle to use a congested road space at a certain time, cordon tolls allow entry to a particular geographical area upon payment. Electronic pricing systems can identify vehicles in two ways: externally (or 'outside the vehicle' measurement) and internally ('inside the vehicle' measurement). The methods supporting the external identification of a vehicle circulating in an area subject to the charge have been evolving, with technological advances that range from scanners built into windshields to radio signals that allow vehicles to be read without their slowing down. In any case, the information is transmitted to a central system where it is stored and the toll charged to the user is determined; the tolls can be settled through pre-payment or post-payment systems. The main problem in applying these collection devices is that they identify the user, which is a clear intrusion of privacy and which was instrumental in the development of other, methods, also electronic, that would guarantee anonymity. In fact, the lack of guarantees of privacy involved in this system's application was crucial to the 'failure' of Hong Kong's proposed electronic pricing scheme in the mid-1980s.

In contrast, internal identification, based on the use of technologies that enable identification by smart cards incorporated into the vehicle, avoids personalizing collection. It functions as a computer integrated into a vehicle, which automatically discounts the amount of the tax each time the vehicle circulates through a point in which the pricing applies. Although it holds an advantage over the previous systems, it can also pose a problem in case of theft, given the non-ownership of the card.

As seen, the range of possibilities is broad. However, in line with the purpose of this study, the idea is to select the measures that best allow for internalization in the face of a specific externality.

---

[18]   Specifically, the Benelux countries, Germany, Austria, Sweden and Denmark. In recent years, Germany (2005) and Austria (2004) have modified their infrastructure use pricing systems on the basis of Directive 38/2006, which introduced a differentiation in tolls according to distance travelled. France envisaged implementation for 2011 and the system is intended to be operational in France by 2013.

[19]   The introduction of the system responded to the objective of reducing the tax differences borne by these types of vehicles and their effects on competitiveness within the context of the single market.

A CRITICAL REVIEW OF TAXATION FROM THE VIEWPOINT OF ITS CORRECTIVE EFFECTIVENESS ON DIFFERENT EXTERNALITIES

A tax's internalizing effectiveness depends not only on the tax rate, but also the on relationship between the property subject to the tax, the tax base and the change in behavior pursued (Palmer and Riera 2003). All of these elements allow the validity of the instruments applied in practice within the EU to be analyzed in terms of correcting the different externalities associated with road transport.

Correcting Atmospheric Externalities

By definition, fixed taxes have a weak relationship to vehicle use, which is clearly a more relevant factor than acquisition and ownership when taxing atmospheric externalities (given the clear relationship between kilometers travelled and emissions). However, incorporating the factors that determine the emissions level per kilometer driven (influenced by vehicle characteristics in terms of technology, fuel use and so on) into the current design of registration and road taxes greatly improves environmental intentionality. Thus, a tax scheme differentiated according to distance travelled and/or vehicle emissions would allow agents to choose either to degrade the environment and pay a price for it or to avoid payment by purchasing cleaner vehicles, keeping vehicles better maintained, or simply curbing vehicle use.

As summarized in Table 16.3, a review of the tax bases of taxes associated with vehicle purchase and ownership in the European Union confirms that although several countries are differentiating taxes on the basis of number of kilometers driven (associated with fuel consumption) or CO_2 emissions, the weak corrective intent of the taxes continues to prevail.

Thus, the environmental effectiveness of the fixed tax instruments is dubious, given the weak relationship with the characteristics that define an optimal tax, both in terms of estimated tax rate (in no case related to marginal damage in the optimal tax) and the determination of the tax base—in this case, volume of emissions.

In turn, variable taxes penalize vehicle use, which is one of their main advantages from the environmental standpoint. Indeed, arguments to defend fuel taxes (and their increase) are founded on their efficiency in combating the problems of climate change and air pollution,[20] given the direct relationship between fossil fuel consumption and CO_2 emissions and the indirect relationship between fuel consumption and other types of emissions through distance travelled, as well as low administrative costs. Increasing these taxes has positive impacts on energy efficiency, since it incentivizes reducing energy consumption per kilometer travelled (Hoeller and Wallin 1991).

Despite these advantages, the fuel taxes' low differentiation in terms of the environmental impact of fuel—derived from the higher or lower proportion of pollutants emitted

---

[20] Fullerton and West (2002) demonstrate how a combination of taxes on products such as fuel and engine type, together with subsidies for emissions reducing equipment, act as the perfect substitute for a direct tax on emissions.

Table 16.3   Tax base of fixed taxes

Country	Registration Tax	Ownership Tax
Austria	Fuel consumption	Kilowatt (Kw)
Belgium	Cylinder capacity (cc) plus age	Cylinder capacity (cc)
Bulgaria	None	Kw
Cyprus	Cc plus CO_2 emissions	Cc plus CO_2 emissions
Czech Republic	None	None
Denmark	105% up to DKK 79 000 180% on the remainder	Fuel consumption, weight
Estonia	None	None
Finland	Price plus CO_2 emissions	Time fuel, weight
France	CO_2 emissions	None
Germany	None	Cylinder capacity (cc), CO_2 emissions, exhaust emissions
Greece	Cc plus emissions	Cylinder capacity (cc)
Hungary	Emissions	Weight
Ireland	CO_2 emissions	CO_2 emissions
Italy		Kw, exhaust emissions
Lithuania	None	None
Latvia	373 Euros	Weight
Luxembourg	None	CO_2 emissions
Malta	Price, CO_2 emissions, vehicle length	Cylinder capacity (cc)
Netherlands	Price plus CO_2 emissions	Weight, province
Poland	Cylinder capacity (cc)	None
Portugal	Cc plus emissions	Cylinder capacity (cc), CO_2 emissions
Romania	Cc plus emissions plus CO_2	Cylinder capacity (cc)
Slovakia	None	None
Slovenia	None	None
Spain	CO_2 emissions	Horsepower
Sweden	None	CO_2 emissions, weight
United Kingdom	None	CO_2 emissions, Cylinder capacity (cc)

upon combustion—significantly softens the taxes' potentially disincentivizing effect. For greater environmental effectiveness to be achieved, the tax differentiation between the fuels and each one's true environmental cost must be adjusted so the taxes can act as a proper incentive for the consumption of cleaner fuels.[21]

Since the payment of road use taxes theoretically varies according to distance travelled, they are a possible instrument that can come close to being optimal in correcting environmental externalities. Obviously, the incorporation of a per kilometer emission factor into these taxes improves their environmental characterization. However, in practice,

---

[21]   In practice, the existing variation in rates between the different fuels is explained by commercial and not environmental motives, because of the higher use of diesel and other types of fuels in professional transport. Nevertheless, in environmental terms, it makes no sense to encourage diesel consumption, which, although it produces fewer CO and VOCs emissions, has a greater environmental impact in terms of NO_x, particles and CO_2 because of its higher carbon content.

one of the main criticisms of the yearly infrastructure use tax, or Eurovignette, was its limited real relationship to distance travelled. Thus, for the external costs caused by heavy vehicles to be properly internalized, kilometer-charging systems that effectively penalize road use would need to be developed. In fact, the directive adopted in 2006 envisages the possibility of using an electronic road pricing system to vary toll payments for goods-transporting vehicles over 3.5 tons according to different factors (distance travelled, location, vehicle characteristics and so on) (European Parliament and Council 2006). This proposal seeks to improve the Eurovignette's corrective nature by internalizing all the costs related to infrastructures, the environment, accidents and congestion that heavy vehicles cause.

Several countries, including Switzerland, Germany and Austria, have implemented tax systems linked to distance travelled. Since 2001, the Swiss system has been gradually introducing a charge, which varies according to kilometers travelled, weight and emissions (kilometer and weight-related charge), on the heavy vehicles that circulate on the national road network. This change replaced the yearly fixed tax that the so-called 'Swiss vignette' represented for the use of all of the country's motorways. Its application requires the installation of an on-board unit with vehicle data (number of axles, engine type and so on) and a GPS satellite system linked to a tachograph that measures the kilometers travelled. Meanwhile, in 2004 Austria replaced the Eurovignette's time-based charge (where payment may be daily or yearly) with a distance-based charge by implementing an electronic collection system. Since payment differs according to route travelled,[22] the system ensures a stronger relationship between infrastructure use and deterioration. Furthermore, since 2005 Germany has been implementing a pricing system with kilometric rates to replace the Eurovignette. The rate per kilometers varies according to the category of vehicle emissions, number of axles and time of day.

These distance-travelled systems are restricted to freight transport, which is why an extension to passenger vehicles appears to be a recommendable option for internalizing external atmospheric costs and transport costs in general.

Lastly, although taxes on the direct use of congested areas involve vehicle use, payment does not differ according to the individual emissions factor. This differentiation could be introduced by including a vehicle's environmental characteristics on the smart card in the electronic pricing systems, although this requires a technological advance in communications systems. In this sense, the launch of the European Galileo system at the EU level—slated for 2014—may be a key element in an efficient transport pricing framework.[23]

Correcting Noise Externalities

As recommended by the European Commission (1996), it would be desirable to introduce some form of differentiation in fixed charges on the basis of noise characteristics or type of noise related to a vehicle. Specifically, additional charges (or subsidies) could be

---

[22] The tax level will be determined by three features of the route: distance, topography and road quality, which depends on the presence of bridges, tunnels and so on.

[23] The European Galileo system is separate from the US GPS satellite navigation system, although they are compatible and interoperable. A Galileo receiver can simultaneously exploit the signals received from both satellites.

applied when a vehicle is purchased (registration tax), or a system of supplements to the yearly road tax could be articulated according to noise category. In terms of effectiveness, the best annual supplement option seems to be the one that incentivizes agents to reduce noise levels and hence, the potential tax burden. Payment of this supplement could be linked to an annual examination to check vehicle status in terms of noise contamination, which would encourage owners to maintain their vehicles properly, introduce equipment that helps reduce noise levels (dynamic efficiency) or even use their vehicles less, if the payment were linked to distance travelled.

With respect to fuel charges, any differentiation in terms of noise impact is clearly inoperative. Therefore, the application of fuel taxes is related primarily to reducing atmospheric externalities, particularly those linked to the problem of climate change. That the tax leads to shorter distances travelled is considered only an indirect attenuation of noise externalities.

As for charges associated with infrastructure use, the Eurovignette and taxes linked to circulating in congested areas do not currently differentiate according to a vehicle's noise characteristics, although this possibility may arise in the future as the technology evolves.

Correcting Accident Externalities

The costs of accidents—and external costs as a result—depend on factors such as risk or likelihood of accidents, which in turn are influenced by vehicle characteristics, type of motorist, road design and distance travelled, among other variables. An approximation to the optimal instrument would thus require a tax to be differentiated in each of these areas, as well as variable according to distance travelled. If a design with these character-istics were feasible, the resulting tax would incentivize better driving, the incorporation of enhanced safety technologies, improved motorist preparedness and awareness, circula-tion in less risky areas and even less vehicle use.

The EU member states' experiences do not reflect practices aimed at internalizing marginal accident costs in this regard. In fact, although the yearly road taxes on vehicles may vary according to vehicle type, and partially according to motorist, they are entirely independent of distance travelled and so are poor approximations of the real costs of accidents, which prevents them from acting as an incentive for safer behaviors.

Furthermore, although fuel taxes are levied on distance travelled, and hence the higher or lower likelihood of accidents, they do not allow for differentiation according to indi-vidual motorist characteristics, vehicle type or route used, which distances the instrument from the optimal in the internalization of external accident costs. The only option is to introduce a degree of differentiation in charges related to infrastructure use. Thus, the modification of the 2006 Eurovignette envisages the possibility of incorporating accident costs not covered by insurance by differentiating tolls according to location (the likeli-hood of accidents differs between urban and rural areas and population density), type of infrastructure, speed (which affects the accident rate) and distance travelled.[24]

---

[24]   In this sense, the new directive broadened the sphere of application to vehicles weighing over 3.5 tons used in freight transport, because they contribute to the same degree as heavy lorries do to increasing accident rates and congestion on road networks.

Correcting Congestion Externalities

As noted, marginal external congestion costs depend on the relationship between speed, traffic flow and time value, which differ according to time of day and location. Thus, any instrument that seeks to correct congestion externalities must achieve spatial and time differentiation. Indeed, this dual condition explains fixed taxes' failure within this context. Taxes on vehicle purchase (registration) and ownership (circulation) only indirectly correct congestion externalities to the extent to which they reduce the number of vehicles in circulation. However, this means that the number of cars not only falls in congested areas, but falls in underserved areas as well, which leads to lower gains in well-being compared with the implementation of an optimal system.

Differentiating for time and space is complicated, if not impossible, with regard to fuel taxes, which makes them far from optimal in reducing congestion externalities.[25] In this sense, like circulation, registration and parking taxes, fuel taxes are figures linked indirectly to the use of congested areas. Although parking price allows for differentiated payments according to space and time of day, it does not tax vehicle circulation *per se* in a congested area, but rather only parking. Thus, the cost of vehicles circulating but not parking in an area is not internalized. In any case, as suggested by Calthrop et al. (2000), parking price can serve as a complementary instrument to other charges directly related to using a space with congestion problems.

Thus, internalizing congestion costs requires specific measures such as circulation licenses or access tolls to be developed and applied in congested areas. However, for a circulation license system to be effective, its payment should be related to the area's period of greatest congestion and should not be applied during periods of reduced congestion, thus enabling the required time differentiation. The circulation license system is also a remarkably flexible system, since it allows for differentiating vehicles according to their higher or lower congestive effect. The adaptability involved in being able to modify the size of areas subject to licenses should not be overlooked. However, despite these advantages, there are several drawbacks, such as the inability to vary payment according to an area's intensity of use, since the system entails a fixed rate that does not distinguish between distances travelled within the space taxed, and the difficulty of establishing refined differentiation by time in practice (which requires different licenses according to circulation time to approach the 'peak' period). The practical challenges have led to the implementation of tax schemes that encompass relatively large-sized taxed areas and timetables, with the corresponding lost efficiencies.

The first practical experience in this regard can be found in Singapore's Area Licensing Scheme of 1975. It exclusively applied to passenger cars, which had to show a card certifying license payment when they wanted to enter the congested zone during the morning. In 1989, the list of vehicles to which it applied was expanded and the obligation extended to the afternoons, with only the public transport system being excluded. Singapore's example is a demonstration of the incompatibility between designing an effective system and designing an administratively simple system. Achieving administrative efficiency

---

[25]   In fact, fuel taxes would act as an adequate proxy only if congestion took place through the entire day (World Bank 1996).

involves a low differentiation between times and zones, which obviously significantly weakens the instrument's efficiency as a means of internalizing external congestion costs. The tendency to tax congested periods the same as periods of free movement means lower gains in social well-being, given each one's different marginal social costs.[26] Since February 2003 London has been applying a similar system in the city center, charging a daily fee for vehicles circulating through the priced area during the period of heaviest traffic. The reduced congestion levels since its establishment (around 30 percent) led the administration to propose its expansion to the western part of the city.

The administrative efficiency of access tolls to certain zones through 'rings' is also related to the question of manual or automatic payment systems.[27] This instrument taxes the right of entry to a certain space, as opposed to the licensing system, which taxes the right to use an area subject to pricing. The problem with manual collection mechanisms is that they require heavy investments in fixed facilities and employee salaries, which means higher direct operating costs, in addition to the opportunity costs of the physical space occupied by these facilities. Furthermore, the need to stop to pay fees may exacerbate the problem that access tolls attempt to solve, that is, congestion.[28] If the congested space is large, more collection points are needed, with the consequent costs, if avoiding wasted time and increased user operating costs is the objective. Finally, vehicles belonging to area residents do not pay for the congestion they cause.

The collection system for this type of tax is being implemented to allow entry to the centre of several Norwegian cities such as Oslo, Bergen and Trondheim. However, these taxes' null differentiation for time reveals a predominantly collection-related intent to finance new road infrastructure, with the exception of Trondheim, which differentiates prices according to time of day, allowing us to assert that its system truly taxes congestion (Larsen 1995). However, recent studies recommend turning these systems into an effective mechanism for congestion pricing in light of the potential socioeconomic benefits (Odeck and Brathen 2002).

As for electronic collection systems, they have several advantages: first, they allow moving vehicles to be charged, which avoids several of the problems involved in previous systems, and secondly, they allow for a greater differentiation in charges according to roads travelled, time of day and even type of vehicle, as introduced by the Eurovignette directive.

This advantage is enhanced in the case of electronic pricing through the use of 'smart cards.' The sound emitted when the card deducts the amount allows users to be aware of the cost of circulating in an area and acts as an incentive for modifying behavior to avoid payment. In 1998, through an electronic short-range wave mechanism, Singapore successfully implemented a variant of this system, which automatically taxes users when they enter congested areas. This instrument's effectiveness can be verified by measuring

---

26   In 1998, the pricing system applied in Singapore based on an area licensing scheme was turned into an electronic pricing scheme. See Khan 2001 or Goh 2002.

27   Payment can also be made electronically, which would situate the system within those called electronic pricing. For simplicity's sake, it has been framed in this second group in the explanation.

28   Automatic collection machines would not significantly solve the problem of stopping and queue formation. Nor would it allow for a differentiation in payment according to vehicle type, a possibility that exists in the case of manual collection.

the volume of traffic in the area and average velocity, as well as by the steady decline in tax collected (Khan 2001).

Lastly, using these instruments may help reduce, although laterally, other externalities by decreasing vehicle use. In fact, several studies have analyzed the use of congestion mechanisms as an alternative to emission taxes and have shown the environmental benefits stemming from their application (Daniel and Bekka 2000; Santos et al. 2000; Beevers and Carslaw 2005).

CONCLUSIONS

Practical experience shows that all the OECD countries use a tax system based on fuel taxes (OECD 2001b), together with fixed charges on vehicles. Although fuel taxes are an effective instrument for correcting the climate change problem by reducing CO_2 emissions, they do not adequately reflect other types of external costs. To the degree in which they affect distance travelled, only indirectly do they reduce other pollutant emissions, congestion or accident problems.

Thus, making road transport pricing more efficient requires changing the current tax structure and adjusting the price to reflect the true cost of vehicle use. In this sense, one of the recommendations made by the proposal of the European Commission's directive (2005) consists in differentiation in the circulation tax and fuel taxes according to different environmental impact, particularly CO_2 emissions. However, a closer approximation to the optimal instrument for correcting all transport externalities would also require differentiation according to the characteristics of individual motorists or vehicle type—reflecting the higher or lower risk of driving—as well as according to time and space. Furthermore, in addition to differentiation policies, variability must be increased by introducing a higher proportion of variable charges versus fixed taxes, in order to enhance the relationship between the tax base and the marginal damage generated by vehicle use.

Hence, establishing a harmonized EU transport pricing system strategy to replace the different mechanisms used in the member states is imperative for reasons relating to both efficiency and equity. To this end, electronic collection for road infrastructure use—in terms of kilometers driven and the differentiations mentioned—emerges as the instrument closest to optimal for correcting external road transport costs. In fact, several studies (EEA 2001) define these instruments as those that come closest to the so-called Pigouvian tax.

Yet this proposal is not without difficulties. Applying taxes equivalent to marginal external costs requires the prior identification and subsequent monetary valuation of all costs an additional trip incurs. Using economic valuation methods in regard to external transport costs is still in the early stages, which is why government generally will not have the information needed to define objectives optimally. Furthermore, when government has this information, it should introduce it into the corresponding decision-making process, forcing motorists to take it into account. This involves applying technological advances that are today still in the development stage.

REFERENCES

ACEA European Automobile Manufacturer's Association (2009), *Annual Tax Guide,* Brussels, Belgium: European Automobile Manufacturers' Association.

Acutt, M. and J. Dodgson (1997), 'Controlling the environmental impacts of transport: matching instruments to objectives', *Transportation Research: Part D, Transport and Environment,* **2D** (1), 17–33.

Babisch, W. et al. (2005), 'Traffic noise and risk of myocardial infarction', *Epidemiology,* **16** (1), 33–40.

Banfi, S. et al. (2000), *External Costs of Transport. Accident, Environmental and Congestion Costs in Western Europe,* Zurich, Switzerland: INFRAS/IWW.

Beevers, S.D. and D.C. Carslaw (2005), 'The impact of congestion charging on vehicle emissions in London', *Atmospheric Environment,* **39**, 1–5.

Bickel, P. et al. (1997), *External Costs of Transport in ExternE: Externalities of Energy, a Research Project of the European Commission,* Brussels, Belgium: European Commission.

Bickel, P. and R. Friedich (2005), *ExternE. Externalities of Energy: Methodology 2005 Update,* Brussels, Belgium: European Commission.

Borger, B. and S. Proost (2001), *Reforming Transport Pricing in the European Union. A Modelling Approach,* Cheltenham, UK: Edward Elgar.

Button, K. (1993), *Transport, the Environment and Economic Policy,* Cheltenham, UK: Edward Elgar.

Calthrop E. and S. Proost (1998), 'Road transport externalities', *Environmental and Resource Economics,* **11** (3–4), 335–48.

Calthrop, E., S. Proost and K. Van Dender (2000), 'Parking policies and road pricing', *Urban Studies,* **37** (1), 63–76.

Carthy, T. et al. (1999), 'On the contingent valuation of safety and the safety of contingent valuation: part 2— the CV/SG 'chained' approach', *Journal of Risk and Uncertainty,* **17** (3), 187–213.

Chapman, L. (2007), 'Transport and climate change: a review', *Journal of Transport Geography,* **15**, 354–67.

Daniel, J.I. and K. Bekka (2000), 'The environmental impact of highway congestion pricing', *Journal of Urban Economics,* **47**, 180–215.

De Borger, B., J. Peirson and R. Vickerman (2001), 'An overview of policy instruments', in B. De Borger and S. Proost (eds), *Reforming Transport Pricing in the European Union: A Modelling Approach,* Cheltenham, UK: Edward Elgar, pp. 37–50.

European Commission (1995), 'Towards fair and efficient pricing in transport. Policy options for internalizing the external costs of transport in the European Union', COM (95) 691, Brussels, Belgium: European Commission.

European Commission (1996), 'Commission's green paper on noise', COM (96) 540, Brussels, Belgium: European Commission.

European Commission (1998), 'White paper. Fair payment for infrastructure use: a phased approach to a common transport infrastructure charging framework in the EU', COM (1998) 466, Brussels, Belgium: European Commission.

European Commission (2000), *Fair and Efficient Pricing in Transport: The Role of Charges and Taxes,* Brussels: Belgium: European Commission.

European Commission (2001), 'White paper. European transport policy for 2010: time to decide', COM (2001) 0370, Luxembourg: Office for Official Publications of the European Communities.

European Commission (2002), 'Fiscal measures to reduce CO_2 emissions from new passenger cars', final report, report no 4, issue no 3.

European Commission (2005), 'Proposal for a Council directive on passenger car related taxes', COM (2005) 261 final, Brussels.

European Commission (2007), 'Green paper on market-based instruments for environmental and related policy purposes', COM (2007) 140 final, Brussels, Belgium: European Commission.

European Conference of Ministers of Transport and INFRAS Consulting Group for Policy Analysis and Implementation (ECMT and INFRAS) (2000), *Variabilisation and Differentiation Strategies in Road Taxation,* Zurich, Switzerland: INFRAS.

European Environment Agency (EEA) (2001), *Environmental Signals 2001,* Luxembourg: Office for Official Publications of the European Communities.

European Environment Agency (EEA) (2008), *Climate for a Transport Change. TERM 2007: Indicators Tracking Transport and Environment in the European Union,* EEA Report No. 1/2008, Luxembourg: Office for Official Publications of the European Communities.

European Environment Agency (EEA) (2009), *Transport at a Crossroads. TERM 2008: Indicators Tracking Transport and Environment in the European Union,* EEA Report No. 3/2009, Luxembourg: Office for Official Publications of the European Communities.

European Environment Agency and World Health Organization Regional Office for Europe (EEA and

WHO) (1997), *Topic Reports: Air and Health*, Luxembourg: Office for Official Publications of the European Communities.

European Parliament and Council (1999), Directive 1999/62/CE on the Charging of Heavy Goods Vehicles for the Use of Certain Infrastructures (EUROVIGNETTE), 1999 O.J. (L 187) 42–50.

European Parliament and Council (2006), Directive 2006/38/CE of the European Parliament and of the Council of May 17th Amending Directive 1999/62/CE on the Charging of Heavy Goods Vehicles for the Use of Certain Infrastructures (EUROVIGNETTE), 2006 O.J. (L 157) 8–23.

Fullerton, D. and S. West (2002), 'Can taxes on cars and gasoline mimic an unavailable tax on emissions?', *Journal of Environmental Economics and Management*, **43** (1), 135–57.

Gago, A. and X. Labandeira (1999), *La Reforma Fiscal Verde: Teoría y Práctica de los Impuestos Ambientales* [Green Tax Reform: Theory and Practice of Environmental Taxes], Madrid, Spain: Mundi-Prensa.

Goh, M. (2002), 'Congestion management and electronic road pricing in Singapore', *Journal of Transport Geography*, **10**, 29–38.

Hau, T. (1992), 'Congestion charging mechanisms for roads: an evaluation of current practice', Policy Research. Working Papers. Transport, Washington, DC, US: World Bank.

High Level Group on Transport Infrastructure Charging (HLG) (1999), *Final Report on Estimating Transport Costs*, Brussels, Belgium.

High Level Group on Transport Infrastructure Charging (HLG) (1999a), *Calculating Transport Congestion and Scarcity Costs, Final Report of the Expert Advisors to the High Level Group on Infrastructure Charging*, Brussels, Belgium.

High Level Group on Transport Infrastructure Charging (HLG) (1999b), *Calculating Transport Environmental Costs, Final Report of the Expert Advisors to the High Level Group on Infrastructure Charging*, Brussels, Belgium.

High Level Group on Transport Infrastructure Charging (HLG) (1999c), *Calculating Transport Accident Costs, Final Report of the Expert Advisors to the High Level Group on Infrastructure Charging*, Brussels, Belgium.

Hoeller, P. and M. Wallin (1991), 'Energy prices, taxes and carbon dioxide emissions', *OECD Economic Studies*, **17**, 91–105.

Ison, S. (1998), 'A concept in the right place at the wrong time: congestion metering in the city of Cambridge', *Transport Policy*, **5**, 139–46.

Jansson, J.A. and G. Lindberg (1998), 'Transport pricing principles', Pricing European Transport Systems deliverable 2, Leeds, UK: Institute for Transport Studies.

Kageson, P. (2000), 'Bringing the Eurovignette into the electronic age: the need to change directive 1999/62 to allow kilometre charging for heavy goods vehicles', T&E 00/4, European Federation for Transport and the Environment (EFTE, T&E).

Kageson, P. and J. Dings (1999), 'Electronic kilometer charging for heavy goods vehicles in Europe', T&E 99/6, European Federation for Transport and the Environment (EFTE, T&E), Brussels.

Khan, A. (2001), 'Reducing traffic density: the experience of Hong Kong and Singapore', *Journal of Urban Technology*, **8** (1), 69–87.

Krzyzanowski, M., B. Kuna-Dibbert and J. Schneider (2005), *Health Effects of Transport-related Air Pollution*, Geneva, Switzerland: World Health Organization.

Larsen, O. (1995), 'The toll cordons in Norway: an overview', *Journal of Transport Geography*, **3** (3), 187–97.

Litman, T.A. (2009), *Transportation Cost and Benefit Analysis: Techniques, Estimates and Implications*, Victoria, Canada: Victoria Transport Policy Institute.

Maibach, M. et al. (2008), *Handbook on Estimation of External Costs in Transport Sector*, Delft, Netherlands: DGTREN.

Mayeres, I. and S. Proost (1997), 'Optimal tax and public investment rules for congestion type of externalities', *Scandinavian Journal of Economics*, **99** (2), 261–79.

Mayeres, I. and K. Van Dender (2001), 'External costs of transport', in B. Borger and S. Proost, *Reforming Transport Pricing in the European Union*, Cheltenham, UK: Edward Elgar, pp. 135–69.

Nash, C. (Project Coordinator) (1998), 'Pricing European transport system', final report, PETS, Leeds, UK: Institute for Transport Studies, University of Leeds.

Nash, C. (2001), 'Concerted action on transport pricing research integration', CAPRI, Leeds, UK: Institute for Transport Studies, University of Leeds.

Nellthorp, J. et al. (2001), 'Valuation conventions for UNITE: unification of accounts and marginal costs for transport efficiency', Leeds, UK: University of Leeds.

Newbery, D. (1990), 'Pricing and congestion: economic principles relevant to pricing roads', *Oxford Review of Economic Policy*, **6** (2), 22–38.

Oberholzer-Gee, F. and H. Weck-Hannemann (2002), 'Pricing road use: politico-economic and fairness considerations', *Transportation Research Part D, Transport and Environment*, **7**, 357–71.

Odeck, J. and S. Brathen (2002), 'Toll financing in Norway: the success, the failures and perspective for the future', *Transport Policy*, **9** (3), 253–60.

OECD (2001a), *Environmental Outlook*, Paris, France: OECD Publishing.
OECD (2001b), *Environmentally Related Taxes in OECD Countries: Issues and Strategies*, Paris, France: OECD Publishing.
OECD (2003), 'External costs of transport in Central and Eastern Europe', study by INFRAS and HERRY for OECD Environment Directorate and Austrian Ministry for Agriculture and Forestry, Vienna, Austria.
Palmer, T. and A. Riera (2003), 'Tourism and environmental taxes. With special reference to the Balearic ecotax', *Tourism Management*, **24** (6), 665–74.
Pearce, D. and A. Markandya (1989), *The Benefits of Environmental Policy*, Paris, France: OECD Publishing.
Proost, S. and K. Van Dender (1999), *TRENEN II STRAN Final report for publication, Models for Transport, Environment and Energy—version II—Strategic Transport Policy Analysis*, Project Coordinator Centre for Economic Studies, Leuven, Belgium: Katholieke Universiteit.
Raux, C. (2004), 'The use of transferable permits in transport policy', *Transportation Research Part D: Transport and Environment*, **9** (3), 185–97.
Rennings, K., A. Ricci, C. Sessa and S. Weinreich (2001), *CAPRI, Annex B: Valuation of Transport Externalities*, Reino Unido: Project Coordinator ITS University of Leeds.
Rouwndal, J. and E. Verhoef (2006), 'Basic economic principles of road pricing: from theory to applications', *Transport Policy*, **13**, 106–14.
Santos, G., L. Rojey and D. Newbery (2000), 'The environmental benefits from road pricing', DAE Working Paper 0020, Cambridge, UK: Department of Applied Economics, University of Cambridge.
Schreyer, C. et al. (2004), 'External costs of transport. Update study', INFRAS/IWW, Zurich, Switzerland: University of Karlsruhe.
Small, K.A. and J.A. Gomez-Ibañez (1998), 'Road pricing for congestion management: the transition from theory to policy', in K.J. Button and E.T. Verhoef (eds), *Road Pricing, Traffic Congestion and the Environment*, Cheltenham, UK: Edward Elgar, pp. 373–403.
Tol, R.S.J. (2005), 'The marginal damage costs of carbon dioxide emissions: an assessment of the uncertainties', *Energy Policy*, **33**, 2064–74.
Verhoef, E. and K. Small (2004), 'Product differentiation on roads: constrained congestion pricing with hetero-geneous users', *Journal of Transport Economics and Policy*, **38**, 127–56.
Verhoef, E., P. Nijkamp and P. Rietvelt (1995), 'Second-best regulation of road transport externalities', *Journal of Transport Economics and Policy*, May, 147–67.
Verhoef, E., P. Nijkamp and P. Rietvelt (1997), 'Tradeable permits: their potential in the regulation of road transport externalities', *Environmental and Planning B: Planning and Design*, **24**, 527–48.
Wardman, M. (1997), 'A review of evidence on the value of travel time in Great Britain', Working Paper No. 495, Leeds, UK: Institute for Transport Studies, University of Leeds.
World Bank (1996), *Sustainable Transport Policies: Priorities for Policy Reforms*, Washington, DC, US: World Bank.
World Health Organization (WHO) (1999), *Health Costs due to Road Traffic-related Air Pollution*, World Health Organization, Regional Office for Europe.

17 Environmental taxation in China: the greening of an emerging economy
Yan Xu

INTRODUCTION

According to some measures, China has achieved a 'miracle' in economic development since the late 1970s, when the 'open door' policy was launched in China. In 1994, China's tax law system underwent a major overhaul to facilitate economic growth and to increase the government's revenue-raising strength. The 1994 tax reform established a system that put indirect taxation, in particular the value added tax (VAT), at the pivot of the tax system, formulated a relatively comprehensive direct and indirect taxation regime, separated the state's tax sources into central and local exclusive taxes, shared taxes between central and local governments, and split the state's tax administration into central and local levels accordingly. This system remains in use today, though there have been various reforms of specific taxes in recent years.

The tax law system can be viewed as a success in terms of generating revenues.[1] But as it was designed, its major function is to exact money, while the role of allocating resources and thereby helping to protect the environment is relatively marginal. However, as a result of the economic boom, China's environmental and ecological problems have become increasingly critical. China's domestic environment has deteriorated rapidly, as the air and water have become polluted, and the land degraded and scarce. China has become the world's largest producer of CO_2 over the course of the last three decades.[2] China has also changed from a major oil exporter in the 1980s to a net importer since 1993, and has become the biggest oil importer in the world in very recent years.[3]

---

[1] In China, tax revenues have experienced a steadfast growth since 1994. Total tax revenue in 2009 was RMB 5.95 trillion, and in 2010 was RMB 7.32 trillion. *See* STATE ADMIN. OF TAXATION (SAT), PEOPLE'S REPUBLIC OF CHINA (PRC), STATISTICAL DATA OF TAX REVENUES FROM 1994 TO 2008 (2009), *available at* http://www.chinatax.gov.cn/n8136506/n8136593/n8137633/n8138817/index.html; *see also* TAX POLICY DEPARTMENT, PRC MINISTRY OF FINANCE (MOF), ANALYSIS ON THE INCREASE IN TAX REVENUE IN 2009 (2010), *available at* http://szs.mof.gov.cn/zhengwuxinxi/gongzuodongtai/201002/t20100211_270552.html; TAX POLICY DEPARTMENT, MOF, PRC, ANALYSIS ON THE INCREASE IN TAX REVENUE IN 2010 (2011), *available at* http://szs.mof.gov.cn/zhengwuxinxi/gongzuodongtai/201102/t20110201_436195.html.

[2] *See China Overtakes U.S. in Greenhouse Gas Emissions*, N. Y. TIMES, June 20, 2007, *available at* http://www.nytimes.com/2007/06/20/business/worldbusiness/20iht-emit.1.6227564.html?_r=1.

[3] *See* ZHIDONG LI, INST. OF ENERGY ECON., JAPAN, ENERGY AND ENVIRONMENTAL PROBLEMS BEHIND CHINA'S HIGH ECONOMIC GROWTH (2003), *available at* http://eneken.ieej.or.jp/en/data/pdf/188.pdf; *see also* JEFFREY LOGAN, ENERGY OUTLOOK FOR CHINA: FOCUS ON OIL AND GAS, EIA'S ANNUAL ENERGY OUTLOOK FOR 2005, *available at* http://www.iea.org/speech/2005/jl_china.pdf; S. Swartz & S. Oster, *China Tops U.S. in Energy Use*, THE WALL STREET JOURNAL, June 18, 2010, *available at* http://online.wsj.com/article/SB10001424052748703720504575376712353150310.html.

Without question, the Chinese government is facing critical heavy pressures, from within and without, to solve its environmental problems efficiently.

The government has used various means, primarily the traditional command-and-control regulations, to address the issue.[4] These traditional measures are, however, insufficient and limited in their effects. Many researchers believe that the lack of market-based instruments such as taxation has constrained the government's ability to efficiently combat environmental problems.[5] The government needs to expand the role of taxation and adopt more efficient tax law and policies to cost-effectively reduce pollution and pro-hibit environmentally harmful activities. Taxation, as a market-based instrument, along with other instruments such as regulation, could help the government meet environmen-tal protection targets, which have been either enshrined in its national development plan or set by the government.[6]

The topic of environmental taxation has received much attention from researchers and policymakers in many jurisdictions. A great deal of research on environmental taxation has been done in economics, law, political science and other related fields.[7] The subject, however, has only recently been discussed by researchers and policymakers in China. Although there has been limited research in recent years,[8] more comprehensive and sys-tematic research is needed for critical thinking about the question of how to efficiently

---

[4] The term 'command and control' has replaced the traditional term 'direct regulation' to indicate direct government intervention as compared to market based instruments in restricting environmentally harmful activities. *See* N.D. Gunningham et al., *Instruments for Environmental Protection, in* Smart Regulation: Designing Environmental Policy 37–91 (N.D. Gunningham et al. eds, 1998).

[5] For example, Asian Dev. Bank, Country Environmental Analysis for the People's Republic of China 88–89, 120 (2008), *available at* http://www.adb.org/Documents/Produced-Under-TA/39079/39079-PRC-DPTA.pdf.

[6] In China's 12th five-year plan (2011–2015), the targets to reduce energy intensity by 16 percent and CO_2 emissions per unit GDP by 17 percent by 2015 are set up. The reduction targets for chemical oxygen demand (COD) and SO_2 are 8 percent, while ammonia nitrogen and nitrogen oxides are 10 percent. *See* PRC Nat'l Dev. and Reform Comm'n, The Outline of the Twelfth Five Year Plan for National Economic and Social Development of the PRC (2011), approved by the PRC Nat'l People's Cong. on 14 March 2011. The central government also set up an emissions target on 26 November 2009. It aims to reduce its 'carbon intensity of the economy' by 40–45 percent by 2020, compared with 2005 levels. *See China Unveils Emissions Targets ahead of Copenhagen*, BBC World News, Nov. 26, 2009, http://news.bbc.co.uk/2/hi/8380106.stm.

[7] *See, e.g.*, A.C. Pigou, The Economics of Welfare (1932); L.H. Goulder, *Environmental Taxation and the Double Dividend: A Reader's Guide*, 2 Int'l Tax & Pub. Fin., 157–84 (1995); D. McCoy, *Reflections on the Double Dividend Debate, in* Ecotaxation 201–14 (T. O'Riordan ed., 1997); K. Määttä, Environmental Taxes: An Introductory Analysis (2006); William Nordhaus, *To Tax or Not to Tax: Alternative Approaches to Slowing Global Warming*, 1 Rev. Envtl. Econ. and Pol'y 26–44 (2007); Janet Milne, *Environmental Taxation: Why Theory Matters, in* 1 Critical Issues in Environmental Taxation 3–26 (Janet Milne et al. eds, 2003).

[8] For example, Z.M. Lu, Conservatism and Transcendence: Innovation on Environmental Law for Sustainable Development (2003); R.W. Yang, China's Resource Tax System (unpublished dissertation) (on file with China Doctoral and Master Theses Electronic Database); J.N. Wang et al., Policy and Implementation Strategy of the Environmental Taxes (2006); H.L. Li, The Legal System of Environmental Taxes and Charges (2007); X.H. Guan, A Study on Tax Policies Promoting the Development of Circular economy (2008); S.Y. Chen, Ecological Tax Law (2008).

employ the instrument of environmental taxation for the aim of protecting China's environment and natural resources. This chapter examines, on the basis of the existing research literature, the problems and prospects of environmental taxation in China. While the chapter focuses on the current environmentally related tax and charge system and its effects in China, it also deals with the issue of whether it is possible to apply a particular tax type, such as environmental taxes, under the Chinese tax law regime, and if so, how to design such a system.

The chapter is organized as follows. It firstly examines the current environmentally related tax and charge system in China. It then considers the effects of the current system from the perspectives of taxation, the environment, and administration, and demonstrates how the uncoordinated mesh of existing rules does not effectively achieve the goal of reducing pollution and other environmentally harmful activities. Building on this assessment, the chapter analyzes the possibility of introducing a particular, focused environmental taxation system in China. An evaluation of major difficulties and opportunities is followed by a discussion of proposals from both government and researchers on how to apply such a system in China.

THE ENVIRONMENTALLY RELATED TAX AND CHARGE SYSTEM IN CHINA

Currently, China does not have environmental taxes in a strict sense. There has been, however, an environmentally related tax and a nationwide pollution charge system that has played a role in protecting China's environment and natural resources.[9]

The Concept of Environmental Taxes

Environmental taxes, also called green taxes, ecological taxes, Pigouvian taxes and the like, have yet to be defined unambiguously and unanimously. This Handbook adopts a definition from research conducted by the Organization for Economic Co-operation and Development (OECD).[10] 'Environmental taxes' are viewed as synonymous with 'environmentally related taxes,' which are distinct from environmental charges that are paid by individuals and companies to authorities in return for services received.

Under China's existing tax law system, the term 'environmental taxes' is used as a generic term for taxes associated with the environment and resources. As in many other jurisdictions, taxes and charges are considered two different concepts in China. A tax is imposed on the community as a whole and its revenue is incorporated into the general

---

[9]   *See* J.N. Wang et al., *Taxation and the Environment in China: Practice and Perspectives in the OECD, in* Environmental Taxes: Recent Developments in China and OECD Countries 61–105 (1999); *see also* Guan, *supra* note 8, at 164–73; X. Wang & Y.F. Zhou, *Greening Taxation System in China, in* 7 Critical Issues in Environmental Taxation 569–86 (Lin-Heng Lye et al. eds, 2009); China Council for Int'l Cooperation on Env't and Dev. (CCICED), CCICED Policy Research Report 2009 (2009).

[10]   OECD, The Political Economy of Environmentally Related Taxes 26 (2006).

budget, while a charge is levied on specific persons in proportion to services rendered, and its revenue is used for defined purposes.

In China, the legal authority to impose taxes lies with the national legislature, that is, the National People's Congress (NPC) and its Standing Committee (NPCSC).[11] The NPC and NPCSC, however, can delegate to the State Council the power to enact administrative regulations with respect to matters regarding which no national law has been enacted. In any event, the legislative power regarding taxes, including central, local and shared taxes, is centralized in the central government.[12] Nonetheless, local governments have the authority to enact administrative rules[13] and to impose fees or charges as long as such imposition is not identified as a tax.

Environmentally Related Taxes in China

Currently, there are 17 tax types in China, among which the resource tax, the consumption tax, vehicle (and vessel) taxes, the urban construction and maintenance tax, and land use taxes have a direct or indirect relationship with environmental protection.

The resource tax, which applies broadly to salt and mineral resources, was introduced in 1984 and was reformed in 1994 by new legislation.[14] Taxable mineral products include crude oil, natural gas, coal, metal mineral products and other nonmetal mineral products.[15] The amount of tax owed by a specific taxpayer, for example a coal mine operator, is dependent mainly on the resource type but is independent of the environmental effects of resource uses, such as the atmospheric pollution caused by combustion of high-sulphur coal.[16] Revenue related to resource taxes collected from offshore oil enterprises is taken by the central government, while all other resource tax revenue belongs to the local governments.[17] From an environmental perspective, the major problems with this tax are that the tax base is too narrow, the tax rates are too low, its volume-based calculation method on the majority of taxable items is too simple and the tax-sharing arrangement is inappropriate.[18] Indeed, pricing of resource products does not reflect their scarcity levels,

---

[11]   Legislation Law of the PRC (promulgated by the Nat'l People's Cong., Mar. 15, 2000, effective July 1, 2000), arts 7–8 (China) (hereinafter Legislation Law).

[12]   State Council Resolution on the Application of a Tax-sharing Fiscal Administrative System in China (promulgated by the State Council, Dec. 15, 1993, effective Jan. 1, 1994), § 2, art. 3 (China).

[13]   Legislation Law, art. 73.

[14]   Provisional Regulations on Resource Tax (promulgated by the State Council, Dec. 25, 1993, effective Jan. 1, 1994) (China) (hereinafter RT Regulations). The RT Regulations were amended by the State Council on November 1, 2011. For more details, see relevant discussion in the part on 'recent tax reforms' below.

[15]   *Id.*, Schedule of Resource Tax Items and Tax Amount Range.

[16]   Before the 2011 amendment, tax payable on all taxable items was computed on the basis of assessable volume of taxable product and the applicable tax amount per unit. After the 2011 amendment, tax payable on crude oil and natural gas is based on sales rather than the assessable volume. All else remains the same.

[17]   China is a unitary state. The terms, 'central government' and 'local governments' are typically used to mean the central government in Beijing, and local governments at and below the provincial level.

[18]   As a study found, the resource tax only covers mineral resources and all other resources such as water are not included. The tax on all taxable resources before the 2011 amendment was

the supply and demand conditions or the external costs of pollution since it is calculated only on the basis of volume and price adjustment is inflexible. These problems prevent the tax from effectively motivating energy conservation activities.

The consumption tax (CT) was introduced in China, along with the VAT, during the 1994 reform. The CT was amended when the VAT was amended at the end of 2008, with the intent to constrain consumption of certain goods as well as modify behavior and at the same time raise tax revenues.[19] The tax is imposed on 14 types of consumer goods.[20] Taxable items related to the environment include petrol, diesel, aviation kerosene, automobile tires, motorcycles, cars, yachts, disposable wooden chopsticks, and tobacco, wine and liquor.[21] Among them, the CT on fuel and vehicles has a direct impact on energy consumption and vehicle use, which are closely tied to China's air pollution problem. According to tax law, both the CT and the VAT apply to petrol, diesel and vehicles.[22] Although the amended tax rates on fuel products have been increased and a differential rate has been applied to leaded and unleaded petrol,[23] they remain low compared with those of other countries. The pricing of domestic refined oil has begun to be linked with global prices, but this is under the government's control.[24] CT rates on vehicles have also been changed to varying degrees:[25] the amended rates schedule now encourages the purchase and use of cars with a lower emission capacity and discriminates against cars with a higher emission capacity. For example, the CT rate on cars with a capacity of more than four liters has increased to 40 percent while the CT rate on cars with a capacity of less than one liter has decreased to 1 percent. The revenue from CT belongs to the central government.

Vehicles are subject to vehicle taxes in addition to the CT. Vehicle taxes are composed of the vehicle acquisition tax and the vehicle (and vessel) tax. The former[26] applies to vehicles purchased that are specified as taxable vehicles. This tax is administered by the

---

simply calculated according to the volume exploited rather than sale price. The highest rate of taxable items is only RMB 60 per ton and the lowest RMB 0.3 per ton. The tax coexists with other taxes and charges on taxable resources. The central government cannot effectively implement its macroscopic management measures on those resources which are subject to local tax administrations. *See* X.L. Zhang, *Improvement Measures on the Resource Tax Law System* (in Chinese), 1 COMMERCIAL TIMES, 76–77 (2010).

[19]   *See* Z. LIU, TAXATION IN CHINA 148, 169 (2006); *see also* Wang et al., *supra* note 9, at 69. Provisional Regulations on Value-added Tax and Provisional Regulations on Consumption Tax (promulgated by the State Council, Dec. 13, 1993, amended Nov. 5, 2008, effective Jan. 1, 2009) (China) (hereinafter VAT Regulations, and CT Regulations, respectively).

[20]   *See* CT Regulations, Schedule of Consumption Tax Items and Tax Rates.

[21]   *Id.*

[22]   In China, CT is imposed on certain specific consumer goods which are subject to VAT also.

[23]   CT Regulations, Schedule of Consumption Tax Items and Tax Rates, item 7; PRC State Council, Notice of Implementing the Reform on Fuel Taxation and Pricing (hereinafter SC Notice), No. 37, § 2, art.1 (3) (2008); MOF & SAT, Notice of Increasing the Consumption Tax Rates on Fuel Products, No. 167, art. 1 (2008).

[24]   SC Notice, § 2, art. 2.

[25]   VAT Regulations, arts. 2 and 12; CT Regulations, Schedule of Consumption Tax Items and Tax Rates, item 9.

[26]   Provisional Regulations on Vehicle Acquisition Tax (promulgated by the State Council, Oct. 22, 2000, effective Jan. 1, 2001) (China) (hereinafter Vehicle AT Regulations).

State Administration of Taxation, China's central tax agency, and, accordingly, the tax revenue belongs to the central government, which uses it specifically for road construction and traffic management work.[27] The applicable tax rate is 10 percent of the vehicle's value and the tax is paid in one lump sum.[28] This tax, however, seems to have had little impact on the rapid growth of private car ownership in China. The vehicle (and vessel) tax is an annual tax administered by local tax bureaus.[29] Its main purpose is to provide funds for local governments to upgrade local public roads and maintain infrastructure.[30] Passenger vehicles and motorcycles are taxed per item depending on the specific size of the vehicle,[31] while cargo vehicles and motor-tricycles are taxed per ton of net capacity.[32] Before the recent new Law on Vehicle and Vessel Tax, tax payable for passenger vehicles carrying fewer than nine passengers was not determined by engine capacity, but by how many passengers a vehicle can carry, which means the tax had no direct relationship with the actual intensity of vehicle use, such as the number of kilometers driven or the amount of petrol consumed. Overall, the tax has represented a small portion of the cost for using vehicles, and hence has had little effect on user behavior.

The urban construction and maintenance tax has been in effect since 1985.[33] It is levied for the purpose of expanding and stabilizing the source of funds for urban infrastructure such as housing, road and bridge maintenance and environmental sanitation.[34] Those who are obliged to pay VAT, CT and business tax (BT) are subject to this tax.[35] Tax rates, which are based on the actual amount of VAT, CT and/or BT paid, vary according to whether the taxpayers are located in cities (7 percent), counties and towns (5 percent) or other areas (1 percent).[36] The tax is a kind of 'green' tax because revenues from the tax have become an important source for investment in environmental protection, particularly in the improvement of urban air and water quality undertaken by local authorities.[37]

The land use taxes include the city and township land use tax and the farmland occupation tax. Revenues from these taxes belong to local governments.[38] Tax payable under

---

[27] Implementation Rules on Transportation and Vehicle Tax and Charge Reform, art. 4.

[28] Vehicle AT Regulations, at arts 5 and 8. The tax rate on cars with a capacity of less than 1.6 liters was reduced to 5 percent in 2009 and 7.5 percent in 2010 according to the central government's decisions.

[29] Law on Vehicle and Vessel Tax (promulgated by the NPCSC, Feb. 25, 2011, effective Jan. 1, 2012), art. 9 and Schedule of the Tax Items and Tax Amount (China) (hereinafter LVVT). The LVVT replaced the previous Provisional Regulations on Vehicle and Vessel Tax issued by the State Council on December 29, 2006. Local tax agencies include tax agencies at provincial, municipal or regional, and county levels as well as tax stations (branches) below the county level.

[30] *See* Wang et al., *supra* note 9, at 71.

[31] LVVT, Schedule of the Tax Items and Tax Amount.

[32] *Id.*

[33] Provisional Regulations on Urban Construction and Maintenance Tax (promulgated by the State Council, Feb. 8, 1985, effective Jan. 1, 1985) (China) (hereinafter UCMT Regulations).

[34] *Id.* at arts 6 and 7.

[35] *Id.* at art. 2.

[36] *Id.* at arts 3 and 4.

[37] *See* Wang et al., *supra* note 9, at 72–73; *see also* Wang & Zhou, *supra* note 9, at 577.

[38] Provisional Regulations on City and Township Land Use Tax (promulgated by the State Council, Sept. 27, 1988, amended Dec. 31, 2006, effective Jan. 1, 2007), art. 10 (China) (hereinafter

them is based on the area of land or farmland actually occupied by the taxpayers, and the applicable rate per unit.[39] The city and township land use tax is aimed at promoting effective use of urban land resources and at adjusting differential rents of urban land.[40] Taxpayers are the enterprises and individuals who use land in cities, counties, towns and dedicated industrial and mining areas.[41] This tax is calculated on an annual basis and paid in installments,[42] and the time limit for payment is determined by local governments at the provincial level.[43] The tax has generated less than 1 percent of overall tax revenue since its imposition.[44]

The farmland occupation tax, introduced in 1987 and reformed in 2007,[45] is paid in one instance. The average tax rate varies across provincial regions according to the local average occupation of farmland and the level of economic development.[46] Although the revenue accounts for a very small proportion of total revenues, the tax has proved effective in controlling, to a degree, arbitrary occupations and misuse of farmland.[47]

It is worth noting that VAT in China applies to a wide range of goods and certain services and, as such, the tax may have an indirect relationship with environmental protection. There are three tax rates: standard (17 percent), low (13 percent) and zero. From an environmental perspective, items subject to a low rate include two types: gas and coal products for residential use, and fertilizers and similar goods used in agriculture.[48] The low rate is likely to remain in the short- and medium-term. Certain preferential VAT policies have been provided for environmentally friendly industries and enterprises, such as exempting from VAT enterprises dealing with waste materials and refunding VAT paid for the exploitation and sale of coalbed gases.[49]

The Pollution Charge System in China

As mentioned earlier, a nationwide pollution charge system has been in place for over two decades in China. This system was reformed in 2003.[50]

CTLUT Regulations); Provisional Regulations on Farm Land Occupation Tax (promulgated by the State Council, Apr. 1, 1987, reformed Dec. 1, 2007, effective Jan. 1, 2008), art. 12 (China) (hereinafter FLOT Regulations).

[39] CTLUT Regulations, art. 4; FLOT Regulations, art. 5, para. 1.
[40] CTLUT Regulations, art. 1.
[41] *Id.* at art. 2.
[42] *Id.* at art. 8.
[43] *Id.*
[44] *See* SAT, PRC, STATISTICAL DATA OF TAX REVENUES FROM 1994 TO 2008 (2009), *available at* http://www.chinatax.gov.cn/n8136506/n8136593/n8137633/n8138817/index.html.
[45] FLOT Regulations, art. 16.
[46] *Id.* at art. 5, paras 2 and 3.
[47] *See* Wang et al., *supra* note 9, at 77.
[48] VAT Regulations, art. 2.
[49] For detail, *see* Wang & Zhou, *supra* note 9, at 571–72.
[50] In 1982, the State Council promulgated the Provisional Method on the Imposition of Pollution Charges. In 1988, the State Council issued the Provisional Method on the Paid Use of Special Funds on Abatement of Pollutant Sources. These two administrative regulations have been replaced by the Regulations on the Collection and Use of Pollution Charges (promulgated by the State Council, Jan. 2, 2003, effective July 1, 2003), art. 26 (China) (hereinafter CUPC Regulations).

The pollution charge can be considered a quasi-tax on the basis of the 'polluter-pays' principle.[51] It is applied to waste water, waste gas, solid waste and noise pollution.[52] The current system is based not only on the amount of emissions that exceed the relevant national or local pollution discharge standard, but also on the total amount and concentration of pollution discharged.[53] The charge rates have been increased by the 2003 reform, with the purpose of moving from a low-cost system for polluters to one that offsets environmental protection agencies' pollution abatement costs.[54] Paying pollution charges does not exempt polluters from all liability for preventing and abating pollution and compensating for pollution damages, nor from other liabilities provided for by administrative regulations.[55] Environmental protection agencies above the county level are responsible for the collection of charges.[56] All pollution charges are remitted to the State Treasury, incorporated into the general fiscal budget, listed as special funds for environmental protection,[57] and allocated to the central government and local governments at the ratio of one to nine.[58]

Despite its reforms, the pollution charge system is still problematic. The rate schedules applied to major pollutants are too low to fully meet the government's pollution abatement costs and the low rates result in a low cost of violation for the polluters.[59] For example, the SO_2 rates were increased from RMB 0.21/kg to RMB 0.63/kg,[60] and the rates have been increased further to varying degrees by the local governments in recent years.[61] Nevertheless, the payment of the SO_2 pollution charge constitutes, very often, a

---

[51]   *See* Wang et al., *supra* note 9, at 78; *see also* T.B. Qin & P. Chen, *The Environmental Fee-for-Tax Reform in China: A One-Size-Fits-All Solution for Environmental Problems?, in* 7 CRITICAL ISSUES IN ENVIRONMENTAL TAXATION 568 (Lin-Heng Lye, et al. eds, 2009).

[52]   CUPC Regulations, art.12, para.1.

[53]   *Id.; see also* Measures for the Administration of the Rates for Pollution Charges (promulgated by the MOF, National Development and Reform Commission (NDRC), State Economic and Trade Commission, and the Former State Environmental Protection Administration (SEPA, which was elevated to the Ministry of Environmental Protection, MEP, in 2008, Feb. 28, 2003, effective July 1, 2003), art. 3 (China) (hereinafter MARPC).

[54]   *See* NAT'L DEV. & REFORM COMM'N OF THE PRC, CHINA'S POLLUTION CHARGE SYSTEM (2007), *available at* http://www1.ndrc.gov.cn/jggl/jgqk/t20070404_126543.htm. 'Pollution abatement cost' here refers to the government's cost of cleaning up the resulting pollution. The NDRC is an institution that is unique to China. It is a macroeconomic management agency under the State Council, which studies and formulates policies for economic and social development, maintains a balance of economic aggregates and guides the overall economic system restructuring. It has taken the lead with related ministries in the area of environmental protection, energy and resource conservation, development of recycling economy and so on. *See Brief Introduction of the NDRC*, NAT'L DEV. AND REFORM COMM'N OF THE PRC, http://en.ndrc.gov.cn/brief/default.htm (last visited Feb. 25, 2011); *Main Functions of the NDRC*, NAT'L DEV. AND REFORM COMM'N OF THE PRC, http://en.ndrc.gov.cn/mfndrc/default.htm.

[55]   CUPC Regulations, art.12, para.2.

[56]   CUPC Regulations, arts 3, 6, 7, 13 and 19.

[57]   CUPC Regulations, art.18, para.1.

[58]   *See* Qin & Chen, *supra* note 51, at 562–63.

[59]   *See*, for example, OECD, OECD ENVIRONMENTAL PERFORMANCE REVIEWS: CHINA (2007).

[60]   MARPC, appendix, § 2, art. 1.

[61]   For example, in Anhui province, the SO_2 rate was increased to RMB 0.84/kg in 2008, RMB 1.05/kg in 2009, and RMB 1.26/kg in 2010 and onwards. *See* Notice on Adjusting SO_2 Charge Rates (promulgated by the Anhui Provincial Price Bureau, Finance Department and

rather small portion of the polluters' (mostly enterprises) total tax and charge burdens.[62] The pollution charge can be reduced, eliminated or postponed, which has led to considerable variation in regional enforcement practices.[63] Some local governments remove or hoard funds from pollution charges for purposes other than environmental protection.[64] It would be desirable, therefore, for most if not all pollution charges to be converted to pollution taxes based on volume, usage, and similar factors.

EFFECTS OF THE SYSTEM

Roughly, the double-dividend hypothesis suggests that increased taxes on polluting activities can provide two kinds of benefits.[65] First, there is an improvement in the environment, a dividend of environmental protection. Second, there is an improvement in economic efficiency from the use of environmental tax revenues to reduce other taxes, such as income taxes, that distort labor supply and decisions regarding saving. This is a dividend of economic benefits that result from increased tax efficiency. Does the hypothesis apply in the case of China? Below is an examination of the effects of the current system in China.

Taxation Effects: Lowering Pre-existing Tax Distortions?

Turnover-related taxation, including VAT, CT and BT, is the mainstay of China's tax regime. Revenues from these taxes have accounted for more than 50 percent of total tax revenue since 1994,[66] while revenues from the enterprise income tax and individual income tax have accounted for 17–20 percent and 6.7 percent, respectively, during the same period. The enterprise income tax rate of 25 percent is comparatively moderate,[67]

Environmental Protection Bureau, June 30, 2008, effective June 30, 2008). The SO_2 rate has been increased to RMB 1.26/kg in Guangdong province since 2010 and an experiment of applying for a differential SO_2 rate on different industrial sectors is under way in the province as well. *See* the Notice on Adjusting SO_2 and COD Charge Rates and Trying out the Deferential Rates Imposition Method (promulgated by the Guangdong Provincial Price Bureau, Finance Department and Environmental Protection Bureau, Mar. 11, 2010, effective Apr. 1, 2010).

[62] C.F. Yang, *Thinking about the Issue of 'Fee to Tax' and Moving towards a Revolutionary Reform on the Pollution Charge System* (in Chinese), 20 ENVTL. PROTECTION 8–12 (2010).

[63] OECD, OECD ENVIRONMENTAL PERFORMANCE REVIEWS: CHINA (2007).

[64] NAT'L DEV. & REFORM COMM'N OF THE PRC, CHINA'S POLLUTION CHARGE SYSTEM (2007), *available at* http://www1.ndrc.gov.cn/jggl/jgqk/t20070404_126543.htm.

[65] *See* Goulder, *supra* note 7; McCoy, *supra* note 7; D. Fullerton & G.E. Metcalf, *Environmental Taxes and the Double-Dividend Hypothesis: Did You Really Expect Something for Nothing?*, 73 CHI.-KENT L. REV. 221, 221–56 (1998); A.L. Bovenberg, *Green Tax Reforms and the Double Dividend: An Updated Reader's Guide*, 6 INT'L TAX & PUB. FIN., 421, 421–43 (1999).

[66] *See* STATE ADMIN. OF TAXATION, *supra* note 1.

[67] Enterprise Income Tax Law (promulgated by the Nat'l People's Cong., Mar. 16, 2007, effective Jan. 1, 2008), art. 4 (China) (hereinafter EIT Law). There is a reduced tax rate, 20 percent, for non-resident enterprises and small low profit enterprises meeting certain conditions, and a lowest tax rate, 15 percent, for important high- and new- enterprises that are to be supported by the state, EIT Law, art. 4, paras 2 and 28. The tax rate for non-resident taxpayers has been further reduced

and enterprises have no deductible social security contributions or expenses related to employees' basic social security programs.[68] As to the individual income tax, although a progressive tax applies to wages and salaries, most people pay tax at the rate of 3–20 percent.[69] The burden from the double-dividend hypothesis' so-called distorting taxes, mainly income taxes, is not so great in China. The current income tax system imposes limited distorting effects on labor supply, due to, among other reasons, the fact that the labor supply in China is comparatively abundant. Even though there is a tax on labor, the substitute effect of this tax is not substantial because most workers would not choose leisure and reduced work solely because of a tax change.

This demonstrates that in China, tax distortions related to labor and capital are not typically as common as one finds in many other developed jurisdictions that rely on income taxes to fund government. There is, however, a certain distortion in the VAT system. Because revenues from China's environmentally related taxes and charges are not significant, and are mainly used for environmental protection programs, the current system seems to have little effect on lowering preexisting tax distortions and has led to no particular economic gain.

Environmental Effects: Lowering Negative Externalities of the Environment?

The current system is, above all, a revenue-raising device, not a set of serious environmental policy instruments. The lack of an effective environmental taxation system has contributed to pollution and other environmental problems in China.

Consider, for example, air pollution. Vehicular emissions have become the number one source of air pollution in urban areas in China. The combined burden of the VAT and CT on the consumption of transport fuel is approximately 23 percent of China's fuel prices, lower than comparable rates applied in many other jurisdictions.[70] The fuel pricing mechanism—partially market-determined and partially government-controlled—may have added to the steady expansion of private vehicles in China, as the fuel price that applied to all transport fuel consumption was adjusted lower than international prices during the time of the spike. The underpricing of fuel would amount to an indirect

---

to 10 percent and could be even further reduced to varying degrees by tax treaties. Implementation Regulations of the EIT Law (issued by the State Council, Dec. 6, 2007, effective Jan. 1, 2008), art. 91 (China).

[68] EIT Law, art. 8; Regulations on the Implementation of the EIT Law, art. 35.

[69] Individual Income Tax Law (promulgated by the Standing Comm. Nat'l People's Cong., Sept. 10, 1980, amended Oct. 31, 1993 for the first time, Aug. 30, 1999 for the second time, Oct. 27, 2005 for the third time, June 29, 2007 for the fourth time, Dec. 29, 2007 for the fifth time, and June 30, 2011 for the sixth time, effective Sept. 10, 1980), Schedule 1 Individual Income Tax Rates (Applicable to Income from Wages and Salaries) (China). Due to the low tax threshold, many ordinary workers are included in the taxpayers' category.

[70] For instance in the third quarter of 2010, the fuel tax in Norway was 63 percent of its fuel price. In the Netherlands, 64.3 percent of the total price of petrol was taken for taxes. By comparison, the tax share in the petro price in the U.S. was only 18.2 percent. *See* International Energy Agency, Energy Prices and Taxes: Quarterly Statistics Fourth Quarter 2010, at xxxii (2010), *available at* http://www.oecd-ilibrary.org/docserver/download/fulltext/6210041e.pdf ?expires=1303638181&id=id&accname=ocid194359&checksum=5E618C3BAAF0CB98B523948 86C902C5.

subsidy, which does not help advance China's energy security and efficiency. The air pollution charge only applies to fixed emission sources, not to mobile sources such as vehicles in cities. These have to some extent led to low energy prices for a relatively long time and have contributed significantly to energy waste and air pollution in China.[71]

Another example is the resource tax system. The current tax rates are too low to reflect the social costs of resource exploitation and to discourage destructive exploitation behavior. The contribution of the tax to total tax revenue has been very small (0.57 percent in 2010, for example).[72] This very limited amount of resource tax revenue has been unable to provide sufficient funds for restoring environmental damage.

There are problems with other environmentally related taxes as well. Government expenditures for pollution abatement, though they have increased since 2001, have accounted for only around 1.2 to 1.5 percent of gross domestic product (GDP), which means the investment in environmental protection falls short of the real and pressing need for funds.[73] In short, the green element of China's tax regime is too small to help lower negative environmental externalities and create incentives to change behavior. The still severe environmental problems in China may imply that there is little environmental gain from the existing system.

Other Effects

The current system has some effect on the issue of how different authorities at different levels of government interact with respect to taxation and the environment.

There is a certain overlap of functions between the State's environmental protection agencies and tax administration agencies. Pollution charges are collected and administered by the environmental protection agencies above the county level. If they are to be incorporated into the formal tax regime, the roles of the two agencies need to be clearly redefined. As to the use of pollution charges, while 80 percent of the revenue and income from fines is used to fund pollution abatement projects, the remaining 20 percent is used mainly for covering the administrative costs of charge collection and local capacity building.[74] Polluting activities are therefore tolerated to a certain extent by environmental protection agencies for purposes of stabilizing their financial resources.[75]

The intergovernmental relationship is also worth noting. The interests of the central government and the local governments may be in conflict, and the central government's environmental protection policies—including its taxation policy—may be compromised by the local governments' lack of funds or their zeal for developing the economy. A number of local governments, especially those in underdeveloped regions, are short

---

[71]   *See* Y.F. Bai, *Understanding the Puzzle of Transforming Road Charges to Fuel Tax in China* (in Chinese), 4 ECON. & MANAGEMENT 77–82 (2009).

[72]   TAX POLICY TAX DEPARTMENT (2011), *supra* note 1.

[73]   For data, see the PRC MINISTRY OF ENVTL. PROT. (MEP), STATISTICAL REPORT OF THE NATIONAL ENVIRONMENT 2001 TO 2008 (2009), *available at* http://www.mep.gov.cn/zwgk/hjtj/qghjtjgb/.

[74]   *See* Wang et al., *supra* note 9, at 80.

[75]   *See* Guan, *supra* note 8, at 189.

of funds to finance environmental protection projects due to limited local tax sources resulting from the tax-sharing system.[76] Local governments' strength and their incentives to efficiently reduce pollution and solve environmental problems are consequently constrained. Worse, many local governments have employed charges (since, as noted earlier, they cannot enact taxes) as a useful means of raising revenues for various needs, including the need to address local environmental problems. The environmentally related charges are collected by various governmental departments and fall outside formal budget control. This not only erodes formal tax bases but also creates opportunities for corruption and poses difficulties for the coordination of governmental efforts in environmental protection.

APPLYING AN INDEPENDENT ENVIRONMENTAL TAXATION SYSTEM IN CHINA

As shown above, the current environmentally related tax and charge system in China cannot act as an efficient market-based instrument to help deal with serious environmental problems. The government is expected to enhance the role of taxation as an important fiscal means of meeting reduction targets in the short term and protecting the environment for sustainable development in the long term.

Government Concerns and Recent Developments in the Tax System in China

Challenges from within and without

China's environmental problems pose a real threat to its own economic development and exert a profound impact on the world. The central government is aware of the urgent need to reduce pollution and solve other environmental problems, though neither is an easy task.

The tension between three conditions, namely, economic development, limited natural resources, and social distinctions and changes in people's demands, is particularly relevant to this task. An oversupply of coal relative to limited, cleaner natural resources, combined with low energy efficiency,[77] render China's sustainable economic development problematic. The fast economic development has led to increasing wealth disparities among individuals and regions across China. With rapid urbanization, the cities in China are facing problems in delivering infrastructure and services.[78] New challenges are arising with the ageing population, increased unemployment, and the inadequacy of social security. Poor people tend to concentrate on ecologically fragile areas with a low capacity to cope with environmental degradation and to pay for the health costs of pollution.[79]

---

[76]   *See* Wang et al., *supra* note 9, at 81, 89; *see also* Guan, *supra* note 8, at 185; B.H. Wang, *Some Thoughts on Enacting an Environmental Taxation System in China* (in Chinese), 8 PRESENT-DAY LAW SCI. 47, 47–52, 58 (2010).

[77]   *Id.*; *see also* CHINA COUNCIL FOR INT'L COOPERATION ON ENV'T AND DEV., *supra* note 9.

[78]   *See* ASIAN DEV. BANK, *supra* note 5, at 6–8.

[79]   *See* ASIAN DEV. BANK, *supra* note 5, at 48–51.

China cannot afford to ignore the importance and urgency of environmental protection, since doing so would negatively affect its economic development interests. If it does not take open and clear economic measures to control pollution, its exported goods may be subject to a border tax imposed by countries that put in place either a carbon tax or a permit trading system.[80] China would have to endure pollution and related problems on its own while losing money to competitive countries and losing face in the global political arena.[81]

China must strike a balance between the environment and the economy. It is not the only country facing this challenge, but due to the magnitude of its growth and the rate at which social and environmental consequences occur, China's decisions and its strategy for environmental protection will have an enormous impact both nationally and worldwide.

Recent tax reforms

In 2007, the central government issued an announcement, making clear its plans to introduce an environmental taxation system.[82] In recent years, it has developed significant policies and has formulated a variety of domestic programs to address environmental and development issues.[83]

Since 2008, certain preparation work has been done in areas such as CT on fuel and vehicles, vehicle taxes, and the resource tax. Following CT reform and subsequent fuel taxation and pricing reform in 2008, six types of administrative charges relating to road and water transportation were waived[84] in order to offset increased fuel tax burdens and to streamline the transport and taxation departments of government.[85] The vehicle (and vessel) tax was amended in 2011, as mentioned earlier. The new Law on Vehicle and Vessel Tax has begun to link the tax with vehicle's engine capacity for passenger vehicles

---

[80] *See* X.T. Zhang, *Legislating Carbon Tax in China* (in Chinese), 2 LAW SCI. MAGAZINE 98–100 (2010); L.Z. Sheng, *Prospects of a Carbon Tax* (in Chinese), 1 ENV'T. 45–47 (2010); Li T., *Imposing Carbon Tax to Resist 'Foreign Aggression' and Pacify the Interior* (in Chinese), 2 BUS. REV. 20 (2010); W.Q. Gu & Y.Q. Li, *Implicit Intentions of France's Proposal for Carbon Tax* (in Chinese), 4 AGRIC. PRODS. MKT. WEEKLY 28–29 (2010); M. Su et al., *Designing China's Carbon Tax under the New Circumstance* (in Chinese), 1 LOCAL FISCAL RESEARCH 9–13 (2010).

[81] *See id.*

[82] PRC STATE COUNCIL, COMPREHENSIVE WORK PLAN ON ENERGY CONSERVATION AND EMISSIONS REDUCTION (2007).

[83] *See* PRC NAT'L DEV. AND REFORM COMM'N, *supra* note 6. It advocates a new economic model in which growth is guided by resource conservation not by continued expansion of resource use. It calls for the development of a pricing mechanism which could reflect supply and demand and the scarcity value of resources so that market forces could play a critical role in allocating resources. *See also* OECD, *supra* note 59.

[84] These charges are road maintenance fee, channel maintenance fee, administration fee of highway transportation, highway transportation surcharges, administration fee of water transportation, and water transportation surcharges. SC Notice, § 2, art. 1(1).

[85] *See* T.B. Qin, *Energy Tax: How Far Is It from Idea to Practice? Lessons Learned from the Experience in China*, in 6 CRITICAL ISSUES IN ENVIRONMENTAL TAXATION 867 (2009). Before the reform, the Ministry of Transportation (MOT) was in charge of all types of charge related to construction, maintenance, and management of highways. The imposition of tax on oil products and vehicles by the SAT might overlap or even conflict with the collection of charges by the MOT.

carrying fewer than nine passengers. The resource tax was also amended by the government on November 1, 2011 after a pilot reform in Xinjiang Province on June 1, 2010. Under the amendment, crude oil and natural gas are taxed on the basis of sales value, and coking coal and rare earths are subject to higher tax rates.[86] According to government officials, a reasonable resource tax level and a proper resource tax calculation method are prerequisites for the efficient distribution of natural resources.[87] The government also plans to introduce a carbon tax on enterprises by the end of the 12th FYP (2011–2015).[88] Resource tax reform is indeed a prologue for the imposition of a carbon tax.

Notwithstanding this progress, introducing an independent environmental taxation system may still not be easy in China.

Difficulties in Opting for an Independent Environmental Taxation System

There are a number of general difficulties in introducing a new environmental tax category in China. According to some studies,[89] these difficulties include: (1) concern about inflation resulting from the increased costs of energy and main raw materials; (2) discounted emission effects, as enterprises producing such products as coal, electricity and fertilizers with high emissions might transfer their tax burdens to others due to demand exceeding supply; (3) increased administrative costs from imposing new taxes; and (4) resistance from enterprises and individuals.[90]

Opposition likely will also come from local governments.[91] Under economic and financial pressures, some local governments are anxious to escape poverty and set out for prosperity. They would prefer economic projects that have immediate benefits over environmental programs that require long-term investments but do not generate immediate results.[92] If the central government attempts to introduce an independent environmental taxation system, it must collaborate with local governments in allocating tax resources and sharing responsibilities. Introducing such a system will involve departmental relationships as well, particularly the relationship between tax administration agencies and

---

[86]   RT Regulations (amended by the State Council, Sept. 30, 2011, effective No. 1, 2011), art. 4 and Schedule of Resource Tax Items and Tax Amount Range. MOF and SAT Notice on Issuing the Rules of Resource Tax Reform on Crude Oil and Natural Gas in Xinjiang Province, No. 54, June 1, 2010, art. 3.

[87]   *See Opportunity to Carry out Resource Tax Reform Arrives*, PEOPLE'S DAILY ONLINE, Apr. 23, 2010, *available at* http://english.peopledaily.com.cn/90001/90778/90862/6961125.html.

[88]   W. Tian, *Officials Weighing Green Benefits of Carbon Taxation*, CHINA DAILY, Jan. 6, 2012, *available at* http://www.chinadaily.com.cn/business/2012-01/06/content_14391943.htm.

[89]   *See* G. Sun, *Difficulties and Suggestions for Imposing Environmental Taxes in China* (in Chinese), 8 TAXATION RESEARCH 45–47 (2008).

[90]   D. PENG, CHINESE TAX INST., ANALYSIS AND PROPOSALS OF APPLYING AN ENVIRONMENTAL TAXATION SYSTEM IN CHINA (2008).

[91]   Many local governments in China have been primarily concerned with developing their own economy at any cost, even though the central government has included environmental protection into macroeconomic policies. The fact that performance and promotion of local officials are closely related to local GDP growth rate motivates them to ignore or divert environmental protection policies from the Centre. *See* ASIAN DEV. BANK, *supra* note 5, at 25–26.

[92]   *Id*; *see also* D.M. Guo et al., *Preliminary Thoughts on Developing China's Low Carbon Economy and Related Tax Policies* (in Chinese), 58 REV. OF ECON. RESEARCH 2–8, 40 (2009).

environmental protection agencies. Cross-institutional coordination and support from other departments such as the National Development and Reform Commission (NDRC) would be greatly needed.[93] Essentially, then, there are no significant legal impediments but there are major political and financial obstacles to applying such a system in China.

Nevertheless, opportunities may exist in the midst of difficulties. Applying such a system would help transform China's economic development model of exports, high input, high consumption, high pollution, and low output[94] into a more sustainable one and help facilitate industrial structural adjustment.[95] A commitment to emissions reduction may attract capital investors who are increasingly concerned with fostering a low-carbon economy. For enterprises, increasing energy efficiency means lowering costs and efficient products mean premium values. For individuals, public expenditure on infrastructure, services and environmental protection projects could create opportunities for poverty alleviation and an improvement in living conditions. Applying environmental taxes, including a carbon tax, could help China avoid international trade disputes and expand export opportunities. There are other supporting factors provided by the macro-economic and tax reforms.[96]

Given the urgent need for emissions reduction and the country's long-term development interests, China is likely to introduce some form of an environmental taxation system in the foreseeable future.

Designing a Sound Environmental Taxation System

There are various proposals from government and researchers as to how to effectively apply an environmental taxation system in China.[97]

In 2005, a research institute under the former State Environmental Protection Administration (SEPA) completed detailed research on how to design China's environmental taxes and related tax policies, as well as a roadmap for implementation.[98] This research put forward three choices: an independent environmental taxation system, a greening of the existing tax regime or a system combining environmental taxes and

---

[93]   *See* ASIAN DEV. BANK, *supra* note 5, at 28–29, 61–68. The responsibility of environmental protection and resources management is shared between multiple central governmental agencies including the MEP. The NDRC has played a leading role in resource pricing and formulating the national socioeconomic development plans that cover natural resource and environment.

[94]   *See* ASIAN DEV. BANK, *supra* note 5, at 27.

[95]   *See* Guo, et al., *supra* note 92. China has relied too much on the secondary industry (approximately manufacturing) for economic development. In developing the secondary industry, it has depended too heavily on energy- and capital-intensive new technology industries. The central government has decided since the 10th FYP to optimize and upgrade the industrial structure and to strengthen China's international competitiveness. *See* PRC NAT'L DEV. AND REFORM COMM'N, THE OUTLINE OF THE TENTH FIVE-YEAR PLAN FOR NATIONAL ECONOMIC AND SOCIAL DEVELOPMENT OF THE PRC (2000); *see also* PRC NAT'L DEV. AND REFORM COMM'N, *supra* note 6.

[96]   *See* Wang et al., *supra* note 9, at 101; *see also* Chen, *supra* note 8, at 218.

[97]   For a general summary, *see* Li, *supra* note 8, at 259–66.

[98]   *See* Wang et al., *supra* note 8. The SEPA was promoted to the ministerial level and renamed the Ministry of Environmental Protection during the 1st Session of the 11th National People's Congress in 2008. *See* Xi Yang, *SEPA Gets Stronger*, CHINA.ORG.CN (Mar. 10, 2008), *available at* http://www.china.org.cn/environment/news/2008-03/10/content_12143406.htm.

charges.[99] In 2007, a tax research institute of the Ministry of Finance conducted another similar research project.[100] This research proposed three options: general environmental taxes according to the 'beneficiary-pays' principle,[101] taxes on pollution or emissions based on the 'polluter-pays' principle or taxes on polluting products following the 'user pays' principle.[102] In the view of the Ministry, greening the current tax system—that is, increasing the environmental tax burden that can possibly be offset by lowering other tax burdens—will be a more urgent task and a more realistic way of dealing with environmental problems at present. Increasing the environmental tax burden on consumption of goods with negative externalities and natural resources can be done by, for example, expanding the scope of CT to include more polluting products such as coal, increasing CT rates on fuel products, enlarging the base of the resource tax to include such resources as water, land and forestry and modifying the procedure for the tax's collection, and removing certain adverse preferential tax treatments on polluting goods.[103]

Though greening the current tax regime is needed, a number of researchers still favor introducing a particular environmental taxation system.[104] They argue that an independent system can help change polluters' and users' behavior, motivate the production and use of environmentally friendly goods, provide financial sources for governments to meet the costs of environmental protection, avoid potential international trade disputes, improve public understanding and public involvement, and so on. Establishing such a system may be the last stage of China's green tax reform.[105] Some proposals suggest that the independent tax system can cover several sub-tax categories, such as a pollution tax

---

[99]   Wang et al., *supra* note 8, at 2–15. The independent environmental taxation scheme includes general environmental tax which is based on the income with the purpose of collecting money for environmental protection, direct pollution tax which is based on the amount of pollutants' emissions, and polluting product tax which is imposed on the products with potential pollution effect. 'Greening of the existing tax regime' means reforming and improving current tax categories and cooperating with the environmental charge system as well. *See also* Wang et al., Chinese Acad. for Envtl. Planning, Design on the Framework of China Environmental Taxation Policy and Its Implementation Strategy (2006), *available at* http://www.caep.org.cn/english/paper/A-Framework-Design-of-Environmental-Tax-Policy-in-China.pdf.

[100]   This was completed by Sun et al., in November 2007. *See* Sun et al., *Necessity of Imposing the Environmental Taxes*, Cai Jing Magazine, Apr. 1, 2008, *available at* http://www.caijing.com.cn/2008-01-04/100044123.html.

[101]   *Id.* This means that the general environmental taxes are applied to all entities or individuals based on the amount of certain taxes that they have paid, for example, enterprises income tax or city construction and maintenance tax. It is to raise capital for environmental protection. The improved environment can be regarded as a kind of public good and the benefits are prevalent. Therefore, government can impose such taxes on beneficiaries who benefit from the improving of environment.

[102]   *Id.*

[103]   *Id.*; *see also* C.Y. Wang, Chinese Soc'y for Envtl. Econ., Take-off of the Environmental Taxes in China from 2008 (2008) (in Chinese), *available at* http://www.csfee.org.cn/ReadNews.asp?NewsID=24; *see also* Lu, *supra* note 8, at 329–32.

[104]   For example, see Guan, *supra* note 8, at 190–91; *see also* Gao et al., *Modes and Legislative Concerns of Establishing an Environmental Taxation System in China* (in Chinese), 1 Taxation Research 36–40 (2010); H.S. Fu & L.W. Yu, *A Legal Analysis of Enacting Environmental Taxes in China* (in Chinese), J. Nanchang U. Human. and Soc. Sci. Ed. 69–72, 77; and Peng, *supra* note 90.

[105]   *See* Wang et al., *supra* note 8.

on pollution goods, a carbon tax on fuel products and a polluting products tax on items like ozone-depleting substances.[106] At the beginning stage, the tax system can focus on major pollution goods and polluting activities in order to reduce public resistance and facilitate administration, but the scope should be expanded gradually[107] by a clear agenda announced well in advance.

Imposition of any new system needs to mesh with the existing environmentally related taxes and charges.[108] For example, if carbon tax is to apply to fuel products, a consumption tax on fuels would not be needed. Resource tax can be moved into the category of environmental taxes. Some pollution charges can be converted into pollution taxes. However, not all types of environmentally related charges are suitable for mutation.[109] One reason is that the collection of certain charges requires specific technology and professional expertise for monitoring pollutants, which would place a heavy burden on tax administration agencies.[110] The charge-to-tax reform also entails significant work on how to distribute responsibilities and budgets among governmental agencies.[111] Some studies suggest that the coexistence of a tax and charge system may be necessary, at least in the transitional period.[112]

There has also been detailed research on the design of environmental tax incentives and policies,[113] greening of other taxes,[114] and imposition of a carbon tax[115] or other specific environmental taxes in China.[116]

Issues about tax administration equally attract attention. It is argued that, although environmental taxes are best administered centrally,[117] certain autonomous power needs to be given to local governments in order to suit local conditions.[118] Environmental tax revenues can be split between the central government and local governments, with more revenues and responsibilities assigned to the local.[119] Public acceptance is vital for introducing the new tax category, which can be encouraged by extensive education programs and other administrative and economic methods.[120]

---

[106]   *See* Gao et al., *supra* note 104; *see also* Li, *supra* note 8, at 282–83.
[107]   *See* Gao et al., *supra* note 104.
[108]   *See* Chen, *supra* note 8, at 221–25; *see also* Gao et al., *supra* note 104.
[109]   *See* Qin & Chen, *supra* note 51; *see also* Li, *supra* note 8, at 314–17; Gao et al., *supra* note 104.
[110]   *Id.*
[111]   *See* Wang & Zhou, *supra* note 9, at 584; *see also* Y. Hong & H.B. Luo, *Aim and Design of China's Environmental Taxes* (in Chinese), 8 TAXATION RESEARCH 51–54 (2008).
[112]   *See* Qin & Chen, *supra* note 51, at 566–68.
[113]   *See* Z.J. Deng & Y. Han, *Designing Environmental Taxes to Promote Circular Economy* (in Chinese), 3 TAXATION RESEARCH 7–12 (2008); *see also* Fu & Yu, *supra* note 104; Guan, *supra* note 8, at 196–204; CCICED Report, *supra* note 9.
[114]   *See* Li, *supra* note 8, at 317–28.
[115]   *See* M. Su et al., *Studies on the Imposition of Carbon Tax in China and 'Related Issues'*, 72 REV. ECON/RESEARCH 2–28 (2009); *see also* Y. Yang & J. Tu, *Abroad Experience of Carbon Tax and Lessons for China* (in Chinese), 1 INT'L TAXATION IN CHINA 41–44; CCICD, *supra* note 9; R.N. COOPER CLIMATE POLICY CENTER, A CARBON TAX IN CHINA? (2004).
[116]   *See*, for example, Li, *supra* note 8, at 286–93.
[117]   *See*, *e.g.*, Gao et al., *supra* note 104; Hong & Luo, *supra* note 111.
[118]   *See* Chen, *supra* note 9, at 227–28.
[119]   Gao et al, *supra* note 104.
[120]   *See* Peng, *supra* note 90; *see also* Wang et al., *supra* note 9, at 101.

CONCLUSION

Environmental taxes in a strict sense have not been applied in China, though an environmentally related tax and charge system has existed in China for some time. The current tax and charge system is, above all, a revenue-generating device, not a set of environmental policy instruments, and therefore its effect on lowering negative externalities and achieving economic gain is limited.

Taxation reform and pricing reform of major energy resources have taken place in recent decades in China. Although coal and crude oil prices are now completely linked with the international market, the pricing of electricity and oil products remains controlled by the government.[121] The questions of how to transit further to a market mechanism and how to efficiently apply environmental taxes in countries with price regulations deserve serious research. Given the urgent need to meet emissions reduction targets and realize China's long-term development interests, the central government intends to increase the role of taxation as an efficient market-based instrument to supplement regulation. An independent environmental taxation system is likely to be introduced in China in the foreseeable future.

Although there are various proposals for how to apply environmental taxes in China, more comprehensive and detailed research is needed. Introducing a new tax category in so large a country as China will involve numerous technical, economic, legal and administrative difficulties. However, greening China's tax regime by applying an independent environmental taxation system will be conducive to the sustainable development of the country—and the world.

---

[121]   CHINA COUNCIL FOR INT'L COOPERATION ON ENV'T AND DEV. TASK FORCE, ASSESSMENT ON CURRENT POLICIES FOR ENERGY PRODUCTIVITY IN CHINA (2008).

18 A review of selected databases on market-based instruments

*Hans Vos**

A wide variety of audiences can benefit from access to information about environmental taxation instruments and other market-based instruments (MBI) that are operating around the world. This chapter explores the evolution of surveys of economic instruments and selected current databases. It offers criteria that can be used to evaluate and guide the development of databases and thoughts on the challenges of database design.

INTRODUCTION

In 1989 the Organisation for Economic Cooperation and Development (OECD) published an overview and assessment of the use of 'economic instruments for environmental protection,' based on case studies from six OECD member countries.[1] This was one of the first attempts to obtain a more comprehensive overview of the role of environmental taxes and other market-based instruments (MBI) and of what they achieve. The report concludes with five research recommendations, three of which concern the need for collecting more data. Data are lacking with regard to, among other things, the actual implementation of these instruments and changes therein, the variables that influence MBI and that are influenced by MBI, and (changing) policy contexts. The report ends with an appeal to prepare an update of its content in 'five or ten years' and to continually collect relevant information to fuel such a new appraisal.[2]

OECD's pioneering role in creating a broader knowledge of MBI is further accentuated by OECD's publications on how such instruments should be applied[3] and how they should be evaluated for their environmental effectiveness and their economic efficiency.[4] The latter report makes very clear how heavy the data requirements are for a correct evaluation, and that an assessment of the counterfactual ('What would have happened otherwise?') should be included.

The more prominently MBI feature in environmental policymaking, the louder the calls

---

* The author worked at the European Environment Agency when writing this chapter. This contribution has been written on a personal title, and represents his opinion alone.
[1] OECD, Economic Instruments for Environmental Protection (1989). The six countries were France, Germany, Italy, the Netherlands, Sweden and the United States. For eight more countries information was received through questionnaires.
[2] Two updates have been published: OECD, Managing the Environment: the Role of Economic Instruments (1994); OECD, Economic Instruments for Pollution Control and Natural Resources Management in OECD Countries: A Survey (1999).
[3] OECD, Environmental Policy: How to Apply Economic Instruments (1991).
[4] OECD, Evaluating Economic Instruments for Environmental Policy (1997).

for 'data' sound. How will instruments in the pipeline perform? Under what conditions will they perform as expected? Will instruments operated in one country work similarly in another country? Have implemented instruments played the role they were expected to play? There is a vast literature describing ex ante and ex post assessments of MBI. The data sections in these publications always play a prominent part, listing the data sources but also the simplifications needed and assumptions made to get the assessment model running. Politically, international policy learning may help improve the potential of MBI through mutual exchange of data. For example, the ENVECO group of environmental economic experts regularly meeting under the auspices of the European Commission's Directorates-General for the Environment and for Economic and Financial Affairs frequently exchanges such information.

In its Green Paper on MBI (published in 2007),[5] the European Commission states: 'There may be scope to improve the structured exchange of information between Member States on their best practices in the area of MBI in general and environmental tax reform in particular. While specialised structures exist in some areas there is no horizontal forum available. In this respect, one option could be the establishment of an MBI Forum.'

Recently the European Commission published a proposal for a regulation on European environmental economic accounts.[6] The proposal includes setting up an account module for environmentally related taxes organized by economic activities (government, corporations and households). This regulation could provide an important motivation for the collection of relevant MBI data.

Clearly, data requests vary according to their purpose. One can distinguish three levels, moving from light to heavy data needs:

- Informative: general description of an MBI for general information, for instance to inform government officials about the existence of a scheme.
- Descriptive: detailed description of an MBI to inform officials and analysts, for instance to support policy preparation.
- Analytical: detailed description supported by quantitative data to allow for empirical analysis, to support both policy preparation and policy evaluation.

Data collections may generally be expected to attempt to be descriptive and to serve analytical purposes.

In response to data requests, initiatives to develop data collections have sprung up around the world. This chapter does not intend to present a full overview of these systems. It will select a few systems, based on the author's European-focused experience, and describe their main characteristics in an attempt to assess whether and to what extent they meet these data requests and other criteria of usability and accessibility. It will not go so far as to rank databases according to their quality.

---

[5]   *Commission Green Paper on Market-Based Instruments for Environment and Related Policy Purposes*, at 5, COM (2007) 140 final (Mar. 28, 2007).
[6]   *Commission Proposal for a Regulation of the European Parliament and of the Council on European Environmental Economic Accounts*, COM (22010) 132 final (Apr. 9, 2010).

Environmental taxes are commonly seen as one tool out of a range of instruments of environmental policy that have in common their use of the market. Data collections either contain solely environmental taxes or deal with them as one of a broader group. Since policy instruments seldom work in isolation, an indication in such data collections of the policy environment in which they feature would be useful.

Data collections exist in many forms. Only a few could be characterized as true databases according to common definitions,[7] but some of the earlier data collections on MBI that do not comply with the criteria of common definitions have had an important role in setting up MBI data services. We will therefore not concern ourselves only with formal criteria. The assessment criteria developed later in this chapter will be applicable in full to only a few of such data collections.

The remainder of this chapter is organized as follows: It first deals with databases (data collections) providing information on MBI. Some will be taken for further analysis. It appears that databases providing a full range of MBI do not exist in multitude. Databases providing information on government support seem to have a majority share in the total population. In the next section, the chapter further specifies several criteria for such collections in order to serve the several kinds of data requests that are made for retrieval. Then, it assesses the selected data collections against the formulated criteria and suggests their usefulness for varied data requests. In the final section, it offers conclusions and recommendations.

DATABASES

OECD's inventory reports of the use of MBI in the OECD area, described above, can be considered as early data collections that could be labeled as 'descriptive,' given that they contain an incomplete overview of instrument details, purpose and significance. Evidence of their effectiveness has been meager, although it does increase from the first to the third inventory.[8]

The European Environment Agency published a triad of MBI reports from 1996 through 2005.[9] They broaden in scope from environmental taxes in the European Union (1996) to market-based instruments in the wider European area (2005).

These six OECD and EEA publications, spanning the period 1989 through 2005, appear to evolve from inventory-based reports to more assessment-focused reports. The 1989 OECD report aimed to come up with a first inventory of instruments in play and contains very little impact assessment, whereas the 2005 EEA report is focused on

---

[7]   For example, according to the EEA Glossary, a 'database' is 'a computerized compilation of data, facts and records that is organized for convenient access, management and updating.' *See* EEA Multilingual Environmental Glossary, ENVTL. TERMINOLOGY & DISCOVERY SERV., EUROPEAN ENV'T AGENCY, http://glossary.eea.europa.eu/EEAGlossary/.

[8]   OECD, MANAGING THE ENVIRONMENT (1999), *supra* note 2.

[9]   EUROPEAN ENVT. AGENCY, ENVIRONMENTAL TAXES—IMPLEMENTATION AND ENVIRONMENTAL EFFECTIVENESS (1996); EUROPEAN ENVT. AGENCY, ENVIRONMENTAL TAXES—RECENT DEVELOPMENTS IN TOOLS FOR INTEGRATION (2000); EUROPEAN ENVT. AGENCY, MARKET-BASED INSTRUMENTS FOR ENVIRONMENTAL POLICY IN EUROPE (2005).

instrument performance and has very little detailed description of individual MBI. It signaled the emergence of other data collections developed in the meantime, giving its authors the opportunity to focus on answering increasingly pressing policy questions on what MBI actually achieve and under what conditions. The 1999 OECD inventory formed the basis for populating the database that OECD, in collaboration originally with the European Commission and later with the European Environment Agency, started to develop in 1997.

Two pioneering data collections not presently maintained provided an early overview of MBI (basically taxes and charges) in a large part of Europe. The first, set up by the University of Keele in 1997 and commissioned by the European Commission, was the database on environmental taxes in EU Member States plus Norway and Switzerland, which covered 17 countries.[10] This data collection was maintained and regularly updated up to the year 2000.

The second data collection, built under the Sofia initiative on economic instruments, was the database on environmental taxes and charges, covering 14 countries in Central and Eastern Europe.[11] The last update of this database occurred in 1999.

The data collections mentioned so far cover Europe and the OECD area, but there are numerous publications covering the use of MBI in environmental and sustainable development policies in other parts of the world. In particular the World Bank and the OECD have published a number of reports on MBI in areas such as Eastern Europe, the Caucasus and Central Asia,[12] China,[13] Latin America[14] and Africa.[15] There are also data collections in the OECD area that store and provide data on financial support for environmentally related activities. Two examples include the Queensland (Australia) national resources management incentives database[16] and the US federal database of state incentives for renewables and efficiency.[17] We will include the latter in the review.

---

[10]   P. EKINS & S. SPECK, EDS., DATABASE ON ENVIRONMENTAL TAXES IN EU MEMBER STATES PLUS NORWAY AND SWITZERLAND 1997–2000 (2001).

[11]   *See* Database on Environmental Taxes and Charges, REGIONAL ENVTL. CTR. FOR CENTRAL & EASTERN EUROPE, http://archive.rec.org/REC/Programs/SofiaInitiatives/EcoInstruments/ Database/SIEI_database.html. *See also* J. KLARER ET AL., SOURCEBOOK ON ECONOMIC INSTRUMENTS FOR ENVIRONMENTAL POLICY IN CENTRAL AND EASTERN EUROPE (1999).

[12]   OECD, THE USE OF ECONOMIC INSTRUMENTS FOR POLLUTION CONTROL AND NATURAL RESOURCE MANAGEMENT IN EECCA (2003), http://www.oecd.org/dataoecd/37/18/26732337.pdf.

[13]   OECD, APPLYING MARKET-BASED INSTRUMENTS TO ENVIRONMENTAL POLICIES IN CHINA AND OECD COUNTRIES (1998).

[14]   R. Huber et al., *Market Based Instruments for Environmental Policymaking in Latin America and the Caribbean: Lessons from Eleven Countries* (World Bank Discussion Paper No. 381, 1998), http://www.bvsde.paho.org/acrobat/market2.pdf.

[15]   T. Panayotou, *Economic Instruments for Environmental Management and Sustainable Development*, (United Nations Env't Programme, Envt'l Econ. Series Paper No. 16, 1994), http://classwebs.spea.indiana.edu/kenricha/Classes/V600/Spring%202009%20Class%20Readings/ Frameworks/panyouto_econ_instru.pdf.

[16]   Natural Resource Management Incentives Database, STATE OF QUEENSLAND, http://www. regionalnrm.qld.gov.au/get_involved/incentives/.

[17]   Database of State Incentives for Renewables & Efficiency, DSIRE, http://www.dsireusa. org/.

A somewhat different form of data collection is provided by annual reports, most often on single instrument schemes. Examples include the IEA/OECD periodical on energy taxes and prices[18] and the regular publication of energy excise tables by the European Commission.[19]

In this chapter we will review five data collections that can be considered to be databases:

1) The OECD/EEA database of instruments used in environmental policy and natural resources management;[20]
2) Economicinstruments.com—Economic instruments in environmental policy, University College Dublin;[21]
3) Environmental fiscal reform database, FÖS Green Budget Germany;[22]
4) Taxes in Europe database, European Commission Taxation and Customs Union;[23] and
5) US federal database of state incentives for renewables and efficiency.[24]

This quintet is not the result of a formal selection procedure. The purpose of this chapter is to review a few databases with a fairly wide geographical coverage and assess them against a set of criteria that will be discussed in the next section.

Table 18.1 provides an overview of some characteristics of these databases. A short description of these data collections is included in the section on Performance of Databases later in the chapter.

REQUIREMENTS OF DATABASES

Literature from the field of environmental valuation offers some insights into criteria for reviewing MBI databases. McComb et al. (2006)[25] assess a couple of the most important valuation databases, which store the results of primary research of nonmarket values of environmental goods and services. The assessed data collections all state more or

---

[18] IEA Energy Prices and Taxes Statistics, OECD, http://data.iea.org/ieastore/product.asp?dept_id=101&pf_id=401.

[19] Taxation and Customs Union of the European Comm'n, Excise Duty Tables (July 2011), http://ec.europa.eu/taxation_customs/taxation/excise_duties/energy_products/rates/index_en.htm.

[20] Database on Instruments Used for Environmental Policy and Natural Resources Management, OECD & European Env't Agency, http://www2.oecd.org/ecoinst/queries/.

[21] Economic Instruments in Environmental Policy, economicinstruments.com, http://www.economicinstruments.com/index.php/home.

[22] Forum Ökologisch-Soziale Marktwirtschaft, FÖS Green Budget Germany, http://www.foes.de/themen/oekologische-steuerreform-1999-2003/eu-datenbank/?lang=en.

[23] Taxes in Europe Database, Taxation and Customs Union of the European Comm'n, http://ec.europa.eu/taxation_customs/taxation/gen_info/info_docs/tax_inventory/index_en.htm.

[24] Database of State Incentives for Renewables & Efficiency, DSIRE, http://www.dsireusa.org/.

[25] G. McComb et al., *International Valuation Databases: Overview, Methods and Operational Issues*, 60 Ecological Econ. 461–72 (2006).

Table 18.1 Some characteristics of selected data collections

Name	Purpose/target group	Scope	Geographic coverage	Web access; free of charge	Administrator
OECD/EEA database on instruments used in environmental policy and natural resources management	Not mentioned	Broad; environment	OECD + EEA + 3 other countries; 49 countries in total	√	OECD/EEA
Economicinstruments.com	'The objective of the site is to present, in a non-technical fashion, information on the practical use of economic instruments in environmental policy. It is envisaged that the site will be of interest to policymakers, members of the public, academics and students.'	Broad; environment	Not mentioned	√	University College Dublin
Ecological reform database	Not mentioned	Environmental taxes	EU-25 + Switzerland and Norway	√	FÖS Green Budget Europe
Taxes in Europe database	'This information tool is "user friendly" and "citizen-oriented." It gives citizens, business, tax professionals, researchers and the press direct access to information that was until today only available piecemeal.'	General taxation, including environmental taxes	EU-27	√	EC Taxation and Customs Union
Federal database of state incentives for renewables and efficiency (DSIRE)	Not mentioned	Financial aid; energy	USA	√	North Carolina State University

less explicitly their purpose: to provide primary data for benefit transfer.[26] The authors evaluate how the databases perform in facilitating benefit transfers in a hypothetical case, which can be seen as an effectiveness test.

Lantz and Slaney (2005)[27] present a set of quality criteria for valuation databases. They discern two main groups of criteria, ease of use, and content, each of which contains several elements. 'Ease of use' is broken down into usability and accessibility, while 'content' relates to the purpose of valuation databases: to facilitate benefit (function) transfer and to provide a bibliography of studies for researchers, teachers and government officials. All of these elements are further specified by means of indicators. For ease of use, indicators include searching capabilities and the presence of a help file or tutorial (usability), and ease in finding and accessing the database, and user costs (accessibility). The content indicators largely relate to the specific purpose of valuation databases, namely facilitating benefit transfer. The bibliography element indicators include the number of studies and datedness.

We will adapt Lantz and Slaney's set of criteria for our review of selected MBI databases. Where the valuation databases generally clearly state their purpose, the databases in this review mostly do not. Interestingly, only one of the five databases in this review has explicitly stated its purpose on its website (http://www.economicinstruments.com). The other four data collections mention why they have been constructed ('to provide data . . .') but are silent about their views on the contexts in which the data could be used. We will however suggest content-related criteria along the lines of the general functions of MBI data collections introduced earlier, and will attempt to label the databases accordingly: informative, descriptive and analysis-facilitative. As regards the 'bibliographic' element, we look to the number of MBI schemes and datedness, and we add the element of reliability.

The 'ease of use' criteria we will use are ease of navigation, help function, search options (custom search or predefined querying) and reporting options; those for accessibility are ease of finding the database and ease of accessing it. We note that all databases in the review can be accessed free of charge, hence there is no need to include a cost criterion. Table 18.2 provides an overview of the criteria, followed by a brief discussion of these criteria.

Content/Type of Purpose

Reviewing data collections against qualitative criteria is obviously a somewhat subjective undertaking. The purpose criteria of informative, descriptive and analytical may jointly or severally apply to the data collections under review. Neither is there a sharp distinction

---

[26] Benefit transfer—or value transfer, as it is applicable to costs as well—concerns the practice of using values of environmental goods and services from primary research for the appraisal of cases with comparable attributes. See for a concise introduction to the issue: EUROPEAN ENV'T AGENCY, SCALING UP ECOSYSTEM BENEFITS—A CONTRIBUTION TO THE ECONOMICS OF ECOYSTSTEMS AND BIODIVERSITY (TEEB) STUDY (2010).

[27] V. Lantz & G. Slaney, *An Evaluation of Environmental Valuation Databases around the World, in* BENEFITS TRANSFER AND INTERNATIONAL VALUATION DATABASES: ARE WE HEADING IN THE RIGHT DIRECTION? (Abt Associates, Inc. eds., 2005).

Table 18.2   Criteria tree for reviewing MBI databases and short descriptions

Content	Type of purpose	Informative	General description to inform government officials
		Descriptive	Detailed description to inform policy analysts
		Analytical	Quantitative data to facilitate empirical analysis
	'Bibliography'	Number of schemes	(not relevant because of differences of scale)
		Datedness	
	Reliability	Correctness of data	
Ease of use	Usability	Ease of navigation	Number of steps to get results
		Help function	Q&A; tutorial
		Search options	Custom search; predefined queries
		Reporting options	Fixed or adaptable formats: spreadsheets
	Accessibility	Ease of finding	Prominence in web search
		Ease of accessing	Usability without help

among the three adjectives. Moreover, any of these may be intertwined with one or more of the other criteria. When, for example, a government official wants an update of the MBI in his policy area, he will want it quickly (usability without help), and he will want it to be topical (datedness) and reliable (correct), and all in a concise report (reporting options), provided he doesn't leave the data search to a policy analyst. A policy analyst probably will want more detail in the context of a broader view on MBI, perhaps in a historical context and across borders (scope and geographical coverage). A researcher may look for hard data, probably in time series.

Content/'Bibliography'

The number of schemes obviously cannot be used as a quality criterion, because this depends on the geographical coverage of the database. This 'bibliography' criterion hints, though, at another more important aspect of databases: their completeness. Evaluating this aspect goes beyond the scope of this chapter, and is difficult in any case. Databases are what one consults to get an overview, in particular where policy competence is fragmented. There is an element of reliability connected to completeness apart from the correctness of the data: can we trust that all schemes are included? This may be more of a concern for government officials and policy analysts than for researchers who may concentrate on one scheme or a small set, and who will usually need to check and top up their data from other sources anyway.

For example, Persson[28] uses the OECD/EEA database to draw up a list of instruments

---

[28]   A.M. Persson, Choosing Environmental Policy Instruments: Case Studies of Municipal Waste Policy in Sweden and England (Sept. 2007) (unpublished Ph.D. dissertation, London School of Economics), http://sei-international.org/mediamanager/documents/Publications/Policy-institutions/PhD_thesis_Asa_Persson.pdf.

in Sweden and England in a comparative waste management study and found it incomplete after checking it against other sources. Bräuer et al.[29] use the same database in a review of instruments for preserving biodiversity in Europe. They warn against possible biases in the way countries enter information in the database, observing that many countries in the EU apply agri-environmental schemes without having those schemes stored.

Datedness requires precise registration. The usual information on a website indicating when the latest update occurred may not be relevant. What exactly has been updated—data, or just layout? Nor will a general indication of the latest update of the data in the database be sufficient. Have all schemes been updated, or only a selection? Checking individual schemes may also not be reliable. For example, a tax rate dated 2008 may still be relevant in 2010, or may be out of date because the rate is being adapted every year.

Box 18.1 shows a little experiment wherein the updating of a single scheme (waste tax in the Netherlands) was checked in four of the five databases under review.

Content/Reliability

The reliability criterion, which evaluates the 'correctness of data,' relates closely to how the database is managed and where the data come from. Proper quality assurance and reliable sources may be expected as a minimum but do not guarantee 100 percent reliability. Sources may vary, from government institutions to interested individuals. Quality assurance can be done under the aegis of a formal platform, by the managers of the database or by the concerned community itself (wiki form).

Ease of Use/Usability

Criteria include ease of navigation (for instance the number of steps necessary to get results, or the availability of hyperlinks), availability of forms of help (Q&A, tutorial, pop-up information), search options (custom search, predefined queries) and reporting options (fixed or adaptable formats, ease of data processing). This is probably a decisive criterion for the success of a database. A first-time visitor not able to find what he looks for (even though it may be there somewhere) will probably not return. The layout and functioning of the home page of the database therefore are a crucial element, as they represent the entrance to the stored information. Ideally the home page should contain links to everything the database has in store to accommodate the diversity of the visitors' demands: for example MBI by type, by theme, by country or by year. As regards help options, the website should be self-evident to the greatest extent possible. Easily available information on definitions (firstly of the several MBI themselves) will help to make clear what the data actually mean.

The search and reporting options of a database further define a database's ease of use. Well-developed options streamline the search. Making quantitative data directly downloadable in a spreadsheet helps to simplify and quicken a session, which is helpful when an analyst needs many sessions for his or her work.

---

[29]　I. Bräuer et al., *The Use of Market Incentives to Preserve Biodiversity* (Ecologic, Jul. 2006), http://ec.europa.eu/environment/enveco/biodiversity/pdf/mbi.pdf.

BOX 18.1   DATEDNESS OF THE RATES OF THE DUTCH
WASTE TAX: FOUR DATABASES COMPARED

The Netherlands introduced a waste tax in 1995 with the aim to divert waste from landfills. The tax is levied on the owner of a waste site and has a nil tax rate when waste is incinerated. The tax has been adapted every year since the start of the scheme and has increased from €13.25 in 1995 to €108.13 in 2011, per ton of waste.

The author twice checked the tax rate of this scheme in four databases, first in August 2008, then in March 2012. The results are presented in the table. Rates are in €/ton.

Database	Rate found 8/2008	Is rate of	Rate found 3/2012	Actual rate 2011[1]
OECD/EEA	85.54	2006	85.54	108.13
Economicinstruments.com	64.28	2000	64.28	108.13
Ecological reform database	78.81	2002	78.81	108.13
Taxes in Europe database	88.21	2008	108.13	108.13

Only the Taxes in Europe database was fully up-to-date both in mid-2008 and in mid-2011 as regards the rate of the Dutch tax on waste. The OECD/EEA database is an example of partial updating. The website indicated a last update for the Netherlands in March 2010, although it offers the caveat that 'Most of the information has been updated.' The other two databases have probably not updated this particular information after having stored the scheme for the first time.

Note: [1] The waste tax has been abolished as per 01.01.2012. This is mentioned in the Taxes in Europe database.

Ease of Use/Accessibility

We will test the ease of finding the reviewed databases in the largest search engine on the Internet (Google) against several search questions. Assessing ease of use without help is a somewhat subjective determination that may work out differently for different visitors depending on their exact questions and their prior experience in working with databases in general.

PERFORMANCES OF DATABASES AGAINST SOME CRITERIA

We take the databases under review in this chapter one by one and confront them with the criteria developed in the preceding section. We do this in a narrative form rather than taking the criteria of Table 18.2 one by one. Assessing the databases against the 'type of purpose' criterion is done by way of a conclusion after the review of the other criteria.

OECD/EEA Database on Instruments Used in Environmental Policy and Natural Resources Management

This database was established in 1997 by the OECD in collaboration with the European Commission. In 2002 the European Environment Agency joined in this work and added to the database information on 13 European countries that were not OECD member countries. On line since 2003, the database contains environmental taxes and charges, emissions trading instruments, environmentally motivated subsidies, deposit-refund systems, and voluntary or industry agreements. Today it covers 49 countries.

The home page does not mention the purpose of the database, but states that it provides information on market-based instruments including voluntary approaches in the OECD and EEA member countries (as indicated in Table 18.1).[30] It explains what has been stored and how it can be found. The evident search option is a list of (predefined) queries available further down the home page but navigable via a link in the first window. The queries give different forms of access to the information.

The first option is retrieval of all information for a specific instrument, which is done via a pull-down menu to select a country, which in turn produces a list of all instruments for that country. Selecting a specific scheme then provides all available general information (on name, country, year of introduction, governing aspects, contact options and so on) and specific information that differs according to the type of instrument one has selected. The result is a long list of all possible aspects and characteristics of the selected scheme, which requires some studying to pin down the single detail one may be interested in. This query is clearly meant to present everything the database has in store for that specific instrument; other predefined queries give access to details in a better-ordered way.

The second option provides two pull-down menus of economic activities, one for economic production sectors and one for household expenditure categories. The economic sectors list follows the UN's ISIC Rev 3.1 classification,[31] and the household list follows the UN's COICOP classification.[32] Selecting any of these categories provides a list of MBI that are related to that economic activity. This is a unique facility that is meant to accommodate research on the role that market-based instruments may play in affecting the economy in a more sustainable way. However, the list does not provide URLs as a shortcut to the instruments' information.

The third option is a list of predefined queries giving access to several aspects of the stored instruments, either to general information on instruments by domain (eight environmental, three economic), or to specific characteristics by type of instrument

---

[30]   The database's name (. . . database on instruments used . . .) suggests it also provides information on other environmental policy tools (of a direct regulation type), but the home page does not confirm that, nor are there predefined queries pointing to that category.

[31]   UNITED NATIONS STATISTICS DIVISION, INTERNATIONAL STANDARD INDUSTRIAL CLASSIFICATION OF ALL ECONOMIC ACTIVITIES, REVISION 3.1 (2002), *available at* http://unstats. un.org/unsd/cr/registry/regcst.asp?Cl=17.

[32]   UNITED NATIONS STATISTICS DIVISION, CLASSIFICATION OF INDIVIDUAL CONSUMPTION ACCORDING TO PURPOSE (2002), *available at* http://unstats.un.org/unsd/class/family/family2. asp?Cl=5.

(environmentally related taxes, fees, charges; tradable permit systems; deposit-refund systems; environmentally motivated subsidies; voluntary approaches). Clicking on any of these options leads the user to a flag page for choosing a country or group of countries for which that information is requested. Countries are also pre-grouped: one can choose all countries, or countries according to their membership in the OECD, the EEA or the European Union. The flags are arranged in two groups: OECD countries and EEA countries that are not OECD members. Knowing the membership situation of a single country may make selecting it easier. If this information is not known, an alphabetic order would be more convenient.

All queries produce information for all schemes of the selected instrument for the selected country. A further zooming in is not possible. The data are provided in a table format that can be converted to a spreadsheet as well, which is convenient for numerical data. This makes processing data of tax revenues easy, for example, but the data for the tax rates is put in cells in the text format, as it also contains information on such things as the exact tax base, dimensions, or pay period. This precludes arithmetic handling. Financial information is presented in local currencies, and in Euros (tax rates), or in US dollars (revenues). It is not immediately clear which exchange rates have been used. The first window of the home page contains a link to a table of bloc-memberships of the countries, which provides the exchange rate of the local currencies to the Euro for one specific year in line with the most recent general update, but not all information has been updated to that same year. That is somewhat problematic for floating rates such as those for the US dollar and the British pound.

The home page also provides links to a couple of reports that clarify and process information from the database, in particular for taxes: definitions of taxes, charges and fees, and tax revenue; comparisons of tax rates over time; and CO_2 tax differentiations for motor vehicles, with time series information in graphs. This is very useful information in empirical research. Clicking the tax revenues graph produces a table with countries in rows and years in columns (1994–2007). Copying and pasting this data into a spreadsheet puts all of the information in a single column, which makes processing very awkward if not impossible.

This database contains numerous instrument schemes, the exact number of which is not known. This makes the database a rich source of information, although its value to specific groups of users depends on datedness, correctness and ease of use.

Box 18.1 indicated the relative value of information on general updates. For example, despite a general update of information for the Netherlands by 31 January 2012, most energy and transport tax rates and many other taxes are not up to date, and there is no clear indication of the year of validity.

Another prerequisite for reliability is the correctness of the data. The website provides some information on the process of acquiring and managing information before it is stored, in particular when the database was populated for the first time. The information was sent to the OECD's Environment Policy Committee's Working Party on National Environmental Policy and the EEA's National Focal Points (non-OECD countries) for verification, update and completion. Yearly updates can be introduced online, but are checked by the database managers before publication.

The website is easily navigable. Finding the data is straightforward. The home page explains how everything works, and a further help facility is not missed. A button to return to the home page from the top of each web page would further increase ease of navigation.

The ease of navigation also brings a certain lack of search and reporting options. The only custom search option available is the two-step selection of all information for a specific country and a specific scheme. A further narrowing down of required information would greatly enhance the database's usefulness but this is not yet possible because of the format of the stored data. Likewise, a more dedicated reporting facility including numerical data retrieval options would improve its utility.

The absence of such options is felt most for those MBI schemes that include numerous sub-schemes, for instance in the area of transport taxes. The German motor vehicle tax counts 78 separate sub-schemes due to the way the tax is calculated. The Danish motor vehicle weight tax counts 213 different sub-schemes. None of the numerical data (tax rates) of these schemes can be arithmetically processed.

The database is quickly found in a Google search. Searching with 'database economic instruments environmental policy' returns the link to the database as the first item on the first page with search results. The search term 'database market based instruments' does not provide the exact link in the first three pages, but a number of websites are returned that include the link or the reference to the database, with the European Commission's DG Environment web page on environmental economics at the top of the page.

To conclude, the database has limited options for searching and reporting its wealth of information. The datedness of the information is variable, rendering the database partially incomplete as seen from the perspective of time. The discerned purpose of the database may be characterized as descriptive rather than informative, with elements that will serve analysts.

Economicinstruments.com[33]

'Information ... in a non-technical sense on the practical use ... of interest to policy makers, members of the public, academics and students.' These elements of the stated purpose of this database, established in 2000, indicate on the home page that its goal is to serve a broad informative purpose and to provide descriptions and data for analysis.

The home page provides in one window a transparent overview of the database's possibilities. Although the text suggests options for searching the database by environmental theme, instrument, country and sector, links are provided only for environmental themes. The theme links provide lists of instruments with links to entries (called 'articles') describing the instrument in more or less exhaustive form.

A general search box on the home page provides alternative search options. However, the search query 'air quality,' for instance, returns only six instruments, whereas clicking 'air quality' returns a long list of schemes. Hence using the search box does not seem to assure a full list of instruments.

---

[33]   Personal communication in August 2010 with the database manager, Dr. Louise Dunn (UCD), revealed that the database is under reconstruction, but that nevertheless new information continues to be included when it arrives.

Articles on individual instruments offer the option of leaving a comment. After acquiring a username and password users can log in, the only advantage of which seems to be a marginally quicker procedure for leaving a comment. A nice feature of these articles is the possibility of sharing its content with a number of scientific or social communities, including Facebook.

The home page furthermore contains small lists of the most viewed, most recent and highest-rated articles. It also contains a link to a Frequently Asked Questions (FAQ) page that appears to be in a testing phase. Extra help for navigation however hardly seems necessary.

The datedness of the information is difficult to assess. The homepage mentions a last update in January 2011.[34] All (or almost all) entries seem to have been posted within a very restricted time window (June 2008). There are however entries in the database up to 2010. Most if not all entries do not provide information on any updates. Glancing through the articles leaves the impression (although certainly not an evidentiary conclusion) that they are seldom adapted to new information (see also Box 18.1). The database does not seem to be formally supervised, but is managed solely by the database administrator.

The database does not offer reporting options apart from simply printing the articles. Tables can be pasted into a spreadsheet, and data are processable when in numerical format.

Google finds the database easily with the search term 'database economic instruments environmental policy.' It appears in the first page of search results. The term 'database market based instruments' does not give a result within the first three pages. However, the second item on the first page, a website of the European Environment Agency, contains a link to this database.

To conclude, this database contains many articles that provide an in-depth description of MBI. These articles do not generally seem to be updated, nor does the database create the impression that it aims at completeness. The database could serve as a discussion platform, in particular for academics, policy analysts and the informed public. In its current state it does not seem to perform as such, as evidenced by the very small number of comments given on the articles and the lack of a central discussion page. The actual purpose could be described as informative or descriptive, keeping in mind the observation made regarding datedness.

The home page shows the actual number of visitors to the database at any given time, which varies between five and ten at any moment of the working day (Central European time).[35]

Environmental Fiscal Reform Database

This database is embedded in the website of FÖS Green Budget Germany, a nongovernmental organization. As regards its goals, the web page introducing the database simply

---

[34]   Last check 22 March 2012.
[35]   The author drafted this text in the summer of 2010 and visited the website frequently in late July and early August. Other periods of the year may show a larger number of visitors.

states that it provides information 'about ecotaxes and environmental fiscal reforms of all EU Member States.'[36] The web page mentions the database's sources, of which the OECD/EEA database seems the most important one.

The database is found after expanding 'Topics' and then 'Environmental tax reform' on the FÖS Green Budget Germany's home page, or with the help of the search box. A list of 25 EU member states appears, with links to short descriptions of the environmental taxation practices of each country. Many of these descriptions contain links to 'tax rates' and 'tax revenues.' Clicking the links returns tables with the indicated information. These tables have been copied from the OECD/EEA database.

The website does not give any indication of the datedness of the information. Box 18.1 above shows that the rate of the Dutch waste tax applied to the year 2002. As another example, the country description for Latvia mentions that the country increased its diesel tax from €154 to €246 before accession to the EU in 2004, in order to comply with the minimum EU standard. The table behind the link to 'tax rates,' however, indicates a diesel tax rate of €149. A clear indication of the lack of datedness is found in the tables for tax revenues, where the most recent year listed is 2002.

Whether this data collection is in fact a database in the sense of the definition in footnote 8 is questionable. The website explicitly points to the OECD/EEA database for further information. Due to limited options navigation is very easy. Apart from entry access via countries, no search options are available, nor are there reporting options other than printing what is presented.

The database is not found with the search term 'database economic instruments environmental policy' in the first three pages of Google results. Nor is it returned by Google when using 'database market based instruments.' Since the database does not pretend to cover a broad area of all instruments we have also used the terms 'database environmental taxes' and 'database environmental tax reform,' but with these too produced no results.

In summary, this data collection has an informative character and offers a useful introduction to the ways in which countries have dealt with environmental tax reform, although the lack of recent updates is a serious obstacle for wide use. The database does allow connection to Facebook.

Taxes in Europe Database

This database is 'the European Commission's on-line information tool covering the main taxes on consumption, labor and capital, including social security contributions, in use in the EU Member States.' These include the more important environmental taxes in terms of revenues, with a cut-off of 0.1 percent of GDP. The database however does contain a number of minor environmental taxes, provided in a separate file. The earliest overview of taxes in Europe is for 2007.

'This information tool is "user friendly" and "citizen-oriented." It gives citizens, business, tax professionals, researchers and the press direct access to information that was until today only available piecemeal.'[37] Hence its purpose is to inform a broad target

---

[36]   This was prior to the accession of Bulgaria and Romania.

[37]   Press Release, European Comm'n, Taxation in Europe: the European Commission Launches

group. Interestingly, policymakers are not explicitly mentioned, perhaps because the information is obtained from national authorities (basically the Ministries of Finance).

The home page of the database provides access to a web page with two search facilities: a simple search and an advanced search. The web page actually suggests a third facility, a historical search, but that option is meant to refine the use of the other two options.[38] Searching for 2007, for example, returns all records in the database for the active countries. This is the quickest way to get an overview of all taxes in a certain country or group of countries for the specified year.

The result of any search is a table of selected tax schemes that contains at least a document title, the year and the country for each scheme. A view/print button then gives access to the selected document. These documents contain a large number of data, such as the year of introduction, the tax base, authority, beneficiary, due date for payment, the legal base, the tax rate, its economic function and the revenues in a time series starting in 2000.

The advanced search option provides a custom search menu that allows selecting many combinations of records. Boolean operators and wild cards help to refine the search. It is however not possible to produce an overview of all environmental taxes in the database. A search for the three types of environmental taxes for 2010 (energy, transport, pollution/resources) produces a list of 120 schemes, but that list contains duplicates because three tax schemes belong to more than one types. The results of an advanced search can be exported to a spreadsheet. Arithmetic operations with the data are possible, as there are a few numerical fields. These include annual revenues, revenues as percentage of GDP and as a percentage of total tax revenues.

The datedness of the database is very good. Most schemes have been updated to 2012. Correctness of data is secured because they are provided by the relevant national authorities.

Finding your way in the database is quite simple, but the search options require some practice if you are not used to custom searching. A manual provides most of the answers, however. There is also a Q&A page explaining some of the (tax) terms. If all of the above fails, a question can be sent to the database administrators.

Google searches of the terms 'database economic instruments environmental policy' and 'database market based instruments' do not return any results in the first three pages, nor can references been found. The database is of relatively recent data and focuses on taxes only. A search for 'database environmental taxes' produces the website on the first page of Google results.

In conclusion, this database has two very strong qualities: its datedness and the reliability of its results. As only major taxes are included, many environmental taxes are missing, but the major schemes in terms of revenue-raising and economic impact—energy and transport taxes—are there. Revenues are presented in time series from 2000. Tax rates are available only from 2007 onward, but the history will grow with time. Tax rate time series need to be manually constructed due to the text fields used for

---

a New Online Information Tool on the Taxes in the Member States (May 11, 2011), http://europa.eu/rapid/pressReleasesAction.do?reference=IP/07/662.

[38]   In fact, the simple and advanced searches return no records if no year is indicated in the historical search box.

description. The database contains detailed descriptions and is a useful tool for analysis, and one that is improving.

Federal Database of State Incentives for Renewables and Efficiency (DSIRE)

This is not an environmental policy instrument database *sensu stricto*, but the objectives of the banked policy tools come close enough for it to be included. It is also the only fully non-European data collection in this assessment. The financial schemes regard federal, state and local incentives and are presented in a state-by-state way. The database also contains some non-financial incentives such as efficiency standards.

The home page of the database (using DSIRE as an acronym) presents as a first selection the option to search either for renewables or for efficiency incentives, or for both. Then there are several search options: a map of the US for selection of specific states, summary maps indicating which states apply selected incentive programs, and the initiators and summary tables that divide the data collection into four parts—financial and non-financial incentives for renewables and for efficiency—and return tables indicating which states apply which incentives, the number of schemes at what institutional level, and where they intervene.

There is a custom search option as well. Schemes can be selected according to the criteria of the eligible sector, the state, the technology, the implementing institution and the type of policy.

For each scheme information is available as indicated above, as are data on the amount of subsidy, the maximum amount, eligible technologies, the year of introduction and of expiration, and the legal base and authority.

There are no particular reporting formats available apart from the summary maps and tables.

The database provides a large number of schemes; its completeness cannot be checked. The home page features a disclaimer stating that the database presents an 'unofficial overview of financial incentives and other policies.' It also indicates that 'it should not be used as the only source of information.' The information is largely up to date, with most of the schemes updated to 2012. An extra feature is a list of schemes that have been added to the database or updated in the last two months.

For help, the homepage offers a Q&A section, covering many possible questions on the schemes and on the database.[39] There is little direct search help, but that is not missed, as the database functioning is rather self-evident.

As this database presents instruments for energy policy, the two to four search terms we have used for checking the ease of finding the other databases in this review do not work in this case. The term 'database economic instruments energy policy' has no result either. The term 'database incentives energy policy' shows the website as the second item on the first page of Google results.

In summary, DSIRE is a useful, up-to-date collection of financial schemes, and can be regarded as informative and descriptive.

---

[39] Including: 'How do you pronounce DSIRE?' Answer: 'We say "desire" but others have it pronounced much more creatively.'

DISCUSSION

We suggested above that different users of databases on market-based instruments may have different demands, ranging from light (informative) to heavy (data needs). In addition to easy access, all users will require up-to-date, reliable and complete information. In particular the datedness of information is a point of concern and attention for three out of the five databases discussed. Up-to-date information of course requires frequent maintenance, which may put a considerable burden on the owner. Easy access to sources may help keep data relevant. The performance of the small sample of databases discussed here does not suggest that one type of organization is better-suited to this task than other types. The two well-maintained databases are owned by a government organization (Taxes in Europe, owned by the European Commission) and a university, supported by a government grant (DSIRE, owned by the NCSU). The three databases for which maintenance is a concern are owned by (semi-)government organizations (the OECD/EEA database), a university (economicinstruments.com, owned by UCD) and an environmental nongovernmental organization (Environmental fiscal reform database, owned by FÖS).

Another issue in the demand for maintenance concerns the range of instruments included in the database. The broader the range of instruments in the database, the better it can function as a 'one-stop shop,' but the more time-consuming maintenance will be. Not only the range but also the type of instrument may determine the amount of work needed for the database to remain up to date. Environmental taxes, for example, are commonly embedded in the government's fiscal policy, updated and reported in the annual budget.

As regards tradable emission permits, the European Union Emissions Trading System (EUETS) has a full monitoring system based in legislation. Other (national) systems are not reported according to a central system.

Environmental subsidies are dispersed and are managed by national or local governments. At either level, environmentally relevant subsidies may be created by various ministries or departments as they can be found in the fields of the environment, energy conservation, transport and nature management, to mention four. Moreover, subsidies may not always fit in an annual cycle of (re)appraisal. Some have a fixed budget and cease when exhausted, while others may be abolished when overridden by other legislation.[40]

Another issue important to the lasting success of maintenance of a database is its being embedded in a proper institutional network. The European Commission has established a relationship with the national finance ministries, including annual reporting, to maintain its Taxes in Europe database that is restricted to fiscal taxes. That database also contains concise information (the name of the scheme only) on environmental charges, which are not commonly managed by national governments, and thus not so easy to come by. The OECD/EEA database receives its information from the national permanent representatives, who have a much broader task than delivering data on taxes and charges. Other administrators such as universities and NGOs will be dependent on a flow of information delivered by volunteers to top off information collected by its own staff.

---

[40] For example, temporary financial support for the sales of cleaner cars is removed when new legislation on more stringent standards is adopted.

There seem to be two conditions for a database's being able to live up to its overall promise of delivering timely, reliable, up-to-date and complete information, and at the same time limit the required work to manageable proportions. The first is knowing what users expect to find, and the second is defining a clear and practical purpose for the database, taking into account the desires of its clients, and sticking to that purpose. As regards clients' desires, to the author's knowledge no market research has ever been conducted to find that out. As regards the purpose of databases in this review, only two out of five have explicitly included theirs on their home pages.

Without a clear purpose and knowledge of their clients, database administrators tend to collect everything they can find about a particular instrument, instead of restricting themselves to information that clients appreciate most. One could speculate that researchers expect that a database on taxes will provide data on the tax base, rate, the target group, the exemptions and the revenues, preferably in long time series. They are probably less interested in institutional data on who governs the scheme at which government level and by which department exactly. Those who are interested in subsidy schemes may primarily be interested in knowing who administers the scheme, in order to obtain a contact for real-time information.

One might imagine that database administrators define priority data as a selection of information made available, which needs to be of high quality at any cost.

Finally, what would a database look like that could serve the information needs of a possible MBI Forum, as mentioned in the introduction? Based on the concerns discussed in this section, first and foremost there is the need to establish who would populate such a forum and what their wishes would be. Given the position of such a forum on the research-policy interface, one could expect a keen interest in one aspect that is badly if at all covered in any of the databases reviewed, namely the impact of MBI as a policy tool. The OECD/EEA database contains a record with relevant information, and the economicinstruments.com database (UCD) gives a prominent place to articles on instruments, of which several deal with the policy performance of these instruments.

OECD launched an important endeavor when it published its early overviews of environmental taxes and other MBI. Existing databases are adding in valuable ways to the scope of knowledge but there is a need to continue to develop and refine databases in order to serve the needs of researchers and the policy community.

PART V

IMPACT

19 Decoupling: is there a separate contribution from environmental taxation?

*Adrian Muller, Åsa Löfgren and Thomas Sterner**

INTRODUCTION

> The term decoupling refers to breaking the link between 'environmental bads' and 'economic goods.' Decoupling environmental pressures from economic growth is one of the main objectives of the OECD Environmental Strategy for the First Decade of the 21st Century, adopted by OECD Environment Ministers in 2001.
>
> (OECD 2002)

Decoupling is a crucial topic in the analysis of sustainable development. Without decoupling, continuing and increasing economic growth in developed and developing countries would come with ever-increasing environmental pressures, unavoidably destroying the carrying capacity of ecosystems with corresponding detrimental effects on the environment and societies. The prime example today is climate change. If we do not succeed in drastically decoupling greenhouse gas emissions from economic growth, the mitigation goals necessary to avoid catastrophic impacts will never be reached. Due to the importance of decoupling, it is thus essential to know how different policy instruments may support its achievement.

The aim of this chapter is to address the question of whether environmental taxation makes a separate contribution to decoupling and to offer researchers some guidance on how to optimally address this question.

Key to achieving this goal is to assess the effects of environmental taxes on environmental pressures and the economic variables, such as emissions and output. Distributional aspects of the tax burden (such as the regressiveness versus progressiveness of a tax), and questions about the optimal tax rate, environmental tax reforms, the double dividend, leakage and pollution havens, and the relative performance of different policy instruments play a minor role here and are covered in other chapters in this book. We also focus on methodological and statistical aspects here and address theoretical considerations only occasionally.

We differentiate several fields of analysis. First, there is the empirical question of whether there is decoupling or not. Decoupling occurs when the growth rate of an environmental pressure is less than that of its economic driving force (e.g. GDP) over a given period. Decoupling can be either absolute or relative. Absolute decoupling is said to occur when the environmentally relevant variable is stable or decreasing while the economic driving force is growing. Decoupling is said to be relative when the growth rate

*   This chapter was written within the INDIGO program funded by the Swedish Fund for Strategic Environmental Research (MISTRA). We thank the editors for very useful remarks.

of the environmentally relevant variable is positive, but less than the growth rate of the economic variable (OECD 2002).

Decoupling most often refers to decreasing emissions per unit of welfare, for example country level GDP, but similarly to OECD (2002) we explicitly use it also in relation to emissions per unit of monetary or physical output of an industrial sector. A wealth of empirical studies addresses whether there is decoupling for whole economies or single sectors and for a range of pollutants, as discussed in the next section. Several problems arise, however. The level of aggregation greatly matters. What looks like decoupling on an all-industry level may exhibit different patterns in a sector analysis, for example if the decrease in aggregate emissions in a context of continuing growth is not due to an increase in technical efficiency in all sectors but to an increase in the size of sectors with low emissions at the expense of the emissions intensive sectors. In this case, no decoupling would have taken place on the sector level, while the opposite holds for the aggregate. One task of the empirics of decoupling is to separate patterns of decoupling in a context of economic growth from patterns in a context of economic decline, which clearly has very different welfare effects. Further complications for the basic empirics stem from changes in prices if output is measured in monetary terms. Such price dynamics can overshadow the 'true,' that is, the physical, respective 'service level' dynamics. Decomposition analysis is one approach that helps identify the presence of decoupling on various levels of aggregation.

Second, we focus on cases where decoupling is observed, and try to identify the drivers behind this and their importance. A tax directly leads to changes in relative prices. There are, however, various ways in which such price changes may support decoupling. A tax can, for example, lead to substitution of the taxed good and/or it may trigger innovations that then drive decoupling. Substitution and innovation in general, however, may or may not be caused by an environmental tax. Identifying the detailed role played by an environmental tax is a daunting task. It is illustrative to think of this in the frame of the cause-and-effect chains as captured in a General Equilibrium (GE) model. The changes in relative prices brought about by the tax will have effects on direct consumption of the goods taxed (such as gasoline) or the goods tightly related to the emissions taxed (such as fossil energy use under a CO_2 tax), on substitutes, on different channels of innovation and so on. It will also have an effect on performance and employment in the sectors adversely affected by a tax (for example, the coal industry under a CO_2 tax) and on sectors gaining from it (such as solar panel manufacturers under a CO_2 tax), and on the demand for inputs used in these sectors. Furthermore, the tax revenues will be used in the economy (for example, to subsidize R&D in green technology or to implement an environmental tax reform, that is, to reduce tax on labor), with corresponding effects. Finally, there are likely other policy instruments in place that may interact with the environmental tax. Different types of regressions of some measure of decoupling on tax levels and several control variables can help reveal the role of the tax in a specific case of empirically observed decoupling. Adequately calibrated Computable General Equilibrium (CGE) models of whole economies can also contribute to identifying and understanding the effects of environmental taxes in concrete cases.

Complexity and data availability, however, may hinder such a contextualized approach that is embedded in the whole economy, and simpler paths must be chosen. Thus, information is also gained from partial analysis, such as estimating price elasticities of demand, e.g. for gasoline under a CO_2 tax. This gives the effect of the tax on gasoline use and thus on emissions, but it does not reveal anything about 'decoupling' directly. For this, further information on the change in 'output' on an aggregate level would be needed, such as information on the effect of the CO_2 tax on GDP. However, such partial analysis can provide different pieces of information that can be combined to form a more complete picture.

This chapter is organized according to these fields of analysis. The next section ('Is there decoupling?') covers the empirics of the presence or absence of decoupling, with a focus on decomposition analysis. The subsequent section ('Does environmental taxation lead to decoupling?') deals with the empirical investigation of the specific role of environmental taxes with regard to the contribution to decoupling, focusing on econometric models. It covers more particular additional information that helps to capture the effect of a tax on decoupling, such as elasticity estimates. It also presents a brief discussion of further complementary approaches, such as case study analysis or CGE modeling. Finally, the chapter concludes by summarizing how these various techniques optimally complement each other and by pointing out some research gaps to be filled in the context of such combined approaches.

We find that decoupling takes place in many cases, but that for many examples the decoupling currently observed is by far not enough to achieve the goals of sustainable development, such as the reduction of greenhouse gases. Methodological findings refer to the necessity to go beyond the simple descriptive empirics of decoupling indicators and to apply more elaborate analysis, such as decomposition analysis, which can reveal underlying patterns. Furthermore, causal analysis of decoupling and its drivers needs to account for the specific structure of the data at hand, employing cointegration and other time series analysis techniques. Optimally, decomposition analysis and econometric analysis are combined. Such combined approaches are rare, however, and currently focus on either decomposition or econometric analysis, not applying state-of-the-art techniques for both these approaches. Finally, additional insights can be gained by complementing these approaches with findings from other types of studies, such as analyses of price and substitution elasticities, and insights from equilibrium models or from firm-level interview surveys.

It should be noted that this chapter does not aim to present an exhaustive assessment of all the different examples of environmental taxes and their contributions to decoupling, but rather to present a set of tools that enables the researcher to address the question. Furthermore, it aims to identify research gaps. Due to the background of the authors, many examples are chosen from the areas of energy use, climate change and air pollution.

IS THERE DECOUPLING?

To answer the question of whether decoupling is present in a certain case, we need indicators to measure decoupling and methods of identifying decoupling in contrast to other patterns. This section shortly presents some indicators, building on the topical publication from the OECD (2002). It then presents approaches to identifying decoupling and concludes with some concrete examples.

Decoupling Indicators

'Decoupling can be measured by decoupling indicators that have an environmental pressure variable for numerator and an economic variable as denominator. Sometimes, the denominator or driving force may be population growth or some other variable' (OECD 2002). Thus, economywide decoupling is measured by indicators such as total CO_2 emissions per unit of GDP (for climate change) or total SO_2 emissions per unit of GDP (for air pollution). Other aspects such as water resource use, material use, waste management or biodiversity can be measured by similar indicators. The quality of these indicators, however, varies largely, as some are more robust and data is more readily available (such as for total CO_2 emissions per unit of GDP), while others face problems of data availability and reliability, or even conceptual problems (for example, the biodiversity indicator based on the Natural Capital Index per unit of GDP, which aims at capturing several types of pressure on biodiversity). One example of a decoupling indicator with population growth in the denominator is water quality, measured by the 'discharges of nutrients from households into the environment versus total population' (OECD 2002, 35). This indicator also demonstrates conceptual problems and problems of reliability and data availability.

In addition to economywide indicators, there are sector-specific indicators such as for transport (for example, passenger car and freight vehicles' combined related emissions of CO_2, NO_x and VOCs per unit of GDP) or agriculture (such as soil surface nitrogen surplus versus agricultural output). Table 1.1 in OECD (2002, 12–13) provides a list of 31 indicators covering a broad spectrum of environmental issues, combined with a judgment of robustness and data availability. Clearly, other institutions and authors also offer sets of or single indicators for specific cases of decoupling. Notable is the fact that the sector-level OECD indicators partly refer to total GDP as the economic variable in the denominator, while sector-level indicators in the academic literature usually refer to sector output (cf. below). The detailed definition of the indicators clearly has to be considered when comparing different assessments of seemingly similar quantities.

Identification of Decoupling

Identification of decoupling is in principle simple. Having chosen a decoupling indicator and given the data available, we need only check whether the decoupling indicator of interest decreases over time. Thus, basic decoupling identification is simple descriptive empirics. However, complications arise due to the effects of aggregation and price changes if the denominator is measured in monetary terms.

A simple and adequate method of further investigating aggregation effects in decoupling analysis is decomposition analysis. Decomposition analysis is not widely used in economics, perhaps because it is purely descriptive and builds neither on economic theory nor on statistical methods. It is based on integral approximation and relates to index theory, and also to the IPAT equation from ecological economics and the Kaya identity. In addition to its application in index theory, it is mainly used in some contexts of environmental, resource and energy economics to better understand energy and resource use and emissions or impacts on the environment, and in development economics to investigate the development of poverty measures (cf. Muller 2008).

Decomposition analysis allows the disentangling of an aggregate picture of decoupling on the level of a whole economy or a sector into several constituents on a sub-economy (such as sector-level) or sub-sector level, and also allows identification of whether the decoupling observed occurs in a context of a growing or declining economy or sector. This is best illustrated by a concrete example. Thus, an observed decoupling of SO_2 emissions from GDP growth for a whole economy can be decomposed into several constituents on the sector level, such as changes in the SO_2 emissions per energy type used (e.g. decreasing sulphur contents of coal), the share of different energy types in the total energy used (e.g. an increasing share of natural gas), the energy intensity of each sector (that is, the energy use per unit of output) and changes in the sector composition (e.g. a decrease of the share of energy intensive sectors in total output).

The most important contribution of decomposition analysis to the mere description of decoupling indicators is its insight into how an observed decoupling in the aggregate translates into different patterns on a more disaggregate level. Often, decoupling cannot be observed for each sector, for example, and sometimes a pattern of decoupling on the aggregate level does not even translate into any decoupling on the sector level but only into effects on sector composition. In such a case, no sector has become 'better' in terms of environmental performance, but the best sectors have become larger at the expense of the worst. Part of the decoupling observed in the aggregate in this case thus occurs in a context of sector-level economic decline.

It is interesting to point out that such decomposition analysis identifies the contributions of, for example, sectoral change and output growth to emissions in a formally well-framed way, accounting for all potential drivers at once. This contrasts with other approaches that account for these drivers by analyzing simple 'growth-' or 'structure-adjusted' emissions. There, total emissions are divided by production volume, or sectoral energy intensity is accounted for prior to summation of sectoral emissions to calculate total emissions. These adjustments, however, can only account for one variable and do not control for the development of other variables not included in the adjustment procedure. These simpler approaches are thus likely to produce biased results (see, for example, the assessment in chapter 9.3 in the otherwise very recommendable book Enevoldsen 2005).

It must be emphasized that decomposition analysis is a purely descriptive method for a detailed ex-post analysis of decoupling indicators. A disadvantage is that no statistical inference can be based on it. On the other hand, data requirements for decomposition analysis are low and it can be undertaken with aggregate data, which is often readily available. One methodological problem is that decomposition analysis is based on the approximation of integrals from unknown functions. The different decomposition methods differ in how they achieve this approximation. Consequently, results of different methods can differ. Löfgren and Muller (2010) and references therein (especially Liu and Ang 2007) can be accessed for a recent methodological discussion of decomposition analysis. Currently, the best method available seems to be the Logarithmic Mean Divisia Index decomposition (for a description, see Löfgren and Muller (2010) and references therein, for example Ang 2004). Specific problems of decomposition analysis in particular involve the level of aggregation, both economic and temporal (for optimal results, the analysis should be undertaken on a level as disaggregate as possible), and the measurement of the economic variables in monetary terms. Changes in prices can disrupt results if interpreted as changes in physical output, though due to a lack of data, there is often no remedy for this. See Löfgren and Muller (2010) for further details.

Decoupling—Concrete Examples

Decoupling is in fact widely observed, although patterns are heterogeneous and the level of analysis should optimally be as disaggregated as possible. OECD (2002, Table 1.2, 14–15), for example, reports decoupling for most of its indicators in most countries where data is available. Absolute decoupling is observed for air pollution and water quality and for most of the sector-level indicators, while the other indicators mostly show only relative decoupling. Most notable are the indicators for climate change, which mainly show only relative decoupling or even no decoupling. The study's coverage is comprehensive but somewhat simplistic in its further decomposition of decoupling indicators into key drivers. It must also be emphasized, that some of OECD's sector indicators relate to GDP while most sector indicators used in decomposition analysis refer to sector output. In some sample comparisons with results from other studies undertaken for the energy sector (for example in Hammar and Löfgren 2001 or Löfgren and Muller 2010), however, this does not make a big difference. Another collection of illustrative examples is given in the Swedish Government's report (Azar et al. 2002), and there are many more examples of governmental and other institutional reports providing evidence of the presence or absence of decoupling for various pollutants, countries and sectors (such as Speck et al. 2006; Speck and Salmons 2007; and Kojima and Bacon 2009).

We give some examples of the types of results to be expected from decomposition analysis and others. Hammar and Löfgren (2001) investigate Swedish SO_2 emissions and report considerable decoupling. Their decomposition analysis reveals that structural change did not play a very important role. Thus, the decoupling observed is not mainly due to shrinking of emissions-intensive sectors, but rather to fuel switching and decreasing energy intensity. Similar are the observations of Liaskas et al. (2000) for industrial EU CO_2 emissions (1983–1993), where structural change is of some importance in a few countries only. This is also shown in the results from Diakoulaki and Mandaraka (2007), who report decoupling for CO_2 emissions (1990–2003), with structural change being of considerable importance in a few countries only. However, specifically for industrial and business CO_2 emissions in Sweden, for example, Löfgren and Muller (2010) find structural change to be important. Similarly to the findings of OECD (2002), decoupling can be observed for the energy sector, but in contrast to the OECD report, no decoupling can be observed in the different transport sectors (land, air and ship). One reason may be the above-mentioned difference in indicators, as the OECD indicators for transportation refer to total GDP in the denominator, while Löfgren and Muller (2010) use sector-specific output measures. Finally, Tunc et al. (2009) and Oh et al. (2010) are two examples of recent LMDI decomposition analysis of energy-related CO_2 emissions for Turkey and South Korea, respectively. Slight decoupling of aggregate energy use is found for Turkey, which is based on considerable decoupling of energy use in the services sector, no decoupling in the industry sector and a strong coupling in agriculture. There is decoupling for South Korea for the manufacturing, services and residential sectors, but not for energy and transportation.

Data for the investigation and evidence of decoupling can also be found in country-level analyses of the Environmental Kuznets Curve (EKC) hypothesis, as the declining part of the EKC corresponds to the signature of decoupling. An example is Markandya et al. (2006) for SO_2 emissions in 12 Western European countries over the past 150 years, where direct descriptive evidence of decoupling is available. Another example is Stern and Common (2001), showing decoupling of SO_2 emissions for developed countries but not for developing ones—which is understandable in the logic of the EKC, as those countries have not yet reached income levels that correspond to the turning point in the EKC. We emphasize that for the decoupling empirics, we are interested in the data only and not in the underlying theory behind the EKC hypothesis itself.

The examples show the importance of disaggregate analysis of decoupling, both temporally and spatially (for single countries, for example) and also in particular regarding sector aggregation. In addition, due attention has to be given to the indicators used, in particular if several studies are compared. We emphasize again that no causal links may be derived from this type of descriptive analysis. Identifying causes of decoupling and quantification of the contribution of a tax is the topic of the next section. Finally, a main issue in identifying decoupling is to clearly separate cases in which decoupling is accompanied with a decrease in the economic variable in the denominator of the decoupling indicator (for example, where decomposition analysis reveals an important contribution from structural change), and cases in which it is not, thus showing contributions from genuine increases in energy efficiency, for example. Although both of these cases correspond to decoupling on an aggregate level, their welfare effects in an economy will be very different. Correspondingly the judgments of the welfare effects of a policy leading to decoupling will differ.

DOES ENVIRONMENTAL TAXATION LEAD TO DECOUPLING?

After the descriptive assessment of the presence and structure of decoupling, we now turn to the purpose of this chapter, namely whether and how a separate contribution from environmental taxation on decoupling may be identified and measured. There are several approaches to answering this question. Ideally, econometric models of a decoupling indicator as a dependent variable with some variable capturing the environmental tax as the explanatory variable, combined with due control variables, can be estimated. This helps to identify the effect of the environmental tax on decoupling, based on an aggregate (economywide), sector- or sub-sector level analysis (see the subsection, 'Aggregate econometric analysis of decoupling' immediately below). Second, firm level analysis can be undertaken, trying to estimate the effect of environmental taxes on emissions or energy intensity or fuel mix (see the subsection, 'Econometric analysis of decoupling based on firm-level data' thereafter). Changes in these variables directly influence measures of decoupling on a more aggregate (e.g. sectoral) level. Third, the effect of an environmental tax on indirect determinants of decoupling, such as innovation or technological change (as potential drivers of increased emissions efficiency) or location choice (as potential drivers of sectoral change), can be estimated. For an assessment of the contribution of a tax on decoupling based on such an analysis, the contribution of these indirect determinants on decoupling would need to be estimated. As these linkages are indirect and the estimation of the more direct cases already poses considerable challenges, we do not further pursue these econometric analyses in this chapter. Some of these issues are a topic in equilibrium models, and some of the linkages between taxation and these indirect determinants (for example, the effect of environmental taxation on innovation) are treated elsewhere in this book. Finally, analysis of some partial effects is possible, such as the estimation of several own- and cross-price elasticities of the consumption of different energy sources, or the energy price elasticity of emissions or output. Also informative are detailed descriptions of the development of key variables embedded in the description of a broader political and economic context after introduction of a policy instrument, or firm-level case study evidence based on interviews. Such more particular or narrative analysis cannot reveal the full contribution of environmental taxation to decoupling, but it can also provide important pieces for an encompassing picture. All of this forms the topic of the third subsection, 'Complementary information.'

This section builds on the work in the previous section. Having chosen the best-suited decoupling indicator for the case at hand, decomposition analysis helps to identify the adequate level of aggregation, the most important sectors and potential patterns of drivers of decoupling (for example, changes in efficiency, sectoral composition and size). This information can then help to improve the causal analysis. We will see that this is usually not done in the current literature, and that an optimal combination of decomposition analysis and econometric approaches is part of the suggested future research presented in the conclusions.

Aggregate Econometric Analysis of Decoupling

Ideally, to answer the guiding question of this chapter, models with a decoupling indicator in dependence of some tax variable should be estimated. In addition to offering insight into the effect of environmental taxation on some aggregate decoupling indicator, which driver of decoupling is influenced to which extent by the tax should also be identified. It should thus be possible to identify whether a tax affects emissions efficiency within several sectors or whether it affects sectoral composition, for example. Those two cases have very different effects in an economy, although an aggregate decoupling indicator may depict them identically. Only a few studies go in the direction of estimating the effects of an environmental tax on decoupling (and do not merely estimate price elasticities used to derive effects of a tax on demand), and no study implements this ideal case, combining both a sound estimation with a detailed decomposition of decoupling.

Enevoldsen et al. (2007a) estimate a demand system for different energy types for ten industrial sectors in the three Scandinavian countries. This estimation aims at addressing the decoupling of CO_2 emissions and energy use, based on the effects of price changes on fuel type shares. The demand system estimation calculates own- and cross-price elasticities. The chosen estimation method (translog demand system estimation for a cross-industry pooled model with fixed effects across industries and time) is motivated and discussed in detail, including often neglected aspects such as the discussion of different energy price discounts and tax exemptions for different sectors and fuels. This study is exemplary for its own- and cross-price elasticity estimation for different fuels. The authors find own-price elasticities of energy demand from -0.35 to -0.44 for Denmark, Norway and Sweden and conclude that environmental taxation will contribute considerably to energy consumption reductions. Despite the 'decoupling' title of their paper, however, this approach cannot estimate the full effect of an energy and CO_2 tax on decoupling. Due to the elasticity estimates, the effects of price changes (and thus also of a tax) on factor use and emissions can be derived. However, elasticity estimates cannot identify individual drivers behind changes in energy demand or emissions. They cannot identify, for example, whether such changes are due to changes in energy efficiency, in emissions efficiency or in output. In addition, due to data availability, elasticity estimates are not sector-specific (sector-specific aspects were captured by fixed effects only). As discussed above, however, decomposition analysis shows that sector-specific differences greatly matter. Thus, this type of study should be complemented by a decomposition analysis of emissions and energy use, which could be done sector-wise with the data available.

Studies like Enevoldsen et al. (2007a) could also be optimally combined with the results of studies like Enevoldsen et al. (2007b), in which the effect of an energy tax on indicators for competitiveness (that is, variables linked to the denominator in a decoupling measure) is estimated on the sector level for eight sectors in seven EU countries between 1990 and 2003. They proceed similarly to Enevoldsen et al. (2007a) with this different but complementary focus.

Enevoldsen (2005, chapter 10) contains a similar analysis as Enevoldsen et al. (2007a) but provides many additional details on the concepts and methods used. The basis of these approaches is the observation that prices, energy consumption and the like (that is, the variables of interest for econometric analysis of decoupling) are nonstationary variables, meaning that 'they meander away from their starting point, thereby giving rise to a moving average instead of returning to a stable, long-term mean' (Enevoldsen 2005, 192). Such variables thus show a 'trend' over time. In addition, one observes that these variables do not move independently in the long run, but rather are 'cointegrated.' Cointegration captures a special type of dependence, namely that variables show the 'same trend.' More technically, two variables are cointegrated if their differenced series (differenced at the same order) are both stationary, that is, 'without trend.' We point out that in this discussion, the potential role of a time trend (leading to trend-stationary variables without unit root that are thus similar to stationary variables) is not addressed, but we will take this up below and in the conclusions. There is a large specialized body of econometric literature that can be employed to estimate models with cointegrated variables (see, for example, the discussion in Enevoldsen (2005) and any textbook on time series econometrics).

Smith et al. (1995) directly estimate energy and emissions intensities and thus directly estimate some decoupling indicator. They first use a similar cointegration approach with an error correction model to account for the short-term dynamics. The problem with this specification is the exogenous technological change. As the influence on technological change is one way in which a tax can affect emissions intensity, they then estimate a new model with endogenous technological change. The drawback to their estimation is their focus on the national level (eight countries), not differentiating for different sectors. However, they do account for different fuel types and estimate substitution and price elasticities. They thus can differentiate between the effect of increased emissions efficiency and the effect of fuel substitution. Sectoral change, however, cannot be captured by their approach. They find that differences between countries greatly matter (without providing further explanation for the differences) and that price elasticity of energy demand is relatively low for some countries. In the short run, gross values for the estimates are −0.05 for Italy; −0.1 for France, Japan and the United Kingdom; and somewhat higher levels for Canada and Germany (−0.3). The United States is at −0.2. In the long run the estimates are −0.1 for Italy; −0.4 for Canada; −0.5 for France, Germany and the United States; and −0.7 for the United Kingdom and Japan. Given the caveats about the methods used, these numbers have to be regarded with caution. We report them as examples only.

Hammar and Löfgren (2001) is an example of a decomposition analysis of SO_2 emissions that is partly complemented by an econometric estimation of the effects of fuel prices on the different drivers, such as fuel-shares of light and heavy oils or substitution of oil for other energy sources. The decomposition analysis reveals a strong contribution to reduced emissions from a switch to cleaner fuels, followed by the contribution from decreased energy intensity. Their regression analysis reveals significant but only small effects of a tax on sulphur emissions (via its effect on changes to oil with less sulphur content and on a switch from oil to other fuels). Their decomposition analysis uses another method than LMDI, but a rerun using LMDI results in small and unimportant changes only.

The regression analysis, however, is done in a very simple manner, as it is not based on a demand system estimation, for example, and does not take into account time trends or structural breaks. The results derived for the effects of a tax on decoupling or on underlying patterns are thus to be interpreted with caution.

Similar caution is warranted by the results of Metcalf (2008), which decomposes US energy intensity into an efficiency and an activity (that is, 'sector composition') part and then runs regressions of those variables on several independent variables, such as energy prices. From the decomposition analysis, the author derives that about three-quarters of the energy intensity decrease from 1970 to 2003 was due to increased efficiency, while shifting to less energy-intensive activities accounted for about one-quarter. The author undertakes this analysis on the national and state levels, but does differentiate between very gross sectors only (residential, commercial, industrial and transportation). He thus cannot account for different developments in different types of industry or transportation, for example. These developments are very important, however, as demonstrated by the studies that can account for them. The regression analysis shows that rising per capita income and also energy prices (thus also a tax) primarily contribute to increasing energy efficiency. The decomposition method is based on a refined Fisher Index and the estimation is done without reference to cointegration techniques. Improving the methods for the same analysis (LMDI for decomposition and cointegration analysis for the estimation) would thus be interesting. The methods chosen may also explain the discrepancy in results to a similar analysis, as noted in the author's footnote 1.

Somewhat stretching the notion of decoupling, we can also count Löfgren and Hammar (2000) as an example of a study directly assessing the impact of an environmental tax on decoupling. They address the specific problem of phasing out leaded gasoline. They estimate the share of leaded gasoline in dependence of the price differential between leaded and unleaded gasoline (that is, the tax level on leaded gasoline) and other variables. This share can be understood as a decoupling indicator, taking leaded gasoline as the environmental pressure variable and total gasoline as the economic activity variable. They identify a significant (but small) contribution of the tax on the reduction of the share of leaded gasoline. More important were the per capita income and the share of catalytic converters. They estimate both fixed and random effects with and without time trends, but undertake no cointegration analysis. Including a time trend leads to lower significance of the theoretically justified variables in their model, and therefore they decide not to include a time trend. Fixed costs are favored, but differences between fixed and random effects are small.

Econometric Analysis of Decoupling based on Firm Level Data

In addition to aggregate data, firm level data can be used for the empirical analysis of decoupling. Although decoupling is an aggregate concept, based on the development of aggregate variables, for example on a global, country or sector level, the analysis of firm level data on the effect of environmental taxation on emissions and energy intensity, input use, output and other quantities can add insight on the effects of taxation on decoupling, as these quantities on firm level are tightly related to patterns of decoupling on a more aggregate level.

The study by Bjorner and Jensen (2002), for example, estimates a translog regression of energy consumption on factor prices and output and control variables, using a single-equation energy demand model with company fixed effects and panel data of single companies in Denmark (1983–1997). Energy consumption is measured as an aggregate of several fuel types (according to energy content). For electricity, specific prices paid by each company are used (based on the prices from each of the 100 different electricity utilities in Denmark), while for the other energy types, general prices are used.

This study estimates price elasticities of energy demand and thus only a part of the decoupling indicator. It finds that the elasticities strongly differ between pooled and company fixed effects estimation and that fixed effects should be used. The elasticity estimates also depend on the level of energy price (in the quadratic functional form that has a better fit). The average energy price elasticity is -0.44, and is lower for energy-intensive companies and higher for energy-extensive ones (with a range between -0.2 and -0.7).

The study does not derive the effects of an energy tax (namely increasing energy prices) on output or on some aggregate variable capturing sectoral change. Due to the aggregation over fuel types, this analysis also lacks the information needed to estimate effects on fuel substitution as one driver of decoupling.

Complementary Information—Elasticity Estimates, CGE Models and Case Studies

Price elasticities
In the previous sections, we have seen that estimation of the effect of taxation on decoupling often is attempted only via some partial analysis, such as the estimation of price elasticities of energy demand. There is a wealth of such elasticity studies for different goods (such as gasoline, industrial energy use), and they contribute to the understanding of the effect of environmental taxes. On the other hand, they do not provide the full picture if not complemented by further analysis. We refer to some of them, as the assessment of environmental taxation's effect on decoupling will at least partly remain a combination of different pieces of evidence—and in such a context, elasticity estimates and the incidence of a tax based on those alone contribute important information.

Huntington (2007) estimates US natural gas demand based on 45 years of time series data. First, he tests the stationarity of the variables involved and concludes that they are stationary (or time-trend stationary). Correspondingly, simpler estimation procedures can be employed. The stationarity of the key variables is in contrast to the findings in the studies referred to in the subsection above on aggregate econometric analysis. One reason hinted at by Huntington (2007) is the short duration of the time series employed in these other studies: the usual test for stationarity is not very powerful with few observations, and due attention should be given to take potential time trends and structural breaks into account. Price and output elasticities of natural gas demand are then estimated, adopting an autoregressive distributed lag relationship with current and lagged values of natural gas consumption and the independent variables. Huntington finds price elasticities for natural gas of −0.25 in the short term and −0.7 in the long term (referring to results from his preferred model). The drawback of this study is the level of aggregation, which does not differentiate for different sectors and is done on a national level. In addition, the drawbacks of mere price elasticity of demand apply, that is, the impossibility of separating structural change from the output effects of a change in prices (namely, of a tax). However, he tries to partly capture structural change effects by employing an aggregate output variable across industries that weights output with energy intensity for each industry. The stationarity of key variables found by Huntington (2007) is of importance as this influences the optimal estimation methods to be used.

Floros and Vlachou (2005) is a further example of a study estimating price and substitution elasticities of industrial fuel demand. They estimate a demand system for the Greek economy and derive the impact of a CO_2 tax based on the elasticities estimated. Again, this study is subject to the drawbacks already mentioned for tax incidence estimations based on elasticities.

A significant portion of studies providing elasticity estimates address gasoline demand. We will not report on them in detail, but we will point out some aspects that can inform the econometric analysis of decoupling. First, given the number of studies on gasoline elasticities, meta-analysis of these results can be undertaken (for example, Brons et al. 2008). Such an analysis helps to integrate differing results from a wealth of studies and will be important for the econometric analysis of tax incidence on decoupling as soon as enough specific studies are available. It also helps to integrate different aspects of the various studies, such as the estimates of price elasticity of demand, as well as this elasticity's determinants (price elasticities of fuel efficiency, mileage per car and car ownership). The recent and detailed meta-study of Brons et al. (2008) found a mean of −0.34 and −0.84, respectively, for the short- and long-run price elasticity of gasoline demand (reporting their estimates from a 'seemingly unrelated regression,' or SUR, model, though standard fixed effects lead to similar results). Changes in fuel efficiency and mileage per car are the most important drivers of the impact of gasoline price on demand. Car ownership is somewhat less important. The elasticity estimates in the studies analyzed strongly depend on study characteristics such as geographic area, time period, and functional form of the demand equation.

Second, there are recent studies that allow for time-varying coefficients and thus for elasticity estimates that vary over time. Given the large differences among price elasticity estimates for gasoline demand for different periods, this is a potentially important differentiation also for the econometric analysis of decoupling (see, for example, Park and

Zhao (2010) on US gasoline demand, reporting values of −0.15 to −0.3 for 1976–1983 and 2006–2008 and 0 to −0.2 for 1984–2005; or Hughes et al. (2008), also on US gasoline demand, reporting −0.034 to −0.077 for 2001–2006, as opposed to −0.21 to −0.34 for 1975–1980, analyzing two periods with similarly high gasoline prices, using somewhat simpler econometrics than did the former study).

As previously mentioned, price elasticities of demand allow for some indication of the incidence of a tax on demand, but do not account for the various ways in which such price signals may be transmitted in an economy. Nor do they allow for an estimate of the incidence on decoupling. Sterner (2007) is an illustrative example of an attempt at such an incidence analysis with simple means for gasoline use in Europe, mainly by building a counterfactual with lower taxes and using elasticity estimates to derive corresponding demand. Sterner concludes, 'Had Europe not followed a policy of high fuel taxation but had low US taxes, then fuel demand would have been twice as large' (Sterner 2007, 3194).

CGE models
Complementary to econometric approaches to particular aspects are economywide models such as CGE models. At the expense of many assumptions—in particular the assumption of a general equilibrium and assumptions on the functional form and the values of relevant parameters of how inputs are combined in the production process, or how utilities for single goods add up to aggregate total utility of consumers—such models can capture some of the complexities of the cause-effect chains in a real economy. There are many examples of such models and corresponding publications.

The accessible description and graphical representation in Bruvoll and Larsen (2004), for example, models the incidence of the Norwegian CO_2 tax on emissions (1990–1999), based on a model run with the real carbon tax and a counterfactual model run without. They find that the carbon tax made only a modest 2 percent contribution to CO_2 emissions reductions. This small effect may be compared with the large effect of fuel taxation identified by Sterner (2007), a difference that can be attributed to the fact that the carbon tax accounts for only a fraction of total fuel taxes. The level of the carbon tax in Norway was thus much lower than the fuel taxes considered in Sterner (2007), and allowed for many exceptions. The key contribution of such models is their ability to provide some insight into how a CO_2 tax, for example, affects the use of inputs (capital, labor, energy, materials and services), intermediate goods and output in various sectors, how it affects technological progress and innovation and how it affects the consumption of goods by individuals. Depending on the focus of interest, different parts of the economy can be depicted in more or less detail. In the end, these different causal chains and linkages all give rise to some aggregate effect on emissions and output and thus on a decoupling indicator. Key inputs therein are price and substitution elasticities and thus the results from the studies described in the previous subsection are relevant.

A drawback of these models is their often very high complexity, which makes them inaccessible to many readers who thus have to accept (or criticize) them as a 'black box'. On the other hand it is impossible to intuitively capture all the complexities of a real economy, and these models offer a simplification and clarification along the lines of well-defined causal chains. It is, for example, difficult to derive the incidence of an environmental tax on emissions or output just by referring to its level and the corresponding price elasticity. Calculating these effects in the framework of a well-built equilibrium model is more reliable, as all the indirect effects are captured as well. If the equilibrium model itself is doubtful, though, the analysis may only lead to wrong confidence. These models are thus to be used with caution. Goulder et al. (1999) present a detailed but relatively accessible example of an equilibrium model, illustrating how it can support the understanding of more complex cause-effect chains in an economy. They address the question of the double dividend on a theoretical/numerical level, but their approach is exemplary of how equilibrium models may be used to identify how and in what ways policy instruments become effective in an economy.

Case studies
A very different type of complementary information is provided by case-study analysis. The empirical analysis of NO_x emissions per GWh in Sweden (Sterner and Höglund Isaksson 2006; Höglund Isaksson 2005) contains some results based on descriptive analysis of single plant data combined with interview results and information on the timing of the policy instrument. This simple analysis provides strong evidence that the refunded emission payments (that is, a tax with refund) were the main cause of the extensive emissions reductions observed (−40 percent in mean emission rates).

    Another example is found in chapter 11 in Enevoldsen (2005). The chapter is based on interviews with persons from industrial firms, branch associations, industry and labor associations, industrial energy technology expert organizations, government agencies and academics. Such an approach gives case study-like evidence that can complement a statistical analysis with concrete 'stories' of how environmental taxation may affect single firms, in particular allowing some assessment of intra-firm aspects such as internal decision structures and barriers. Enevoldsen finds that energy decision-making is well organized and professional in energy-intensive firms and that the overriding goal is cost minimization with respect to energy input, but this is at times interpreted from a long-term perspective. The central concern there is the payback time of energy investments. Such interview studies, however, clearly provide only very indirect evidence of the incidence of environmental taxation on decoupling.

CONCLUSIONS

First, we can state that on an aggregate level (for example, a nation level) considerable decoupling takes place according to many indicators: energy use or local air pollutants decouple from GDP or total industrial output. However, this has to be investigated in more detail. For CO_2, for example, no decoupling or only weak decoupling can be identified in most cases, while SO_2 shows a clear pattern of decoupling. Many pollutants also only show relative and not absolute decoupling. This means that the environmental pressures still increase, albeit at a lower rate than economic performance. This can be observed for CO_2 in industrial countries, for example. This is by far not enough to reach certain environmental goals, such as the greenhouse gas emissions reductions necessary to limit climate change to manageable levels, say by keeping warming below 2°C in the twenty-first century. The presence of decoupling is thus by no means an indicator for a sustainable economic development. To attain sufficient decoupling, strong policies may be required.

Second, the simple descriptive empirics of decoupling indicators should be complemented by analysis, such as decomposition analysis, that identifies underlying patterns. This reveals that a disaggregate picture is necessary to understand decoupling in detail. Annual instead of decennial, and sector or sub-sector level analysis instead of national, is necessary to gain a realistic picture.

Third, causal analysis of the effects of environmental taxation on decoupling is notoriously difficult. Ideally, decomposition analysis revealing detailed disaggregate patterns of decoupling should be combined with econometric estimation to identify the contribution of key variables. Such combined studies are rarely undertaken, and when they are, either the decomposition or the econometric aspect is not very elaborate. Decomposition analysis should use the LMDI method. However, further research is still needed on optimal decomposition methods and how they relate to the underlying integral approximation problem. The specific statistical characteristics of the time series analyzed (cointegration, stationary vs. non-stationary, and so on) may be employed to optimize these methods. The econometric estimation should also account for this and cointegration techniques may often be the first choice. Due attention, however, has to be given to several tests for time trends, structural breaks, non-stationarity or unit-roots, and so on, particularly in light of shorter time series.

Fourth, such detailed combined descriptive and econometric analysis can further benefit from more partial insights, for example on price and substitution elasticities or firm-level interview studies. This information should be included more systematically in the assessment of decoupling. In particular the rich knowledge gained from elasticity studies, including newer insights on changing elasticities over time, should be used in such a way as to account not only for the effect of price change on the environmental pressure, but also for the effects of changes in the economic variables. There, complementary analysis with whole-economy models, such as CGE models, can be very informative.

Coming back to our question: does environmental taxation make a separate contribution to decoupling? In some cases, there is automatic decoupling simply through technological progress or other forces. In many cases, however, particularly when abatement or decoupling implies bigger costs, it will not happen without strong policy instruments. These instruments may be either taxes or conceivably some other policy instrument such as tradable permits. In many cases, the tax has been crucial to make decoupling happen, while in others, taxation makes a big contribution to emissions reduction, but analysis does not directly address decoupling. However, employing complementary information on GDP development, for example, sometimes points to a crucial contribution to decoupling as well (such as in the case of gasoline taxation). Further cases show only a weak contribution of taxation to decoupling. In parts, other drivers are more important. For some cases, though, the tax level is low and higher taxes likely would lead to decoupling. Detailed answers can be derived employing the methods described in this chapter.

REFERENCES

Ang, B. (2004), 'Decomposition analysis for policymaking in energy: which is the preferred method?', *Energy Policy*, **32**, 1131–9.

Azar, C., J. Holmberg and S. Karlsson (2002), *Decoupling—Past Trends and Prospects for the Future*, Stockholm, Sweden: Environmental Advisory Council, Ministry of the Environment, Sweden.

Bjorner, T. and H. Jensen (2002), 'Energy taxes, voluntary agreements and investment subsidies—a micro-panel analysis of the effect on Danish industrial companies' energy demand', *Energy and Resource Economics*, **24**, 229–49.

Brons, M., P. Nijkamp, E. Pelsand and P. Rietveld (2008), 'A meta-analysis of the price elasticity of gasoline demand. A SUR approach', *Energy Economics*, **30**, 2105–22.

Bruvoll, A. and B. Larsen (2004), 'Greenhouse gas emissions in Norway: do carbon taxes work?', *Energy Policy*, **32**, 493–505.

Diakoulaki D. and M. Mandaraka (2007), 'Decomposition analysis for assessing the progress in decoupling industrial growth from CO_2 emissions in the EU manufacturing sector', *Energy Economics*, **29**, 636–64.

Enevoldsen, M. (2005), *The Theory of Environmental Agreements and Taxes: CO_2 Policy Performance in Comparative Perspective*, Cheltenham, UK: Edward Elgar.

Enevoldsen, M., A. Ryelund and M. Andersen (2007a), 'Decoupling of industrial energy consumption and CO_2-emissions in energy-intensive industries in Scandinavia', *Energy Economics*, **29**, 665–92.

Enevoldsen, M., A. Ryelund and M. Andersen (2007b), 'The impact of energy taxes on competitiveness, output and exports: a panel regression study of 56 European industry sectors', in M.S. Andersen et al. (eds), *Competitiveness Effects of Environmental Tax Reforms (COMETR). Final Report to the European Commission*, Aarhus, Denmark: National Environmental Research Institute, University of Aarhus, http://www.dmu.dk/Pub/COMETR_Final_Report.pdf.

Floros, N. and A. Vlachou (2005), 'Energy demand and energy-related CO_2 emissions in Greek manufacturing: assessing the impact of a carbon tax', *Energy Economics*, **27**, 387–413.

Goulder, L., I. Parry, R. Williams and D. Burtraw (1999), 'The cost-effectiveness of alternative instruments for environmental protection in a second-best setting', *Journal of Public Economics*, **72** (3), 329–60.

Hammar, H. and A. Löfgren (2001), 'The determinants of sulfur emissions from oil consumption in Swedish manufacturing industry, 1976–1995', *The Energy Journal*, **22** (2), 107–26.

Hilton, F.G.H. and A. Levinson (1998), 'Factoring the environmental Kuznets curve: evidence from automotive lead emissions', *Journal of Environmental Economics and Management*, **35**, 126–41.

Höglund Isaksson, L. (2005), 'Abatement costs in response to the Swedish charge on nitrogen oxide emissions', *Journal of Environmental Economics and Management*, **50**, 102–20.

Hughes, J., C. Knittel and D. Sperling (2008), 'Evidence of a shift in the short-run price elasticity of gasoline demand', *The Energy Journal*, **29** (1), 113–34.

Huntington, H. (2007), 'Industrial natural gas consumption in the United States: an empirical model for evaluating future trends', *Energy Economics*, **29**, 743–59.

Kojima, M. and R. Bacon (2009), *Changes in CO_2 Emissions from Energy Use—A Multicountry Decomposition Analysis*, Extractive Industries for Development Series No. 11, Washington, DC, US: The World Bank.

Liaskas K, G. Mavrotas, M. Mandaraka and D. Diakoulaki (2000), 'Decomposition of industrial CO_2 emissions: the case of European Union', *Energy Economics*, **22**, 383–94.

Liu, N. and B.W. Ang (2007), 'Factors shaping aggregate energy intensity trend for industry: energy intensity versus product mix', *Energy Economics*, **29**, 609–35.

Löfgren, A. and H. Hammar (2000). 'The phase out of leaded gasoline in the EU countries. A successful failure?', Transportation Research Part D, *Transport and Environment*, **5D** (6), November, 419–31

Löfgren, A. and A. Muller (2010), 'Swedish CO_2 emissions 1993–2006: an application of decomposition analysis and some methodological insights', *Environmental and Resource Economics*, **47** (2), 221–39.

Markandya, A., A. Golub and S. Pedroso-Galinato (2006), 'Empirical analysis of national income and SO_2 emissions in selected European countries', *Environmental and Resource Economics*, **35**, 221–57.

Metcalf, G. (2008), 'An empirical analysis of energy intensity and its determinants at the state level', *The Energy Journal*, **29** (3), 1–26.

Muller, A. (2008), 'Clarifying poverty decomposition', Scandinavian Working Papers in Economics 217, available at http://ideas.repec.org/p/zbw/gdec08/30.html.

OECD (2002), *Indicators to Measure Decoupling of Environmental Pressure from Economic Growth*, SG/SD(2002)1/Final, Paris, France: OECD.

Oh, I., W. Wehrmeyer and Y. Mulugetta (2010), 'Decomposition analysis and mitigation strategies of CO_2 emissions from energy consumption in South Korea', *Energy Policy*, **38**, 364–77.

Park, S. and G. Zhao (2010), 'An estimation of U.S. gasoline demand: a smooth time-varying cointegration approach', *Energy Economics*, **32**, 110–20.

Smith, C., S. Hall and N. Mabey (1995), 'Econometric modelling of international carbon tax regimes', *Energy Economics*, **17** (2), 133–46.

Speck, S. and R. Salmons (2007), 'Leakage Analysis within a Decoupling Framework', in M.S. Andersen et al. (eds), *Competitiveness Effects of Environmental Tax Reforms (COMETR). Final Report to the European Commission*, Aarhus, Denmark: National Environmental Research Institute, University of Aarhus.

Speck, S., M. Andersen, H. Nielsen, A. Ryelund and C. Smith (2006), *The Use of Economic Instruments in Nordic and Baltic Environmental Policy 2001–2005*, Aarhus, Denmark: National Environmental Research Institute, University of Aarhus.

Stern, D. and M. Common (2001), 'Is there an environmental Kuznets curve for sulfur?', *Journal of Environmental Economics and Management*, **41**, 162–78.

Sterner, T. (2007), 'Fuel taxes: an important instrument for climate policy', *Energy Policy*, **35**, 3194–202.

Sterner, T. and L. Höglund Isaksson (2006), 'Refunded emission payments theory, distribution of costs, and Swedish experience of NO$_x$ abatement', *Ecological Economics*, **57**, 93–106.

Tunc, G., S. Türüt-Asik and E. Akbostanci (2009), 'A decomposition analysis of CO$_2$ emissions from energy use: Turkish case', *Energy Policy*, **37**, 4689–99.

20 The role of environmental taxation in spurring technological change

Herman Vollebergh*

INTRODUCTION

Do environmental taxes change the use and even the invention of new technologies? This simple question has not generated much interest in the literature until recently. For a long time, since the seminal contribution by Baumol and Oates (1971), the focus in most contributions, in particular by economists, has been on the static cost-effectiveness or efficiency of such taxes. So-called Pigouvian taxes guarantee cost efficiency because agents, like consumers or firms, select the lowest-cost options when they are confronted with a price on environmental pollution.[1] For this simple theorem to hold, variety in the cost of different existing abatement options is enough, and new technological options are not at all necessary.

Despite this focus on cost-effectiveness potential, dynamic impacts have always generated some interest. Kneese and Schulze, for instance, pointed out long ago that 'Over the long haul, perhaps the most important single criterion on which to judge environmental policies is the extent to which they spur new technology toward the efficient conservation of environmental quality' (Kneese and Schulze 1975, 38). Indeed, it is hardly disputed nowadays that environmental taxes can be of critical importance to the inducement and diffusion of new technologies, or 'technological change' for short. Imposing an environmental tax on a polluting activity is likely to increase efforts to generate new ideas about abatement options, subsequent filings of new patents, pilots of new technologies, changes in process and product characteristics, and, finally, a reduction in emissions at lower cost.

Since its start in the 1970s, the focus in environmental regulation was almost entirely on standard-setting, for example uniform reduction percentages across pollution sources, input restrictions, product requirements and technology-specific prescriptions (Downing and Hanf 1983; Opschoor and Vos 1989). Much has changed since. Clearly the tide has turned for market-based environmental policy instruments such as environmental taxes (see Stavins 2003). Whereas these market-based instruments usually address specific pollution problems, like water or air pollutants, the growing attention for climate change calls attention to economy-wide taxes such as energy or carbon taxes.

*   The author is grateful to Nils Axel Braathen, Paul Koutstaal, Edwin van der Werf and the editors of this Handbook for their useful comments.

[1]   The necessary condition for static efficiency is that marginal abatement costs are equalized across firms, and in this respect instruments like emission taxes or tradable emission permits are generally preferred to quotas, performance standards and investment subsidies (Baumol and Oates 1988).

Interestingly, this change in perception of pollution as a problem at the periphery of economic activity (water pollution) to a problem that may affect the economy as a whole (climate change) has also induced more interest in the link between environmental taxes and technological change. In particular when environmental quality is perceived as an indispensible input for production (Smulders 2005), it also makes sense to consider shifts in the production possibility curve and how environmental policies, like environmental taxes, affect these shifts. Moreover, if technological change becomes part of the solution to environmental problems, it is also important to consider the incentive structures that affect this change (see Jaffe et al. 2003; Popp et al. 2009). Finally, environmental tax expenditures may have a role on their own because they specifically address well-known positive externalities in the decision-making processes that drive technological change.[2]

To discuss technological change without understanding its driving role in capitalism is impossible. Following the famous work by Schumpeter (1934 and 1942), the literature on technological change typically distinguishes among three main phases. The first phase is the invention and initial development of new ideas usually embodied in new technology and/or product design. This phase not only includes research and development (R&D) in large firms, but also lone inventors. In the second or innovation phase some of those new ideas are elaborated into new technologies or products to be applied in the world. In this phase, new inventions and ideas are tested and screened for their market potential. Only in the third phase do new ideas reach firm ground. In this phase they typically diffuse across society and become widely implemented.[3]

The relatively recent and new economic literature on these effects is the subject of this chapter. I discuss what is currently known about the impact of environmental taxation, as well as environmental tax expenditures, on technological change. In framing the main subject this way I stay away from at least three related topics. First, I do not review the literature that compares environmental taxes relative to other instruments in a dynamic perspective.[4] Second, no attention is paid to the effectiveness of both tax instruments as emission-reducing devices. Third, what we know about resource taxation, i.e. taxes on nonrenewable minerals or fossil fuel extraction, is also not reviewed.[5]

---

[2] Note, however, that subsidies (including environmental tax expenditures) have received relatively little attention in the environmental economics literature. Indeed, from recent surveys of the adoption literature (Requate 2005) and market-based instruments (Stavins 2003), it is clear that the economics profession has focused predominantly on the analysis of pollution taxes, tradable pollution permits and quotas.

[3] This distinction associates learning with diffusion of technology and/or knowledge across agents (firms, households).

[4] Magat (1978) compares effluent taxes and standards using an innovation possibilities frontier model of induced innovation. Interesting follow-ups are Fischer et al. (2003) and Requate and Unold (2003). Requate (2005) and Vollebergh (2007) review the theoretical respectively empirical literature from this perspective.

[5] Newbery (2005) shows that this restriction may be far from innocent. However, the dynamics involved here justify a wholly separate discussion. See also Smulders (2005) for a discussion of insights obtained from the analysis of nonrenewable resources and endogenous technological change.

DYNAMIC INCENTIVES OF ENVIRONMENTAL TAXES

As noted in the introduction, the main criterion by which the economics profession has evaluated tax instruments is that of static efficiency, i.e. the extent to which these instruments can achieve a specified environmental objective at minimum cost. However, static efficiency is just one of many criteria for instrument choice, and it is not necessarily the most important one (Jaffe and Stavins 1995; Jaffe et al. 2003). Accordingly, one would expect the introduction of environmental taxes and tax expenditures also to be fundamental drivers of an increase in R&D investment in abatement technologies, subsequent filings of new patents and, finally, a reduction in emissions.

To assess the likely impacts of tax measures on innovation, it is useful first to distinguish explicitly between the incentive mechanisms induced in a static setting, i.e. with given technologies, before considering generalizations to a dynamic setting. As a starting point, consider the following substitution channels for evaluating different taxes from a regulatory perspective (Smulders and Vollebergh 2001; Fullerton 2002):[6]

- First, end-of-pipe *emission abatement* separates emissions from input use and output;
- Second, *input substitution* implies the substitution of emission-intensive inputs for emission-extensive inputs, such as switches in composition in fuels;
- Third, *factor substitution* involves the replacement of dirty inputs by clean inputs, such as for labor for fossil fuel energy;
- Fourth, *output substitution* accounts for the substitution between dirty and clean products, and also includes what could be called *output characteristics substitution*, applying to changes in the characteristics of products.

Taxes typically differ depending on what and how these different mechanisms are triggered.[7] Note that the prototype Pigouvian emission tax exploits all four mechanisms at the same time, which explains its efficacy (and, by implication, its emission-reduction efficiency). The alternative of an input tax, however, does exploit three channels but not the emission abatement channel of reducing emissions. With input taxation, the firm can no longer reduce tax payments directly by reducing emissions. An output tax can also be exploited as an alternative for an emission tax. For instance, an ad valorem output tax is a very indirect and therefore costly instrument for reducing emissions. A firm facing such an output tax has no incentive to abate emissions directly because that would not reduce its tax burden. The classification of these substitution mechanisms in a static setting identifies options for how firms might react to different types of tax policy measures. The static analysis typically classifies substitution channels along a given technology frontier, however, which implies—conceptually—that these substitution mechanisms only exploit already known and available products or technologies. Accordingly, the focus in such an analysis is on the promotion of their diffusion. In other words, these mechanisms

---

6   These channels also apply to policies that aim to dispose of or reduce waste. See, for instance, Fullerton and Kinnaman (1995) and Aalbers and Vollebergh (2008).

7   See Vollebergh (2008) for an application to Dutch energy and climate taxation.

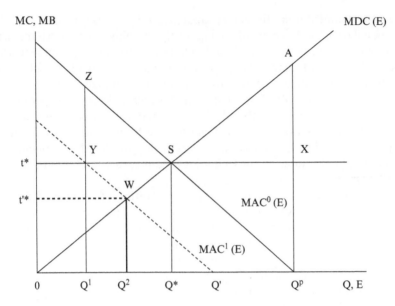

Figure 20.1   Dynamic incentives from environmental regulation

represent shifts *along* the technology frontier, but they do not describe shifts *of* the frontier. Long-run dynamic incentives induce entirely new technologies that may or may not be implemented in practice.

The dynamic impact of an environmental tax on technological change can be represented as an inward shift of the marginal abatement cost curve (MAC) and represents a shift of the abatement technology frontier.[8] The idea behind this shift is as follows: assume a profit-maximizing firm produces output Q^p in the status quo and faces the introduction of tax t^* on its emissions in order to internalize the marginal damage associated with its production (MDC).[9] As is well-known the 'classic' social optimum in a world without changes in technology or ecology is point Q^*. Starting in a polluted world with output Q^p and associated marginal damage A, welfare increases after introducing a Pigouvian tax on pollution equal to t^* in order to guarantee the optimal social level of pollution at point Q^*. The reason that this optimum will be 'produced' by firms and consumers in this market is simple. With such a tax in force, rational firms avoid paying the full initial tax amount $0t^*XQ^p$ by reducing waste or adopting currently available and relatively inexpensive add-on technologies. The marginal abatement cost curve $MAC^0(E)$ describes these options.

---

[8]   Note that the inward shift of the marginal abatement curve is exactly similar to the shift in the technology frontier as described by Newell et al. (1999). Less elastic abatement in the status quo corresponds with few options to reduce emissions without reducing output. New inventions are likely to make abatement more elastic, whereas learning is typically more linked to diffusion processes rather than new inventions. See also OECD (2010, 123ff) for a useful discussion of the relevant mechanisms involved and how this might be related to the design of a tax (or rebate).

[9]   Figure 20.1 is based on the assumption that each unit of output yields one unit of emission.

With an environmental tax firms face, apart from their abatement costs, additional payments equal to 0t*SQ*. To avoid paying for the remaining emissions, the firm could also invest in invention or innovation to develop new abatement equipment with lower remaining emissions and therefore incur lower tax payments. If successful, the production possibility set is shifted outwards (higher emissions abatement for a given input), which induces an inward shift of the abatement cost curve (lower costs per unit of emissions abated). This technology, labeled $MAC^1(E)$, reduces tax payments substantially, to 0t*YQ^1. So it would always be beneficial for the firms to invest in creating a new invention, as long as the expected average costs of the additional investment (including the cost of any capital equipment the technology requires) are lower than the average tax savings Q^1YSQ*.[10]

Note that these incentives for invention and innovation of a new environmental tax do not exist if a firm expects future command-and-control regulations to remain similar. If firms comply with current standards and abatement costs, $MAC^0(E)$ are 'sunk'; no additional benefits can be expected from investing in new abatement equipment labeled $MAC^1(E)$. However, if not all costs are sunk, for example because of maintenance and operating costs or because the firm expects future regulations to be stricter, incentives remain to invest in the development of new technologies.[11] For instance, the firm would save $Q^1ZSQ*-Q^1YWQ^2$ from the new technology under this new regulation, which could represent even more than savings under a tax (or auctioned tradable permit scheme) would.

ENVIRONMENTAL TAX EXPENDITURES INTERNALIZING POSITIVE EXTERNALITIES

Environmental tax expenditures can be evaluated in a similar way. Tax expenditures may (re)establish a social optimum in the context of technology spillovers. Instead of paying some 'fine' for generating pollution, such tax expenditures in fact provide a bonus to do more of a 'good' activity because it has positive 'spillovers.' A key issue in the economics of innovation, however, is that agents' willingness to invest time or money in research or learning is fraught with public good aspects, i.e. the problematic appropriation of their social value. Since the seminal paper of Arrow (1962), the standard view here is that the inventor is often unable to get a full return on his investment because new knowledge, once available, is non-rival and only partially excludable through instruments such as patents. Moreover, diffusion of new knowledge is less likely to be instantaneous across a heterogeneous population because of all sorts of information failures (see also Popp et al. 2009).

Due to the inability to fully exploit new knowledge privately, rational firms are likely to underinvest in this type of investment. Without stimulus a firm would invest in R&D

---

[10]   Note that the graph disregards dynamic aspects of investment decisions as well as the potential benefit of selling the technology to other firms in a similar situation.

[11]   Firms might also anticipate that investment in new (cost-efficient) technologies could be observed by the regulator, who in turn could respond with tougher regulation. Such expectations clearly make innovation and diffusion more costly.

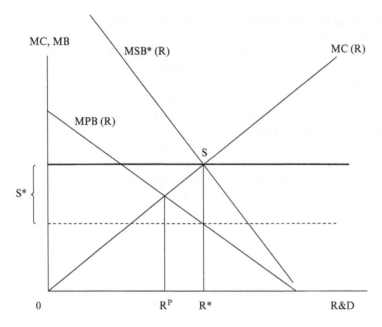

Figure 20.2   Tax expenditures for positive R&D spillovers

up to where its private return MPB(R) would be equal to its private cost MC(R), which is at the level R^P (see Figure 20.2). This level is below what is socially optimal, because the knowledge generated by the firm's activity may easily spill over to other firms. For instance, inventors may leave the firm while knowledge protection, such as through patents, cannot prevent the inventor from taking his knowledge with him. Accordingly a firm cannot fully appropriate its returns privately and therefore is likely to underinvest in this R&D activity. An optimal response from a social welfare perspective would be to stimulate the market for new knowledge by using a subsidy or an equivalent tax expenditure to guarantee a socially optimal amount of R&D spending R^* or diffusion by firms (see Figure 20.2). Ideally this tax expenditure or subsidy should be equal to the difference between the social and private return to R&D in the social optimum, which is equal to s^*.

Similar reasoning applies to adoption decisions. Adoption decisions are typically firm- or household-specific choices and usually require new knowledge for the adopter. Indeed, reschooling of existing staff or hiring of new personnel are but two examples of the additional costs involved. Moreover, one firm's investing in a specific technology might induce learning effects that in turn may benefit all firms that have not yet adopted the new technology.[12] Such investment externalities may provide justification for regulators to stimulate adoption of new technologies with subsidies as well. It is not uncommon to design such incentives as environmental tax expenditures. Incentives

---

[12]   If firms are heterogeneous, for instance with respect to the technology currently in use or with respect to capital (or borrowing) constraints, the adoption of a particular technology is likely to follow a gradual pattern over time, or a so-called penetration curve.

that induce investment commonly include investment credits, accelerated depreciation, partial expensing and exemptions.

Note that these spillover considerations apply to all R&D and adoption investment decisions and not only to environmental R&D decisions. Thus no specific environmental tax expenditure for R&D or adoption seems to be required. This conclusion is, however, preliminary. Viewed from a different angle, R&D and adoption are input-neutral only under very exceptional circumstances and usually depend on relative prices of inputs (see also the section below on the empirical analysis of environmental taxes). Both types of investment decisions apply to specific technologies and products. Technologies and products usually differ in terms of their characteristics, such as in the use of energy or the amount of pollution (see Newell et al. 1999). Some technologies and products therefore have beneficial characteristics relative to others. Due to information or other market failures, firms or households may not always be aware of such differences and their associated positive external benefits. This provides justification for regulators to stimulate R&D activity and adoption of cleaner technologies and products with additional subsidy as well. Thus environmental tax expenditures can come on top of a subsidy that already compensates for the general spillover (see also the section below on the empirical analysis of environmental tax expenditures). Indeed many such expenditures actually exist in practice (Jenkins and Lamech 1992; Price et al. 2005; OECD 2006).

The theoretical literature on the dynamic impact of the tax expenditure instrument has been remarkably limited, however. Only a small amount of literature focuses on the adoption decisions of technologies with beneficial environmental characteristics and how the government could stimulate their penetration (see Wirl 2000; Van Soest 2005). In this analysis a decision-maker adopts a new technology or product after comparing the future benefits and investment costs of the available options.[13] In this framework the predicted effect of a tax expenditure is straightforward. Defining the net adoption costs as the actual adoption costs minus the investment subsidy provided, technologies with lower net adoption costs are likely to obtain a higher ordering in the ranking of available alternative technologies. Therefore the subsidized technology will be adopted more readily than it would in the expenditure's absence. If firms are heterogeneous, for instance due to technology currently in use or capital (or borrowing) constraints, the adoption of a particular technology follows a gradual pattern over time. A subsidy will shift this pattern, whereas the overall penetration will be lifted somewhat due to the lower net cost of this particular technology.[14]

So the idea behind additional incentives for environmentally friendly technologies is to reduce the net R&D and adoption costs to stimulate a higher ordering in the financial ranking of potential research avenues or available alternative technologies among firms or households. Therefore the subsidy may direct R&D in specific directions, and more

---

[13]   This method is the Net Present Value (NPV) framework and simply computes the discounted net benefit streams of a typical investment option by subtracting the discounted investment cost from the discounted benefits associated with the economic lifetime of the option at a given discount rate (such as the market interest rate).

[14]   Note that this line of reasoning holds even if firms belong to different risk classes, that is, if they differ with respect to the discount rate they apply to their investment decision (DeCanio and Watkins 1998).

environmentally productive technologies and products will be adopted more readily than they would be in the absence of the environmental expenditure. These expenditures stimulate inventions as well as earlier adoption due to the lower net cost of the subsidized options. Note that this analysis applies to both firms and household decisions. Household investment decisions, such as buying a new refrigerator or other electric or energy-consuming appliances, are also adoption decisions of new technology already available at the market. Consequently, the diffusion phase typically also includes the penetration of new technologies or products to households.

ENVIRONMENTAL TAXES SHIFTING TECHNOLOGICAL CHANGE

For a long time the analysis of pollution mainly focused on emission abatement, the first of the substitution channels mentioned earlier. Specifically the whole concept of 'abatement technology' reflects the idea that emissions are 'additional' to (or 'separable from') the production process. Examples of such add-on technologies are water purification installations and scrubbers. Figure 20.1 clearly reflects this idea, with its focus on an environmental tax that regulates a specific emission in a specific market ('partial equilibrium').

Two main developments have changed this perspective. First, both firms and governments realized at some point that environmental policy would be irreversible and in several areas would become more and more stringent. After an initial phase of retrofitting and the development of add-on technologies, firms started to engage in the development of entirely new add-on technologies, including what is sometimes called 'integrated technology' (Kemp 1997). This process can be observed in many areas of environmental control, such as water sanitation and purification, air pollution control (smog, acid rain particles, etc.) and waste management. Second, the growing concern about climate change and other energy-related issues contributed to the acknowledgement that some pollution problems are more fundamentally rooted in our economic system. Indeed, many problems relate to production processes that are both directly and indirectly responsible for emissions, such as electricity-generating technologies or energy-consuming technologies and products.

Around the same time, economists started to pay more attention to a better understanding of the role of technological change as the engine of economic growth. For instance, Nelson and Winter (1982, 275ff) built on the fundamental contributions of Schumpeter in their effort to better understand the dynamics of capitalism through the role of technological change. However, it took until the end of the 1980s for these and other pioneers to shift the attention of mainstream economists to a more explicit investigation or 'endogenization' of the dynamics of technological change (Romer 1990; Aghion and Howitt 1992). Application of these new mechanisms to environmental issues started, for instance, with Gradus and Smulders (1993).

Instead of exogenous technological change, which arrives as 'manna from heaven,' the endogenous growth literature acknowledges that technological change is a complex process that is dependent on more than just the passage of time. The key modeling assumption is to include a knowledge stock in the production function of the economy.

As a consequence, a society that is willing to spend enough on R&D can realize a steady state of technological change sufficiently strong to offset the diminishing returns from capital-resource substitution. Accordingly, sustainable long-run growth is now possible in this framework. Opportunities and incentives for R&D are determined by costs and benefits to innovation. Investment in R&D, for instance, competes with investments in physical assets or consumption, whereas the return equals the required rate of return for the other assets.

It is one thing to show that R&D is key to understanding the dynamics and economic growth in capitalism. Quite another thing is whether this dynamics also benefits the environment.[15] Smulders (2005) explains why this is not obvious at all. Without regulation, new technology improves environmental quality only under two conditions. First, the new technology should decrease the unit production cost (which excludes the environmental cost if the environment is not priced). Second, the new technology must substantially reduce the marginal productivity of polluting inputs.[16] If this reduction is not strong enough, it is unlikely that compensation can be found for the expansion in the scale of output induced by the new technology. So an improvement may only happen by coincidence in this case.

Environmental policy, such as environmental taxes, can shift the balance toward better environmental quality. With such a policy, firms have an explicit incentive to avoid pollution not only by reducing output or emissions per unit of output, but also by shifting their R&D investments to change the technology frontier. For instance, Goulder and Schneider (1999) use a small partial equilibrium model to study the cost and benefits of endogenous technological change modeled as investments to lower the cost of abatement. In the case of an emission tax, they show that the net social benefits rise once technological change is endogenized. Compared to the case of exogenous abatement technology, both optimal pollution and output are lower. Thus in this model the possibility of reducing costs in abatement may improve the trade-off between environmental quality and production in favor of the environment.

The study by Goulder and Schneider (1999) shows that the dynamic impact of an environmental tax is not only to lower the cost of abatement, but also to affect the optimal stringency of the tax. This is illustrated in Figure 20.1, where the ex post social optimum, i.e. after the new abatement technology becomes available, is Q^2. Because the new technology reduces the opportunity cost of environmental regulation, also a lower optimal tax t'^* ex post is justified! Note that this feedback still reflects the fundamental insight that technological change improves cost efficiency of environmental policy: emission reduction is cheaper along the whole new abatement technology frontier.

These results are not obtained in an endogenous growth approach proper, however. In the paper by Goulder and Schneider (1999), technological change is reduced to improve-

---

[15]   Note the fundamental difference between (nonrenewable) resource scarcity, which is more or less properly marketed, and environmental scarcity, which is prone to fundamental market failures. See Smulders (2005) for a clear distinction between these two scarcity issues.

[16]   If the first condition is not met the firm is better off using the old technology and would not adopt the new one. If the second condition is not met the firm would either increase pollution per unit of output or decrease pollution per unit of output, but due to the expansion of the scale of output, total pollution still increases (rebound effect).

ments in abatement technology, and no interactions with other markets are taken into consideration. The endogenous growth literature studies also allow the production technology for the whole economy to adapt. Indeed, one could reach the opposite conclusion using a general-equilibrium model where R&D reduces production costs (Smulders 2005). In such a model the effect of endogenous technological change is to lower optimal abatement because spending resources on abatement crowds out investment in total factor productivity improvements. In other words, endogenous technological change also allows for increases in the opportunity cost of abatement itself.

By now quite a large body of literature has explored the role of technological change in theoretical as well as applied general equilibrium models, in particular in the area of climate change. These models not only focus on R&D, but also consider learning-by-doing, learning-by-using, the role of vintages in current physical capital, and lock-in in existing technological paradigms (see also next section). The interested reader could consult several older and more recent reviews of this literature (for example Clark et al. 2006; Popp et al. 2009).[17]

One key issue in this literature is the role of the knowledge stock that governs the overall level and direction (i.e., input-bias) of technological change. As noted by Popp et al. (2009, 7), the difficulty lies in determining how this stock accumulates and affects future input use and emissions. In particular, Acemoglu (2002) has shown how the trade-off among innovation in different directions, which is inherent in the innovation possibility approach, results endogenously from a firm's dynamic optimization. In deciding how much and where to invest in the generation of new ideas ('R&D'), firms also consider changes in the relative input prices. Higher prices for certain inputs directly affect the expected returns of a specific invention, which is likely to generate a bias of new inventions away from the more expensive input.[18]

This so-called induced innovation hypothesis has been applied to environmental externalities recently by Sue Wing (2006), Gerlagh et al. (2009) and Acemoglu et al. (2012). This literature explicitly combines the two previously mentioned market failures.[19] First, pollution creates a negative environmental externality, which requires an environmental tax to induce polluters to abate emissions up to the social optimum. Second, knowledge spillovers characterize endogenous technological change and a subsidy could compensate for potential social loss of underinvestment in R&D. Sue Wing (2006), for instance, finds that environmental taxes indeed bias production away from the dirty good toward the clean good. To what extent research will be biased toward the clean good, however, depends on the substitutability of the clean and dirty inputs. Only if the environmental tax is large enough do innovators tend to compensate for the hump-shaped profile of the dirty R&D.

I conclude from this literature that the ability to judge environmental taxes from a cost

---

[17]   There are also a number of special issues of journals like *Ecological Economics, Environmental and Resource Economics* and *Energy Journal* specifically devoted to this literature.

[18]   The overall direction of technological changes balances market size and price effects. Market size encourages innovation toward the larger input sector, while the price effect directs innovation toward the sector with the higher price. The overall effect is determined by input substitutability and elasticity between the dirty and clean sectors.

[19]   Note, however, that other market failures like monopolistic competition play a role too.

efficiency point of view is limited. Environmental taxes not only exploit the available substitution mechanisms at a given production possibilities frontier, but also induce a shift of the frontier. This, in turn, contributes to lower abatement costs for a given reduction commitment, but also has indirect effects on the optimal reduction level itself as well as on R&D effort and its direction. As for the interaction between environmental taxes and R&D subsidies for the 'clean sector,' the analysis with endogenous technology confirms results obtained from partial equilibrium analysis. As Jaffe et al. (2005, 169) argue, the rate of investment in the clean technology is usually below the socially optimal level in cases where environmental externalities have not been fully internalized. Therefore they maintain that it is unlikely that environmental policy alone creates sufficient incentives for first-best levels of adoption. So investment subsidies should be used not as a substitute for environmental policy, but as a complement to it.

EMPIRICAL ANALYSIS OF ENVIRONMENTAL TAXES

Studies of the actual impact of Pigouvian tax instruments on technological change are still very limited. Much of our early knowledge comes from some typical case studies and anecdotal evidence (Opschoor and Vos 1989; Andersen 1994). Moreover, the early studies also focus more on short-run dynamic impacts and less on long-run impacts. One of the oldest examples to date is Bressers' (1988) analysis of the impact of an earmarked water charge implemented in the Netherlands in 1970.[20] The original purpose of this charge was a full-cost recovery scheme to finance public sewage treatment measures. Its design was such that 'polluters had to pay:' firms and households paid a fee roughly in relation to the amount of organic pollution they created. A remarkable drop in oxygen-consuming industrial pollution in industrial wastewater relative to the amount of industrial production was observed in the Netherlands. Based on a small sample of regions, Bressers (1988) found that the water levy, and in particular the increase in its rate between 1975 and 1980, contributed strongly to this change in the level of pollution. However, this study does not make the effect of the charge on technological change explicit at all.

Kemp (1998) more closely focuses on this dynamic impact. Specifically, he studied whether the average rate of this water charge in the Netherlands had an impact on the diffusion of biological effluent treatment plants in the Dutch food and beverage industry between 1974 and 1991. His empirical estimation fits diffusion equations to the average rate at each period in time and finds that the adoption of this technology was strongly influenced by the effluent tax rate.[21] His result confirms the idea that prospective adopters trade off the costs of effluent treatment against the savings on effluent tax payments. Kemp also finds that adoption strongly depends on firm-specific characteristics, such as the use of investment selection criteria that cannot be directly controlled by the regulator. Note, however, that the study by Kemp also does not study whether this charge contributed as well to the rise of *new* knowledge.

---

[20]   For an update of this case see http://economicinstruments.com/index.php/water/article/165-.
[21]   This result is also confirmed by specification of diffusion based on the epidemic model of technological diffusion.

Another well-known measure of a potential dynamic impact is shifts in abatement cost functions over time. Höglund Isaksson (2005), for instance, studied changes in Swedish nitrogen oxides' (NO_x) abatement cost functions in response to the Swedish NO_x charge (and which operates as a tax) implemented in 1992. The revenues from this charge were refunded, net of administrative cost for the government, and firms received output-based instead of emissions-based refunds. The drawback of output-based refunding, however, is that diffusion of abatement technology is hampered because firms may strategically prevent information disclosure to other firms. Looking at pollution abatement cost changes for 162 NO_x abatement measures implemented in 114 firms during the period 1990–1996, Höglund Isaksson (2005) observes that firms were very active in complying with the charge on emissions of NO_x. She observes that many of the analyzed plants had options for reduction at a very low or even zero cost. Furthermore, she also finds that learning and technological development in abatement are present because the range of options tends to widen over the analyzed period.

Clearly these studies tend to focus on short-run impacts of the use of environmental taxes and at best indirectly analyze impacts on new knowledge. For instance, the decline in abatement costs over time may be due to learning effects associated with diffusion of an already existing technology, but could also be the result of new knowledge. Identification of this impact, however, is quite complex due to data limitations as well as the limited use of such taxes in practice. One approach taken in the literature is to explore variation in energy prices as a proxy of variation in the stringency of tax instruments. Indeed, the theoretical literature suggests that higher (tax-inclusive) energy prices are likely to shift technological change toward less energy-intensive technologies, which, in turn, reduces emissions as long as energy and emissions are complements. Greene (1990) is an early example that followed this approach. He studied the practical experiment provided by the CAFE standards imposed on the fuel efficiency of cars in the US while controlling for energy price variation. Greene finds that the CAFE standards had perhaps twice as much influence as gasoline prices. Accordingly, this suggests that the responsiveness of fuel efficiency to prices is significant, but also that binding standards are an important driver behind changes in the car market. Also, recent advances in the literature that report evidence for dynamic shifts in the car market still do not explicitly control for a potential difference between energy prices and taxes (see Knittel 2009).

A major step forward in identifying long-run dynamic impacts of policy is to use explicit measures of new knowledge, such as patents. In particular Popp (2002) is the first paper to date that offers clear econometric evidence that the filing of US patents is sensitive to changes in relative prices, in particular between 1970 and 1994. Specifically, Popp shows that rising fossil fuel prices, in particular oil and gas prices, raise the cost of this type of energy use (and its associated emissions) and induce patents (and citations) for energy-saving technologies. Technology groups such as fuel cells, use of waste as fuel or for heat production, and coal gasification have clearly benefited from the changes in energy prices over time.

Another recent study is Johnstone et al. (2008), who evaluate the impact of different environmental policy instruments on patents in an international context. Using country data for a panel of OECD countries, they evaluate which instruments have the strongest impact on the number of renewable energy patents for wind, sun, ocean, biomass and waste for 25 countries between 1978 and 2003. In this paper, again environmental taxes are studied only indirectly, through changes in energy prices. These authors find a positive effect only for covenants on waste but not for the other renewables, while taxes, standards and tradable permits stimulate patents for all renewables.

Energy prices are not the same as energy or environmental taxes, however. Firms and households may react differently to market prices or taxes. Moreover, tax-to-price ratios differ enormously across products which will cause these reactions to be different across products as well. Studies that explicitly analyze the impact of energy or environmental taxes on new knowledge have not yet been published. Only a very recent report by the OECD (2010) contains some interesting recent material based on some underlying studies that have tried to identify this role explicitly. One of these studies is Martin and Wagner (2009), who evaluate whether the UK climate levy in connection with a tax rebate for those firms that participate in a so-called Climate Change Agreement (CCA) has stimulated new invention as measured by patents. They report that participating firms began to patent less after the introduction of this policy. This suggests that a tax incentive on its own would provide stronger incentives to engage in innovative activity than do negotiated targets under CCA.

THE EMPIRICAL ANALYSIS OF ENVIRONMENTAL TAX EXPENDITURES

The available empirical evidence on the impact of environmental tax expenditures on technological change is also rather bleak. Again the available studies focus on short-run behavioral responses and typically neglect the impact on new knowledge. Much of our insight is derived from the Demand Side Management (DSM) program operated by US electric utilities in the 1990s, which aimed to entice households to adopt high-efficiency appliances, typically via a tax rebate. Empirical evidence from this program seems to support the belief that such subsidies are ineffective and inefficient. For instance, some studies (such as Malm 1996 and Wirl 2000) report that the behavior of many agents was not affected by the subsidy.

In a somewhat neglected study, however, Hassett and Metcalf (1995) provide some counterevidence, showing that those energy conservation rebates actually have been effective in stimulating the penetration of modern energy-saving technologies. Using much better panel data at the household level, they first reproduced previous results showing no effects, or even adverse effects. But when they included unobservable individual characteristics, such as 'taste' for conservation, they actually found that US households invested in energy-saving technologies, such as insulation and replacing furnace burners, and therefore responded in a rational way to the energy conservation incentives of the tax rebate.

That the design of a tax rebate significantly affects its impact has been shown in a study by Revelt and Train (1998). They studied the relative importance of rebates or loans to the adoption of high-efficiency appliances by households in the US. To study the potential effect of loans, stated-preference data were collected to estimate the effect of loans relative to the effect of rebates. Using 6081 choice experiments of 401 customers, they also concluded that DSM is effective but that loans have a larger impact than rebates. This is surprising because a rational individual would prefer the rebate over a loan (of equivalent money) if upfront costs were the basic problem. As explained by Revelt and Train (1998, 652), individuals may not be indifferent and may see the subsidy as a signal. It is clear for a loan that the lender makes money from it, but a rebate is a 'giveaway' and customers may wonder what its motivation is. If individuals start wondering about its motivation, their behavior is likely to be affected. For instance, if an individual is suspicious about the benefactor, he or she might not buy the appliance, just for that reason.

Further and recent evidence that a rebate on an energy-efficient technology actually changes adoption behavior by firms is provided by Aalbers et al. (2009). They analyze the impact of technology adoption subsidies on investment behavior in an individual choice experiment, with managers of real firms as participants.[22] The authors constructed the decision environment of agents in such a way that they all faced essentially the same investment decision. Moreover, to mimic decision situations in small and medium-sized enterprises, decision-makers also faced binding time constraints. The findings are remarkable. Subsidies are highly effective as an incentive mechanism even if only a small, expensive subset of available technologies is subsidized and the subsidy does not make these technologies profitable. The managers realize much higher energy savings in the treatment with subsidy than in the treatment without subsidy. Furthermore, the subsidies seem to induce more radical choice behavior: either managers adopt very early or they do not purchase a technology at all.

Clearly all of these studies focus on adoption behavior of existing technologies that are not yet widely used or not used at all. Despite widespread use of tax expenditures like investment credits, accelerated depreciation, partial expensing and exemptions, we know little or nothing about their long-run impact. Whether and how these subsidies have had an impact on, for instance, R&D expenditures or the availability of entirely new knowledge as measured by patents, has only been studied in some of the background studies as reported in OECD (2010).

RESEARCH AGENDA

Recent advances in both theory and applied general equilibrium analysis illustrate that environmental taxes are likely to have an impact in all stages of technological change, i.e. invention, innovation and diffusion of new products and technology. Some of this literature is also a warning against simple, sometimes too-positive receptions of this dynamic impact. Cheaper abatement also has an opportunity cost and therefore requires changes in regulatory behavior by the regulator as well as induce rebound effects. Directed clean technology may also crowd out other R&D activities that could be helpful in other areas of human life.

Empirical studies of the link between environmental taxes and technological change are remarkably scarce. Studies that pass the test of modern identification requirements usually exploit proxies of taxes using energy price changes. Others are restricted to case studies and do not always account for econometric pitfalls such as the identification

---

[22] Note that this paper studies tax expenditures for investments but not other types of tax expenditures.

of proper controls, including the use of multiple instruments at the same time. Further efforts should be made to exploit the much better data sets that have become available recently, such as patent data, and to collect new ones. Typical promising areas of research are energy and waste. One example is the impact that energy taxes may have had on new ideas or the adoption of new technology relative to the role of energy prices and other instruments. Similar questions apply to water and waste charges.

Some other topics deserve wider study as well. One example is the role of tax design, i.e. the choice of the tax (expenditure) rate and base, in the development of new ideas or the adoption of existing but not yet applied technology. Keen (1998), for instance, has shown the different impacts that ad valorem or specific taxes may have in the context of monopolies. Also selection effects should be studied more systematically to better understand the dynamic effectiveness of taxes and tax expenditures. The study by OECD (2010) is a good example of how to proceed and contains valuable material that merits further scrutiny. Furthermore, current empirical assessments have the tendency to be biased toward observable information, such as changes in abatement costs, number of patents (citations), physical characteristics of technologies, so we may miss effects on organization design, changes in attitudes, etc. How taxes affect soft practices, like the use of internal monitoring systems, also deserves further attention (e.g. Frondel et al. 2008). There is also some evidence that decisions of households, apart from the scale of the investment, are quite different from those of firms (DeCanio and Watkins 1998). Finally, behavioral economics may be a promising area for future studies. The findings in this literature are a warning against simple conjectures based on theoretical propositions, even if they come from the 'enlightened' endogenous technological change literature.

REFERENCES

Aalbers, R. and H.R.J. Vollebergh (2008), 'An economic analysis of mixing wastes', *Environmental and Resource Economics*, **39**, 311–30.
Aalbers, R., E. van der Heijden, J. Potters, D.P. van Soest and H.R.J. Vollebergh (2009), 'Technology adoption subsidies: an experiment with managers', *Energy Economics*, **31**, 431–42.
Acemoglu, D. (2002), 'Directed technical change', *Review of Economic Studies*, **69**, 781–809.
Acemoglu, D., P. Aghion, L. Bursztyn and D. Hemous (2012), 'The environment and directed technical change', *American Economic Review*, **102** (1), 131–66.
Aghion, P. and P. Howitt (1992), *Endogenous Growth Theory*, Cambridge, MA, US: MIT Press.
Andersen, Mikael Skou (1994), *Governance by Green Taxes: Making Pollution Prevention Pay*, Manchester, UK and New York, US: Manchester University Press.
Arrow, K. (1962), 'The economic implications of learning by doing', *Review of Economic Studies*, **29**, 155–73.
Baumol, W.J. and W.E. Oates (1971), 'The use of standards and prices for protection of the environment', *Swedish Journal of Economics*, **73**, 43–54.
Baumol, W.J. and W.E. Oates (1988), *The Theory of Environmental Policy*, 2nd ed., Cambridge, UK: Cambridge University Press.
Bressers, H. (1988), 'A comparison of the effectiveness of incentives and directives: the case of the Dutch water quality policy', *Policy Studies Review*, **7** (3), 500–518.
Clark, L., J. Weyant, and A. Birky (2006), 'On the sources of technological change: assessing the evidence', *Energy Economics*, **28**, 579–86.
DeCanio, S.J. and W.E. Watkins (1998), 'Investment in energy efficiency: Do the characteristics of firms matter?', *Review of Economic Studies*, **80**, 95–107.
Downing, P.B. and K. Hanf (1983), *International Comparisons in Implementing Pollution Laws*, Boston, MA: Kluwer.
Fischer, C., I.W.H. Parry, and W.A. Pizer (2003), 'Instrument choice for environmental protection when technological innovation is endogenous', *Journal of Environmental Economics and Management*, **45** (3), 523–45.

Frondel, M., J. Horbach and K. Rennings (2008), 'What triggers environmental management and innovation? Empirical evidence for Germany', *Ecological Economics*, **66** (1), 153–60.

Fullerton, D. (2002), 'A framework to compare environmental policies', *Southern Economic Journal*, **68**, 224–48.

Fullerton, D. and T.C. Kinnaman (1995), 'Garbage, recycling and illicit burning or dumping', *Journal of Environmental Economics and Management*, **29**, 78–91.

Gerlagh, R., S. Kverndokk and K.E. Rosendahl (2009), 'Optimal timing of climate change policy: interaction between carbon taxes and innovation externalities', *Environmental and Resource Economics*, **43** (3), 369–90.

Goulder, L.H. and S. Schneider (1999), 'Induced technological change and the attractiveness of CO_2 abatement policies', *Resource and Energy Economics*, **21**, 211–53.

Gradus, R. and J.A. Smulders (1993), 'The trade-off between environmental care and long-term growth—pollution in three prototype growth models', *Journal of Economics*, **58** (1), 25–51.

Greene, D.L. (1990), 'CAFE or price? An analysis of the effects of federal fuel economy regulations and gasoline price on new car MPG, 1978–89', *The Energy Journal*, **11** (3), 37–57.

Hassett, K.A. and G.E. Metcalf (1995), 'Energy tax credits and residential conservation investment: evidence from panel data', *Journal of Public Economics*, **57**, 201–17.

Höglund Isaksson, L. (2005), 'Abatement costs in response to the Swedish charge on nitrogen oxide emissions', *Journal of Environmental Economics and Management*, **50**, 102–20.

Jaffe, A.B. and R.N. Stavins (1995), 'Dynamic incentives of environmental regulations: the effects of alternative policy instruments on technology diffusion', *Journal of Environmental Economics and Management*, **29**, 43–63.

Jaffe, A.B., R. Newell and R.N. Stavins (2003), 'Technological change and the environment', in K.-G. Mäler and J. Vincent (eds), *Handbook of Environmental Economics*, vol. 1, Amsterdam, Netherlands: Elsevier, pp. 461–516.

Jaffe, A.B., R. Newell and R.N. Stavins (2005), 'A tale of two market failures', *Ecological Economics*, **54**, 164–74.

Jenkins, G.P. and R. Lamech (1992), 'Fiscal policies to control pollution: international experience', *Bulletin for International Fiscal Documentation*, **46**, 483–502.

Johnstone, N., I. Hascic and D. Popp (2008), 'Renewable energy policies and technological innovation: evidence based on patent counts', NBER Working Paper 13760, Boston, MA, US: NBER.

Keen, M. (1998), 'The balance between specific and *ad valorem* taxation', *Fiscal Studies*, **19**, 1–37.

Kemp, R. (1997), *Environmental Policy and Technical Change*, Cheltenham, UK: Edward Elgar.

Kemp, R. (1998), 'The diffusion of biological waste-water treatment plants in Dutch food and beverage industry', *Environmental and Resource Economics*, **12**, 113–36.

Kneese, A.V. and C.L. Schulze (1975), *Pollution, Prices, and Public Policy*, Washington DC, US: Brookings Institution.

Knittel, C.R. (2009), 'Automobiles on steroids: product attribute trade-offs and technological progress in the automobile sector', NBER, Working Paper 15162, Boston, MA, US: NBER.

Magat, W.A. (1978), 'Pollution control and technological advance: a dynamic model of the firm', *Journal of Environmental Economics and Management*, **5**, 1–25.

Malm, E. (1996), 'An actions-based estimate of the free-rider fraction in electricity utility DSM programs', *Energy Journal*, **17**, 41–8.

Martin, R. and U. Wagner (2009), 'Climate change policy and innovation', mimeo.

Nelson, R.R. and S.G. Winter (1982), *An Evolutionary Theory of Economic Change*, Cambridge, MA, US: Harvard University Press.

Newbery, D.M. (2005), 'Why tax energy? Towards more rational policy', *The Energy Journal*, **26** (3), 1–39.

Newell, R.G, A.B. Jaffe, and R.N. Stavins (1999), 'The induced innovation hypothesis and energy-saving technological change', *Quarterly Journal of Economics*, **114**, 941–75.

OECD (2006), *The Political Economy of Environmentally Related Taxes*, Paris, France: OECD.

OECD (2010), *Taxation, Innovation and the Environment*, Paris, France: OECD.

Opschoor, J.B. and H. Vos (1989), *Economic Instruments for Environmental Protection*, Paris, France: OECD.

Popp, D. (2002), 'Induced innovation and energy prices', *American Economic Review*, **92**, 160–80.

Popp, D., R.G. Newell, and A.B. Jaffe (2009), 'Energy, the environment and technological change', NBER Working Paper 14832, Boston, MA, US: NBER.

Price, L., C. Galitsky, J. Sinton, E. Worrell, and W. Graus (2005), 'Tax and fiscal policies for the promotion of industrial energy efficiency: a survey of international experience', Paper LBNL-58128, Berkeley, California, US: Lawrence Berkeley National Laboratory.

Requate, T. (2005), 'Dynamic incentives by environmental policy instruments: a survey', *Ecological Economics*, **54**, 175–95.

Requate, T. and W. Unold (2003), 'Environmental policy incentives to adopt advanced abatement technology: Will the true ranking please stand up?', *European Economic Review*, **47**, 125–46.

Revelt, D. and K. Train (1998), 'Mixed logit with repeated choices: households' choices of appliance efficiency level', *Review of Economics and Statistics*, **80**, 647–57.

Romer, P.M. (1990), 'Endogenous technical change', *Journal of Political Economy*, **98**, S71–S102.

Schumpeter, J.A. (1934), *The Theory of Economic Development*, Cambridge, MA, US: Harvard University Press.

Schumpeter, J.A. (1942), *Capitalism, Socialism and Democracy*, London, UK: George Allen & Unwin.

Smulders, J.A. (2005), 'Endogenous technological change, natural resources and growth', in R.D. Simpson, M.A. Toman, and R.U. Ayres (eds), *Scarcity and Growth Revisited: Natural Resources and the Environment in the New Millennium*, Baltimore, MD, US: RFF Press.

Smulders, J.A. and H.R.J. Vollebergh (2001), 'Green taxes and administrative costs: the case of carbon taxation', in C. Carraro and G.E. Metcalf (eds), *Behavioral and Distributional Effects of Environmental Policy*, Chicago, IL, US: University of Chicago Press, pp. 91–125.

Stavins, R. (2003), 'Experience with market based environmental policy instruments', in K.G. Mäler and J.R. Vincent (eds), *Handbook of Environmental Economics*, vol. 1, Amsterdam: Elsevier Science, pp. 461–516.

Sue Wing, I. (2006), 'Representing induced technological change in models for climate policy', *Energy Economics* **28**, 539–62.

Van Soest, D.P. (2005), The impact of environmental policy instruments on the timing of adoption of energy-saving technologies', *Resource and Energy Economics*, **27** (3), 235–47.

Vollebergh, H.R.J. (2007), 'Lessons from the polder: energy tax design in the Netherlands from a climate change perspective', *Ecological Economics*, **64**, 660–72.

Wirl, F. (2000), 'Lessons from utility conservation programs', *Energy Journal*, **21**, 87–108.

21 Impacts on competitiveness: what do we know from modeling?

Paul Ekins and Stefan Speck

INTRODUCTION TO THE ISSUES

In recent years, as trade and globalization have become perceived as increasingly important sources of economic growth and development (Mongelli et al. 2006, 88), concern with regard to the implications of more stringent environmental policies within the EU on the competitive situation of European industry as compared to their main foreign competitors has intensified, in particular in the context of the EU energy and climate policy plans. This chapter is intended to explore this concern. The chapter focuses on the European context because European experiences with energy and carbon taxes have provided the opportunity to analyze competitiveness impacts of environmental tax policies. Nevertheless, the competitiveness principles and methodology discussed here can apply to other parts of the world as well and therefore are of broader interest.

While on first consideration the concept of competitiveness seems straightforward, in fact its meaning varies with the level at which it is being considered. Most simply, for the firm it relates to whether the firm's products can be sold in competitive markets. Thus OECD (2003, 5) defined competitiveness at the business/firm level as 'primarily a matter of being able to produce products that are either cheaper or better than those of other firms.' The markets in question in an economy open to international trade may be domestic or foreign.

An industrial sector consists of many firms, some of which will be more competitive than others. The sectoral competitiveness of a given country therefore relates to whether the sector as a whole can retain or expand its share of markets. Again, the markets may be domestic or international.

At the national level the concept is different again. In its annual competitiveness report, the European Commission defines national competitiveness as 'a sustained rise in the standards of living of a nation and as low a level of involuntary unemployment as possible' (EC 2007, 6). The OECD less succinctly defines national competitiveness as the 'degree to which a country can, under free and fair market conditions, produce goods and services which meet the test of international markets, while simultaneously maintaining and expanding the real incomes of its people over the longer term' (OECD 1993, 237).

Many factors affect competitiveness at the firm, sectoral and national levels. The international dimension of competitiveness is affected by factors such as the existence and the nature of trade barriers between countries and exchange rate variations (for example between the US dollar and the Euro). In contrast, at the national level such factors as real wage rates, factor prices and national policies, taxes and regulations, and their interactions, are significant. Although it may be thought that these factors are common for all businesses in the same industrial sectors, in fact differences in the competitiveness of individual firms still exist, as the ability to produce the most output using a given quantity of inputs depends on factors, such as the quality of human capital and the application of the latest technological innovations in the production process. The economic performance of an entire industrial sector is a reflection of the performance of individual firms, some of which overperform and others of which underperform compared with the average firm.

There is no single measure of competitiveness. Factors found in the literature to be relevant in assessing competitiveness are costs of production, market share (share of global production), and import and export intensity, as well as sector profitability. What all these factors have in common is that they are quantifiable, unlike non-price factors such as the quality of the workforce, infrastructure, corruption, and the legislative, fiscal and regulatory framework (how it is implemented and whether it is adhered to) and so on, which can also affect the competitiveness of firms, sectors or nations.

Assessments of competitiveness impacts in response to carbon/energy taxes must not only take into account the carbon/energy tax burden, but should also consider total energy prices, which are composed of factors including the import price (import prices of the same energy product can vary between EU member states (Ekins and Speck 2008), and are of course affected by exchange rate movements) and how final end-user electricity prices are set (because of the relatively big differences in the network tariffication between European countries (Speck and Mulder 2003)). The competitive situation of an industry is also determined by nonprice elements, such as production methods and regulations (see EC 2004 and Baranzini et al. 2000).

The logic behind the fear of loss of competitiveness caused by carbon/energy taxes is simple: such taxes make energy for production processes more expensive and therefore, other things being equal, lead to an increase in production costs. If these taxes, or indeed any other taxes on business, are implemented unilaterally (either at the national level or at the EU level), the extra production costs may impair the international competitiveness of the affected firms and industrial sectors. However, other things are typically not equal.

First, one result of the tax increase may be to cause firms to discover and implement cost-effective energy efficiency measures which they had previously overlooked. Contrary to what might be surmised from economic theory, there is substantial evidence that firms do not routinely operate at the efficiency frontier in relation to their energy use. For example, the experience with the UK Climate Change Agreements (CCAs), under which numerous economic sectors met supposedly demanding targets a full eight years early, suggests that the extra incentive of the tax rebate associated with the CCAs was required for companies to discover significant opportunities for energy efficiency which already existed (Ekins and Etheridge 2006).

Second, it is possible that increasing the costs of environmental damage or resource use will stimulate industrial innovation. This may even increase competitiveness (Porter and van der Linde 1995), as companies seek to develop less environmentally intensive products and processes, and environmental industries are created to help other companies reduce their environmental impact. A number of studies suggest that environmental industries are likely to be a fast-growing sector of the economies of many European countries, and will make a substantial contribution to their national incomes (Ernst and Young 2006; UKCEED 2006). However, such processes of innovation and industrial development may take time to become established and bear fruit, suggesting that analysis of competitiveness effects from environmental taxes or environmental policy generally should distinguish between the long and the short term.

Third, the taxes may be imposed as part of an environmental tax reform (ETR), such that the overall tax change is broadly revenue-neutral, and the overall tax burden is unchanged. Thus the European Environment Agency has defined ETR as 'a reform of the national tax system where there is a shift of the burden of taxes from conventional taxes such as labour to environmentally damaging activities, such as resource use or pollution' (EEA 2005, 84). So ETR is a tax *shift*, rather than a tax increase. In this case the effect of ETR on competitiveness depends on which taxes have been reduced to compensate for the increase in environmental taxes. If they are business taxes, then this will tend to directly offset any competitiveness effect on businesses. Of course, different firms will be affected differently: some will emerge from the tax shift as net gainers, others will be worse off. If, for example, the tax increase is on energy and the tax decrease is on the business costs of employment (such as a reduction in employers' social security contributions), then winning sectors and companies will be those with relatively high labor-, rather than energy-, intensity. Losing sectors and firms will have the opposite characteristic.

If the country undertaking the ETR has involuntary unemployment, then the reduction in the cost of labor may stimulate increased labor demand and cause unemployment to fall and output to increase—the so-called 'double dividend' effect. The extent of this effect is likely to be limited, and may be offset by complex interactions between the taxes (see Ekins and Barker 2001 for a discussion), but there is general agreement that recycling revenues in this way will reduce the net cost of environmental improvement compared with other ways of revenue recycling. These competitiveness effects of ETRs are explored in some detail later.

Competitive considerations are the major reason why EU member states have granted special tax provisions in the form of partial tax exemptions to industries, in particular when they have introduced special carbon-energy taxes—normally as part of an ETR— during the last two decades (see Ekins and Speck 1998, 1999, 2008; Speck and Jilkova 2009). These special tax provisions can have serious implications for the efficiency and effectiveness of the ETR.

It is clear, therefore, that despite its apparent simplicity, the competitiveness concept is actually rather complex. Environmental taxes, like other taxes on business, may have effects on competitiveness, an outcome that will depend crucially on what is done with the revenues from the taxes. That is why this chapter focuses on the competitiveness effects of ETR, which is revenue-neutral. Even so it is no simple matter to find evidence as to whether past ETRs have damaged competitiveness, or whether they might do so in the future. In order to address these questions, the evidence at the national level, the firm level and the sectoral level will be examined in turn.

ETR AND NATIONAL COMPETITIVENESS

Since the early 1990s several European countries have made more widespread use of economic instruments in environmental policy. Some have also embraced the concept of ETR by either launching new environmental taxes or revising already existing ones, and by reducing other taxes—often those levied on labor—simultaneously.

As noted above, the economic effects of ETR are felt in a number of ways at a number of different levels. Most obviously the increases in energy or environmental taxes will increase the prices of the affected fuels or activities. Producers will be able to pass on a greater or lesser proportion of those price increases depending on whether they are in less or more competitive markets.

The revenue-recycling mechanism will also affect prices, perhaps directly by reducing the cost of other inputs into production when this might reduce the prices of goods and services, therefore wholly or partly offsetting the inflationary effect of the tax increase. Another possibility, where the revenue recycling is through a reduction in employers' social security contributions, is that this will increase the demand for labor. Where there is involuntary unemployment, this could increase employment and output over what they would otherwise be. As noted above, in a situation of full or near-full employment, this may act to increase wages, which would then add to the inflationary effect of the tax increase, with further knock-on effects throughout the economy.

Another possible economic impact of the tax increase is that firms would seek to reduce their energy use by purchasing energy-efficient intermediate or investment goods from appropriate companies. This would have multiple economic effects. First, it would reduce the energy use of the company making the investment, which would serve to offset wholly or partly the increased tax expenditures (so that company energy expenditure may actually be lower than before the tax increase). Second, it would add to the output of the energy-efficiency companies, serving to offset wholly or partly any reduction in output from the increased taxes on energy. Thirdly, the investment would stimulate technical change more generally, especially over the longer term. More energy-efficient equipment is often more productive in other ways as well.

All of these effects act in different ways on different companies (depending on how their managements respond to the tax increase), different sectors (depending on, among other things, their energy intensities and openness to international trade) and different countries (depending on their overall economic structure). Moreover, there is continuous interaction and feedback at all levels among these effects and all the other influences on economic activity. The effects of ETR on international competitiveness are therefore multifaceted and complex. One way that insights into such effects in a complex system like a national economy can be generated is through economic modeling. Another way is to identify whether, due to ETR (or environmental policy in general), those economic activities that are most affected tend to relocate away from countries with relatively stringent policy toward less regulated countries, a phenomenon that is sometimes called the 'pollution haven effect' (because it is likely to be the relatively polluting activities that are relocating). Where the policy measures are intended to reduce carbon emissions, relocation may cause what is called 'carbon leakage,' a situation in which 'part of the CO_2 reduction that is achieved by countries that abate CO_2 emissions is offset by an increase in CO_2 emissions in non-abating countries' (Sijm et al. 2004, 11), because of the non-abating countries' increased relative competitiveness. Pollution haven effects and carbon leakage are collectively called 'spillover effects.'

In this section, there follows a brief review of the literature on modeling related to national competitiveness concerns, and then a more detailed examination of a modeling exercise of the effects of European ETRs which have been implemented to date. The subsequent section looks in more detail at the firm- and sectoral-level issues.

A Brief Review of the Literature

In the literature, there has been a particular emphasis on the spillover effects on the rest of the world of carbon mitigation polices implemented by old industrial countries (those in Annex I of the Kyoto Protocol). The effects may be divided into price effects (on international competitiveness and overall CO_2 emissions—the carbon leakage effect) and nonprice effects, sometimes called technological spillovers.

While much of the literature recognizes the existence of spillovers, different models produce different conclusions with varying level of uncertainties, with the added complication that the effects may be displaced over time. The measurement of the effects is made more difficult because they are often indirect and secondary, although they can also accumulate to make local or regional mitigation action either ineffective or the source of global transformation. It is important to emphasize the uncertainties in estimating spillover effects. In the modeling of spillovers through international trade, researchers rely on different modeling approaches (such as bottom-up or top-down, econometric or general equilibrium), assumptions of perfectly homogeneous versus differentiated products, and estimates (of substitution parameters, for example) whose signs and magnitudes are disputed. Many of these models focus on substitution effects in estimating costs and do not consider the induced development and diffusion of technologies, as well as information, policy and political changes brought about by the originating mitigation actions. For example, Grubb et al. (2002) argue that spillovers from Annex I action, via induced technological change, could have substantial effects on sustainable development, with emissions intensities of developing countries at a fraction of what they would be otherwise. 'However, no global models yet exist that could credibly quantify directly the process of global diffusion of induced technological change.' (Grubb et al. 2002, 302).

There is general agreement in the literature that the international competitiveness of economies and sectors *may* be affected by mitigation actions (see surveys by Boltho 1996; Adams 1997; and Barker and Köhler 1998) such as ETR. In the long run, exchange rates change to compensate for persistent loss of national competitiveness, but this is a general effect and particular sectors can lose or gain competitiveness. In the short run, higher costs of fossil fuels may lead to a loss in sectoral price competitiveness especially in energy-intensive industries, which, as noted above, may lead to the relocation of industry.

Recent years have seen a number of new empirical studies of carbon leakage, at least some of which suggest that it is potentially a serious threat to the effectiveness of mitigation policies. However, such results are not found in the empirical studies of carbon leakage as a general response to mitigation under the Kyoto Protocol. Sijm et al. (2004, 14) summarize these modeling results. 'Models provide a useful, but abstract tool for climate policy analysis; they are faced by several problems and limitations with regard to practical policy decision making, including problems such as model pre-selection, parameter specification, statistical testing or empirical validation.' Moreover, the potential beneficial effect of technology transfer to developing countries arising from technological development brought about by Annex I action is substantial for energy-intensive industries, but has so far not been quantified in a reliable manner. 'Even in a world of pricing CO_2 emissions, there is a good chance that net spillover effects are positive given the unexploited no-regret potentials and the technology and know-how transfer by foreign trade and educational impulses from Annex I countries to Non-Annex I countries.' (Sijm et al.

2004, 179). The conclusion from this review is that, in practice, carbon leakage is unlikely to be substantial because transport costs, local market conditions, product variety and incomplete information all favor local production, and the cost effects of environmental regulation are found to be small.

Modeling the Economic Impacts of ETR

Economic models are constructed using both theoretical insights about the relationships between different economic variables (for example, it is normally assumed that the quantity of a good demanded is reduced if its price is increased, and vice versa), and statistical estimation of the parameters of these relationships. There are different kinds of economic models which make different theoretical assumptions and therefore have different structures. That is one reason why different models can give different outcomes in their modeling of economic interventions such as ETR. This is not the place to go into a detailed comparison of different models, the literature concerning which is now voluminous (for example, see Ekins and Barker 2001). This chapter reports the results of the most comprehensive modeling of European ETRs, which was carried out as part of the European research project COMETR.[1] The model used was a macroeconometric European model (including the 25 member countries of the EU in 2006, plus Norway and Switzerland) called E3ME, which is described in some detail in Barker et al. (2009a).

Modeling ETR with E3ME: methodology and approach
As discussed earlier, the notion of ETR typically involves the modification of the national tax system to move the burden of taxes from conventional taxes, for example those imposed on labor and capital, to environmentally related activities, such as taxes levied on resource use, especially energy use, or environmental pollution. To counterbalance the possible adverse effects of an increase in green taxes, other taxes are reduced using the revenues generated by the ETR implementation (called 'revenue recycling'). The implementation of a revenue-neutral policy is designed to ensure that the tax burden falls more on 'bads' than on 'goods' by ensuring that price signals, as a result of the introduction of ETR, give an incentive to households and industries to alter behavior.

The revenue recycling may take effect through reductions in:

- Direct taxes (income tax, corporation tax);
- Social security contributions
  - paid by employers;
  - paid by employees;
- Other measures
  - Support schemes for investment expenditure (and depreciation); and
  - Benefits or other compensatory measures.

---

[1]   'COMETR—Competitiveness effects of environmental tax reforms' (2004–2006), FP6 Proposal 501993 funded by DG Research of the European Commission, the support of which is gratefully acknowledged—the findings of the projects are published in Andersen and Ekins (2009).

An ETR can, in principle, provide complete tax exemptions for economic sectors or reduced tax rates for different energy fuels and economic sectors in combination with some form of negotiated agreements with targets to improve energy efficiency or carbon emissions. Tax ceilings may also be established to limit the total tax burden faced by individual companies. However, such special measures may reduce the economic efficiency of the ETR overall.

In order to model the effects of ETR, a number of scenarios were generated by E3ME over the period 1995 to 2012 (the projection period therefore includes Phase 2 of the EU Emission Trading System [EU ETS][2]), the main two of which are reported here:

- the Reference Case (R), which is a counterfactual projection without the ETR, but including current and expected developments in the EU economy, for instance the EU ETS;
- the Baseline Case (B), which is an endogenous solution of E3ME over the period 1995–2012. This scenario includes the ETR implemented in each member state covered by the project, exemptions or special treatment for the industries most affected and the compensating reduction in another tax. This scenario is calibrated closely to the observed outcome through using historical data which include the effects of ETR implementation.

Modeling ETR with E3ME: results
This section discusses the simulation results from the COMETR scenarios by looking at the Baseline solution and taking an overview of the results from the countries that pursued ETR in the 1990s. The results for the Baseline case are compared with the Reference case. In summary, this illustrates the difference between what did happen and what would have happened had there been no ETR (with both cases projected to 2012). Revenue neutrality is assumed in each case through the revenue-recycling mechanisms. Exemptions, nonpayments and negotiated agreements are included as accurately as possible as they happened, subject to the total revenues matching the published figures in each case (for a detailed discussion see Barker et al. 2009a).

As the taxes included in the analysis increased fuel prices, we would expect the primary effect to be a reduction in the demand for energy. The scale of the reduction will depend on the tax rates, how they are applied to the various fuels and fuel user groups, how easy it is for fuel users to alternate among the different fuel types and nonfuel inputs, and the scale of the secondary effects from resulting changes in economic activity.

All of the six European countries (Denmark, Finland, Germany, the Netherlands, Sweden and the UK) that have implemented an ETR show a reduction in fuel demand from the ETR (Barker et al. 2009a). In most cases the reduction was in the region of 4 percent, although it was slightly larger in Finland and Sweden than in the other regions.

A key feature of the results is the recovery in fuel demand in several of the examined countries over 2004–2005 in the Baseline case relative to the Reference case, due to higher world energy prices, included in both the Baseline and Reference cases. In most

---

[2]　See for further information concerning the EU ETS: http://ec.europa.eu/clima/policies/ets/index_en.htm

of the ETRs, the environmental taxes were not raised in line with fuel prices (and in some cases may have been reduced), so the relative change in fuel prices becomes less in 2004–2005.

We would expect to see a reduction in atmospheric emissions from lower consumption, but total emissions will also depend on the relative consumption levels of each fuel type. For example, a tax system that encourages the use of coal is likely to produce higher emissions than one which encourages the use of natural gas or biofuels. E3ME includes explicit equations for fuel shares of hard coal, heavy oil, natural gas and electricity. Assumptions are made about the other fuel types linking them to the closest modeled alternative (for example, other coal is linked to hard coal, crude oil to heavy oil). For middle distillates (petrol, diesel, etc.) demand is linked to total fuel demand by that sector. The reason for this is that demand for these fuels is dominated by the transport sectors. These sectors do not generally use any other fuels, so fuel share equations are not required.

The scenario results show that the ETR led to reductions in greenhouse gases in all six ETR regions (Barker et al. 2009a). The effects closely follow the results for total fuel consumption, with the largest reductions occurring in regions with the highest tax rates. The largest reduction in emissions occurred in Finland and Sweden. It should be noted that in most cases the decrease in emissions is relatively larger than the decrease in fuel demand, indicating that the tax policies, by inducing fuel switching as well as a reduction in energy demand, are efficient at reducing emissions.

The Porter hypothesis suggests that environmental regulation can induce efficiency and innovation and improve competitiveness as efficiency gains partially, or more than fully, offset the costs of complying with the regulation (Porter and van der Linde 1995). In the COMETR context, environmental regulation has been more narrowly defined, however, as energy taxation implemented to encourage households and industries to behave in an environmentally sustainable manner. Using this definition, the results show, contrary to the Porter hypothesis, that in the absence of revenue-recycling mechanisms, energy taxation leads to a net loss of output in all examined countries (except Finland). However, when there is revenue recycling, ETR, as modeled within E3ME and as shown in Figure 21.1, produces a small double-dividend effect in every country, with GDP increasing by up to 0.5 percent compared to the Reference case. In Sweden, the effects take slightly longer to come through, as the very large increase in household electricity taxes depresses real incomes in the short run. Finland has a short-term boost to GDP from the effects of the taxes on fuel demand, because a reduction in the demand for imported fuel improves the country's trade balance.

As the ETRs result in higher fuel prices it is likely that there will be an increase in the overall price level. The degree of this is likely to be dependent on the scale of the increase in fuel costs, how easy it is for industry and consumers to switch fuels and use cheaper alternatives (and non-energy inputs) and how much of the cost is passed on by industry to consumers (which is dependent on the level of competition in the industry, estimated econometrically for each region and sector). It should also be noted that the revenue recycling may have a deflationary effect when the revenues are recycled through reductions in employers' social security contributions (i.e. labor costs).

Figure 21.2 shows the effect of the ETR on the Consumer Price Index of each country. In Denmark and the UK, there were no significant increases in the overall price index (so they are not shown in the chart). In the UK this is because the tax is relatively small and

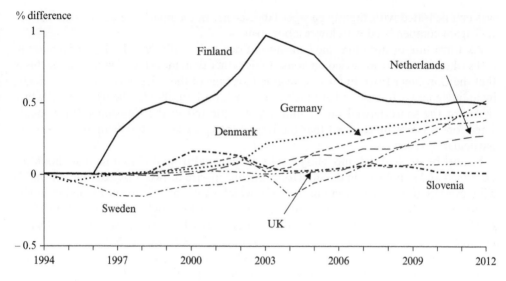

Note: % difference is the difference between the base case and the counterfactual reference case.

Source: Barker et al. 2009b, Charts 3, 12.

Figure 21.1 The effect of ETR on GDP

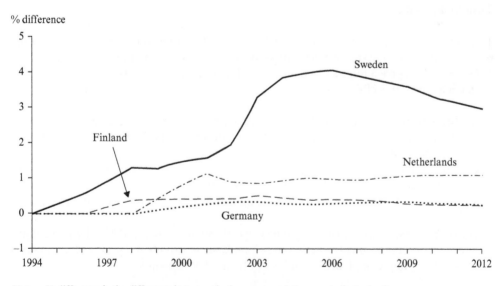

Note: % difference is the difference between the base case and the counterfactual reference case.

Source: Barker et al. 2009b, Charts 7, 16.

Figure 21.2 The effect of ETR on the Consumer Price Index

was compensated with slightly cheaper labor costs. In Denmark the tax was larger, but was again compensated with lower labor costs.

As a measure of inflation, the Consumer Price Index will record a larger increase in cases where the taxes are levied on households rather than industry. The reason for this is that the Consumer Price Index is a weighted average of the price of consumer products, including energy. In cases where the tax is levied on households, the whole tax, rather than just the share passed on by industry, is reflected in the Consumer Price Index. Therefore it is not unexpected that the largest increases are in the Netherlands and, in particular, Sweden.

It must be stressed that modeling results of this kind from different models should be examined and compared in detail before conclusions are drawn. For example, the modeling exercise of Oxford Economics (2007), which shows a 0.5 percent reduction in EU GDP by 2023 from a carbon price of €25 per ton of CO_2, might seem to contradict the E3ME results above, until inspection reveals that the carbon price is not matched by any revenue recycling but rather is an exogenous shock to the economy that simply increases the price level. It is hardly surprising that this leads to a loss in output, and E3ME also shows this, as discussed earlier. The revenue-recycling effect, which reduces taxes elsewhere, plays a key role in compensating for the increased price of carbon/energy.

COMPETITIVENESS AT THE FIRM AND SECTORAL LEVELS

Firm Competitiveness

In principle, as already stated, it is clearly possible for environmental policy, including environmental taxes, to reduce the competitiveness of firms. Christainsen and Tietenberg (1985, 372–373) give a number of environmental tax-related reasons why environmental policy may have this effect:

- Investments in pollution abatement may crowd out other investment.
- Pollution abatement requires labor to operate and maintain the relevant equipment with no contribution to saleable output.
- Compliance with environmental policy absorbs managerial and administrative resources with no contribution to saleable output.
- Uncertainty about present and future environmental policy may inhibit investment.

However, reasons have also been put forward (Smart 1992, 3) as to why progressive environmental management, whether in response to environmental policy or as part of a strategy of 'beyond compliance,' can benefit firms. These include:

- Pollution prevention can save money in materials and end-of-pipe remediation, and minimize future risks and liabilities.
- Being on top of the environmental agenda can make it easier to respond cost-effectively to new regulations.
- New green products and processes and increase consumer appeal and open up new business opportunities.

- An environmentally progressive reputation can improve recruitment, employee morale, investor support, acceptance by the host community and management's self-respect.

Porter and van der Linde (1995, 98) go further, with their hypothesis of 'innovation offsets' stimulated by well designed environmental policy: 'Detailed case studies of hundreds of industries, based in dozens of countries, reveal that internationally competitive companies are not those with the cheapest inputs or the largest scale, but those with the capacity to improve and innovate continually. ... Properly designed environmental standards can trigger innovation that may partially or more than fully offset the costs of complying with them.' Later in the same article, the authors make clear that '[w]here possible, regulations should include the use of market incentives, including pollution taxes' (Porter and van der Linde 1995, 111). They give a range of reasons why well designed regulations may stimulate innovation:

- They may draw attention to resource inefficiencies and potential technological improvements.
- They may stimulate information gathering and raise corporate awareness.
- They may increase investor confidence about the regulatory environment, encouraging investment.
- They provide external pressure to innovate in response to the regulation.
- They make environmental investment less risky by making all firms subject to the same rules.

Christie et al. (1995, xi) draw the same conclusions from their study of UK-based businesses:

> The main benefits reported from investments in cleaner production systems were cost savings through improved waste management, improved public image for the company and staff motivation, cost savings through better energy management, improved process efficiency, and increased profitability. Substantial savings could be made through energy management systems and relatively simple 'housekeeping' modifications to production processes. Longer term gains in competitiveness were expected by many firms, mainly large corporations with sophisticated strategies for environmental management.

Two sets of case studies (reported in EFILWC 1998) sought to investigate in some detail, through comparative analysis of firms in the same sector, the impacts of environmental regulations on firm performance. The sectors chosen for analysis included dairy and meat processing, ceramics, foundries and engineering, power generation, chemicals, tanning and furniture. The conclusions from the analysis were:

- Marginal firms may find environmental regulations a serious extra cost which may, in the extreme, drive them out of business, but on average competitive firms tend to be able to take even quite stringent environmental regulations in their stride.
- Well-managed firms tend to respond more innovatively to environmental regulations, and 'innovation offsets' in these circumstances are not an exceptional occurrence.

However, the notion that environmental regulation can lead to 'win-win' outcomes of economic as well as environmental improvement runs clearly counter to economists' normal assumptions of efficient, competitive markets. It has been attacked as being at best a marginal phenomenon with regard to the costs of environmental regulation as whole. Palmer et al. (1995, 127–128) estimate that Porter and van der Linde's 'innovation offsets' amount to only a few percent of the total costs of conforming to environmental regulations. They contend that the vast majority of these costs conform to the standard economic trade-off model, whereby environmental benefits are gained at the expense of growth and competitiveness.

It is unlikely that this debate will ever reach a definitive resolution, because it is clear that environmental regulations have different impacts on different firms, and it will always be possible to find case studies that show regulation as having net costs or, because of innovation offsets, net benefits (see Lehr et al. 2009). Moreover, most of the above analysis was carried out in relation to environmental regulations rather than environmental taxes, and, in a way, environmental taxes raise more serious competitiveness issues than regulations for firms that are in environmentally intensive sectors. This is because, after compliance with regulations, firms may use the environment without further payment. With environmental taxes, firms pay for *all* use of the environment (which is why environmental taxes provide an incentive for continuous environmental improvement), which may result in the costs imposed by environmental taxes on firms being higher than the costs of regulation. (This is quite different from the costs imposed on the economy overall, which were discussed above.)

On the other hand one of the principal advantages of economic instruments such as environmental taxes, as opposed to regulation, is the prospect of achieving dynamic efficiency gains as 'taxes create a continual incentive for firms to further reduce polluting emissions, through cost-effective abatement, innovation of cleaner production techniques and better abatement technologies, and through industrial restructuring' (OECD 2001, 23).

Because of the differing impacts on different firms, it may therefore be more fruitful to seek to identify the competitiveness impacts of environmental policy in general, and environmental taxes in particular, on particular economic sectors. There is now a substantial literature concerning this; it is the subject of the next section.

Sectoral Competitiveness

With the advent of environmental policy in the 1970s, and its increasing stringency over the years, a 'pollution haven hypothesis' emerged to the effect that this policy would cause 'dirty' industrial sectors to migrate from countries with relatively high environmental standards to those that were less regulated. The literature that has since emerged, like that on firms, has arrived at some conflicting conclusions but an overall consensus that, if there are such displacement effects, they are not very great.

To give a flavor of this literature, Lucas et al. (1992, 80) found that the growth rate of the toxic intensity of manufacturing both was higher in the poorest countries and increased through the 1970s and 1980s. The authors consider that this is consistent with the hypothesis that 'stricter regulation of pollution-intensive production in the OECD countries has led to significant locational displacement, with consequent acceleration of industrial pollution intensity in developing countries.' This result showing the absolute and relative growth of pollution-intensive industry in poor countries is confirmed by Low and Yeats (1992) through quite different noneconometric analysis of trade statistics. However, while Low and Yeats agree that the result is consistent with the Lucas displacement hypothesis, they stress that there are a number of other possible explanations, including that the strong growth of 'dirty' industries is a normal occurrence at an early stage of development.

Other studies, surveyed by Dean (1992, 16–20), give conflicting results, but overall do not suggest that the forces for displacement are very great. In the same vein, the overall review of the literature by Jenkins (1998) suggested that 'there was no strong universal relationship between environmental pressures and competitive performance, either at the firm level or the industry level' (Jenkins 1998, 38). Meanwhile his empirical work (Jenkins 2001) found no relationship between pollution intensity and foreign ownership in the manufacturing sectors of Malaysia and Indonesia, suggesting that foreign direct investment in such developing countries is not disproportionately driven by the quest for pollution havens. Moreover, if it is true that environmentally intensive sectors are also capital-intensive, as suggested by Nordström and Vaughan (1999, 31), comparative advantage theory suggests that these industries would tend to be located in capital-abundant (i.e. industrialized) countries. In fact, the authors present World Bank data which shows that high-income countries do indeed export more pollution-intensive goods than they import, while the reverse is true for upper-middle-income, lower-middle-income and low-income countries (Nordström and Vaughan 1999, 32).

Jaffe et al.'s (1995, 157) review concluded that 'studies attempting to measure the effect of environmental regulation on net exports, overall trade flows, and plant location decisions have produced estimates that are either small, statistically insignificant or not robust to tests of model specification.' This is very similar to the OECD's conclusions on the competitiveness impacts of environmental policy, namely that '[t]he trade and investment impacts which have been measured empirically are almost negligible' (OECD 1996, 45). Smarzynska and Wei (2001) made strenuous efforts to improve on previous studies in terms of data, measures of the stringency of environmental policy and pollution-intensity, and controls for corruption. Their best evidence in support of the pollution haven hypothesis came 'when participation in international environmental treaties is used as a measure of a host country's environmental standard,' when 'there is some evidence that investment from pollution-intensive multinational firms as a share of total inward FDI is smaller for host countries with a higher environmental standard [sic]. However, these findings do not survive various extensions and robustness checks. Therefore, our overall message is a caution against drawing strong conclusions based on selective evidence.' (Smarzynska and Wei 2001, 5). A few years later, Sijm et al. (2004, 165) also concluded on this subject that 'existing studies cannot provide a clear picture about the effect of environmental policy on the relocation of energy-intensive industries; but they do indicate that—if a relation between environmental policy and relocation should exist—it is statistically weak.' Specifically in relation to carbon reduction policies, the IPCC concluded that 'reported effects on international competitiveness are very small . . . at the firm and sector level, given well-designed policies, there will not be a significant loss of competitiveness from tax-based policies to achieve targets similar to those of the Kyoto Protocol' (IPCC 2001, 589). Even more recently, Oikonomou et al. (2006,

3663) concluded that the 'prevailing conclusion of the pollution haven literature is that environmental requirements have a small or negligible effect on relocation.'

MITIGATION OF COMPETITIVENESS EFFECTS

Policymakers have listened to the concerns of businesses about the threat of environmental taxes and ETR to competitiveness, and have implemented these policy measures quite differently from the recommendations of environmental economic theory. Tax rates are generally set at different rates for different energy users, with energy-intensive users usually facing lower tax rates (Ekins and Speck 1998, 1999, 2008; Bach 2005; Kohlhaas 2003; Speck and Andersen 2006). In addition, the carbon-energy tax rates are regularly not set according to the energy or carbon content of the energy products (for example under the UK Climate Change Levy, natural gas is taxed more heavily in terms of carbon content than coal).

European countries have adopted quite different strategies for reducing the effective tax burden for industries when either new carbon-energy taxes have been introduced or existing ones increased. These policies all have in common that they are aiming to protect domestic industries because of the fear of a loss of competitiveness caused by the unilateral introduction of carbon-energy taxes.

The different approaches of granting special tax provisions to industries are extremely complex, and details may be found in the references in the previous paragraph, but they can be summarized as follows:

- Tax subject—tax provisions with regard to a specific energy product:
  - Energy products have been exempt from energy taxes in the past. However, this option of tax differentiation is no longer available following the adoption of the EU Energy Taxation Directive (ETD, Directive 2003/96) in 2003.[3]
- Tax level—tax provisions with regard to setting of tax rates:
  - Granting tax reductions or complete tax exemptions to economic sectors. Again the adoption of the ETD brought the complete tax exemption of economic sectors more or less to a standstill. However, the granting of reduced energy tax rates to economic sectors (as with the UK CCL and associated Climate Change Agreements) is still permitted under the new directive but only when special regulations are taken into account, in particular when the tax rates are higher than the minimum rates as laid down in the ETD.
  - Implementing some form of refund systems for economic sectors. A small number of EU member states, including Germany, Sweden and Finland, make use of this option. Article 17 of the ETD provides some leeway to EU member states in establishing such refund systems but these refund systems are permitted only under the condition that the minimum rates are being paid by those economic—mainly energy-intensive—sectors. Energy intensity is normally

---

[3]   Council Directive 2003/96/EC of 27 October 2003 restructuring the Community framework for the taxation of energy products and electricity.

expressed in terms of a ratio between the total energy bill and the economic performance of an industry using the production value or valued added as an indicator.

o   Reducing tax rates for higher consumers. This option is widely used in the Netherlands: higher consumption of natural gas and electricity is levied with a lower tax rate (Speck and Jilkova 2009).

•   Tax provisions based on the quantities of energy products to be consumed:

o   Provision of a tax ceiling: Again this scheme was applied in the Netherlands and was abolished because of EU regulations. The basic approach was that all energy consumed exceeding a predetermined level is not subject to carbon-energy taxes.

o   Provision of tax-free allowances: This scheme was used in the 1990s in the Netherlands: a basic amount of energy products is not subject to any energy taxation. However, this tax differentiation was not in accordance with EU regulations and was therefore terminated.

All these policies can be classified either as mitigation measures or as compensation measures (OECD 2001). The key difference is that the former provide for reductions of tax rates or some form of modifications of tax bases, while the latter are outside of the realm of taxes. Compensation measures can include revenue recycling and the granting of subsidies, and could also include the provision of border tax adjustments (see below). One of the differences between mitigation and compensation measures concerns environmental effectiveness, as with the OECD's stating, 'Mitigation measures reduce the environmental effectiveness of the tax by cancelling out some of the incentives to change consumption and investment behaviour' (OECD 2001, 29).

There are two possible approaches to mitigating competitiveness impacts that do not have the effect of blunting the efficiency and effectiveness of the policy measure. One is to adjust import and export taxes at the border, or to make some other 'carbon equalization' provisions (EC 2008, 8) for international trade in the output of vulnerable sectors. The first issue is discussed in the literature under the term 'border tax adjustment' and is high on the political agenda (WTO UNEP 2009), particularly in the context of the failed implementation of the French CO_2 tax in early 2010. The then French government was a keen proponent of the policy of imposing a carbon tariff on imports of countries which are not part of a global agreement on reducing greenhouse gases, and was joined in this position by the then Italian Prime Minister in April 2010.[4]

The second option, discussed in detail in Bodansky (2007), is to arrive at some global agreement for the limitation of carbon emissions from vulnerable sectors, which would ensure that sectors from Europe subject to the EU ETS were not at a competitive disadvantage, because the same sectors in other countries were committed to similar levels of effort. Negotiations on such agreements were part of the Bali negotiating process under the UN Framework Convention on Climate Change, as a result of which international sectoral approaches to and agreements on greenhouse gas (GHG) management are more

---

[4]   See http://www.euractiv.com/en/climate-environment/italy-joins-french-calls-for-eu-carbon-tariff-news-450643.

widely discussed at different political stages and between stakeholders. Such agreements are coming to be seen as a policy option for reducing GHG emissions and dealing with competitiveness concerns simultaneously. These agreements would be international in scope and are assumed to prevent carbon leakage, as they would allow companies in countries with stringent carbon regimes to obtain emission reduction credits within sector-specific agreements. The Cement Sustainability Initiative (CSI), coordinated by the Geneva-based World Business Council on Sustainable Development, is at the forefront of this policy development (WBCSD 2009). Numerous questions, in particular with regard to including this policy option in the international climate negotiation process, are still outstanding (OECD-IEA 2009).

CONCLUSIONS

A number of conclusions can be drawn from the extensive work to date on the competitiveness implications of environmental policy, including environmental taxes and ETRs. The first is that there is no convincing evidence of a widespread pollution haven effect. It is clear that other factors influence location more than environmental policy does. The second is that possible international competitiveness effects are limited to relatively few vulnerable sectors. With respect to carbon/energy taxation, these are the sectors which simultaneously exhibit the characteristics of high energy intensity and share of energy expenditures in costs, low market power (and therefore a low ability to pass costs through to consumers), and high trade intensity. For such sectors, as with the simulations with regard to the steel and cement sectors in a recent OECD report (OECD 2006), the conclusion may be that the use of economic instruments 'is likely to have negative impacts on the international competitiveness position of some industrial sectors' (OECD 2006, 75). Even so, it may be pointed that the low trade intensity of cement is likely to limit the extent of these impacts.

For the ETRs that have been introduced so far, no adverse sectoral competitiveness effects have been discovered by research, but this may be due to the very great efforts which most countries have made to shield their vulnerable sectors from these effects by giving them tax rebates or making other tax provisions, as discussed above. In addition to reducing effects on competitiveness, these special provisions are likely to have reduced the effectiveness and efficiency of the policy instrument. Two other ways of mitigating competitiveness effects have been briefly mentioned—border tax adjustments and international sectoral agreements—but these are still in an early phase of discussion and it is not clear whether they will ever be introduced.

National competitiveness is quite different from sectoral competitiveness, because it takes into account all the impacts of revenue recycling in non-energy-intensive sectors, and the effects of investments in energy efficiency and low-carbon energy supplies which are missed by sectoral studies. The modeling reported here suggests that the effects on national GDP of ETRs aimed at carbon abatement are small and, if anything, positive. In fact, this is not surprising. There is no theoretical reason why a modest shift in the taxation of factor inputs should have a large or negative impact on GDP.

If future efforts at carbon abatement are more stringent than they have been in the past, which seems likely, the competitiveness implications for vulnerable sectors are more pronounced, and either these sectors are likely to be exempted from some of the provisions of measures like the EU ETS, or other arrangements such as border tax adjustments or international sectoral agreements will be put in place to mitigate competitiveness effects.

At the same time, faced with the prospect of increasingly stringent carbon reduction, governments are looking more and more to new competitiveness advantages that might be gained through the development of new, low-carbon industries. A case in point is the report from the UK Government's Commission on Environmental Markets and Economic Performance (CEMEP). First, the CEMEP report notes that a 'transition to a low-carbon, resource-efficient economy is needed to meet the global challenges of climate change and sustainable development' (CEMEP 2007, 5). This transition can be achieved only by large investments in new technologies, processes and products. With respect to these investments, 'There will be a trade-off between short-term costs and the potentially huge but uncertain longer-term economic benefits in the form of higher growth and greater job creation than might have been achieved otherwise' (CEMEP 2007, 5).

It is clear that CEMEP expects business, rather than government, to make the investments. The role of government is first to support the innovation process: 'Innovation support is needed because setting a price for carbon and other environmental impacts high enough to create the conditions for business investment in environmental innovation on the scale needed is politically difficult, and may not in practice be sufficient, or quick enough to create competitive advantage' (CEMEP 2007, 6). Governments' second role is to establish the market conditions that stimulate the investment. 'Goals will only become meaningful to individual businesses when translated into the price signals against which investment decisions are made, through market interventions such as environmental taxation and "cap and trade" schemes' (CEMEP 2007, 7).

It is this role that provides the rationale for the kind of ambitious ETR that was explored in the research project 'Resource Productivity, ETR and Sustainable Growth in Europe,' funded by the Anglo German Foundation (Ekins and Speck 2011) and promoted by the Green Fiscal Commission in the UK (Green Fiscal Commission 2009). For example, the Shell corporation's Vice President of Business Environment is reported to have stated that a carbon price of $100 per ton of CO_2 is required before industry will invest in carbon capture and storage schemes (Macalister 2008), considerably higher than current carbon prices or those projected for the EU ETS by most observers for 2020. The key issue now for climate policy is whether governments will now price carbon so that high-carbon investments become economically unviable, and low-carbon investments become businesses' first choice and the foundation for competitiveness in the future. What this chapter has shown is that while such a policy may be challenging for energy-intensive sectors in the short term, these challenges can be addressed by a mixture of mitigation and compensation measures, and more far-reaching international measures in the future. It is difficult to see how the kind of ambitious carbon targets that are now being accepted, by European countries at least, can be reached in any other way.

REFERENCES

Adams, J. (1997), 'Globalisation, trade, and environment', in *Globalisation and Environment: Preliminary Perspectives*, Paris, France: OECD, pp. 179–98.

Andersen, M.A. and P. Ekins (eds) 2009, *Carbon Energy Taxation Lessons from Europe*, Oxford, UK: Oxford University Press.
Bach S. (2005), 'Be- und Entlastungswirkungen der Ökologischen Steuerreform nach Produktionsbereichen' [The net financial impact by sector of the ecological tax reform], Berlin, Germany: Deutsches Institut für Wirtschaftsforschung (DIW), http://www.ecologic.de/download/projekte/1850-1899/1879/1879_1_sektoral.pdf.
Baranzini, A.B., J. Goldemberg and S. Speck (2000), 'A future for carbon taxes', *Ecological Economics*, **32**, 395–412.
Barker, T. and J. Köhler (1998), *International Competitiveness and Environmental Policies*, Cheltenham, UK: Edward Elgar.
Barker T., S. Junankar, H. Pollitt and P. Summerton (2009a), 'The effects of environmental tax reform on international competitiveness in the European Union: modelling with E3ME', in M.S. Andersen and P. Ekins (eds), *Carbon Energy Taxation Lessons from Europe*, Oxford, UK: Oxford University Press, pp. 147–214.
Barker, T., P. Ekins, S. Junankar, H. Pollitt and P. Summerton (2009b), 'The competitiveness effects of European environmental fiscal reforms', *European Review of Energy Markets*, **3** (1), 1–33.
Bodansky, D. (2007), 'International sectoral agreements in a post-2012 climate framework', Working Paper, Arlington, VA, US: Pew Center on Global Climate Change.
Boltho, A. (1996), 'Assessment: international competitiveness', *Oxford Review of Economic Policy*, **12**, 1–16.
Christainsen, G. and T. Tietenberg (1985), 'Distributional and macroeconomic aspects of environmental policy', in A. Kneese, A. and J. Sweeney (eds), *Handbook of Natural Resource and Energy Economics*, Vol. 1, Amsterdam, Netherlands: Elsevier Science Publishers, pp. 345–93.
Christie, I., H. Rolfe and R. Legard (1995), *Cleaner Production in Industry: Integrating Business Goals and Environmental Management*, London, UK: Policy Studies Institute.
Commission on Environmental Markets and Economic Performance (CEMEP) (2007), 'Report to Department for Business Enterprise & Regulatory Reform (BERR), Department for Innovation, Universities & Skills, Department for Environment Food and Rural Affairs (Defra)', London, http://www.co2sense.org.uk/uploads/public/cemep-report.pdf.
Dean, J. (1992), 'Trade and the environment: a survey of the literature', in P. Low (ed.), *International Trade and the Environment*, World Bank Discussion Paper No.159, Washington, DC, US: World Bank, pp. 15–28.
Ekins, P. and T. Barker (2001), 'Carbon taxes and carbon emissions trading', *Journal of Economic Surveys*, **15** (3), 325–76.
Ekins, P. and B. Etheridge (2006), 'The environmental and economic impacts of the UK Climate Change Agreements', *Energy Policy*, **34**, 2071–86.
Ekins, P. and S. Speck (1998), 'The impacts of environmental policy on competitiveness: theory and evidence', in T. Barker and J. Köhler (eds), *International Competitiveness and Environmental Policies*, Cheltenham, UK: Edward Elgar, pp. 33–69.
Ekins, P. and S. Speck (1999), 'Competitiveness and exemptions from environmental taxes in Europe', *Environmental and Resource Economics*, **13** (4), 369–95.
Ekins P. and S. Speck (2008), 'Environmental tax reform in Europe: energy tax rates and competitiveness', in N. Chalifour et al. (eds), *Critical Issues in Environmental Taxation*, Vol. V, Oxford, UK: Oxford University Press, pp. 77–105.
Ekins, P. and S. Speck (eds) (2011), *Environmental Tax Reform (ETR): A Policy for Green Growth*, Oxford, UK: Oxford University Press.
Ernst & Young (2006), 'Eco-industry, its size, employment, perspectives and barriers to growth in an enlarged EU, Final Report to DG Environment, European Commission, Brussels', http://ec.europa.eu/environment/enveco/industry_employment/ecoindustry2006.pdf.
European Commission (EC) (2004), *A Comparison of EU Air Quality Pollution Policies and Legislation with other Countries—Review of Implications for the Competitiveness of European Industry*, Brussels, Belgium: DG Enterprise, http://www.pedz.uni-mannheim.de/daten/edz-h/gdb/04/study1.pdf.
European Commission (EC) (2007), 'Raising productivity growth: key messages from the European Competitiveness Report 2007', COM (2007) 666 final, Commission Staff Working Document SEC(2007)1444, Brussels, Belgium, http://ec.europa.eu/enterprise/enterprise_policy/competitiveness/doc/compet_report_2007/comprep_2007_sec_1444.pdf.
European Commission (EC) (2008), 'Proposal for a directive of the European Parliament and of the Council amending Directive 2003/87/EC so as to improve and extend the greenhouse gas emission allowance trading system of the Community', 23 January, Brussels, Belgium.
European Environment Agency (EEA) (2005), *Market-Based Instruments for Environmental Policy in Europe*, Technical Report No 8/2005, Copenhagen, Denmark: European Environment Agency.
European Foundation for the Improvement in Living and Working Conditions (EFILWC) (1998), 'Environmental economic policies: competitiveness and employment', Report on the Conference 16–17 October 1996, Dublin, Ireland: EFILWC.

Green Fiscal Commission (2009), 'The case for green fiscal reform. Final report of the UK Green Fiscal Commission, London', UK: Green Fiscal Commission, http://www.greenfiscalcommission.org.uk/index.php/site/about/final_report/.

Grubb, M., J. Köhler and D. Anderson (2002), 'Induced technical change in energy and environmental modelling: analytical approaches and policy implications', *Annual Review of Energy and the Environment*, **27**, 271–308.

IPCC (2001), *Third Assessment Report of the Intergovernmental Panel on Climate Change*, Cambridge, UK: Cambridge University Press.

Jaffe, A, P. Peterson, P. Portney and R. Stavins (1995), 'Environmental regulation and the competitiveness of US manufacturing: What does the evidence tell us?', *Journal of Economic Literature*, **XXXIII** (March), 132–63.

Jenkins, R. (1998), 'Environmental regulation and international competitiveness: a review of literature and some European evidence', UNU/INTECH Discussion Paper #9801, Maastricht, Netherlands: UNU/INTECH.

Jenkins, R. (2001), 'Trade, investment and industrial pollution: lessons from South-East Asia', in N. Adger, M. Kelly and N. Huu Ninh (eds), *Living with Environmental Change*, London, UK and New York, NY, US: Routledge.

Kohlhaas M. (2003), 'Energy taxation and competitiveness—special provisions for business in Germany's environmental tax reform', DIW Berlin (German Institute for Economic Research), Discussion Paper 349, Berlin, Germany: DIW Berlin, http://www.diw.de/documents/publikationen/73/40455/dp349.pdf.

Lehr, U., C. Lutz and R. Salmons (2009), 'Eco-innovation: literature review on eco-innovation and ETR and modelling of ETR impacts with GINFORS', part of the project 'Tax reform in Europe over the next decades: implications for the environment, for eco-innovation and for household distribution' commissioned by the European Environment Agency, Copenhagen, Denmark.

Low, P. and A. Yeats (1992), 'Do "dirty" industries migrate?', in P. Low (ed.), *International Trade and the Environment*, World Bank Discussion Paper No.159, Washington DC, US: World Bank, pp. 89–103.

Lucas, R., D. Wheeler and H. Hettige (1992), 'Economic development, environmental regulation and the international migration of toxic industrial pollution: 1960–88', in P. Low (ed.), *International Trade and the Environment*, World Bank Discussion Paper 159, Washington DC, US: World Bank, pp. 67–86.

Macalister, T. (2008), 'Firms will act on CO_2 only if its cost triples, says Shell', *The Guardian*, 15 February, http://www.guardian.co.uk/business/2008/feb/15/royaldutchshell.oil.

Mongelli, I., G. Tassielli and B. Notarnicola (2006), 'Global warming agreements, international trade and energy/carbon embodiments: an input-output approach to the Italian case', *Energy Policy*, **34**, 88–100.

Nordström, H. and S. Vaughan (1999), 'Trade and Environment', *Special Studies*, **4**, Geneva, Switzerland: World Trade Organization.

OECD (1993), *Environmental Policies and Industrial Competitiveness*, Paris, France: OECD.

OECD (1996), *Implementation Strategies for Environmental Taxes*, Paris, France: OECD.

OECD (2001), *Environmentally Related Taxes in OECD Countries: Issues and Strategies*, Paris, France: OECD.

OECD (2003), *Environmental Taxes and Competitiveness: An Overview of Issues, Policy, Options, and Research Needs*, Stephen Smith, COM/ENV/EPOC/DAFFE/CFA(2001)90/FINAL, Paris, France: OECD.

OECD (2006), *The Political Economy of Environmentally Related Taxes*, Paris, France: OECD.

Oikonomou, V., M. Patel and E. Worell (2006), 'Climate policy: bucket or drainer?', *Energy Policy*, **34**, 3656–68.

Organisation for Economic Co-operation and Development and International Energy Agency (OECD-IEA) (2009), *Sectoral Approaches and the Carbon Market*, R. Baron, B. Buchner (IEA) and J. Elllis (OECD), COM/ENV/EPOC/IEA/SLT(2009)3, Paris, France.

Oxford Economics (2007), 'Report on modelling the macroeconomic competitiveness impacts of EU climate change policy', a report to DTI/BERR, Oxford, UK: Oxford Economics, http://www.berr.gov.uk/files/file41682.pdf.

Palmer, K., W. Oates and P. Portney (1995), 'Tightening environmental standards: the benefit-cost or the no-cost paradigm?', *Journal of Economic Perspectives*, **9** (4), 119–32.

Porter, M. and C. van der Linde (1995), 'Toward a new conception of the environment-competitiveness relationship', *Journal of Economic Perspectives*, **9** (4), 97–118.

Sijm, J.P.M. et al. (2004), 'Spillovers of climate policy. An assessment of the incidence of carbon leakage and induced technological change due to CO2 abatement measures', Netherlands Research Programme on Climate Change Scientific Assessment and Policy Analysis, Netherlands: ECN.

Smart, B. (ed.) (1992), *Beyond Compliance: A New Industry View of the Environment*, Washington, DC, US: World Resources Institute.

Smarzynska, B. and S.-J. Wei (2001), 'Pollutions havens and foreign direct investment: dirty secret or popular myth?', World Bank, Policy Research Working Paper 2673, Washington, DC, US: World Bank.

Speck, S. and M.S. Andersen (2006), 'Environmental tax reform and competitiveness', in A. Cavaliere et al. (eds), *Critical Issues in Environmental Taxation*, Vol. III, Richmond, UK: Richmond Law & Tax, pp. 285–97.

Speck, S. and J. Jilkova (2009), 'Design of environmental tax reforms in Europe', in M.S. Andersen and P. Ekins (eds), *Carbon Energy Taxation Lessons from Europe*, Oxford, UK: Oxford University Press, pp. 24–52.

Speck, S. and M. Mulder (2003), 'Competition on European energy markets between policy ambitions and practical restrictions', CPB Document No. 33, The Hague, Netherlands: CPB.

UKCEED (2006), *Emerging Markets in the Environmental Sector*, Report to DTI and DEFRA, Peterborough, UK: UKCEED, http://www.ukceed.org/files/downloads/emergingmarkets_full.pdf.

World Business Council for Sustainable Development (WBCSD) (2009), *The Cement Sustainability Initiative–A Sectoral Approach: Greenhouse gas mitigation in the cement industry*, Geneva, Switzerland: WBSCD, http://www.wbcsdcement.org/pdf/WBCSD%20rev%20final%20low.pdf.

World Trade Organization and United Nations Environment Programme (WTO UNEP) (2009), *Trade and Climate Change*, Geneva, Switzerland: WTO UNEP, http://www.wto.org/english/res_e/booksp_e/trade_climate_change_e.pdf.

PART VI

POLICY MIX

22 The role of environmental taxation: economics and the law
Michael G. Faure and Stefan E. Weishaar

INTRODUCTION

Environmental taxation is different from other forms of taxation. It is not designed primarily for revenue-raising or as an instrument directed to marginally influence behavior, but rather strives for fundamental and structural changes in the behavior of economic actors (Backhaus 1999). Since altering behavior is not easily achieved, it is not surprising that incentive mechanisms have to be designed within a particular socio-political context where actors will seek to influence policymaking.

Environmental pollution associated with economic activity also gives rise to benefits. The optimal level of pollution is therefore normally not zero, but positive. A crucial question that environmental law and economics scholars have is thus how to usefully determine the desired level of environmental protection. In a related question, these scholars are also interested in the optimal design of institutions and instruments to ensure efficient and effective environmental protection.

The economic literature suggests the use of incentive-based (or economic) instruments that specify a particular environmental goal but subsequently leave it (via financial incentives) to market participants to decide how to reach these environmental goals. Examples of such instruments are environmental taxes and emissions trading systems. Since legal policy instruments such as liability rules are also 'incentive based' through their use of sanctions, the division between economic instruments and command-and-control instruments is not clear-cut. To be effective, both require a particular form of legal design and regulation as well as enforcement. Since the various instruments have specific strengths and weaknesses, much of the recent environmental policy literature pays attention to optimal mixes of policy instruments. This chapter provides an overview of taxation and other incentive-based regulations from an environmental law and economics perspective by addressing their strengths and weaknesses. Issues such as flexibility and cost-effectiveness, and also their susceptibility to lobbying at the legislative level and to regulatory capture, are examined. Such a comparative perspective is useful given the different and at times seemingly contradictory approaches to environmental policy design. We will show that it is not surprising that there are differing approaches since none of the policy instruments (taxes, contracts, liability rules, regulation or economic instruments) may alone be optimal to provide adequate incentives for pollution control. As can often be found in policy practice, a combination may be necessary, ideally making optimal use of the advantages of each particular policy instrument. To show the relevance of these instruments in practice we also address how particular instruments (environmental liability, emissions trading) have been implemented in European environmental policy, discuss these evolutions from an economic perspective and examine the linkages between environmental taxation and other elements of the 'policy mix'.

This chapter is structured as follows. First the Coase theorem is briefly presented since it constitutes an important framework for comparing the various policy instruments. Next, the potential of environmental liability as an incentive-based instrument is explained. Subsequently the particular weaknesses that may make a regulatory intervention necessary are examined. The traditional instrument proposed by environmental economists to govern environmental issues is environmental taxation, which the chapter then considers. It also examines emissions trading. Increasingly, there is also experience with the model of emissions trading that may complement taxation in the area of climate change. Both in the US and in Europe, emissions trading is used to control greenhouse gases. Experience shows that notwithstanding its incentive-based character, legal design issues are crucial to its success. Having discussed these seemingly different approaches to environmental policy design issues, the question of course arises as to whether it is useful to determine which instrument is 'best', or whether one could opt instead for a combination of particular types of instruments. The final section of the chapter addresses this question and the need for future research.

THE COASE THEOREM

Reciprocal Nature of Harm

Economists have advocated that externalities such as environmental pollution could be internalized optimally by imposing a tax on the polluting activity (as discussed later in this chapter). However, in his seminal article 'The problem of social cost' Ronald Coase (1960) opposed this idea. Coase stressed the reciprocal nature of harm, i.e. that pollution is caused by emitters and the presence of neighbors. Coase holds that if the transaction costs are 'zero' (i.e. sufficiently low, see also Coase 1990), an optimal allocation of resources will always take place, irrespective of the contents of the governing legal rule. This is usually known as the Coase theorem. The actors will thus negotiate how pollution is to be reduced. To prevent pollution, policymakers should thus ask which actors (polluters or victims) should be limited in their property rights. The answer to this question will be dependent on which of the various actors can take precautions to reduce or prevent the harm.

The Coase Theorem: A Few Constraints

The theorem merits a few comments. First, the actual price to be paid for abatement will depend on the bargaining power of the actors. If a 'right to pollute' is assigned, most benefits could be reaped by polluters if they are tough bargainers. Second, the efficient outcome can be undermined by strategic behavior. Third, the victims must have resources to pay for abatement.

Fourth, the Coase theorem only considers the efficiency aspects of pollution, not its distributional effects. While legal liability may not matter from an efficiency point of view, the victims having to bear the costs will matter from a distributional perspective.

This may explain the legislature's intervening even when the conditions of the Coase theorem are fulfilled.

Fifth, although many law and economics scholars and environmental economists use the Coase theorem as a starting point for discussing the role of environmental law and, more generally, the need for legal instruments to control environmental pollution (Frey 1992; Baumol and Oates 1979; Oates 1983; Schulze and D'Arge 1974; Mishan 1971b), two drawbacks are obviously that the Coase theorem is based on the assumption of zero (or at least low) transaction costs and that full information about costs and damages is available. In most large-scale pollution cases the number of victims will be too large and transaction costs will be prohibitive (see Mishan 1971a; Kapp 1970).

Sixth, another questionable assumption is that both property rights and damages are clearly defined and that negotiations take place on the basis of this allocation of rights. In reality, subjective valuations may hinder an efficient negotiated solution and can therefore also be considered transaction costs.

Practical Value of the Coase Theorem

Critics could argue that the zero-transaction costs hypothesis will never be realized in the environmental context, so that one could question its usefulness. Although many settings in which pollution occurs involve prohibitive transaction costs, that does not necessarily imply that the Coase theorem would not be useful.

First, there may be many small-scale pollution cases in which factories cause nuisances that have effects limited to a restricted neighborhood. In that situation Coasean bargaining may be possible.

Second, if transaction costs prevent efficient solutions through bargaining, one could reduce these costs. Through mandatory disclosure of information, transaction costs could be lowered, making Coasean bargaining possible. Coase therefore teaches that prohibitive transaction costs should not necessarily lead to regulation determining the standard of safety; the policymaker could opt instead for a regulatory solution that facilitates bargaining. Such a solution is obviously less interventionistic, and it is also more likely that efficient outcomes will occur through these efficient agreements than through mandatory regulation.

Third, even if intervention is unavoidable, the Coase theorem is still useful since it provides an indication to the legislator of the efficient solution, so that the legislative solution can 'mimic' the market. Lastly, it bears mentioning that Coase himself acknowledged that transaction costs exist and that high transaction costs related to the administration of schemes such as environmental taxation could be a reason for preferring more liability-based schemes.

ENVIRONMENTAL LIABILITY AS INCENTIVE INSTRUMENT

Economic Principles of Accident Law

The economic analysis of accident law starts from the belief that liability will give actors incentives for careful behavior. Economists stress the deterrent function of tort law and thereby take an ex ante perspective.

From an economic perspective the main goal of liability rules is the minimization of 'primary accident costs' (Calabresi 1961; Calabresi 1970): the costs of accident avoidance and the damage expected from an accident. Indeed, from a social point of view as well, investments in accident avoidance are costs associated with accidents. Clear examples include investments in safety controls, but also less visible costs such as taking special care in dangerous operations. A difference is further made between so-called unilateral accidents, in which only the care taken by one of the parties (the injurer) can influence the accident risk, and bilateral accidents, in which the behavior of both parties can influence the accident risk (Shavell 1987). In a bilateral accident situation the goal of accident law should therefore be to give incentives to minimize the total costs of care taken by the potential injurer and the potential victim and the expected damage that will occur in case of an accident.

Economists use classic cost/benefit analysis to determine the level of care that will minimize the social costs of accidents. Such 'optimal or efficient care levels' (Landes and Posner 1981; Polinsky 1983) are found at the point at which the marginal costs of care-taking equal the marginal benefits for accident reduction (Shavell 1987). This is true for a risk-neutral setting. Risk-averse actors may prefer a higher investment in care.

Strict Liability versus Negligence

Basic model

Having defined the regulatory function of liability rules, our next question is which liability rule will provide appropriate incentives to optimally prevent environmental damage. The two legal rules are the classic fault or negligence rule and the strict liability rule. Under the former, the risk creator compensates the victim only when his behavior falls short of a certain level of due care as determined by the court. Strict liability, on the other hand, places upon the injurer a duty to compensate the victim irrespective of the injurer's behavior, provided there is a causal relationship between the activity and the damage.

Economic literature holds that if a negligence rule is adopted, the injurer will take optimal care, provided the due care required in the legal system is equal to the optimal care as defined in the model (Shavell 1987; Calabresi 1975). Since an individual will minimize costs by complying with this due care standard, the negligence rule will lead to an efficient outcome.

Also, a strict liability rule will lead to the optimum in a case in which only one party can influence the accident risk because the injurer will bear all the social costs of accidents, namely his own costs of care-taking and the expected damage (Polinsky 1983; Shavell 1987). An injurer will minimize his total expected accident costs by comparing marginal costs of care-taking to the marginal benefits of accident reduction.

Refinements

Considering only the influence of the injurer's care on accidents, both negligence and strict liability can provide incentives for taking optimal care. However, there are important nuances. Administrative (court) costs for strict liability seem higher, since a legal case will follow with every accident given that the injurer is always bound to compensate. On the other hand, the negligence rule seems to have high information costs for the judge, since he will have to determine the marginal costs and marginal benefits of care-taking (Brown 1973; Calabresi 1975; Shavell 1987).

In bilateral accident situations, a contributory or comparative negligence defense has to be added to a strict liability rule to give victims as well an incentive to take optimal care. In such situations a negligence rule will induce victims to take due care. A fully informed victim will assume that the injurer will take due care to avoid liability, hence the victim will avoid accidents in order not to be left with his loss. Further refinement can be found in the literature, which *inter alia* focuses on activity levels of dangerous operations (Adams 1989; Diamond 1974; Shavell 1980).

Strict Liability for Environmental Harm?

Environmental pollution can in most cases be considered a unilateral accident situation. Since the victim cannot influence the accident risk, strict liability seems to be the first best solution to give the potential polluter incentives for adopting optimal activity levels and for taking efficient care (see Faure 1995).

In cases in which parties other than the polluter could influence the risk of environmental degradation (for example, when private actors are responsible for managing a natural resource area), liability should set incentives for appropriate preventive measures. In such cases environmental pollution would constitute a bilateral risk, if one considers that third party a victim. However, the case would probably be more one in which multiple parties can influence the accident risk (and should therefore be given appropriate incentives) since the actors, as in the example given, cannot be considered traditional victims who suffer the loss personally (Niezen 2000). A strict liability rule is warranted to give the party who has most influence on the accident risk (the polluter) the incentive to take preventive measures. In bilateral cases a defense should always be added for victims as well. Moreover, if parties other than the polluter can influence the accident risk, they might be held liable for the amount of their contribution to the loss. That is, however, not an argument against the strict liability of the polluter.

Applying the criteria for determining the choice between negligence and strict liability to the environmental cases, there seem to be strong arguments in favor of an introduction of strict liability. In many cases environmental pollution will be truly unilateral in the sense that only the injurer's activity can influence the accident risk, which constitutes a strong case for strict liability. Nevertheless, in some cases it will be the victim's activity that caused the harm, such as if the victim knowingly came to the nuisance. This may then lead to a denial of a claim on compensation (see Wittman 1980).

Another important difference between negligence and strict liability bears mentioning. Negligence requires judges to set care standards, and information is costly and difficult to obtain. Strict liability shifts all costs to the injurer, who will then have to define the optimal care level. If information on optimal precaution is better available to industry, strict liability may be preferred. In cases in which regulators have an information advantage regulation is desirable, but this is not an argument against strict liability.

If risk aversion is introduced and the potential injurer is risk-averse, Endres and Schwarze (1991) correctly argue that strict liability is only efficient if risk can be removed from the risk-averse injurer, for instance through insurance. Moreover, we assume that the judge has accurate information regarding the amount of the damage. If courts err in assessing damages, strict liability will lead to underdeterrence. In other words, if courts can more easily observe the socially desirable level of precaution than the exact amount of external harm, a negligence rule should be favored (Cooter 1984).

REGULATION

Environmental Liability versus Regulation

Although environmental liability is an important instrument for preventing environmental damage, it has serious limitations. Some scholars therefore qualify the public law approach as 'the preferred approach' for preventing environmental damage (Bergkamp 2001). If the conditions for the application of liability law are not fulfilled, such as when victims and injurers or causal relationships between an activity and the damage cannot be determined, instruments other than liability law will have to be used.

Law and economics literature has closely examined whether safety in society can best be reached through liability rules or through regulation. An important contribution comes from Shavell, who examined the choice between liability rules and regulation (Shavell 1984a; Shavell 1984b; Shavell 1987). Both liability rules and regulation can be used to optimally prevent environmental harm, but their approaches differ. Tort law sets incentives for taking optimal risk prevention measures by inducing risk creators to pay damages or compensation, but it leaves the choice of measures to the risk creator. Under regulation the government imposes a standard ex ante. Non-compliance with this standard can lead to administrative or criminal sanctions. Regulation is thus considered as an ex ante system aimed at prevention, whereas liability rules mainly intervene ex post after the damage has occurred. The criteria advanced by Shavell that influence the choice between safety regulation and liability are described below.

Criteria for Choosing

Information asymmetries
Information deficiencies, as a cause of market failure and justification for government intervention (Stigler 1961; Schwartz and Wilde 1979; Mackaay 1982), are crucial for the proper operation of a liability system. Parties in an accident setting generally have better information on the accident risk than regulatory bodies (Shavell 1984a) and are consequently better able to determine optimal preventive action. This assumption is reversed if risks are not appreciated by the parties. This is especially a problem if costs are external and cannot be assessed by the parties.

Insolvency
If the potential damages exceed the wealth of the individual injurer, liability rules will not provide optimal incentives since the injurer will consider the accident as having a magnitude only equal to his wealth, and will thus take suboptimal precautionary measures (Shavell 1984a). This gives rise to underdeterrence (Shavell 1986). Insolvency especially causes problems under strict liability rules, but less so under negligence.

Environmentally oriented safety regulation can overcome this insolvency problem (as could insurance, provided that the moral hazard problem associated with insurances is cured). Under safety regulation the efficient care level is determined ex ante and will be affected by enforcement instruments compelling compliance with the standard, irrespective of the injurer's wealth. If safety regulation is introduced to address potential insolvency problems, non-monetary sanctions should be employed to avoid reoccurrence of the problem (Shavell 1985).

Underdeterrence of tort law

Some activities cause considerable damage, but are unlikely to face a lawsuit. In the absence of a liability suit, liability rules will not be effective and regulation setting efficient care standards is desirable (Shavell 1984a).

An injurer can escape liability if the damage to each individual is small (for instance, if the damage is caused to common property), if the damages take time to arise and evidence has been lost, or if the injurer has already gone out of business. Proving causal links between activities and damages can also be difficult (Landes and Posner 1984; Kunreuther and Freeman 2001). The burden of proof of a causal relationship becomes more difficult as time passes and often victims will not recognize that harm originates from tort, but may think it has a natural cause. For such reasons, a liability suit might not be brought, thus making environmentally oriented safety regulation necessary to ensure that the potential polluter takes efficient care (Bocken 1987 and 1988).

Empirical Evidence

Liability rules alone therefore cannot suffice to prevent environmental harm. Instruments other than the command-and-control type of regulation can be used. Taxes are an alternative but are also publicly imposed.

Some studies examine the effectiveness of safety regulation in controlling environmental harm. They do not address the quality of environmental law, but whether regulation has been more important in reducing environmental harm than have liability rules. Dewees (1992a, 1992b) demonstrated that in North America the quality of the environment has improved substantially as a result of regulatory efforts, and not so much in response to legal action in tort. This empirical evidence of the success of regulation compared to tort law has also been supported by Dewees, Duff and Trebilcock (1996). These authors also point to the importance of other non-regulatory factors (economic growth, the weather) that influence environmental quality.

Necessity to Combine Liability and Regulation

According to Shavell's criteria there is a strong argument for controlling environmental risk through ex ante regulation (or taxes). Yet liability rules are an important complement, for example regarding individual damage cases. Furthermore, the effectiveness of regulation is dependent upon enforcement, which may be weak and is susceptible to lobbying. Regulation also lacks flexibility and can become outdated. The complementary relationship between tort law and regulation has been examined in detail by Rose-Ackerman (1992 and 1996), Faure and Ruegg (1994), Kolstad, Ulen and Johnson

(1990), Arcuri (2001) and Burrows (1999). For a comparison of the US and Europe see Rose-Ackerman (1995 and 1996).

Therefore, although there is a strong case for safety regulation to control environmental risk, tort rules will still play an important role as well (Schmitz 2000). These interdependencies between regulation and tort law raise a number of interesting questions that have been extensively addressed in the literature (Schmitz 2000).

COMMAND-AND-CONTROL VERSUS MARKET-BASED INSTRUMENTS

'Market-based' or 'Economic' Instruments

Traditionally environmental law largely consisted of a 'command-and-control' type of regulation. Economists increasingly pointed to several disadvantages of imposing pollution standards via government regulation (Faure, Peeters and Wibisana 2006). Thus, they have in recent years picked up Pigou's message of the 1920s that taxation could be used to internalize externalities. Moreover, since the 1960s Dales also pointed out that social welfare could be increased by trading in pollution rights. The literature calls these economic or market-based instruments. Such instruments have been advanced for a number of years by policy analysts as a reaction to (command-and-control) regulation. Using the market instead of relying on regulation sounds modern and flexible, and hence politicians also increasingly argue that environmental policy should be market-oriented instead of merely relying on top-down regulation by government.

Terminology can, however, be misleading. One could argue that all legal and policy instruments can be considered 'economic' as long as they give appropriate incentives to polluters for an efficient reduction of the externality caused by the pollution. Hence, liability rules are also 'economic' in the sense that liability gives incentives to polluters to prevent environmental harm. Nevertheless, liability rules are traditionally not included among 'economic' instruments, a concept that usually refers to instruments whereby only the environmental targets are defined, but whereby it is largely left to the polluters to find the optimal instruments for reaching the particular targets. Hence integral parts of economic instruments are incentive drivenness and flexibility.

Weaknesses of Command-and-Control

Before looking at environmental taxes and emissions trading this section summarizes the criticisms of the command-and-control approach.

First, traditional command-and-control systems focusing on permits and licensing have been criticized since the 1970s for focusing on controlling emissions while they disregarded the total effect of the emissions on environmental quality. As a result, the effect was that notwithstanding severe emission controls, total environmental quality was seriously reduced. It is indeed striking that within the US context, emissions trading could more particularly develop within the context of the Clean Air Act, which had set target emissions standards referred to as National Ambient Air Quality Standards (NAAQS) (Hahn and Hester 1989). Hence, the focus should be on target standards or environmental quality standards. This criticism does not invalidate *per se* a command-and-control approach, since this instrument could also be used within a system that would focus largely on target standards. However, there are several other criticisms that can be formulated (Faure and Ubachs 2003).

Second, command and control requires optimal standards and optimal enforcement entailing high information and enforcement costs. If enforcement is suboptimal, profits can be earned by polluting more (see Tietenberg 2000). Although enforcement and information costs can be reduced by relying on industry information, the private interest theory of regulation suggests that industry can benefit from distorting information.

Third, compliance with regulatory standards (such as of a permit) does not provide continuous incentives for reducing pollution or investing in environmentally friendly technology. Fourth, and relatedly, polluters bear the costs of complying with regulatory standards but may not be required to pay for residual damages associated with the pollution created while in compliance with the standard.

Fifth, command and control cannot ensure equalization of marginal pollution costs among different polluters. Given prohibitively high information and regulatory costs, administrative agencies will not (normally) determine the efficient emissions for each polluter and may demand comparable reductions by polluters. This is inefficient, and it increases social welfare losses if the possibilities for pollution abatement differ (Rosen 1999). Polluters that have the possibility to abate the pollution above the regulatory standard do not have any financial incentive to do so.

This shows that there are considerable disadvantages to the traditional command-and-control approach: regulatory standards are often too general and not sufficiently flexible and differentiated. An optimal environmental policy needs adaptable instruments (hence often referred to as market-based) that on the one hand provide more flexibility (taking into account each polluter's individual possibility of optimal pollution abatement) and on the other hand provide optimal incentives toward environmental technological innovation and not merely compliance with a regulatory standard. Having addressed the disadvantages of the traditional command-and-control approach, we thus better understand why environmental policy analysts are increasingly interested in the so-called economic instruments.

ENVIRONMENTAL TAXATION

Basic Principles

The Pigouvian tax for environmental pollution was first developed by Arthur C. Pigou. This concept states that pollution can be reduced to socially desirable levels by increasing a firm's marginal private costs by means of a tax to reflect the marginal costs incurred by society (that is, costs reflecting all negative externalities). Since polluters' production costs are increased by the tax to reflect society's costs, firms maximize profits by reducing activity levels to the social optimum (Groosman 1999; see also Turner, Pearce and Bateman 1994). Some authors recast Pigou's ideas in terms of costs of pollution abatement. Here the marginal costs of pollution abatement for the firm are compared to the marginal external costs of abatement. (See Pindyck and Rubenfield 2001. See also Perman et al. 2003, 17 ff.)

Potential Advantages of Environmental Taxes

First, a pollution tax entails fewer total abatement costs than the emissions standard does. However, total compliance costs for firms may be higher with environmental taxes if polluters will not only have to abate emissions, but are also liable to pay the tax for non-abated emissions. This could be avoided by ensuring revenue neutrality of the environmental tax by reducing another existing tax.

Second, pollution taxes levied on inputs via existing authorities have a lower risk of evasion than fixed emission standards that are controlled via irregular onsite inspections. Pollution taxes that use emissions as the tax base require sufficient control and monitoring to limit the risk of evasion. Unfortunately, such control and monitoring are not cheaper and less demanding than the control and monitoring under regulatory standards.

Third, pollution taxes provide continuous incentives for abatement to reduce the tax burden and abatement costs. Fourth, taxes induce investment in research and development. Finally, taxes may induce substitution of inputs that reduce other environmental harmful substances.

Critical Issues

Failure to set an appropriate tax rate equaling marginal benefits and marginal costs of pollution would undermine the effectiveness of the tax in achieving a full internalization of external costs. The Pigouvian tax is a simple incentive-based mechanism capable of inducing behavioral changes. To set an optimal tax rate, governments require optimal information, which is not always likely to be available (see Fullerton, Leicester and Smith 2010 for an elaborate criticism). The effectiveness of taxes also depends heavily on demand and supply functions. Only if the functions are flat (elastic) will a price increase lead to a significant change in the consumption or supply patterns and render the tax effective.

Environmental taxes require that emissions are monitored as closely as possible to ensure their effectiveness, even if that is difficult and if pollution contains different substances. To avoid such a difficulty, 'proxy variables' are sometimes employed, although their use is not consistent with the idea of Pigouvian tax.

Taxes have regressive effects on some income categories and although it is highly debatable, the effects of taxes on distribution must be considered appropriately.

It also bears mentioning that other approaches toward environmental taxes could be developed that do not have anything in common with Pigovian taxes: Albrecht (2006) proposes a pragmatic classification of sustainable products that benefit from low VAT levels to green the tax system (see Kosonen and Nicodème 2009 for a comparison).

Empirical Evidence

Most empirical evidence concerning the effectiveness of environmental taxes comes from Europe rather than from the US (see Oates 1994). Dewees, Duff and Trebilcock (1996) note that taxes are rarely introduced 'in the textbook form'. The evaluation of environmental taxes is further complicated by the fact that they are frequently applied in conjunction with other instruments such as regulations, which makes it difficult to determine the exact impact of a tax (OECD 2006, 50).

Hahn (1989) moreover claims that most emission taxes are misused as a revenue-raising instrument rather than a policy tool. Closely associated with the element of revenue raising is the aspect of distributional effects and equity. Studies show that direct effects of electricity and heating taxes—a prominent area of environmental taxation—tend to be regressive (see also Brännlund and Nordström 2004). The regressiveness tends to be softened if the analysis allows for indirect distributional effects from price increases of taxed products, compensation measures and the resulting environmental benefits (OECD 2006, 143).

Success stories in which taxes were used to reduce environmental harms such as water pollution are found in the Netherlands (Dewees, Duff and Trebilcock 1996) and Germany (Brown and Johnson 1984, 929 ff.). Since Germany (like most European countries) combines effluent taxes and emission standards, it is hard to argue that the reductions are mainly attributable to taxes and not to administrative and/or criminal sanctions associated with emission standards. These findings comply with Frey's reports that the environmental taxes led to a considerable reduction of emissions into the aqua system and into the air (Frey 1992). Bongaerts and Kraemer (1987, 12–19) compare water pollution taxes in France, the Netherlands and Germany, and similarly conclude that effluent taxes provide a strong incentive to invest in water pollution abatement equipment, but also contend that it is impossible to disentangle the separate effects of levies and emission standards. Bressers (1988) uses a regression analysis of multiple time series to disentangle the effects of economic and regulatory impacts. He concludes that effluent charges have been a quite effective instrument of Dutch water quality policy. Not surprisingly, in the area of greenhouse gas emission abatement, taxes also have been successfully used to reduce emissions, for example in the UK or Sweden (Richardson and Chanwai 2003; Natur Vårds Verket 2006). Bruvoll and Larsen (2004) present evidence that environmental taxation in Norway has led to a significant reduction in greenhouse gas emissions per unit of GDP—attributable to reduced energy intensity, adaptations in the energy mix and reduced process emissions—while overall emissions increased. The limited effect of the tax was attributable to extensive tax exemptions and the inelastic demand in the sectors covered by the tax. Fullerton et al. (2008) show that in the UK environmental taxes in the area of energy, road transport, aviation and household waste could significantly contribute to the efficiency of environmental policy. Morley (2010) suggests that the recent introduction of environmental taxes in the EU has had a significant negative effect on pollution while only a limited one on the use of natural resources. A study on the usage of environmental taxes on building material (EEA 2008) in the Czech Republic, Italy and Sweden shows us that different tax rates can give rise to negative cross-border effects and that setting the tax in light of the actual damages is non-trivial.

Influence of Private Interest

Economists belonging to the 'public choice' school argue that regulation is not always based on public interest. Rent-seeking behavior can explain why 'economic prescriptions' (Hahn 1989) are not always followed with regard to taxation (see Lee 1985, 731–44 and Brooks and Heijdra 1987, 335–42, but also Bretteville and Aaheim 2004). Taxes, unlike environmental standards, do not constitute barriers to entry and are not protecting incumbents (Buchanan and Tullock 1975; Coelho 1976, 976–78; Yohe 1976, 981–82).

As a result of the influence of private interest, there are also clear examples of regulatory failure as far as environmental taxation is concerned. For instance in the Netherlands in 1996, a regulatory energy tax was introduced in tax law on an environmental basis. It is a regulatory levy, meaning a tax that has as its primary goal the realization of certain ecological goals. However, this energy tax is only addressed toward small consumers, since it imposes a system of digressive taxes. It simply means that the larger the energy use, the lower the tax will be. This curious model hence seems to give incentives for increasing the use of energy instead of decreasing it (see Faure and Ubachs 2002, 321–22, and Faure and Ubachs 2005, 521–32).

However, a study by Barker et al. (2009) shows that, despite its unfortunate design, econometric analysis suggests that overall impacts have been to reduce energy use and GHG emissions.

EMISSIONS TRADING

Basic Principles

The lack of flexibility and incentives is often considered a disadvantage of traditional command and control approaches, which in the form of standards are too general to allow for a differentiation between polluting firms' abatement potential. Worse, fine-tuned regulation, like traditional permit schemes, asks for expensive and burdensome bureaucratic work. This could be overcome by the increasingly popular marketable permits as introduced by Dales (1968) (for example the National Sulfur Dioxide Trading Program and Regional Nox Trading Programs (see Nash and Revesz 2001; Oates 1990, 290–93; Barde 1995, 218–20; Stavang 2005; Freestone and Frenkil 2009).

Marketable emission permits are issued to polluters up to the amount predetermined by policymakers. The market price and willingness to pay determines which actors will pollute. Many different distribution schemes are possible. Permits can for example be auctioned or distributed for free (for a comparison see Weishaar 2007a).

Marketable emission permits have major advantages: first, the regulator determines directly the quantity of emissions; second, contrary to the tax system, they automatically adapt to inflation (though it bears mentioning that several legislators have indexed their environmental tax rates); third, marketable permits may gain more acceptance because regulators are already familiar with permits. Marketable permits also have a number of disadvantages. First, initially permits are usually allocated via grandfathering according to past emissions records (and are thus free of charge). Hence it can be assumed that initial rights to use the environment are assigned to the polluters. Second, there are concerns that the pollution will be transferred to another region. Third, volatility of permit prices causes uncertainty about future price developments and results in sub-optimal investment in energy supply, particularly renewables. Fourth, marketable permits are criticized because polluters' profits can increase while pollution levels remain the same. Taxes by contrast will not only improve the level of pollution but will also raise revenue for the government. Since taxes are increasingly considered and employed alongside emissions trading to curb greenhouse gas emissions, a close examination of the former is in order.

Design Issues

Despite its theoretical appeal, emissions trading encounters problems regarding its legal and institutional design that are underestimated by economists (Woerdman 2004).

Allocation method

From an economic perspective, auctioning is the preferred allocation method. In practice, however, free allocation rewarding old polluters (grandfathering) and hindering new entries is often employed in practice (Ogus 1999, 226). Turner, Pearce and Bateman (1994, 184) argue that marketable permits can be used to create entry barriers if incumbents start hoarding them. The relationship between interest groups lobbies and the emissions trading system is discussed by Svendsen (1998, 133–44). Early actors as well as cleaner companies might need to buy rights from firms that have polluted more and can therefore be disadvantaged. Another objection is that grandfathering runs counter to the basic meaning of the polluter-pays principle (Nash 2000; Peeters 2003) though Woerdman et al. (2008) on the contrary argue that grandfathering is compatible with an efficiency interpretation of the polluter-pays principle. Alternative allocation criteria should also respect the legitimate expectations of firms based on traditional permits. The (partial) revocation of traditional permits must correspond to legal criteria, such as ensuring reasonable transition periods. Additional design details could be considered to mitigate the undesirable effects of grandfathering; the setting of a maximum price on the tradable rights could be analyzed (Victor 2001, 102 ff.).

Enforcement

Also, marketable permits require effective control. Much of the debate on emissions trading concerns its compatibility with the existing legal system and initial allocation. Even Dales did not pay much attention to the enforcement aspects of emissions trading, but nowadays we know about the enforcement deficit of environmental legislation. Policymakers should be very alert to the enforcement task that is part of an emissions trading system, since it could be attractive for firms to camouflage the real emissions data in order to minimize emissions control costs, receipts or expenditures from permit market transactions, as well as expected penalties from reporting and emissions violations (Stranlund, Chavez and Field 2002, 343–61).

The EU Emissions Trading Scheme

Scope of the EU ETS

It is interesting to address briefly the European Emissions Trading System. The EU ETS entered into force on 1 January 2005 and covers the main sources that emit CO_2 (see Dornau 2005), encompassing some 12 000 installations representing close to half of Europe's emissions of CO_2. As of 2012 it also covers aviation activities (Directive

2008/101/EC). The EU ETS is the biggest domestic emissions trading system established thus far. The first trading period ended in 2007; the second trading period will run till the end of 2012. After the revision of the EU ETS Directive (Directive 2003/87/EC was amended by Directive 2009/29/EC only three years after the system's introduction) in the third trading period (2013–2020), auctioning will be phased in while grandfathering gradually declines. Specific provisions for industries facing international competition are made. Furthermore, the trading system's scope is enlarged, incorporating additional greenhouse gases and sectors (Massai 2009).

Allocation method

Although many different legal design issues and institutional questions could be addressed, it is interesting to review some issues associated with allocation and enforcement. The economic literature has stressed the superiority of auctioning as an allocation mechanism since it prevents overrepresentation of industry's emissions projections (Baldwin 2008). The European Commission, however, limited auctioning to 5 percent in the first trading phase and 10 percent in the second. In the third trading phase auctioning will be gaining importance.

This free allocation (grandfathering) has given rise to a number of interesting legal and economic questions. For example the question of whether free allocation constitutes state aid has been examined. Although the European Commission considers free allocation to be state aid, the academic literature is much more divided on the issue (Weishaar 2007b; De Sepius 2007). The reason why free allocation rather than auctioning was chosen is that free allocation serves the interests of incumbents and may help to make the system more acceptable to industry.

Enforcement

The EU ETS Directive 2003/87/EC lays down specific provisions relating to monitoring and enforcement. Member states are expected to impose a 100 Euro penalty per allowance (see Art. 16 of Directive 2003/87/EC as amended) that is not surrendered to cover emissions. Operators remain obliged to surrender allowances for illegal emissions. In addition, a 'naming and shaming' provision has been introduced, meaning that Member States shall ensure publication of the names of operators who are in breach of requirements to surrender sufficient allowances (Art. 16 (2) of the Directive).

Also, a 'market-based' instrument like emissions trading needs adequate information about the actual emissions and enforcement measures taken against violators, so as to mitigate any incentive for free-riding and to ensure the system's environmental effectiveness (Baldwin 2008; Peeters 2006a; Peeters 2006b).

Effectiveness of the EU ETS?

Assessing the effectiveness of the EU ETS is a non-trivial enterprise because opinions could significantly diverge on the definition of an effectiveness test. Theoretical studies and empirical analysis are rather enthusiastic about emissions trading systems as an environmental policy tool, and yet questions could be asked with respect to the suitability of emissions trading in the particular case of developing countries (Faure, Peeters and Wibisana 2006). Also on the particular design of the EU emissions trading system, much criticism has been raised that *inter alia* is related to accountability and fairness (see Baldwin 2008; Endres and Ohl 2005).

If one narrows the broad effectiveness question somewhat, one could ask to what extent the EU ETS has contributed to achieving a behavioral change in industry as a result of which CO_2 emissions will be reduced to the extent required by the Kyoto Protocol (see Cló 2009). In that narrow sense one could examine whether the EU ETS has been effective in reaching the Kyoto targets or at least contributing to reaching them (though the effectiveness, or efficiency, of the Kyoto Protocol as such is also questioned (see Victor 2001). Based on an evolution of the price of allowances (which dropped during the first trading phase, even to below 10 Euro cents per allowance), many scholars have argued that member states have over-allocated allowances. Less clear, however, is whether the over-allocation as such means that the EU ETS therefore has been necessarily ineffective in providing incentives for emissions reductions. Over-allocation could also be (at least partially) the result of drastic investments in technological and other innovations causing emission reductions. If that was the case, the introduction of the EU ETS would have had the desired incentive effect of reducing emissions. The fact that emissions were lower than predicted should not then solely be considered as a negative outcome, but also as the result of the introduction of the EU ETS. Hence, one cannot conclude from the simple fact that the price of an allowance dropped below meaningful levels at the beginning of 2007 that the EU ETS would have had no incentive effect on innovation and thus would in that sense be ineffective. To the contrary, it seems that the EU ETS has actually been influencing operational and strategic decisions, more particularly in the EU's energy-intensive industry (Point Carbon 2011). After significantly reducing the amount of allowances allocated in the second trading phase, the price of emission allowances currently lies above 15 Euros per ton of CO_2 (June 2011), so as to stimulate investment in emission abatement technology.

Still, notwithstanding these relatively enthusiastic evaluations, one has to remain cautious. One problem is that merely by analyzing whether there has been any emission reduction effect on firm behavior, one does not take into account whether additional reductions could have been equally achieved with other instruments (taxation, for instance). The conclusion that the EU ETS is effective (in the sense of having some effect) does not therefore imply that it is optimal. Indeed, Baldwin recently argued that the transaction costs of trading systems can be high, referring to the EU ETS as 'an administrative nightmare' (Baldwin 2008, 15). Without taking into account the relative costs of EU ETS, one cannot argue that the system would be cost-effective. The mere fact that the EU ETS may have been effective in providing incentives for technological change leading to emission reductions does not therefore mean that there is no room for improvement that would increase the effectiveness. It consequently bears mentioning that the use of emissions taxes or energy taxes in sectors covered by the EU ETS has received scholarly attention that will surely intensify with the recent European Commission proposal on amending the Energy Tax Directive (see below). Authors appear to be rather cautious about the desirability of such complementary approaches, particularly if they represent unilateral action by member states (Böhringer, Koschel and Moslener 2007; Eichner and Pethig 2009). Further improvements in the legal and institutional design of the emissions trading system may well reduce its costs and thus increase its effectiveness.

THE ROLE OF ENVIRONMENTAL TAXATION IN THE POLICY MIX

The central question of this chapter is, given the specific properties of different instruments, which (combination of) instruments could lead to a cost effective reduction of environmental pollution. Indeed, the issues of cost-benefit analysis and environmental standard-setting give indications as to what level the pollution should be internalized, but they do not explain through what kind of instruments these optimal standards should be implemented. The role of environmental taxation will therefore often lie in the harmonious concert with other instruments.

Not One Single Optimal Instrument

Depending upon particular circumstances, all reviewed instruments have their specific strengths and weaknesses; no system is perfect. Environmental liability, for example, can provide excellent incentives to reduce pollution while still leaving industry sufficient flexibility. The duty to compensate victims under liability prevents polluters from taking care below the required standard even without governmental intervention. Optimal standards are determined by the judge (under a negligence setting) or by the potential polluter himself (under strict liability). Consequently continuous incentives for adaptation and innovation to a changing environment are offered to reduce pollution (especially under strict liability). Liability rules are moreover relatively cheap, since no standards are determined ex ante through government agencies and enforcement takes place via private parties (the victims) and not via government.

Liability rules will have this incentive effect only if the potential polluter has money at stake and hence the expected harm is not greater than his wealth. Furthermore, liability will give rise to optimal behavior only if victims can identify polluters and establish causal relationships between activities and damages caused. If this cannot be ensured, as is often the case, there is a justification for regulation. Yet regulation cannot be idealized either, since it is insufficiently flexible (too static), is not able to adapt quickly to changing circumstances, does not provide enough incentives for innovation, and (probably most importantly) can be subject to the influence of private interest groups, which gives rise to the setting of inefficient care levels.

Market-based instruments look promising and theoretically have many advantages over regulation. Yet legal and institutional design issues may reduce the efficiency of these so-called economic instruments: environmental taxes never reflect marginal environmental costs correctly and are used only to a limited extent, and emissions trading may suffer from grandfathering and other design issues that can reduce their effectiveness. These economic instruments are susceptible to lobbying that also affects instrument choice and design.

Search for 'Optimal Mixes'

A tax is generally capable of affecting the total amount used of a given type of product, and is also able to impact the choice between different product varieties. Yet due to *inter alia* monitoring and enforcement reasons, taxes appear to be less suited to address how a given product is used, when it is used, where it is used, etc. (see OECD 2006). Therefore, other instruments are needed to complement environmental taxes.

There is an abundant law and economics literature on this optimal combination of various policy instruments that discusses the comparative benefits of various instruments in a given situation. Polinsky (1979) (building upon Calabresi and Melamed 1972) argues that when the government has full information about the externality problem, only tax subsidies control externalities efficiently and protect both parties' entitlements, even in a transaction-cost world. In the presence of limited information, Polinsky (1979, 1–48; Brown and Holahan 1980, 165–78) claims that a tax is often inferior to the liability rules but that the property rights approach best protects entitlements, thus drawing a distinction between remedies based on property rights and liability rules on one hand and incentive-based mechanisms such as taxes and charges on the other.

Some attention has also been paid to the problem of combining tort recovery and effluent fees or tradable rights. Rose-Ackerman, for example, argued that incentive-based regulatory statutes should preempt tort actions: if fee schedules were set to reflect social costs, tort actions would be redundant or even counterproductive (Rose-Ackerman 1992, 128). This underlines the usefulness of combining instruments to attain complementary benefits. If, on the other hand, both instruments in fact reach the same goal, applying two instruments may only lead to increased administrative costs or to overdeterrence. A rich body of law and economics literature examines the combined use of such instruments to realize complementary benefits (see Hansson and Skogh 1987, 132–44; Skogh 1982, 67–80; Skogh 1989, 87–101; and Gravelle 1987, 115–31, and see more particularly Gunningham and Grabosky 1998).

Optimal Instrument Mixes in Practice

In practice as well, environmental policy may be based on a combination of economic instruments and regulatory solutions (see Gunningham and Grabosky 1998, 422–53). In many legal systems, environmental pollution is controlled primarily via command-and-control regulation, but liability rules still apply, along with incentives for meeting optimal care levels even beyond regulatory standards.

Undoubtedly there is more potential in actual environmental policy to make optimal use of efficient combinations of policy instruments. Regarding climate change, for example, the EU chose emissions trading without employing other classic instruments such as taxation. There is undoubtedly room to examine whether, also in the EU, environmental taxation could achieve (instead of or in combination with the ETS) similar or even better results than emissions trading. In this context it bears mentioning that the European Commission proposed to amend the rules on taxation of energy products and electricity (Council Directive 2003/96/EC) in order to restructure and target their carbon emissions and energy content (European Commission 2011). An interesting combination of environmental taxation and emissions trading can also be found in the UK in the form of the climate change levy that recycles money back to industry (Richardson and Chanwai 2003). In Switzerland, by contrast, companies participating in an emissions trading scheme are exempted from the domestic CO_2 tax. Since emission levels will be contingent on individual firms' cumulative responses to incentives, the environmental effectiveness is less predictable (Baldwin 2008, 6). Nevertheless, environmental taxation could be employed effectively in those sectors that are not subject to the EU ETS—not necessarily on the EU level but on the national level.

Limits of Instrument Mixes

Due to political choices and influences by interest-group politics, optimal mixes of policy instruments may not always be used. This was, for example, undoubtedly the case regarding the EU Emission Trading System, which was selected over environmental taxation. However, it also bears mentioning that for introducing taxation unanimous agreement in the Council of Ministers would have been needed (see Art. 192 (2)(a) TFEU).

Frey (1997) provides us with yet another relevant dimension of the choice of policy instruments: intrinsic motivation of citizens in the form of 'environmental morale'. This intrinsic motivation of citizens to behave environmentally responsibly is weak in the context of regulation since it reduces citizens' self-determination. Moreover, complex and abstract regulations are unlikely to improve the environmental morale. According to Frey, however, the same is true for tradable emissions rights, in which citizens purchase a 'license to pollute'. In the short term, environmental morale is best promoted by appeals and participation procedures, and in the long run by education. Moreover, when legal regulations have an expressive function, this supports the environmental morale. This is the case with easily comprehensible regulations whose punishments fit exactly the damage done to nature.

Frey equally holds that complementary policies are best, provided they are not overly ambitious and that they exploit the strengths of the various instruments (Frey 1999, 395–417; Frey 1997, 56–79). An important lesson from this literature is therefore that an optimal combination should thus not result in an imposition of all instruments at the same time, which may lead to an ineffective and costly overdeterrence and potentially adverse results.

Recommendations for Areas of Further Interdisciplinary Research

In order to better understand the effectiveness of environmental policy instruments, a close cooperation between various scholars interested in 'environmental social engineering', such as lawyers and economists (preferably brought together in the law and economics discipline) is of crucial importance. The experience with the EU ETS shows the importance of multidisciplinary research and cooperation to a better understanding of the strengths and weaknesses of an instrument like emissions trading, which rests on both complex economic incentive structures and equally complex 'legal details' that may be fully comprehended only if a holistic view is taken.

The example of the EU ETS makes this clear: even though there is some empirical evidence concerning the effectiveness of this scheme in reducing emissions (see Kuik and Oosterhuis 2008), it is equally clear that even in the case of compliance with the EU ETS, greenhouse gases will continue to an extent that they can cause climate change that can lead to substantial damage. This hence raises the question of whether there is room for a carbon tax in addition to an emissions trading scheme. The European Commission seems to answer this question in the affirmative since it recently proposed an amendment to the Energy Tax Directive (Council Directive 2003/96/EC) that will take a strong account of CO_2 emissions (European Commission 2011). Closely examining such options is necessary not only from a prevention perspective, but also for addressing the issue of compensation. Since climate change may (notwithstanding the EU ETS) still cause substantial damage, the question arises as to whether a compensation fund should be created to compensate for the damage caused by climate change. When it comes to the financing of such a scheme, again thoughts may go in the direction of levies or taxes. These examples show that, even though the EU may have chosen emissions trading as primary tool to fight climate change, the debate on the optimal mix of instruments is not over yet. Especially when it becomes clear that further-going measures are necessary, or when questions are asked concerning effective compensation mechanisms, the role of taxation again comes into the picture. The question of how a carbon tax could then be combined in an effective way with other instruments (such as emissions trading, but also liability rules) is a fascinating one that surely merits further interdisciplinary research.

REFERENCES

Adams, M. (1989), 'New activities and the efficient liability rules', in M. Faure and R. Van den Bergh (eds), *Essays in Law and Economics. Corporations, Accident Prevention and Compensation for Losses*, Antwerpen: Maklu uitgevers.

Albrecht, J. (2006), 'The use of consumption taxes to re-launch green tax reforms', *International Review of Law and Economics*, **26**, 88–103.

Arcuri, A. (2001), 'Controlling environmental risk in Europe: the complementary role of an EC environmental liability regime', *Tijdschrift voor Milieuaansprakelijkheid* [*Journal of Environmental Liability*], 39–40.

Backhaus, J. (1999), 'The law and economics of taxation: when should the ecotax kick in?', *International Review of Law and Economics*, **66**, 117–34.

Baldwin, R. (2008), 'Regulation lite: the rise of emissions trading', *Regulation & Governance*, **2** (2), 3–215, http ://www3.interscience.wiley.com/journal/119423171/issue.

Barde, J.-P. (1995), 'Environmental policy and policy instruments', in H. Folmer, H.L. Gabel and H. Opschoor (eds), *Principles of Environmental and Resource Economics: A Guide for Students and Decision-Makers*, Aldershot, UK: Edward Elgar Publishing, pp. 218–20.

Barker, T. et al. (2009), 'The effects of environmental tax reform on international competitiveness in the European Union: modelling with E3ME', in M.S. Andersen and P. Ekins (eds), *Carbon Energy Taxation: Lessons From Europe*, Oxford, UK: Oxford University Press, pp. 147–214.

Baumol, W.J. and W.E. Oates (1979), *Economics, Environmental Policy and the Quality of Life*, Englewood Cliffs, NJ, US: Prentice Hall.

Bergkamp, L. (2001), *Liability and Environment*, The Hague, Netherlands and London, UK: Kluwer Law International.

Bocken, H. (1987), 'Alternatives to liability and liability insurance for the compensation of pollution damages', *Tijdschrift voor Milieuaansprakelijkheid* [*Journal of Environmental Liability*], 83–87; and (1988), *Tijdschrift voor Milieuaansprakelijkheid*, 3–10.

Böhringer, C., H. Koschel and U. Moslener (2007), 'Efficiency losses from overlapping economic instruments in European carbon emissions regulation', *Journal of Regulatory Economics*, DPI 10.1007/S11149-007-9054-8.

Bongaerts, J.C. and R.A. Kraemer (1987), 'Water pollution charges in three countries. Control through incentives', *European Environment Review*, **1** (4), 12–19.

Brännlund, R. and J. Nordström (2004), 'Carbon tax simulations using a household demand model', *European Economic Review*, **48**, 211–33.

Bressers, H.Th.A. (1988) 'A comparison of the effectiveness of incentives and directives: the case of Dutch water quality policy', *Policy Studies Review*, **7** (3), 500–518.

Bretteville, F. and C.H. Aaheim (2004), 'Sectoral opposition to carbon taxes in the EU – a myopic economic approach, international environmental agreements', *Politics, Law and Economics*, **4**, 279–302.

Brooks, M.A. and B.J. Heijdra (1987), 'Rent-seeking and pollution taxation: an extension', *Southern Economic Journal*, **54** (2), 335–42.

Brown, G. and R. Johnson (1984), 'Pollution control by effluent charges: it works in the Federal Republic of Germany, why not in the US?', *Natural Resources Journal*, **24**, 929–66.

Brown, J.P. (1973), 'Toward an economic theory of liability', *Journal of Legal Studies*, **2** (2), 343.
Brown, J.P. and W.L. Holahan (1980), 'Taxes and legal rules for the control of externalities when there are strategic responses', *Journal of Legal Studies*, **9**, 165–78.
Bruvoll, A. and B.M. Larsen (2004), 'Greenhouse gas emissions in Norway: do carbon taxes work?', *Energy Policy*, **32**, 493–505.
Buchanan, J. and G. Tullock (1975), 'Polluters' profits and political response: direct controls versus taxes', *American Economic Review*, **65**, 139–47.
Burrows, P. (1999), 'Combining regulation and liability for the control of external costs', *International Review of Law and Economics*, **19**, 227–42.
Calabresi, G. (1961), 'Some thoughts on risk distribution and the law of torts', *Yale Law Journal*, **70**, 499–553.
Calabresi, G. (1970), *The Costs of Accidents. A Legal and Economic Analysis*, New Haven, CT, US: Yale University Press.
Calabresi, G. (1975), 'Optimal deterrence and accidents', *Yale Law Journal*, **84**, 656–71.
Calabresi, G. and D. Melamed (1972), 'Property rules, liability rules and inalienability: one view of the cathedral', *Harvard Law Review*, **85**, 1089–128.
Cló, S. (2009), 'The effectiveness of the EU Emissions Trading Scheme', *Carbon Policy*, **9** (3), 227–41.
Coase, R.H. (1960), 'The problem of social cost', *Journal of Law and Economics*, **3**, 1–44.
Coase, R.H. (1990), *The Firm, the Market and the Law*, Chicago, IL, US: The University of Chicago Press.
Coelho, Ph.R.P. (1976), 'Polluters' profits and political response: direct control versus taxes: comment', *American Economic Review*, **66**, 976–78.
Cooter, R. (1984), 'Prices and sanctions', *Columbia Law Review*, **84**, 1343–523.
Dales, J. (1968), *Pollution, Property and Prices: An Essay in Policy*, Toronto, Canada: University of Toronto Press.
De Sepius, J. (2007), 'The European Emission Trading Scheme put to the test of state aid rules', NCCR Trading regulation working paper 2007/34, http://papers.ssrn.com/so3/papers.cfm?abstract_id=1088716.
Dewees, D. (1992a), 'The comparative efficacy of tort law and regulation for environmental protection', *The Geneva Papers on Risk and Insurance*, **17** (4), 446–67.
Dewees, D. (1992b), 'Tort law and the deterrence of environmental pollution', in T.H. Tietenberg (ed.), *Innovation in Environmental Policy, Economic and Legal Aspects of Recent Developments in Environmental Enforcement of Liability*, Aldershot, UK: Edward Elgar Publishing, pp. 139–64.
Dewees, D., D. Duff and M. Trebilcock (1996), *Exploring the Domain of Accident Law: Taking the Facts Seriously*, Oxford, UK: Oxford University Press.
Diamond, P. (1974), 'Single Activity Accidents', *Journal of Legal Studies*, **3**, 107–64.
Directive 2003/87/EC of the European Parliament and of the Council of 13 October 2003, establishing a scheme for greenhouse gas emission allowance trading within the Community and amending Council Directive 96/61/EC, 2003 O.J. (L 275/32), 25 October 2003.
Directive 2009/29/EC of the European Parliament and of the Council of 23 April 2009 amending Directive 2003/87/EC so as to improve and extend the greenhouse gas emission allowance trading scheme of the Community, 2009 O.J. (L 140/63), 6 May 2009.
Dornau, R. (2005), 'The Emissions Trading Scheme of the European Union', in D. Freestone and C. Streck (eds), *Legal Aspects of Implementing the Kyoto Protocol Mechanisms*, Oxford, UK: Oxford University Press, chapter 23.
Eichner, T. and R. Pethig (2009), 'EU-Type carbon emissions trade and the distributional impact of overlapping emissions taxes', CESifo Working Paper No 2579.
Endres, A. and C. Ohl (2005), 'Kyoto, Europe? An economic evaluation of the European emissions trading directive', *European Journal of Law and Economics*, **19**, 17–39.
Endres, A. and R. Schwarze (1991), 'Allokationswirkungen einer Umwelthaftpflichtversicherung' [Allocative effects of environmental liability insurance], *Zeitschrift für Umweltpolitik und Umweltrecht* [*Journal for Environmental Policies and Environmental Law*], **14**, 1–25.
European Commission (2011), 'Proposal for a Council Directive amending Directive 2003/96/EC restructuring the Community framework for the taxation of energy products and electricity', Brussels, COM(2011) 169/3.
European Environment Agency (EEA) (2008), 'Effectiveness of environmental taxes and charges for managing sand, gravel and rock extraction in selected EU countries', No 2/2008.
Faure, M. (1995), 'Economic models of compensation for damage caused by nuclear accidents: some lessons for the revision of the Paris and Vienna Conventions', *European Journal of Law and Economics*, **2** (1), 21–43.
Faure, M. and M. Ruegg (1994), 'Standard setting through general principles of environmental law', in M. Faure, J. Vervaele and A. Weale (eds), *Environmental Standards in the European Union in an Interdisciplinary Framework*, Antwerpen-Apeldoorn, Netherlands: Maklu uitgevers, pp. 39–60.
Faure, M. and S. Ubachs (2002), 'Environmental taxation in the Netherlands: a Dutch treat?', in L.A. Kreiser et al. (eds), *Critical Issues in International Environmental Taxation. Insights and Analysis for Achieving Environmental Policy Goals through Tax Policy*, Chicago, US: CCH, pp. 301–29.

Faure, M. and S. Ubachs (2003), 'Comparative benefits and optimal use of environmental taxes', in J. Milne et al. (eds), *Critical Issues in Environmental Taxation: International and Comparative Perspectives*, Vol. I, Richmond, UK: Richmond Law and Tax, pp. 29–49.

Faure, M. and S. Ubachs (2005), 'Harmful tax measures and greying of taxation in the Netherlands: what went wrong?', in H. Ashiabor et al. (eds), *Critical Issues in Environmental Taxation: International and Comparative Perspectives*, Vol. II, Richmond, UK: Richmond Law and Tax, pp. 521–32.

Faure, M., M. Peeters and A. Wibisana (2006), 'Economic instruments: suited to developing countries?', in M. Faure and N. Niessen (eds), *Environmental Law in Development. Lessons from the Indonesian Experience*, Cheltenham, UK: Edward Elgar Publishing, pp. 218–62.

Freestone, D. and D. Frenkil (2009), 'Emissions trading in the US: a new regime approaching?', in M. Roggenkamp and U. Hammer (eds), *European Energy Law Report VII*, Antwerp, Belgium: Intersentia, pp. 75–94.

Frey, B.S. (1992), *Umweltökonomie* [Environmental Economics], Göttingen, Germany: Van den Hoeck & Ruprecht.

Frey, B.S. (1997), *Not Just for the Money: An Economic Theory of Personal Motivation*, Cheltenham, UK: Edward Elgar Publishing.

Frey, B.S. (1999), 'Morality and rationality in environmental policy', *Journal of Consumer Policy*, **22**, 395–417.

Fullerton, D., A. Leicester and S. Smith (2008), 'Environmental taxes', NBER Working Paper Series, Number 14197.

Fullerton, D., A. Leicester and S. Smith (2010), 'Environmental taxes', in Institute for Fiscal Studies (ed.), *Dimensions of Tax Design*, Oxford, UK: Oxford University Press.

Gravelle, H.S.E. (1987), 'Accidents, taxes, liability rules and insurances', *Geneva Papers on Risk and Insurance*, **12**, 115–31.

Groosman, B. (1999), '2500 Pollution Tax', in *Encyclopedia of Law and Economics, Common Property and Regulation of the Environment*, pp. 538–68.

Gunningham, M. and P. Grabosky (1998), *Smart Regulation. Designing Environmental Policy*, Oxford, UK: Clarendon Press.

Hahn, R.W. (1989), 'A new approach to the design of regulation in the presence of multiple objectives', *Journal of Environmental Economics and Management*, **17**, 195–211.

Hahn, R.W. and G.L. Hester (1989), 'Where did all the markets go? An analysis of EPA's emissions trading program', *Yale Journal on Regulation*, **6**, 109–53.

Hansson, I. and G. Skogh (1987), 'Moral hazard and safety regulation', *The Geneva Papers on Risk and Insurance*, **12**, 132–44.

Kapp, K.W. (1970), 'Environmental disruption and social costs: a challenge to economics', *Kyklos*, **23**, 833–48.

Kolstad, Ch.D., Th.S. Ulen and G.V. Johnson, 'Ex post liability for harm vs. ex ante safety regulation: substitutes or complements?', *American Economic Review*, **80**, 888–901.

Kosonen, K. and G. Nicodème (2009), 'The role of fiscal instruments in environmental policy', CESifo Working Paper No. 2719.

Kuik, O. and P. Oosterhuis (2008), 'Economic impact of the EU ETS: preliminary evidence', in M. Faure and M. Peeters (eds), *Climate Change and European Emissions Trading. Lessons for Theory and Practice*, Cheltenham, UK: Edward Elgar, pp. 208–22.

Kunreuther, H. and P. Freeman (2001), 'Insurability, environmental risks and the law', in A. Heyes (ed.), *The Law and Economics of the Environment*, Cheltenham, UK: Edward Elgar Publishing, pp. 304–5.

Landes, W. and R. Posner (1981), 'The positive economic theory of tort law', *Georgia Law Review*, **15**, 870.

Landes, W. and R. Posner (1984), 'Tort law as a regulatory regime for catastrophic personal injuries', *The Journal of Legal Studies*, **13**, 417.

Lee, D.R. (1985), 'Rent-seeking and its implications for pollution taxation', *Southern Economic Journal*, January, 731–44.

Mackaay, E. (1982), *Economics of Information and the Law*, Boston, MA, US: Kluwer Nijhoff Publishing.

Massai, L. (2009), 'The revision of the EU Emissions Trading System', in M. Roggenkamp and U. Hammer (eds), *European Energy Law Report VII*, Antwerp, Belgium: Intersentia, pp. 3–25.

Mishan, E.J. (1971a), 'Pangloss on pollution', *Swedish Journal of Economics*, **73** (1), 113–20.

Mishan, E.J. (1971b), 'The post war literature on externalities: an interpretative essay', *Journal of Economic Literature*, **9** (1), 1–28.

Morley, B. (2010), 'Empirical evidence on the effectiveness of environmental taxes', Bath Economics Research Papers, No 02/10.

Nash, J.R. (2000), 'Too much market? Conflict between tradable pollution allowances and the "polluter pays principle"', *Harvard Environmental Law Review*, **24**, 465–535.

Nash, J.R. and R.L. Revesz (2001), 'The design of marketable permit schemes to control local and regional pollutants', *Ecology Law Quarterly*, **28**, 559–661.

Natur Vårds Verket (2006), 'The Swedish charge on nitrogen oxides—cost-effective emission reduction', http://www.naturvardsverket.se/Documents/publikationer/620-8245-0.pdf.

Niezen, G.J. (2000), 'Aansprakelijkheid voor milieuschade in de Europese Unie' [Liability for environmental damage in the European Union], in G.J. Niezen, M.J.G.C. Raaijmakers and A.J.S.M. Tervoort (eds), *Ongebonden Recht Bedrijven, Bedrijfsjuridische opstellen op de grens van het derde millennium bij gelegenheid van het 70-jarig bestaan in 2000 van het Nederlands Genootschap van Bedrijfsjuristen* [Unbound issues of company law, Company law essays on the brink of the third millennium at the occasion of the 70th anniversary of the Dutch Association of Company law lawyers in 2000], Netherlands: Genootschap van Bedrijfsuristen.

Oates, W.E. (1983), 'The regulation of externalities: efficient behaviour by sources and victims', *Public Finance*, **38** (3), 362–75.

Oates, W.E. (1990), 'Economics, economists, and environmental policy', *Eastern Economic Journal*, **16** (4), 289–96.

Oates, W.E. (1994), 'Environment and taxation: the case of the United States', in OECD Documents, *Environment and Taxation: The Cases of the Netherlands, Sweden and the United States*, Paris, France: OECD.

OECD (2006), *The Political Economy of Environmentally Related Taxes*, Paris, France: OECD.

Ogus, A. (1999), 'Evaluating alternative regulatory regimes: the contribution of "law and economics"', *Geoforum*, **30**, 223–29.

Peeters, M. (2003), 'Emissions trading as a new dimension to European environmental law: the political agreement of the European Council on greenhouse gas allowance trading', *European Environmental Law Review*, **12**, 82–92.

Peeters, M. (2006a), 'Enforcement of the EU greenhouse gas emissions trading scheme', in K. Deketelaere and M. Peeters (eds), *EU Climate Change Policy: The Challenge of New Regulatory Initiatives*, Cheltenham, UK: Edward Elgar Publishing, pp. 169–87.

Peeters, M. (2006b), 'Inspection and market-based regulation through emissions trading: the striking reliance on self-monitoring, self-reporting and verification', *Utrecht Law Review*, **2** (1), 177–95.

Perman, R., Y. Ma, J. McGilvray and M. Common (2003), *Natural Resources and Environmental Economics*, Essex, UK: Longman.

Pindyck, R.S. and D.L. Rubenfield (2001), *Microeconomics*, New Jersey: Prentice Hall.

Point Carbon (2011), 'Carbon 2011', report published at Point Carbon's 7th annual conference, Carbon Market Insights 2011 in Amsterdam, 1–3 March, www.pointcarbon.com.

Polinsky, A.M. (1979), 'Controlling externalities and protecting entitlements: property right, liability rule and the tax-subsidy approaches', *Journal of Legal Studies*, **8**, 1–48.

Polinsky, A.M. (1983), *Introduction to Law and Economics*, Boston, MA, US and Toronto, Canada: Little, Brown & Co.

Richardson, B. and K. Chanwai (2003), 'The UK's climate change levy: is it working?', *Journal of Environmental Law*, **15** (1), 39–58.

Rose-Ackerman, S. (1992), *Rethinking the Progressive Agenda. The Reform of the American Regulatory State*, New York, NY, US: Free Press.

Rose-Ackerman, S. (1992), 'Environmental liability law', in T.H. Tietenberg (ed.), *Innovation in Environmental Policy, Economic and Legal Aspects of Recent Developments in Environmental Enforcement and Liability*, Cheltenham, UK: Edward Elgar Publishing, pp. 223–43.

Rose-Ackerman, S. (1995), *Controlling Environmental Policy: The Limits of Public Law in Germany and the United States*, New Haven, CT, US: Yale University Press.

Rose-Ackerman, S. (1995), 'Public law versus private law in environmental regulation: European Union proposals in the light of United States experience', *Review of European Community and International Environmental Law*, **4** (4), 312–32.

Rose-Ackerman, S. (1996), 'Public law versus private law in environmental regulation: European Union proposals in the light of United States and German experiences', in E. Eide and R. Van den Bergh (eds), *Law and Economics of the Environment*, Oslo, Norway: Juridisk Forlag, pp. 13–39.

Rosen, H.S. (1999), *Public Finance*, Chicago, IL, US: Irwin.

Schmitz, P.W. (2000), 'On the joint use of liability and safety regulation', *International Review of Law and Economics*, **20** (3), 371–82.

Schulze, W. and R. D'Arge (1974), 'The Coase proposition, information constraints, and long run equilibrium', *American Economic Review*, **64**, 763–72.

Schwartz, A. and L. Wilde (1979), 'Intervening in markets on the basis of imperfect information: a legal and economic analysis', *University of Pennsylvania Law Review*, **127** (3), 630–82.

Shavell, S. (1980), 'Strict liability versus negligence', *Journal of Legal Studies*, **9**, 1–25.

Shavell, S. (1984a), 'Liability for harm versus regulation of safety', *Journal of Legal Studies*, **13**, 357–74.

Shavell, S. (1984b), 'A model of the optimal use of liability and safety regulation', *Rand Journal of Economics*, **15** (2), 271–80.

Shavell, S. (1985), 'Criminal law and the optimal use of non-monetary sanctions as a deterrent', *Columbia Law Review*, **85**, 1232–62.

Shavell, S. (1986), 'The judgement proof problem', *International Review of Law and Economics*, **6**, 43–58.

Shavell, S. (1987), *Economic Analysis of Accident Law*, Cambridge MA, US: Harvard University Press.

Skogh, G. (1982), 'Public insurance and accident prevention', *International Review of Law and Economics*, **2**, 67–80.

Skogh, G. (1989), 'The combination of private and public regulation of safety', in M. Faure and R. Van den Bergh (eds), *Essays in Law and Economics. Corporations, Accident Prevention and Compensation for Losses*, Antwerp, Belgium: Maklu, pp. 87–101.

Stavang, E. (2005), 'Property in emissions? Analysis of the Norwegian GHG ETS with references also to the UK and the EU', *Environmental Law and Management*, **17**, 209–17.

Stigler, G. (1961), 'The economics of information', *Journal of Political Economics*, **69** (3), 213–25.

Stranlund, J.K., A.C. Chavez and B.C. Field (2002), 'Enforcing emissions trading programs: theory, practice and performance', *Policy Studies Journal*, **30** (3), 343–61.

Svendsen, G.T. (1998), *Public Choice and Environmental Regulation: Tradable Permit Systems in the United States and CO₂ Taxation in Europe*, Cheltenham, UK: Edward Elgar Publishing.

Tietenberg, T. (2000), *Environmental and National Resource Economics*, Reading, MA, US: Addison–Wesley.

Turner, R.K., D. Pearce and I. Bateman (1994), *Environmental Economics: An Elementary Introduction*, New York, NY, US: Harvester Wheatsheaf.

Victor, D.G. (2001), *The Collapse of the Kyoto Protocol and the Struggle to Slow Global Warming*, Princeton, NJ, US: Princeton University Press.

Weishaar, S. (2007a), 'CO₂ emission allowance allocation mechanisms, allocative efficiency and the environment: a static and dynamic perspective', *European Journal of Law and Economics*, **24** (1), 29–70.

Weishaar, S. (2007b), 'The European CO₂ Emission Trading System and state aid: an assessment of the grandfathering allocation method and the performance standard rate system', *European Competition Law Review*, **28** (6), 371–81.

Wittman, D. (1980), 'First come, first served: an economic analysis of "coming to nuisance"', *Journal of Legal Studies*, **9** (3), 557–68.

Woerdman, E. (2004), *The Institutional Economics of Market-Based Climate Policy*, Amsterdam, Netherlands: Elsevier.

Woerdman, E., A. Arcuri and S. Cló (2008), 'Emissions trading and the polluter-pays principle: do polluters pay under grandfathering?' *Review of Law and Economics*, **4** (2), 565–90.

Yohe, G. (1976), 'Polluters' profits and political response: direct control versus taxes: comment', *American Economic Review*, **66**, 981–82.

23 Regulatory reform and development of environmental taxation: the case of carbon taxation and ecological tax reform in Finland

Rauno Sairinen

During the 1990s, regulatory reform experiments offered an impressive range of new environmental policy tools, classified as economic, coregulation and planning instruments. This chapter discusses the role of environmental taxation in the trend (or turn) toward regulatory reform. The case of the development of carbon taxation and ecological tax reform in Finland during the last two decades (from the beginning of the 1990s through 2010) offers an interesting example of how regulatory reform can be complex and full of conflicts but still go forward continually.

REGULATORY REFORM AND ENVIRONMENTAL TAXATION

Regulatory Reform and the Shift Toward New Policy Instruments

Originating in the late 1960s, the first generation of environmental policies in the western world primarily followed the so-called command-and-control approach, which has been characterized by direct regulation: the government prescribes uniform environmental standards across large regions, mandates the abatement methods required to meet such standards, licenses production sites that adopt the required methods, and assures compliance through monitoring and sanctions (Golub 1998, 2).

In particular, Northern European countries, such as Germany, the Netherlands and the Nordic countries, boast relatively strong environmental records and had extensive direct regulation covering air, water, waste and noise in place by the end of the 1970s (Golub 1998, 2). For a long time, this approach was seen as the most appropriate and also the most efficient way to handle the increasing environmental problems.

During the 1990s, the limitations and regulatory failures of the traditional command-and-control approach sparked a search for a second generation of instruments that would offer greater flexibility, efficiency, effectiveness and legitimacy. In 1996, Francois Leveque (1996a, 18) noted that there was a general regulatory reform taking place worldwide in environmental policymaking. During the early 1990s, the number of ecological taxes, tradable permits and voluntary agreements was increasing in industrialized countries.

Significant changes were seen in the EU. In the introduction to his book *New Instruments for Environmental Policy in the EU*, Jonathan Golub (1998, 1) wrote, 'European environmental policy is currently undergoing a major transition. At the supranational level, both the Maastricht treaty and the Fifth Environmental Action Programme herald a new era dominated by the search for more flexible and efficient instruments to replace traditional forms of regulation.' In addition, the private sector itself developed so-called 'self-regulation' instruments (Leveque 1996b; Glasbergen 1998). In the environmental policy literature, the widening of the scope of policy instruments was also described as the trend toward NEPIs ('new' environmental policy instruments) (Jordan et al. 2003b).

The economic instruments included several types of environmental taxes and charges, comprehensive ecological tax reform, tradable pollution permit systems, government subsidies for environmental improvement and deposit/refund schemes. The economic instruments also included instruments that tried to alter liability and insurance rules in a manner that benefited the environment. Economic incentives seek to correct market failures directly by changing the costs faced by private decision-makers to reflect the full social costs of their actions. It is believed that, if the incentives are properly designed, private actions can more closely approximate the socially optimal use of environmental resources (EPA 1991).

Coregulation was often seen as a relative approach to economic instruments but was still a different new instrument category. Coregulation covers cases in which the interactive relationships between public authorities and firms are especially pervasive and close. This group consists of voluntary agreements, ecolabels, ecoaudits and conflict-resolution models (JEP 1998).

In the field of environmental policy, the new instruments were expected to perform many kinds of policy-related tasks (see Golub 1998, 6–8):

- to provide efficiency by using market mechanisms and target-specific governing;
- to reduce the regulatory burden on firms (deregulation);
- to provide positive incentives instead of negative ones (win-win option);
- to harness the market power of 'green consumerism;'
- to rely on consultation rather than open confrontation;
- to open up the policy process for third parties (openness, participation); and
- to develop the public legitimacy of environmental governing.

In practice, these varying objectives are largely independent of and also frequently in conflict with each other. Moreover, different policy actors have their own expectations concerning the new instruments, and the use of these new policy instruments varies widely among the countries, as do the reasons for their introduction.

In the literature, it is often claimed that industry and other polluters, such as agriculture, support most alternatives to direct regulation, arguing that other options will improve environmental protection while reducing compliance costs. However, the polluters have usually been critical of environmental taxation and new kinds of environmental planning requirements. Thus, the polluters have in practice exhibited some ambivalence toward the shift, because of the uncertainty and transaction costs they face by abandoning a well-understood regulatory approach over which they probably exercise considerable influence (Golub 1998, 6–7). In addition, the polluter perspective on new instruments may involve mixed motives, for instance when dealing with free-rider problems, or when the interests of large and small firms diverge. In any case, the polluters have certainly expressed strong preference for coregulation and self-regulation instruments over other types of new tools.

Regulatory Reform as a Turn in Governance

The regulatory reform was influenced by general changes in the modes of governance as well as by new forms of socio-political interaction. According to the analysis by Kooiman et al. (Kooiman, ed. 1993), new kinds of interaction between government and society in terms of governance and governing were developing. Public governing after this governance turn typically not only involves singular actions but is also a process in which several actors may participate. According to Kooiman (Kooiman, ed.1993, 4), the new forms of governance differed from more traditional ones in that they 'take complexity, dynamics and diversity much more seriously than their predecessors who often regarded these characteristics as nasty side effects, which unfortunately did not fit in the applied models . . .. The shift seems to be away from "one-way steering and control" to two- or multi-way "designs.'''

The ideas of regulatory reform in environmental policymaking secured especially drastic influence inside the EU, where the new trend was accompanied by several institutional changes. The Maastrict Treaty on European Union in 1992 vigorously enhanced the involvement of the Community in the area of the environment, but also modified environmental rulemaking. The broadening of the set of policy instruments was one of the key orientations of the new EU approach, as defined in the fifth action program 'Towards Sustainability' (COM 1993). Another key orientation of the new EU approach was dialogue and consultation with the concerned parties (Leveque 1996a).

The Deregulation and Ecological Modernization behind the Choice of Policy Instruments

The choice of a policy instrument is always influenced by economic, political and ideological factors that generally also have an effect on the changing of governance modes. Behind the regulatory reform of environmental policy there are at least two larger societal trends: deregulation and ecological modernization.

The emergence of the new environmental policy instruments has often been associated with the idea of 'free-market environmentalism' and the more general deregulative policies (Collier, ed. 1998; Eckersley, ed. 1995). Since the 1980s, the dominant feature of public policy in many countries has been a reduction in direct governmental intervention, both financial and regulatory (Määttä 1997). This trend of deregulation has created an ideological basis for adopting new styles of public management and policy instruments in all sectors of policy.

On the other hand, the regulatory reform has been linked to the theory and/or strategy of ecological modernization (JEP 1998; Liefferink and Mol 1998). In its different modes, the ecological modernization theory has stressed the increasing importance of economic and market dynamics in ecological reform, and the role of innovators, entrepreneurs and other economic agents—in addition to state agencies and new social movements—as social carriers of ecological restructuring.

The Role of Environmental Taxation in Regulatory Reform

Paradoxically, environmental taxes may be called an 'old yet new' instrument, because the idea was first suggested in 1920 (Andersen 1994). In practice, however, environmental taxes were first applied on a wider scale in the 1980s.

Environmental taxes have generally been defined as market-based instruments. Määttä (1997, 187) criticized this view as too simple:

> Discussion about market-based instruments may give an impression that there is no need for legislative measures with respect to environmental taxes, although the situation is actually the reverse. According to the legality principle, the power to levy an environmental tax rests upon the legislator, and in order to be valid the legislation should contain all essential elements of a tax. By contrast, regulatory instruments can be enacted through framework laws which leave much discretionary power to the environmental authorities.

Thus, from this perspective, environmental taxes are intervention norms, and they do not necessarily follow deregulative ideas. Such taxes usually require very precise and strong hard-law regulation and are often applied as complementary to other instruments. Thus, far from acting as tools of deregulation, they have represented additional intervention norms in society.

Regardless, environmental taxation represents the trend of regulatory reform, because it brings a new governing mechanism to the agenda, influencing markets and prices instead of directly regulating them. It also represents a new policy instrument insofar as it has not been used in real life before.

The forms and usage of market-based instruments and environmental taxes have been developing continually. The periods of environmental tax policy can be divided into the following stages (Määttä 1997; Jordan et al. 2003c, 210–11):

- *An ad hoc stage*, which lasted until the mid-1980s, included individual experiments in different countries without any general policy or strategy. Japan adopted one of the very first environmental taxes (on sulphur dioxide) in 1974. The Nordic countries, the Netherlands and France followed soon after with charges on water and air pollution.
- *An expansionary stage*, which began in the mid-1980s and continued throughout the 1990s, brought a significant increase in the number of environmental taxes and the shift toward the use of incentive taxes and energy and carbon taxes. Notably, the Scandinavian countries have to an extent been pioneers in this field (Andersen and Liefferink 1996 and 1997). The UK initiated national environmental taxes in the beginning of the 1990s. Here, policymakers also began to experiment with hypothecation; that is, earmarking a certain portion of the revenue stream for particular forms of environmental spending. For example, the UK decided on the landfill tax and Finland on the oil waste levy (Jordan et al. 2003c, 210–11).
- *Environmental tax reform* is the most advanced form of developing environmental taxation. There are clear forerunners, such as Finland, the Netherlands, France, Germany, and the UK, which adopted some programs in this field in the late 1990s (Jordan et al. 2003c, 211). During the 2000s, environmental tax reform has advanced in many countries, but at the same time at the political level it has been in competition with the development of tradable permits systems. The idea of environmental tax reform is to tax fossil fuels and nuclear energy, water consumption, raw materials (especially those that are likely to end up as toxic pollutants or hazardous waste), and also possibly emissions and waste, and to reduce other taxes instead. A revenue-neutral tax reform would stipulate that the overall fiscal

burden on business must not increase. Revenue neutrality has a politically important terminological implication: that one should not talk about environmental or
'green' taxes but rather environmental tax reform. This is likely to meet with greater
political acceptance than the term 'green taxes,' which could be understood as
representing an additional burden. Unlike earmarked charges, environmental tax
reform requires no scientific proof of the causal link between the taxed commodity
or emission and the environmental damage (von Weizsäcker and Jesinghaus 1992).
Environmental tax reform is also sometimes referred to as ecological tax reform, as
is frequently the case in Finland.

THE FINNISH EXPERIENCE

The International Need of Carbon Tax Development and the Finnish Case

During the last two decades, climate policy issues have come to be defined as top-priority
questions on the environmental agenda on the global, national and even local levels.
Carbon taxation as a measure for decreasing CO_2 emissions was developed because traditional direct regulation is somewhat problematic (Bragge 1997, 16–17; ME 1994). There
is a huge number of small emitters (such as cars and residential houses) rather than just
a few large ones, which means that regulation and monitoring would be inflexible and
far too costly compared to the potential reductions in emissions. Moreover, with current
technology, it is not economically feasible to clean the CO_2 emissions from exhaust gases.
Consequently there exist two main alternatives for abating the emissions in the short run:
reducing the use of energy by saving and by increased energy efficiency, and substituting
energy sources with a low carbon content for those with a high carbon content.

During the 1990s, while awaiting international agreements on energy taxes, some EU
countries, such as Finland, Sweden, Denmark and the Netherlands, introduced their
own models. It was argued that the favorable experiences of the 'pioneering' countries
might be an effective way of contributing to the advancement of international agreements
(Andersen and Liefferink 1996).

The following text describes the four phases that can be distinguished in the development of the Finnish carbon tax and of ecological tax reform from the end of the 1980s
to the year 2010 (Sairinen 2000; Tikkanen 2005). As a starting point, it is reasonable to
note that the price of energy has always been very important for Finnish industrial policymaking. In Finland, the total consumption of energy has been somewhat higher than
the OECD average (ME 1996). Because of the country's northern location, its climate is
the coldest in Europe. In addition, the country is sparsely populated, economic activity is
hampered by long transport distances, and the structure of the manufacturing industries
(forest and paper) is energy-intensive. In this kind of policy context, the goal of increasing
energy taxation is not easily achievable politically.

The First Phase (1989–1990): The World's First Carbon Tax

During the first phase (1989–1990), the carbon tax was added to the political agenda and
the first version of the carbon tax was introduced. Previously, in 1986, the Ministry of the

Environment established the Committee on Environmental Economy (KM 1989), which represented several stakeholders and studied in general terms the economic approaches to environmental protection, but which also made some proposals concerning environmental taxes. It also proposed that the feasibility of introducing a charge on carbon dioxide emissions should be studied.

From the very beginning, the industry was critical of environmental taxation (see Tommila 1989), as it feared that its tax burden would be increased and its competitiveness weakened. In their dissenting opinion for the Committee on Environmental Economy, the representatives of the industry argued:

> It is not well-founded to aim at economic steering as an end in itself . . .. Changes in corporate behaviour would be possible to reach also by true incentives, for example by precisely focused subsidies or other supporting measures . . ..The best scopes for the application of economic instruments are those in which numerous decisions are made, mainly on economic grounds. (KM 1989, 123–30).

At the political level, the Parliament was active. In April 1989, the Green League seized upon the environmental tax initiatives of Member of Parliament Esko Seppänen (socialist) and began to organize the environmental tax cooperation of the opposition parties.[1] It soon became evident that the parties in government, the Social Democratic Party (SDP) and the Coalition Party (CP), were unwilling to give the opposition, especially the Greens, an asset for the next elections. Therefore, the environmental tax debate launched by the opposition soon resulted in tangible results. Both Prime Minister Harri Holkeri (CP) and Finance Minister Erkki Liikanen (SDP) adopted a positive attitude toward environmental tax proposals. In June 1989, Liikanen made a deal with the Greens: he promised to establish environmental taxes if the Greens would support some cuts in income taxes. The general political atmosphere and mentality was also suitable for taking new steps in environmental policy governing. The economic boom and the new debate on sustainable development provided favorable conditions for this.

In 1990, Finland was the first country in the world to introduce the carbon dioxide tax on fossil fuels on environmental grounds (KM 1993, 27). The tax covered light fuel oil, heavy fuel oil, coal, natural gas and peat. At the same time, the excise taxes on liquid transportation fuels were also renewed on environmental grounds. The scaling of these taxes was not based on the carbon content of the fuels, as in the case of other fossil fuels, but on the lead content. At first, the CO_2 tax was relatively low, approximately FIM 7/ tCO_2 [1,3 euros/tCO_2] (FIM 24.5/tC [4,6 euros/tC]). Of all the possible energy-related environmental taxes, the CO_2 tax was introduced first because it was easy to enact and technically easy to implement. Emission taxes, such as the sulphur tax or the nitrogen tax, would have been much more difficult to measure and control. The Finnish CO_2 tax was a share tax, not an emission tax, and was based on the carbon content of the fuel.

---

[1]   The Finnish Greens were forerunners in the international field. The Green Group of the European Parliament presented a proposal for a 20-dollar EU-wide tax on nonrenewable energy two years later, in July 1991.

The Second Phase (1991–1994): Raising the Level of Carbon Tax

During the second phase (1991–1994), the carbon tax was raised in 1993 and in 1994 it faced a structural change. The 75/25 tax model was established: 75 percent of the tax was based on the carbon content of the primary energy source and 25 percent on the energy content. An important reason for introducing an energy tax component into the tax system was to take into account the externalities involved in nuclear power. The problem of a pure carbon tax is that it confers a fiscal advantage on nuclear power production. This structural change, which was later considered very advanced by environmentalists, took place after a relatively short political conflict and successful broad-based committee work. At that time, environmental taxes were a popular trend in Finnish politics and the state was facing serious fiscal difficulty in the middle of an economic crisis. Thus, it is interesting to note that general energy and environmental policy was moving toward the normalization of environmental taxation in conditions of deep economic depression.

In April 1993, the Environmental Economics Committee presented its statement on energy taxation (KM 1993). The statement proposed the gradual increase of environment-related energy taxes within the limits of international development and the competitive position of the industry. The level of taxation was not specified explicitly. Above all, it was assumed that the EU would introduce a similar tax within the next few years.

Because the proposal of the committee was unanimous and the result of high-level civil servant preparation, the proposal was widely supported in the Government. This time, industry also supported the model presented by the committee. In May 1993, the Government proposed the '75/25 tax model' for 1994. The only alteration to the committee's proposal involved the taxation of electricity generated by nuclear power and of imported electricity. An additional tax, similar to an excise tax, would be levied on these electricity sources—but not on others. As a result, it imposed the equivalent of the energy tax under the 75/25 model. In February, the Government made a decision on principle that proposed that peat, as a domestic energy source, should be exempted from the CO_2 component of the tax due to regional and employment policy as well as for security policy reasons.

In the autumn of 1993, the proposed tax model ran into political difficulties because of the nuclear power issue. In Government, the Coalition Party heavily promoted the fifth nuclear power plant.[2] Attempts were made to persuade the members of the Centre Party, who opposed nuclear power in the Parliament, to back nuclear power by promising tax relief and subsidies to domestic energy (peat and wood). This 'consensus package' was most strongly advocated by Foreign Minister Väyrynen (Centre Party). The plan fell through, however, because the Parliament voted down the nuclear power plant initiative. After that, the Conservative Party was much more reluctant to establish the energy taxes. After a minor political crisis in the Government, the structure of the energy tax remained unaltered, but peat was not totally exempted from the CO_2 tax. The amount of the tax came to about 30 percent of the corresponding tax on coal. The new energy tax, which was rather radical from the viewpoint of environmental policy, came into force at the beginning of 1994.

---

[2]   In Finland, four nuclear power plants were already in operation.

During the same years, voluntary agreements (VAs) concerning energy savings and efficiency were put into use for the first time in Finland. The Government's first extensive energy conservation program was launched in 1992. The program presented VAs between the state and energy consumers as a new policy instrument. The main governmental approach emphasized simultaneous use of both carbon taxation and the voluntary agreements, so these new instruments were seen not as alternatives to each other but rather as complementary tools in the toolbox. There could also be seen some division of labor between these instruments: environmental taxes were thought to influence the modes of energy production and voluntary agreements the modes of energy consumption.

During the mid-1990s, the promotion of energy efficiency became a stronger, more official and more consistent goal in Finnish energy politics. All governing activities, such as new policy strategies, voluntary agreements and rising energy and carbon taxation, gave a clear signal to the energy markets and consumers that energy conservation was necessary. In December 1995, the Government made a decision in principle regarding energy policy and energy conservation (VN 1995). Its goal was to slow down, without new policy instruments, the predicted growth of energy consumption by 15 percent by the year 2010. In this program, the VAs played a more significant role.

The Third Phase (1994–1996): Decreasing the Role of Carbon Tax

During the third phase (1994–1996), the structure of the energy taxation was altered by decreasing the role of carbon taxes. A definite turn took place in 1994, when many Finnish policy actors lost their hope for an EU energy tax. Simultaneously, the EU Commission started to criticize the Finnish system, claiming that the Finnish tax imposed on imported electricity violated trade agreements. After hearing about the critique of the Commission, the Outokumpu company filed a complaint with the EU Court of Justice regarding the taxes it paid on imported electricity. To the state, the matter was a serious question. If Outokumpu should win the case, other companies might also file complaints and Finland would have large reimbursements to pay. In practice, this claim meant that the whole energy tax system would have to be reformed.[3] However, mainly because of the insistence of the Greens inside the Government, the reform of the energy and carbon tax was done in a manner wherein parts of the carbon tax were preserved and the total level of the taxes was increased remarkably.

The development of the carbon dioxide tax and its increase in 1993 had gained the approval of the Parliament and the Government, but obtaining the backing of the majority of the Parliament was quite difficult. The tax had been actively opposed, and the industry had continuously criticized it. The industry considered the best model to be an electricity tax not based on carbon content, and which exempted the electricity used by heavy industry. Now, the Ministry of Trade and Industry (MTI) and the Ministry of Finance (MF) doubted also the feasibility of the new '75/25 tax model.' This doubt existed during the Government of Aho (in 1995), but doubts about the tax system became concrete during Lipponen's first Government (1995–1999).

---

[3] http://eur-lex.europa.eu/smartapi/cgi/sga_doc?smartapi!celexplus!prod!CELEXnumdoc&lg =en&numdoc=61996J0213.

In addition to energy taxes, the central energy policy reform of the 1990s addressed the liberalization of the energy markets in Finland. The new Electricity Market Act came into force on June 1, 1995, opening the Nordic electricity markets as of November 1995. Simultaneously, the opening of the markets and the divergent energy tax systems of different countries raised questions about the suitability of the Finnish carbon tax in common markets. The big power companies tried to raise problems that the tax would likely cause. In the spring of 1995, two Finnish industrial enterprises, Outokumpu and Enso-Gutzeit, agreed to purchase electricity from the Swedish company Vattenfall. The agreements came into force at the beginning of November 1995, just as the electricity transmission obligation enacted in the Finnish Electricity Market Act took effect. In connection with this, Imatran Voima (IVO), the biggest power company in Finland, stressed that the reason it lost these clients was the Finnish CO_2 and energy taxes, and that because of these taxes, IVO's own coal-condensing capacity had been out of use. According to the IVO representatives, the Finnish CO_2 tax was excessive and would lead to an increase in imported electricity and indirectly to the use of Danish coal power.

In June 1995, a working group (VM 1995) consisting of representatives from the MF, the energy department of the MTI and the National Board of Customs recommended a combined electricity and CO_2 tax in which the energy tax would be completely abolished for electricity production and the CO_2 component would be reduced by 50 percent. An electricity tax would compensate for the changes. The work of the group was based on the following opinions: (1) the Finnish export industry paid considerably more taxes than the export industries of rival countries; (2) domestic electricity production was not competitive with foreign production; (3) the taxation of imported electricity violated international regulations; (4) the tax refund procedure for exported electricity was not neutral for the various power-generation sources; and (5) the taxation of imported electricity complicated the functioning of the Nordic electricity pool.

On December 21, 1995, the Government made a decision in principle on energy policy (VN 1995), stating, 'The problems related to energy taxation will be amended by transferring the focal point of electricity taxation from production fuels to the end product, that is electricity.' In practice, the suggestion meant that the focus of taxation would be moved from production to consumption. At the same time, the energy tax burden on industry would be reduced gradually to bring it closer to the level of rival countries.

At this stage, various environmentalists were already very worried about the course of events. Environmental organizations strongly criticized Minister of the Environment Pekka Haavisto (Greens) for his low profile and his politics of compromise. Although environmental taxes had been provided for in the government program, none were developed. On the contrary, even existing environmental taxes were going to be abolished.

In August 1996, the budget negotiations for the following year took place. The income taxes were intended to be cut down. Here, the Greens brought up the environmental tax targets and threatened to withdraw from the Government unless the matter was advanced. In the wee hours of the morning, an agreement was reached. It was evident that Prime Minister Lipponen wanted to keep the Greens in the Government (perhaps partly because of the future EMU decisions), so the Government decided to reduce the income tax and simultaneously covered FIM 1.1 billion [0.2 billion euros] of this cut via new electricity taxes, following the Greens' demand. The Government decided to aim the new electricity taxes at households, not at industry. The carbon tax was removed from electricity production, but at the same time heat production was now to be taxed completely (100 percent) according to carbon content. Reliefs were allowed for natural gas and peat.

The decision of the Government was a very complex compromise and provided room for various interpretations. The Chairman of the Green League, Tuija Brax, spoke of a historical turn toward ecological tax reform: the focal point of taxation had been transferred from labor to energy. At the same time, environmental groups criticized the weakening of the carbon tax system.

The Fourth Phase: Developing the Ideas of Ecological Tax Reform

The Finnish basic energy and air pollution tax system has been more or less unchanged since 1997; only the tax rates have been adjusted somewhat (Lindhjem et al. 2009, 12). The revised energy tax legislation in 1998 introduced a refund scheme for special energy-intensive industries.[4]

The major change with regard to economic instruments has been the introduction of the European emissions trading scheme (ETS) at the beginning of 2005 (Lindhjem et al. 2009, 39). The ETS can be seen as a main instrument for carrying out energy and climate policy actions in Finland. The introduction of emissions trading has not led to any major changes in the carbon tax system for those emissions that are part of the trading system. However, the tax on electricity paid by industry has been lowered and the tax on peat has been abolished.

In 1999, a government working group on environmental taxation assessed the effects of environmental taxes (Talousneuvosto 2000). The results showed that energy and carbon taxes reduced carbon emissions by over 7 percent (57 million tons) during 1990–1998. The attitudes of main policymakers toward further use of environmental taxes in the energy sector were nonetheless dubious. The main reasons for this attitude were the costs of structural changes of production, the narrow tax base of environmental taxes and the problems for international competitiveness (Talousneuvosto 2000, Tikkanen 2005, 112). In addition, there was not very much trust that energy taxes would be used to further international climate policy. These viewpoints provided the main basis of the tax-related decisions made by Paavo Lipponen's second Government 1999–2003 (Tikkanen 2005), wherein environmental and energy taxes and ecological tax reform were not considered in the political arena as a serious matter, although the Greens inside the Government tried to make some noise about them.

A clear change in these attitudes happened during 2003. At first, the Ministry of the Environment ordered an inquiry called 'Environmentally-based taxation and the pre-conditions of sustainable development—vision to the year 2020' ('*Ympäristöperusteinen verotus ja kestävän kehityksen edellytykset—visio vuoteen 2020*') (Honkatukia and

---

[4]   The refund scheme is only applicable to companies when the total burden of excise duties on energy exceeds 3.7 percent of the value added of the given company. The company is then entitled to a refund of the taxes paid, and it can apply for a refund of up to 85 percent of the taxes paid exceeding 50000 euros. This means that a very limited number of industrial facilities can claim a tax refund.

Kiander 2003). In the first Government of Prime Minister Vanhanen (2003–2007), ecological tax reform was first mentioned as a policy tool for sustainable development (Tikkanen 2005). After this, the Ministry of Finance issued a report called 'Sustainable development and ecological tax reform' *(Kestävä kehitys ja ekologinen verouudistus)* (VM 2004), in which the Ministry assessed various ways of implementing the tax reform. The Ministry stated that the implementation of ecological tax reform is extremely challenging if one tries to balance simultaneously the benefits of environment, welfare and employment. Therefore, the double dividend was seen as very hard to achieve.

The inquiries continued in the second Government of Prime Minister Matti Vanhanen (2007–2010). The climate policy debate made environmentally-based energy taxes again very relevant, and simultaneuously the need to improve the tax base for the future provided room for a general rethinking of the tax system. The car registration tax system was changed in 2008, and differentiated according to the specified fuel consumption of the car. Tax rates were generally cut by one sixth. Since 2010 the annual car owner's tax has been based on the car's CO_2 emissions.

The taxation working group, appointed by the Ministry of Finance in 2008 and led by Mr. Hetemäki, proposed key changes to taxation in its intermediate report (VM 2010a). The main themes of the intermediate report were widening the tax base, lightening the taxation of work and shifting the focus from direct taxes to consumption taxes. The group set a target of increasing the consumption tax burden on activities harmful to health and the environment. In its final report at the end of 2010 (VM 2010b), the group stated that 'significant increases of excise duties on heating fuels and electricity will come into force at the beginning of 2011.'

The state budget proposal for the year 2011 called for a hike in energy taxation, which brought in 750 million euros in revenue. Taxes on fuel for heat and power plants and energy taxes on electricity were raised in connection with structural tax reforms, to help offset the tax revenue losses incurred by the abolition of the employers' national pension contribution. The taxation of earned income was left unchanged, given the economic depression and the need to balance the budget.

Ecological tax reform has been ongoing for a decade now in the contents of policy programs and administrative inquiries. The concrete changes in the tax system have been gradual, but through this some real alteration in the balance of tax system is happening. Since the 1990s, the emphasis of taxation has been gradually shifted from taxation of labor to taxation of activities polluting the environment. The most important taxes for environmental purposes are excise taxes on fossil fuels and electricity, the tax on waste and the registration tax on passenger cars.

During 2010, the public debate on environmental taxation was active, and even had some new emphasis. In earlier times, the Conservative Party used to be against environmental taxes, but now it was supporting ecological tax reform along with the Greens. The biggest critique of energy and carbon taxation came not from industry but from opposition parties such as the Social Democrats and the growing populist party, True Finns. The main criticism concerns the effects of ecological tax reform on social equality, social justice and the division of income among social groups. Environmental taxation is changing the tax system from a foundation of progressive principles toward one of equal taxes (flat tax). The critics are afraid of the possible costs that environmental taxes are imposing on, for example, low-income people, mobility or rural areas. The supporters of ecological tax reform have thought of some possibilities for compensating for these losses through other changes in the tax system. The debate was continuing actively during winter and spring 2011, because Finland had parliamentary elections in April 2011.

In June 2011, the new coalition government (the so-called six-pack including the Conservatives, the Social Democrats, the Greens, the Left Alliance, the Christian Democrats and the Swedish People's Party) decided in its program to raise excise taxes in order to bring in about an additional 660 million euros (Government Programme 2011). Excise taxes are levied on electricity, heating fuels, petrol and diesel oil, tobacco, alcohol, sweets, ice cream, and soft drinks. The SDP agreed to this, seeing it as preferable to a higher VAT. In addition, the coalition decided to decrease the energy taxes from energy-intensive industry (Government Programme 2011, 41). Despite the Social Democrats and Left Alliance's doubts, the general policy targets of environmental tax reform are still mentioned in the government program. The program states as a normative target that '[t]he focus of the taxation will be moved towards environmental- and health-based taxation from the growth harmful taxes of labour and entrepreneurship' (Government Programme 2011, 14).

CONCLUSIONS

The new environmental policy instruments do not represent similar ideas or approaches, but in fact very different ones. Their goals can be to utilize market mechanisms, voluntariness, negotiation, preventive action, participation, self-regulation, etc. Because of this, the concept of regulatory reform incorporates very different aspects and can be misleading. At a certain level, the only common matter is perhaps the critique of the traditional command-and-control approach; and today even hard-law regulation is taking steps toward new ideas. In addition, policy instruments differ from one country to the next in the way they are calibrated and implemented. As Jordan et al. (2003a, 4) have noted, what may be a 'new' instrument in one country may already be part of established practice in another. Nevertheless, environmental taxation represents the trend of regulatory reform. It is bringing a new governing mechanism to the agenda and influencing markets and prices instead of regulating them directly.

The two decades of regulatory reform have witnessed an evolution toward more approbative attitudes among various policy instruments. Supporters of hard regulation more often accept that economic instruments and taxes may offer both cost savings and environmentally effective outcomes, while economists on the other hand have realized that the use of economic instruments poses many challenges they did not originally foresee (Lindhjem et al. 2009, 17). This realization has sharpened public debate and academic research and has led to a better understanding of the complex role of environmental regulation in the political economy. As Lindhjelm et al. (2009) have noticed, in no other region is this perhaps more true than in the Nordic countries (including Finland), which adopted economic instruments, mostly taxes, at an early stage, but which currently have rather complex regulation systems shaped by a multitude of considerations.

Normalization and Intensification of Environmental Taxation

The Finnish case of carbon taxation and ecological tax reform tells a story about how one new environmental policy instrument, environmental taxation, gradually became a normalized matter for the state administration. The potential aspects of Finland's environmental taxation were first developed by the means of committees. Through the committee work, different ministries and interest groups were themselves committed to the new governing approach.

The amount of environmental energy taxes increased significantly in Finland in 1990–1996 (Sairinen 2000). The total revenue was FIM 0.5 billion [0,1 billion euros] in 1990 and 2.8 billion [0,5 billion euros] in 1996. At the same time, fiscal energy taxes also increased quite rapidly. During the years 1994–1996, the carbon tax was disputed and reformulated. In 1996, after six years of development work, Finland made major changes in energy taxation, which meant turning away from active carbon tax policy. The changes in policy-strategy were so significant that we may almost speak of 'the rise and fall of the CO_2 tax,' although there still existed a heavy CO_2 tax (100 percent) for the production of heating energy. The changes meant a clear increase in electricity taxation. The state's income tax relief partly compensated for this. As a political solution, the result was the first step toward ecological tax reform. This policy solution tells us how tax solutions can be complex and how the ecological steering mechanisms can be many-sided. In addition, it tells us how situational policy contexts (here, the Green group's veto-power in the government) can influence the design of environmental taxation.

After this, development was slow, but the concept of ecological tax reform was there to stay and was further developed during the 2000s. On the one hand, it must be remembered that situational factors such as the economic circumstances of the state and the governmental coalition were influential in the final decisions in autumn 1996. On the other hand, it can be argued that using the idea of ecological tax reform as a tool for solving the fiscal problems of the state is a clear step toward normalization of environmental taxation. Following this experience, the whole idea has been much easier to discuss and develop at the governmental level. However, normalization does not imply an automatic consensus concerning the further development of policy. If the economic situation of the state were better, increases in energy or carbon taxation similar to those made in 1996 would probably be politically very difficult to reach without some progress at the European level.

Role of the EU in Finnish Carbon Tax Policy

The role of the EU has been influential but also contradictory in the phases of Finnish carbon taxation's development. During the entire policy process, the supporters of the carbon tax noted the imminent EU-wide carbon tax. The idea was that Finland would be among the forerunners of the effective use of the carbon tax, and the rest of the EU countries were supposed to follow the 'good' example. This kind of policy development was intended to provide benefits for improving international eco-competitiveness. From the year 1994, negative attitudes toward the carbon tax emerged among many stakeholders. The reasons behind the general frustration lay partly in the contradictions of the EU policy. The EU-wide carbon tax policy gave rise to drawn-out disputes, and simultaneously the EU Commission started to criticize the Finnish tax model. Finally, the political and economic pressures against the carbon tax model were so widespread that the tax system was changed. Only the veto power of the Green party in the Government rescued the basic ideas of ecological tax reform in energy taxation.

During the 2000s, the EU concentrated on the ETS system and carbon and energy taxation have been given little attention. In any case, the strengthening of the EU's climate policy has provided new room for developing environmental taxation at the national level. Together with the economic depression, budget problems and the need for developing new sources of state incomes, this has meant active debate over ecological tax reform in Finland. The European Commission on April 13, 2011 presented its proposal to overhaul the outdated rules on the taxation of energy products in the European Union. The new rules aim to restructure the way energy products are taxed to remove current imbalances and take into account both their CO_2 emissions and energy content.[5] This proposal has not yet significantly influenced the energy tax discussions in Finland.

Regulatory Reform, Policy Instrument Mix and Social Legitimacy

In Finland, the regulatory reform in environmental policy and the development of national climate policy have had the same influence on the level of policy instrument use. Both have emphasized the adoption of new environmental policy instruments and an instrument mix. There have been several policy instruments in use, such as environmental taxes, ETS, voluntary agreements, building regulations, eco labels, subsidies and information to promote renewable electricity production.

When we look at the progression from the end of the 1980s to the year 2010, we can see regulatory reform going forward little by little, and the policy instrument mix becoming a routine or normalized context for the policy instrument choices. The development has been more an evolution than revolution. Finland was one of the forerunners in the world for using and developing carbon taxation and various models of it.

Although carbon taxes have become normal matters and routine, this development has not been an easy path. The use of environmental taxation has been continually a target of policy conflicts, but in the long run ecological tax reform has been going forward. The energy-intensive industry has favored voluntary agreements and achieving some lowering of the environmental tax burden. But the general strengthening of climate policy and the need for balancing the state budget have made room for developing environmental taxation and ecological tax reform at the same time that other policy instruments such as ETS have been put into use. From the standpoint of climate policy, the ongoing challenges are whether the changes in tax systems and other governing principles are too slow to be sufficiently influential, and how the other policy instruments are used in relation to environmental taxation.

In addition, recent developments have meant that the issue of environmental taxation is widening from one of industrial policy toward concerns about social justice. When looking at the Finnish case, it seems that Roger Piehlke Jr. (2010, 221) is right by saying

---

[5] http://ec.europa.eu/taxation_customs/taxation/excise_duties/energy_products/legislation/index_en.htm.

that people might be willing to accept some increases in their energy costs, but this willingness has its limits. In the conditions of welfare societies, the legitimacy of developing environmental taxation further is dependent on general features of the taxation system, for instance the level of progressivity. The conflicts between long-term environmental and climate policy targets and short-term economic and social targets linked with questions of income distribution effects will certainly become more explicit. It seems that in order to be developed further, the environmental taxation system needs to be balanced with the social targets.

One way of going forward is to make more explicit connections between new energy technological innovations and increasing energy and environmental taxation. Piehlke, Jr. (2010, 228–31) calls for 'earmarking' of energy taxation, which could build better public support necessary to sustain investments over decades and longer. Piehlke, Jr. (2010, 228) argues that 'it is important to emphasize that the point of a carbon tax at this level is not to change people's behavior, to restrict economic activity, or to price fossil fuels at a level higher than alternatives. The purpose of a low carbon tax is to raise revenues for investments in innovation.'

In Finland, environmentally oriented tax reform will probably be developed further in the future, but this means that the benefits of environmental taxation should be made more concrete (for example by using earmarking) and that the social issues should be managed in a legitimate way. In welfare societies such as Finland, the features of progressivity of taxation are fundamental elements of the legitimacy of the whole taxation system. This legitimacy and historical balance cannot be changed too radically by environmental tax reform. Keeping political support for environmental tax reform needs continual societal creativity and balancing of different societal goals.

REFERENCES

Andersen, Mikael Skou (1994), *Governance by Green Taxes. Making Pollution Prevention Pay*, Manchester, UK: Manchester University Press.

Andersen, Mikael Skou and Duncan Liefferink (1996), *The New Member States and the Impact on Environmental Policy, Draft Final Report to the Commission (DG-XII)*, Part I, Aarhus, Denmark: Institut for Statskundskap, Aarhus Universitet.

Andersen, Mikael Skou and Duncan Liefferink (1997), 'Introduction: the impact of the pioneers on EU environmental policy', in Mikael Skou Andersen and Duncan Liefferink (eds), *European Environmental Policy: The Pioneers*, Manchester, UK: Manchester University Press, pp. 1–39.

Bragge, Johanna (1997), *Premediation Analysis of the Energy Taxation Dispute in Finland*, Acta A-130, Helsinki, Finland: Helsinki School of Economics and Business Administration.

Collier, Ute (ed.) (1998), *Deregulation in the European Union: Environmental Perspectives*, London, UK: Routledge.

Commission of the European Communities (COM) (1993), *Towards Sustainability: Fifth Environmental Action Programme*, O.J. C 138, 17 May, Luxembourg.

Eckersley, Robin (ed.) (1995), *Markets, the State and the Environment: Towards Integration*, London, UK: Macmillan.

Environmental Protection Agency (EPA) (1991), *Economic Incentives: Options for Environmental Protection*, Report of the US Environmental Protection Agency, Economic Incentives Task Force, Washington, DC, US.

Glasbergen, Pieter (1998), 'The question of environmental governance', in Peter Glasbergen (ed.), *Co-operative Environmental Governance*, Dordrecht: Kluwer Academic Publishers, pp. 1–20.

Golub, Jonathan (1998), 'New instruments for environmental policy in the EU', in Jonathan Golub (ed.), *New Instruments for Environmental Protection in the EU*, London, UK: Routledge, pp. 1–32.

Government Programme (2011), Government Programme of Prime Minister Jyrki Katainen's Government, 22 June, http://www.vn.fi/hallitus/hallitusohjelma/en.jsp.

Honkatukia, Juha and Jaakko Kiander (2003), *Ympäristöperusteinen verotus ja kestävän kehityksen edellytykset—visio vuoteen 2020* [Environmentally-based Taxation and Requirements of Sustainable Development Vision for 2020], Helsinki, Finland: Valtion taloudellinen tutkimuskeskus VATT-Muistioita, http://www.ymparisto.fi/download.asp?contentid=24939.

Joint Environmental Policy-Making (JEP) (1998), *New Interactive Approaches in the EU and Selected Member States. Final Report*, Vol. I, Netherlands: Wageningen Agricultural University, Environmental Sociology.

Jordan, Andrew, Rudiger Wurzel and Anthony Zito (eds) (2003a), *'New' Instruments of Environmental Governance*, London, UK: Frank Cass.

Jordan, Andrew, Rudiger Wurzel and Anthony Zito (2003b), '"New" instruments of environmental governance: patterns and pathways of change', in Andrew Jordan et al. (eds), *'New' Instruments of Environmental Governance*, London, UK: Frank Cass, pp. 1–26.

Jordan, Andrew, Rudiger Wurzel and Anthony Zito (2003c), '"New" environmental policy instruments: an evolution or a revolution in environmental policy', in Andrew Jordan, Rudiger Wurzel and Anthony Zito (eds), *'New' Instruments of Environmental Governance*, London, UK: Frank Cass, pp. 199–224.

KM [Committee Report] (1989), *Ympäristönsuojelun Taloudellinen Ohjaus* [The Economic Steering of Environmental Protection], Ympäristötalouskomitea. Komiteanmietintö [Committee Report] 1989:18, Helsinki, Finland: Valtion Painatuskeskus.

KM [Committee Report] (1993), *Ympäristötaloustoimikunnan Mietintö* [The Report of the Environmental Economy Working Group], Komiteanmietintö [Committee Report] 1993:35, Helsinki, Finland: Painatuskeskus & Ympäristöministeriö.

Kooiman, Jan (ed.) (1993), *Modern Governance: New Government—Society Interactions*, London, UK: UKL Sage.

Leveque, Francois (1996a), 'The European fabric of environmental regulations', in F. Leveque (ed.), *Environmental Policy in Europe*, Cheltenham, UK: Edward Elgar, pp. 9–30.

Leveque, Francois (1996b), 'The regulatory game', in F. Leveque, *Environmental Policy in Europe*, Cheltenham, UK: Edward Elgar, pp. 31–52.

Liefferink, Duncan and Arthur Mol (1998), 'Voluntary agreements as a form of deregulation? The Dutch experience', in Ute Collier (ed.), *Deregulation in the European Union: Environmental Perspectives*, London, UK: Routledge, pp. 181–97.

Lindhjem, Henrik et al. (2009), *The Use of Economic Instruments in Nordic Environmental Policy 2006–2009*, TemaNord 2009:578, Copenhagen, Denmark: TemaNord and Nordic Council of Ministers.

Määttä, Kalle (1997), *Environmental Taxes: From an Economic Idea to a Legal Institution*, Kauppakaari Oy, Helsinki, Finland: Finnish Lawyers' Publishing.

Ministry of the Environment (ME) (1994), *Interim Report of the Environmental Economics Committee. Environment Related Energy Taxation*, Working Group Report 1994:4, Helsinki, Finland: Painatuskeskus Oy.

Ministry of the Environment (ME) (1996), *Finland's Natural Resources and the Environment 1996*, Report no. Environment 1996:10C, Helsinki, Finland.

Piehlke Jr., Roger (2010), *The Climate Fix*, New York, NY, US: Basic Books.

Sairinen, Rauno (2000), *Regulatory Reform of the Finnish Environmental Policy*, Helsinki, Finland: Yhdyskuntasuunnittelun tutkimus- ja koulutuskeskus [Centre for Urban and Regional Studies], Serie A 27, Helsinki University of Technology: Espoo.

Talousneuvosto [The Council of Economy under the Prime Minister Office] (2000), *Ympäristö- Ja Energiaverotuksen Käyttö Suomessa* [The Usage of Environmental and Energy Taxation in Finland], Työryhmäraportti [Report of the Working Group], Valtioneuvoston kanslian julkaisuja [Publications of the Prime Minister's Office] 3/2000, Helsinki, Finland.

Tikkanen, Sarianne (2005), *Ekologisen Ferouudistuksen ituja Hallinnollis-poliittisella Kentällä* [The Beginnings of Ecological Tax Reform in Finnish Politics], Lisensiaatintutkielma, Yhteiskuntapolitiikan laitos, Helsingin yliopisto [Licentiate thesis, Department of Soical Policy, University of Helsinki], Helsinki, Finland.

Tommila, Esa (1989), 'Ympäristöverojen teoria kaunis ja käytäntö vaikea' [The nice theory of environmental taxation—but the difficult reality], *PTT Katsaus* 4/1989, 13–6.

Valtioneuvosto (VN) (1995), Valtioneuvoston periaatepäätös energiapolitiikasta [Government's decision in principle on energy policy], December 21, Helsinki, Finland.

Valtiovarainministeriö (VM) [Ministry of Finance] (1995), Energiaverotyöryhmän muistio III [The memorandum of energy taxation working group III], Valtiovarainministeriön työryhmämuistioita [Memoranda of the working groups of the Ministry of Finance] 1995:19, Helsinki, Finland.

Valtiovarainministeriö (VM) [Ministry of Finance] (2004), Kestävä kehitys ja ekologinen verouudistus [Sustainable development and ecological tax reform], Helsinki, Finland.

Valtiovarainministeriö (VM) [Ministry of Finance] (2010a), Verotuksen kehittämistyöryhmän väliraportti [Interim Report of the Working Group for Developing the Finnish Tax System], Valtiovarainministeriön julkaisuja [Ministry of Finance publications] 35/2010, Helsinki, Finland.

Valtiovarainministeriö (VM) [Ministry of Finance] (2010b), Final Report of the Working Group for Developing the Finnish Tax System, Ministry of Finance publications 51/2010, Helsinki, Finland.

von Weizsäcker, Ernst Ulrich and Jochen Jesinghau (1992), *Ecological Tax Reform: A Policy Proposal for Sustainable Development*, London, UK, and Atlantic Highlands, NJ, US: Zed Books, http://esl.jrc.it/dc/etr/ecological_tax_reform.htm.

24 Bounded rationality in an imperfect world of regulations: what if individuals are not optimizing?

Helle Ørsted Nielsen

INTRODUCTION

Environmental economists have increasingly persuaded policymakers that market-based instruments are preferable to the more traditional command-and-control approach to environmental regulation (OECD 2001; Tietenberg 1990; Speck et al. 2006). Taxes appear to remain the first instrument of choice among market-based policy instruments, at least as calculated by the number of schemes (OECD 2010). According to economic theory, environmental taxes have several benefits: firstly, they effectively regulate the behavior of producers and consumers through economic incentives to either consume more environmentally sustainable products, switch to more sustainable production methods, reduce waste or consume less natural resources. Secondly, environmental taxes produce such changes in a more cost-effective manner than other types of policy instruments, as the taxes ensure that those economic actors who face the lowest abatement costs will undertake a larger share of abatement than those with higher abatement costs (Sprenger 2000; Andersen 2000a; Perman et al. 1999). Thirdly, economic theory also holds that environmental taxes are a welfare-efficient way toward environmental improvements, as the price mechanism ensures that the levels of environmental damage and environmental abatement costs reflect the preferences of a given community (Sprenger 2000; OECD 2001; Kolstad 1999). In fact, the tax serves to set a price on the externality costs of pollution and thus compensates for market failure, ensuring that the new market equilibrium represents a higher level of social welfare than the market that does not incorporate preferences for a cleaner environment. These effects are both short-run and long-run. Environmental taxes provide continuous incentives for businesses to reduce their pollution abatement costs; in order to avoid tax payments they will change production in a more sustainable direction. At the macro level the economy will restructure as less environmentally damaging industries gain competitive advantages (Speck et al. 2006; OECD 2001).

Environmental economists draw their foundation from neoclassical economics. The theoretical expectations outlined above rest on a set of behavioral assumptions embodied in the proverbial model of homo oeconomicus. In the short version the model assumes that economic actors are profit maximizers, or in the case of consumers, utility maximizers, and that their choices are fully rational. These assumptions are hotly contested both by behavioral economists and cultural theorists, who argue that this is a highly unrealistic depiction of human beings and their organizations (see for instance Conlisk 1996; Jones 2001; Monroe 1991; Green and Shapiro 1994; Simon 1997a). But the academic debate has turned mostly on the epistemological question of whether assumptions must be accurate for a model to have scientific merit (Friedman 1953; Moe 1979; Simon 1997a, 1978; Conlisk 1996; van den Bergh et al. 2000). Neoclassical economists argue that a theory should be judged by its parsimony and ability to generate testable hypotheses rather than by how well it matches real-world behavior (Friedman 1953 delivered the classic argument). Critics argue that the assumptions cannot be separated from the theory; without the assumption of full rationality, the theory generates no testable predictions (Moe 1979 in Nielsen 2009). Interesting as this discussion is—and it has occupied scholars for decades—it should be beyond dispute that when the neoclassic economic models provide prescriptions for environmental policy, model assumptions do matter. If the behavioral assumptions do not hold, the claimed benefits of economic instruments may not materialize; environmental taxes may be less effective than modeled in theoretically-based policy analyses.

This contribution applies the theoretical perspective of the behavioral tradition, which has demonstrated shortcomings in the neoclassical economic model when applied to real-world behavior. A central theme in behavioral economics is that decision-makers, be they individuals or organizations, tend toward boundedly rational behavior due to cognitive limitations (Simon 1997d, 291–4). Bounded rationality has implications for the use of economic instruments in environmental policy, suggesting that human agents respond less efficiently to economic incentives than assumed in environmental economics; it does not by any means rule out their use but it offers suggestions as to how such instruments could be designed or combined with other types of policy instruments for greater effectiveness. The objective of the present contribution thus is to review the competing behavioral models and discuss the implications for the use and design of environmental taxes if individuals are boundedly rational rather than fully rational.

BEHAVIORAL ASSUMPTIONS OF ENVIRONMENTAL ECONOMICS

The driver in environmental economic models is the profit- or utility-maximizing actor, who is constantly tuned in to price changes. Thus, when a tax is levied on natural resources, energy or emissions producers, consumers will reduce their activities in response to the cost increase. Likewise, charges on public utilities such as water or waste will reduce demand for these services and induce users to be more resource-conscious. This very simple dynamic flows from a simple conceptualization of agents—be they individuals, households or business organizations—as economic. The model involves three aspects: motivation, the structure of preferences and the process of choice.

It has been said that 'the first principle of Economics is that every agent is actuated only by self-interest' (Edgeworth 1881 quoted in Sen 1977, 317). Leaving aside for now the discussion as to whether agents may also be motivated by forms of social interest, the self-interest assumption does not in itself offer much information. However, economic modeling of businesses assumes that business organizations pursue the singular goal of profit (see any microeconomics textbook). In neoclassical models of the consumer, self-interest is conventionally translated into more rather than less of preferred material goods, and within a given budget the consumer will pursue the bundle of goods that gives him the highest total utility. An environmental tax on any good will affect the composition of goods within the bundle as consumption of the taxed good will decrease.

Neoclassical economics further assumes that all agents are equipped with an underlying utility function that represents a consistent ordering of preferences. A weak order of preferences as theorized by Arrow (Sen 1986) involves two consistency requirements. The ordering is complete, which implies that agents are able to make pair-wise comparisons among alternatives and consistently rank them regardless of how they are presented; and the ordering is transitive, which means that the ranking among several alternatives must be consistent, so that if A is preferred to B and B to C, then A would also be preferred to C. This ensures that agents will always make the choice that maximizes utility, given available alternatives. It also ensures predictability of the model because preferences are not shaped in the situation of choice, but are fixed (Whitehead 1991). Faced with the same alternatives, agents will consistently make the same choice.

These aspects concern the 'why' of any given choice. But choice also involves a 'how.' Economic theory assumes that agents are capable of maximizing profit or utility in a manner that fully reflects their preferences in any given situation. They are fully rational decision-makers. In the words of Nobel Laureate Amartya Sen, rational behavior can be described as '*reasoned* pursuit of self-interest' (1987, 69).

While not typically spelled out in economic textbooks, the implicit model of decision-making mirrors the classic consumer choice, which involves comparing a number of alternatives across a range of attributes, weighing the importance of each attribute and synthesizing this into one measure that denotes optimal utility (Jones 2001; Payne, Bettman and Johnson 1993; McFadden 1999). To illustrate: a person choosing among travel by car, bus or train may evaluate these alternatives by his values on attributes such as convenience, time and price; weigh the importance of each attribute; and then calculate the optimal choice. A road tax or a gasoline tax would affect the relative prices of the transport alternatives and thus might change the decision. The same applies to more complex choices, say among business strategies or production decisions. The model thus assumes virtually unlimited computational skills. Additionally, this model of choice assumes that agents can make smooth trade-offs between different alternatives and attributes; in other words the consumer knows the value of one good relative to other goods and is able to determine the exact combination of alternatives that will yield optimal profit or utility under given prices (Douma and Schreuder 1998; Bettman, Luce and Payne 1998; Jones 2001). To continue the transport example, the commuter would know exactly how much more he is willing to pay for gas in order to save commuting time.

In order to choose rationally, the actor also must have perfect information about each alternative, be it a good for purchase or a course of action. Given the impossibility of this condition, economists and rational choice scholars tend to interpret the information requirement somewhat leniently; rational decision-making involves making full use of the information available (Opp 1999, 175; Jones 1999). But the assumption of full information also involves constant updating of decisions as new information becomes available (Jones 2001, 94). This implies that businesses and consumers would notice a price change when an environmental tax is introduced and incorporate the new prices into their choices and actions. Such decision-making is fully adaptive to the circumstances (Jones 2001).

These behavioral assumptions are critical components of the neoclassical economics framework. Firstly, if motivation is not materialistic or even self-interested, prices may become a less powerful regulatory tool. Secondly, stable, consistent and exogenous preferences ensure the predictive power of economic modeling, which is important for ex ante policy assessments (van den Bergh et al. 2000). If preferences are not exogenous or invariant, the effect of environmental taxes is harder to predict. Finally, the behavioral assumptions establish the link between choice and welfare: if agents are capable of adjusting to marginal price changes and if choice reflects underlying preferences then the resulting market equilibrium expresses an optimal allocation of resources in an economy. Conversely, if the assumptions do not hold, this link is broken and the normative claim that price-based mechanisms lead to a welfare-efficient allocation of resources is undermined (Whitehead 1991; van den Bergh et al 2000).

It follows that the theoretical foundation for environmental taxes turns on the soundness of this description of individuals or organizations as fully rational. As indicated, not everyone buys this description. A significant theoretical alternative maintains that bounded rationality is a more appropriate model of behavior than is full rationality.

BEHAVIORAL MODEL EMBODIED IN BOUNDED RATIONALITY THEORY

The bounded rationality approach emanates from organizational studies but has developed its key theoretical concepts from cognitive psychology, and its focus is on individual and organizational decision processes (key works are Simon 1947; March and Simon 1958; Cyert and March 1963; Kahneman, Slovic and Tversky 1982; for overviews see Jones 2001; Nielsen 2009; Conlisk 1996). What has been observed in the laboratories of cognitive psychologists and studies of public and business organizations differs significantly from the fully rational model of choice. But bounded rationality scholars and scholars in related behavioral traditions also question the neoclassical conceptualization that all action stems from self-interested pursuit of profit or utility. They argue that choice could just as well be motivated in altruistic concern or other forms of social interest, including concern for the environment (Simon 1993 and 1997, 264; Ostrom 1998; Monroe 1991).

Self-interest and Social Motivation

Behavioral research has demonstrated social or altruistic behavior that cannot be construed as purely self-interested or materialistic. Classic experimental game studies such as 'divide the dollar' often find that the appointed leader shares a bigger part of the dollar with other participants than would be necessary or predicted from a strictly rational calculation. The leader acts out of fairness or a desire to cooperate (for a review of such games, see Camerer and Thaler 1995; Mullainathan and Thaler 2000). Similar tendencies to cooperate are found in political studies of coalition formation, which also lead to bigger coalitions than strictly necessary and therefore to a greater division of political influence (Jones 1999; Green and Shapiro 1994).

Nobel Laureate Amartya Sen, in an analytic critique of neoclassical economics, argues that the self-interest assumption is 'wholly arbitrary' and unduly ignores the social context in which human behavior unfolds. Lest humans be 'social morons,' they must take into account the welfare of others or at least follow social norms. He introduces a distinction between sympathy, which implies behavior that incorporates the welfare of others into the utility function of the agent, and commitment, which implies that the agent chooses a course of action out of a sense of duty or moral consideration regardless of how it affects his personal welfare (1977, 326–29). Thus, to use an evocative example, rescuers who at their own peril helped get Jewish refugees to safety during World War II would be acting out of commitment rather than social welfare (unless they were paid large sums of money, of course) (Monroe 1991). Choosing to spend several hours on public transit instead of driving one's car in order to reduce one's CO_2 emissions might also be interpreted as an act of commitment.

The benefits of environmental taxation are clearest with self-interested utility maximizers. The price change affects utility calculations and results in a welfare-efficient market equilibrium, incorporating the price of externalities. Thus, an environmental tax on gasoline works because an individual's relative utility from driving is diminished when gasoline prices increase. An externality tax would appear less strong in the face of social preferences motivated by sympathy. In that case the utility calculation is driven by the environmental benefits to oneself and others of driving less, but the utility of others does not depend on the cost function of the decision-maker. Hence, the effect of the price incentive would be lesser. In the case of behavior driven by commitment, environmental taxes might even be futile because such behavior is unrelated to prices but follows from moral inclinations.

These considerations do not in any way rule out self-interest as a source of action or even assign primary status to socially motivated behavior. Instead the behavioral tradition assumes that choice can be driven by multiple sources of motivation, and treats the issue of motivation as an empirical question to be determined in the specific context (Simon 1997a).

Bounded rationality theory furthermore questions the neoclassical notion of a fixed and underlying utility function's ensuring consistency of choice. A whole field within bounded rationality has been devoted to uncovering the 'heuristics and biases' in human decision-making that defy the notion of consistent choice (Kahneman, Slovic and Tversky 1982). Such biases include framing effects that indicate that choice is molded by the specific presentation of alternatives. For instance, in a study of environmental valuation, Payne et al. (2000) found that the order of presentation of different alternatives affected the willingness to pay for different environmental goods. Another very consistent framing effect is the tendency of humans to value an option higher when it represents a loss than when it represents a gain, even when the two options are of equal monetary value (see for instance Tversky and Kahneman 1974; Kahneman 2002; McFadden 1999; Shafir and LeBoeuf 2002); this has been termed an endowment effect and implies that people value a good more highly once they have it and might lose it than they do before they actually have it (Kahneman, Knetsch and Thaler 1991, 194n). One consequence is that it leads to a bias in favor of the status quo, which may delay or hinder the adoption of new technologies and by extension hamper the realization of dynamic efficiencies of environmental taxation (Venkatachalam 2008). Framing effects are found so frequently in studies that behavioral economists have concluded that they are not simply arbitrary errors or artifacts of the research setting but reflect cognitive properties. The outcome is that choice cannot be interpreted as expression of a set of fixed and consistent preferences. Rather, in the bounded rationality approach, preferences are seen as molded by the social and institutional context in which choice is made and are therefore also prone to change.

Cognitive Constraints on Decision-making

Above all, the bounded rationality school offers insight into how decision processes unfold and how this might condition the response to economic incentives. Cognitive studies have demonstrated physiological constraints on the speed with which humans can perceive and compute information; information processing is slow compared to the amount of stimuli directed at decision-makers at any given moment or in any situation (Simon 1990, 7). The short-term memory in particular is a limiting factor in decision processes, as humans can attend to just a few pieces of information at a time (Simon 1985). The short-term memory thus acts as a bottleneck for the amount of information stimuli an organism can attend to. Furthermore, the computational capacity, that is, the ability to handle complex information in the algorithmic manner implicit in the neoclassic model, is also limited (Conlisk 1996; Simon 1990). In contrast to the neoclassical assumption this means that agents may not comprehend or use all information available to them. In the bounded rationality approach, attention is the scarce resource. If key information is ignored, the decision-maker may not choose the strategy that would be optimal had he used this information. Moreover, information updating is incomplete and disjointed and it is therefore far from given that agents even notice price changes that follow from introduction of an environmental tax. Also in contrast to the neoclassical model, humans have difficulties making trade-offs, particularly when objectives conflict or are incommensurate (Jones 2001; Simon 1997b). When trade-offs are difficult, choices may be deferred or agents may aim for a satisfactory rather than an optimal outcome, a process that will be discussed in greater detail below. Altogether these features suggest that adaptation to environmental taxes would be much less smooth than predicted by economic models.

But boundedly rational organisms also possess cognitive features that enable decision-making. Individuals and organizations draw on a number of learned strategies, including information cues heuristics, routines and standard operating procedures that serve to simplify information processing and choice (Jones 2001).

In the face of information overload, boundedly rational actors are cued in to important information through frames, that is, the way they perceive a given task or choice. For instance, a decision may be viewed primarily through a production lens or through sales lenses or even through environmental management lenses. Consequently, information related to production or sales or pollution would be selected while information related to other types of frames are excluded from consideration. Frames are often formed in context, such as the subdivision of a business, which may have a local focus rather than a focus on the overall business strategy or even profit objective (March 1994). While frames compensate for information overload, they also lead to inattention to some kinds of information. For instance, a study of Danish farmers found that many were more likely to frame decisions about fertilizer in terms of getting the best crop possible rather than in terms of maximizing monetary earnings from the crop. As a consequence they paid relatively little attention to the economics of fertilizer decisions but focused instead on cultivation techniques (Nielsen 2009).

Routines and standard operating procedures also represent information-efficient behavioral strategies. They provide information and ready-made solutions to tasks based on past experience. But routines also lock behavior into certain patterns where new information and opportunities may be ignored. Thus, frames and routines provide information but also ensure that some information goes unnoticed; the effect of a tax incentive would thus depend on the extent to which price information was incorporated into frames and routines.

Likewise, decision-makers use social cues to zoom in on what is important and what isn't. Information passed on through social leaders may be much more influential than information not picked up by those who are, literally, agenda-setters. Similarly, an emphasis on environmentally conscious behavior may be augmented if it gains popularity with trendsetters, or it could be ignored if the social cues suggest that driving an SUV is high-status. Jones (2001, 8) refers to information cascades and bandwagon effects; both entail behavior that is different from what it would have been if each decision-maker had made his choice from an individual consideration of facts against preferences. Sociological institutionalists say that decision-makers are guided by what is appropriate by social norms rather than by a rational calculation of utility that uses consequentialist logic (March and Olsen 1989; Hall and Taylor 1996). With regards to environmental taxes, the effect of social cues may be that adjustment to prices may be filtered through social norms; reactions might then either be larger or smaller than model predictions based on rational utility calculation economics (see also Fehr and Tyran 2005 for a discussion of the effects of institutions on aggregate behavior).

In lieu of comprehensive calculations, humans may *satisfice*, a term invented by Herbert Simon in *Administrative Behavior* (1947). Used in a general sense it denotes a choice in which the decision-maker settles for a satisfactory outcome rather than optimal yield. More specifically, satisficing describes a type of decision process that Simon observed in his studies of public administrative organizations. It is a process in which, for each of the sub-goals pursued as part of a given decision, decision-makers predefine a target, referred to as an aspiration level (Bendor 2003; March 1994). Different courses of action are then evaluated until an alternative that meets all the pre-specified goals has been found. As the decision process stops once a satificing solution has been identified, it is quite likely that alternatives that would yield even higher utility go unexplored. Satisficing helps decision-makers who cannot make trade-offs among multiple and perhaps conflicting objectives, which arise in the absense of a complete and consistent utility function (Jones 2001).

One implication of satisficing is that businesses contrary to the neoclassical model do not use resources efficiently; they operate 'inside the boundary of efficiency' or with slack (Leibenstein 1966 refers to x-efficiency; Cyert and March 1963; March 1994). As long as the organizational performance of a given course of action fulfills the aspiration level, the organization will stick with it, failing to realize the efficiency gains from optimal use of resources. Porter and van der Linde (1995, 98–99) likewise reject the neoclassical proposition that there are no sidewalk dollars to be picked up, because if there were, profit-optimizing companies would have already done so. Instead it takes some external stimulus such as impending failure, competitive pressure or an economic downturn (Leibenstein 1966) or maybe environmental regulations (Porter and van der Linde 1995) to prompt a stronger focus on cost minimizing and slack reduction.

The bounded rationality approach does not claim that decision-makers do not intend to act rationally, nor does it claim that they never do; it also does not claim that human decision-makers are irrational. But it claims that human rationality is bounded, meaning that behavior 'is shaped by the interaction between the environment and the computational capabilities of the actor who is trying to adapt to that environment' (Simon

1997a, 325). Sometimes this leads to decisions that approximate fully rational decisions as modeled in economics; often, the decision differs from this ideal. Whereas in the neoclassical framework, the agent is capable of utility-maximizing in any decision environment, the bounded rationality framework holds that decision-makers perform better by rational standards in some environments than in others (Jones 2001; Simon 1997a). The cognitive constraints on information processing affect behavior most when decisions are made under time pressure, when information is abundant, complex and frequently changing, and when decision-makers are uncertain about the outcome of their decisions, conditions that sum up to a high degree of complexity (Simon 1978, 353). On the other hand, humans and organizations learn over time, and experience thus may cushion the effect of complex circumstances (Simon 1997c, North 1990).

Moreover, deviation from fully rational decisions is more likely when using an intuitive decision mode, relying on routines and rules of thumb, as opposed to a synoptic, rational, decision mode (Simon 1990; Jones 2001; Payne et al. 1993; Thaler and Sunstein 2008 distinguish between automatic and reflective thinking). The rational mode is more likely when decision-makers are highly motivated to pay attention to a given decision or problem (North 1993; Denzau and North 2000). A high degree of motivation may stem either from the fact that the decision at hand is important for the self-assessment of the decision-maker or from confidence that he can affect the outcome (Denzau and North 2000). Marcus and MacKuen (1993) found that anxiety will also prompt decision-makers to switch into a more attentive decision style. This underpins the findings that businesses need a jolt to reduce slack and operate closer to the profit frontier.

Even so, it is noteworthy that many anomalies or systematic errors have been uncovered in the field of behavioral finance, which is a field of highly trained and highly motivated economic experts (Thaler and Sunstein 2008).

Organizations as Coalitions of Cognitively Limited Agents

While much of the bounded rationality approach is phrased in cognitive and therefore individualistic terminology, its origin is with organizational studies, notably Herbert Simon's *Administrative Behavior* (1947). Organizations are as challenged by complexity as individuals are. Likewise, the organizational response to complexity is to simplify decisions and decision-making structures. This may be in the form of standard operating procedures or in the subdivision of the organization into smaller units (Cyert and March 1963). But subdividing turns the organization into a coalition of participants each with his or her own focus and objectives (ibid.). The behavioral approach disputes the assumption of the neoclassical theory that all units of a firm pursue one single goal, namely, profit.

Firstly, it is questioned whether participants in the organization, employees at lower levels, focus on an overall goal such as profit (Cyert and March 1963; Simon 1997d). Studies of professionals find that they are often guided by professional values and standards rather than overall organizational goals (see for instance Goodrick and Salancik 1996; Andersen et al. 2006).

Secondly, overall objectives such as profit must be divided into operational objectives for each unit (Cyert and March 1963). If each division focuses on achieving its own objectives it may lose sight of the overall objective of the organization, leading to a lack of coordination or even conflicts among sub-units when vigorous pursuit of one objective may undermine the achievement of other objectives. Organizational structure defines the boundaries of attention for each sub-unit. The discussion as to whether effective environmental management in an organization is best furthered by establishing a separate environmental management unit or by integrating this function into other departments reflects the notion that structure and attention are integrated. An evaluation of the Danish waste taxation scheme serves to illustrate this point. The tax scheme primarily affected the behavior of the waste-intensive companies, such as construction companies. In other companies the organizational structure turned out to be a barrier to the effect of the tax precisely because of differential attention. Waste bills were paid by accounting personnel in a routine manner while those who were responsible for the handling of waste were not exposed to the incentive and therefore did not make any changes (Andersen 2000b, 249).

Thus, if an environmental tax is not consequential, either because it is a low tax rate or because it is levied on an unimportant production input, chances are that the predicted marginal adjustment will not occur.

Implications for Use of Environmental Taxes

If, as behavioral economics suggest, agents are boundedly rational rather than fully rational, there are implications both for environmental economic theory and for the policy recommendations that flow from it.

First and foremost, if agents do not adjust to marginal prices, price-based policies such as environmental taxes may be less effective than is modeled by standard equilibrium models; certainly the effect of such policies could be predicted with much less certainty and precision (van den Bergh et al. 2000). The departure from environmental theory relates to motivation as well as to decision processes.

Taxes will not work as effectively if prices are not the main driver in business and household decisions, that is, when other types of motivation prevail or significantly affect behavior. For instance, a study of Danish farmers found that professional pride in a nice-looking crop would cause farmers to apply more fertilizers than would be economically optimal (Nielsen 2009). This matches the findings from other studies of professionals, which have shown that professional norms have a stronger impact on behavior than do economic incentives (Goodrick and Salancik 1996; Andersen et al. 2006). Likewise one may surmise that if travelers are preoccupied with time and convenience, it may take more than a gasoline tax to see a significant switch to public transportation. The effect of the tax, in other words, depends on how decision-makers handle potentially conflicting objectives. Furthermore, some would be motivated more strongly to reduce environmental impact out of concern for the environment than because of environmental taxes. It has been argued that in such cases economic incentives may crowd out an otherwise strong inclination toward environmentally benign behavior (Frey and Oberholzer-Gee 1997). In such cases the economic incentive becomes inefficient because the same behavior conceivably could have been achieved for free or at least without the tax.

But even when decision-makers are primarily profit- or utility-motivated, decision processes may derail a smooth adjustment to price changes. For taxes to work, decision-makers must pay attention to the tax as expressed in prices. This is in no way a given, as has been outlined above. For instance, gasoline prices may go up, but once the tank has been filled drivers may continue along familiar paths, driving the same trips as always or speeding even if a different driving pattern might conserve gas. And, where energy taxes are made part of routine payments for utilities, households or businesses may continue in routine ways without paying attention to the tax. As indicated by the example of the Danish waste tax above, there may not be an overlap between those who pay and those who handle the waste, whose behavior is the target of the extra bill, and therefore the tax may not register at the appropriate place. The point is that if adaptation to the price signal requires changes in individual or organizational routines, competition for attention will affect the response and may delay or impede such adaptation.

Still, claiming that decision-makers are boundedly rational does not lead to the conclusion that environmental taxes cannot work. But it follows that greater consideration should be given to where and how incentive-based policies will be effective. Furthermore, the behavioral framework offers suggestions for how the design of environmental taxes may be improved or how they may be combined with other instruments to enhance their effect. Finally, it points to contexts where other types of instruments might be more effective.

REGULATING BEHAVIOR IN A WORLD OF BOUNDED RATIONALITY

Bounded rationality theory suggests that incentive-based policies, in order to regulate behavior, should be designed with three objectives in mind: they must motivate, they must draw attention and they must make for simple decision-making.

Motivate

One lesson from the bounded rationality school is that an environmental tax is more likely to make an impact when the taxed activity or resource is economically important. In that case the agent is strongly motivated to keep an eye on prices, breaking the barrier of attention deficits. Hence, a review of waste tax schemes in the Nordic countries concluded that the tax schemes were primarily effective with waste-intensive companies or with heavy waste fractions such as construction waste, while other companies were less likely to heed the taxes at least until tax rates were increased significantly (Speck et al. 2006 citing Andersen 2000b; Plancenter 2005; Hiltunen 2004).

In another example, pesticide taxation in Denmark has been much less effective than predicted by ex ante modeling that was based on profit maximizing; in fact current calculations suggest the tax on insecticides should be increased by about 400 percent (Miljøministeriet et al. 2007, 4). The lack of effect is due in part to changing prices on crops, which have altered the economic optima. But recent studies also suggest that some farmers at least downplay economic considerations and aim instead for a high yield, which offers professional satisfaction because generally the costs of pesticides do not make or break budgets (Nielsen 2009; Pedersen et al. forthcoming).

One way to overcome both motivational and attentional barriers to achieve a target effect would be to set tax rates much higher than a marginal economic calculation would suggest. A high tax rate would more likely gain attention from decision-makers as it would provide the cognitive jolt necessary to reduce slack; moreover, a larger price increase may reduce conflicts among different objectives as the economic objectives gain more weight. The drawback to this approach is that if the tax rate is set much higher than what would be necessary if agents were economic maximizers, incentive-based policies may lose in cost-effectiveness comparisons. In a different context, Baumol and Oates (1988) argue that tax rates required to control pollution levels under emergency conditions may be so high that they would offset static efficiency, hence taxes may not always come out more efficient in comparisons with rule-based regulation.

Another approach would be to reserve incentive-based policies for economic sectors or activities where the taxed input or activity truly matters economically; for example, energy taxes could be applied to energy-intensive sectors of the economy. In such cases it is quite likely that the tax would overcome attention deficits. In effect, the opposite has often been the case, as such industries have been able to negotiate exemptions based on the hardship and competitive disadvantages that would beset the affected companies (Speck et al. 2006; Nielsen 2009). As for households, it would appear that utilities would be appropriate for taxing, although the effect of the taxes might be more pronounced on households with a tighter budget constraint, which raises the issue of equity but also effect. Presumably high-income households would have a higher consumption of, say, electricity, but they might be less motivated to change consumption patterns if and when they can afford not to notice the price changes.

Some scholars suggest that environmental taxes and other incentive-based policies may be more effective when directed at producers rather than consumers, because businesses resemble the model of profit maximization more than consumers resemble the model of utility maximization (van den Bergh et al. 2000). All things being equal, businesses are more likely to focus attention on economic incentives.

Catch their Attention

But if lack of attention to prices is the main factor limiting adaption to the tax, it is possible that also consumers can be made to respond to incentives. Instant and continuous feedback on the monetary or consumption effects of behavior may help direct attention toward these effects and break routine behavior. To illustrate, in Denmark a green tax is levied on energy and electricity consumption, but for most households these utilities are paid in the form of a constant monthly rate, except once a year when the annual consumption is tallied and the account settled either by a return or an extra payment. While the effect of this tax has not been evaluated in a systematic and reliable manner, from a bounded rationality perspective it is likely that such a system will not achieve its potential effects because the economic incentive does not feature prominently in everyday decision-making. The green tax incentive may lose out to more prominent information and hard-to-break habits. If utilities were paid frequently and reflected current and fluctuating consumption, the price incentive would be more closely tied to actual behavior and thus might better serve to overcome attention barriers. In fact, new research indicates the power of immediate feedback mechanisms. In one study, 20 families were equipped with a screen, placed in a central location of their homes, that gave ongoing information about electricity consumption, split into different uses (Thøgersen and Grønbæk 2010).

This device reduced the families' electricity consumption by 8 percent, and the authors estimate the potential savings of such immediate feedback at about 15 percent, as some of the larger appliances including dryers were not included due to technical difficulties. The mechanism makes visible the effect of behavior, and the information appeals both to those motivated by cost savings and to those wanting to conserve resources for environmental reasons. Likewise, a California utility provided users with a device that flashed red when energy consumption was high, leading to energy savings of up to 40 percent (Thompson 2007 in Thaler and Sunstein 2008). The aforementioned study of decision processes among Danish farmers also suggests the potential in using such feedback devices as a reinforcement of economic incentives (Nielsen 2009). Comparing different types of decisions, it showed that farmers were more likely to apply a fully rational decision mode when immediate and quantitative feedback was available; by contrast, decision domains characterized by uncertainty and lack of feedback information tended to beget more intuitive decisions and habit-prone behavior.

Richard Thaler and Cass Sunstein, in a much-acclaimed book, refer to feedback and similar mechanisms as 'nudges,' small prods that help people overcome cognitive limitations to act more in line with their preferences (Thaler and Sunstein 2008). They point to the US fuel economy sticker as such a nudge, one that may help people select fuel efficient automobiles; they also suggest that the sticker would work even more effectively if it included information about annual or even five-year cost savings—in other words, a monetary value (ibid., 193). Again, in the world of neoclassical economists the potential of cost savings should do the trick, but behavioral scholars suggest that a nudge that serves to highlight relevant information may be necessary to unleash the full potential of the economic incentive.

Likewise, a labeling scheme may enhance the effect of an environmental tax (OECD 2007, 159). For instance, a labeling scheme on appliances easily identifies the more energy-efficient appliances and thus simplifies for the consumer the calculation of the more economically beneficial decisions. Moreover, the labeling scheme generally increases awareness of environmental taxes and thus improves price elasticity on energy, which improves effectiveness and efficiency of the environmental tax and perhaps allows for a smaller incentive altogether (OECD 2007, 159). On the other hand, evaluations of Nordic energy taxes indicated that tax incentives themselves may work as much by drawing attention to energy consumption as through their price signal. For instance, a Norwegian study found that energy taxes drew industry's attention to the possible economic gains of investing in pollution abatement technology, regardless of the fact that these gains also existed before the introduction of taxes (ECON 2004).

Another way to enhance the effect of tax schemes is by earmarking the tax revenue and returning it to the taxed industries as investment support for environmental improvements. Such schemes have contributed a significant add-on effect to Danish carbon and energy taxes (Enevoldsen 2005, 174). Earmarking thus serves to increase the dynamic efficiency of a tax scheme, as the subsidies serve to increase the motivation of businesses and possibly also simplify decisions. Instead of earmarking, a similar effect might be achieved through tax expenditures, that is, a tax credit on investments in pollution abatement. Endowment effects suggest that the effect of an environmental tax, which represents an economic loss, would be stronger than the effect of a tax credit, which represents a gain. But when the two are combined that would be less important.

Make it Simple

Finally, if the barrier to a full response to an environmental tax lies with the computational capabilities, policymakers might combine economic incentives with decision-support tools. Labeling schemes, as mentioned above, provide simple mechanisms for identifying economically optimal solutions. Agricultural policy in Denmark uses more elaborate but still simple computer programs that help farmers calculate optimal responses to different decision parameters.

Generally, behavioral research indicates the potential for aids that help structure decisions. Thaler and Sunstein (2008) point to the effectiveness of designing policy instruments so that the desired behavior is the default option. The point is to help shape routines so that they are in line with the objectives of a policy. For instance, waste taxes may be reinforced through different size waste bins, which would make both visible and simple the effect of waste reductions. In contrast, some cities collect regular refuse but require citizens to take their recycling to collection sites. This represents a default option that would undermine the objectives of most municipal waste policies.

Finally, it is possible to reinforce the effect of an environmental tax by deliberately working to influence norms, be they professional or social. Professional norms may be shaped through education and professional associations and may help point attention to environmentally benign behaviors or resource awareness as standards of the profession. By establishing such behavior as professional routines, one barrier to the effectiveness of environmental taxes would be lowered. Thaler and Sunstein cite experimental studies that show the agenda-setting power of defining tax compliance as normal behavior (2008, 66).

If Taxes will not Work

However, if taxes cannot motivate or catch the attention of boundedly rational agents, other market-based mechanisms may. Hence emissions trading schemes and similar tradable quotas make for quite visible price signals and establish regular market decisions. The trading system differs from environmental taxation, where the tax is an integral part of the price, at least where the price is levied on production resources such as energy. With a trading scheme the economic incentive is quite visible. Moreover, it makes clear the trade-off between higher production and emissions on the one hand and costs on the other. Hence a tradable quota may serve to overcome both motivation and attention deficits more effectively or with greater precision than a tax. Thus, if it is important to achieve a certain policy objective, such as an emission ceiling, the quota may work better. Likewise if agents are not strongly motivated by economics, the tradable quota provides an inescapable incentive.

Danish fertilizer regulation uses a non-tradable nitrogen quota which is based on a set of economically optimal nitrogen norms.[1] As such the quota has forced farmers to reduce fertilizer levels, thus overcoming motivational barriers. Before the regulation farmers would apply fertilizers in amounts considerably above economic optima. But

---

[1] The current regulations have reduced the norms so that they are now *below* economically optimals levels.

the fertilizer norms also implicitly take into account the bounded rationality of decision-makers, as they make it simple to identify economically optimal fertilizer levels. This policy instrument has been effective, if not loved by farmers (Nielsen 2009).

The quota is closer in nature to command-and-control regulation and shows that there may still be a place for such policies as well. Baumol and Oates (1988, 200) suggest that rule-based regulation may be relevant if 'unforeseeable variability' in conditions would require a high tax rate in order to ensure that pollution levels do not exceed certain levels.

CONCLUSION

Replacing neoclassical assumptions of behavior with a model of boundedly rational actors has implications for policy recommendations regarding the use of tax incentives to shape behavior. Boundedly rational actors may be motivated by economic incentives but also by other types of motivation; they do not appear to have fixes and stable preferences that ensure predictable responses to taxes, and they may pay attention to price incentives, but not always, and if they do, they may go on with their usual routines without adapting to the incentive. All of this suggests some modifications to the use of environmental tax policies.

It suggests, first of all, that policymakers should know the motivation structures of target populations. In some cases this means that the tax incentive should be designed in accordance with a set of motivations broader than pure economic incentives. This may be done by combining the tax with other types of policy instruments. In some cases the tax incentives may have to be set at a high level to gain attention. In other cases, the tax-based policy might not be the best choice altogether.

Furthermore, the design of tax incentives would benefit from knowledge of the decision processes and professional decision rules applied by the actors in different sectors. It is possible to adapt incentive structures to different types of decision modes or to design the tax in line with the need for simplifying decisions, for instance by providing labeling schemes or targeted tax expenditures for environmentally friendly production schemes. And in the longer term it may even be possible to affect professional decision rules so that they automatically consider environmental policy objectives.

However, so far the application of insights from bounded rationality to policy decisions has been scant; one obvious reason for this is the fact that the more complex models of decision-making are not well suited to precise predictions about the outcomes of different policy choices (for instance, they cannot calculate ex ante the precise effect of environmental taxes). The research agenda linking bounded rationality and environmental policy analysis therefore requires more research into the systematic features of decision-making at the level of individuals, but just as importantly of the interaction among individuals and organizations in complex systems. One promising venue for such research would be the coupling of research on decision-making with agent-based modeling. Agent-based models are computational models for simulating the behavior and interactions of any number of decision-makers in a dynamic system. Interaction is modeled through a set of empirically based rules (Farmer and Foley 2009). The simulation incorporates the specific situation of each decision-maker, his perception of the problem and the decision context, and the rules governing his decisions; the latter may include different types of motivation (Farmer and Foley 2009, 685). Furthermore, the model can take in both learning effects and nonlinear behavior (ibid.). Based on such information, the model simulates patterns of behavior and outcomes over time, for instance the consequences of different environmental tax designs. Agent-based models are therefore better suited than are general equilibrium models for capturing behavior patterns of complex systems. At the same time, research in bounded rationality and behavioral economics has already yielded many insights that could inform the modeling with regard to the behavioral rules. Bounded rationality research therefore could ensure realistic modeling while the agent-based modeling approach enhances the predictive value of behavioral modeling, as it can handle the complex and dynamic character of the systems into which an environmental tax would be introduced.

Thus, objections to the neoclassical behavioral model do not spell the end for environmental taxation; rethinking environmental policy in the context of bounded rationality merely suggests when and how to use such policy instruments. Furthermore, extending the behavioral research agenda into agent-based modeling may lead to more realistic as well as more operational policy analyses.

REFERENCES

Andersen, L.B., C.B. Jacobsen, A.L. Møller and T. Pallesen (2006), 'Arbejder forskere just for the money? En analyse af ny løn på universiteter og sektorforskningsinstitutioner' [Do scientists work just for the money? An analysis of new wage policies in research institutions], *Politica*, **38** (4), 380–91.

Andersen, M.S. (2000a), 'Designing and introducing green taxes: institutional dimensions', in M.S. Andersen and R.-U. Sprenger (eds), *Market-based Instruments for Environmental Management: Policies and Institutions*, Cheltenham, UK: Edward Elgar, pp. 27–48.

Andersen, M.S. (2000b), 'The Danish waste tax: the role of institutions for the implementation and effectiveness of economic instruments', in M.S. Andersen and R.-U. Sprenger (eds), *Market-based Instruments for Environmental Management: Policies and Institutions*, Cheltenham, UK: Edward Elgar, pp. 231–59.

Baumol, W.J. and W. Oates (1988), *The Theory of Environmental Policy*, Cambridge, UK: Cambridge University Press.

Bendor, J. (2003), 'Herbert A. Simon: political scientist', *Annual Review of Political Science*, **6**, 433–71.

Bettman, J., M.F. Luce and J. Payne (1998), 'Constructive consumer choice processes', *The Journal of Consumer Research*, **25** (3), 187–217.

Camerer, C. and R. Thaler (1995), 'Anomalies: ultimatums, dictators and manners', *The Journal of Economic Perspectives*, **9** (2), 209–19.

Conlisk, J. (1996), 'Why bounded rationality?', *Journal of Economic Literature*, **34**, 669–700.

Cyert, R.M. and J.G. March (1963), *A Behavioural Theory of the Firm*, Cambridge, UK: Blackwell Business; 2nd ed. (1992).

Denzau, A.T. and D.C. North (2000), 'Shared mental models: ideologies and institutions', in A. Lupia, M.D. McCubbins and S.L. Popkin (eds), *Elements of Reason. Cognition, Choice and the Bounds of Rationality*, Cambridge, UK: Cambridge University Press, pp. 23–46.

Douma, S. and H. Schreuder (1998), *Economic Approaches to Organizations*, London, UK: Prentice Hall.

ECON (2004), 'Evaluering av miljøavgifter' [Evaluation of environmental taxes], Rapport 2004-123, available at http://www.econ.no/search_all.asp?mnusel=a185a190a.

Enevoldsen M. (2005), *The Theory of Environmental Agreements and Taxes*, Cheltenham, UK: Edward Elgar.

Farmer, J.D. and D. Foley (2009), 'The economy needs agent-based modelling', *Nature*, **460** (6), 685–86.

Fehr, E. and Tyran, J.-R. (2005), 'Individual irrationality and aggregate outcomes', Discussion Papers, pp. 1–30, Copenhagen, Denmark: Department of Economics, University of Copenhagen.

Frey, B. and F. Oberholzer-Gee (1997), 'The cost of price incentives: an empirical analysis of crowding-out', *American Economic Review*, **87**, 746–55.

Friedman, M. (1953), 'Introduction', in *Essays in Positive Economics*, Chicago, IL, US: University of Chicago Press, pp. 3–43.

Goodrick, E. and G. Salancik (1996), 'Organizational discretion in responding to institutional practices: hospitals and Cesarian births', *Administrative Science Quarterly*, **41**, 1–28.
Green, D.P. and I. Shapiro (1994), *Pathologies of Rational Choice Theory*, New Haven, CT, US: Yale University Press.
Hall, P.A. and R. Taylor (1996), 'Political science and the three new institutionalisms', *Political Studies*, **XLIV**, 936–57.
Hiltunen M. (2004), *Economic Environmental Policy Instruments in Finland*, Helsinki, Finland: Finnish Environment Institute.
Jones, B.D. (1999), 'Bounded rationality', *Annual Review of Political Science*, **2**, 297–321.
Jones, B.D. (2001), *Politics and the Architecture of Choice. Bounded Rationality and Governance*, Chicago, IL, US: University of Chicago Press.
Kahneman, D. (2002), 'Maps of bounded rationality: a perspective on intuitive judgment and choice', Nobel Prize Lecture, 8 December, in Stockholm, available at http://nobelprize.org/economics/laureates/2002/kahneman-lecture.html.
Kahneman, D., J. Knetsch, and R. Thaler (1991), 'The endowment effect, loss aversion, and status quo bias', *Journal of Economic Perspectives*, **5**, 193–206.
Kahneman, D., P. Slovic and A. Tversky (eds) (1982), *Judgement under Uncertainty: Heuristics and Biases*, Cambridge, UK: Cambridge University Press.
Kolstad, C. (1999), *Environmental Economics*, Oxford, UK: Oxford University Press.
Leibenstein, H. (1966), 'Allocative efficiency vs. x-efficiency', *The American Economic Review*, **56** (3), 392–415.
March, J.G. (1994), *A Primer on Decision-making: How Decisions Happen*, New York, NY, US: The Free Press.
March, J.G. and J.P. Olsen (1989), *Rediscovering Institutions*, New York, NY, US: Free Press.
March, J.G. and H.A. Simon (1958), *Organizations*, Cambridge, MA, US: Blackwell Publishers; 2nd ed. (1993).
Marcus, G.E. and M. MacKuen (1993), 'Anxiety, enthusiasm and the vote: the emotional underpinnings of learning and involvement during presidential campaigns', *American Political Science Review*, **87** (3), 672–85.
McFadden, D. (1999), 'Rationality for economists?', *Journal of Risk and Uncertainty*, **19** (1–3), 73–105.
Miljøministeriet, Finansministeriet, Fødevareministeriet (2007), 'Rapport fra et tværministerielt udvalg. Analyse af virkemidler til opfyldelse af af Pesticidplan 2004 – 2009 mål om en behandlingshyppighed på 1,7' [Report from a cross-ministerial committee. Analysis of policy instruments for achievement of the objective of a pesticide treatment frequency of 1.7 in Pesticide Action Plan], available at http://www.mst.dk/NR/rdonlyres/ECF073BF-D1D6-41C4-8928-61CF38128A2D/0/Bilag2Virkemiddelrapport1101073.doc.
Moe, T.M. (1979), 'On the scientific status of rational models', *American Journal of Political Science*, **23** (1), 215–43.
Monroe, K.R. (1991), 'The theory of rational action: origins and usefulness for political science', in K.R. Monroe (ed.), *The Economic Approaches to Politics. A Critical Reassessment of the Theory of Rational Action*, New York, NY, US: HarperCollins Publishers.
Mullainathan, S. and R. Thaler (2000), 'Behavioral economics', Working Paper 7948, Cambridge, MA, US: National Bureau of Economic Research.
Nielsen, H.Ø. (2009), *Bounded Rationality in Decision-making. How Cognitive Shortcuts and Professional Values May Interfere with Market-based Regulation*, Manchester, UK: Manchester University Press.
North, D. (1990), *Institutions, Institutional Change and Economic Performance*, Cambridge, UK: Cambridge University Press.
North, D. (1993), 'What do we mean by rationality', *Public Choice*, **77**, 159–62.
OECD (2001), *Environmentally Related Taxes in OECD Countries – Issues and Strategies*, Paris, France: OECD.
OECD (2007), *Instrument Mixes for Environmental Policy*, Paris, France: OECD.
OECD (2010), OECD/EEA database on instruments used for environmental policy and natural resources management, http://www2.oecd.org/ecoinst/queries/, accessed May 10 2010.
Opp, K.-D. (1999), 'Contending conceptions of the theory of political action', *Journal of Theoretical Politics*, **11** (2), 171–202.
Ostrom, E. (1998), 'A behavioural approach to the rational choice theory of collective action. Presidential address, American Political Science Association 1997', *The American Political Science Review*, **92** (1), 1–22.
Payne, J.W., J.R. Bettman and E.J. Johnson (1993), *The Adaptive Decision Maker*, New York, NY, US: Cambridge University Press.
Payne, J.W., D.A. Schkade, W.H. Desvousges and C. Aultman (2000), 'Valuation of multiple environmental programs', *Journal of Risk and Uncertainty*, **21**, 95–115.
Pedersen, A.B., H.Ø. Nielsen, T. Christensen and B. Hasler (forthcoming), 'Barrierer i landmændenes beslutningsmønster vedrørende ændret pesticidanvendelse. Rapport til Miljøstyrelsen' [Barriers for different pesticide practices due to decision patterns of farmers. Report to the Environmental Protection Agency of Denmark], Aarhus, Denmark: National Environmental Research Institute, Aarhus University.
Perman, R., Y. Ma, J. McGilvray and M. Common (1999), *Natural Resource & Environmental Economics*, Essex, UK: Pearson Education Limited.

Plancenter Ltd. (2005), 'A study of the efficiency of the waste tax in Finland. English summary of report commissioned by Finland's Ministry of Environment, Helsinki', Finland: Plancenter Ltd.

Porter, M.E. and C. van der Linde (1995), 'Toward a new conception of the Environment–Competitiveness Relationship', *The Journal of Economic Perspectives*, **9** (4), 97–118.

Sen, A. (1977), 'Rational fools: a critique of the behavioural foundations of economic theory', *Philosophy and Public Affairs*, **6** (4), 317–44.

Sen, A. (1986), 'Behaviour and the concept of preference', in J. Elster (ed.), *Rational Choice*, New York, NY, US: New York University Press.

Sen, A. (1987), 'Rational behaviour', in J. Eatwell, M. Milgate and P. Newman (eds), *The New Palgrave: A Dictionary of Economics*, London, UK: Macmillan.

Shafir, E. and R.A. LeBoeuf (2002), 'Rationality', *Annual Review of Psychology*, **53**, 491–517.

Simon, H.A. (1947), *Administrative Behaviour. A Study of Decision-Making Processes in Administrative Organizations*, New York, NY, US: The Free Press; 3rd ed. (1976).

Simon, H.A. (1978), 'Rational decision-making in business organizations', Nobel Memorial Lecture, 8 December, http://nobelprize.org/nobel_prizes/economics/laureates/1978/simon-lecture.pdf.

Simon, H.A. (1985), 'Human nature in politics: the dialogue of psychology with political science', *The American Political Science Review*, **79** (2), 293–304.

Simon, H.A. (1990), 'Invariants of human behaviour', in M. Rosenzweig and L. Porter (eds), *Annual Review of Psychology*, **41**, 1–19.

Simon, H.A. (1993), 'Altruism and economics', *The American Economic Review*, **83** (2), 156–61. Papers and Proceedings of the Hundred and Fifth Annual Meeting of the American Economic Association.

Simon, H.A. (1997a), 'Methodological foundations of economics', in *Models of Bounded Rationality: Vol. 3: Empirically Grounded Economic Reason*, Cambridge, MA, US: MIT Press, pp. 319–35.

Simon, H.A. (1997b), 'Satisficing', in *Models of Bounded Rationality: Vol. 3: Empirically Grounded Economic Reason*, Cambridge, MA, US: MIT Press, pp. 295–98.

Simon, H.A. (1997c), 'A mechanism for social selection and successful altruism', in *Models of Bounded Rationality: Vol. 3: Empirically Grounded Economic Reason*, Cambridge, MA, US: MIT Press, pp. 205–16.

Simon, H.A. (1997d), 'Organizations and markets', in *Models of Bounded Rationality: Vol. 3: Empirically Grounded Economic Reason*, Cambridge, MA, US: MIT Press, pp. 217–40.

Speck, S., M.S. Andersen, H.Ø. Nielsen, A. Ryelund and C. Smith (2006), *The Use of Economic Instruments in Nordic and Baltic Environmental Policy 2001–2005*, TemaNord 2006:525. Copenhagen, Denmark: Nordic Council of Ministers.

Sprenger, R.-U. (2000), 'Market-based instruments in environmental policies; the lessons of experience', in M.S. Andersen and R. Sprenger (eds), *Market-based Instruments for Environmental Management*, Cheltenham, UK: Edward Elgar, pp. 3–24.

Thaler, R. and C. Sunstein (2008), *Nudge. Improving Decisions about Health, Wealth and Happiness*, New Haven, CT, US: Yale University Press.

Thøgersen, J. and A. Grønbæk (2010), 'Sladrehank får familier til at spare på elforbruget' [Tattle-tale makes families save on electricity], News release, Aarhus School of Business, Aarhus University, http://www.asb.dk/news.aspx?pid=16479&focus=25454, accessed 17 May 2010.

Tietenberg, T.H. (1990), 'Economic instruments for environmental regulation', *Oxford Review of Economic Policy*, **6** (1), 17–33.

Tversky, A. and D. Kahneman (1974), 'Judgment under uncertainty: heuristics and biases', *Science*, **185** (4157), 1124–31.

van den Bergh, J.C.J.M, A. Ferrer-i-Carbonell and G. Munda (2000), 'Alternative models of individual behaviour and implications for environmental policy', *Ecological Economics*, **32**, 43–61.

Venkatachalam, I. (2008), 'Behavioral economics for environmental policy', *Ecological Economics*, **67**, 640–45.

Whitehead, J.W. (1991), 'The forgotten limits: reason and regulation in economic theory', in K.R. Monroe (ed.), *The Economic Approach to Politics*, New York, NY, US: Harper Collins, pp. 53–73.

25 Global environmental taxes
Philippe Thalmann

INTRODUCTION

Other chapters of this Handbook show that environmental taxes are very interesting instruments for environmental regulation. The question addressed in this chapter is whether they are still interesting when the environmental problem is a global one. Are they still effective and efficient? Are they feasible and acceptable? First, however, a few definitions are needed: what are global environmental problems and how could taxes help address them?

A global environmental problem is an environmental problem to which nearly all countries contribute and that affects nearly all countries of the world. This implies that nearly all countries should participate in resolving it. However, individual countries contribute in different amounts and are affected in different ways. They also face different abatement costs, or costs for reducing their share of environmental harm. This implies that national contributions toward resolving the problem should be modulated. Clearly, making sure that all countries participate and allocating abatement efforts efficiently across all countries will be key issues for global environmental problems, particularly as there exists no global authority that could force participation and impose abatement efforts on sovereign countries (Carraro 1999).

The main global environmental problems are climate change, ozone depletion and biodiversity loss.[1] The atmosphere and the oceans, with their absorptive capacity and the species they host, and even outer space with the room it offers, are common property resources of humanity. Everyone who uses such a resource reduces others' ability to use it. No one can prevent or regulate this in the absence of enforceable property rights.

Ozone depletion has been combated quite successfully through treaties banning dangerous substances. The success of this approach has been attributed to the possibility of rapidly replacing the chemicals. Similar bans on greenhouse gases are obviously much less feasible. Therefore, a more gradual approach is advocated for climate policy, one that leaves much more freedom to individual emitters about how and when they reduce their emissions of greenhouse gases and which gases they abate primarily. The international approach relies mainly on voluntary measures such as information, persuasion (see Baranzini and Thalmann 2004), technology transfer, and bilateral mitigation projects (clean development mechanism, joint implementation) that generate 'credits' to be used against some mitigation obligation or objective. The main internationally coordinated

---

[1] The depletion of mineral resources could be added to this list, with some precautions. Indeed, contrary to the atmosphere and the oceans, ownership rights are often well defined for mineral resources (but not always, viz. deep ocean resources). However, their owners may over-exploit them, at the expense of future generations of the world population. Their depletion at an inefficient rate is similar to the depletion of natural resources without ownership.

action is the European Union's Emission Trading System (EU ETS), a cap-and-trade system for large carbon dioxide emitters. In addition, nearly all countries have implemented some climate policy, drawing on a mix of these instruments, augmented with regulation, subsidies and taxes.

Based on the experience with domestic carbon taxes and economists' long-standing promotion of this instrument, the question of whether that potentially very effective and efficient instrument could also be used at the international level naturally arises, particularly as its environmental- and cost-effectiveness could grandly be augmented by international coordination.

Since climate policy is the area in which a global environmental tax has received the greatest attention by the political and scientific community, this chapter concentrates on the carbon tax. However, the assessment of the global carbon tax can easily be carried over to other global environmental taxes. A good part of the assessment of the global carbon tax also extends to a broader approach, that of global carbon pricing (advocated by the OECD, among others (OECD 2009, Chapter 4)), which includes reductions in subsidies to fossil fuels and a market for carbon dioxide emission certificates.

THE DESIGN OF A GLOBAL CARBON TAX

Two possible formats for a global carbon tax have been discussed extensively: harmonized taxes and an international tax (Hoel 1992). In the first, a set of countries agree to raise their carbon prices. They might agree on the same tax rate or on different rates in different countries, for instance lower rates in less developed countries. The rates could be set with a quantity objective or at a level corresponding to external costs. Tax revenues accrue to each country but a part could be put into a common fund and used for international transfers.

With the international tax design, each country is taxed on its national emissions,[2] and each has to pay into a common fund an amount that is proportional to its total CO_2 emissions. At the Toronto Conference on the Changing Atmosphere of 1988, the creation of a World Atmospheric Fund was recommended. Under that proposal, the revenues are returned to the participating countries in fixed shares. Each country is free to decide how it finances its net contribution to the common fund, whether by a domestic carbon tax or by any other means.

Apart from these overarching schemes, one can imagine all sorts of combinations of national carbon taxes with other instruments that would create international links. For instance, firms could be exempted from the domestic carbon tax if they deliver foreign ETS permits for their emissions.[3] OECD (2009, 120) even envisages the reverse option, namely that a firm could avoid buying domestic ETS permits by paying the carbon tax

---

[2]   Whalley and Wiggle (1991a, 1991b) estimated the effects of a variant where the carbon tax is collected on a production basis. In that case, large producers of fossil fuels such as the OPEC countries and Russia would collect the highest tax revenues or contribute most into the common fund. Absent compensating redistribution of the revenues, there is of course an enormous difference between harmonized taxes on carbon extraction and those on CO_2 emissions.

[3]   Such a model is in preparation in Switzerland, where large CO_2 emitters could buy permits

enforced in a foreign country. In that case, the foreign carbon tax would place a lid on domestic permit prices. Alternatively, a country with an emissions-reduction target could use a domestic carbon tax to try to meet it and could plan to buy foreign permits if the tax turned out to be too low. It could even try to sell its own permits abroad if domestic mitigation overshot the target, provided of course that other countries accepted its permits. Such mechanisms lead to some international harmonization of carbon prices and transfers of funds.

In the following sections, we will assess the two 'pure' global tax schemes: harmonized taxes and an international tax.

ASSESSMENT OF THE GLOBAL CARBON TAX

The first question to ask is: what are the criteria for assessment? The standard criteria for an environmental policy instrument are its target effectiveness (does it achieve its goal, such as a desired environmental improvement or a target revenue), cost-effectiveness (does it achieve that goal at minimum resource costs), practical feasibility (legal conditions, administrative and compliance costs), fairness (is the burden fairly shared), and, finally, acceptability.

The assessment of the global carbon tax in this chapter will emphasize the international dimensions, i.e. its effectiveness in meeting a global environmental or income target, its ability to allocate efforts across countries in a manner that minimizes total costs of meeting that target, and the way it shares the burden among countries.

The assessment criteria are not independent. Participation is more likely if countries perceive an agreement to be fair. Wide participation is necessary for target- and cost-effectiveness. Feasibility constraints may reduce effectiveness.

The global carbon tax can be assessed on its own, i.e. in comparison with no international policy, or in comparison with other instruments designed to achieve the same environmental or revenue goal, such as tradable emission quotas.[4]

ENVIRONMENTAL-EFFECTIVENESS AND PARTICIPATION

An incentive tax can, in theory, be designed to meet any environmental target. Its effectiveness is reduced, however, when it is set at a low rate or when important sources are exempted for political reasons (Ekins and Speck 1999). In the case of a global environmental tax, effectiveness is threatened by nonparticipation of countries that are large emitters. Consider for instance CO_2 emitted by the consumption and flaring of fossil fuels. China and the United States together account for 41 percent of world emissions of

---

on the European ETS, of which Switzerland is not a member. In practice, Swiss and EU permits would become fungible, at least for Swiss firms.

[4] For comparisons between a global carbon tax and a system of tradable quotas, see for example Cooper (2000), Green, Hayward and Hassett (2007) McKibbin, Morris and Wilcoxen (2009) and Nordhaus (2007), who all conclude in favor of the tax, and Wiener (1999), who concludes in favor of quotas.

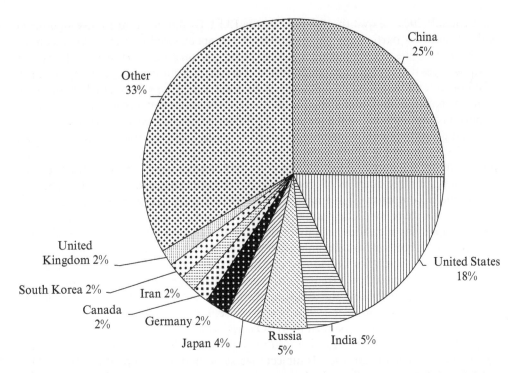

Figure 25.1   *Shares of main emitters in 2009 world CO₂ emissions from the consumption and flaring of fossil fuels, U.S. Energy Information Administration, International Energy Statistics*

this type. Ten countries account for two thirds of world emissions (Figure 25.1). Clearly, an agreement among these ten would have the potential to lower world CO_2 emissions substantially. Note that three of them—China, India and Iran—are not in Annex I of the Kyoto Protocol, the list of countries with an emissions-reduction target. The European Union accounts for about 12 percent of world emissions.

A global environmental tax will be effective only if at least the main emitters participate, and they must participate voluntarily as there is no world authority to impose participation. This concerns not only current large emitters but also future ones. Jacoby, Prinn and Schmalensee (1998) argue that even if all industrialized countries listed in Annex I of the Kyoto Protocol reduced their net greenhouse gas emissions to zero by the end of this century, that would have only a small impact on the climate, due to rapid emissions growth in the developing world. Still, the lowest-income countries might be given time for economic growth before they take over mitigation objectives. Nordhaus (2006) suggests a threshold for participation of US$10 000 per capita.

Nonparticipating countries ('pollution havens') could use the resulting competitive advantage to increase their world market shares and possibly even attract some production facilities from participating countries. As a result, global emissions would decrease less than those of the participating countries, a phenomenon known as carbon leakage. There exists a sizable empirical literature on the magnitude of carbon leakage, as this argument is often advanced against unilateral climate policy (OECD 2009, Chapter

3). Reinaud (2009) shows that phase I of the EU ETS did not lead to any significant leakage, even for particularly carbon-intensive sectors exposed to international competition, contrary to the pessimistic forecasts of simulation studies. However, the author acknowledges that the generous distribution of emission certificates did not impose much of a burden and that it might be too early to draw conclusions. Nevertheless, this confirms the results of earlier studies that showed that environmental regulation was not as important a determinant of the location of production as labor costs, taxes, or exchange rate and political risks (Cropper and Oates 1992; OECD 1993). Even so, the European Commission drafted a controversial list of sectors exposed to serious risk of carbon leakage under full auctioning of ETS permits that includes nearly one half of all sectors, accounting for three quarters of greenhouse gas emissions covered by the EU ETS.

Gaining a competitive advantage by not participating versus running the risk of losing market share by participating are strong incentives for free-riding. Hence the call for accompanying measures, mainly in the form of border adjustments: a country that imposes the carbon tax would reimburse it to its exporters and charge it on imports from nonparticipating countries. Obviously, measuring the contents of untaxed carbon in each imported product would be extremely difficult, but the number of carbon-intensive goods is not that large, so limiting the adjustments to these goods would yield a feasible and satisfactory solution (Goulder 1992). This measure, however, looks very similar to protectionist measures that are banned by WTO rules, which suggests that it must be drafted very carefully (Holzer 2010). Another solution is to start with a non-uniform domestic tax that imposes a higher rate on goods subject to less international competition (Hoel 1996).

Carbon leakage is not the only deterrent against participation in a global carbon tax scheme. Each country also weighs the burden the tax represents against the expected benefits. When the revenues of the tax are recycled in the country, its burden is equal, as a first approximation, to abatement costs. It is less, in fact, due to the ancillary domestic benefits of carbon mitigation (such as less damage due to air pollution, and terms-of-trade gains on fossil fuels imports), and even less if the revenues are well recycled ('second dividend'). Still, there could remain a net burden of the carbon tax, which might or might not be offset by the expected benefits of climate change mitigation. Indeed, countries will be affected quite differently by climate change. Some might even gain, although this is increasingly doubted. Still, some countries might make this argument in order to stay out of conjoint abatement efforts.

Even if environmental benefits exceed total net burdens in the world aggregate when the mitigation target is well set (Stern 2007), that may not be the case for each individual country. It is generally admitted that participation in a global carbon tax scheme, and in efficient global climate mitigation as a general matter, would be particularly burdensome for developing countries. OECD (2009, 59) attributes this to the 'higher carbon-intensity of their economies.' On the other hand, developing countries are also expected to gain the most from avoided climate change because of their greater exposure. Nevertheless, with their great difficulties in addressing the current needs of their populations, developing countries generally attach less priority to preserving the environment and discount the future at much higher rates than developed countries do, which is understandable if they expect stronger consumption growth rates than the latter (Dasgupta, Mäler and Barrett 1999). For both reasons the balance of carbon abatement costs and benefits is strongly tilted toward the costs side.

The fact that total abatement costs will be inferior to the cost of no action when the target is appropriately set implies that climate mitigation generates a global 'surplus' potentially sufficient to compensate countries for which abatement costs exceed benefits. This potential compensation may well have to become real to make at least all major emitters participate. The UNFCC (Article 11) provides for such a financial mechanism, which is operated by the Global Environment Facility (GEF) created in 1990. Remember, however, that the benefits from mitigation will accrue in the distant future in the form of avoided damages, not an easy source of funds for compensatory payments today! Alternatively, the global carbon tax might be part of a wider international environmental agreement, which might provide for different forms of conditional side-payments, technology transfer, trade sanctions and so forth (for a survey, see Wagner 2001).

If redistribution of funds is a condition for participation, some of the revenues of the harmonized national taxes would have to be put into a common pool. The international tax would automatically direct huge revenues into the common pool if the tax is designed to induce significant mitigation. Most of those revenues would be contributed by the richer countries. It is, however, doubtful that these countries would participate and entrust huge funds to an international body.[5] Neither is it clear that their electorates would support large payments to countries where they might raise governance issues (OECD 2009, 59).

These concerns could be addressed by imposing the international tax above some national quota of tax-free emissions, i.e. participating countries would pay only the tax on emissions exceeding their quota. If the quota were too generous, exceeding the level of emissions the country would choose in the face of the tax, the tax would be entirely ineffective. It would be effective if it could turn into a subsidy for countries that emitted less than their quota. This is illustrated in Figure 25.2. The high-income country optimally decides to abate the amount A^* of its CO_2 emissions under the tax, because beyond A^* the marginal cost of the additional abated ton would cost more than paying the tax. Therefore, its residual emissions are equal to $E^0 A^*$, E^0 being total emissions without any abatement, or the maximum abatement volume. With a regular carbon tax, this country would have to pay an amount equal to the surface of the rectangle of which one side is the segment $E^0 A^*$ and the other is equal to the tax rate. With a quota of free emissions E^f, the country effectively only pays the tax on its excess emissions, or $E^0 E^f A^*$. The amount of that tax corresponds to the darkened rectangle. With the same reasoning, the low-income country, which emits little and has low marginal abatement costs and a generous quota, chooses residual emissions below its quota. It is rewarded by the amount represented by the darkened rectangle. Under this scheme, both high- and low-income countries have the same incentive for mitigation: the amount that the former pays into the common fund are limited, and the latter is clearly rewarded for its efforts by an amount that covers a good part of its abatement costs (the surface under the MAC curve).

In spite of its attractive features, this solution does not simplify the negotiation process. It is still necessary to agree on the tax-free quota for each participating country. On the other hand, the international tax design leaves each nation its sovereignty over how it

---

[5]   Schelling (1991, 215) had estimated the contribution of the United States at some US$100 billion per year, a figure that is confirmed below.

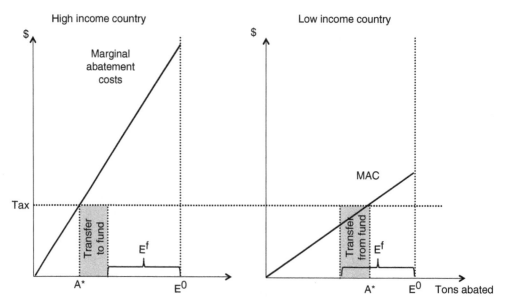

Figure 25.2   Illustration of international tax scheme with small net contributions by industrialized countries and transfers to developing countries

finances its contribution to the common fund, infringing much less on the delicate matter of tax systems than does the harmonized tax scheme.[6]

REVENUE-EFFECTIVENESS

That its revenues can be used for compensation payments is of course the attractive feature of a global tax, compared to tradable quotas allocated for free. The amounts involved are potentially huge. Not surprisingly, some have proposed to reverse the perspective: to raise a global environmental tax for its revenue potential, the environmental improvement being the welcome side-effect. A revenue target would be set and the effectiveness of a global environmental tax in meeting this target would take the place of environmental-effectiveness as the main purpose. This would have the practical implication that the tax rate would be set not to attain a mitigation target or to internalize external costs but to raise a desired amount of revenue.

Many different revenue targets have been proposed for global environmental taxes, with corresponding hypothecation of the tax revenues. Earmarking of revenues is fundamentally a constraint on spending that ought to be avoided, but it is often necessary in order to make a tax acceptable. This seems to be particularly the case for global

---

[6]   Loss of tax sovereignty was the killer argument against the European project of a centralized mixed carbon and energy tax, particularly as unanimity was required for its adoption (Zhang and Baranzini 2004).

environmental taxes. The international community seems more likely to accept such taxes if their revenues are earmarked for international spending, especially spending related to the nature of the taxes. Such earmarking of the revenues may also be needed when the main purpose of the global tax remains environmental-effectiveness.

Thus, it has been proposed to dedicate the revenues of carbon taxation to international development funding (Atkinson 2004), with the argument that climate change threatens the economic growth of the poorest countries, both through the burdens of mitigation and adaptation and the remaining impacts of climate change (Sandmo 2004). The World Bank estimates annual mitigation costs in developing countries between US$140 billion and $175 billion by 2030, but since this requires mostly up-front investments, the financing needs in the early years are two to three times larger. To that must be added some US$30 billion to $100 billion every year for adaptation, which would not avoid all damages (World Bank 2010, 259–60). In the Copenhagen Accord and reinforced at the 16th Conference of Parties in Cancun in December 2010, the developed countries committed to mobilizing jointly US$100 billion per year by 2020 for mitigation and adaptation actions in developing countries. A 'Green Climate Fund' is to be created, but there is no agreement yet on how the money would be raised. There exists already a 2 percent tax on certified emission reductions created through the clean development mechanism of the Kyoto Protocol. Its revenues feed the Adaptation Fund and could reach between US$1 billion and $2 billion in 2020 depending on the restrictions imposed on the purchase of credits (Fankhauser and Martin 2010).[7]

What would the revenue effectiveness of a global carbon tax be? Worldwide CO_2 emissions from energy consumption amount to some 30 billion tons, of which about 15 billion tons come from high-income countries (US Energy Information Administration, International Energy Statistics). Thus, every dollar of tax per ton of CO_2 emissions in high-income countries would generate US$15 billion in revenues for the global fund. The middle range of the estimates of mitigation and adaptation costs in developing countries presented above, about US$220 billion, could be financed by a tax of US$15 per ton CO_2 in high-income countries.[8]

Such back-of-the-envelope calculations ignore the incidence of the tax on its tax base. Revenue effectiveness is controversial for environmental taxes precisely because those taxes are initially designed to discourage a polluting activity, which is their own tax base. Of course, the kinds of global taxes considered in this chapter are not designed to eliminate the polluting activity entirely, but the tax base erosion effect ought to be taken into account. This is done in simulations with computable general equilibrium (CGE) models. Altamirano-Cabrera et al. (2010) start from different estimates of climate change impacts and adaptation costs in the literature. They retain climate change impacts of US$223 billion in 2040 for developing countries, or about 1 percent of their GDP.

As of January 31, 2011, the Adaptation Fund, which was established in 2011 but really began operations after 2008, had received US$138 million from the CER tax and US$86 million from donors and other sources (AFB/EFC.4/10/rev.2).

[8]   These estimates assume full compliance and they ignore the incentive effect of the tax. CO_2 emissions can be estimated to decrease by some 10 percent in developed economies for a tax of US$15 (Bicchetti et al. 2007, 25). We express all tax rates per ton CO_2. They can be converted into tax rates per ton carbon by multiplying them by 3.66.

Financial compensation could be funded with a global tax of US$6.80 per ton CO_2 if all countries participated, or US$20 if participation were restricted to OECD countries. In the first case, world CO_2 emissions would decline as a side effect by 19 percent and in the second case by only 3.6 percent relative to baseline.[9] As a matter of fact, the tax restricted to OECD countries has CO_2 emissions growing by 2 percent relative to baseline in non-OECD countries due to lower demand for fossil fuels in the OECD, resulting in lower prices, and to some relocation of industrial production. The details of the simulation show the difficulties a tax restricted to the OECD will have in paying for worldwide climate change impacts. It would impose welfare losses on Australia, New Zealand and Canada equivalent to close to 2 percent of their total household consumption and it would imply annual transfers of about US$100 billion from the United States mainly to India and other emerging countries in Asia aside from China. These economic impacts can be divided approximately by five if the global carbon tax is designed to cover adaptation costs in developing countries instead of their costs from climate change.

Financing adaption in developing countries is also the aim of the Swiss proposal to the Conference of Parties to the UNFCC: an international carbon tax of US$2 per ton CO_2 with a basic tax exemption of 1.5 ton of CO_2 per capita. Its estimated annual revenues of about US$18 billion would go into the Adaptation Fund.[10] This proposal beats other proposals that make the tax rate depend on the income level of each country in that it maintains the cost-effectiveness of climate mitigation (see below).

Another reference for financing needs is that of the additional resources required to reach the Millennium Development Goals, estimated at around US$50 billion per year on top of the US$57 billion provided currently under official development assistance, or ODA (Atkinson 2004). The fact that the revenues of the CO_2 tax would have to come on top of existing ODA hints at an important threat to this proposal: countries might see their carbon-based contribution to the global fund as a substitute for their existing ODA and lower it (Sandmo 2004). The fact that the carbon tax would crowd out domestic tax revenues by eroding their tax base adds to the likelihood of such considerations.

COST-EFFECTIVENESS

When several sources contribute to a common pool of pollution and each has the ability to lower its emissions, it seems to be desirable that those sources that can lower their emissions at the smallest cost provide the greatest reductions. This minimizes the total cost

---

[9]   The revenues are paid lump-sum to the populations of the affected countries in proportion to their costs of climate change. This has only a marginal impact on emissions reduction. Emissions reduction is obtained by the incentive effect of the tax.

[10]   In the preparation of this proposal, Bicchetti et al. (2007) simulated an international carbon tax that would be sufficient to finance adaptation needs in the developing countries, estimating it at about US$10 billion in 2010 and rising to US$45 billion by 2040. The required tax would start at US$1 per ton CO_2 in 2010 and rise to US$4 in 2040. If the tax were restricted to OECD countries, it would have to start at US$3 and rise to US$13. In this case, world CO_2 emissions would decrease by less than 1 percent, whereas the worldwide tax generating the same revenues would obtain a decrease in CO_2 emissions by 6 percent in 2040.

for a target amount of emissions reduction or, equivalently, allows the greatest reduction for the same budget. This will be discussed on a theoretical level before addressing the challenges of implementation.

For well-defined marginal abatement costs (MAC), total abatement cost is minimized when each source abates to the point where its MAC is equal to that of all other sources. So long as MACs are different, total cost can be lowered for the same mitigation result by having a source with lower MACs abate a little bit more and letting a source with higher MAC abate correspondingly less.

Of course, it is extremely difficult to estimate a national MAC, let alone a global MAC. Indeed, doing so would involve ranking all possible measures available to abate emissions, from the cheapest to the dearest. For simulation purposes, this is done by examining each measure individually (often a technology or a type of resource substitution), estimating the cost of abating different quantities of emissions with each measure (its MAC), and then constructing the outer envelope of these MACs, which defines the mix of measures that minimizes costs for each desired level of abatement. Setting a common mitigation target for several countries increases the portfolio of possible mitigation measures, which generally lowers the costs of reaching that target. Estimating MAC is necessary for setting optimal targets, based on a comparison of mitigation costs and benefits. The beauty of economic instruments such as environmental taxes is that they do not require any centralized knowledge of MAC. Indeed, they confront emitters with a common price for emissions, which induces each to compare her own mitigation options (i.e. MAC) with that price, thereby comparing them indirectly with the mitigation options of all other emitters facing the same price.

Equalization of MAC could be obtained by regulation if some authority were able and allowed to impose upon each source that amount of abatement that equates all MACs. It can be obtained much more easily by making sources pay a unit price for their emissions. Sources minimize their total cost—abatement plus tax on residual emissions—by selecting the quantity of abatement that equates their MAC to the unit price. Since that price is the same for all sources, all MACs are equated and least-cost mitigation obtains.

The uniform carbon price has the further attractive feature of rewarding continuous improvement. Indeed, as sources pay on residual emissions, contrary to regulation, they have an incentive to find new ways to reduce their emissions. This promotes the development, diffusion and adoption of innovation. Cost minimization at any point in time is called 'static cost-effectiveness,' while the pressure to improve continuously leads to 'dynamic cost-effectiveness.'

Transposed to a global environmental problem like CO_2 emissions, this suggests that global mitigation cost minimization can be enforced with a uniform carbon price. Every source of CO_2 emissions in the world should be charged the same price for each ton of CO_2 it emits (more precisely, for each quantity of greenhouse gases that has a warming potential equal to that of a ton of CO_2). If a global carbon tax allows the achievement of this, then it can be considered as efficient.[11] Any deviation from a uniform global carbon price would imply inefficient mitigation.

Full tax harmonization naturally obtains a uniform carbon price for all sources. In

---

[11]   The uniform carbon price could also be achieved, in theory, by subsidizing emitters for

the case of the international tax, where countries are charged proportionally to their CO_2 emissions, a uniform carbon price for all sources obtains only if each country passes those costs down to all domestic sources. That means that in each country each source is made to contribute to the national bill in proportion to its contribution to national emissions. This amounts, in effect, to each country's introducing a domestic carbon tax at a rate equal to the international tax, which ends up being the same as tax harmonization.

The global costs of mitigation can be lowered substantially by its efficient division among all countries. Early simulations with four world models found cost savings in the range of 30 to 40 percent compared to a case where each country abates by itself (Weyant 1993). Later simulations with 13 improved integrated assessment models found even greater cost savings. Just allowing for the efficient apportionment of mitigation across the Annex I countries of the Kyoto Protocol lowers the required carbon tax by half compared to the tax if each country meets its target on its own (Weyant and Hill 1999). If developing countries are included, the required world tax, which measures the burden of mitigation indirectly because it is the common MAC, is four to nine times smaller than the stand-alone US tax for instance, depending on the model used (ibid.). The required carbon tax can be further reduced by 15 to 55 percent by including noncarbon greenhouse gases (Weyant, de la Chesnaye and Blanford 2006).

The substantial cost savings derived from including all countries in the global mitigation effort arise from the fact that developed countries are 'locked' in carbon-intensive infrastructures such as power plants, which cannot be replaced rapidly at low cost, whereas developing countries could follow a low-carbon growth path. However, these estimates do not account for many practical issues and market imperfections that stand in the way of cost-efficient sharing of the mitigation burden (Kolstad and Toman 2005).

There are many reasons to revise this ideal picture of the global carbon tax, even aside from its feasibility.[12] The first is related to fixed costs, which the comparison of MACs ignores. Forcing many small sources to reduce their emissions when each faces a fixed cost to start doing so may end up costing more than forcing large sources with possibly higher MACs to mitigate more. It could even cost more than the damage avoided. Administrative and compliance costs contribute to fixed costs. If these costs vary by source, they should be taken into account in the comparison of MACs.[13] The ideal picture also breaks down when large or numerous small sources do not minimize their total costs—abatement plus tax. One can imagine many situations where they would not: nonoptimizing behavior, imperfect information, split incentives (whoever decides is not

---

emissions reduction or by forcing them to acquire emission permits on an efficient (i.e. single-price) market, provided the subsidy or the price of permits were the same worldwide.

[12]   Baumol and Bradford (1970) show that optimal taxation of externalities differs from the internalization of those externalities under a budget constraint. Baumol and Oates (1988, Chapter 7), show further real-world interferences with the first-best ideal of equal MACs. In particular, the local (marginal) comparison of gains in abatement costs when they are reallocated between sources may not be representative of the global comparison of the actual production patterns with the social optimum.

[13]   OECD (2009) cites deforestation and methane emissions resulting from pipeline leakage as sources with high monitoring and enforcement costs.

the one who pays, for instance in rental housing), market power, or subsidies (including public or semipublic enterprises).[14]

Further problems with the ideal picture appear at the international level. The model assumes that abatement costs can be compared worldwide, as though there existed a single world market with a single world price for the resources needed for abatement. That might be true for commodities such as oil and gas, which are traded worldwide, but not for less mobile resources such as physical capital and labor. Barriers to trade and the diffusion of technologies and know-how jeopardize static and dynamic cost-effectiveness. Suppose it took one man-hour to abate one ton of CO_2 in the United States and two man-hours to do it in China. Should one conclude that more mitigation ought to be performed in the United States? United Nations Industrial Development Organization (1972) and Dasgupta (1972) recommend using domestic shadow prices, reflecting opportunity costs in terms of foregone domestic consumption, to assess projects.

Even if abatement costs were perfectly comparable across countries, it is not obvious that the kind of total abatement cost minimization that a uniform tax would bring corresponds to a welfare optimum (Chichilnisky and Heal 1994; Chichilnisky 1994; Hourcade, Helioui and Gilotte 1997). If any country were to set its carbon tax in autarky, it would compare the marginal cost of mitigation, in terms of foregone consumption utility for its population, with the marginal benefits of smaller (future) climate change. Every one of these determinants of the optimal domestic carbon tax differs between countries. In low-income countries, the balance tilts strongly on the side of mitigation costs, so they would select a much lower tax than would high-income countries.[15] A uniform world carbon tax would be too high for low-income countries and too low for high-income countries. It seems that the only way to agree on the total abatement cost minimization solution of the uniform tax is to transfer revenue from high- to low-income countries. The transfers would not need to equate income levels but they would need to compensate for the differentials in burdens imposed by the cost-minimizing solution. Absent such transfers, a solution with differentiated carbon taxes is closer to a second-best option (Sandmo 2004).

A further complication derives from the fact that the greenhouse effect is not the only motive for taxing fossil fuels. Their burning generally causes local damage, mainly through air pollution. In addition, many countries tax fuels for revenue purposes, whether because they cannot impose less distorting taxes or because they want to link payment to the use of public goods (such as a tax on gasoline and diesel to pay for roads). With preexisting fuel taxes, a uniform carbon tax such as the harmonized carbon tax does not equate marginal abatement costs (Haugland, Olsen and Roland 1992). Hoel

---

[14]   OECD (2009, 100) estimates that 'removing environmentally harmful fossil fuel energy subsidies, especially in non-OECD countries is an important first step. This would reduce greenhouse gas (GHG) emissions drastically in the subsidized countries, in some cases by over 30 percent relative to business-as-usual (BAU) levels by 2050 and it would also raise GDP per capita in most of the countries concerned. A multilateral removal of energy subsidies would cut GHG emissions globally by 10 percent by 2050 relative to BAU and this cut could be increased if developed countries adopt binding emission caps. The removal of energy subsidies would lower the cost of achieving a given mitigation target.'

[15]   This argument is equivalent to the personalized Lindahl contributions to the costs of a public good (Hinchy and Fisher 1999).

(1993a) has shown how the other motives ought to be taken into account in determining the optimal national taxes on fossil fuels. As a result, the full optimal taxes on fossil fuels are quite different from country to country, even when the part that corresponds to the greenhouse effect, the carbon tax, is harmonized. It is not even the case that the harmonized carbon tax should simply be added on top of the preexisting taxes, because the higher tax reduces emissions, moving the country down the marginal damage curve for local pollution, and increases the deadweight loss. It is therefore quite defendable to lower preexisting fuel taxes when introducing the carbon tax. Of course, it is extremely hard to distinguish that adjustment from a country's compensating reductions because it would rather free-ride on other countries' carbon mitigation than pass the full cost of the carbon tax onto its citizens.

The design with the international tax is not exempt from similar problems. Indeed, it determines only how much each participating country must contribute to the common fund in proportion to its emissions, not how it finances this contribution. It might for instance exempt its trade-exposed sectors and impose taxes more heavily on the emissions of sheltered sectors. That would destroy both gains from trade and cost-effective mitigation. Although this is a clear breach of trade principles, it remains that it is not necessarily optimal for a country to impose a uniform tax on all its emissions sources equal to the international tax, for the same reasons that the harmonized carbon tax does not imply equal optimal domestic taxes on fossil fuels (Hoel 1993b).

FAIRNESS

Focusing on environmental- and cost-effectiveness is acceptable for small national environmental taxes because other social mechanisms or the potential redistribution of the net gains from the policy can be invoked to address their burden on low-income households. Such an argument is much harder to defend at the international level, where the disparity in incomes is even greater and where there are very few redistributive mechanisms (Wiener 1999). On the other hand, actual redistribution and compensation is much more likely with a global tax because countries must be made to participate voluntarily.

It is necessary to consider three elements in assessing the fairness of a global environmental tax: (1) the direct economic burden for each country, (2) the revenue share received by each country, and (3) the environmental benefits for each country. The last impact is of course the hardest to estimate, as still very little is known about the likely costs of climate changes and about how and at what costs they could be mitigated by adaptation measures. The direct economic burden is estimated with the use of general equilibrium models, which are designed to capture the many channels through which a carbon tax could affect a nation's production and consumption, including international effects such as impacts on terms of trade. Early estimates on such an issue are those of Whalley and Wiggle (1991a), and, in more detail, Whalley and Wiggle (1991b), which show that the burden on each region (three world regions in the first paper, six in the second) depends very much on the format of the global carbon tax and the rules for revenue redistribution. Countries that are significant net exporters of fossil energy (such as OPEC countries) would benefit strongly from harmonized taxes levied at the well, with no international redistribution of the revenues, because that would amount to a coordinated price increase. Symmetrically, net importers of fossil energy would benefit from harmonized taxes levied on emissions, with no international redistribution, because that would improve their terms of trade, like a buyers' cartel. Finally, an international tax with revenues redistributed to countries in proportion to their populations would greatly benefit the least developed ones, thanks to huge transfers from North to South. Those countries would suffer from the harmonized tax regimes.

The importance of compensatory redistribution is made evident by the large differences in abatement costs across regions if a harmonized carbon tax is imposed, even if its revenues stay in each country. Figure 25.3 shows estimates of those net costs, taking into account general equilibrium effects such as terms-of-trade changes and trade flows (TOCSIN research team 2009). The simulations were performed with a state-of-the-art model coupling the worldwide computable general equilibrium model GEMINI-E3 and the bottom-up technology model TIAM after carefully updating them with the best available data for China and India. The costs of mitigation are those obtained with a harmonized tax on all greenhouse gas emissions that would control them so that radiative forcing never exceeds 3.5 W/m². All countries are assumed to participate and to recycle their tax revenues in lump-sum fashion to their population. The costs of mitigation are measured in terms of GDP, consumption and consumer surplus loss.[16] Climate change impacts and adaptation are not considered. Mitigation costs are greatest for the fossil-fuel exporters Russia and the Middle Eastern countries, but they are also relatively high for Africa, while the most advanced Asian and European countries bear no net costs at all.

A well-drafted global environmental tax creates surplus relative to the no-policy alternative, which can be used for the actual compensation of the losers. This global surplus is the difference between avoided environmental damage and adaptation costs on the one hand and mitigation costs on the other hand. However, avoided damage costs are a hard-to-mobilize source of transfers, particularly when they occur in the distant future. Many countries, particularly the least developed ones, place much greater weight on current mitigation costs rather than on future avoided climate change costs. They call for a fair sharing of mitigation costs. Figure 25.3 does not suggest that mitigation costs are shared fairly under a global carbon tax, whatever one's definition of fairness is. The kind of redistribution needed to ensure voluntary participation ought to make sure that no participant is worse off under the global tax regime, a minimal condition of fairness.

COMPLIANCE

A global environmental tax raises new compliance issues compared to the textbook national tax. To begin with, it might have to be enforced by developing countries that might lack the required institutions. Second, the global tax would be imposed without

---

[16]   GDP loss is the sum of discounted GDP losses relative to the no-policy baseline until 2100. Consumption loss is the sum of discounted variations in household consumption. Surplus loss is the sum of discounted annual consumer surplus divided by the present value of household consumption in the baseline.

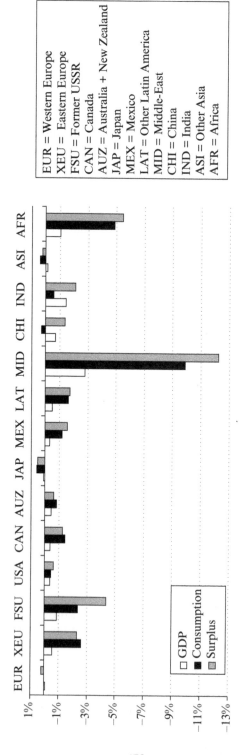

EUR = Western Europe
XEU = Eastern Europe
FSU = Former USSR
CAN = Canada
AUZ = Australia + New Zealand
JAP = Japan
MEX = Mexico
LAT = Other Latin America
MID = Middle-East
CHI = China
IND = India
ASI = Other Asia
AFR = Africa

Figure 25.3   Burden of global cost minimizing greenhouse gas mitigation for 14 regions of the world

any superior authority that could ensure compliance, even though each country would have an incentive to free-ride on other countries' efforts. A country might have decided to participate, maybe in exchange for some compensatory transfer or other advantage granted by other countries, but it might still want to cheat on its commitments. In the case of the international tax design, it must agree to contribute to the global fund based on its actual emissions. In the case of the harmonized tax design, it must agree to tax all of its domestic sources even though it might wish to protect some sectors.

Developing countries might be even further away from the textbook model of optimal Pigouvian taxation than are developed countries. Their markets are less efficient; they have greater difficulty in preventing tax evasion and making sure that effective and statutory tax rates coincide; and they typically lack the means to offset the adverse distributional consequences of environmental taxes (Blackman and Harrington 2000; Sandmo 2004). Nonetheless, a carbon tax is not the most difficult environmental tax to implement because it need not be charged on actual emissions. It can be levied at the border, on the imports of fossil fuels, and, if applicable, at the point of extraction.

This does not address, however, the issue of the heavy burden falling on particularly fragile households or firms. Participating countries might want to protect them against the hardships of the global tax. They also might want to protect particularly polluting or resource-intensive sectors, especially if those sectors are exposed to international competition. These are strong motives for noncompliance with the harmonized tax. The hidden means for such 'domestic cushioning strategies' (Wiener 1999, 785) are numerous: offsetting tax cuts, indirect subsidies such as free land rights, and so forth. In the case of carbon taxation, almost all countries apply other direct and indirect taxes and subsidies on fossil energy, which can be perfectly justified by the internalization of local external effects or revenue purposes and which can easily be modified by arguing that those motives changed (Hoel 1992; Hoel 1993a). They actually do change when a carbon tax is introduced!

Clearly, international enforcement of compliance with harmonized taxation would be extremely difficult and would imply deep scrutiny into domestic tax practices.[17] The incentives for cushioning and the difficulty of detecting it are greater under the harmonized tax regime than under a quota regime, which would force countries to compensate for the exemptions granted to some sectors and which would not impose a burden on polluters beyond the mitigation costs (Wiener 1999, 786). On the other hand, a country that is lenient with its polluters under a system of internationally tradable quotas allows them to sell more permits for foreign cash, which increases the risk of corruption (Nordhaus 2006, 34).

The international tax design faces compliance difficulties too. It requires precise monitoring on national emissions. For CO_2, countries already contribute data to national emissions inventories, which is not very complicated (the algorithm is thus: measure the extraction of fossil fuels plus imports minus exports). Things are more complicated when carbon sequestration and the emissions from cement production are to be taken into

---

[17] Cooper (1998) argues that the IMF could monitor enforcement of the harmonized tax, as it holds annual consultations with nearly all countries in the world on their macroeconomic policies, including their tax revenues.

account, and even more so when the tax is extended to other greenhouse gases. These issues are not different, however, for the international tax than for an agreement on quantities or a cap-and-trade regime.

CONCLUSION: PROSPECTS FOR IMPLEMENTATION

There are two main formats for a global tax: a harmonized tax, which each participant country imposes at the same rate on all its domestic emitters, and an international tax, which each participant country pays into a common fund in proportion to its total emissions. We have assessed global taxes and have compared the two formats with respect to five criteria: environmental-effectiveness, revenue-effectiveness, cost-effectiveness, fairness and compliance. The main results are summarized in Table 25.1.

Where does this leave us with respect to the likelihood of implementation? Clearly there are great challenges related to all criteria, but also great potential, in particular for generating the large revenues that developing countries will increasingly need in order to address the effects of climate changes. Should revenue generation become the main argument for a global environmental tax on which all countries can agree, then the international tax would be the natural design. Most likely it would be a small tax and it would be levied mostly on higher-income countries, or possibly on all countries as they pass an income-per-capita threshold. Such a tax would not do much for climate change mitigation.

If climate change mitigation remains the main purpose of the global tax, then harmonized national taxes would be the more natural and likely design.[18] It is much easier for countries to agree on a set of actions, in particular harmonized carbon taxes, than on quantitative targets such as national emission targets (Cooper 2000). Tax harmonization is flexible in that it can start with a nucleus of first movers who simply align their internal carbon taxes at a common rate, without the need to create new institutions or conduct controversial negotiations about such things as emission quotas. New participants can join at any time by simply introducing the same carbon tax. This might lead the coalition to revise its climate policies and modify technology and financial transfer rules, in accordance with the 'bottom-up approach' of Bodansky et al. (2004). Complete adherence of all countries is not necessary, but the circle of participants ought to be extended gradually to increase environmental- and cost-effectiveness. Dedicating part of the revenues of the harmonized carbon tax to a common pool that helps newcomers would accelerate adherence.

This progressive approach can draw on the international diplomatic experience with the harmonization of tariffs (Nordhaus 2006).[19] It is similar to the EU's 'opting out' and 'flexible geometry' rules. EU climate policy, in particular its emissions trading scheme,

---

[18]   OECD (2009) sees the most promising way toward a global carbon price in the linking of domestic and regional emission trading schemes. This approach would suffer, however, from the new skepticism in global financial markets, which have shown that they spread shocks around the globe, and the new skepticism in a common currency, since emission permits would be a common currency.

[19]   Incidentally, tariff harmonization could lead to the harmonization of domestic carbon taxes. Indeed, countervailing import tariffs (border tax adjustments) require equivalent carbon

Table 25.1   Assessment of a global environmental tax in general and the two main formats in particular

	Global tax in general	International tax	Harmonized tax
Environmental-effectiveness & Fairness	Main emitter countries must participate voluntarily, which requires transfers or other compensation for fair burden sharing.	Revenues flow into a common fund that can be used for compensation payments, but the amounts would be very large, unless countries are allowed a volume of tax-free emissions.	Revenues accrue nationally, so some of them would have to be redistributed. Border adjustments could oppose free-riding.
Revenue-effectiveness	Potentially large tax base to generate revenues needed for the large financial needs for mitigation, adaptation and damage compensation in developing countries.	This is the natural format for international income redistribution.	Revenues accrue in each country, but not enough in developing countries, so some redistribution is needed.
Cost-effectiveness	As a first approximation, a global tax can lead to global mitigation at minimum global cost thanks to a uniform price on all emissions, without regard for who bears the costs.	This format only obtains a uniform price on all emissions if each national contribution is financed through a harmonized emissions tax.	This is the natural format for a uniform price on all emissions.
Compliance	Compliance by sovereign countries is difficult to monitor and enforce.	Since countries pay taxes on their total emissions, this is relatively easy to monitor.	This format would require deep scrutiny of national tax systems to make sure that all sources are taxed.

shows that (groups of) countries are willing to take a first step to address climate change even when other big emitters opt out (such as the United States) or are allowed to not participate (developing countries). Similar unilateral first moves, later followed by cooperation, have been observed in other areas: trade, disarmament, phasing-out of ozone-depleting substances, etc. (Pizer 2009). There are advantages for first movers in a repeated game context where there is a good chance that some cooperation will ultimately ensue.

---

taxes on domestic production under WTO regulation. When these import tariffs are harmonized, this leads automatically to harmonized domestic carbon taxes.

The first movers might be countries for which the balance of benefits (including internal benefits such as reduced pollution and terms-of-trade gains) and costs is more favorable. More research might be needed on such gradual implementation of a global environmental tax and the conditions for 'coalitions of the willing' to emerge.

The EU is probably the best place to experiment with harmonized national taxes. It has experience with tax harmonization, in particular value-added taxation (Padilla and Roca 2004). On the other hand, the EU has tried and failed in the past to agree on a common carbon tax. The Commission of the European Communities had put such a proposal to the Council in 1992, a tax starting at about US$7 per ton CO_2 and rising gradually to US$22 (Delbeke 1994). This shows that it is easier to harmonize taxes that all countries already have in some form or other, which is not the case with carbon taxation (Baranzini, Goldemberg and Speck 2000).[20] As a result, passing carbon tax legislation is a first step that each country must take on its own before it can join the coalition.

The harmonized tax format faces the problem of preexisting taxes on fossil fuels and compensating subsidies on complements. This problem is not negligible, as countries use a wide array of significant taxes and subsidies related to fossil fuels. The only practical solution seems to be to agree on some minimum tax on fossil fuels and let each country decide how it wants to incorporate financing motives or the internalization of local external effects, and how it wants to compensate the users of fossil fuels for the income effects. Lower carbon tax rates in developing countries can be defended following second-best arguments as long as large transfers from developed countries do not compensate them for the heavy mitigation burden imposed on them (Sandmo 2004). Here again, more research is warranted to find practical rules for differentiated harmonized taxes that replace the uniform-emissions-price mantra by taking into account all the subtleties of the real world.

One interesting attempt at harmonization originates again in the European Union. In May 2011, the European Commission issued proposals to regulate transport and heating fuel taxation in the Union, not just by setting minimum rates but also by defining a common tax base. By these proposals, fuel taxes should be the sum of a component based on energy content and a component based on CO_2 emissions. The latter would be a uniform 20 Euros per ton from 2013, close to the expected carbon price in the EU ETS.

In the meantime, there should be some agreement to gradually phase out all forms of harmful subsidies to fossil fuels. This could be achieved in a multilateral fashion, similar to the removal of barriers to trade. Non-OECD countries are the most concerned. The removal of these subsidies could lower greenhouse gas emissions from fossil fuels combustion by 30 percent relative to business-as-usual levels by 2050 (OECD 2009).

---

[20]   The OECD maintains a database on environmentally related taxes and other instruments: http://www.oecd.org/env/policies/database.

REFERENCES

Altamirano-Cabrera, J.-C., D. Bicchetti, L. Drouet, P. Thalmann and M. Vielle (2010), 'A global carbon tax to compensate damage and adaptation costs', *Climate Economics at the NCCR Climate Research Paper* 2010/03, Berne, Switzerland.

Atkinson, A.B. (2004), 'Innovative sources to meet a global challenge', in A.B. Atkinson (ed.), *New Sources of Development Finance*, Oxford, UK: Oxford University Press for UNU-WIDER, pp. 1–16.

Baranzini, A. and P. Thalmann (eds) (2004), *Voluntary Approaches in Climate Policy*, Cheltenham, UK: Edward Elgar.

Baranzini, A., J. Goldemberg and S. Speck (2000), 'A future for carbon taxes', *Ecological Economics*, **32** (3), 395–412.

Baumol, W.J. and D.F. Bradford (1970), 'Optimal departures from marginal cost pricing', *American Economic Review*, **60** (3), 265–83.

Baumol, W.J. and W.E. Oates (1988), *The Theory of Environmental Policy*, 2nd ed., Cambridge, UK: Cambridge University Press.

Bicchetti, D., L. Drouet, P. Thalmann and M. Vielle (2007), 'The feasibility of a world-wide tax on anthropogenic emissions of greenhouse gases: levels and impacts of world-wide taxes on greenhouse gases', *Climate Economics at the NCCR Climate Research Paper* 2007/04, December, Berne, Switzerland.

Blackman, A. and W. Harrington (2000), 'The use of economic incentives in developing countries: lessons from international experience with industrial air pollution', *The Journal of Environment & Development*, **9** (1), 5–44.

Bodansky, D., E. Diringer, J. Pershing and X. Wang (2004), *Strawman elements: an assessment of possible approaches to advancing international climate change efforts*, Pew Center on Global Climate Change, Washington, DC, US.

Carraro, C. (1999), 'The structure of international environmental agreements', in C. Carraro (ed.), *International Environmental Agreements on Climate Change*, Dordrecht, Netherlands: Kluwer Academic, pp. 9–25.

Chichilnisky, G. (1994), 'Commentary on J. Coppel: "Implementing a global abatement policy: the role of transferts"', *The Economics of Climate Change. Proceedings of an OECD/IEA Conference*, Paris, France: OECD, pp. 159–69.

Chichilnisky, G. and G. Heal (1994), 'Who should abate carbon emissions? An international viewpoint', *Economics Letters*, **44** (4), 443–49.

Cooper, R.N. (1998), 'Toward a real global warming treaty', *Foreign Affairs*, **77** (2), 66–79.

Cooper, R.N. (2000), 'International approaches to global climate change', *The World Bank Research Observer*, **15** (2), 145–72.

Cropper, M.L. and W.E. Oates (1992), 'Environmental economics: a survey', *Journal of Economic Literature*, **30** (2), 675–740.

Dasgupta, P.S. (1972), 'A comparative analysis of the UNIDO guidelines and the OECD manual', *Bulletin of the Oxford University Institute of Economics and Statistics*, **34** (1), 33–51.

Dasgupta, P.S., K.-G. Mäler and S. Barrett (1999), 'Intergenerational equity, social discount rates, and global warming', in P.R. Portney and J.P. Weyant (eds), *Discounting and Intergenerational Equity*, Washington, DC, US: Resources for the Future, pp. 51–77.

Delbeke, J. (1994), 'Carbon taxes: the European Community proposal', *The Economics of Climate Change. Proceedings of an OECD/IEA Conference*, Paris, France: OECD, pp. 187–90.

Ekins, P. and S. Speck (1999), 'Competitiveness and exemptions from environmental taxes in Europe', *Environmental and Resource Economics*, **13** (4), 369–96.

Fankhauser, S. and N. Martin (2010), 'The economics of the CDM levy: revenue potential, tax incidence and distortionary effects', *Energy Policy*, **38** (1), 357–63.

Goulder, L.H. (1992), 'Carbon tax design and U.S. industry performance', *Tax Policy and the Economy*, **6**, 59–103.

Green, K.P., S.F. Hayward and K.A. Hassett (2007), 'Climate change: caps vs. taxes', *Environmental Policy Outlook. The American Enterprise Institute for Public Policy Research*, **2007** (2).

Haugland, T., Ø. Olsen and K. Roland (1992), 'Stabilizing CO_2 emissions. Are carbon taxes a viable option?', *Energy Policy*, **20** (5), 405–19.

Hinchy, M. and B.S. Fisher (1999), 'Negotiating greenhouse abatement and the theory of public goods', in C. Carraro (ed.), *International Environmental Agreements on Climate Change*, Dordrecht, Netherlands: Kluwer Academic, pp. 27–36.

Hoel, M. (1992), 'Carbon taxes: an international tax or harmonized domestic taxes?', *European Economic Review*, **36** (2–3), 400–406.

Hoel, M. (1993a), 'Harmonization of carbon taxes in international climate agreements', *Environmental and Resource Economics*, **3** (3), 221–31.

Hoel, M. (1993b), 'How should international greenhouse gas agreements be designed?', in P.S. Dasgupta,

K.-G. Mäler and A. Vercelli (eds), *The Economics of Transnational Commons*, Oxford, UK: Oxford University Press, pp. 172–91.

Hoel, M. (1996), 'Should a carbon tax be differentiated across sectors?', *Journal of Public Economics*, **59** (1), 17–32.

Holzer, K. (2010), 'Proposals on carbon-related border adjustments: prospects for WTO compliance', *Carbon and Climate Law Review*, **1**, 51–64.

Hourcade, J.-C., K. Helioui and L. Gilotte (1997), 'De quelques paradoxes autour de la fixation d'une taxe internationale sur le carbone' [On a few paradoxes about the setting of an international carbon tax], *Revue Economique*, **48** (6), 1509–28.

Jacoby, H.D., R. Prinn and R. Schmalensee (1998), 'Kyoto's unfinished business', *Foreign Affairs*, **77** (4), 54–66.

Kolstad, C.D. and M. Toman (2005), 'The economics of climate policy', in K.-G. Mäler and J.R. Vincent (eds), *Handbook of Environmental Economics*, Vol. 3, Amsterdam, Netherlands: Elsevier North-Holland, pp. 1561–618.

McKibbin, W.J., A. Morris and P.J. Wilcoxen (2009), 'Expecting the unexpected: macroeconomic volatility and climate policy', in J.E. Aldy and R.N. Stavins (eds), *Post-Kyoto International Climate Policy. Implementing Architectures for Agreement*, Cambridge, UK: Cambridge University Press.

Nordhaus, W.D. (2006), 'After Kyoto: alternative mechanisms to control global warming', *American Economic Review Papers and Proceedings*, **96** (2), May, 31–4.

Nordhaus, W.D. (2007), 'To tax or not to tax: alternative approaches to slowing global warming', *Review of Environmental Economics and Policy*, **1** (1), January, 26–44.

OECD (1993), *Environmental Policies and Industrial Competitiveness*, Paris, France: OECD.

OECD (2009), *The Economics of Climate Change Mitigation: Policies and Options for Global Action Beyond 2012*, Paris, France: OECD.

Padilla, E. and J. Roca (2004), 'The proposals for a European tax on CO_2 and their implications for intercountry distribution', *Environmental and Resource Economics*, **27** (3), 273–95.

Pizer, W.A. (2009), 'Economics versus climate change', in R. Guesnerie and H. Tulkens (eds), Cambridge, MA, US and London, UK: MIT Press.

Reinaud, J. (2009), 'Trade, competitiveness and carbon leakage: challenges and opportunities', Chatham House, *Energy, Environment and Development Programme Paper* 09/01, January, London, UK.

Sandmo, A. (2004), 'Environmental taxation and revenue for development', in A.B. Atkinson (ed.), *New Sources of Development Finance*, Oxford, UK: Oxford University Press for UNU-WIDER, pp. 33–57.

Schelling, T.C. (1991), 'Economic responses to global warming: prospects for cooperative approaches', in R. Dornbusch and J.M. Poterba (eds), *Global Warming: Economic Policy Responses*, Cambridge, MA, US: MIT Press, pp. 197–221.

Stern, N. (2007), *The Economics of Climate Change: The Stern Review*, Cambridge, UK: Cambridge University Press.

TOCSIN research team (2009), *Technology-oriented cooperation and strategies in India and China: reinforcing in EU dialogue with developing countries on climate change mitigation*, EU Framework Program 6, EPFL Swiss Federal Institute of Technology, Lausanne, Switzerland.

United Nations Industrial Development Organization (1972), *Guidelines for Project Evaluation*, ID/SER.H/2, New York.

Wagner, U.J. (2001), 'The design of stable international environmental agreements: economic theory and political economy', *Journal of Economic Surveys*, **15** (3), 377–411.

Weyant, J.P. (1993), 'Costs of reducing global carbon emissions', *The Journal of Economic Perspectives*, **7** (4), 27–46.

Weyant, J.P. and J. Hill (1999), 'The costs of the Kyoto Protocol: a multi-model evaluation—introduction and overview', *The Energy Journal*, **Special Issue**, May, vii–xliv.

Weyant, J.P., F.C. de la Chesnaye and G.J. Blanford (2006), 'Overview of EMF-21: multigas mitigation and climate policy', *The Energy Journal*, **Special Issue—Multi-Greenhouse Gas Mitigation and Climate Policy**, November, 1–32.

Whalley, J. and R. Wiggle (1991a), 'Cutting CO_2 emissions: the effects of alternative policy approaches', *Energy Journal*, **12** (1), 109–24.

Whalley, J. and R. Wiggle (1991b), 'The international incidence of carbon taxes', in R. Dornbusch and J.M. Poterba (eds), *Global Warming: Economic Policy Responses*, Cambridge, MA, US: MIT Press, pp. 233–63.

Wiener, J.B. (1999), 'Global environmental regulation: instrument choice in legal context', *Yale Law Journal*, **108** (4), January, 677–800.

World Bank (2010), *Development and Climate Change*, World Development Report 2010, Washington, DC, US: The World Bank.

Zhang, Z. and A. Baranzini (2004), 'What do we know about carbon taxes? An inquiry into their impacts on competitiveness and distribution of income', *Energy Policy*, **32** (4), 507–18.

PART VII

CONCLUSION

26 The future agenda for environmental taxation research
Mikael Skou Andersen and Janet E. Milne

INTRODUCTION

Nearly a century has passed since the idea of introducing taxes with a tax base related to emissions and other environmental burdens was first proposed by Pigou (1920). There was for several decades a disinclination for his innovative idea, widely perceived as impractical. It remained a footnote in economics textbooks for a long time and Ronald Coase (1960, 1988) even developed a formal theorem to explain why the idea would not be appropriate. Still, several economists, particularly of US origin, began from about 1960 to explore theoretically the principles of environmental taxation.

With challenges of industrialization and increases in the associated pollution and material flows gaining momentum in the aftermath of World War II, the idea also attracted more serious attention among decision-makers. In France new framework water legislation, Loi sur l'eau, was presented in 1959, and it included the introduction of effluent charges to raise funding for pollution abatement purposes (Barraqué 2000). When it was finally implemented in 1971, similar systems of effluent charges on water pollution were also agreed on and adopted in the Netherlands (1971) and Germany (agreed on in 1971 and implemented beginning in 1976). It appears that local Dutch water boards, with prerogatives for taxing water users, had individually pioneered effluent charges starting in the 1950s, hence their being the first to implement the idea in practice. In the beginning, introduction of effluent charges was a pragmatic approach to settling the costs of abatement and overcoming political inertia (Kneese and Bower 1968).

Ambitious environmental legislation was also introduced in the United States and Japan from about 1970 (Vogel 1993). In Japan, where air pollution was a concern, a significant levy on SO_2 was introduced in 1974 to finance compensation payments for pollution victims suffering from respiratory diseases and poisoning (Committee 1997; Matsuno and Ueta 2000). Japan's scheme was a solution to the problem of finding an appropriate way to issue a health bill to polluters, rather than to the general taxpayer. So too was the levy on chemicals instituted under the US Superfund scheme in 1985 to finance the cleanup of hazardous waste sites, and the first tax on municipal landfill waste introduced by Denmark in 1986 to sponsor measures for recycling and cleaner technology (Rahm 1998). Both the European water effluent charges and Japan's air pollution levy proved nevertheless highly effective in curbing emissions, which helped stimulate further reflections and proposals for making use of economic instruments around the world. The waste-related measures were also significant in their own way.

Beginning around 1990, attention shifted from viewing such taxes as useful instruments for environmental policy purposes, and toward their potential under the consideration of more fundamental changes in taxation policies, whereby environmentally related taxes could substitute for other taxes. In this process far more complex public finance questions appeared. Also a broader set of taxes became relevant, as tax bases relating to energy, transport and natural resources are significant in their potential for raising revenues. Under this new discourse it became apparent that long-established excises and taxes, for instance on petrol, and sometimes dating back to the days of Pigou, would be equally relevant for consideration, even if questions regarding the exact match between their tax base and Pigouvian principles of internalizing externalities can be raised. Supportive of this new broader perspective on environmentally related taxes were concerns about carbon emissions and the greenhouse effect, which, following the first IPCC report, moved center stage in global environmental policy deliberations. The idea of introducing a price on carbon fuelled a new wave of interest in how to align the broad set of excises and taxes on energy and transport under these new perspectives.

The opportunity to reform tax systems using this kind of taxation to replace other more distorting taxes immediately began to catch the imagination of academics, tax administrators and policymakers and also gradually to transform into policymaking. Over the past 10–15 years an international community of experts who study, explore and address the specific principles and practices of environmental taxation from the perspectives of economics, law and policy studies has emerged, and their efforts have been reflected in an expanding literature as well as in specific conferences dedicated to the study of environmental taxation. The annual Global Conference on Environmental Taxation has passed its thirteenth gathering, having resulted in numerous conference volumes and journal articles.

The field of environmental taxation research is by now a distinct area of study, which from a range of disciplines addresses questions that are normative as well as positive in nature. Basic theoretical frameworks within economics, law and behavioral sciences are being applied to explore environmental taxation, while the testing of normative propositions against positive observations in turn is generating new ideas and theoretical reflections on the tax system and its possible 'greening.' While the very first literature on environmental taxation was inherently economic in the neoclassical tradition, scholars coming from the law and economics tradition challenged and expanded that framework for research. With environmental taxation transcending from the world of ideas into one of legislative action, the issues and challenges with administrating the law and examining specific cases in fact opened an entirely new area of research to legal scholars. A separate behavioral approach rooted in policy sciences emerged too, addressing broader questions that go beyond the purely economic efficiency criterion, in particular relating to equity implications and ultimate policy effectiveness. Scholars traditionally preoccupied with concerns about optimal taxation design, in particular from public finance, have also subjected environmental taxation principles to investigation. Policy questions spurred by concerns about optimality in turn have led to the involvement of environmental engineers with tools that enable estimates of what might be suitable rates of environmental taxes reflecting external costs.

The study of environmental taxation is closely linked with studies of other policy instruments applied in the area of environment, energy and climate. It belongs to the family of market-based policy instruments, which seek to take advantage of the dynamics of signals that originate in the marketplace. The inverse of an environmental tax is an environmental subsidy, which places a premium on specific actions with presumably favorable implications. Subsidies can be granted directly with transfers and favorable loans, or indirectly with tax expenditures that allow polluters to offset their costs against tax liabilities. While taxes and subsidies are price-based policy instruments, their shared contrast is with quantity-based policy instruments, which place a cap on emissions and require markets with an exchange of pollution rights to be established. Where quantity-based allowances are handed out for free, they imply a subsidy to polluters, whereas allowances that become available only upon auctioning share the features of an environmental tax.

The entire basket of market-based policy instruments, price- or quantity-related, is different from the more conventional basket of 'command-and-control' policy instruments that do not speculate in provision of incentives, but merely prescribe what behavior is required by regulators under the law. 'Command and control' imposes standards, prescribes bans and requires procedures to be adhered to under a juridical perspective where compliance is an issue that may be resolved ultimately in the court. A third category consists of informal voluntary arrangements, based on more or less negotiated understandings between regulators and polluters. Obviously much of the research relating to environmental taxation addresses differences from and similarities to these other types of policy instruments. As such the environmental-tax-related research on policy instruments is very much part of the wider research agenda outlined here. Suggestions for further research have been indicated in most of the contributions to this Handbook. The present chapter attempts a bird's-eye view on the involved disciplines and the research frontier.

ECONOMICS: FROM MICROECONOMIC TO MACROECONOMIC PERSPECTIVES ON ENVIRONMENTAL TAXATION

The microeconomics of environmental taxation was a hallmark of the pioneering environmental economics literature. By using the available neoclassical toolkit, it was fairly straightforward to show how one could use a tax to limit environmental free-riding and achieve an 'optimal' balance between pollution abatement and environmental quality, and hence secure better and more efficient solutions than with conventional command-and-control policy. Many efforts went into exploring environmental taxation within the neoclassical paradigm in the decade that featured the publication of Baumol and Oates' *The Theory of Environmental Policy* (1975). Differences and similarities between using price and quantity instruments were widely explored, mainly identifying the common ground for these two instruments to attain an optimal level of pollution. During the period 1960–1990, economists focused almost entirely on the microeconomics of environmental taxes. There have been a few returns to microeconomics for exploring the differences and possible interplay between emissions trading and taxation, but it is by now becoming fairly difficult to point out any obvious lacunas in microeconomic neoclassical economics research on the topic.

Macroeconomics has moved center stage following the upsurge in climate mitigation policy and tax reform proposals, featuring many attempts to model with computerized tools the implications of environmental tax reforms (see Ekins and Speck, this volume). The main approach has been to employ or develop computerized general equilibrium models, or CGE models, with different levels of sectoral disaggregation. In

CGE macroeconomic models the behavior of economic agents is modeled according to microeconomic principles. Sometimes the environmental tax is simply represented with an exogenous carbon price to drive simulations or define scenarios with the models. Other modeling exercises have more specifically explored outcomes for different designs of environmental tax reforms (for an overview see Bergman 2005). An obvious challenge is that many of these CGE tools have been developed for other purposes and so often do not offer adequate resolution of fuel carriers and sectors to capture relevant substitution effects from environmental taxes. CGE models are best suited to analyzing important changes over the long run, rather than predicting short-run transition paths in a realistic way. For this reason another line of research has resorted more to macroeconomic demand models, which are considered to be more realistic over the short run, because their equations have been estimated from time-series data (Barker and Köhler 1998). The latter approach is far more data-demanding but better suited to identifying short-term imbalances for which policymakers would consider mitigation efforts. While better-grounded research is always preferable, we would like to stress here in particular the need for extending and developing more such econometric modeling frameworks.

Modeling has explored competitiveness effects and carbon leakage from carbon-energy taxation introduced under numerous different conditions, probing the implications of various approaches to revenue recycling and mitigation (see Braathen, this volume). The research frontier is moving toward exploring ambitious levels of carbon pricing, as required for phasing out fossil fuels, and the number of assumptions that need to be made are challenging to the predictive capacity of available modeling frameworks (Barker et al. 2011). Many of these exercises are now more in the nature of a conditional prediction, where care is required to present findings in view of the specific assumptions made. Many modelers are not explicit about their use of learning curves, for instance, or about the other ways in which technological progress is represented in modeling. Key assumptions generally seem to deserve more careful explanation when findings are being reported.

Labor market effects have attracted attention in view of questions raised in public finance literature (see below) over how wage earners may respond to changes in tax burdens, even if these changes are revenue-neutral (Kratena 2002). Wage earners may respond to higher marginal costs of energy and transport, even when these are partly offset by income tax reductions, with demands for compensation—as there will be secondary effects from a carbon tax when costs are passed on to general consumer goods. Although the magnitude of these effects may have been exaggerated, modeling factoring in the labor market reaction is desirable, and research needs related to environmental taxes are becoming tied in with an improved understanding of labor market effects. There is debate over specific elasticities of significance for final results, for instance relating to how wage earners will respond to a lowering of their real income (Goodstein 2003). Unfortunately many modeling studies have not taken into account that when recycling revenues reduce employers' social security contributions, the pass-on effect will be greatly diminished. As pointed out by Nordhaus (1993, 317) almost 20 years ago, the 'tail of revenue recycling would seem to wag the dog of climate-change policy.'

Macroeconomics has been almost entirely devoted to transport and energy. While many of the other environmental emissions may be too insignificant—or too complex— to warrant development of separate modeling frameworks (such as conventional air pollution, which can be linked to carbon for instance), it is surprising that water resources have not been the subject of more research interest. Since macroeconomic modeling was applied in the Netherlands for a pioneering study on the implications of introducing water effluent charges (MTPW 1975), there have been few further efforts in this important area. It seems to be an obvious candidate in building similar macroeconomic modeling frameworks. Although water increasingly is becoming a scarce resource, it seems that this scarcity, apart from a few attempts, has not yet been translated into pricing to an extent that would trigger interest and funding for such research.

Perhaps it would also be useful if future research, whether relating to energy, transport or water, were complemented with more bottom-up, sector-oriented studies. The business economics approach, in which case studies explore implications to strategies and responses at the level of the firm (Porter 1991), has been criticized for relying mainly on anecdotal evidence (Palmer et al. 1995), but now that environmental taxation has been introduced in many places around the world and companies have had to find ways to cope with it, opening up the black box of company responses to research offers a potential for new and significant insights (cf. the early and rigorous exploration of Canadian breweries in Smith and Sims 1985).

As mentioned by Morgenstern (1995) many economists were caught by surprise when public finance literature raised questions about what has since been dubbed the 'strong' double dividend hypothesis: that environmental taxes would be welfare-increasing by offering the prospect of reducing other distorting taxes on labor and capital. The basic argument of public finance economists has been that environmental taxes might exacerbate pre-existing distortions in the tax system or distortions caused by environmental regulations in place to internalize or remedy externalities. Jaeger (this volume) reviews the difficult theoretical debate over the strong double dividend and presents findings that indicate a possible oversight in the public finance literature relating to the so-called 'tax interaction effect.'

Goulder (1995) has suggested that the presence of tax interaction effects might be dependent on specific properties of the tax switch in question—hence the relevance of an 'intermediate' double dividend—but the implicit plea to move forward from what has emerged as a highly theoretical debate to investigations that are more specific in nature has been largely ignored. Hence a persistent fog and much controversy hang over questions related to the double dividend. Actual environmental tax reforms, for instance in European countries, have shifted revenues of generally less than 1 percent of GDP, so expectations as to what second dividends might be created at this level of ambition are perhaps slightly exaggerated. Even ambitious schemes of carbon taxation would face difficulties in increasing the scale of revenue-shifting in question, and hence more research attention ought perhaps to be devoted to the first dividend, emphasizing the environmental potentials of non-carbon-related taxes as well.

LEGAL RESEARCH: EXPLORING THE LEGAL BOUNDARIES

Legal scholars gradually began to pick up the theme of environmental taxation, and research interest seems to have been triggered especially where environmental taxes and other economic instruments have found their way into actual legislation or legislative debates. Whereas economics research in the field has been intense for half a century, tax law and environmental law have been addressing environmental taxation only over the past 30–35 years. Three different strands can be identified in particular in the legal literature on taxation.

First, there has been a focus on specific schemes featuring some element of environmental taxation; for instance, the US Superfund scheme seems to represent one of the early topics that became subject to intense legal research (Hedeman et al. 1987). The early legal studies of the Superfund, where taxes on chemicals were used pragmatically to finance the cleanup of sites contaminated with hazardous waste, focused on broader issues of liability and paid limited attention to efficiency issues. The Superfund was an attempt to institute a polluter-pays principle, even if the tax burden was pragmatically shifted from the polluters of the past to the potential polluters of the present. Secondly, legal scholars have more generally addressed the relative virtues of taxation as a policy instrument vis-à-vis other types of policy instruments, providing different perspectives and sometimes reaching other conclusions than economists and policy scientists (Westin 1992; Suprak 1995; Määttä 1997). Thirdly, within the framework of international law, environmental taxation issues related to trade law and WTO disputes have become an emerging field of inquiry in their own right (Kometani 1995; Wiener 1999).

Legal principles and rules can shape the details of environmental taxation and result in litigation, highlighting the need for more research to help define the legal parameters of environmental taxation. For instance, in 1994 the German Constitutional Court declared the coal levy on electricity (Kohle-pfennig) unconstitutional, holding that electricity consumers should not finance subsidies for domestic coal production. In 2009 the High Court in France scrapped a proposed carbon tax, as the exemptions had become too extensive. The European Court of Justice has made several pathbreaking decisions related to environmental taxes, such as in the case of the Finnish electricity tax (see Sairinen, this volume). We need more research to address how and why specific environmental taxation schemes might violate legal principles. These issues can include the legal distinction between taxes and fees and allocations of power among different levels of government.

The legal discipline is involved not only in defining the legal limits on environmental taxation but also as a participant in the legislative process of shaping the policies and legal design features of environmental taxation. Those engaged in the law often bring different views to the table. Legal scholars have been pointing out that next to cost-effectiveness several other objectives are equally relevant to legislators, in particular equity considerations and overall policy effectiveness. The broader set of evaluation criteria favored by legal scholars has been reflected in the debate over the general properties of economic instruments versus other, more traditional, standard-oriented policy instruments. Whereas environmental economists will tend to view the equity issue as a question simply of appropriate compensation mechanisms and transfers, once Pareto optimality has been achieved, legal scholars tend to study equity issues through other conceptual lenses to describe the degree of vertical (ability-to-pay) and horizontal (similarly situated) equity. Equity is about who wins and who loses, and so the topic cannot easily be escaped; indeed the entire acceptability of an environmental tax scheme may depend on whether equity and fairness implications are considered legitimate or are being challenged. One of the obvious issues with the Superfund scheme, for example, was how it made present purchasers of chemicals liable for the cleanup costs of past polluters.

These equity and fairness principles may rest in law or policy. The above mentioned ability-to-pay principle in some countries is a law codex that has institutionalized equity and legitimacy considerations. Legal requirements to this effect differ among different legal systems but comparative legal studies remain rare. Although tax law is perhaps not always explicit about its approach, the exploration of such deeper jurisprudential principles and their implications will often go to the core of dilemmas and challenges associated with environmental taxation.

Trade and competitiveness issues in a way are an extension of the equity and fairness issues, but they arise in a wider international and global domain. While economics research can phrase these aspects in terms of lost output and market opportunity, it takes legal research to comprehend and disentangle the powerful forces in play when international trade agreements are creating barriers for unilateral initiatives with environmental taxation. These trade agreements range from the regional level of the EU and NAFTA to the global level of WTO, and understanding the implications for environmental taxation of their complex legal frameworks is no small challenge. Within the European Union, for instance, taxation powers remain with member states, and introducing environmental taxes for the EU requires unanimity. Yet because of treaty restrictions on state aid, member states are constrained in their ability to adapt their taxation systems. State aid is considered from a functional perspective, and offering reduced energy taxes, for instance, will often qualify as state aid, which implies that EU member states are prevented from setting tax rates according to their own priorities. Although there has been substantial legal research on state aid issues, more comprehensive legal research on the implications for environmental taxation of the framework and the doctrines is required to fully understand how member states can act. The same can be said for WTO law. As reflected in Olsen (this volume) there is debate over how important concepts can be interpreted, which will be key to any border-tax-adjustment measures, for instance with respect to CO_2.

The significance of institutions and institutional arrangements for the functioning and manipulation of the market mechanism was perhaps most clearly identified by Ronald Coase in 'The Problem of Social Cost' (1960). Coase showed how definitions of property rights matter importantly as to who can be said to be causing the externality in the first place, and claimed that under the circumstances it is not important for the outcome whether it is the polluter or the victim who becomes liable for a payment—for which reason he proposed to consider also the relevance of a victim-pays principle. Today Coase's property rights approach features not only in emissions-trading schemes, but also in several other environmentally relevant settings, such as take-back obligations for packaging producers. Whereas economists widely perceive the differences between Pigou and Coase mainly under the price-versus-quantity approach, there is also a more fundamental institutional framework of differences relating to the allocation of property rights to which legal scholars could devote more attention. These institutional and legal issues play heavily into the question of the relative merits of property-based and tax approaches.

POLICY SCIENCES' RESEARCH: IMPLEMENTATION AND EX POST STUDIES

Policy sciences are the youngest subdiscipline to have addressed environmental taxation, with the first comprehensive study emerging in the 1980s (Bressers 1988). In addition to actual environmental taxation legislation, several years of experience with environmental taxation were required before policy sciences could address implementation and outcome. Actually Baumol and Oates had grappled with many of the policy issues in their quite neglected nontechnical companion volume to *The Theory of Environmental Policy* (1975) entitled *Economics, Environmental Policy and the Quality of Life* (1979). So had other economists in previous writings (Kneese and Bower 1968), but it was not feasible at the time to establish and research time-series reflecting actual environmental taxation experiences. In contrast to the ex ante perspective prevailing in economics, policy sciences offer an ex post approach to the study of environmental taxation. It is more explorative in nature and does not make strong assumptions about individual rationality and the perfect clearing of markets. As such it challenges to some extent the neoclassical theoretical framework and seeks to factor in institutional constraints and conditions influencing incentives of environmental taxation, while also exploring the interplay with other policy instruments.

Three strands of research within the policy sciences deserve mentioning. First there are the specific implementation studies, focusing on the environmental and economic outcomes of a specific environmental tax arrangement, which try to separate out the impact of the tax from other influences on trends in the tax base, whether of emissions, natural resources or products. A few of these studies have been pursued by scholars looking for elasticities for economic modeling purposes, but far more significant are the dedicated implementation studies in their own right (such as Bressers 1988). Secondly there are more behavioral studies exploring within a broader analytical framework the functioning and effectiveness of environmental taxation for public policy purposes (Eckersley 1995; Enevoldsen 2005). These studies tend to rely more on a theoretical framework different from the neoclassical and mainly belong to the discipline of political science. Finally a third and distinct line of research has emerged, addressing more specifically the politics of environmental taxation, taking a mainstream political science perspective on decision-making processes and the role of vested interests in suboptimal designs of environmental taxation schemes (Daugbjerg 2003). In this category we also find studies exploring the international politics of carbon taxation in particular.

Studies from policy sciences are potentially useful for improving our understanding of how environmental taxation schemes operate in the imperfect second-best world with which we are confronted. There are good political reasons why the optimal environmental tax is not likely to be the first choice of policymakers—as economists in the US will be the first to confirm. Even if introduced, tax rates are frequently too insignificant to reflect appropriately the external costs and to offer sufficient incentives, while tax bases are being distorted by vested interests and by tax administrations keen to assure stable revenue flows from inelastic items. Despite these constraints policy sciences have nevertheless been able to identify in several instances impacts of environmental taxation and also to identify mitigation mechanisms that have allowed administrators to get more behavioral response from schemes than a neoclassical perspective might have suggested.

Hybrid approaches that combine tax designs that might be able to survive the political decision-making process with supplementary policy measures deserve more research interest from the ex post perspective. Hybrid approaches are required to transcend institutional constraints in the market, for instance between producers and sellers, as well as the constraints of policymaking within the framework of individual nation states, vulnerable to international competition and trade laws. While conventional emissions taxes are fairly well researched, the more complex areas of product design and waste disposal deserve more scrutiny in the policy sciences. Deposit-refund systems, for instance, are different from a tax, but the specific approach for returning a deposit can be modulated in several ways to provide incentives similar to an environmental tax with a subsidy. Palmer and Walls (1999) have shown that from the theoretical perspective, an 'upstream combination tax-subsidy' (UCTS) has several attractive features similar to deposit-refund systems, and its consistency with principles of extended producer responsibility means it will feature more dynamic impacts than the take-back obligations prevailing in many countries today. The UCTS concept looks in actual fact like a promising return to a Pigouvian tax-bounty scheme. Taxes relating to natural resources more broadly are often closely related to reuse and recycling options for specific material streams (aggregates for instance) and also deserve more careful attention in future research.

Starting from a paradigm of behavioral assumptions based on bounded rationality and the notion of commitment (Sen 1977; Nielsen, this volume), policy sciences is the branch of research that could be expected to contribute to improving the framework for understanding the interplay of environmental taxation with other policy instruments and institutions, building on insights from psychology and sociology (Frey 1993). We would hope to see more of this research in the years to come, as it would seem strategically significant for improving our basic understanding of environmental taxation as a regulatory instrument.

INTERDISCIPLINARY RESEARCH ON ENVIRONMENTAL TAXATION

Interdisciplinary collaboration to explore environmental taxation has only rarely emerged, but would seem important to expand for a number of reasons (see for a promising example Metcalf and Weisbach 2009). The three research branches reviewed here appear to be relatively distinct, and scholars are clearly not taking sufficient advantage of insights coming from other disciplines. Economists tend to ignore legal constraints and institutions, regarding them as undesired barriers rather than as inevitable circumstances that must be integrated into research and analysis. Legal scholars, on the other hand, sometimes might be able to improve their juridical analysis by paying attention to economic principles penetrating the regulatory framework and underlying certain principles encoded in law, such as with the polluter pays principle, which reflects in particular a desire to avoid trade distortions from subsidies. Policy sciences, finally, while having devoted more effort to comprehending the basics of environmental economics and law as a basis for ex post research, often stumble when matching realities to economic and legal theory, and only rarely manage to frame findings in a way that would enable their uptake in those other disciplines.

Collaboration is made difficult for all the well-known reasons of requirements for merit-seeking within the ranks and files of the disciplines, but these constraints should not be exaggerated. There are many established scholars who have taken an interest in environmental taxation and who could afford to pursue more interdisciplinary projects and see what insights they might achieve. Opportunities for such research arise frequently, as research is commissioned by government agencies and foreign aid organizations to review and examine schemes of environmental taxation for policy support, for instance, and seem to require only some follow-up with dedicated research publications. There have been numerous capacity-creating projects on environmental tax reform in developing countries (see Rodi et al., this volume), but only few attempts to revisit them with systematic analysis. Differences in institutional background would nevertheless make interesting cases for explorations of the potential for environmental taxation to prevail in quasi-planned economies of developing countries and emerging economies.

Emissions trading of certificates for carbon has emerged as an important approach for restricting further increases in emissions and is the dominant instrument in several countries. Still, taxes and excises remain in place on fuels, and so the question of the interactions between environment-related taxation and emissions trading arises. These interactions are poorly understood, both from the theoretical and from the practical perspective. Under the impact of budgetary crisis some countries have with separate taxes introduced a floor for the carbon price, while others have instituted a safety valve to prevent prices from exceeding certain thresholds. A number of institutional constraints arise from the emissions-trading schemes, due to the limitations of specified commitment-periods or restrictions on the quantities of certificates that can be used to offset domestic emissions in relation to agreed reduction targets. These tax-trading interactions not only call for more research, but due to the very nature of the complexities, seem a strong candidate for more interdisciplinary collaboration.

A Pigouvian tax is one that equals marginal external costs. What exactly these costs are have, for a long time, remained a big question, which may help explain why environmental taxation initially was regarded as a somewhat exotic issue. However, beginning in the late 1990s, and thanks to interdisciplinary research efforts from environmental economists, environmental engineers and health specialists, the first actual estimates were published for the external costs of air pollution (ExternE 1999). These figures have represented a major accomplishment for the ability to carry out economic analyses of environmental policies and also provide a useful benchmark for the level of appropriate environmental taxation (Miranda and Hale 2002). As such they seem to demonstrate that in our investigations interdisciplinary analysis will in fact often be required in order to go beyond the research frontier. The availability of these estimates is now creating spin-offs for analyses in the various disciplines. Under EU law, for instance, estimates of external costs are used to inform decisions about allowable state aid for renewables and will be required for administration of the Eurovignette, the road-user charge for heavy-goods vehicles. There is a huge agenda for research activity, interdisciplinary in nature, aiming at providing more estimates of external costs for other emissions and substances, as well as for water pollution and chemicals.

Global questions and challenges, related in particular to carbon taxation and trade distortions, constitute a further area of research where interdisciplinary collaboration would be likely to yield important new insights. Referring to the questions and issues mentioned in the section on economics above, we think it would be valuable if lawyers, economists and policy scientists were able to address them with a shared conceptual framework. There is little disagreement that carbon pricing will be a crucial policy instrument for phasing out fossil fuels, but in the absence of a global framework of agreement, individual countries are constrained in their actions. For this reason the possible introduction of border tax adjustment (BTA) has been on the agenda for quite some time. There are numerous ways in which BTA can be implemented, but basically the principle is to tax imported products according to their embedded carbon, while rebating products for exports. With BTA a country or region can create a level playing field for products of domestic and foreign origin in its own market. Apart from the important question of WTO conformity to BTA (see the legal section above), there are wider issues relating to the relative economic significance of BTAs for different sectors and products, as well as policy issues relating to the diplomacy required for successful BTA, that usefully could be addressed in interdisciplinary projects. It seems to us that the fragmented disciplinary perspectives on BTA so far have provided only partial insights and that interdisciplinary research providing a broader and consistent understanding of BTA would be potentially of very large significance for carbon mitigation policies.

Finally, we would highlight the need for more research relating to the distributional implications of environmental taxation. Taxation is first of all an instrument intended to serve the purpose of financing public expenditures, and questions about the associated distributional burdens are inevitable. While it is generally understood that environmental taxes can be regressive in the same way as other consumption taxes, there has been very limited research to date exploring to what extent this can be substantiated with empirical data. A couple of studies have found that environmental taxes related to transport tend in fact to be progressive, and one study put the regressiveness of environmental taxes in perspective by showing that a value-added tax (VAT) is three to four times more so, as measured with a Gini coefficient (Kosonen, this volume). Obviously these findings might differ across different tax systems, and so distributional questions and possible mitigation mechanisms seem to be an obvious candidate for future interdisciplinary research projects. At the end of the day there is no legislator who cares only about overall social efficiency—each one cares also for his own constituency and whether it stands to win or lose from the environmental tax measures in question.

FINAL OBSERVATIONS

In acknowledgement of not being in the first-best world of economics, Baumol and Oates (1971) developed their second-best theorem, recommending the establishment of environmental standards, and then the application of economic instruments to support enforcement. This solution became known as the standard-pricing approach. However, we are not in a second-best world either, due to numerous influences from regulatory institutions and the politics of taxation, which are conflicting with textbook recommendations. While this may be disappointing to scholars, it also offers challenges and should be a stimulus for further research on environmental taxation.

As we move away from even the second-best world, we increasingly appreciate the need to reorient research. The double dividend debate and the associated tax interaction effect understandably have been discussed in a highly stylized world of models, but the public finance literature increasingly needs to connect with the 'real' world of environmental challenges and problems, where environmental taxation is being considered as a policy instrument. For example, some of the key findings have been presented under the strict assumption that externalities have been internalized with existing regulations, but it is reassuring that there are now estimations available from another branch of the environmental economics literature, allowing for a check on theoretical assumptions. In addition, the public finance and other literature has often addressed carbon for very valid reasons, but the time has come to expand findings in relation to the long-standing problems of air quality, water and waste, where many governments have experiences with the use of environmental taxation and where huge challenges still prevail.

Doing away with harmful subsidies has often been mentioned as a precursor to environmental taxation, as subsidies are distorting the desired internalization. However, the role of subsidies is ambiguous in several ways. Pigou, in *A Study of Public Finance* (1928), suggested that the proceeds from internalizing taxes could be disbursed as subsidies to reward positive externalities (Pigou 1947, 99–101). There is a category of environmental taxes, known in Germany as lenkungs-abgaben (literally, 'linked taxes'), where the legal requirement is that taxation revenues specifically are matched to the needed expenditures (the equivalence principle) for a particular purpose. Due to the legal and institutional context, often with collection by specific-purpose entities rather than the state, they seem to be distinct from what is understood by Anglo-Saxon scholars under the term 'hypothecation,' and some observers even regard them as payment vehicles for common-property regimes of the Ostrom type (Ostrom 1990). One prominent example is Poland's National Environmental Fund, which was established during the 1989 events and which has played a key role in the environmental transition. Similar special-purpose funds are in place in several other countries. Unfortunately there are only few examples in the literature of scholars who have researched these approaches theoretically and empirically, but they would seem to deserve more careful attention.

Subsidies are also in play under a different name: tax expenditures. According to Kleinbard (2010, 18) the use of tax expenditures in general has become significant because they can be presented to taxpayers as 'targeted tax cuts,' while in reality they are promoting new expenditures that policymakers favor. Even if they are not always immediately visible in the budget, they become subject to the same ambiguity of subsidies more generally (Surrey 1973) and represent substantial expenditures (Hungerford 2011). Tax expenditures accounted for about two-thirds of energy-related expenditures in the US federal budget in 2007, for instance (EIA 2008, xii). Environmentally harmful tax expenditures would naturally be inadvisable under our environmental perspective, but to the extent that tax expenditures are available as rewards for positive environmental behavior—for instance, in the case of renewables—the implications might be different (Milne 2009), and there seems to be a lacuna in the literature deserving serious attention. Still, tax expenditures might actually be more distorting than direct budget expenditures, because they hollow out the respective tax bases and call for higher marginal tax rates. They also tend to favor higher-income groups and so distort the income redistribution of the tax system. We think that the role and effect of tax expenditures warrants more research attention.

Environmental taxes are a hybrid tool with both revenue-raising and regulatory properties. Electronic databases (Harzing's publish or perish) return several thousand academic references published after 1990 to a search on the simple term 'environmental tax,' and many more references can be identified when exploring research on synonyms such as 'resource tax,' 'green tax,' 'eco-tax,' and so on. The amount of practical and academic interest in the topic has become overwhelming and it seems to represent perhaps the most important potential for innovation of our tax systems in the 21st century, with a revenue potential several times exceeding that of a possible Tobin tax on stock exchange transactions. While OECD countries have introduced environmentally related taxes to an average extent of 2 percent of GDP, there are individual countries that have managed to double that level to 4–5 percent, implying that such taxes now constitute 8–10 percent or more of their total taxes. Analysis has shown that it would be possible to further double that level simply by adopting what is best practice in environmental taxation across the world, for instance, to use the environmentally related taxes to substitute for other more distorting taxes on labor and capital. Naturally there would be many challenges and difficulties to consider, and so research is likely to play an important role for a qualified transition of our tax systems. As this Handbook has demonstrated, there are implications in many different domains to take into consideration. To progress in our understanding of these implications, closer and more advanced types of research cooperation among scholars from different disciplines will be required. We hope that this Handbook, by offering a comprehensive overview of ongoing research on environmental taxation, will be a useful tool to this purpose.

We think there are good reasons to address environmental taxation, first and foremost from the perspective of pressing environmental challenges that are requiring a huge effort to reconcile them with our economic, legal and political systems. While the conventional approach is to apply an established theoretical framework to the investigation of a specific issue, we recommend keeping in mind that some of these environmental challenges now have multiple, complex dimensions, which responsible researchers must also carefully tend. We will close this chapter with a quote from Pigou (1920, 4–5), who reminded us nearly a century ago that

> One who desired knowledge of man, apart from the fruits of knowledge, would seek it in the history of religious enthusiasm, of martyrdom or of love; he would not seek it in the marketplace. When we elect to watch the play of human motives that are ordinary—that are sometimes mean and dismal and ignoble—our impulse is not the philosopher's impulse, knowledge for the sake of knowledge, but rather the physiologist's, knowledge for the healing that knowledge may help to bring.

REFERENCES

Barker, T. and J. Köhler (1998), *International Competitiveness and Environmental Policies*, Cheltenham, UK: Edward Elgar.

Barker, T., C. Lutz, B. Meyer and H. Pollitt (2011), 'Models for projecting the impacts of ETR', in P. Ekins and S. Speck (eds), *Environmental Tax Reform (ETR)—A Policy for Green Growth*, Oxford, UK: Oxford University Press, pp. 175–203.

Barraqué, B. (2000), 'Assessing the efficiency of economic instruments: reforming the French Agences de l'Eau', in M.S. Andersen and R.U. Sprenger (eds), *Market-based Instruments for Environmental Management: Politics and Institutions*, Cheltenham, UK: Edward Elgar.

Baumol, W.J. and W.E. Oates (1971), 'The use of standards and prices for protection of the environment', *Swedish Journal of Economics*, **73** (1), 42–54.

Baumol, W.J. and W.E. Oates (1979), *Economics, Environmental Policy and the Quality of Life*, New Jersey, US: Prentice-Hall.

Baumol, W.J. and W.E. Oates (1988), *The Theory of Environmental Policy*, Cambridge, UK: Cambridge University Press (first published 1975).

Bergman, L. (2005), 'CGE modelling of environmental policy and resource management', in K.G. Mäler and J. Vincents (eds), *Handbook of Environmental Economics*, Vol. 3, Amsterdam, Netherlands: Elsevier.

Bressers, H. (1988), 'A comparison of the effectiveness of incentives and directives: the case of the Dutch water quality policy', *Policy Studies Review*, 7 (3), 500–518.

Coase, R.H. (1960), 'The problem of social cost', *Journal of Law and Economics*, **3**, 1–44.

Coase, R.H. (1988), *The Firm, the Market and the Law*, Chicago, IL, US: Chicago University Press.

Committee on Japan's Experience in the Battle Against Air Pollution (1997), *Japan's Experience in the Battle Against Air Pollution*, Japan: Committee on Japan's Experience in the Battle Against Air Pollution.

Daugbjerg, C. and G.T. Svendsen (2003), 'Designing green taxes in a political context: from optimal to feasible environmental regulation', *Environmental Politics*, **12** (4), 76–95.

Eckersley, R. (1995), *Markets, the State and the Environment: An Overview*, Melbourne, Australia: Palgrave Macmillan.

Energy Information Administration (EIA) (2008), *Federal Financial Incentives and Subsidies in Energy Markets 2007*, Washington, DC, US: Energy Information Administration.

Enevoldsen, M. (2005), *The Theory of Environmental Agreements and Taxes: CO₂ Policy Performance in Comparative Perspective*, Cheltenham, UK: Edward Elgar.

ExternE (1999), *External Costs of Energy*, Vol. 1–8, Brussels, Belgium: Community Research.

Frey, B. (1993), 'Motivation as a limit to pricing', *Journal of Economic Psychology*, **14** (4), 635–64.

Goodstein, E. (2003), 'The death of the Pigovian tax: policy implications from the double dividend debate', *Land Economics*, **79** (3), 402–14.

Goulder, L. (1995), 'Environmental taxation and the double dividend: a reader's guide', *International Tax and Public Finance*, **2** (2), 157–83.

Hedeman, W.N., P.E. Shorb, and C.A. McLean (1987), 'The Superfund amendments and reauthorization act of 1986: statutory provisions and EPA implementation', *Hazardous Waste and Hazardous Materials*, **4** (2), 193–210.

Hungerford, T.L. (2011), 'Tax expenditures and the federal budget', RL34622, Washington, DC, US: CRS Report for Congress, http://www.fas.org/sgp/crs/misc/RL34622.pdf

Kleinbard, E.D. (2010), 'The Congress within the Congress: how tax expenditures distort our budget and our political process', *Ohio Northern University Law Review*, **36** (1), 1–30.

Kneese, A. and B. Bower (1968), *Managing Water Quality: Economics, Technology, Institutions*, Washington, DC, US: Resources for the Future.

Kometani, K. (1995), 'Trade and environment: how should WTO panels review environmental regulations under GATT articles III and XX', *Northwestern Journal of International Law and Economics*, **16**, 441–77.

Kratena, K. (2002), *Environmental Tax Reform and the Labour Market*, Cheltenham, UK: Edward Elgar.

Määttä, K. (1997), *Environmental Taxes: From an Economic Idea to a Legal Institution*, Helsinki, Finland: Finnish Lawyers Publishing.

Matsuno, Y. and K. Ueta (2000), 'A socio-economic evaluation of the SOx charge in Japan', in M.S. Andersen and R.U. Sprenger (eds), *Market-based Instruments for Environmental Management: Politics and Institutions*, Cheltenham, UK: Edward Elgar.

Metcalf, G.E. and D. Weisbach (2009), 'The design of a carbon tax', *Harvard Environmental Law Review*, **33** (2), 499–556.

Milne, J.E. (2009), 'US climate change policy: a tax expenditure microcosm with environmental dimensions', in L. Philipps et al. (eds), *Tax Expenditures: State of the Art*, Proceedings of the 2009 Osgoode conference.

Miranda, M.L. and B.W. Hale (2002), 'A taxing environment: evaluating the multiple objectives of environmental taxes', *Environmental Science and Technology*, **36** (24), 5289–95.

Morgenstern, R. (1995), 'Environmental taxes: dead or alive?', Discussion paper 96-03, Washington, DC, US: Resources for the Future.

MTPW (Ministry of Transport and Public Works) (1975), *The Combat Against Surface Water Pollution in the Netherlands*, The Hague: MTPW.

Nordhaus, W. (1993), 'Optimal greenhouse gas reductions and tax policy in the DICE model', *American Economic Review*, **83** (2), 313–17.

Ostrom, E. (1990), *Governing the Commons*, Cambridge, UK: Cambridge University Press.

Palmer, K. and M. Walls (1999), 'Extended product responsibility: an economic assessment of alternative policies', Discussion paper 99-12, Washington, DC, US: Resources for the Future.

Palmer, K., W. Oates and P. Portney (1995), 'Tightening environmental standards: the benefit-cost paradigm or the no-cost paradigm?', *Journal of Economic Perspectives*, **9** (4), 119–32.

Pigou, A.C. (1920), *Economics of Welfare*, London, UK: Macmillan.

Pigou, A.C. (1947), *A Study in Public Finance*, London, UK: Macmillan (first published 1928).

Porter, M. (1991), 'America's green strategy', *Scientific American*, **264**, 168.

Rahm, D. (1998), 'Superfund and the politics of US hazardous waste policy', *Environmental Politics*, **7** (4), 75–91.

Sen, A. (1977), 'Rational fools: a critique of the behavioural foundations of economic theory', *Philosophy and Public Affairs*, **6** (4), 317–44.

Smith, J.B. and Sims, W.A. (1985), 'The impact of pollution charges on productivity growth in Canadian brewing', *Rand Journal of Economics*, **18** (3), 410–23.

Suprak, M.A. (1995), 'Environmental tax law: challenge of the 1990s', *Journal of State Taxation*, **14**, 35–51.

Surrey, S.S. (1973), *Pathways to Tax Reform: The Concept of Tax Expenditures*, Cambridge, MA, US: Harvard University Press.

Vogel, D. (1993), 'Representing diffuse interests: environmental policy', in K. Weaver and B. Rockman, *Do Institutions Matter? Government Capabilities in the United States and Abroad*, Washington, DC, US: Brookings Institution.

Westin, R.A. (1992), 'Understanding environmental taxes', *Tax Lawyer*, **46**, 327–62.

Wiener, J.B. (1999), 'Global environmental regulation: instrument choice in legal context', *Yale Law Journal*, **108** (4), 677–800.

Index

abatement costs
  balancing with benefits 460–68
  global carbon tax 460–68
  least-cost abatement theory 20
  marginal abatement cost matching 36–40,
      48–50, 143, 360, 363, 462
  marginal external costs modeling 142–4
  marginal social damage 48, 211–12, 217–18,
      227
  studies 239
  technological change, influences on
      368–70
  studies 371, 373–4
ability-to-pay principle 63–4, 71–2, 96–8
accidents, environmental 10
  economic principles, and 401–2
  negligence 402–3
  optimal/efficient care levels 402–3
  road transport externalities 287
  strict liability for 402–4
  taxes, correctional capabilities of 296
  unilateral/bilateral accidents 402–3
Acid Rain Program, US 39
adoption decisions 365–6
agricultural subsidies 45, 226
air pollution
  air quality research 146
  road transport
    externalities 284–6, 293–5
    proportion from 285
    taxes, correctional capabilities of 293–5
air transport see civil aviation
allowances trading see carbon tax; emissions
    trading
Alm, J. 252–5, 257–8, 261–3
Andersen, M.S. 23, 112, 447
Australia 4, 66–8, 80, 470
Austria 290–91, 294–5

Banzhaf, H.S. 252–5, 257–8, 261–3
Baron, R. 239
Baumol, W. 5, 17–18, 23, 27, 486, 489
Baumol-Oates tax 5, 23
behavioral economics
  behavioral assumptions 440–42
  principles 440–42
  rational choice 441–2
  research trends and opportunities 452–3,

486–7
  self-interest 440–43
  technological change, and 372–4
  see also bounded rationality theory
Belgium 259–60, 290–91, 294
border tax adjustments 79–80, 489
  competitiveness 238, 391
  under GATT 198, 201–2
  purpose 201
bounded rationality theory
  cognitive restraints of 444–6
  earmarking, and 450
  endowment effect 443, 450
  environmental taxes, implications for
      447–53
  instrument design, and 448–53
  organizational responses 446–7
  overcoming barriers 448–52
  policy development, influences on
      448–51
  profit, relevance of 446–9
  research opportunities 452–3
  satisficing 445
  social motivation 442–3
Bovenberg, A.L. 216–17, 220–21, 225, 239
Brazil 65
Bressers, H. 370, 409
British Columbia, carbon tax study see
    Canada
Brundtland Report (1987) (UN) 33
Bruvoll, A. 355, 409
Buchanan, J.M. 108, 231–2
Bulgaria 290–91, 294

Canada
  cap-and-trade policies 179–80, 188
  carbon tax
    background 175–80
    challenges 182–3, 185–7
    design criteria 180–83
    economic efficiency, of 182–3
    lessons from 189–90
    long-term prospects for 187–9
    political context 179–80, 185–9
    purpose 182–3
    revenue-neutrality, and 181–3
    social impacts, of 183–4
    tax unfairness, assessing 183–4

climate change, attitudes to 177–8
CO₂ emissions 459
greenhouse gas mitigation burden 470
transaction costs, studies 280
cap-and-trade policies
    Canada, in 179–80, 188
    preferences for 175
    see also emissions trading
capture theory 231–2
carbon tax
    cap-and-trade, preferences for 175
    carbon equalization provisions 391
    carbon leakage mitigation schemes 381–2,
        391–2
    competitiveness, and 391–3
    compulsory *vs.* noncompulsory taxes
        175–6
    double dividend on 24
    elasticity of supply and demand, and 162
    France, in 52, 56, 72, 241, 392
    modeling 220–22
    social impacts, of 183–4
    tax unfairness, assessing 183–4
    United States, in 177
    see also Canada; Finland; global carbon tax
Cement Sustainability Initiative (CSI) 392
chapeau conditions, under GATT 204–5
charges
    definitions 20–22, 34, 104
    distinction, from taxes 20, 34, 87, 104
Chile 106
China
    CO₂ emissions 459
    economic development trends 303
    environmental challenges 314–15
    environmental taxes 8, 320
        challenges 316–17
        definition 305–6
        design criteria 317–19
        double dividend 311–14
        environmental effects 312–13
        fuel taxes 312–13
        intergovernmental relationships, and 260,
            313–14
        land use taxes 308–9
        pollution charge system 309–11
        research trends 146, 304–5
        resource tax 306–7, 313
        scope and context 305–6
        taxation effects 311–12
        types of 306–9, 312–13
        VAT 307–9
        vehicle taxes 307–8, 315–16
    greenhouse gas mitigation burden 470
    tax distortions 311–12

tax reform, generally 303–4, 315–16
    design criteria 317–19
    tax administration 319
civil aviation taxes 80–81, 264–5
Clean Air for Europe Programme 146
climate change *see* global environmental
    problems
Climate Change Agreement (UK) 372, 390
Climate Change Levy (UK) 105, 114–15, 240,
    372, 390, 415
Coase, R.H. 17, 30, 275, 400–402, 485
Coase's theory on reciprocal nature of harm
    institutional role 485
    Pigouvian taxation, and 10, 17, 30
    practical advantages 401, 485
    theorem 10, 30, 400–401, 479
command and control approach *see* regulation
Commission on Environmental Markets and
    Economic Performance (UK) 393
commodity taxes 162–7
competitiveness
    environmental tax reform, and
        compensation measures 390–92
        complexity of 379–80
        double dividend effect 379
        energy-efficient equipment, role of 380
        exchange rates 381
        at firm level 386–8
        influences on, complexity of 379–80
        modeling 381–6
        partial exemptions 379
        research on 381–2
        revenue recycling 380
        at sector level 388–93
    environmental taxes, and
        carbon tax 391–3
        influence of 378–80
        international trade regimes, and 193, 485
        mitigation policies 381–3, 390–92
        multilevel governance, and 270–71
        negative impact on 237–40
        non-discrimination, WTO policy on
            194–5
        pollution havens, influence on 459–60
        research studies 237–40
        sectoral agreements 391–3
        and tax subsidies, in EU 78–9
    generally
        assessment measures 378
        definition 377
        influences on 2, 5, 377–80
        most-favoured nation principle 195
        national/international influences on 377–8
        national treatment principle 195
        principles of 377

computable general equilibrium (CGE) models
  decoupling, and 162, 355–6, 481–2
  disadvantages 355–6
concentration-response functions (CRF)
  impact pathway approach, and 148, 150–51
Conference on the Changing Atmosphere
  (Toronto, 1988) 457
conflict of laws
  civil aviation taxes 80–81
  constitutional law 69, 72
  international taxes 79–81
  rights and freedoms, and 71–2
congestion
  road transport externalities 288–9, 295,
    297–9
constitutional law
  earmarked taxes, influences on 106–8
  environmental taxes, and
    legal authority for 65–9
    revenue allocation 68–9
  principle of legality 70
  remedies, availability under 63
  retroactivity 71
  substantive law concepts 63–4
  taxing powers 63
consumer prices
  environmental tax impact on 169–70, 172–3
consumers
  economic burden on 162–7
  preference assumptions, and 223–4
  relative consumption effects 223–4
  social impacts, of environmental taxes
    183–4
costs
  least-cost pollution reduction 17–18, 20
  marginal external costs, modeling 142–4
  reductions, in labor markets 24, 110–11,
    164–5
  see also abatement costs; road transport;
    transaction costs
countries in transition
  characteristics of 122–3
  environmental fiscal policy 5, 122–4
  general tax policy in 122–3
  see also Vietnam
Croatia 280
Cyprus 290–91, 294
Czech Republic 278–9, 290–91, 294

databases, of environmental instruments
  advantages 321, 324–5
  characteristics 326
  database criteria 325
    accessibility 329–30
    datedness 328–30, 338–9

instrument coordination 95
  purpose 327–9
  reliability of 328–9, 338–9
  scope of content 328–30, 338
  usability 329–30
database reviews
  Economicsinstruments.com 333–4
  Environmental Fiscal Reform Database
    334–5
  Federal Database of State Incentives for
    Renewables and Efficiency (DSIRE)
    337–8
  OECD/EU Database on Instruments
    Used in Environmental Policy and
    Natural Resources Management
    331–3, 338
  Taxes in Europe Database 335–8
  influences on 321
  information needs, and 322–3
  maintenance concerns 338
  OECD/EU studies of 321–2
de Mooji, R.A. 216–17, 225
decoupling, environmental taxes from other
  taxes
  analysis
    aggregate econometric analysis 350–53
    cause and effect chains 344–5, 357
    challenges 356–7
    computable general equilibrium (CGE)
      models 162, 355–6, 481–2
    context, need for 344–5
    decomposition analysis 343–52
    elasticities of demand/price, and 353–5
    evidence sources for 348–9
    firm level data, as basis for 353
    identification criteria 346–8
    indicators 346, 348
    methods, generally 349–50
    studies 350–56
  generally
    absolute decoupling 343, 348
    challenges 344–5
    definition 343–4
    drivers for 344, 350–53, 356–7
    importance of 343
    research examples 348–9
dedicated taxes *see* earmarked taxes
Demand Side Management Program (DSM)
  372
Denmark
  agricultural taxes and regulation 448, 451–2
  bounded rationality, and 448–52
  economic theory, and 237
  energy consumption tax 353, 449–50
  regressivity, of environmental taxes 167

road transport taxes 290–91, 294
tax reform modeling 383–6
tradable quotas 451–2
waste taxation scheme 447–8
design criteria, for environmental taxes
    administration, responsibility for 5, 95–6,
        270
    agency cooperation, importance of 95–6
    bounded rationality theory, and 448–53
    challenges 100–101
    earmarked taxes 5, 102–6, 116–17
    global carbon tax 457–8
    hybrid approaches 487
    instrument coordination 95
    international trade rules, and 193
    legal criteria 484–5
    non-environmental tax expenditure 94
    polluter pays principle 87–8, 107, 411
    practicability principle 90
    public utilities, as taxpayers 93–4
    tax base 90–91
    tax expenditures 28–9, 97–8, 450–52
    tax rates 5, 91–3
    tax reductions 94–5
    tax shift 40–42, 93–4, 111
    taxable events 89
    taxing powers 88–9
    transaction cost 275
Dewees, D.N. 231, 405
direct taxes, definition 62
double dividend 56–7
    China, application in 311–14
    competitiveness, and 379
    distortionary taxes 164, 212–17, 227
    dynamic efficiency, and 40–41
    earmarked taxes, and 24, 110–11
    environmental effects on productivity, and
        222–3
    fiscal neutrality, and 24–5, 211, 214
    forms of 215–16, 483
    generally 221–2
    individual preference assumptions, and
        223–4
    inefficiency, and 224–5
    labor market influences 24, 110–11, 164–5,
        225
    market failure correction mechanism, as
        211–12
    motivations behind 211–12
    political importance 33
    preexisting inefficient tax programs, and
        224–5
    principles 24, 56–7, 110–11, 164–5
    research 226–7
    special circumstances 221–5

tax interaction effect, and 213–14, 216–21
    algebraic errors 217–18
    benchmark bias 218–19
    benefit-side tax interaction effects 222
    direct/indirect taxes, compounding effects
        219–21
    theory development 213–21, 227
    welfare changes 216–17, 223–4

E3ME, modeling economic impact of
    environmental tax reform 382–6
earmarked taxes
    advantages and disadvantages 105–6,
        108–14
    balancing revenue with efficiency 40–41,
        104, 112–14
    bounded rationality theory, and 450
    choice, influences on 106–8
    constitutional law, and 106–8
    definition 103–6
    design criteria 5, 102–6, 116–17
    double dividend, and 24, 110–11
    examples
        Climate Change Levy (UK) 105, 114–15
        Hazardous Substances Response Fund
            (Superfund) (US) 116
        Oil Spill Liability Trust Fund (US) 116
        Permanent Forest Fund (Portugal)
            115–16
    generally 5, 101–3
    geographic balance, and 113
    negative impact 103
    political acceptance of 109–11
    research focus 108–9, 118
    research opportunities 117–18
    revenue recycling, and 104, 108
    tax-aversion, and 108–9
    transparency 109–10
    see also global carbon tax
Eastern Europe
    earmarked taxes 103
    greenhouse gas mitigation burden 470
    multilevel governance 270
    road transport taxes 290–91, 293–4
ecological tax reform *see* environmental tax
    reform
economic theory
    capture theory 231–2
    environmental taxation, and
        background and development 479–81
        policy, influence on 235–7
    neoclassical economic assumptions 439–40
    statutory and economic incidence of
        taxation, on 162
    use of, reasons for 39, 231–5, 439

see also behavioral economics; bounded
  rationality theory; Coase; Pigouvian
  taxation
The Economics of Welfare 15–16
Economicsinstruments.com 333–4
EcoSenseWeb 147
efficiency
  accidents, optimal/efficient care levels 402
  environmental taxes
    context, role of 37
    double dividend, and 224–5
    dynamic efficiency 40–41
    externalities, balancing negative and
        positive 142–4
    inefficiency 35–6, 224–5
    influences on 231–3, 408–9
    political efficiency 231–3
    static efficiency 36–40
    studies 409
    tax shift 40–42, 93–4, 111
    vs. revenue generation 40–41, 93–4, 111
  pollution optimum level, managing 37–40,
      399–400
elasticity of demand 162, 212–13
  decoupling studies 353–5
electricity production externalities 141–2,
    144–5
emissions charges
  advantages 408
  definition 22–3, 34
  Europe, development in 20
  payment responsibilities 30
  transaction costs 278
emissions trading
  basic principles 30–31, 410–11
  bounded rationality theory, and 451–2
  challenges 47–8, 175
  compulsory *vs.* noncompulsory taxes 175–6
  earmarked taxes, and 118
  enforcement 411
  grandfathering 29–30, 411–12
  interest groups, influence of 411
  misuse of 409, 416
  policy options 175–6, 416–17
  research opportunities 31
  restrictions imposed on 488
  vs. taxes 29–31, 47–50
    choice criteria 48–50, 54–6
    combining 50–52
  see also carbon tax; European Emissions
      Trading Scheme
energy prices 372
energy taxes
  conflict of laws 80–81
  definition 34

distributional impact
  on consumer prices 169–70
  in EU 168–72
  on households 6, 170–73
  research trends 489
  research trends 482–3
  restructuring options 41
  as source of revenue, role 280
  see also carbon tax
Enevoldsen, M. 256, 350–51
enforcement *see* monitoring and enforcement
environmental economics
  basis for 439–40
  behavioral assumptions 440–43
  bounded rationality, implications for 10,
      447–53
  economic assumptions 439–40
  organizational responses 446–7
  profit, relevance of 446–9
environmental federalism 252, 255
environmental fiscal reform
  advantages 26
  in context 4
  in countries in transition 5, 122–4
  definition 26
  harmful subsidy measures 43–7
  research trends and opportunities 43–7,
      480–81
  welfare gains 26
  see also environmental tax reform
Environmental Fiscal Reform Database 334–5
environmental instruments
  choice of 423–4
    influences on 422–3
  design criteria 95
  instrument mixes 95, 414–16
    limitations 416
    research opportunities 416–17
  market-based instruments 19
    advantages 414, 439
    definition 406
    development trends 425–6
    influences on 321
    limitations 406–7
    regulation, compared with 9–10, 232, 235,
        406–10
    studies of 321–5
  new environmental policy instruments
      (NEPI), trends 422–3
  patents, influence on 371–2
  research opportunities 416–17
  studies of
    EU 321–5
    OECD 321, 323–5
  see also databases

environmental liability 10
  accident law, economic principles 401–2
  optimal taxation, and 402–3, 414–17
  regulation, and 404–7
    burden of proof 405
    choice criteria 404–6
    combination, need for 405–6
    incentive effects 414
    information asymmetries 404
    insolvency 404–5
    insurance 404–5
    limitations 404–5
  strict liability
    for environmental harm 403–4
    vs. negligence 402–3
environmental policy
  choices, studies of influences on 235–7
  environmental tax role in 2, 414–17
    common markets, and 74–5
    stages and trends 424–6
  market failure, and 192
  objectives 61
  policy coordination
    competition policy 78–9
    tax policy 74–8
environmental tax reform
  efficiency *vs.* revenue generation 40–42
  generally
    approaches to 175–6, 390–92, 423–4
    definition 26, 379
    economic rationale 26, 33, 35–6, 38–41
    environmentally related taxes, role in
      25–6
    history and development 24–6, 480–81
    influences on 422–4
    purpose 379, 382–3
    revenue recycling 380, 382–3
    stages/trends in 425–6
  incentive taxes *vs.* fiscal taxes 61–2
  policy options 40–43, 48–52
    combination approaches 50–52
    compulsory *vs.* noncompulsory taxes
      175–6
    coregulation 423
    deregulation 424
    development and stages 41–2, 425–6
    EU, in 424–6
    special tax provisions, approaches to
      390–92, 490–91
    tax shift 40–42
  see also environmental fiscal reform;
    Finland; Vietnam
environmental taxation, generally
  background 3–4
  bounded rationality theory, and 10, 447–53

  definition 3
  equity and fairness principles 484–5
  history and development 479–81
  hybrid nature 4, 490–91
  lifecycle approach 1–2
  non-discrimination, WTO policy on 194–5
  purpose 1, 15
  scope of 25–31, 491
  taxation generally, differences from 399
  see also environmental policy; environmental
    taxes
environmental taxes
  advantages 39, 161, 408–9, 439
  characteristics
    dual nature 59, 69
    limitations 408
    price responsiveness 162–3
    principles 70–71
    retroactivity, and 71
    substitution mechanisms 136
    tax base focus 21, 93
    taxing powers 88–9, 98–9
    tax types 33–4
  context
    global 24–6, 79
    historical 33
  definitions 20–23, 33–4, 60–63, 399
    charges 20, 34, 87, 104
    consumer taxes 62
    direct/indirect taxes 62, 163
    emissions trading, whether taxes 29–30
    environmentally related taxes 21–2, 25,
      34, 61, 85–6
    incentive taxes *vs.* fiscal taxes 61–2
    quotas *vs.* taxes 47–52
  economic burden
    ability-to-pay principle 63–4, 71–2, 96–8
    on consumers 162–7
  impact of
    consumer prices, on 169–70
    existing taxes, on 52–4
    households, on 6, 169–73
    labor market effects 24, 110–11, 164–5,
      482
    in Scandinavia, studies 165–7
  influences on
    bounded rationality theory 10, 447–53
    constitutional law 65–9
    interest groups 231–5, 241, 409–11
    international organisations 21, 86, 91
    market forces 52–4
    politics 31–2, 48, 231–5
    rights and freedoms, and 72
  national economic burdens 468–71
  political economy of 7, 48, 240–42

choice of regime, relevance to 31–2, 48
definition 230, 235
equilibrium structure, role of 232–3
external party influences on 231–5
modeling role of 233–4
public choice emphasis 231–2
tax rates criteria 92–3
purpose 41–3, 85–6, 231–5, 612
taxes *vs.* emissions trading 48–50
trends 161
see also carbon tax; double dividend;
earmarked taxes; environmental
instruments; research
environmentally related taxes
certification 100
definition 21–2, 25, 34, 61, 85–6
environmental tax reform, role in 25–6
research focus 31
equilibrium frameworks 162
Estonia 290–91, 294
European Emissions Trading Scheme
allocation method 412
earmarked taxes, and 118
effectiveness 412–13, 472–3
monitoring and enforcement 338, 412
problems 47–8
scope of 411–12
European Union
competition law 78–9, 95
multilevel governance, and 270–71
constitutional law
legislative procedure 69
national tax sovereignty 76
policy coordination 74, 76–8
earmarked taxes 107–8, 112–13, 118
environmental taxation
consumer need, and 209
discrimination, prohibition of 207–10
energy taxation, distributional impact
168–72
exclusion clauses 209–10
externality research projects 144, 146
general framework 205–6
harmonization 205–6, 210, 270–71, 471–4
market-based instruments, studies 322–5
Process and Production Method (PPM)
taxes 206
product substitutability, and 209
reform policy trends 424
research opportunities 488
similar products, and 208
successes of 409
greenhouse gas mitigation burden 470
international trade, and
discrimination, prohibition of 207–10

general framework 205–6
harmonization 205–6, 210
Process and Production Method (PPM)
taxes 206
product substitutability, and 209
similar products, and 208
multilevel governance challenges 264–5
New Energy Externalities Developments for
Sustainability (NEEDS) 146
road transport
accident externalities 287
air pollution externalities 284–6, 293–5
congestion externalities 288–9, 295, 297–9
correctional capabilities, of taxes 293–9
emissions modeling 285–6
fuel taxes 290–91
noise externalities 286–7, 295–6
policy developments 107
taxes 283–4, 289–91
state aid policies, for environmental
protection 78–9, 141, 485
subsidies, controls over 78–9
taxation, generally
and competition 78–9
fiscal controls 48
harmonization 76–7, 205–6, 210, 270–71,
471–4
Member State differences, and 172
tax incidence, influences on 162
see also European Emissions Trading
Scheme
Eurostat 21
Eurovignette 291–2, 295–6
externalities
definition 139–40
efficiency, balancing negative and positive
142–4
energy conversion, due to 153–4
internalization principles 142–4, 490
monetary values of
CRF, per unit of emission, example
151–2
least-cost pollution reduction 17–18
life cycle assessment (LCA) 140–41, 154
modeling 6, 139–42
Pigouvian taxation, and 16–17, 139
polluter pays principle 16–17, 107, 140
research projects
clean air programmes 146
CRF and monetary values per unit of
emission, example 151–2
development of 144–7
impact pathway approach 6, 145, 147–52
opportunities for 154
US–EC Fuel Cycle Externality Study 144

road transport, in
  accidents 287
  air pollution 284–6, 293–5
  congestion externalities 288–9
  emissions modeling 285–6
  influence of 283
  noise pollution 286–7, 295–6
  taxes, correctional capabilities of 293–9
  scale, analysis of 254–5
  technological change, and
    adoption decisions 365–6
    positive externalities 364–7
    R&D expenditure 364–70
ExternE 144–5

Federal Database of State Incentives for
  Renewables and Efficiency (DSIRE)
  337
fees *see* charges
Finland
  carbon tax regime 10
    background 426–7
    challenges 428–30
    criticisms of 427, 429–33
    development stages 426–34
    political influences on 429–35
    revenue trends 434
    scope and features 427–30
  energy consumption trends 426
  environmental taxes, generally
    electricity tax 430, 484
    influences on 431–6
    normalization 431–5
    regressivity of 166
    tax reform 383–6, 431–6
  road transport taxes 290–91, 294
fiscal federalism 251–2, 269
France
  carbon tax 52, 56, 72, 166, 241, 391, 484
  constitutional law 63, 69, 72
  earmarked taxes 103
  economic theory influences 236–7
  road transport taxes 290–91, 294
  success, of environmental taxes 409
  water pollution taxes 479
Frey, B. 409, 416
Fuel Cycle Externality Study (US–EC) 144
fuel taxes
  correctional capabilities 293–7, 299
  decoupling studies 354–5
  earmarked taxes 116–17
  EU, in 290–91
  externality studies 144
  leisure, and 223
  subsidies 241–2

Fullerton, D. 215, 217–18, 222, 268, 278–80,
  409

General Agreement on Tariffs and Trade
  (GATT)
  border tax adjustments 198, 201–2
  chapeau conditions 204–5
George, H. 212
Germany
  CO_2 emissions 459
  constitutional law 63, 66, 69, 70, 72
  environmental taxes
    hybrid subsidies 490
    reform modeling 383–6
    road transport taxes 290–91, 294–5
    successes of 409
    water pollution taxes 479
  transaction cost studies 279
global carbon tax
  adaptation costs 464
  assessment criteria 458
  border tax adjustments 79–80, 198, 201–2,
    238, 391, 489
  challenges 488–9
  competitiveness, and 283, 391, 459–60
  cost-effectiveness 460–62, 464–8, 473
  design criteria 457–8
  earmarking 462–3
  enforcement 469–73
  environmental-effectiveness 458–62, 473
  fairness 458, 468–9, 473
  first mover advantages 473–4
  harmonized tax, as 465–74
  implementation prospects 472–4
  international tax, as 465–74
  international trade, and 468
  marginal abatement costs, calculation
    difficulties 464–8
  Millennium Development Goals, and 464
  mitigation costs, reduction of 464–9
  multiple motives for 467–8
  national economic burdens, and 468–71
  national sovereignty, and 461–2
  national tax-free quotas 461–2
  non-compliance, motives for 470–73
  participation levels 458–62
  pollution havens, influence of 459–60
  revenue distribution 461–2, 468–9
  revenue-effectiveness 462–4, 473
  tax base erosion effect 463–4
  terms-of-trade changes, and 469
  welfare loss calculations 463–4
global environmental problems
  climate change, approaches to tackling
    456–7

international trade liberalization, and 192
ozone depletion 456–7
responsibility for 456
variable impacts of 456
voluntary measures for 456–7
Global Environment Facility (GEF) 461
global environmental taxes *see* global carbon
tax
Goulder, L.H. 216, 220–21, 239, 356, 368–9,
483
grandfathering 29–30, 411–12
Greece 290–91, 294, 354

Hahn, R. 235–6, 409
Hazardous Substances Response Fund (US)
116, 202, 479, 484–5
Höglund Isaksson, L. 240, 371
Hohmeyer, O. 144–5
households, environmental tax impact on 6,
170–73
Hungary 290–91, 294

impact pathway approach
concentration-response functions (CRF)
148, 150–51
general principles 6, 145, 147–8
impact categories, pollutants and burdens
149
monetary values
corresponding 150–53
per unit of emissions 151–2
nonmarket valuation techniques
150–52
willingness to pay 150–51
implementation, of environmental taxes
environmental federalism 7–8, 252, 255
fiscal federalism 251–2, 269
global carbon tax 472–4
research trends 486–7
transaction costs 275–6
see also multilevel governance
incentive taxes
ability-to-pay principle 63–4, 71–2, 96–8
advantages 399, 408
basis for 96
bounded rationality theory, and 444–53
competition, influence on 378–80
context, relevance of 362–4
cost to society, and 28–9
definition 22–3, 27–8, 46, 54, 61–2
effectiveness, influences on 372–3, 458–9
efficiency *vs.* revenue generation 40–42,
93–4, 111
environmental competencies 98–9
environmental liability, and

optimal taxation, and 402–3, 414–17
regulation, and 404–7, 414
environmental tax revenues, and 40–41
equivalence-oriented taxes 98
and fiscal taxes, compared 61–2
and freedoms, conflicts between 72
non-environmental expenditures 94–5
policy conflicts 28–9, 94
polluter pays principle, conflicts with 28–9,
94
purpose 96, 99, 490–91
quantity 99
for R&D 362, 364–70
regulatory incentives, and 35–6
retroactivity 71
tax incidence, factors influencing 162–5
tax procedures 99–100
tax-revenue-oriented taxes 98
tax shift, and 40–42, 93–4, 111
taxing powers 98–9
technological change
influence on 361–2, 372–3, 380
R&D, and 362, 364–70
see also environmental liability; subsidies
India 459, 470
indirect taxes, definition 62
Indonesia 267
inefficiency *see under* efficiency
Informal International Tax Dialogue (ITD)
79
innovation *see* technological change
instrument mixes *see* environmental
instruments
international law
border tax adjustments 79–80, 198, 201–2,
391, 489
competitiveness 238, 391
conflict of laws 79–81
environmental policies, as market failure
192
see also international trade
International Tax Organization (ITO) 79
international trade
environmental taxation, and
competitiveness, and 193, 485
design criteria 193
direct impact 193
global carbon tax 468
Process and Production Method (PPM)
taxes 193–4, 196, 206
General Agreement on Tariffs and Trade
(GATT)
border tax adjustments 198, 201–2
chapeau conditions 204–5
liberalization, global issues 192

WTO, generally
    non-discrimination principles 195–202
    powers and duties 194–5
Iran 459
Ireland 290–91, 294
Italy 290–91, 294

Jaffe, A.B. 370, 389
Japan 146, 459, 470, 479
Johnstone, N. 165–6, 371–2

Kahneman, D. 183, 442–3
Kallbekken, S. 109, 183
Kapp, K.W. 17
Kneese, A.V. 360

labor market effects
    labor costs, reducing 24, 110–11, 164–5
    pollution, of 222–4
    research trends 482
    unemployment 225
Larsen, B. 355, 409
Latin America 268–9, 470
Latvia 290–91, 294
least-cost abatement theory 20
legal authority
    constitutional law
        legislative competencies 65–8
        legislative procedures 69
        policy coordination 74–8
        remedies under 63
        revenue allocation 68–9
        substantive law concepts 63–4
        taxing powers 63
    multilevel governance, and 4, 59
    policy coordination
        common markets, and 74–5
        competition policies 78–9
        environmental policies 73–4
        tax policies 74–8
    principle of legality 70
    proportionality, and 72
    retroactivity 65, 71
    rights and freedoms, conflicts with 71–2
legality, principle of 70
liability, for environmental harm *see*
    environmental liability
life cycle assessment (LCA) 140–41, 154
Lithuania 290–91, 294
lobby groups, influence of 232, 234, 241,
    409–11
Luxembourg 290–91, 294

Määttä, K. 61, 72, 425
Malta 290–91, 294

Manne, A. 53–4, 239
marginal abatement costs
    cost matching 36–40, 48–50, 143, 360, 363,
        462
    global carbon tax, calculation difficulties
        464–5
marginal external costs modeling 142–4
marginal social damage 48, 211–12, 217–18,
    227
Markandya, A. 141–2, 286, 349
market-based instruments *see under*
    environmental instruments
Martin, R. 240, 372
Metcalf, G.E. 352, 372, 487
Mexico 241–2, 470
Middle East 470
Millennium Development Goals 464
monitoring and enforcement
    emissions trading 338, 412
    multilevel governance, and 256
Morgenstern, R.D. 239, 483
most-favoured nation principle 195
multilevel governance 249
    allocation of powers
        principles 254–9
        research 259–63
    challenges 271–2
        integration and coordination 263–6
        inter-level competition 258
    characteristics 250–51
    China, in 313–14
    governance levels
        allocation principles 254–9
        inter-level competition, and 258
        interrelational institutional models 255
        local level taxes 261–3
    implementation
        administration and costs 268–70
        coordination mechanisms 266–8
        horizontal coordination 265–6
        integration and coordination 263–8
        multi-part instruments 269–70
        time coordination 268
        vertical coordination 264
    influences on
        effectiveness 256–7
        excise taxes 262
        geographic scale 254–5
        governance trends 252–3
        mobility of polluting industry 256
        monitoring and enforcement capacity 256
        motor vehicle tax 261
        property taxes 261
        research into 259–63
        revenue need 257–8, 260

surtaxes 262–3
waste taxes 262
legal authority for 4, 59
research
    allocation of powers 259–63
    focus 250–53
    opportunities for 258–9, 263, 272

National Emission Ceilings Directive (EU) 146
national treatment principle 195, 202
necessity test, for ability-to-pay-oriented taxes
    97
negligence, *vs.* strict liability 402–3, 405
Netherlands
    dynamic impact studies 370
    earmarked taxes 103
    environmental tax reform modeling 383–6
    private interest, influence of 410
    road transport taxes 290–91, 294
    success, of environmental taxes 409
    water pollution taxes 479
New Energy Externalities Developments for
    Sustainability (NEEDS) 146
new technologies *see* technological change
New Zealand 470
noise pollution
    road transport
        externalities 286–7
        taxes, correction capabilities of 295–6
Nordhaus, W. 47, 458–9, 482
Norway
    decoupling study 355
    earmarked taxes 114
    economic theory influence on 237
    environmental tax successes 409
    regressivity, of 167
    road transport taxes 298
Nykvist, B. 255, 265–6

Oates, W.E. 17, 27, 214, 230–31, 449, 452, 466,
    486, 489
    Baumol-Oates tax 5, 18, 23
    fiscal federalism 252, 254
Oberson, X. 66
OECD (Organisation for Economic
    Cooperation and Development)
    Database on Instruments Used in
        Environmental Policy and Natural
        Resources Management 331–3
    environmental taxes, role in 21, 86, 91
    environmental tax reform, defining 25, 29
    polluter pays principle, on 18–19, 33, 87
    studies
        competitiveness of environmentally
            related taxes, on 237–8, 389

databases, of environmental instruments
    321, 323–5, 331–3
environmental charges 19
tax-to-price ratios 372
transaction costs 273–5, 279
Oil Spill Liability Trust Fund (US) 116
Olson, M. 183, 234–5
optimal taxation, theory of *see under*
    Pigouvian taxation
Ostrom, E. 490
ozone protection regime, conflict of laws 80

Palmer, K. 388, 487
parking taxes 297
Parry, I.W.H. 214
patents, environmental policy influence on
    371–2
Pearce, D. 24, 214–15
Pigou, A.C. 4, 406–7, 479–80, 485, 490–91
    see also Pigouvian taxation
Pigouvian taxation 491
    criticism of 17, 19, 30, 116–17
    environmental taxation
        charges, and 20, 87
        earmarked taxes, and 112
        externalities, role of 16–17, 139, 212–13
        influence on 11, 15–16
        interpretation 85–6
        optimal taxation, theory of 399
    historical influences on 27
    interpretation 85–6, 488
    optimal taxation, theory of
        environmental liability 402–3, 414–17
        environmental taxes, and 399, 414–17
        marginal social damage, and 211–12,
            217–18
        taxation generally, and 212–13
        dirty goods, and 215, 217–19, 222
    principles 91–3, 407–8
        equivalence principle 87
        extraordinary encouragement principle
            28–9
        polluter pays principle 87–8
        tax bounty/subsidy approach 16–17, 26–9
    purpose 17–20
    tax rates, criteria for 91–3
    taxing powers, and 88–9
    welfare economics, and 15–16
Poland 290–91, 294, 490
policy sciences *see* behavioral economics
politics
    capture theory 231–2
    environmental taxes, and 7, 48, 240–42
        choice of regime, relevance to 31–2, 48
        equilibrium structure, role of 232–3

external party influences on 231–5, 241
modeling role of 233–4
research trends 486–7
tax rates criteria 92–3
political economy, definition 230, 235
see also environmental policy
polluter pays principle
background 17
China, application in 310
conflicts with tax expenditures 94
definition 26
earmarked taxes, and 107, 112–13
emissions trading schemes, and 30, 411
expansion of 18–19
importance 33
introduction of 18, 33
monetary values of externalities 16–17, 107,
140
purpose 18, 87
pollution
air quality research 146
change in perception of 361, 367–70
Coase's theory of reciprocal nature of harm,
and 10, 30, 400–401, 479
economic benefits of 399
externalities
air pollution 284–6, 293–5
noise pollution 286–7, 295–6
road transport 284–6, 293–5
monetary values of 16–17, 107, 140
impact pathway approach 150–53
least-cost pollution reduction 17–18
life cycle assessment (LCA) 140–41, 154
modeling 6, 139–42
per unit of emission, example 151–2
Pigouvian taxation 16–17, 139
polluter pays principle 16–17, 107, 140
optimum level, managing efficiency 37–40,
399–400
polluters
mobility of 256, 388–9
policy support from 423
pollution charge system, China 309–11
pollution havens 388–9, 459–60
right to pollute 400–401
pollution havens 388–9, 459–60
pollution tax *see* emissions charges
polycentricity 251
Porter, M.E. 40, 387–8
Portney, P. 230
Portugal 115–16, 290–91, 294
Poterba, J.M. 163–5
pressure groups, influence of 232, 234, 241,
409–11
price responsiveness 162–3

principle of equality 71–2
principle of legality 70
Process and Production Method (PPM) taxes
193–4, 196–201, 206
proportionality 72, 78–9, 97
'pure steering taxes' 61–2

Ramsey, F.P. 107, 116–17, 212–13, 224, 276
R&D, environmental tax incentives for 364–70
regressivity, of environmental taxes
distributional impact, and 169–72, 174–5,
489
elasticity of supply and demand, and 162–3
generally 161, 172–4
geographical differences 173–4
income concept 163–4
indirect effects 163
mitigation 161
price responsiveness 162–3
revenues, uses for 164–5
in Scandinavia, studies 166–7
regulation
coregulation 423
definition 22–3, 68, 142, 231–2
deregulation 424
environmental tax reform, role in 424–6
equal treatment principle, and 35
limitations of 35–6, 39, 132, 406–8
market-based instruments, compared with
9–10, 232, 235, 406–10
power asymmetries, susceptibility to 35–6
supporters 423
and technological change, response to 36
trends in, development 422–3
see also environmental liability
research, in environmental taxation
opportunities
bounded rationality theory 452–3
earmarked taxes 117–18
emissions trading 31
environmental instruments 416–17
EU, environmental taxation in 488
instrument mixes 416–17
subsidies 31, 43–7, 480–81
trends 491
competitiveness 381–2
distributional implications 489
in European Union 488
interdisciplinary research 487–9
labor market effects 482
legal issues 483–5, 487–8
macroeconomic studies 481–3
microeconomic studies 481
modeling, developments in 482
policy sciences 486–7

subsidies 43–7, 480–81
technological change, influences of
366–74
retroactivity 65, 71
revenue
allocation, legal authority for 68–9
earmarked taxes
efficiency, and 40–41, 104, 112–14
policy relevance of 102–3
revenue recycling, whether 104, 108
efficiency, balancing with 40–41, 93–4, 104,
111–14
global carbon tax
revenue distribution 461–2, 468–9
revenue-effectiveness 462–4, 473
multilevel governance influences on 257–8,
260
as proportion of GDP 41
as purpose, of environmental taxes 40–42,
68–9, 280
revenue recycling 104, 108, 133–4, 380,
382–3
revenue-neutral taxes
advantages 408
carbon tax, in Canada 5–7, 24–5, 181–3
Richels, R. 53–4
rights and freedoms, conflicts with
environmental taxes 71–2
ringfencing *see* earmarked taxes
road transport
costs
accidents 296
congestion 288, 297
Eastern Europe, in 283
monetary value analysis 299
externalities
accidents 287
air pollution 284–6, 293–5
congestion 288–9
emissions modeling 285–6
influence of 283
noise pollution 286–7, 295–6
pollution contribution 283
taxes, correctional capabilities of 293–9
road transport taxes 8
correctional capabilities
accidents 296
air pollution 293–5
congestion 295, 297–9
noise pollution 295–6
electronic collection 297–9
EU, in
Eurovignette 291–2, 295–6
types 283–4, 289–92, 294–9
fixed taxes 289–90, 293, 297, 299

fuel taxes 290–91
infrastructure use charges 291–2
instrument types 283
parking 297
research trends 482–3, 489
tax differentiation, and 72, 290, 292–9
variable taxes 289–90, 293
VAT 289–90
vehicle ownership and regulation 289–90,
297
Romania 290–91, 294
Rose-Ackerman, S. 18, 415
Russia 459, 470

Saelen, H. 118, 183
St Petersburg Guidelines on Environmental
Funds in Economies in Transition
(OECD) (1995) 107
Sandford, C. 276–7, 280
Sandmo, A. 213, 217–19, 463–4
Scandinavia
decoupling studies 350–52, 355
earmarked taxes 114
economic theory, influence on environmental
policy 236–7
multilevel governance 270
regressivity, of environmental taxes 167
tax reform 19, 425–6
Schneider, S. 368–9
segregated accounts/budgets *see* earmarked
taxes
Sen, A. 441–3
Shavell, S. 404–5
Shrim-Turtle case 205
Simon, H. 445–6
Singapore 297–9
Slovakia 290–91, 294
Slovenia 114, 290–91, 294
Smith, Adam 16
Smith, S. 22, 163–5, 173, 269
Smith, V.K. 223
Smulders, J.A. 276, 367–8
The Social Costs of Private Enterprise 17
South Korea 459
Spain 92–3, 260, 290–91, 294
special funds *see* earmarked taxes
spillover effects, and incentives for
technological change 364–70
state aids, compatibility with competition law
78–9, 141, 485
static efficiency 36–40
Stavins, R.N. 47, 230–32, 235
steering taxes 62, 65–6, 70
Sterner, T. 240, 262, 343–56
strict liability

accident law, economic principles 401–2
for environmental harm 403–4
limitations 405
vs. negligence 402–3
subsidies
anti-subsidy measures 17–18, 43–54
definition 27–8, 46, 63, 490–91
disadvantages 27, 43–4, 490
economic effects 52–4
effectiveness 372–3
environmental effects of
detrimental 43–4
long-term *vs.* short-term 44
measuring 46–7
technological change, and 372–3
EU controls 78–9
Pigouvian approach to 16–17, 26–9
policy focus 3, 25, 29, 43, 97
polluter-pays principle 17–18
research trends and opportunities 31, 43–7,
480–81
scope and extent 45–6
as tax rebates, influence of 372–3
use of, attitudes to
changes in 26–9, 490–91
government failures, viewed as 43–4
incentive value of 372–3
justification for 43
substitution mechanisms 362–4
Sunstein, C. 450–52
Superfund (US) 116, 202, 479, 484–5
sustainable development policy 33
Sweden
decoupling study 356
dynamic impact studies 371
earmarked taxes 112
economic theory influences 237
environmental tax reform 19, 383–6
regressivity, of environmental taxes 166–7
road transport taxes 290–91, 294
transaction cost studies 279
Switzerland 66, 106–7, 295

Tamborra, M. 141–2
tax base
definition 90–91
erosion effect 463–4
global carbon tax, of 463–4
tax differentiation
competitiveness in international trade, and
206
road transport taxes 72, 290, 292–9
tax expenditures
ability-to-pay principle, and 96–8
compulsory investments, and 99

definition 27–8
design, influences on 28–9, 97–8, 450–52
and earmarking 450
environmental competencies 98–9
equivalence-oriented taxes 98
interaction with other taxes 28–9
justification for 96
necessity test 97
non-environmental tax expenditures 94–5
Pigouvian taxation, and 28–9
policy approaches involving 28–9
polluter pays principle, and 94
proportionality test 97
quantity 99
research focus and opportunities 31, 372–4
suitability test 97
tax procedures 99–100
tax reductions 94–5
tax-revenue-oriented taxes, in 98
taxing powers 98–9
see also subsidies; tax incentives
tax incentives
ability-to-pay principle 63–4, 71–2, 96–8
advantages 399, 408
basis for 96
bounded rationality theory, and 444–53
competition, influence on 378–80
context, relevance of 362–4
cost to society, and 28–9
definition 22–3, 27–8, 46, 54, 61–2
effectiveness, influences on 372–3, 458–9
efficiency *vs.* revenue generation 40–42,
93–4, 111
environmental competencies 98–9
environmental liability
optimal taxation, and 402–3, 414–17
regulation, and 404–7, 414
equivalence-oriented taxes 98
and fiscal taxes, compared 61–2
and freedoms, conflicts between 72
non-environmental expenditures 94–5
policy conflicts 28–9, 94
polluter pays principle, conflicts with 28–9,
94
purpose 96, 99, 490–91
quantity 99
for R&D 362, 364–70
regulatory incentives, and 35–6
retroactivity 71
tax incidence, factors influencing 162–5
tax procedures 99–100
tax-revenue-oriented taxes 98
tax shift, and 40–42, 93–4, 111
taxing powers 98–9
technological change

influence on 361–2, 372–3, 380
  R&D, and 362, 364–70
  see also subsidies
tax incidence
  definitions 162
  economic incidence 162
  factors influencing 162–5
  statutory incidence 162
tax rates
  design criteria 5, 91–3
  political criteria 92–3
  technical criteria 91–2
tax shift
  efficiency *vs.* revenue generation 40–42,
    93–4, 111
taxable events 89
taxation, generally
  constitutional authority over 64
  distortionary taxes 164, 212–13, 227
  double dividend, and 164, 212–13, 227
  environmental taxation, differences from 399
  harmonization 76–7, 457, 471
    barriers to 192, 270–71
    global carbon tax, and 461, 465–6, 469,
      471–4
  optimal taxation, theory of 212–13
    dirty goods, and 215, 217–19, 222
  without distortions, possibility of 212–13
Taxes in Europe Database 335–7
taxing powers
  environmental competencies, and 98–9
  legal authority 63
  multilevel governance, in
    allocation principles 254–9
    research 254–9
  tax design criteria, and 88–9
taxpayers, public entities as 93–4
technological change
  environmental taxes, influences on 380, 387
    adoption decisions 365–6
    behavioral economics 372–4
    benefit to environment 368
    change as part of solution 361
    dynamic efficiency, and 40–41
    dynamic incentives 362–4
    importance of 360–62
    indirect effects 369–70
    induced innovation hypothesis 368–70
    knowledge spillovers 368–70
    net present value framework 366–7
    patents, as evidence of 371
    R&D incentives, as 362, 364–70
    regulatory response to 36
    research on 366–74
    spillover effects 364–70

tax rate criteria, and 91–2
  tax rebates, and 372–3
  generally
    capitalism, understanding role in 361
    endogenization of 367–8
    phases of 361
  innovation, economics of
    dynamic incentives 362–4
    innovation offsets 387–8
    positive/'spillover' effects 364–7
  integrated technology, development of 367
Terkla, D. 24
Thaler, R. 450–52
Tietenberg, T. 39, 386
trade agreements *see* General Agreement on
  Tariffs and Trade
trading regimes *see* carbon tax; emissions
  trading
transaction costs 8
  environmental taxes
    allowances trading schemes, and 30
    definition 275–7
    implementation 275–6
    measurement 277–8
    studies 279–81
    tax design, and 276
  generally
    definition 273, 275–7
    OECD evaluation framework 273–5
  measurement
    methods 277–8
    size, influences on 278
  research
    opportunities 281
    studies 279–81
    trends 276–7
transport taxes, generally
  civil aviation taxes 80–81
  externalities, modeling costs of 142
  regressivity studies 165–6, 173–4
  subsidies 45–6
  see also fuel taxes; road transport taxes
Tullock, G. 108, 231–2
Turkey 241–2

United Kingdom
  Climate Change Levy 105, 114–15, 240, 372,
    390, 415
  CO_2 emissions 459
  Commission on Environmental Markets and
    Economic Performance 393
  Congestion Charge 298
  earmarked taxes 103, 105, 112, 114–15
  environmental tax reform modeling 383–6
  road transport taxes 290–91, 294, 298

success, of environmental taxes 409
transaction costs studies 279–80
United Nations
  Framework Convention on Climate Change
      (UNFCC) 461, 464
  System of Environmental Economic
      Accounting (SEEA) 21
United States
  Acid Rain Program 39
  bounded rationality, influence on tax design
      450
  carbon tax, in California 177
  CO$_2$ emissions 459
  constitutional law
    legislative procedures 69
    policy coordination 75–7
  decoupling studies 354–5
  earmarked taxes 116, 118
  environmental tax development 479
  externality research projects 144, 146–7
  Federal Database of State Incentives for
      Renewables and Efficiency (DSIRE) 337
  Fuel Cycle Externality Study 144
  governance level, influences on choice of
      260–61
  Hazardous Substances Response Fund
      (Superfund) 116, 202, 479, 484–5
  marginal excess burden 214–15
  Oil Spill Liability Trust Fund 116
  ozone protection regime 80
  proportionality 97

Van der Linde, C. 40, 387–8
vehicle taxes
  conflict of laws 72
  EU, in 289–90, 293–5
  governance level 261
  tax bases 293–4
  vehicle ownership and registration taxes
      289–90, 297

victim-pays principle 30, 485
Vietnam
  economic development 124–5
  environmental tax reform
    advantages of 136–8
    background 5, 124–6
    challenges 131–2
    design features 128–32
    impact of 134–7
    political background 126–8
    revenue allocation and recycling
        133–4
    tax rates under 129–31
Vollebergh, H. 232, 235, 256, 276
von Weizsäcker, E.U. 19, 24, 426

Wagner, U. 240, 372
Walls, M. 487
Weisbach, D. 487
Whalley, J. 457, 468–9
White Papers (EU)
  Competitiveness and Employment (2002)
      24–5
  Fair and Efficient Pricing (1995) 107
  Fair Payment for Infrastructure Use (1998)
      107
  Roadmap to a Single European Transport
      Area (2011) 107
Wiggle, R. 457, 468–9
Williams, R.C. III 222–3
World Atmospheric Fund 457
World Bank 25, 29, 463
World Trade Organization (WTO)
  General Agreement on Tariffs and Trade
      (GATT)
    border tax adjustments 198, 201–2
    chapeau conditions 204–5
  non-discrimination principles
      195–202
  powers and duties 194–5